MARINE ARCHAEOLOGY

A

THE BUTTERWORTH GROUP

ENGLAND:	BUTTERWORTH & CO. (PUBLISHERS) LTD. LONDON: 88 Kingsway, WC2B 6AB
AUSTRALIA:	BUTTERWORTHS PTY. LTD. SYDNEY: 586 Pacific Highway, NSW 2067 MELBOURNE: 343 Little Collins Street, 3000 BRISBANE: 240 Queen Street, 4000
CANADA:	BUTTERWORTH & CO. (CANADA) LTD. TORONTO: 14 Curity Avenue, 374
NEW ZEALAND:	BUTTERWORTHS OF NEW ZEALAND LTD. WELLINGTON: 26/28 Waring Taylor Street, 1
SOUTH AFRICA:	BUTTERWORTH & CO. (SOUTH AFRICA) (PTY) LTD. DURBAN: 152/154 Gale Street

March 1973

ISBN 0 408 70477 2

Made and Printed in England by
J. W. Arrowsmith Ltd., Bristol BS3 2NT and Bound by Webb, Son & Co. Ltd., London

MARINE ARCHAEOLOGY

Edited by

D. J. BLACKMAN

Proceedings of the
Twentythird Symposium of the Colston Research Society
held in the University of Bristol
April 4th to 8th, 1971

LONDON
BUTTERWORTHS

Previous volumes in the Colston Papers are:

Vol. I. 1948 *Cosmic Radiation*—Editor, Professor F. C. Frank (out of print)
Vol. II. 1949 *Engineering Structures*—Editor, Professor A. G. Pugsley (out of print)
Vol. III. 1950 *Colonial Administration*—Editor, Professor C. M. MacInnes (out of print)
Vol. IV. 1951 *The Universities and the Theatre*—Editor, Professor D. G. James
Vol. V. 1952 *The Suprarenal Cortex*—Editor, Professor J. M. Yoffey
Vol. VI. 1953 *Insecticides and Colonial Agricultural Development*—Editors, Professor T. Wallace and Dr. J. T. Martin (out of print)
Vol. VII. 1954 *Recent Developments in Cell Physiology*—Editor, Dr. J. A. Kitching (out of print)
1955 No symposium held this year
Vol. VIII. 1956 *The Neurohypophysis*—Editor, Professor H. Heller (out of print)
Vol. IX. 1957 *Observation and Interpretation*—Editor, Professor S. Körner (out of print)
Vol. X. 1958 *The Structure and Properties of Porous Materials*—Editors, Professor D. H. Everett and Dr. F. S. Stone (out of print)
Vol. XI. 1959 *Hypersonic Flow*—Editors, Professor A. R. Collar and Dr. J. Tinkler
Vol. XII. 1960 *Metaphor and Symbol*—Editors, Professor L. C. Knights and Basil Cottle
Vol. XIII. 1961 *Animal Health and Production*—Editors, Professor C. S. Grunsell and A. I. Wright
Vol. XIV. 1962 *Music and Education*—Editor, Professor Willis Grant (out of print)
Vol. XV. 1963 *Reality and Creative Vision in German Lyrical Poetry*—Editor, Professor A. Closs
Vol. XVI. 1964 *Economic Analysis for National Economic Planning*—Editors, P. E. Hart, G. Mills and J. K. Whitaker
Vol. XVII. 1965 *Submarine Geology and Geophysics*—Editors, Professor W. F. Whittard and R. Bradshaw
Vol. XVIII. 1966 *The Fungus Spore*—Editor, M. F. Madelin
Vol. XIX. 1967 *The Liver*—Editor, A. E. Read
Vol. XX. 1968 *Towards a Policy for the Education of Teachers*—Editor, Professor William Taylor
Vol. XXI. 1969 *Communication and Energy in Changing Urban Environments*—Editor, Professor D. Jones
Vol. XXII. 1970 *Regional Forecasting*—Editors, M. Chisholm, A. E. Frey and Professor P. Haggett.

Foreword

THE name of Edward Colston, the great seventeenth-century philanthropist and educationalist, is associated in Bristol with a number of scholastic and charitable institutions. It was adopted by a group of public-spirited citizens when, in 1899, they established the "University College Colston Society", with the aim of fostering the young and struggling University College. For a decade it played a part in the movement which culminated in the institution of the University of Bristol in 1909.

The Society then changed its name and made its object more precise: it became the "Colston Research Society" and devoted itself to the encouragement of original work in the University. It made grants for the purchase of apparatus and for other expenses of research. As resources increased, activities expanded and, notably, in the later 'thirties the Society financed a full-scale Social Survey of Bristol.

After the war, a new reconsideration of policy led to the decision to devote the major part of the Society's efforts to the promotion of an annual symposium, the first being held in 1948. The rapid growth of the symposium as a means for the advancement of knowledge is one of the remarkable features of the intellectual life of recent years. Usually, such meetings are fostered by bodies interested in one particular field of learning. As the list of titles (on the page opposite) shows, no such limitation applies to the symposia of the Colston Research Society. That the subject should be one at an interesting and active stage of development is the main factor in making a choice. The fact that the symposium is held in one of the younger seats of learning, with its home in an historic city, is a stimulus not only to the University but also, we believe, to the visiting guests who have come from many countries. The publication of the proceedings ensures the communication of the papers and discussions to wider circles.

It was my privilege to be President of the Colston Research Society for the year 1970–1971, during which the twentythird symposium was promoted by the Society. The subject was "Marine Archaeology" and the proceedings are printed here as the twentythird volume of the Colston papers.

C. PITMAN

Preface

MARINE archaeology is the youngest branch of archaeology; indeed, most of its development has taken place since the last war, with increasing momentum in the nineteen-sixties. Like the geologist, the archaeologist has gone into and under the water, and for both the results have been particularly rewarding. In the spring of 1965 the Seventeenth Symposium of the Colston Research Society was devoted to the subject "Submarine Geology and Geophysics", and its published proceedings have become well known; it was therefore fitting that "Marine Archaeology" should form the subject of a Colston Symposium a few years later, for both subjects eminently fulfil the requirement of the Colston Research Society, "that the subject should be one at an interesting and active stage of development."

The Twentythird Symposium was the first long conference on marine archaeology to be held in Great Britain. Thanks to the generous support of the Colston Research Society full publication of the proceedings is assured (one of the main problems facing the organizer of such a conference thus being solved in advance); also the participation of a number of members from Europe and further afield was made possible.

For the formal sessions a number of themes were selected and, in order to provide some coherence, geographical limits were suggested (though these were not applied rigidly): the Mediterranean and British waters. Several of these themes highlighted the interdisciplinary nature of the subject, notably the first three: sea level changes and coastline studies; search and survey; and conservation. The publication in this volume follows in the main the order in which the papers were given, but the opening paper, by P. Throckmorton, has been moved to the end to form the epilogue.

The formal sessions were not, and were not intended to be, the only focus. One of the main aims of all Colston Symposia is to allow plenty of time for private discussion among members, and to facilitate this by restrictions on numbers and by accommodation under one roof; this was certainly one of the most valuable results of the Twentythird Symposium, for many of the members who are active in marine archaeology had the chance to meet for the first time and exchange experiences. This aspect of the Symposium can be only dimly reflected in the published proceedings.

At the Colston Society's Annual Reception, Lt. Cmdr. G. P. B. Naish gave an illustrated address (not published here) on "Marine Archaeology: Present State and Future Prospects", which enthralled a wider audience. Symposium members visited Bristol City Museum for a reception and a preview of the special exhibition on Marine Archaeology—a highlight of the week, and one which did much to strengthen relations between City Museum and University. A visit was made to the City Docks and the SS *Great Britain*, and there were many comments on the suitability of this site for a Maritime Museum, within the wider context of the preserved City Docks. If this project is ever realized, it might be considered to stem at least partly from discussions during the Symposium.

As regards the abbreviation of periodical titles in the lists of references, scientific periodicals have in general been abbreviated in accordance with the World List of

Scientific Periodicals, periodicals and reference works on ancient history and archaeology in accordance with "Notes for Contributors and Abbreviations" in *American Journal of Archaeology*, **74** (1970) 1–8. For the medieval and later periods no such generally accepted list appears to exist. Clarity has been my main aim. Some abbreviations are used without further explanation: O.D. = Ordnance Datum; (M.)H.W.N.T. = (Mean) High Water Neap Tides, etc.

It is my pleasant duty to record my thanks to those who helped me in the organization of the Symposium and the publication of its proceedings: to Mr. C. Pitman, President of the Colston Research Society in 1970–71, and Mr. R. H. Brown, then Secretary of the Society; to the members of the Council and Committee of the Society; to the Vice-Chancellor of the University, Dr. A. W. Merrison, for the interest he took in the proceedings; to Prof. R. F. Peel, University representative on the Colston Society Council, and to my own Head of Department, Prof. J. M. Cook, who was Director of the Symposium, for advice and encouragement; to Nicholas Thomas and the staff of the City Museum, for arranging a reception and organizing the special exhibition; to my colleagues, Keith Branigan and John Betts, for practical help, and also to Douglas Waite, John Tayless and Deborah Quare for help during the actual Symposium; to all the contributors and those who chaired sessions; and to Paul Johnstone for arranging for the showing of some B.B.C. *Chronicle* films. Of many who helped on the secretarial side, I should like to thank especially Miss Linda Martin, who bore the brunt; organization of the Symposium was not made easy by a postal strike in the preceding three months. The Warden, Bursar and staff at Manor Hall made us very much at home, and we are most grateful to them. Last, but not least, I owe much to the patience and help of Mr. F. A. Keedwell of Messrs. J. W. Arrowsmith Ltd; he now knows only too well that archaeologists disappear for months at a time with only the most dubious of forwarding addresses.

David Blackman

Contents

Archaeological evidence for eustatic and tectonic components of relative sea level change in the South Aegean

by

FLEMMING, N. C., CZARTORYSKA, N. M. G., & HUNTER, P. M.

SUMMARY

Seventy archaeological sites were visited on the coasts of the Peloponnese and south-west Turkey in 1967–69. Relative sea level changes were detected at each site by interpreting the function of remains and foundations and attempting to relate these to the original sea level at the site when it was occupied. The age of sites varied from 2000 B.C. to medieval and modern structures of the past 100 years. The relative displacement of sites varied from relative uplift of 3.0 m to submergence of 5.0 m.

There was no simple correlation between age and displacement of site, and therefore the observations could not be explained by steady continuous movement of either the land or the sea. The average displacement of sites increased towards relative depression with increasing age, but the scatter between sites of the same age always exceeded the average displacement for that age, indicating a high incidence of earth movements between sites. This is to be expected in view of the intense faulting and seismicity of the region.

The data for the Peloponnese were treated with surface fitting programmes. The average rate of displacement for each site was correlated with its geographical co-ordinates on an arbitrary local grid. Third-degree surfaces for the east and west coasts independently produced the best fit, and a smoothing equation was computed for the junction between the areas. The contours of rate of relative displacement indicate that the margins of the Peloponnese are being depressed while the centre is being uplifted. A ridge of relative uplift extends through the Elos peninsula, Kythera and Antikythera towards Crete.

The data from Turkey were both recorded and analysed with a more advanced technique. Estimates of the probability of various displacements other than the most probable were made, and the resulting figures were treated for separation of the factors due to earth movement and eustatic change of sea level. It was proposed that the eustatic change of sea level through time could be represented by a third-degree equation, while the geographical distribution of rate of earth movements could be represented by a fourth-degree equation in local geographical co-ordinates. It was proposed that the observed relative displacement at a site should be the sum of these two factors. The expressions were expanded into their algebraic terms, and a stepwise multiple regression fitted to the combined expression. The best fit equation was separated into those terms in time only, those including geographical co-ordinates, and the two equations plotted separately. The eustatic sea level/time curve indicated that sea level was within a few centimetres of present level at 2000 B.C., dropped slowly to about —30 cm in about A.D. 500, and then rose to present level. This is, of course, a smoothed curve and there may have been oscillations about this mean with periods of a few hundred years. The contours of earth movements showed complex warping and faulting of the Turkish coast, with a general depression to seawards and landwards about the mean coastal axis, and regions of uplift stretching westwards over the Ceşme peninsula and west of south from the Cnidus peninsula towards Rhodes.

In the present paper the archaeological observations are presented with sketch maps, and the mathematical and geological interpretation is summarized with reference to other publications.

INTRODUCTION

Coastal archaeological sites provide an excellent sea level indicator in the time span 1–5,000 years, with an accuracy varying from ± 1.0 m to as little as ± 0.1 m. To obtain a reliable sample on which to base deductions about earth movements and eustatic sea level changes, it is necessary to locate a large number of sites in the area; this sometimes leads to the discovery of new sites. Even where sites are previously known, often only the briefest descriptions have been published of ruins on the beach or underwater, and the simple survey needed to establish the magnitude of relative sea level change may have original archaeological value in its own right.

In 1967, 1968 and 1969 surveys were conducted on the coasts of the Peloponnese and south-west Turkey, and a total of 69 sites was studied. In spite of the excellent general archaeological publications on the region (Waterhouse & Hope Simpson, 1961; Hope Simpson, 1965; Bean, 1966; Bean & Cook, 1952; 1957; Newton, 1863; Stark, 1956), and the detailed charts and more specific archaeological reports, it was quite difficult to locate some sites, while others were almost inaccessible. In many cases large areas of ruins were noted both on shore and in the water, but it is beyond the scope of the present study to attempt detailed archaeological surveys. It therefore seems desirable to reproduce the sketch-maps of the sites visited, both to substantiate the exact nature of the evidence used to derive sea levels, and as an aid to archaeologists who may be able to deduce from them those sites which merit more professional study or excavation.

The geological and geophysical results of the survey have been published in interim form (Flemming, 1968*a* & *b*), and a fuller analysis is given by Flemming (1972). In the present paper the archaeological observations will be presented, followed by a summary of the mathematical techniques used to separate local earth movements from eustatic sea level changes. Methods for deducing sea levels from archaeological remains near the shore are given by Flemming (1969).

METHODS

Sites visited are shown in Figures 1 and 2. In most cases surveying methods were extremely primitive. Sites were located either from published literature, or by following up local stories, or by searching the coast with polarizing glasses to cut out the dazzle from the water, or on a topographic basis, that is, by deducing likely sites for harbours from the topography of the coast and the offshore zone. The following sites were surveyed in some detail: Elaphonisos (Harding, Cadogan & Howell, 1969); Gythion, with a sextant and tapes; Asopus, with tapes and rules. The remainder were sketched with the aid of pacing, rules, estimation of distances by eye, and measurements from photographs. In some cases the large-scale Admiralty charts provide a good basis for the outline of a site map. Depths were measured accurately by rule, where less than 3 m, and were measured by a diver's depth gauge or taken from the charts, where greater.

The date attributed to a structure from which a sea level is derived is taken from previously published observations, usually based on historical sources and pottery, modified where necessary by approximate judgements based on styles of masonry. Thus, an obviously medieval structure may be the best indicator of sea level changes at a site where the principal archaeological interest is focussed on a much earlier period. Except at Elaphonisos, where the underwater site was fully surveyed in 1968 (Harding,

Figure 1. Archaeological sites in the Peloponnese studied in 1967 and 1968.

Cadogan & Howell, 1969), no special attempt has been made to obtain dates from pottery or artifacts in connection with determinations of sea levels. Thus, errors in dating are probably of the order of 200–500 years, while errors in estimation of vertical displacement are of the order of 20 cm. In both cases the error is of the order of 10–20% of the value estimated. Probability estimates of the likelihood of different vertical displacements of sites were made for sites on the Turkish coast, as explained in a later section.

For each site visited the following data are given: ancient name or names, modern name or names, latitude and longitude measured on the largest-scale Admiralty chart, Admiralty chart number at the largest scale, classical references, and modern

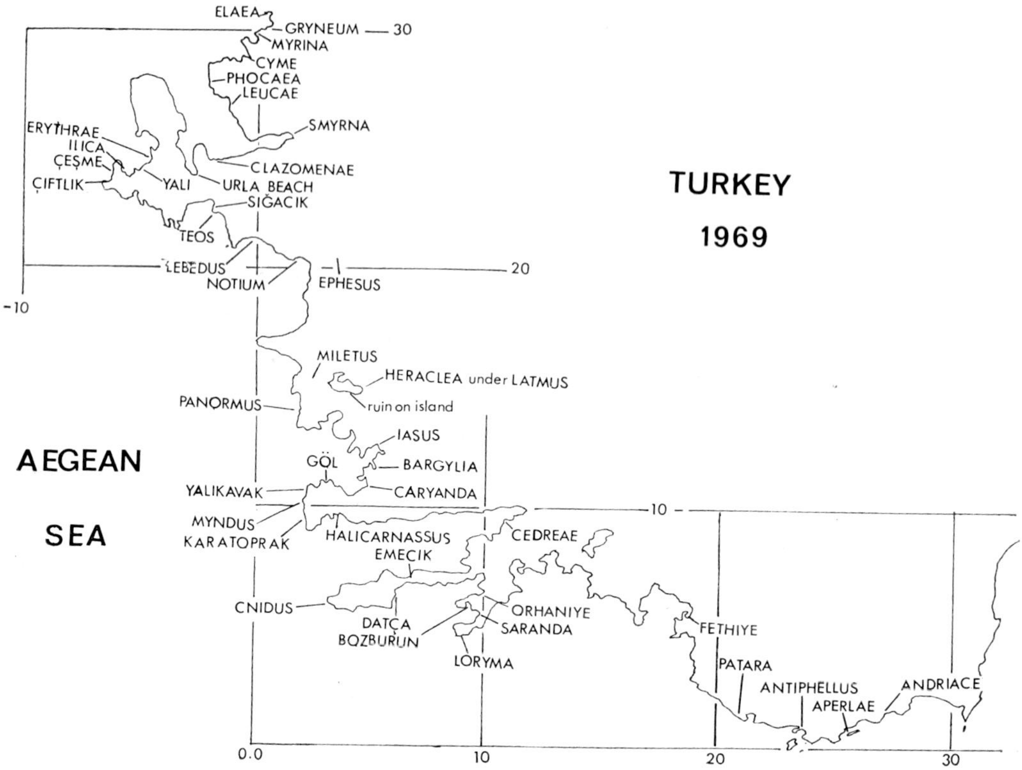

Figure 2. Archaeological sites in South-West Turkey studied in 1969.

archaeological references. This is followed by a brief summary of archaeological observations, with reference to sketch maps, and conclusions about relative sea level change.

SITES IN THE PELOPONNESE

LECHAEUM (near Corinth). 37° 56′ N., 22° 52′ E. Chart 1600.
Pausanias 2.1.5. Fowler & Stillwell (1932). Figure 3.

Areas of blocks on either side of the harbour entrance suggest training moles to prevent silting or provide additional shelter. Slight submergence of tower foundations along the coast to the west, combined with the relation of the water level to the walls of the entrance channel, suggest submergence of not more than 70 cm.

CENCHREAE. Kenchreai. 37° 52′ N., 23° 00′ E. Chart 1657.
Pausanias 2.1.5. Scranton & Ramage (1964), Hawthorne (1965).

The southern mole provides the base for the foundations of a number of buildings and interconnecting tanks, all of which are submerged. In particular, a cross wall supports a flight of steps which begins beneath the water and descends 1 metre to the rubble. It is probable that there has been a relative change of level of up to 2 m.

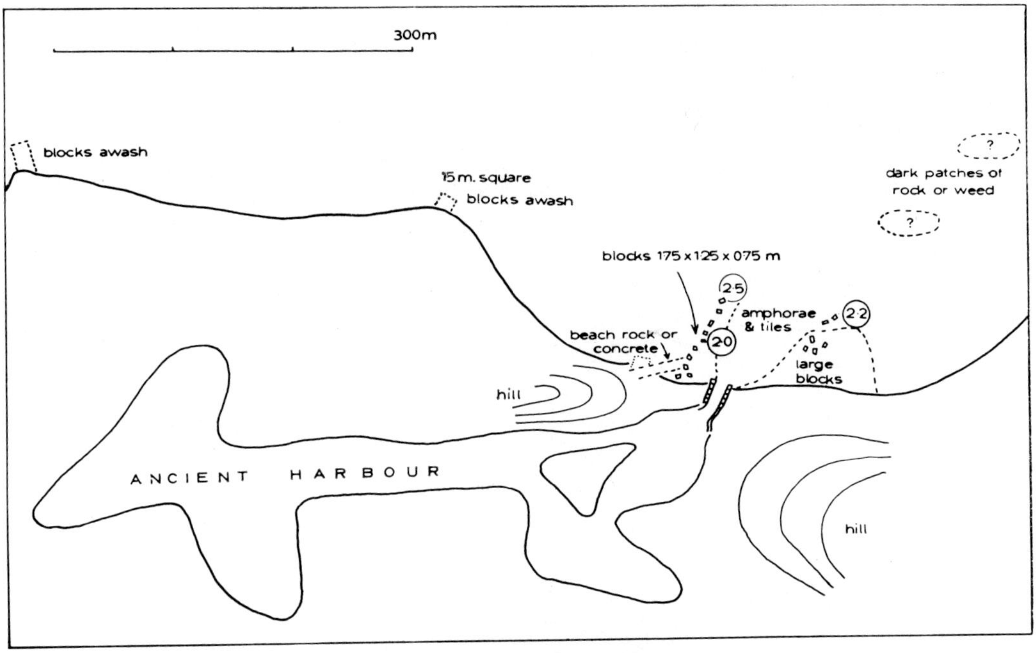

Figure 3. Lechaeum.

EPIDAURUS. Palia Epidavros. 37° 38′ N., 23° 09′ E. Chart 1657.
Pausanias 2.26–9. Figures 4 and 5.

There are foundations underwater on the north and south sides of the peninsula at the points marked A and B. At site A two sets of parallel ashlar walls project at right angles into the sea terminating at a depth of 2 m. At site B a considerable area of house walls is submerged, including a floor *in situ*, and the ashlar foundations of a larger structure. A gutter channel lined with tiles slopes to a depth of 2.5 m near the houses, and there are larger blocks of masonry 75 cm thick, with foundations in 3.0–3.5 m. The gutter must have been above water level when in use, but the thicker walls may have been built in the water as parts of dockside structures rather than houses. The most probable submergence is therefore 2.7 m.

METHANA. Vathi, near Methana. 37° 35′ N., 23° 20′ E. Chart 1518.
Pausanias 2.34.1.

On the west side of the Methana peninsula, south of the fishing harbour of Vathi, is a shallow bay backed by an acropolis heavily built over with large ashlar structures and some rougher stone and mortarwork. At the southern end of the bay a river debouches near a cliff, and there are walls in a depth of 1.0 m. All along the shore of the bay there are cut stones and rubble in the water to a depth of 2.0 m, but no foundations *in situ*. The few modern houses on the shore are partly undercut and collapsing into the water. There is indication of probable submergence by 1.0 m since the classical period.

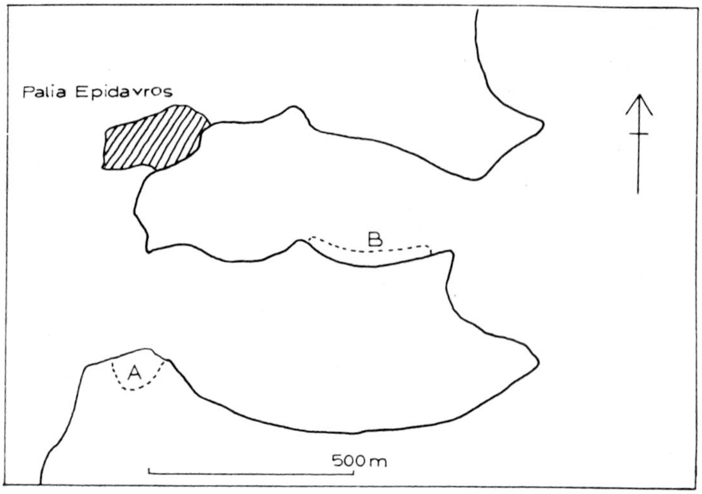

A

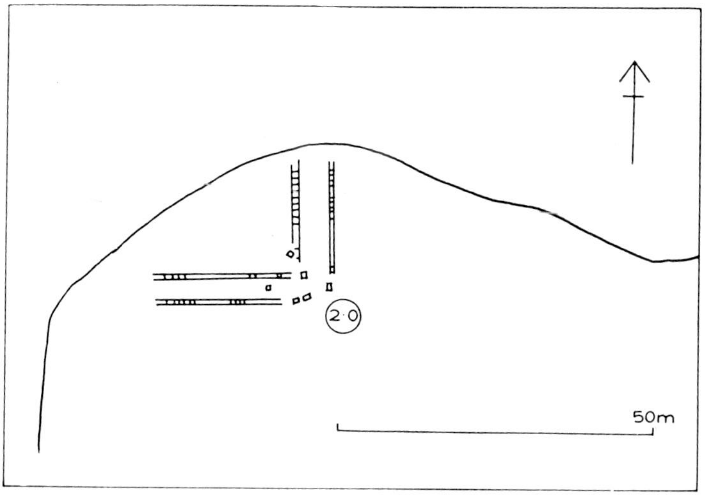

B

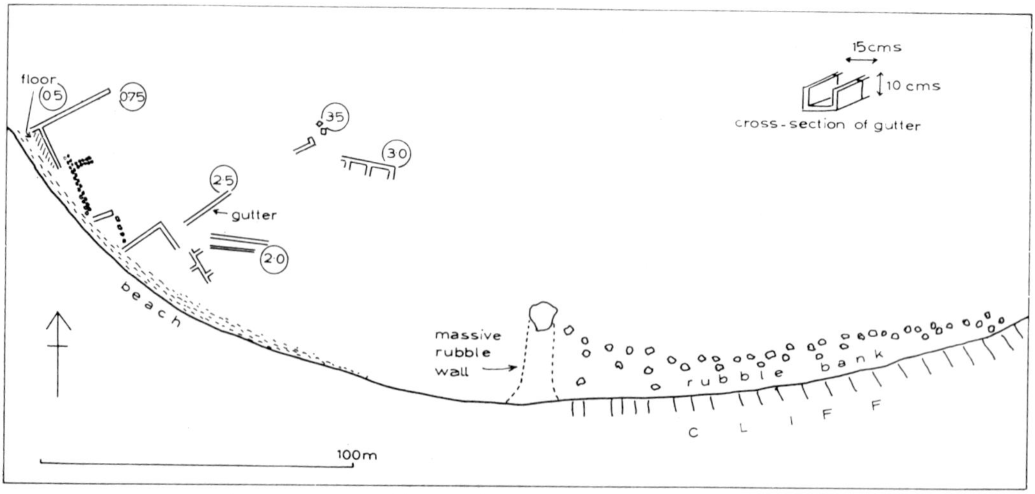

Figures 4, 5. Epidaurus.

HALIEIS. Porto Cheli. 37° 19′N., 23° 09′ E. Chart 1518.
Pausanias 2.36.1. Ervin (1967, 299 & pl. 88), Jameson (1969).

The ruins in the water on the south shore of the bay date from the fifth century B.C. to Byzantine times. There are further fragments of buildings and roads on the north side of the bay. There is extensive indication of submergence by about 5 m.

ASINE. Tolon. 37° 32′ N., 22° 53′ E. Chart 1518.
Pausanias. 2.36.4–5. Frödin and Persson (1938).

In the bay to the south of the headland on which the Mycenaean city is situated are alignments of stones cemented with coralline algae which are probably the remains of walls. The stones are unshaped, and the area enclosed by the wall closest to the shore is marked by Frödin and Persson as a harbour, though this seems unlikely, on account of its small size and shallowness. The supposed walls are on a rocky platform under 2 m of water, beyond which the loose rubble slope drops rapidly to 5 m. Immediately south of the platform is an area of pottery and small stones, and a submerged strip of beach rock. It is not possible to say with any certainty that the beach rock and the walls are of the same date, but there is indicative evidence for submergence by 2.0 m since the occupation of the Mycenaean site.

ZARAX. Limen Ierakas. 36° 47′ N., 23° 05′ E. Chart 712.
Pausanias 3.24.1. Figure 6.

Landward of the modern village the bay is very shallow, but seaward there is a deep harbour. Probably in ancient times the bay was less silted, and ships could off-load

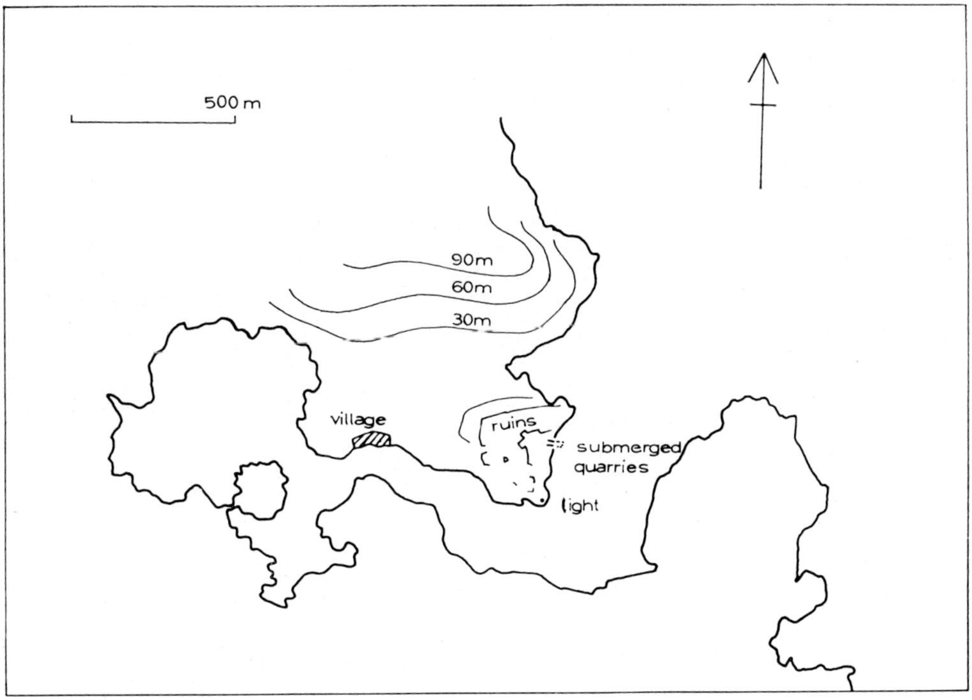

Figure 6. Zarax.

at the back of the bay. Towards the entrance the cliffs are so steep and high on both sides that landing would be almost impossible, especially on the south shore. Beneath the city walls the cliffs descend steep but not sheer, and there is no space for any construction of harbour works. There are, however, some signs of quarrying, and cut recesses suggesting a small landing-place, with cuttings and steps descending 3 m underwater.

MINOA. Monemvasia. 36° 41′ N., 23° 03′ E. Chart 712.
Pausanias 3.23.11. Figure 7.

One kilometre north of Monemvasia and visible from the road is an area of flat rock about 50 m square jutting into the sea and mostly submerged. There are some projections above the water, but most of the platform is awash, and the surface is quarried, with the marks of individual blocks having been removed. There are some depressions which could possibly be for foundations. The depth of water over the cuttings is 75 cm, indicating submergence of at least 1.0 m. Along the southern shore of the island of Monemvasia are numerous ruined houses and foundations, but none of these descends below sea level. An illustration of the city in the eighteenth century shows houses in this area.

Three kilometres north of Monemvasia are the ruins of Epidaurus Limera, on a rocky hill. On the beach below the city, between the mouth of the stream and the foot

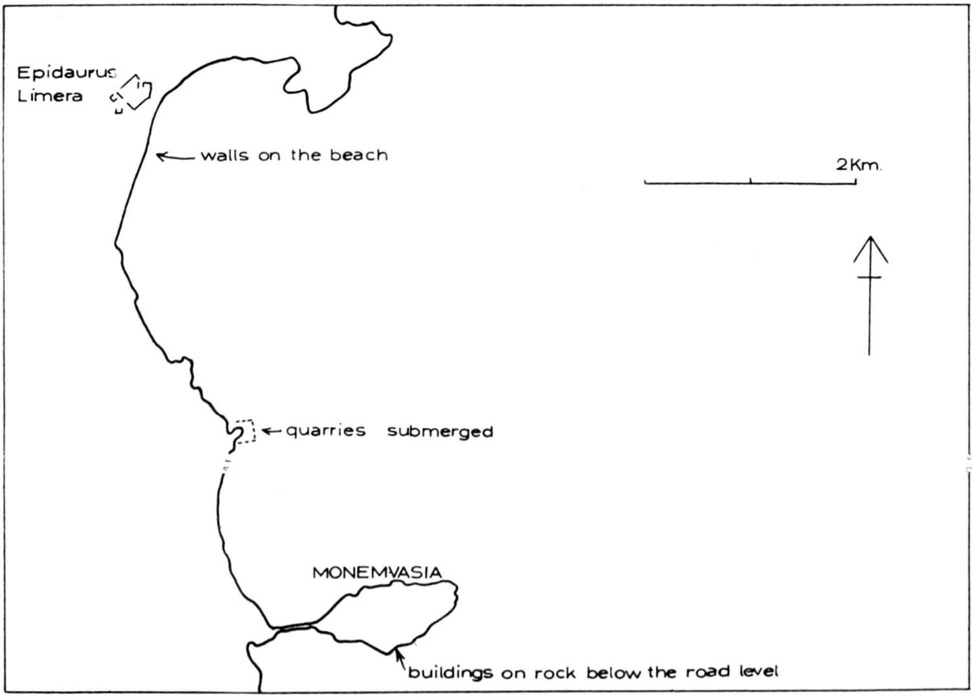

Figure 7. Monemvasia.

of the acropolis, there is a long wall foundation about 1 m above sea level. There were no walls found in the water, and no evidence was found from which a change of sea level could be deduced.

BOEAE. Neapolis. 36° 31′ N., 23° 02′ E. Chart 712.
Pausanias 3.22.11. Waterhouse & Hope Simpson (1961, 142–4).

About 1 km north of Neapolis, where the bathing beach terminates against the rocks, there are cuttings and quarries awash to a depth of 30 cm. At the mouth of the river by the site of ancient Boeae there is an extensive beach rock sloping to a depth of 5 m, indicating a continuous rise of sea level.

ONUGNATHUS. Elaphonisos, Pavlo Petri. 36° 28′ N., 22° 59′ E. Chart 712.
Pausanias 3.22.10. Strabo 8.5.1. Negris (1904), Waterhouse & Hope Simpson (1961, 145–8), Flemming (1968*b*), Harding, Cadogan & Howell (1969). Figure 8.

Obsidian chips and Bronze Age sherds have been found on the beach on either side of the Elaphonisos Strait for many years. In 1967 a search between the mainland shore and the islet of Pavlo Petri revealed an area of Helladic ruins 200 m by 300 m. In 1968 a full survey was made on which the present map is based. In several regions of the site foundations of houses extend out to but not beyond the 3.0 m isobath, suggesting a change of level of the order of 3.0 to 3.5 m. Elaphonisos Island was still connected to the mainland at the time of Pausanias (second century A.D.), and the Strait was still fordable in the seventeenth century.

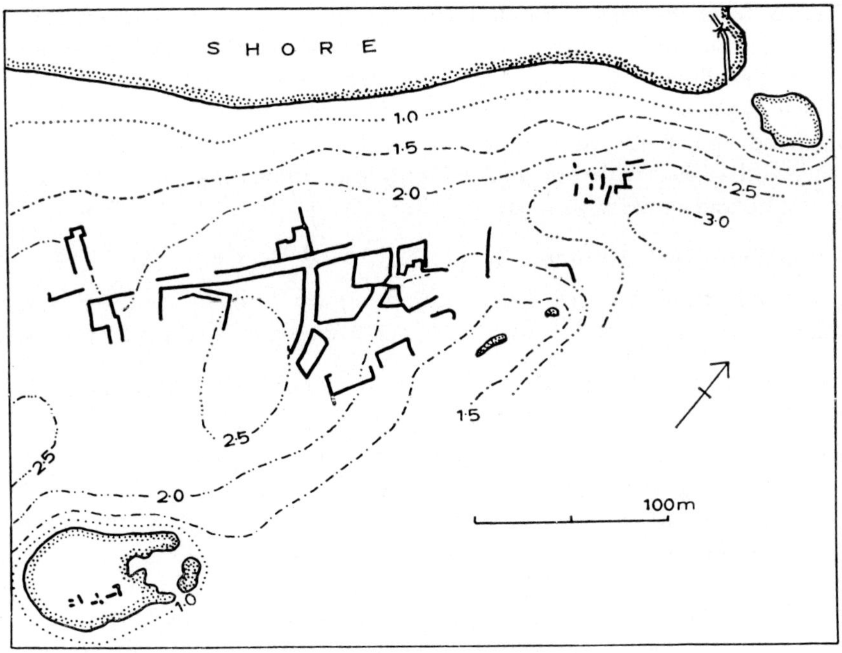

Figure 8. Pavlo Petri.

ARKHANGELOS (modern name). 36° 37′ N., 22° 53′ E. Chart 3372, 712.

On the north side of the rocky promontory about half way along its length are some small quarries submerged by 20 cm. In the village a number of capitals and columns have been found, but there are no harbour works.

ASOPUS. Plitra. 36° 41′ N., 22° 50′ E. Chart 3372, 712.
Pausanias 3.22.9. Figures 9 and 10.

The land site occupies a broad flat peninsula and there is no obvious harbour. The bay to the east is broad and open to the waves, and would only provide shelter from a northerly or easterly wind. Below the water level the promontory swings round to the south-east (see Fig. 9), so that if the sea had been lower the entrance to the bay would have been of less than half the present width. This submerged area of the promontory is covered in ruins of various ages.

At the southern limit of the submerged area is a network of long walls in lengths of 10–20 m, standing up to 1 m high, in a water depth of 3 m. They are of a primitive type, composed of unshaped stones and without mortar. The stones are odd in that they are well rounded from beach or stream action, and are quite white and not covered by marine growth. By analogy with Elaphonisos it is probable that these walls are of Helladic origin, indicating submergence of at least 3.0 m in 3,000 years.

The eastern limit of the submerged area is bordered by a rubble bank composed of stones similar to those in the walls already mentioned. Broken pottery is scattered among stones. It is not clear whether this bank was originally a mole or jetty, or whether it is simply the result of earlier walls having been destroyed by waves as the sea level rose and the stones being swept over the rock ledge into deeper water. A massive concrete pier projecting from the rubble mound and totally submerged suggests that it was a mole or jetty purposefully constructed. Nearer the shore there are areas of well preserved ashlar in shallow water, interspersed with rough walls of mortar, tiles and rubble. There are also tanks and an olive-press. Stretching seaward from the south-east corner of the headland and sheltered by the submerged area, there are large structures of mortar, tile, and stone, with one apsidal building, indicating submergence of 2.0 m since the late Roman or Byzantine period (Fig. 10).

ARAGORA (modern name). Kythera. 36° 13′ N., 23° 05′ E. Chart 1685, 712.

At the Minoan site of Aragora there does not appear to have been any change in sea level, though there is a possibility that there has been a slight relative drop of sea level.

POTAMOS (modern name). Antikythera. 35° 53′ N., 23° 17′ E. Chart 1685, 712.
Figure 11.

In spite of the apparent shelter provided by Ormos Potamos, the prevalence of northerly winds makes it insecure. It is probable that the ancient harbour was in the creek on the east side of the bay, immediately beneath the slope of the acropolis. The bar of large cobbles which rises 4 m above the level of the present stream mouth, the wave-cut notch at +3 m behind the bar, and the numerous solution notches in the cliff up to a height of 3 m on both sides of the creek, all indicate a relative drop in sea level. The most probable explanation is that the island, which is of volcanic nature, has been uplifted discontinuously, but repeatedly, with a notch formed at each standstill.

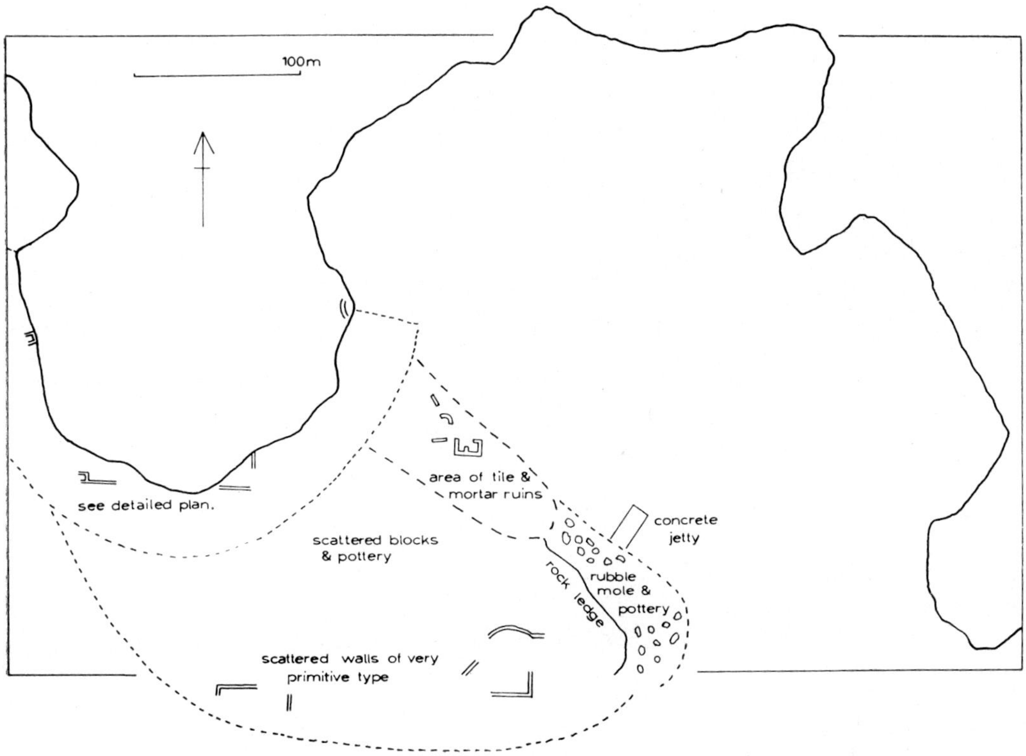

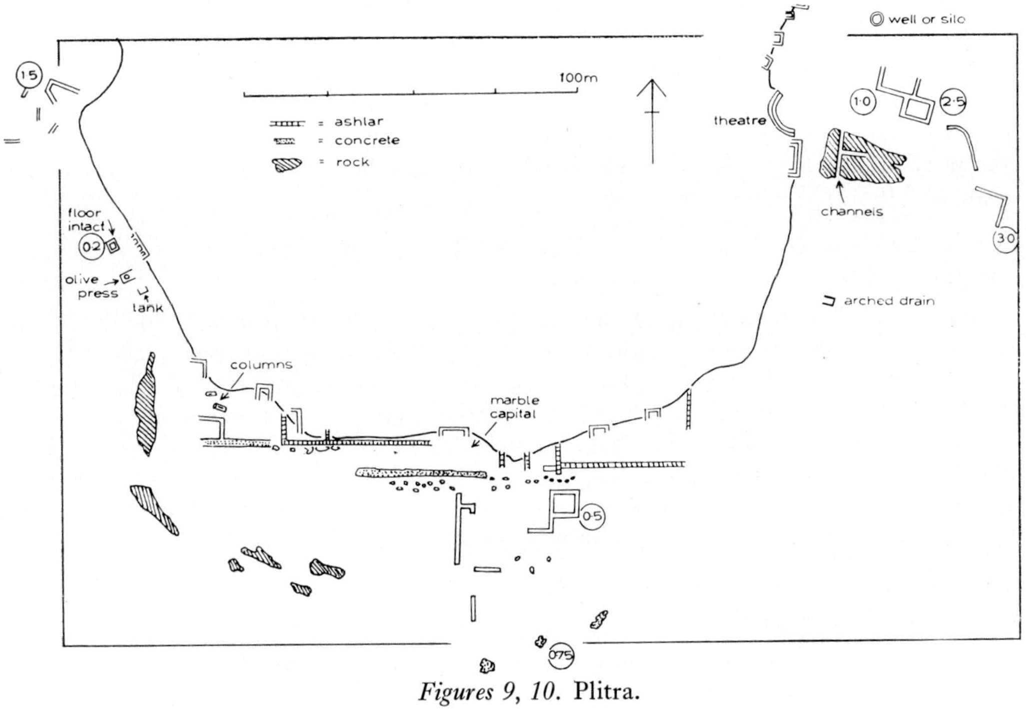

Figures 9, 10. Plitra.

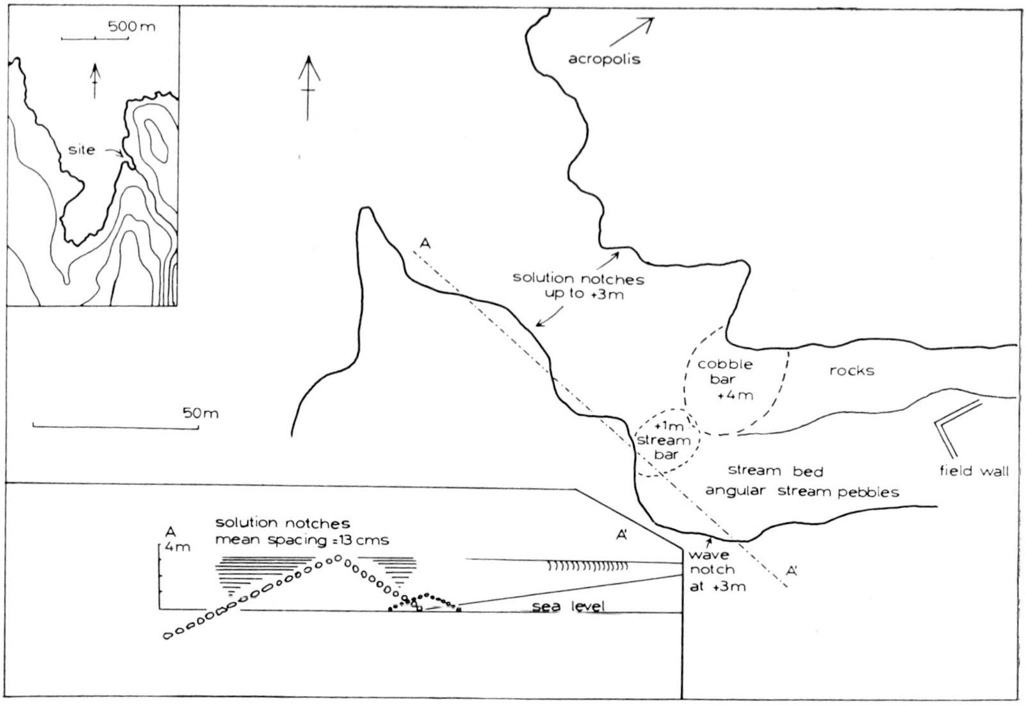

Figure 11. Ormos Potamos.

The spacing between the notches is about 13 cm on average. During the Flandrian transgression the rise of sea level would have been faster than the uplift of the island, but when the eustatic sea level approached its present level in about 3000 B.C. the continued uplift of the island would produce the notches. Thus there is evidence for uplift of 3.0 m in 5,000 years.

ACRIAE. Elea. 36° 44′ N., 22° 48′ E. Chart 3372.
Pausanias 3.22.4.

South of the bay containing the modern harbour of Elea is an area of shallow water and rocky outcrops of breccia, with fragments of pottery wedged in cracks. There is one rectangle of unsquared blocks, similar to those at Plitra, approximately 10 m square. North of the modern harbour, round a small headland, are a number of submerged patches of similar stones, quite distinct from the local rock, at depths of 2 to 4 m. While the purpose and nature of these features is unknown, they may have been solid towers or hollow dwellings which have collapsed. By analogy with Plitra there is evidence for submergence of 2 m in 3 millennia, but this is very approximate.

TRINASUS. Trinisi. 36° 47′ N., 22° 36′ E. Chart 3372.
Pausanias 3.22.3. Figures 12 and 13.

At the southern end of the long sandy bay south of the rocks known as Trinisi, is a medieval church with a domed roof almost completely buried in sand dunes and concealed by bushes and reeds. A wall of mortar, stones, and tiles emerges from the sand 3 m above water level, and continues about 0.5 m above the sand straight into the water for a distance of 10 m at a depth of 1.0 m. About 30 m to the north a similar wall extends into the sea, and the two are partly joined by a cross wall. A length of marble column-drum was found at water level. There is clear indication of submergence by 1.0 m.

The small bay opposite Trinisi rocks (Fig. 13) is almost filled with foundations in the water. The walls are of rough uncut stones and mortar, with some tiles, and are largely embedded in beach rock which is beginning to cover the structure. The remains appear to be those of a house or group of houses surrounding a yard. The deepest wall is in 1.0 m of water, indicating submergence of this amount.

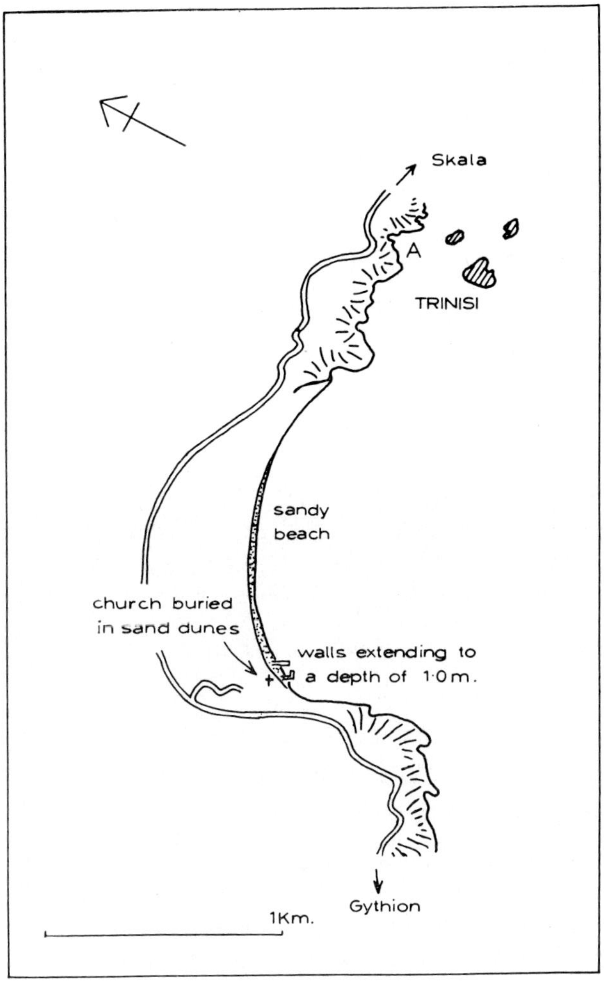

Figure 12. Trinisi.

A

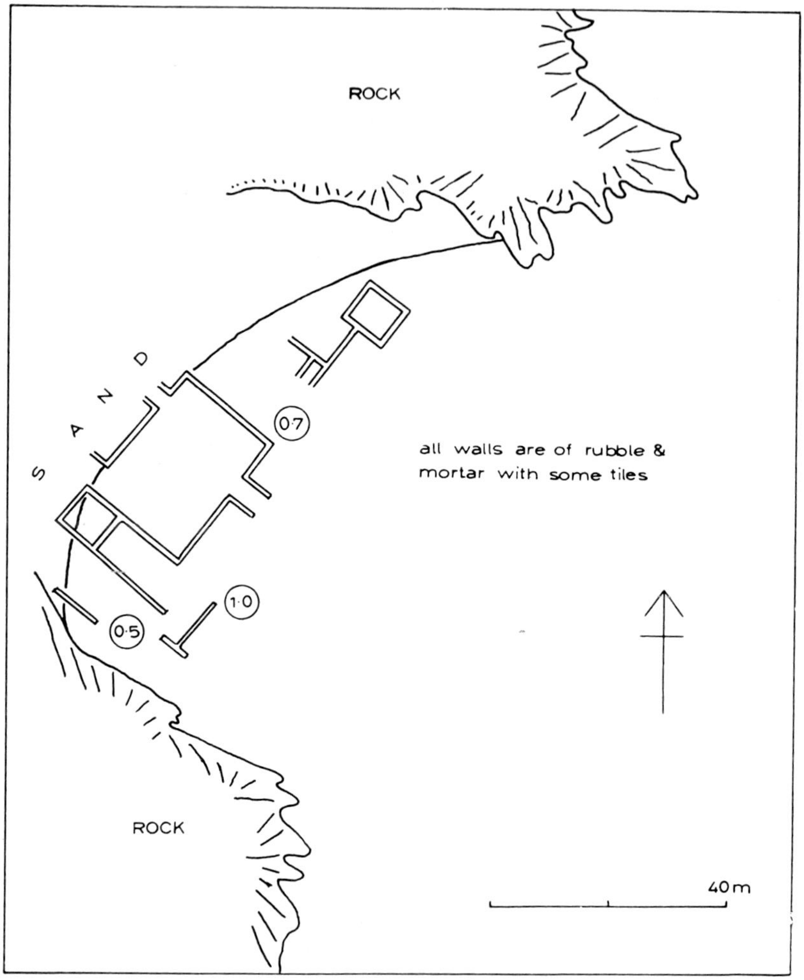

Figure 13. Trinisi.

GYTHEUM. Gythion. 36° 45′ N., 22° 34′ E. Chart 712.
Pausanias 3.21.6–22.2. Giannakopoulos (1966). Figure 14.

The ruins surveyed in the water are adjacent to recovered land at the northern side of the modern harbour. The fill used to reclaim the land from the sea has undoubtedly concealed a further extensive area of ruins. In the zone mapped were found the remains of a mole, a tiled tank, long walls of ashlar, house foundations, and chunks of mortar and tile construction. The deepest land structures are in 2.5 m, indicating submergence by this amount since late Roman times.

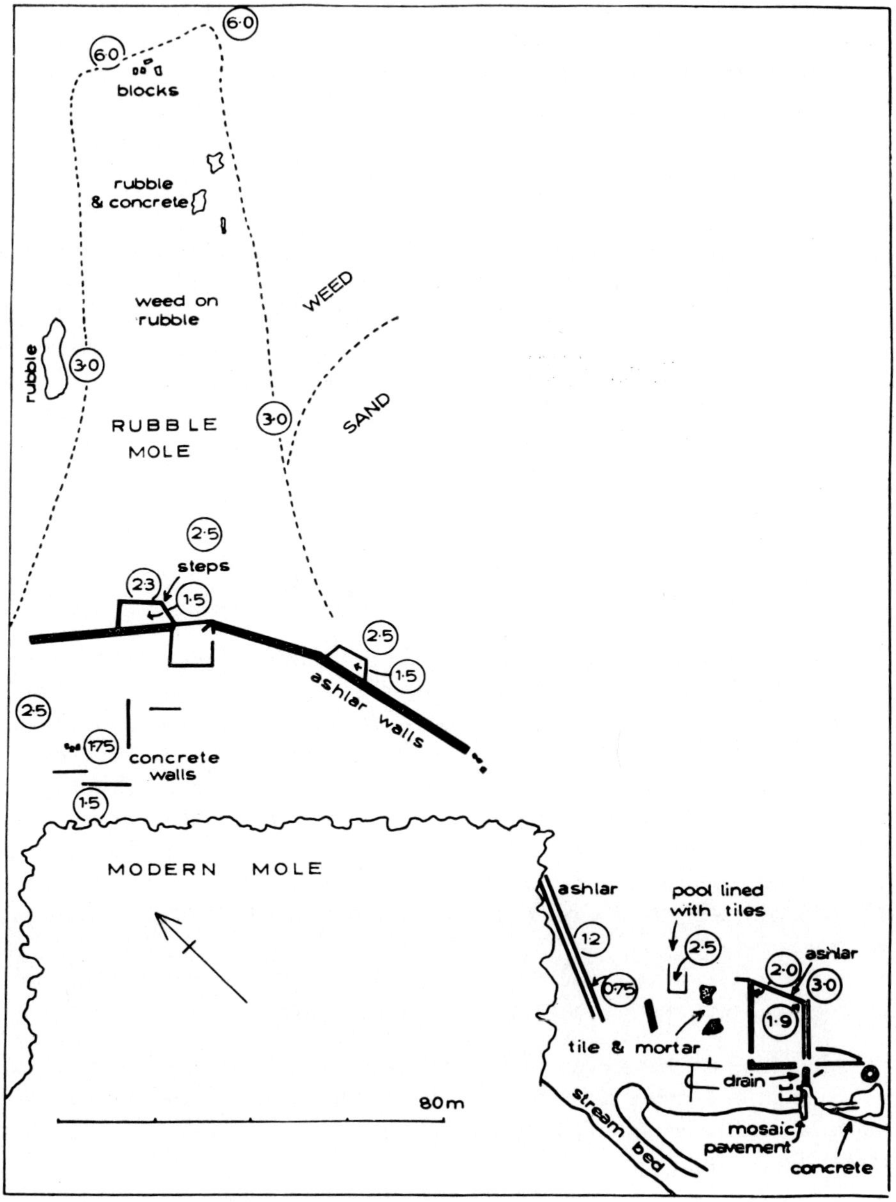

Figure 14. Gythion.

SKOUTARI (modern name). 36° 40′ N., 22° 30′ E. Chart 712.

There is an abandoned church on the beach. One hundred metres directly offshore from the church is a strip of rubble or broken wall in 3.5–4 m of water parallel to the shore. There are several squared blocks about 0.5 m square and one block of 1 × 0.5 × 0.3 m; also some blocks of mortar and tile work. It is not certain whether all this material is *in situ*; it could be the remains of a building which has collapsed owing to erosion, or the remains of a mole made out of debris of earlier buildings. The presence of the mortar and tile work suggests collapsed structures *in situ*, indicating submergence of about 3.5 m.

TEUTHRONE. Kotronas. 36° 37′ N., 22° 29′ E. Chart 3372.
Pausanias 3.21.7,25.4. Figure 15.

On the mainland west of the spit are a number of buildings broken open by the sea, and some rock-cuttings awash. There is a bath with marble floor, and a round room. These buildings date from about the third century A.D. (Delivorias, personal communication). Where the spit joins the island there is a fortified wall and a medieval church. The wall continues into the water, and large fragments of stone and mortar and tile work continue south-eastward for 75 m at a distance of 5–10 m from the shore. The area of rubble extends slightly eastwards, and the deepest masonry is in 3.0 m of water, although the average depth by the wall is only 1.0 m. There is clear indication of submergence by 1.0 m.

TAENARUM. Limen Asomatos. 36° 24′ N., 22° 29′ E. Chart 712.
Pausanias 3.14.2,25.4–8. Figure 16.

Rock cuttings, a road cut in rock, and a number of buildings on shore date from the third century B.C. Foundations and cuttings near the shore are awash by 25 cm, and a well or cistern cut in the rock descends 0.8 m below sea level and has been broken into at the bottom by the waves. A line of ashlar blocks extends across the eastern inlet, joining the eastern side where the rock-cut road comes to the shore. This suggests the foundation of a quay. There has been some submergence, but there must have been at least 1 m of water beside the quay; therefore the total submergence is probably only 1 m. In both bays there is a great quantity of pottery on the sea floor, and this is possibly associated with votive offerings connected with the temple on the median headland.

TIGANI (modern name). 36° 32′ N., 22° 22′ E. Chart 1685.

This headland is near the town of Mezzapos, the ancient Messa (Pausanias 3.25.10). There are ancient and medieval structures on the headland. On the north side of the peninsula in a small bay below the fortress there is a broken tomb awash, indicating submergence by 0.5 m.

PEPHNUS. Selenitsa. 36° 49′ N., 22° 18′ E. Chart 1685.
Pausanias 3.26.2.

On the north side of the modern harbour there is an area of submerged walls and rock-cut basins. Adjoining the mole are four small basins with walls 50 cm high, with longer walls leading seawards in water 1.0 m deep. A quarry with its floor awash marks the end of the walls. The small basins may have been salt-pans, but the function of the remaining walls is uncertain. There has been slight submergence, but less than 1 m.

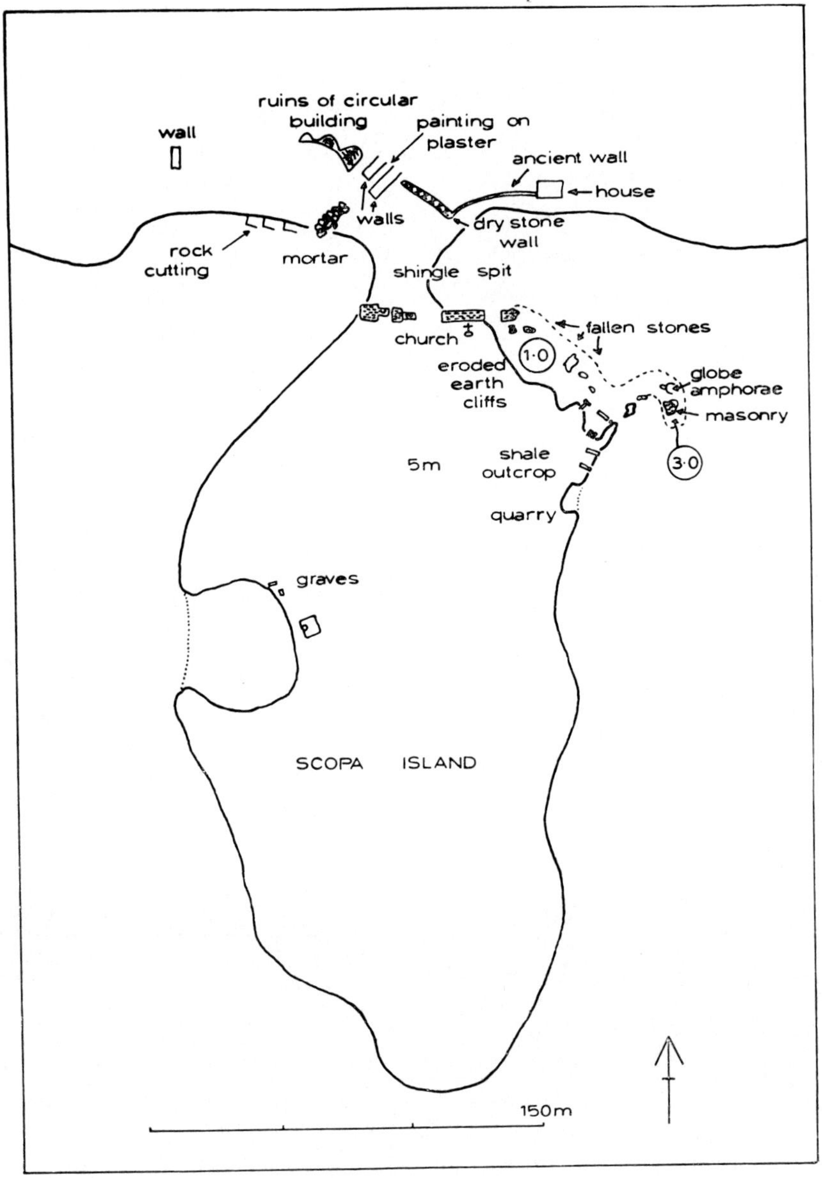

Figure 15. Kotronas.

LEUCTRA. Stoupa. 36° 50′ N., 22° 16′ E. Chart 1685.
Pausanias 3.26.4.

The bay north of the headland of Stoupa contains a central basin about 10 m deep, bordered on both sides by extensive areas 1–2 m deep from which project the apparent remains of two rubble moles. Rock cuttings and walls occur in the shallower areas to depths of 2 m, indicating submergence of the order of 2.5 m.

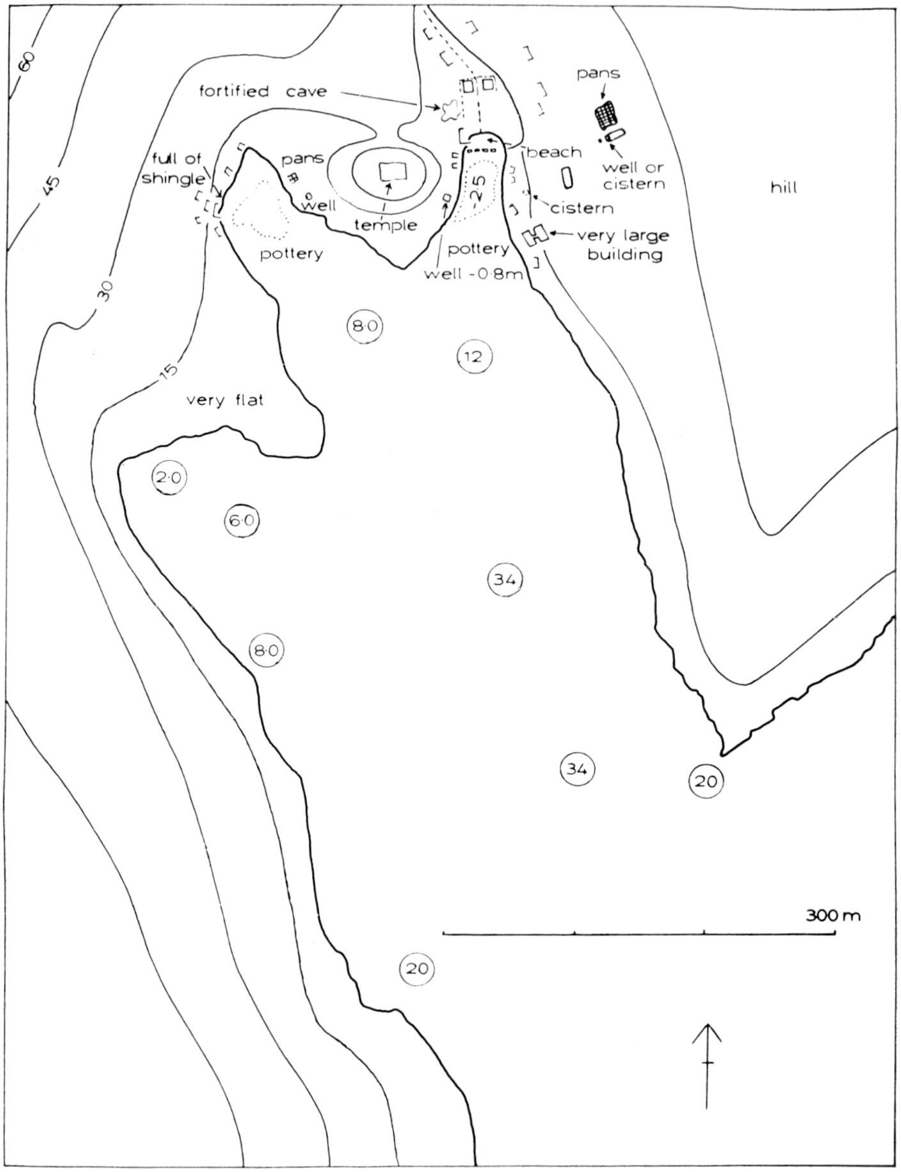

Figure 16. Taenarum.

CARDAMYLE. Kardamyli. 36° 52′ N., 22° 15′ E. Chart 1685. Pausanias 3.26.7.

In the bay north-west of the modern mole there is a rectangular structure of roughly squared masonry, supporting one course of well cut blocks. It appears to be a base of a tower, but is not solid, and there is water within the walls. There is an iron ring on the outer face at the shoreward end, where the water is 1.0 m deep, and the structure has obviously been used as a landing-place, though it was probably not built as such. The outer end is on a rock ledge, from which the depth descends to 3.0 m. There appears to have been a submergence of 1.0 m.

CORONE. Petalidi. 36° 57′ N., 21° 56′ E. Chart 719.
Pausanias 4.34.4. Hope Simpson (1966, 124).

Search of the bay, both inside and outside the modern breakwater, revealed no underwater structures, although there were many pottery fragments and parts of globe amphorae. The ribs of striated rock overlain by beds of beach rock gave the impression of artificiality, but in all cases turned out to be natural geological features. It was not possible to deduce a change of sea level from this site.

ASINE. Koroni. 36° 48′ N., 21° 58′ E. Chart 719.
Pausanias 4.34.9–12. Figure 17.

No remains of the classical period were found in the water. The first defensive wall surrounding the peninsula was built by the Venetians in the thirteenth century A.D., and was subsequently enlarged and modified by the Turks. On the north side of the peninsula there are some walls on the beach extending into 25 cm of water, and below the steep ramparts several thick walls *in situ* standing in 1.0 m of water, and a square building which once had a domed roof lined with plaster standing in 50 cm. The rough stone and mortarwork suggests a chapel outside the fortifications. There is clear indication of submergence by slightly more than 1.0 m.

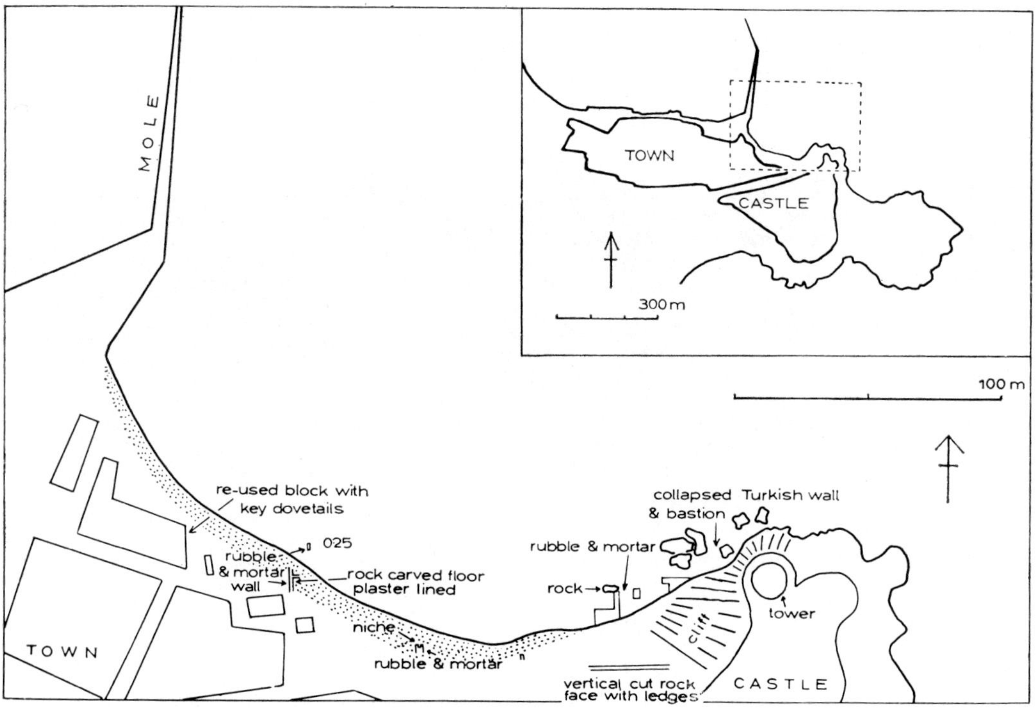

Figure 17. Asine.

METHONE. Methoni. 36° 49′ N., 21° 42′ E. Chart 719.
Pausanias 4.35. Higgins (1966). Figure 18.

There were classical and Byzantine fortresses on this site, and the headland was fortified by the Venetians in A.D. 1206. Further defences were added by successive Turkish and Venetian occupiers. The octagonal tower at the south end was built by the Turks in the sixteenth century. The jetty to the east was built in 1870, and contains

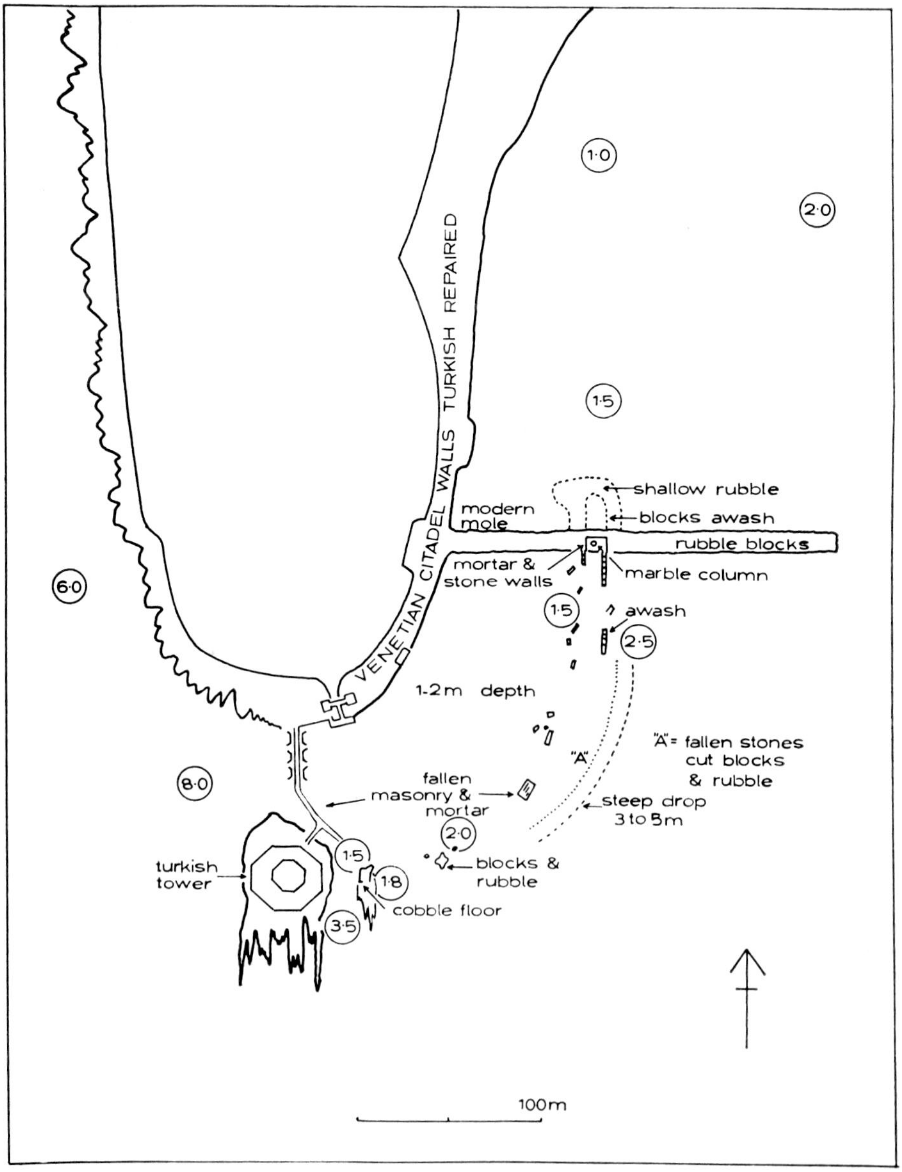

Figure 18. Methone.

an erect marble column which is embedded in masonry which predates the jetty. The area of rubble to the north of the column and the submerged walls to the south of it suggest that the column was a bollard in an earlier jetty. The submerged walls form a continuous arc from the column to the octagonal tower, always about 100 m from the shore, but the area enclosed was not searched in detail. The masonry remains in the arc suggest a double-faced wall with several towers built on the brink of a slope. It seems probable that the fortress extended out to this limit at one period, but that relative submergence forced the defences back to the present circumference. The remains of the wall were probably later modified to form a jetty or landing-place, and the marble column was embedded in the earlier structure to make a mooring-stone. This in its turn was incorporated in the modern jetty. The cobble floor on the rock next to the octagonal tower is just awash, and the walls leading south from the marble column are laid in 1.0 m of water, while other masonry lies broken in 2.0 m. The ruins in the water might be part of a Byzantine fortress, but are more probably of medieval origin, and indicate submergence by about 1.5 m.

PYLUS AD CORYPHASIUM. Navarino Bay. 36° 57′ N., 21° 30′ E. Chart 211.
Pausanias 4.36.1–2. Thucydides IV. 26–41. Grundy (1896). Figure 19.

The ancient city of Pylus was on the hill to the north of the Strait of Sykia at the entrance to the Bay of Navarino, and a small harbour was located just inside the mouth of the Strait, later called Zounchio by the Venetians. A number of walls of various periods break off on the steep shore at the water's edge, but in the back of the bay

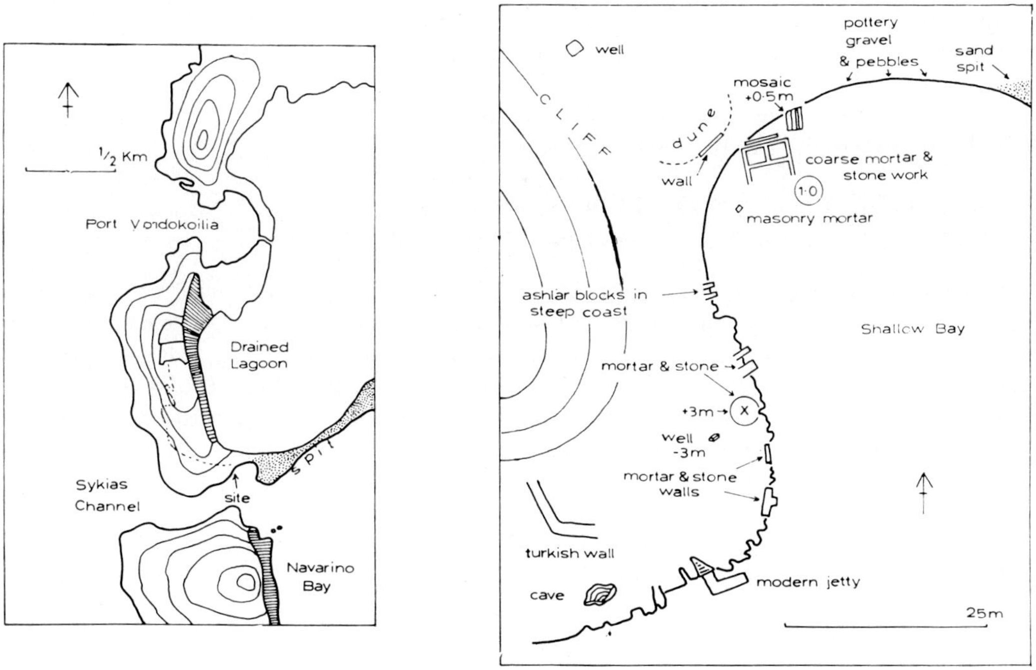

Figure 19. Pylus.

there are the foundations of a house or villa *in situ* in 1.0 m, and some scattered masonry in slightly deeper water. There is indication of submergence by 1.5 m since the Roman period.

PHEA. Katakolon. 37° 38′ N., 21° 20′ E. Chart 270.
Strabo 8.3.12. Hall (1969).

This site has been surveyed underwater by J. Hall of the University of Miami, who has reported that there are walls *in situ* to depths of several metres and that a slump fault appears to cross the underwater site. Investigation in 1968 failed to locate these structures, but a number of ancient quarries with individual block cuttings along the shore indicated submergence by 1.0 m.

TURKISH COAST

Introduction

Conduct of the survey of ruins on the coast between Izmir and Cnidus was greatly assisted by previous discussion with D. J. Blackman, and we wish to express extreme indebtedness for the opportunity of consulting unpublished field notes.

ELAEA. Kazıkbağları, near Reşadiye. 38° 57′ N., 27° 03′ E. Chart 1617.
Strabo 13.1.67. Schuchhardt (1912, 111–13), Bean (1966, 112–14).

Bean (1966) described the early Hellenistic mole, and shows a photograph of it projecting from mud and shallow water. Blackman (personal communication) reports that the mole is at least 204 m long, with keyed blocks bevelled on the outer edge to protect the joints. The mole rises 20–40 centimetres above water level, but the top courses are missing. There is very little evidence for a change of level here, though there may have been slight submergence.

CYME. Namurt Limanı. 38° 46′ N., 26° 56′ E. Chart 1617.
Strabo 13.3.3,6. Schäfer & Schläger (1962), Bean (1966, 103–6).

Schäfer and Schläger (1962) describe a mole of carefully laid blocks, of which the earliest period of construction may be of the sixth century B.C., with additions continuing into Roman Imperial times. From a cross-section of this mole they calculate (p. 53) that the water level change has been 1.60 m, on the assumption that cut blocks were not laid in regular courses below water level. Blackman (personal communication) considers that this assumption is not valid, and that therefore the relative change of the level is of the order of only 1.0 m.

(OLD) SMYRNA. Bayraklı, near Izmir. 38° 28′ N., 27° 11′ E. Charts 1645, 1522.
Strabo 14.1.37. Cook (1959).

Cook (1959, 9) discovered that the level of remains of the beginning of the second millennium B.C. was 3 m below sea level. The level of the fifth century B.C. was depressed relative to sea level by 1–2 m (1959, 11).

CLAZOMENAE. Urla Iskelesi, Karantina Adası. 38° 22′ N., 26° 48′ E. Chart 1645. Pausanias 7.3.9. Strabo 14.1.36. Cook (1954), Bean (1966, 128–36). Figure 20.

The Hellenistic causeway to the island is parallel to the modern road, and extends 20 m in width out from the road on the western side beneath the water. The causeway appears to have consisted of a rubble bank upon which were laid facing-walls of stone and mortarwork, including some large well-cut blocks. The western facing-wall is now flush with the water level, with blocks projecting in places, and the area within the walls which would have included the road surface is submerged by 1–2 m. The road surface is missing, and the height of this above the rubble or the base of the facing-wall is uncertain. It seems probable that the rubble bank originally reached to or above

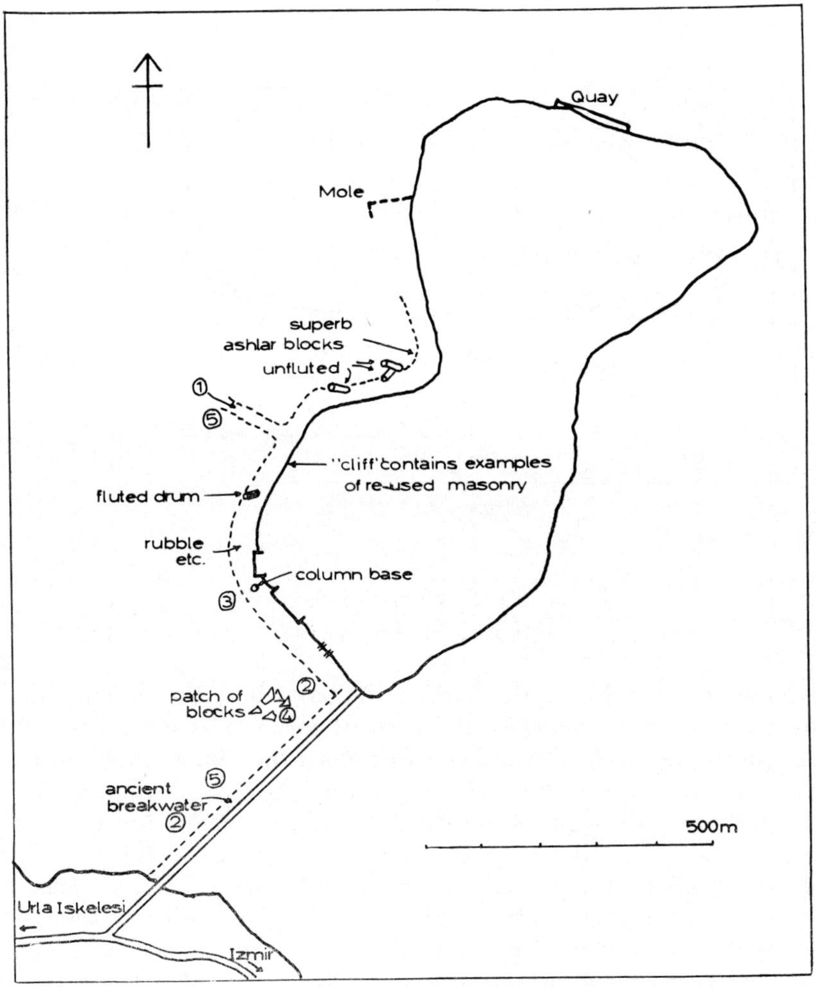

Figure 20. Clazomenae.

the water level, and that submergence has therefore been of the order of 1.0 m. The south and west sides of the island are fringed with rubble and cut blocks, including several column-drums, but no detectable foundations *in situ*. Two rubble moles project westwards, with their upper surfaces submerged by 1–2 m in a total water depth of 5 m. The southern mole has a very flat top and straight sloping sides, suggesting that its original form has been preserved.

URLA BEACH (modern name). 38° 19′ N., 26° 41′ E. Chart 1645. Figure 21.

An old road on the beach parallels the modern one for a distance of 1 km at Urla Beach. The road surface of roughly-cut blocks is awash by 20–25 cm, and broken by the waves in many places. There are two bridges spanning small stream beds, with their piers partly in the sea and partly embedded in the sand of the beach. The road appears to be several hundred years old, and to have been submerged by about 0.5 m since its construction.

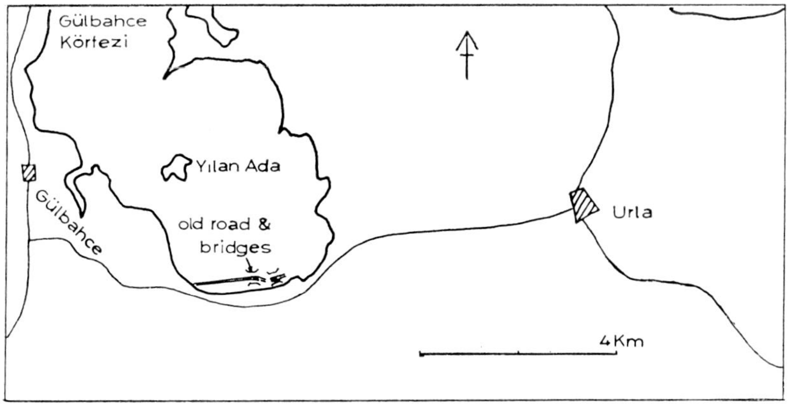

Figure 21. Urla Beach.

ERYTHRAE. Ildır. 38° 23′ N., 26° 30′ E. Chart 1645.
Strabo 14.1.31. Weber (1901), Roebuck (1959, 14–15), Bean (1966, 153–9). Figures 22 and 23.

The harbour was probably in the back of the bay where the stream enters the sea. There are some walls in the marshes, and a small mole 5 m broad just breaks the water on the south side of the stream mouth. Further along the shore on the south side of the bay there are cart ruts in the solid rock, now awash, and some beach rock in a depth of 1.5 m. Where the road through the present town of Ildır comes down to the sea there is an extensive area of ruins in the water. The modern track which continues round the headland to the north-west is partially protected with rows of uncut stones, but nevertheless is awash in places, showing evidence of continuing submergence. On the shore below the circular tower there are a number of house-foundations between the track and the sea. The most modern foundations have a floor level only 20 cm above the water, and appear to have been abandoned within this century. Below this layer, and extending

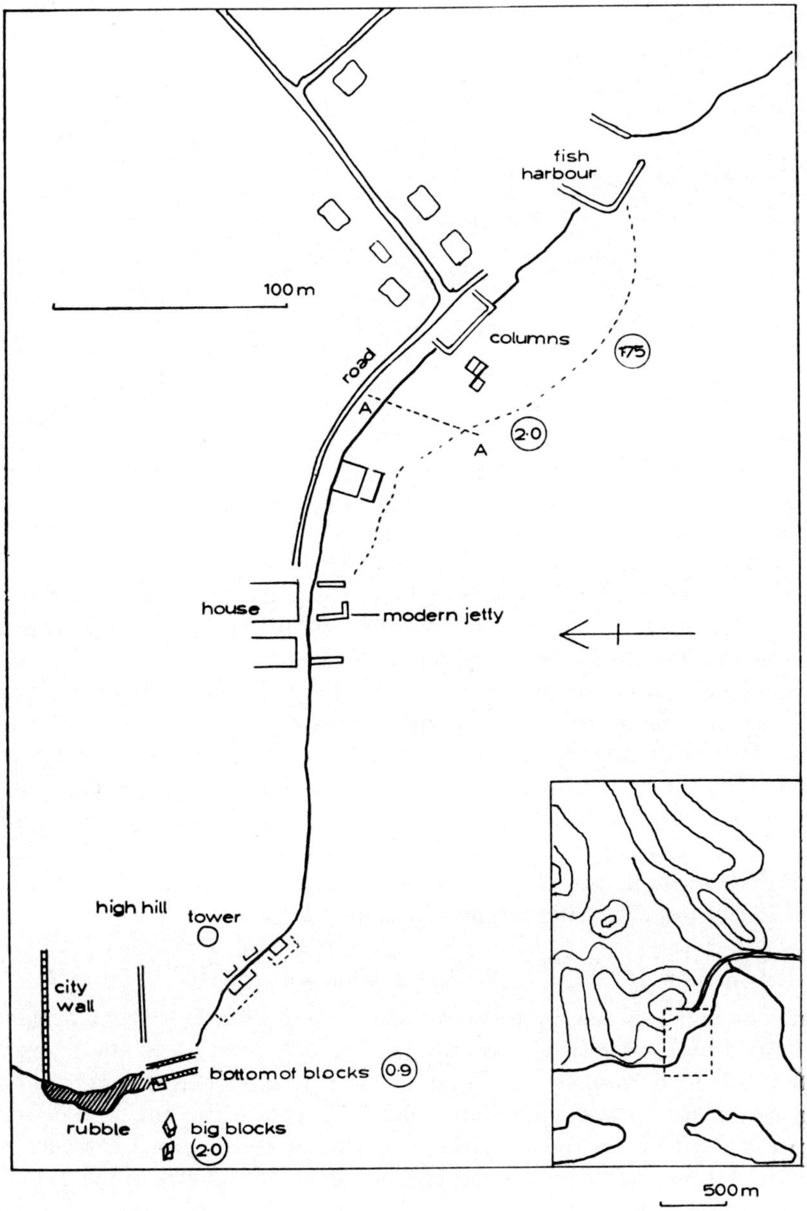

Figure 22. Ildır.

several metres further seawards, are foundations with floors at −20 cm, probably several centuries old. Further round the headland to the north are two parallel lines of cut blocks in 90 cm of water, suggesting an ancient roadway or possibly the seaward wall of the ancient city.

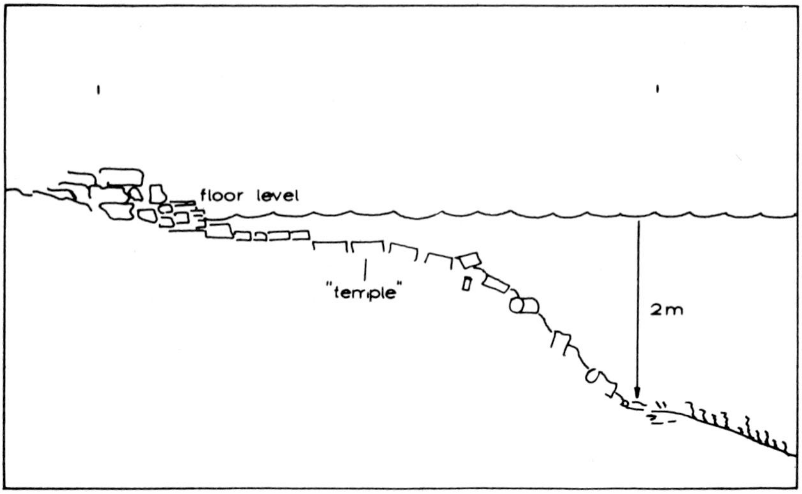

Figure 23. Ildır. Profile A–A.

The section AA on Figure 22 is represented in Figure 23. There is a floor at a depth of 0.5 m, which is broken apart at the brink of a rubble slope which descends to 2.0 m. At the landward edge there are the remains of houses with floor levels just above the present water level. In the shallow water and on the rubble slope there are the remains of a building of some importance: six column-drums of 80 cm diameter and 1 m length; four column-drums of 30 cm diameter; two column-drums of 40 cm diameter, with a bevelled lip at one end; one column-drum of 40 cm diameter and 60 cm length, bevelled at both ends; several carved architraves, fluted column-bases, and rectangular blocks carved with raised keys or recessed slots. The floor level of this building was certainly raised above the ground, and this, combined with the road or wall-foundation now at a depth of 90 cm, indicates submergence of about 1.5 m.

YALI (modern name). 38° 20′ N., 26° 26′ E. Charts 1645, 1087. Figure 24.

No charts or maps of this piece of the coast are accurate. The name given for the group of houses may be only of local use, as it is not marked on the maps. The track through the village terminates at the shore at a point where a field-wall protects a projecting area of land from immediate erosion. Beyond this wall, in a depth of 0.5 m, is an area of several house-walls of rough mortar and more square stones with some ashlar. There has probably been submergence by half a metre since medieval times.

ILICA (modern name). 38° 20′ N., 26° 22′ E. Chart 1645.
Cook (1959, 21), Bean (1966, 159). Figure 25.

Bean (1966) states that there was no ancient city at Ilıca, but that it was the site of important thermal springs. Cook (1959) dates pottery on the site to the fourth century B.C. An unsurfaced road leads from the village along the east shore of Kalem Burun, where there are a number of small jetties for holiday boats. From the tip of the headland

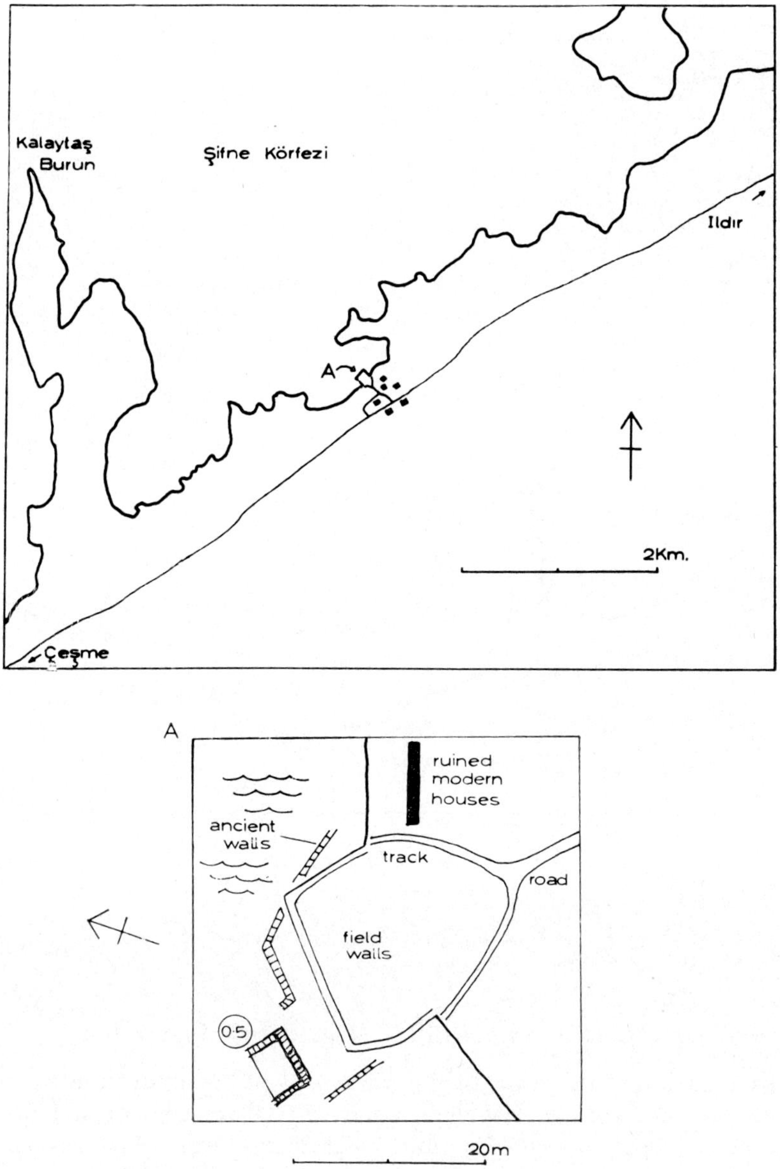

Figure 24. Yalı.

a submerged mole of rubble and cut blocks stretches eastwards, containing many pottery fragments in the interstices. After a gap of 100 m a similar mound extends further on the same alignment, the crest being submerged by half a metre. The water depth at the end of this breakwater is 2–3 m. It is possible that there has been submergence of about 0.5 m.

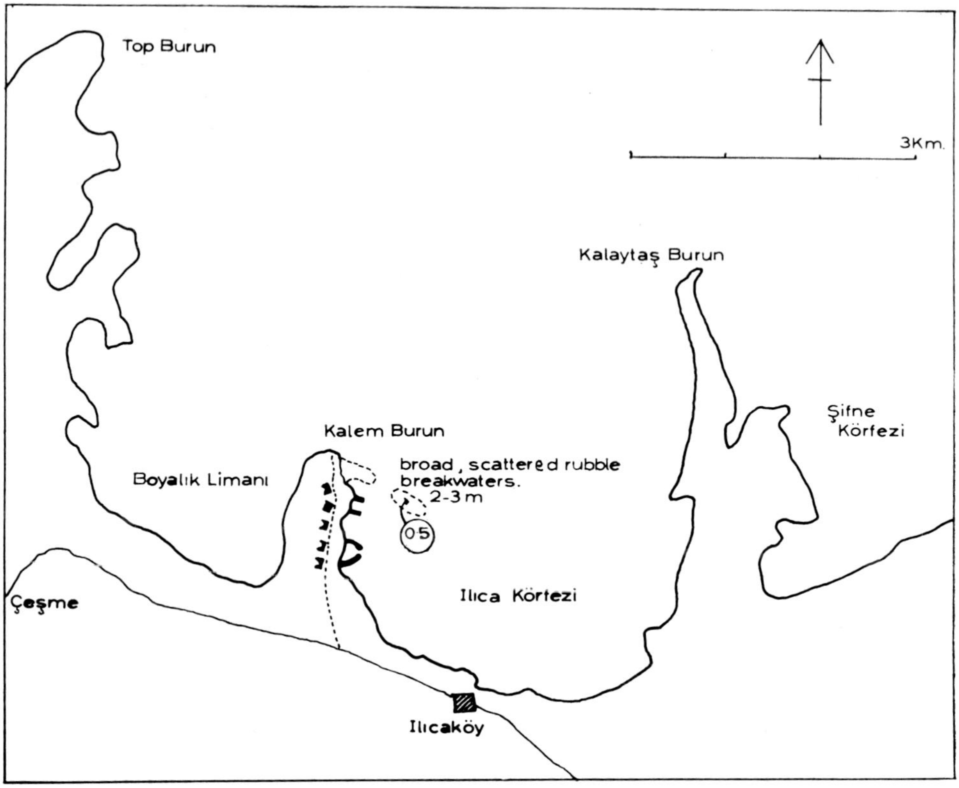

Figure 25. Ilıca.

ÇEŞME (modern name). 38° 20′ N., 26° 19′ E. Chart 1617. Figure 26.

Where the road leaves the town to the south and passes round the bay, there is a broad expanse of mud-flats and shallow water. A wall of cement and uncut stones forms a square of side 20 m, extending into water 20 cm deep. This does not appear to have been a fish-tank or salt-pan, and therefore indicates a submergence of about 20 cm in the last few hundred years.

ÇIFTLIK (modern name). 38° 18′ N., 26° 17′ E. Chart 1645. Figure 27.

The village of Çiftlik is partly abandoned. South of the jetty, field- and garden-walls project into the sea and are being broken by the waves. North of the jetty, a field- or house-wall stretches towards the river mouth in a depth of 20 cm of water. The jetty extends 50 m seawards and consists of walls of cement and uncut stones infilled with gravel. The ends of the walls are broken, and the sea is washing out the gravel. Beyond this there are the remains of a much older mole almost completely destroyed by the sea. There is clear evidence of continuing submergence, with a change of about 10 cm in the last hundred years.

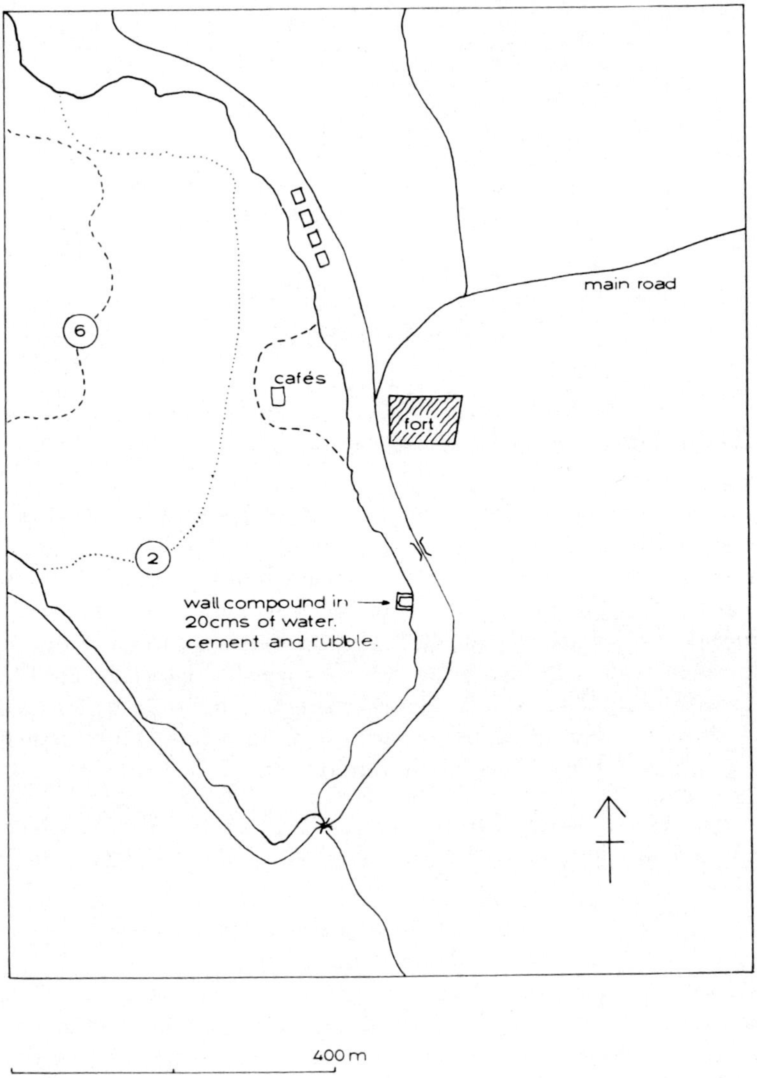

Figure 26. Cesmc.

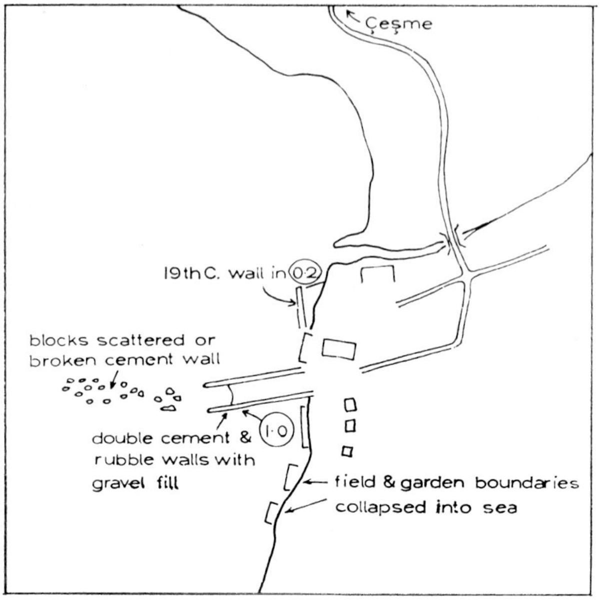

Figure 27. Çiftlik.

TEOS (northern harbour). Sığacık. 38° 12′ N., 26° 48′ E. Chart 1606.
Strabo 14.1.29–30. Béquignon & Laumonier (1925, pl. VII), Bean (1966, 142). Figure 28.

This bay was the northern harbour of Teos. A pathway at the level of the modern quay extends round the walls of the fortress, set with small mooring-rings. A submerged mole consisting of two small walls of ashlar projects into the bay from the seawardmost point of the castle. The difference of level between the modern and ancient jetty surfaces is 80 cm. Another wall of ashlar projects from the western corner of the present quay. These structures indicate a change of 50–80 cm since the classical period. In the mud-flat south-west of the quay there is a disused road, which would be covered by the sea if the level rose only a few centimetres in an onshore wind. This suggests a relative submergence of about 10 cm in the last hundred years.

TEOS (southern harbour). South of Sığacık. 38° 11′ N., 26° 48′ E. Chart 1645.
Strabo 14.1.29–30. Béquignon & Laumonier (1925), Bean (1966, 140–2 & pl. 21). Figure 29.

The walls of the Hellenistic city extend down to a quay protected by a spit of rock and sand at the river mouth. At its western end the quay has subsided completely into the water, but at its eastern end the facing, upper surface, and mooring-stones appear to be *in situ*. The mooring-stones are separated from one another by 3 m, and the centre of the mooring-hole is 20 cm above the present waterline, while the lower edge of the stones is awash. A section of ashlar wall continues to the end of the spit, and breaks off into the water. Rocks projecting from the water on the outer side of the spit give the appearance of masonry, but are all bedrock. If we assume that the centre of

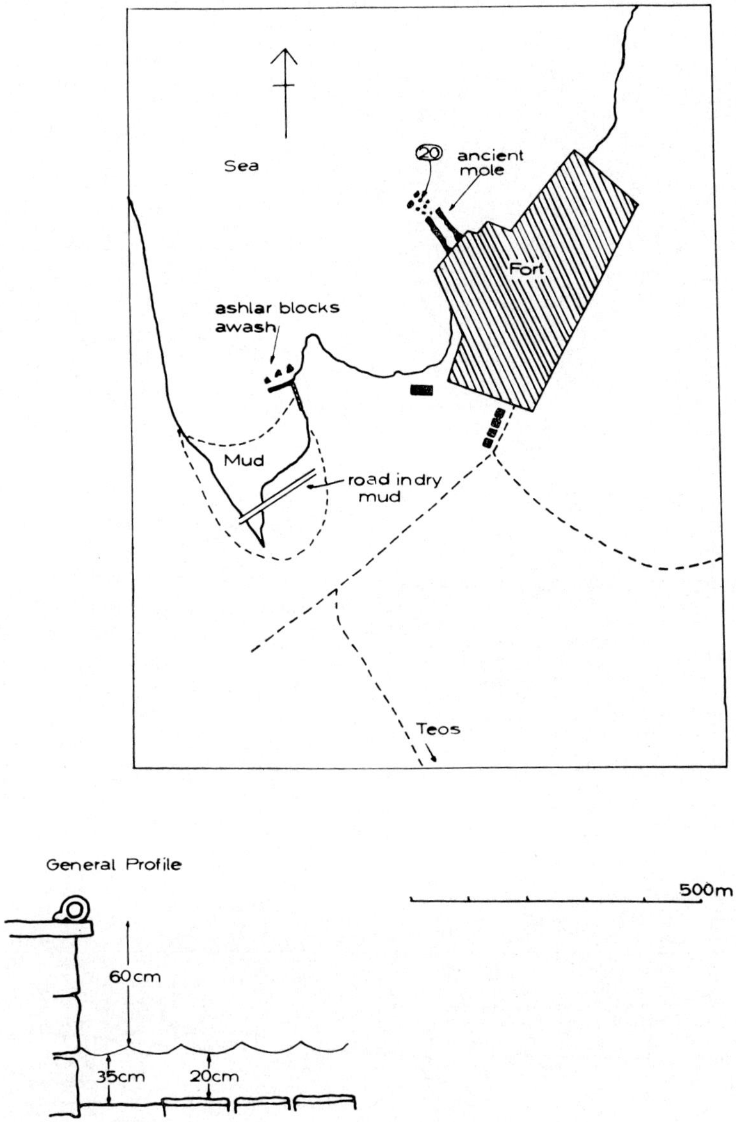

Figure 28. Sığacık.

the mooring-rings was originally 1.0 m above the water (compare Leptis Magna: Bartoccini and Zanelli, 1958), the relative change of level has been 80 cm.

Lebedus. Kısık. 38° 05′ N., 26° 59′ E. Chart 1645.
Bean (1966, 151–3).

The circumference of the peninsula was searched, but no signs were found from which possible changes of sea level could be deduced.

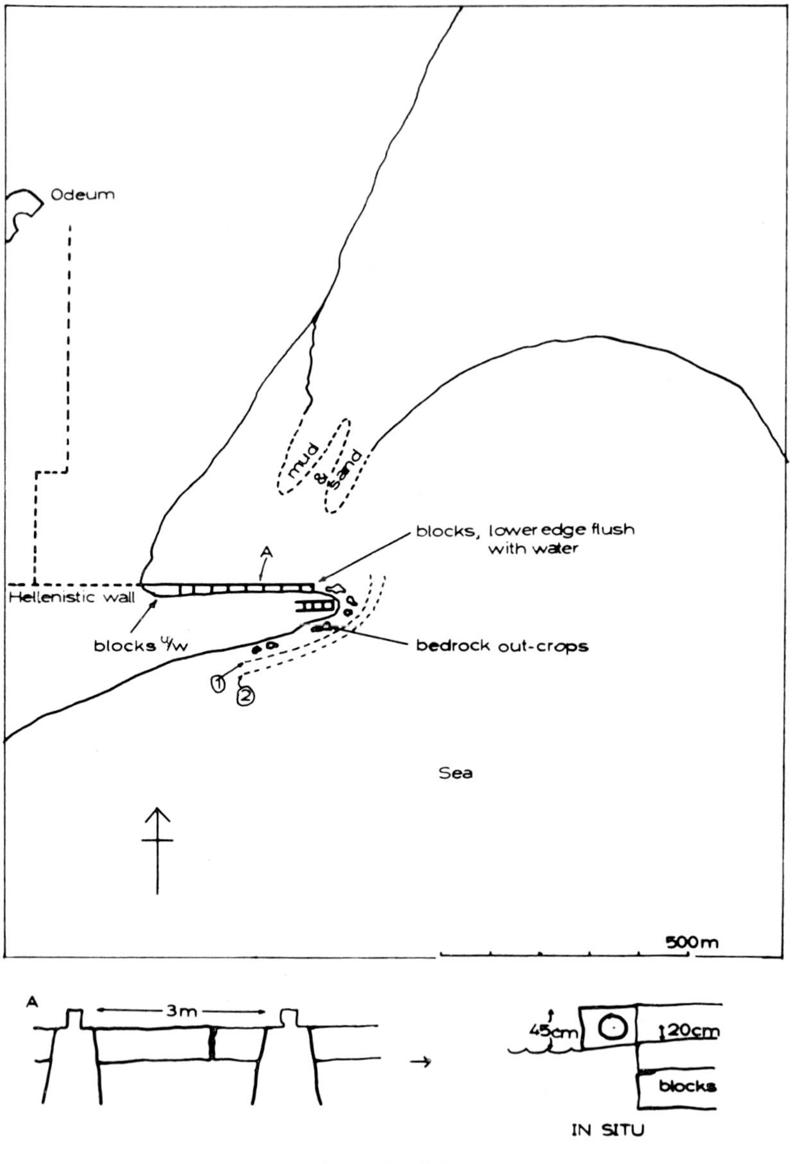

Figure 29. Teos.

NOTIUM. Near Ahmetbeyli. 38° 00′ N., 27° 13′ E. Chart 3346.
Demangel & Laumonier (1923), Bean (1966, 188–90). Figure 30.

The city of Notium is on the summit of the hill on the east side of the valley overlooking the sea. There are steep cliffs and no ruins on the shore. The temple of Claros is 1 km inland in the alluvial river plain; it has, since its construction, been overwhelmed by about 5 m of sediment so that the foundations are at least 1 m below the summer

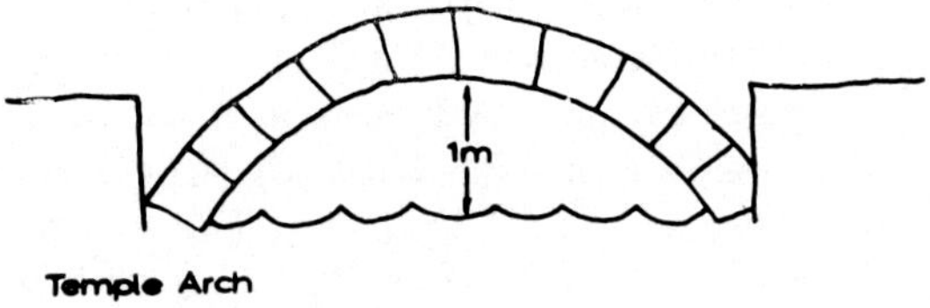

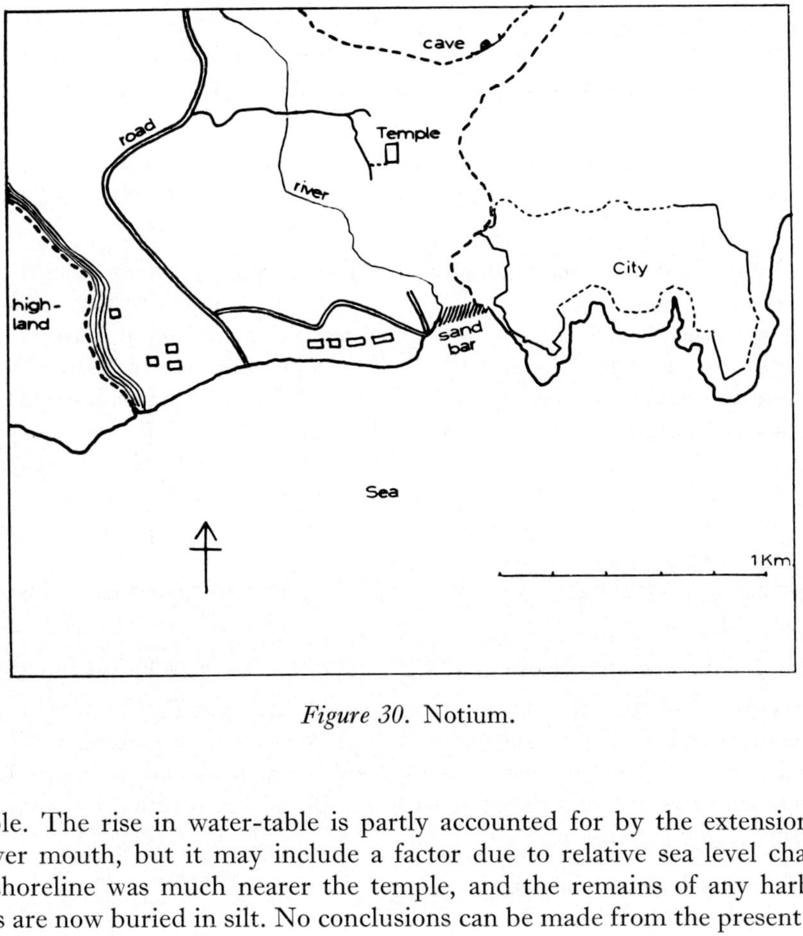

Figure 30. Notium.

water-table. The rise in water-table is partly accounted for by the extension seaward of the river mouth, but it may include a factor due to relative sea level change. The original shoreline was much nearer the temple, and the remains of any harbour constructions are now buried in silt. No conclusions can be made from the present evidence.

EPHESUS. Near Selçuk. 37° 56′ N., 27° 20′ E. Chart 3346.
Pliny, *N. H.* XXXVI. 95. Hogarth (1908), Bammer (1965), Bean (1966, 160–84).

The city of Ephesus is now 7 km from the sea, and the harbour is completely silted up. The principal religious site was the temple of Artemis; it has also been covered by silt, and its foundations are below the modern water-table. Bammer (1965, 126) states that the foundation of the eighth-century B.C. temple lies only 0.6 m above the present sea level. In contrast, the late classical temple was built 2.74 m above present sea level. From this evidence Bammer argues a rapid rise of sea level in the intervening period. While this is not totally impossible, it is probable that the earlier building has indeed been submerged relative to present sea level by $\frac{1}{2}$–1 m, and that the later building was constructed higher for purely architectural reasons. The present level of the water-table is not the same as sea level, owing to the distance from the sea.

MILETUS. Balat. 37° 32′ N., 27° 18′ E. Chart 1546.
Strabo 14.1.6. von Gerkan (1935), Kleiner (1966), Bean (1966, 219–30).

Miletus is now 4 miles from the sea, though it was originally a port. von Gerkan (1935) states that the relative rise of sea level has been 1.5 m since Greco-Roman times. Kleiner (1966) reports Mycenaean levels at and slightly below the ground water level. The change of level since Mycenaean times would probably be more than that since Greco-Roman times.

HERACLEIA UNDER LATMUS. Kapıkırı. 37° 30′ N., 27° 33′ E. Chart 1546.
Strabo 14.1.8. Leake (1824, 237–9), Bean & Cook (1957, 138–40), Bean (1966, 252–8). Figure 31.

Heracleia under Latmus was originally on the sea coast in a deep inlet, but the silt from the Maeander has closed the entrance and formed a lake. At the moment it is not possible to deduce relative changes of level from this site, on account of variations in level of the lake, and the absence of levelling from the lake to the sea. There are ashlar walls in the water between the main city and the island, although these do not appear to link the island to the city circuit. The much later walls on the island itself do not descend below water level. North of the island, on the side of a rock outcrop projecting from the water, is a Carian-type rock-cut grave with its floor at a depth of 1.45 m. Around the necropolis headland there are at least seven graves submerged to depths of 1.45–1.5 m. Erosion marks and encrustations of dried algae on rocks showed that the spring or winter water level was 60–70 cm higher than that observed in the summer.

GHIOURKERI ISLAND (modern name). 37° 29′ N., 27° 31′ E. Chart 1546. Figure 32.

The island is about 100 m from the south shore of Lake Bafa, opposite Heracleia under Latmus. Between the mainland and the island are two parallel walls in 1.5 m of water, and an arch with the centre of the vault only 37 cm above the water. These ruins, which are presumably associated with the Byzantine fortified monastery on the island, are immersed by at least 1.7 m.

PANORMUS. Kovala Limanı. 37° 24′ N., 27° 15′ E. Chart 1546.
Pausanias 5.7.5. Newton (1863). Figure 33.

There was an important temple at Didyma by the sixth century B.C., and the vast temple of Apollo which can still be seen was started in 332 B.C. The pilgrims arrived at the temple by way of the harbour at Panormus and thence along a ceremonial road 6 km in length. About 80 m from the shore the top of a column-drum 2 m in diameter and 2 m in length projects from the water. Two other drums lie nearby on their sides. These materials were probably abandoned at some stage during the construction of

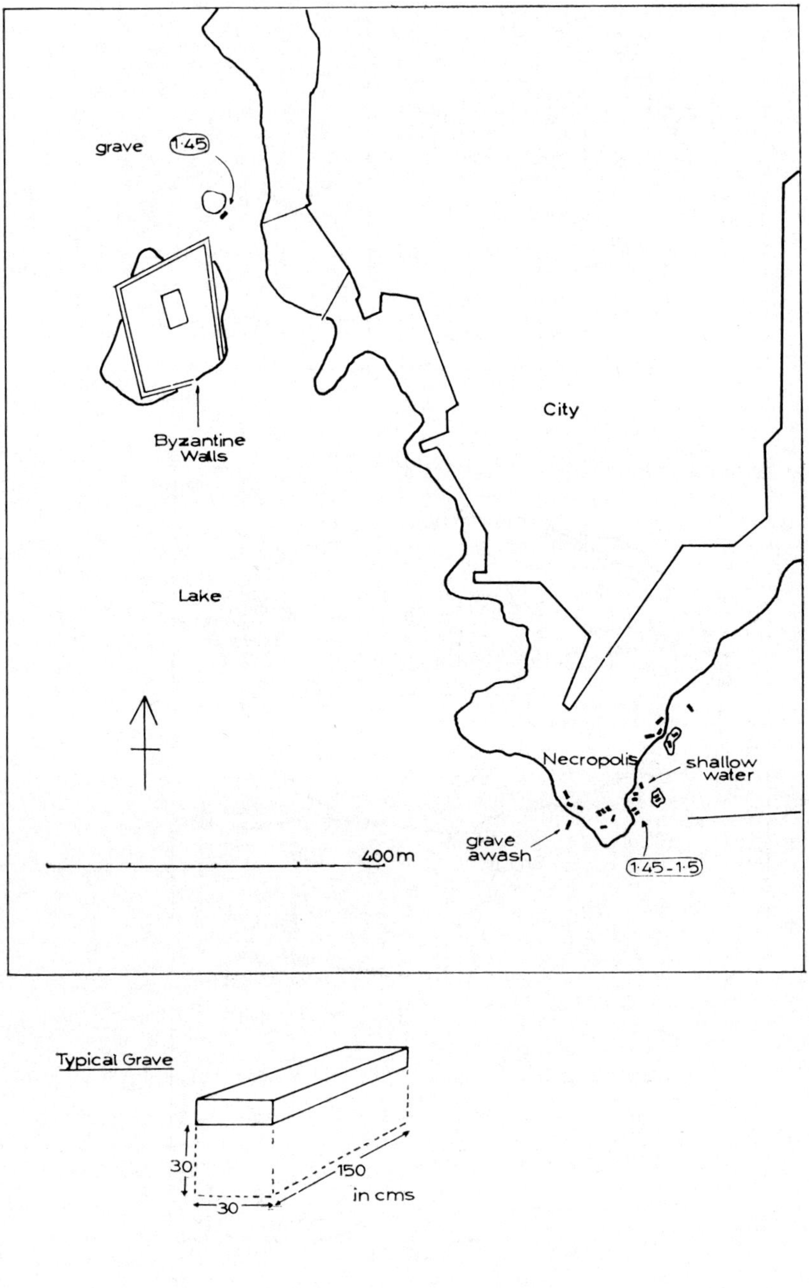

Figure 31. Heracleia under Latmus.

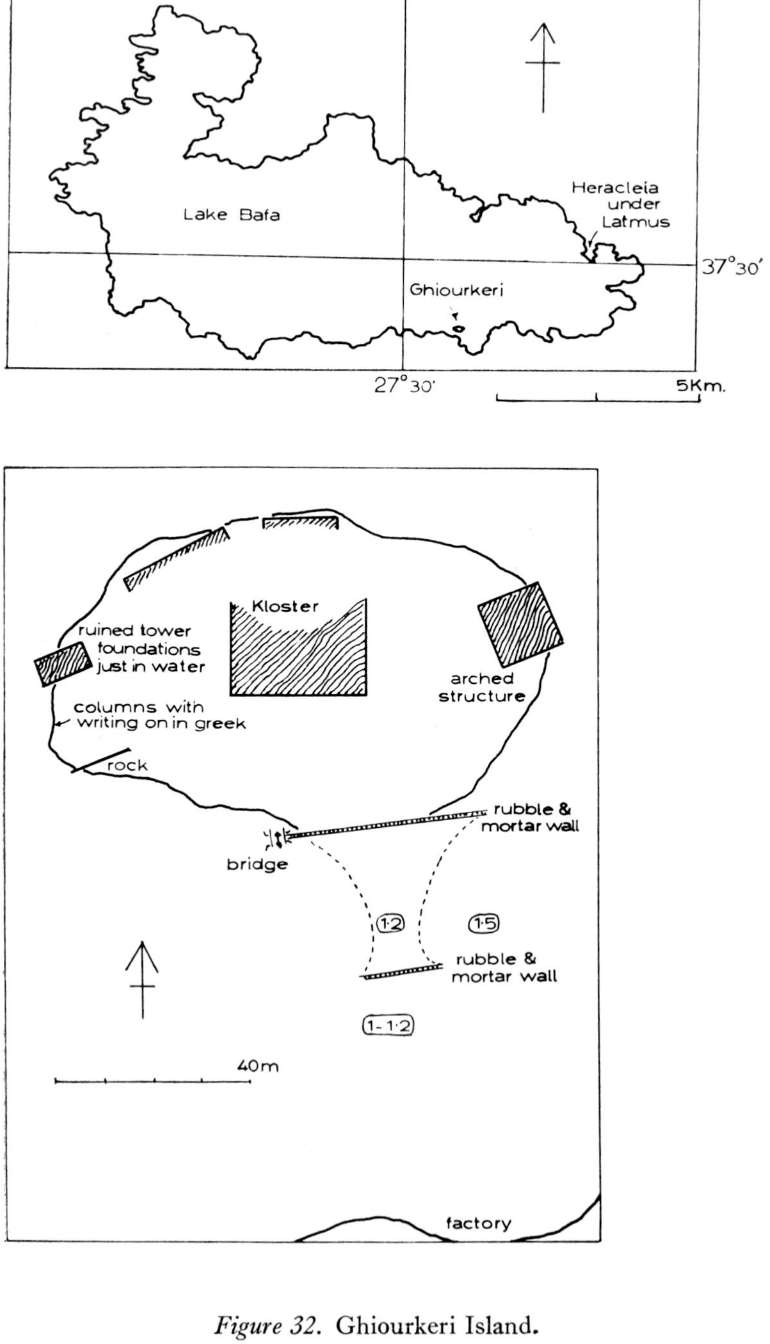

Figure 32. Ghiourkeri Island.

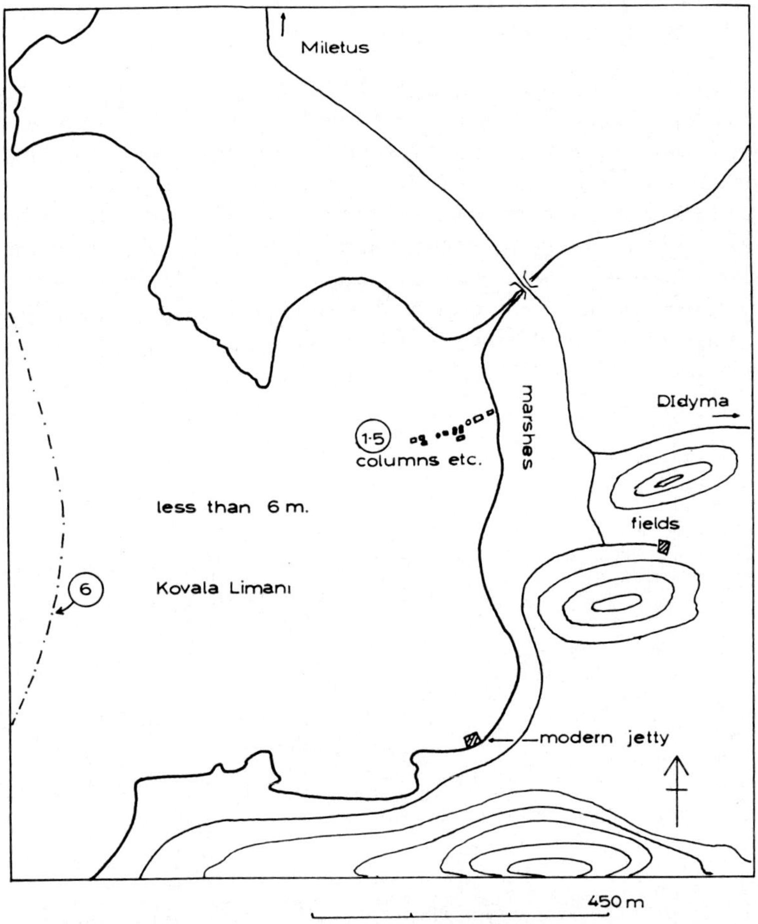

Figure 33. Panormus.

the temple at Didyma, which was never completed. The drums lie in a continuous line with a number of large blocks, 2 by 1.0 by 1.5 m, which are submerged at their upper surface by 20–50 cm, and patches of scattered rubble. The depth at the end of the line, 130 m from the shore, is 1.5 m. Owing to the shallowness of the bay there must have been jetties at which the pilgrims and cargoes were disembarked, but nothing substantial remains. The column-drums were probably unloaded on to a jetty and left on the surface, or dropped in the water near the jetty. It is probable that there has been little silting, because the columns are still exposed; and the jetty must have extended into at least 1–1.5 m of water, so that there can have been little change of water level. Owing to the uncertainties of this site, movement could have been anything between +50 and −50 cm.

Iasus. Asın Kale. 37° 17′N., 27° 37′ E. Chart 1606.
Strabo 14.2.21. Bean & Cook (1957, 100–05). Figure 34.

The rubble mole on the west side of the bay is awash to a depth of 50 cm, but has no foundations on it. The mole on the east side has a single course of ashlar, with its upper surface just awash, resting on the rubble. At the end of this mole there is a medieval fort with its foundations at water level, but the floor is considerably raised. At the tip of the headland there are walls of ashlar seriously undermined by the waves, and on the west side a row of large blocks submerged by 10 cm, suggesting a roadway along the shore. At many points medieval walls come to the beach and stop, or run parallel to the shore, but at no point are walls of this period submerged. Therefore there has been a change in level of 50 cm since the Greco-Roman period, but very little change since medieval times.

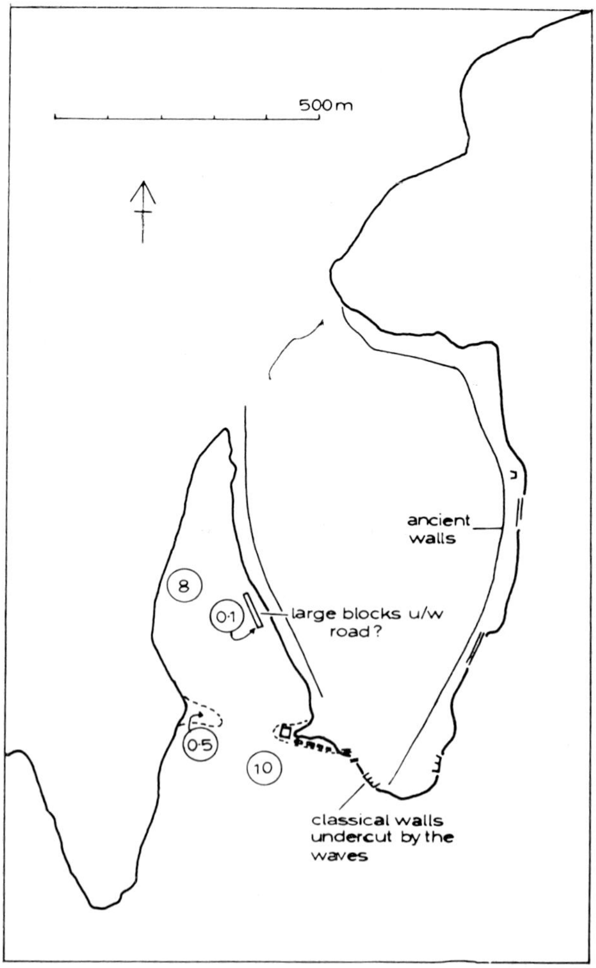

Figure 34. Iasus.

BARGYLIA. Varvil, Asar. 37° 12′ N., 27° 38′ E. Charts 1546, 1531. Polybius 16.24. Leake (1824), Bean & Cook (1957, 96–7). Figure 35.

The harbour has silted up and the mole from the city across to the east side has partly collapsed into the water. This causeway has been continuously remade and repaired, though part is now broken, and it is not possible to deduce any change of level or date from it. The bay to the south of the city dries out as a mud-flat in summer. There are a number of small indentations off the shore facing the mud, and flush with the surface of the mud are various walls and fragments of foundations. Before the bay

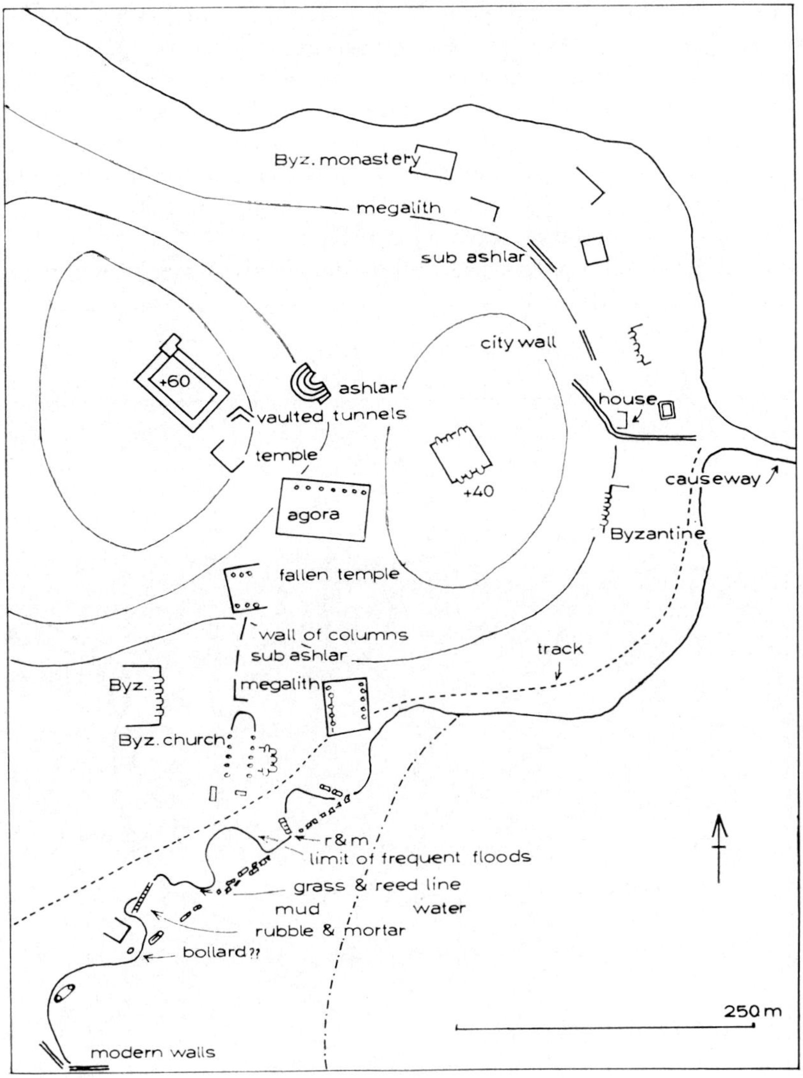

Figure 35. Bargylia.

silted up, this area would have provided a very sheltered quay, and although pillaging may have removed the upper surface, there may have been submergence by about 20 cm.

CARYANDA. Güvercinlik. 37° 08′ N., 27° 36′ E. Chart 1546.
Leake (1824, 227–8), Bean & Cook (1957, 97). Figures 36 and 37.

The headland is scattered with ruins of many periods, including late Roman or Byzantine, medieval, and others up to the nineteenth century, while at the back of the bay there are large vaulted ruins near the beach. In the most sheltered corner of the bay is a broken mole with a paved surface of irregular flat stones resting on a broad bank of loose rubble. The paved surface breaks off before the end of the bank, and at this point (see Fig. 37A) there is an intricately carved architectural block which must have been acquired from a building of some importance. A submerged road fringes the northern side of the headland, marked by a row of uncut blocks 2–3 m seawards of the shore, or the same distance from foundations or walls in the water. Seawards of the road are two loose stone jetties with their upper surfaces submerged by 20 cm. The road is submerged by 10 cm, although the true surface may be missing. On the south side of the headland there are a number of rock cuttings and structures of unshaped stones in the water, but nothing clearly identifiable.

The submerged road and jetties and foundations in the water near the road indicate submergence of about 30 cm since late Roman times. The large mole with paved

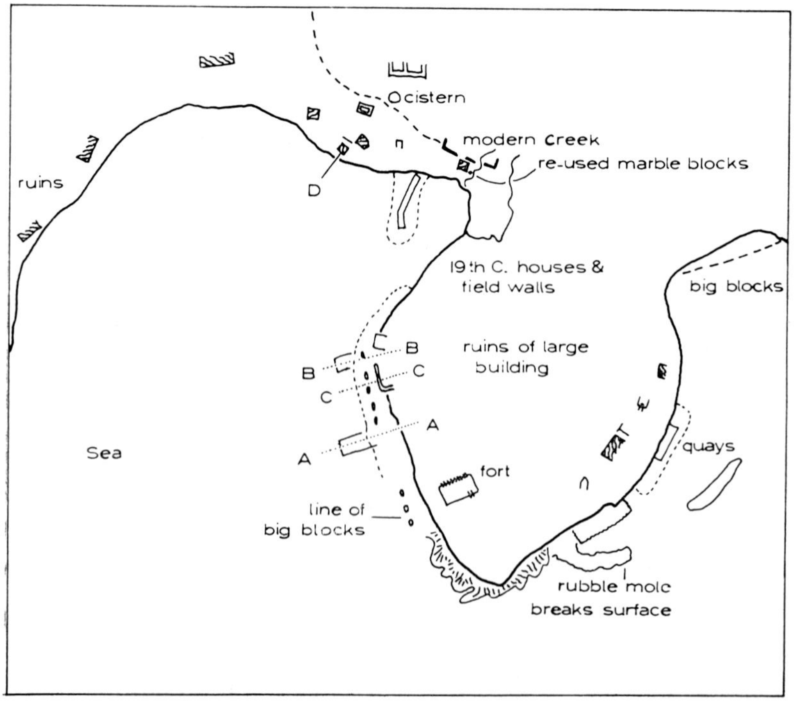

Figure 36. Güvercinlik. North to left.

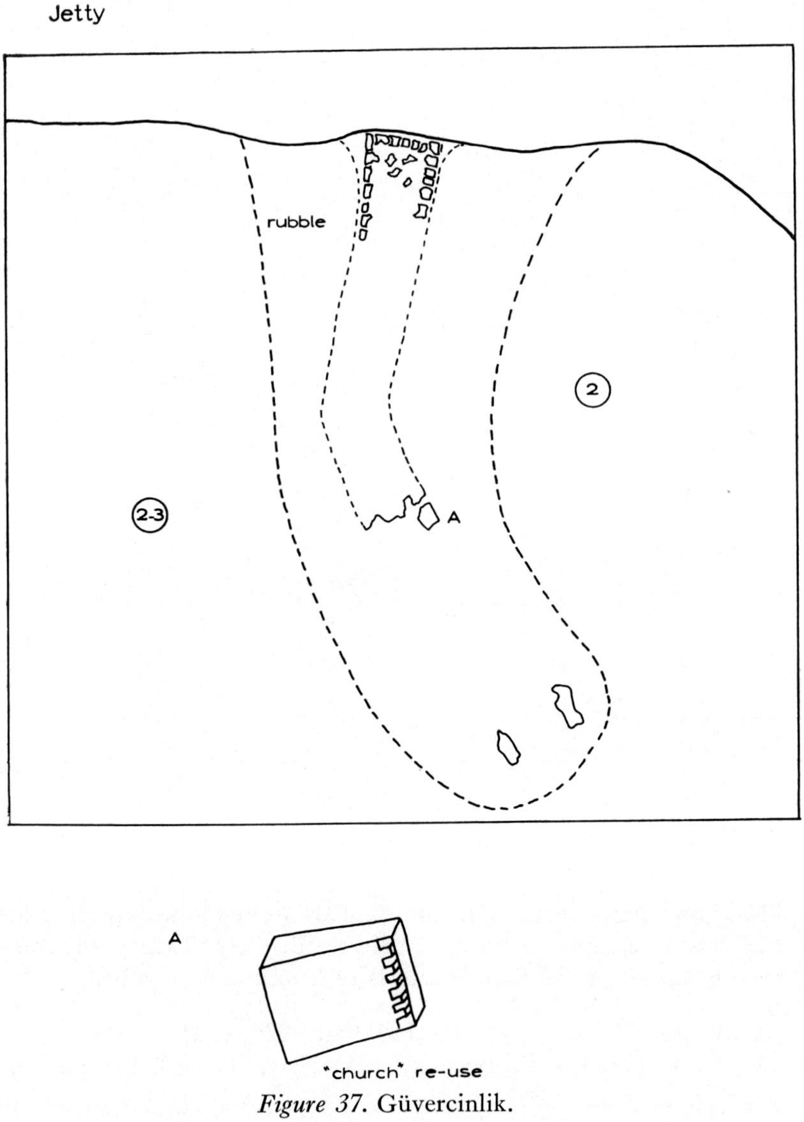

Figure 37. Güvercinlik.

surface has its upper surface complete in places and 20 cm above the water. The mole terminates clearly at the present shoreline. Although the rubble bank may be much older, the paved surface appears to be only a few hundred years old, and a change of level since its construction is not detectable.

GöL (modern name). 37° 08′ N., 27° 26′ E. Chart 1546.
Newton (1863, 595), Bean & Cook (1955, 131). Figure 38.

Between Göl and Türkbükü there are tombs and quarries on the shore with cut surfaces awash to a depth of 20 cm. At Göl there is a small Christian church still standing, though much overgrown, and roadworks in 1969 revealed a number of marble columns

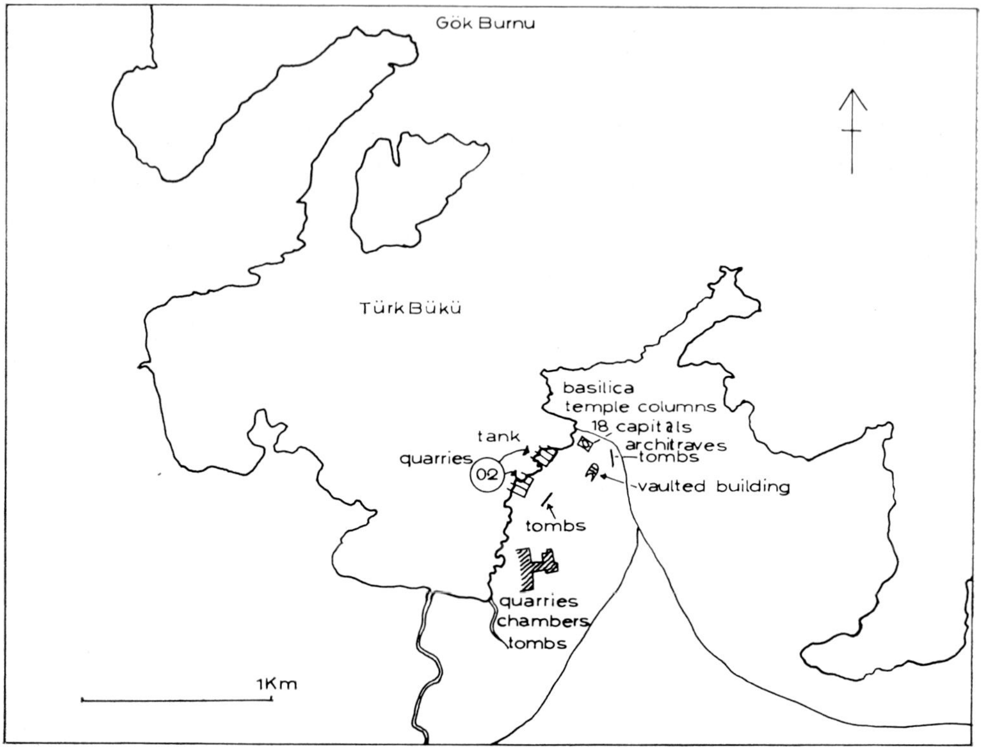

Figure 38. Göl.

and 18 capitals. Some parts of the same building are to be found built into local houses. There are Hellenistic remains on the hills behind. Because of the difficulties of dating the quarries no firm conclusion about changes of level can be reached.

MYNDUS. Gümüşlük. 37° 03′ N., 27° 16′ E. Chart 3924, 1531.
Strabo 14.2.18. Leake (1824, 228), Bean & Cook (1955, 108–11). Figures 39, 40.

On the north side of the isthmus there is a tower foundation with a paved floor flush with the water level over which the waves break. On the east side of the bay near the present village is a rubble mole with the surface 70 cm below the water. On Chart 1531, surveyed in 1837, the presence of a rectangular structure is marked on this mole. On the north side of the harbour entrance is a short rubble mole topped with two parallel walls of ashlar, terminating in a tower base of stepped ashlar construction. The upper surface of the tower is at water level, and the base at −2 m. On the south side of the harbour entrance there is a flight of steps descending the cliff to a rock-cut platform about 6 metres square and 1 m above the water. Along the northern shore of the island there is a broad fringing bank of rubble in the water, including cut blocks and some columns. Between the island and the mainland a curving shingle spit partly conceals Roman quays and breakwaters, and a number of later building foundations

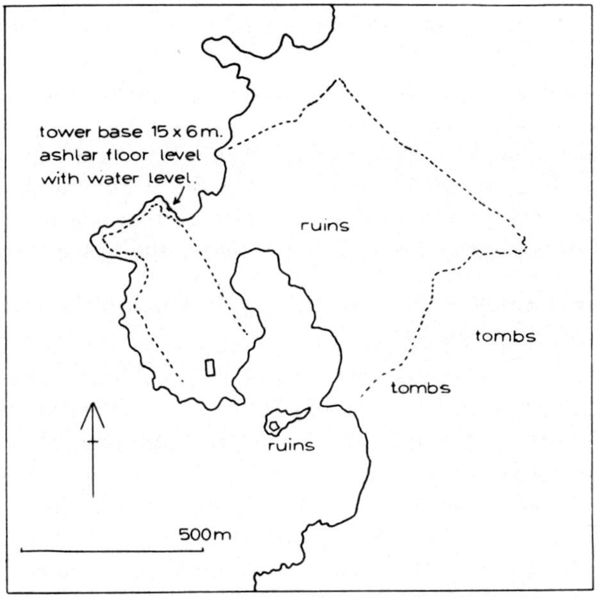

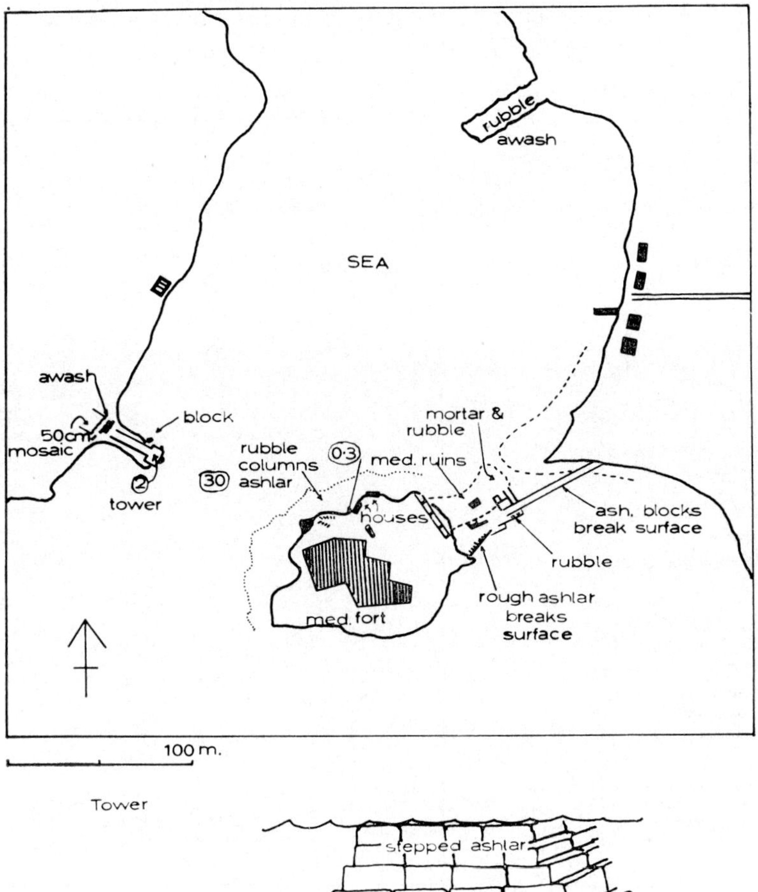

Figures 39, 40. Myndus.

in the water. The main quays of ashlar are heavily corroded on the upper surface, but the highest parts of the stones just project above the water.

When the site was visited in July 1969, waves were breaking over all structures near the shore, including the platform 1 m above the water on the south side of the harbour entrance. In view of the exposed position of this site it is probable that the main quay surfaces were slightly more than 1 m above the water.

KARATOPRAK (modern name). 37° 00′ N., 27′ 17′ E. Chart 3924.
Bean & Cook (1955, 128). Figure 41.

The road south from Karatoprak shows signs of erosion at many points, and there are also tombs and traces of early settlement in the area. There are no ancient remains *in situ* on the shore apart from a well or silo near the lighthouse. The floor surrounding the rim of this is 1 m above sea level. About 100 m north of the northern edge of Karatoprak (A on Fig. 41) the remains of a villa are largely buried by sand, but fragments of wall protrude into the sea. The walls are of rubble and white mortar with a thickness of 0.5 m. Some of the broken material has been piled up to make a small groyne or jetty, but the original walls *in situ* are still clearly visible, with the deepest structure a rectangular room partly covered by the jetty. There is a mosaic floor with a decorated

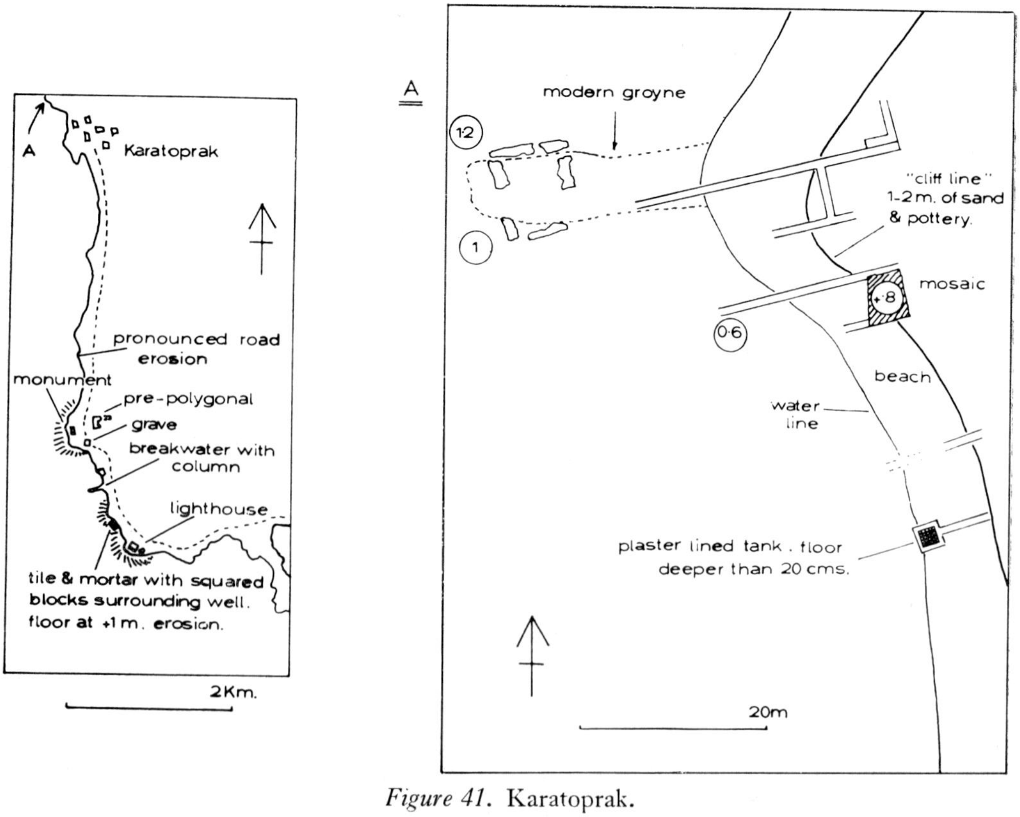

Figure 41. Karatoprak.

border 18 cm above water level. The two long walls running into the water are definitely *in situ* where they are on the dry beach, but in the water they slope seawards with the beach, as if they had been undermined. Thus they may not originally have been based at exactly this level. On the other hand, the rectangular walls at the end of the jetty appear to be exactly *in situ*, and the foundations of the walls on the beach must descend at least to the water level, if not 20 cm below. Thus the change is of the order of 0.5–1.0 m.

HALICARNASSUS. Bodrum. 37° 02′ N., 27° 27′ E. Chart 1606.
Strabo 14.2.16–7. Newton (1863), Bean & Cook (1955, 85–97). Figure 42.

In the north-east corner of the harbour is a submerged rubble mole supporting two ashlar tower foundations. The upper surface of the mole varies from 0.5–1.0 m in depth, while the ashlar upper surface is 40 cm under water. On the west side of this mole is a second parallel rubble wall separated from it by a water base about 5 m wide. The whole structure stands in 2–3 m of water. From the presence of the ashlar foundations and the fact that the narrower rubble wall could not be built any higher on the existing width of the base, it seems that the upper surface of the mole is intact. There may have been a paved surface, but that would not have raised the level more than 10 cm. Thus submergence is about 1.0 m.

CEDREAE. Taşbükü. 37° 00′ N., 28° 14′ E. Chart 1533.
Bean & Cook (1957, 64–5). *Mediterranean Pilot*, Vol. 4 (1918) 339. Figure 43.

The earliest pottery found on the island is of the fourth century B.C. and most of the surviving foundations are Hellenistic, Roman or Christian. On the northern shore of the eastern limb of Castle Island are a number of ruins, including a church with three apses, with foundations in a depth of 10–60 cm of water. The footings of the walls of the church are exactly at water level, and a quay surface between the apses and the water is 20 cm above water level. A mole projecting northwards is submerged by 50 cm, though the upper surface is not intact, and the foundations of it are awash. Since some of the deeper foundations may have been built in shallow water, it is probable that the actual sea level change has been 30 cm.

OLD CNIDUS. Datça. 36° 44′ N., 27° 44′ E. Chart 1604.
Bean & Cook (1952). Figure 44.

On the north shore of the bay 1 km north of Datça there is a considerable area of remains. On the landing beach there are some medieval walls and cisterns. Further round towards the headland of Dalacak, there are walls in the water which appear to enclose two small harbour basins. The masonry is trapezoidal in profile, but the interior surfaces of the blocks are quite irregular. The depth of water beside the easternmost jetty and in the entrance to the eastern basin suggests that there has been no change of relative level. At the tip of the headland is a small hook-shaped promontory enclosing a rectangular basin with a water depth of 1.0 m, and an entrance sill at 0.80 m. This may have been a fish-tank. North of the headland is more trapezoidal masonry of the fifth–fourth century B.C.

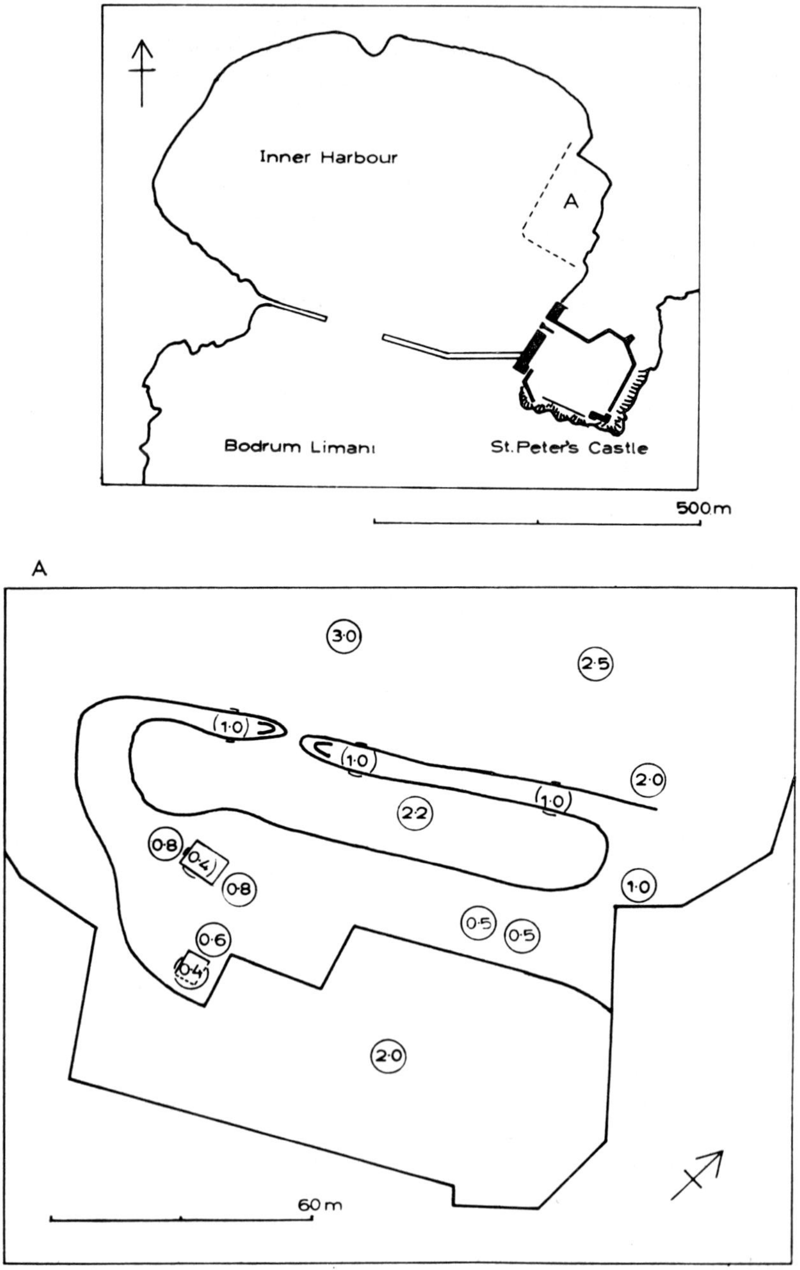

Figure 42. Bodrum.

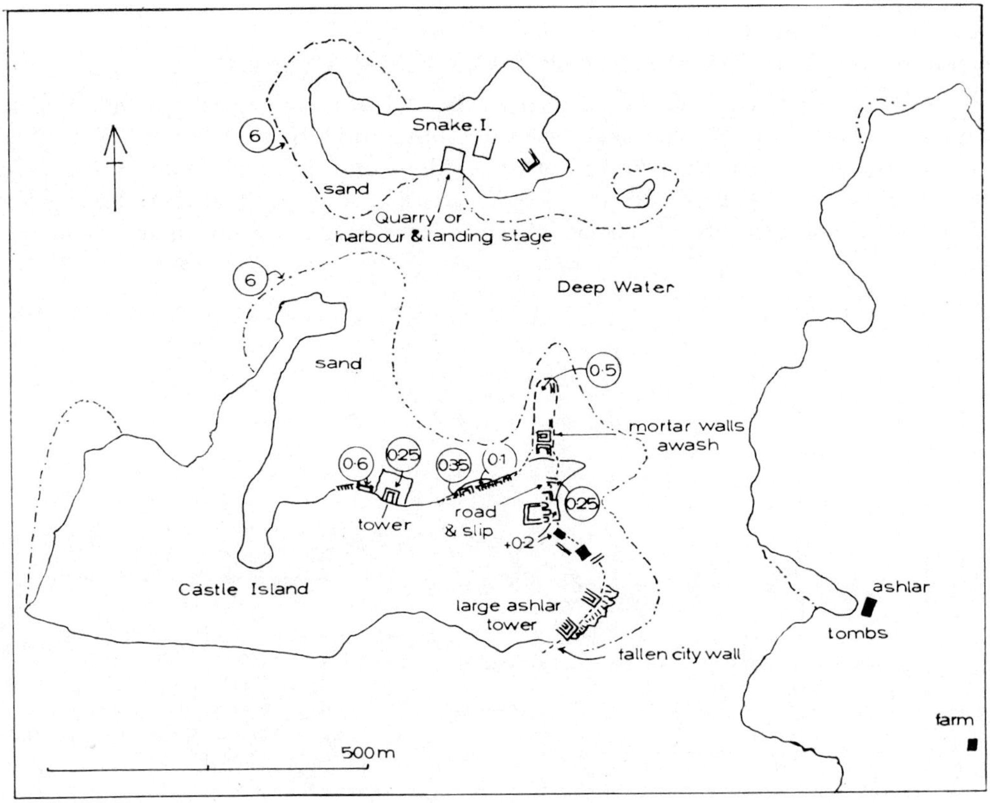

Figure 43. Cedreae.

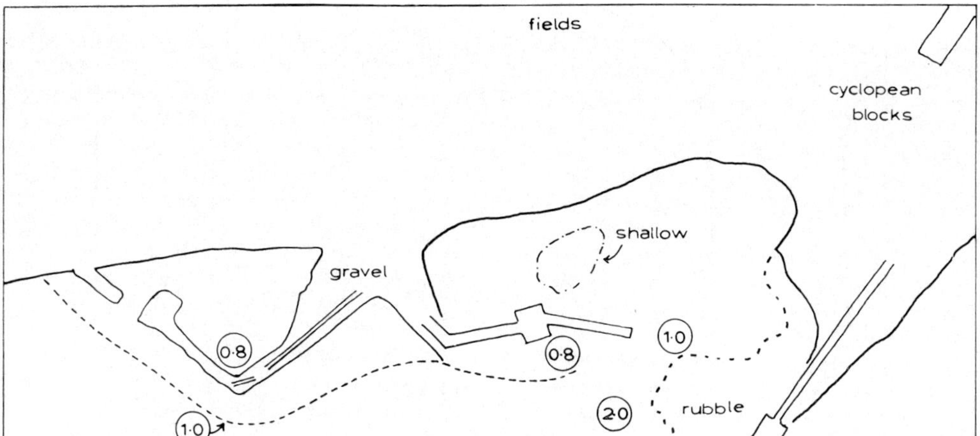

Figure 44. Old Cnidus.

NEW CNIDUS. Tekir. 36° 41′ N., 27° 24′ E. Chart 3924.
Strabo 14.2.15. Leake (1824, 226), Bean & Cook (1952). Figures 45, 46.

The site is at present being excavated by Prof. Iris Love. Specific details relevant to sea level change are the quay surfaces in the southern harbour at 1.0 and 1.7 m above sea level, the vertical mooring-bollard at some 2.0 m, and the stone mooring-rings with the centres of the mooring-holes at +1.0 m. All these indicate that there has been no submergence, and possibly even uplift of a few centimetres. A problem is presented by

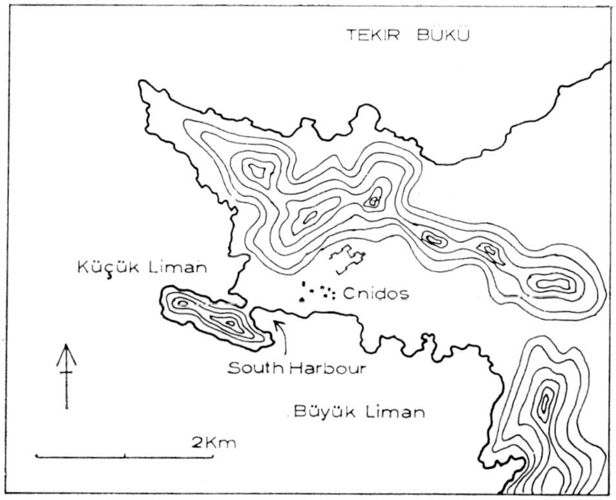

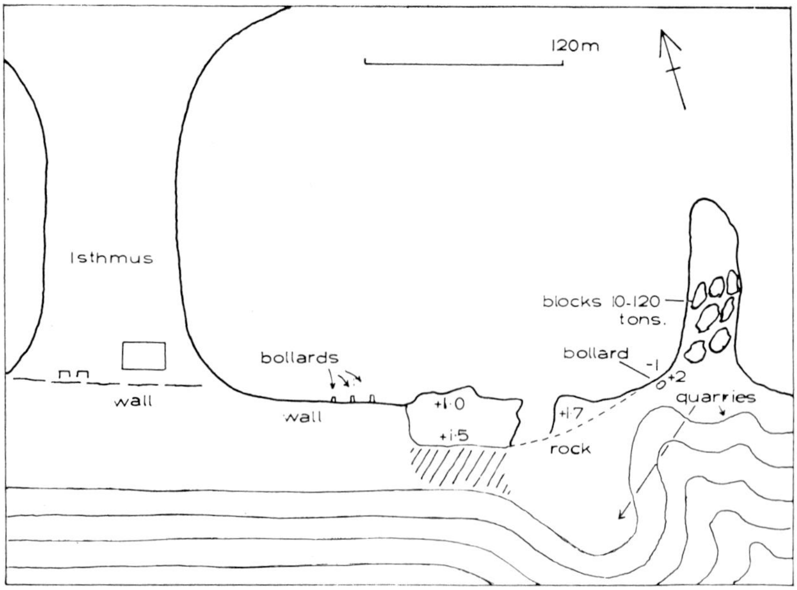

Figure 45. New Cnidus: General Plan. Detail: South Harbour.

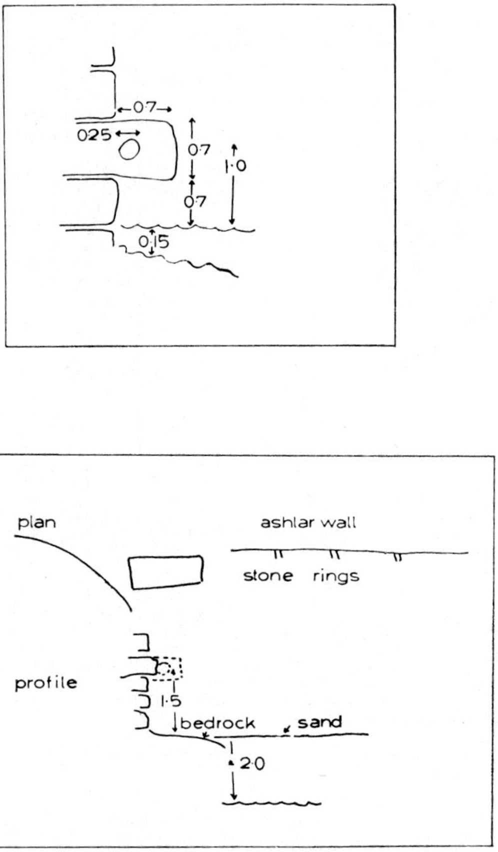

Figure 46. New Cnidus: Mooring-ring, S. Harbour. Mooring-ring, isthmus.

similar mooring-rings on the wall across the isthmus between the two harbours, which appear to be about 3.5 m above present sea level. A possible explanation is that there was a channel between the harbours, now covered by sand, and that this channel was flanked by quay surfaces at the back of which were the mooring-rings. There is no reason to suppose uplift of this part of the site, since the northern (trireme) harbour also seems to be adjusted to the present sea level.

ORHANIYE (modern name). 36° 46′ N., 28° 10′ E. Chart 1604. Figure 47.

Where the sand spit parts from the shore by the road there is an ashlar wall above the road, and on the spit itself a rectangular foundation of mortar and rough stones, and a wall about 25 m long. There is also a remnant of two apses, each about 2 m across. All these structures, though close to the water, indicate a negligible change of sea level, possibly 10 cm, since medieval times.

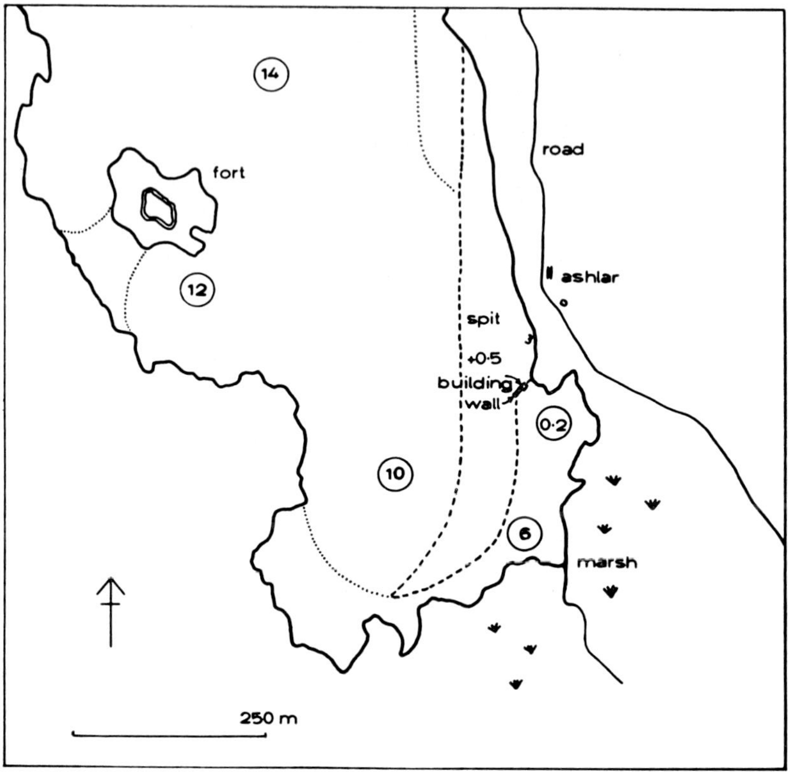

Figure 47. Orhaniye.

BOZBURUN (modern name). 36° 42′ N., 28° 05′ E. Chart 1604. Figure 48.

Ruins are marked on the chart, but none were investigated closely in the present survey. A trip by boat through the bay revealed that the most interesting area was that between the headland on the island marked B, the group of low sandy islands and the mainland shore opposite. The tip of the headland is prolonged by a row of massive irregular blocks, but whether these are natural, or compose a man-made breakwater is not known. There is a church on the larger island, though another island is little more than a sandbank, almost awash. There are walls on the shore and leading into the water, suggesting a change of 0.5–1.0 m.

SARANDA (modern name). 36° 39′ N., 28° 07′ E. Chart 1604. Figure 49.

Saranda is a group of three of four houses by a small jetty. To the east of the modern jetty is a broad rubble mole, now submerged. To the west are four small hooked jetties of rubble, also submerged. In all these cases the rubble may have collapsed, since the original structure may have been retained with a facing of blocks or wooden stakes. About $\frac{1}{2}$ km to the south-west is an anvil-shaped headland of very pronounced shape.

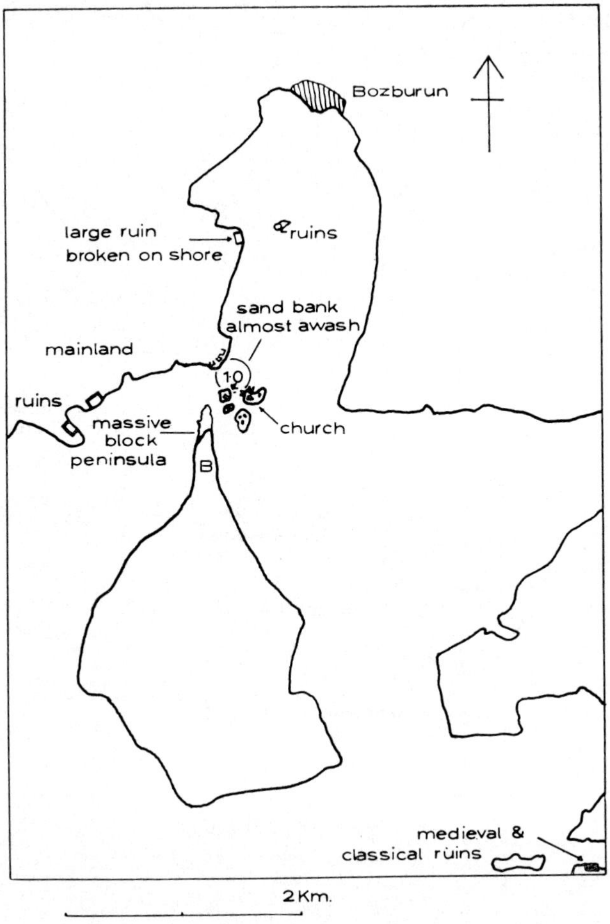

Figure 48. Bozburun.

On the hill behind the headland are rock cuttings and walls of yellow ashlar, almost completely concealed by earth and vegetation. On the headland itself is an olive-press and the foundations of a temple in ashlar, overlain by remnants of a Christian basilica. In the small sheltered bay to the north are two rubble jetties, the outer one submerged, the inner one breaking the surface by 50 cm. On the shore are medieval house-walls extending into a depth of 30 cm of water. From the assemblage of jetties and the house-walls it is probable that there has been a relative change of level of about 30–50 cm.

Extending beyond the jetties is an area of pottery and tiles, which, below the cliff at the tip of the headland, blends into a vast mound sloping at 45° into deeper water. Although some of the pieces may be roof-tiles from the basilica, many appear extremely large, while there are also large numbers of small dishes and bowls. The quantity suggests that they were thrown from the cliff deliberately.

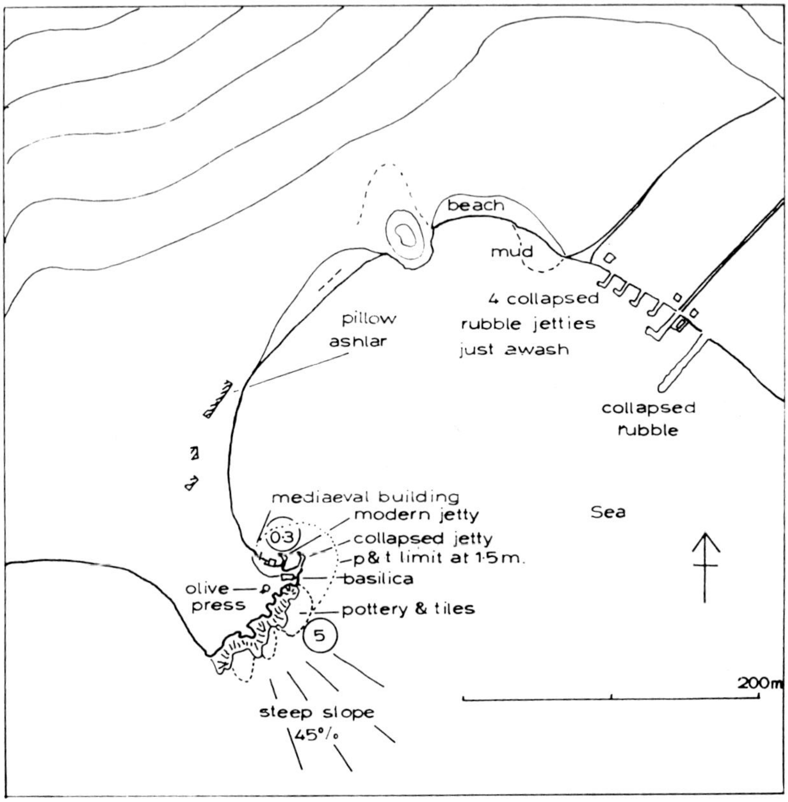

Figure 49. Saranda.

LORYMA. Oplotheke, Bozuk. 36° 35′ N., 28° 03′ E. Chart 1604.
Strabo 14.2.14. Leake (1824, 223). Figure 50.

None of the earlier or Hellenistic remains are near the water level, but there is a row of stones on the beach between the northern temple foundations and the shore which may be part of a road. At the back of the bay is an apsidal building with a number of adjoining rooms, with the walls standing in 60 cm of water. Submergence is about 0.5–1.0 m.

PATARA. Gelemiç. 36° 16′ N., 29° 19′ E. Chart 236.
Strabo 14.3.6. Stark (1956). Figure 51.

At several points on the shore of the lagoon there are large structures remaining to a height of 5–10 m, but they are difficult of access because of scrub, trees and reeds, as well as the waterlogged ground. The sandy beach completely closes the lagoon, which was once the harbour. In winter and spring the lagoon level rises and flows out to the west of the hill over the bar. The only building which might indicate a change of level is the arch on the east shore at the back of the lagoon, but the level of the lagoon itself may be higher than the sea, so this is not conclusive.

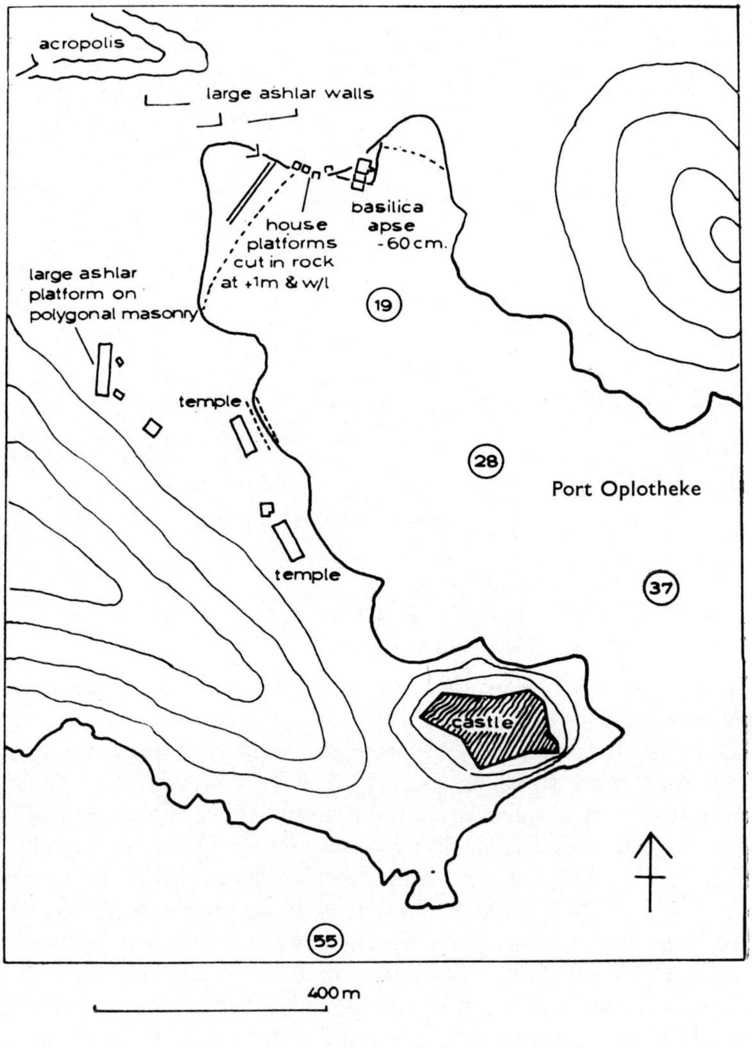

Figure 50. Loryma.

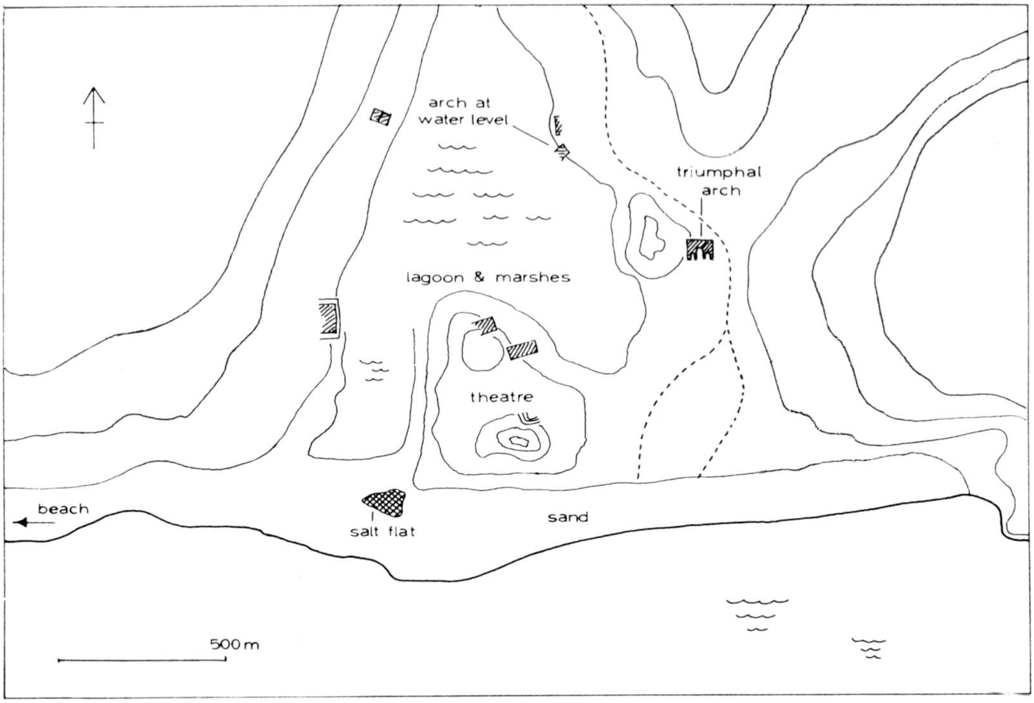

Figure 51. Patara.

ANTIPHELLUS. Kaş. 36° 13′ N., 29° 38′ E. Chart 2188.
Strabo 14.3.7. Leake (1824, 185). Figures 52, 53.

At A on the north side of the promontory there are quarries and tombs on the shore. A particularly fine tomb with a rectangular door and a triangular prismatic superstructure or monumental pedestal is cut from the solid rock and submerged by 2.0 m. The back of the roof of the tomb has been broken by waves.

At B there are rock cuttings and room foundations above the water line and medieval foundations just in the water. The breakwater C (Fig. 53) is cut in solid rock and is now largely submerged. There are a number of cisterns sunk into it, flooded to a maximum depth of 1.4 m (X & Y), and a rock-cut walkway, with its surface submerged by 1.3 m. Near the base of the breakwater beside some modern houses are the remains of crude walls, probably of medieval date, submerged by 18 cm.

In 1971 the nearby sites of Gemili Island and Kekova, the ancient Aperlae, were visited, and found to be submerged by 2·0 and 2·5 m. respectively.

ANDRIACE-MYRA. Kale. 36° 13′ N., 29° 58′ E. Chart 236.
Stark (1956). Figure 54.

Stark (1956, 156) states that Myra probably had a small port on the river at the back of the lagoon and a second at Andriace. The mouth of the lagoon is almost closed by a sand bar, and the narrow entrance is at the extreme eastern edge (Fig. 54). The water

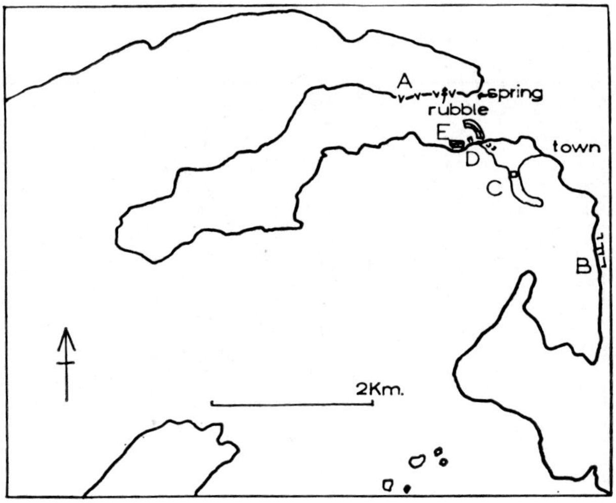

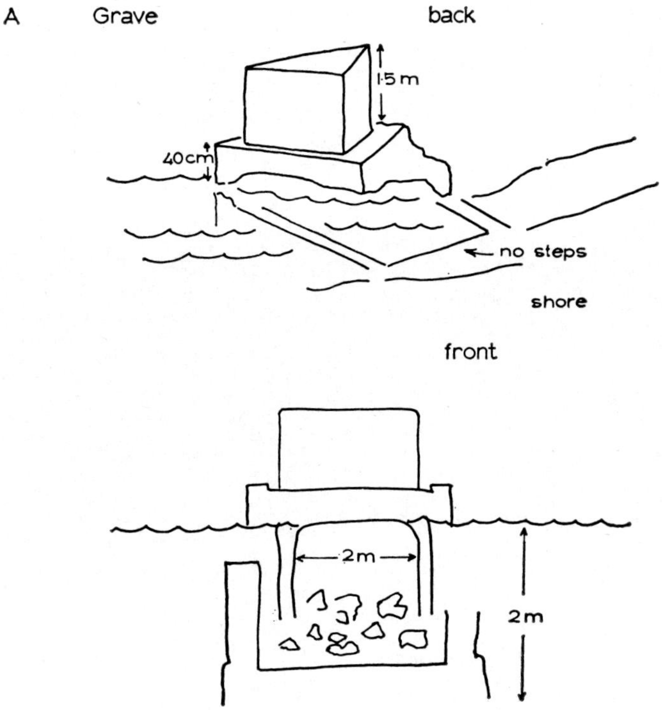

Figure 52. Kaş.

C

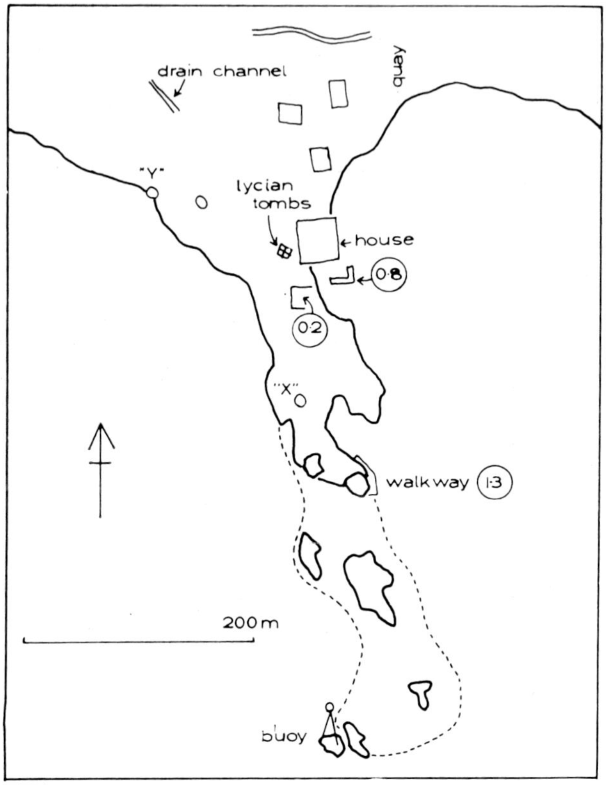

Silos

in metres

Figure 53. Ka,.

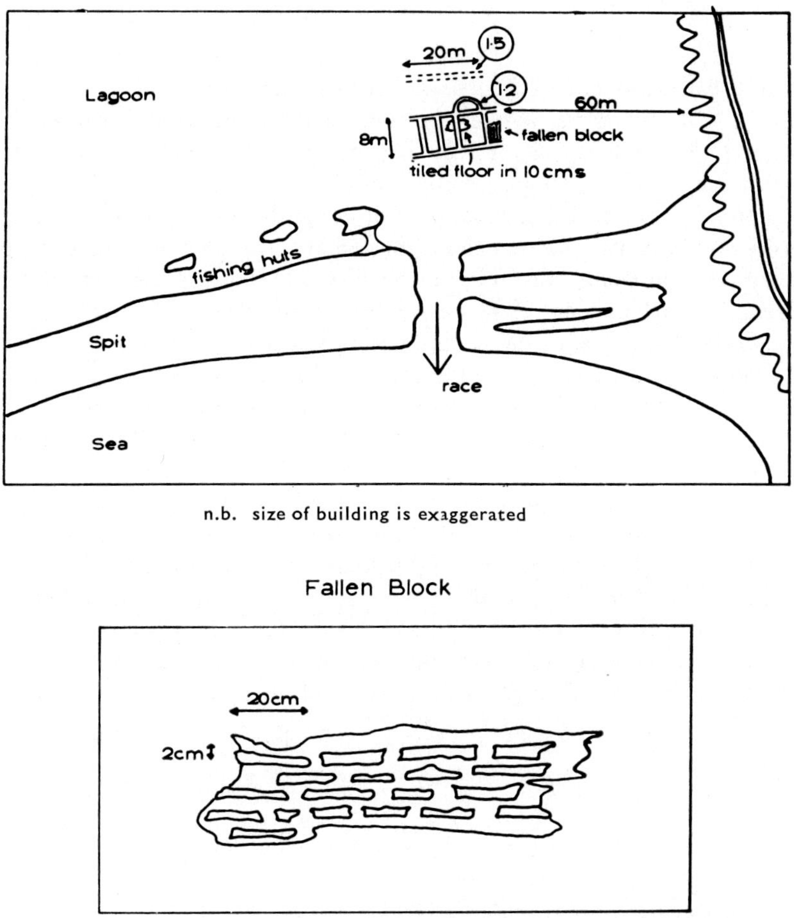

Figure 54. Kale.

flows out of the lagoon in a race and the lagoon level is about 5 cm higher than sea level. Just inside the lagoon entrance is an apsidal ruin with a number of rooms and a tiled floor submerged by 10 cm. Adjoining walls are submerged by 1.2 and 1.5 m, and there is a large fallen block of tile and mortarwork.

ANALYSIS AND DISCUSSION

Discussion of the mathematical, geological and geophysical reasoning behind the analysis of relative and absolute sea level changes is given elsewhere (Flemming, 1972), and a summary will be presented here. From the archaeological data at each site the best estimate of relative change of sea level is obtained, together with estimates of the probability that the change is more or less than the best estimate. In analysis of the Peloponnesian data only the best estimates of change were used, but in the analysis of the Turkish data the probability estimates were used.

In the general case the observed relative change of sea level at each site is made up of the algebraic sum of the world-wide eustatic sea level change since the site was occupied, and the vertical earth movement at the site over the same time. The first factor must be the same for all sites of the same age, but will vary for different periods of occupation of the same site. The second factor will in general be different for every site and will also vary with the age for a single site. Certain simplifying assumptions can be made. Although earth movements occur with varying magnitudes and frequencies at different sites, it is reasonable to assume that the direction and rate of movement at each site has been more or less constant throughout the last 5,000 years. Statistical tests on the Peloponnesian data (Flemming, 1968 *a* & *b*) showed that there was very poor correlation between age and displacement of sites, indicating that an explanation purely in terms of a steadily changing sea level could not account for the variability observed. On the other hand, an equation was fitted which contoured the area in terms of the rate of displacement, and this produced a much better fit (Fig. 55). This implies a variable earth movement from region to region, accounted for in terms of geological structure and gravity anomalies. The study of the Peloponnese did not reveal any consistent eustatic sea level change in the last 2,000 years to within an accuracy of $\pm$ 50 cm.

More detailed analysis was made of the Turkish data. Probability estimates were made of relative change at each site, and these were used as input to the surface fitting programme as if each estimate were a separate observation. In addition, an attempt was made to separate the eustatic and geological factors by purely statistical means. It was proposed that the relative change of level at each site should be best expressed as follows:

$$Z = f(T) + g(x, y)T$$

where

Z = the relative displacement,
$f(T)$ = a third-degree function of time,
$g(x,y)$ = rate of local displacement expressed as a fourth-degree function of arbitrary geographical co-ordinates, x, y.

This expression was expanded, and the values of Z, x, y, and T inserted for each site, and a multiple regression applied to find the best coefficients for the equation. The terms were then separated into those involving x and y only, representing the geological regional factor, and those involving T only, representing the eustatic factor independent of location. The two equations are plotted in Figures 56 and 57.

It will be seen that the deduced eustatic sea level variation is of the order of 30 cm and that sea level 2,000 years ago was very close to present sea level. This is supported by Mörner (1969). The distribution of earth movement shows a folding along the general line of the coast, with anticlinal folds extending westwards over the Çeşme Peninsula and west of south over the Cnidus Peninsula towards Rhodes.

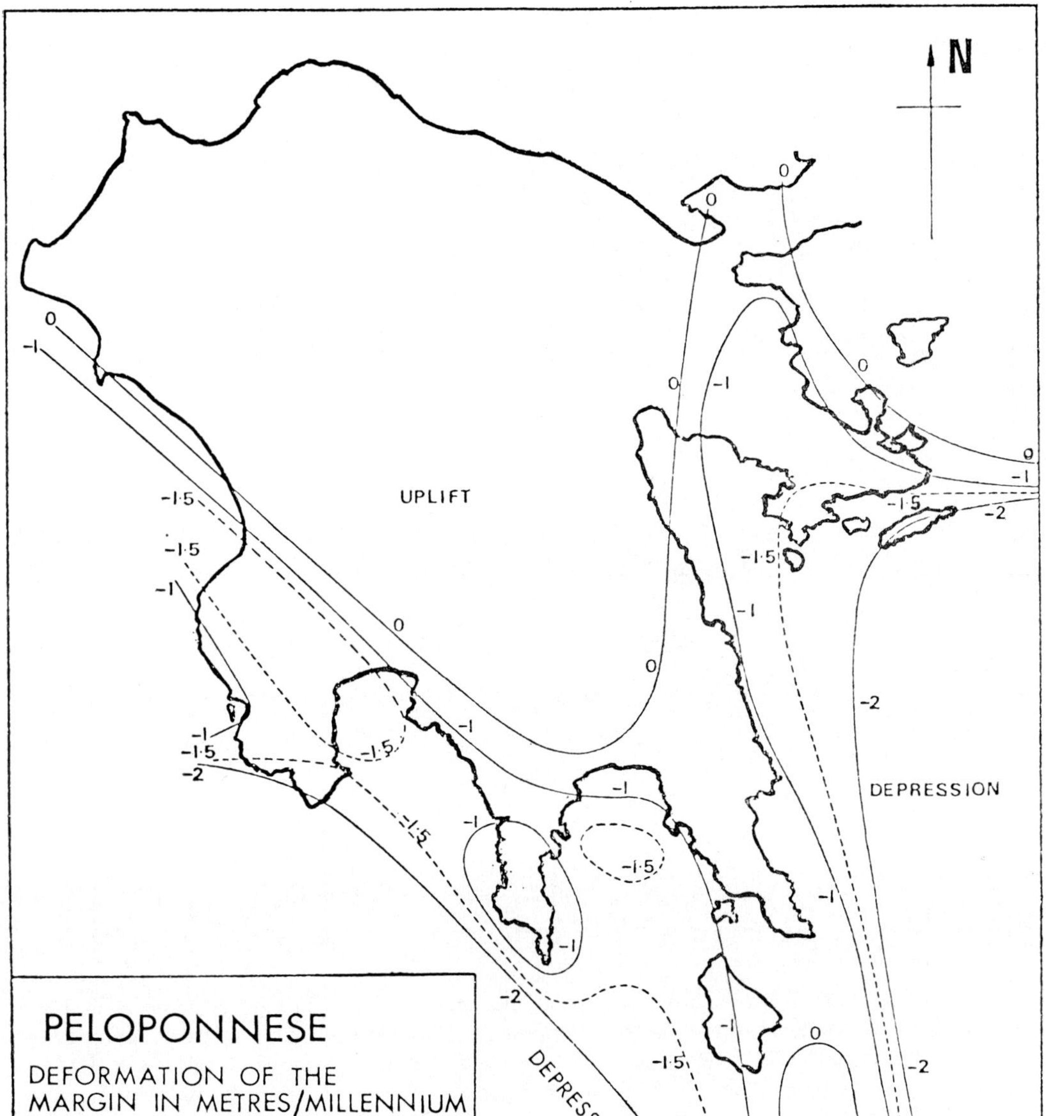

Figure 55. Plot of the relative rate of deformation of the margin of the Peloponnese in metres per millennium. The contour interval is at 1 m/millennium, with the 1.5 m/millennium line added to show the detailed structure in the Gulf of Messenia and the Gulf of Lakonia.

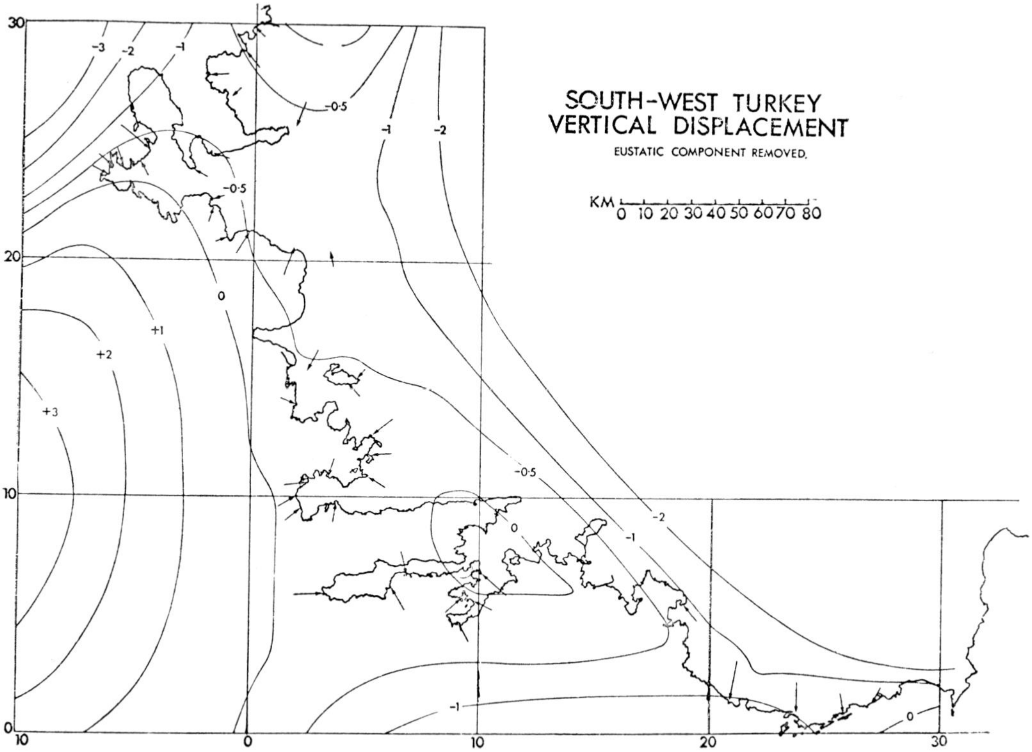

Figure 56. Plot of the relative rate of displacement of the margin of South-West Turkey after removal of the eustatic component. Contour interval is 1 m/millennium, with the 0.5 m/millennium line added to show detailed structure near the coast. In this presentation the contours in the open Aegean suggest uplift, but this is a mathematical fiction generated by the computer programme as there are no field data from this region. Nevertheless, the trend of the contours indicates the possible form which, with the sign reversed, might be taken by a depression.

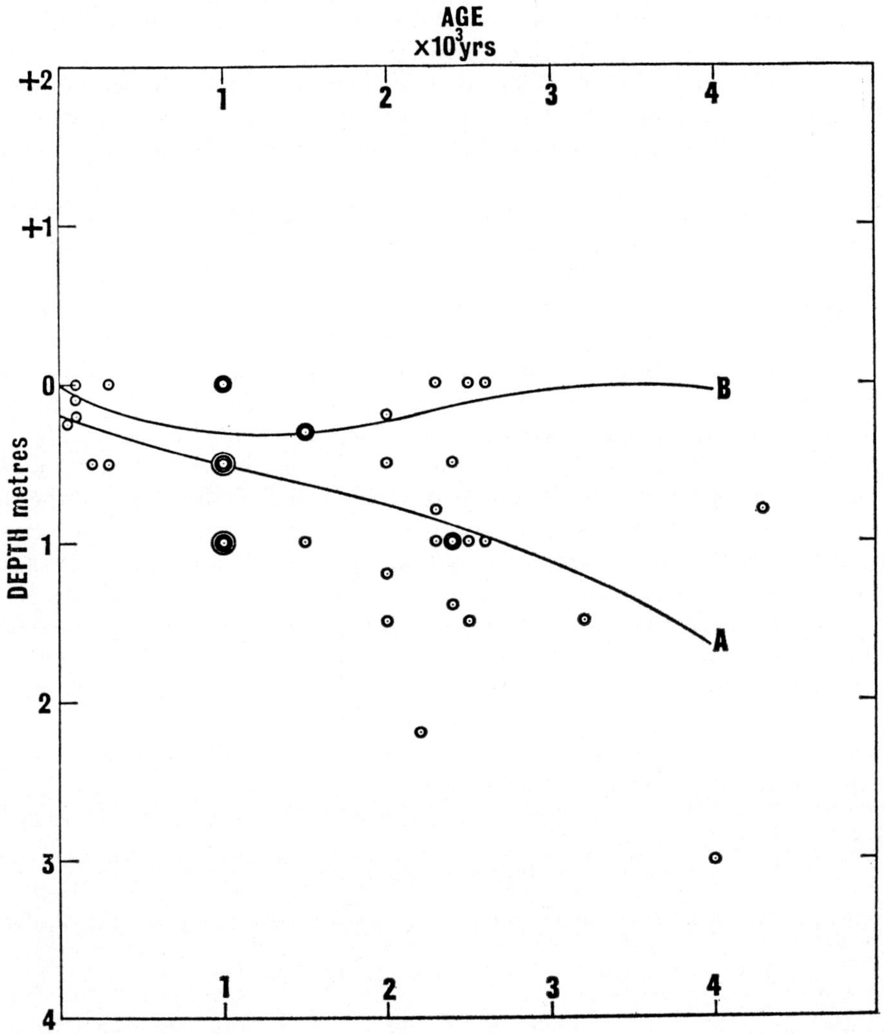

Figure 57. Plot of displacement of sites in S.W. Turkey against age of site in thousands of years. The heavy dots indicate double and triple points. Curve A is the mean displacement of sites of the same age, ignoring the possibility of earth movements. This shows that, as would be expected, older sites are deeper, but this could be due to eustatic or tectonic factors. Curve B shows the eustatic sea level curve obtained after separation of the tectonic factor shown in Figure 56.

CONCLUSIONS

Archaeological sites provide a highly sensitive method for deducing relative sea level changes. In the Aegean the close spacing of sites is such that statistical treatment enables separation of eustatic and tectonic factors over the last 3,000 years. To within the order of accuracy of the method, that is 20 cm and 200 years, the eustatic sea level change has not exceeded 30 cm in the last 3,000 years. There have certainly been deviations from this curve with durations of a few hundred years, but it is unlikely that the total amplitude of sea level change ever exceeded ± 1 m relative to the present sea level in the last 3,000 years.

If one takes the plots of earth movement from the Peloponnese and Turkey together, it is apparent that there is a general down-warping towards the centre of the Aegean basin, with a pronounced anticlinal fold extending east of south from Greece to Crete, and west of south from Turkey towards Crete. This suggests that the Cretan island arc is currently being folded and that the folding extends to the continental blocks at each extremity. The plans put forward in this paper are compatible with the distribution of historical seismicity discovered by Ambraseys (1965, 1970) and broadly compatible with the locations of tectonic plate boundaries put forward by McKenzie (1970).

The proposed eustatic sea level curve is at least compatible with data from other areas, but should not be taken as firmly established. Nevertheless, the fact that the curve is reasonable is a partial vindication of the statistical methods used. This underscores the fact that, in a site less than 3,000 years old, any observed sea level change is more likely to be due to local earth movement than a world-wide eustatic change. If the relative change at a site is more than 30–50 cm, there is certainly a contributory factor of earth movement, but every archaeological site should be treated as a special case, and it is not possible to argue for an 'expected' relative sea level change on the basis of the age of a site, nor is it possible to derive dates of structures from their depth of submergence on the basis of an expected sea level time curve. At all sites totally independent estimates of sea level change must be made.

REFERENCES

Ambraseys, N. N. 1965 A note on the Seismicity of the Eastern Mediterranean. *Studia geophys. geod.* **9**, 405–10.

Ambraseys, N. N. 1970 Some characteristic Features of the Anatolian Fault Zone. *Tectonophysics.* **9**, 143–66.

Bammer, A. 1965 Zum jüngeren Artemision von Ephesos. Die Terrasse des jüngeren Artemisions und eustatische Schwankungen des Meeresspiegels. *Jahreshefte des österreichischen archäologischen Instituts*, **47**, 1964–65, 126–45.

Bartoccini, R. & Zanelli, A. 1958 *Il Porto romano di Leptis Magna* [Bollettino del Centro di Studi per la Storia dell'Architettura, 13, Suppl.], 222 pp. Rome.

Bean, G. E. 1966 *Aegean Turkey: an archaeological guide*, 288 pp. London.

Bean, G. E. & Cook, J. M. 1952 The Cnidia. *BSA*, **47**, 171–212.

Bean, G. E. & Cook, J. M. 1955 The Halicarnassus Peninsula. *BSA*, **50**, 85–171.

Bean, G. E. & Cook, J. M. 1957 The Carian Coast. *BSA*, **52**, 58–146.

Béquignon, Y. & Laumonier, A. 1925 Fouilles de Teos (1924). *Bulletin de Correspondance Hellénique*, **49**, 281–321.

Cook, J. M. 1954 The Topography of Klazomenai. *Archaiologike Ephemeris*, 1953–54 [*Studies in Memory of G. P. Oikonomos*], vol. 2, 149–57.

Cook, J. M. 1959 Old Smyrna. *BSA*, **53–54**, 1958–59, 1–35.
Demangel, R. & Laumonier, A. 1923 Fouilles de Notion (1921). *Bulletin de Correspondance Hellénique*, **47**, 353–86.
Ervin, M. 1967 News-letter from Greece. *AJA*, **71**, 293–306.
Flemming, N. C. 1968*a* Holocene Earth Movements and Eustatic Sea Level Change in the Peloponnese. *Nature, Lond.* **217**, 1031–2.
Flemming, N. C. 1968*b* Archaeological evidence for sea level changes in the Mediterranean. *Underwater Association Report 1968*, 9–12.
Flemming, N. C. 1969 Archaeological evidence for Eustatic Change of Sea Level and Earth Movements in the Western Mediterranean in the last 2,000 years. *Spec. Pap. geol. Soc. Am.* **109**, 125 pp.
Flemming, N. C. 1972 Eustatic and Tectonic factors in Relative Vertical Displacement of the Aegean Coast, *in* Stanley, D. J. (ed.) *Sedimentation of the Mediterranean*. Smithsonian Institution.
Fowler, H. N. & Stillwell, R. 1932 *Corinth, I.1. Introduction, Topography, Architecture*, 239 pp. Cambridge, Mass.
Frödin, O. & Persson, A. W. 1938 *Asine: Results of the Swedish Excavations, 1922–1930*, 452 pp. Stockholm.
Giannakopoulos, P. E. 1966 *Gytheion*, 204 pp. Athens.
Grundy, G. B. 1896 An investigation of the topography of the region of Sphacteria and Pylos. *JHS*, **16**, 1–54.
Hall, J. E. 1969 Ancient Underwater City. *Oceans*, **1** No. 4, 48–51.
Harding, A., Cadogan, G. & Howell, R. 1969 Pavlopetri, an Underwater Bronze Age Town in Laconia. *BSA*, **64**, 113–42.
Hawthorne, J. G. 1965 Kenchreai, Port of Corinth. *Archaeology*, **18**, 191–200.
Higgins, C. G. 1966 Possible disappearance of Mycenaean coastal settlements of the Messenian Peninsula. *AJA*, **70**, 23–9.
Hogarth, D. G. 1908 *Excavations at Ephesus. The Archaic Artemisia . . .*, 344 pp. London.
Hope Simpson, R. 1965 *A Gazetteer and Atlas of Mycenaean Sites* [Bulletin, Institute of Classical Studies, Supplement 16], 200 pp. and 6 maps. London.
Hope Simpson, R. 1966 The Seven Cities offered by Agamemnon to Achilles. *BSA*, **61**, 113–31.
Jameson, M. H. 1969 Excavations at Porto Cheli and Vicinity, Preliminary Report, I: Halieis, 1962–1968. *Hesperia*, **38**, 311–42.
Kleiner, G. 1966 *Alt Milet* [*SB Frankfurt/M*, Vol. 4, No. 1], 26 pp. Wiesbaden.
Leake, W. M. 1824 *Journal of a Tour in Asia Minor*, 362 pp. London.
McKenzie, D. 1970 Plate Tectonics of the Mediterranean Region. *Nature, Lond.* **226**, 239–43.
Mörner, N. A. 1969 Eustatic and Climatic changes during the last 15,000 years. *Geologie Mijnb.* **48**, 389–99.
Negris, P. 1904 Vestiges Antiques Submergés. *Athenische Mitteilungen*, **29**, 340–63.
Newton, C. T. 1863 *A History of Discoveries at Halicarnassus, Cnidus, and Branchidae*, Vol. 2, 835 pp. London.
Roebuck, C. 1959 *Ionian Trade and Colonization* [Monographs on Archaeology and Fine Arts, sponsored by the Archaeological Institute of America and the College Art Association of America, 9], 148 pp. New York.
Schäfer, J. & Schläger, H. 1962 Zur Seeseite von Kyme in der Aeolis. *Archäologischer Anzeiger*, 1962. 1, 40–57.
Schuchhardt, C. 1912 *in* Conze, A. (ed.) *Altertümer von Pergamon*, Vol. I.1, 61–143.
Scranton, R. L. & Ramage, E. S. 1964 Investigations at Kenchreai, 1963. *Hesperia*, **33**, 134–45.
Stark, F. 1956 *The Lycian Shore*, 204 pp. London.
von Gerkan, A. 1935 in Wiegand, T. (ed.) *Milet*, Vol. II.3, 135 pp. Berlin.
Waterhouse, H. & Hope Simpson, R. 1961 Prehistoric Laconia, Part II. *BSA*, **56**, 114–75.
Weber, G. 1901 Erythrae. *Athenische Mitteilungen*, **26**, 103–18 & Pl. VII.

Discussion

Blackman I have been over much of the same ground as Dr. Flemming, also looking for evidence of sea level changes. My conclusions, with respect to the individual sites, are very close to his.

Peel Your application of fairly straightforward statistical techniques is most interesting. Could you describe them in more detail?

Flemming The analysis used on the Peloponnesian data was a conventional surface fitting programme. The technique used for Turkey was an advance on this. First, instead of making a single estimate of the relative change of level at a site, probability weights were allocated to the most probable estimate and to less likely estimates on either side. Ten points were allotted for each site, of which, for example, seven might go for the best estimate, two for an estimate 25 cm more than the best, and one for an estimate 25 cm less than the best. In subsequent analysis each point was treated as a single observation.

The study of the Peloponnese had suggested that tectonic regional variations could reasonably be fitted in terms of third- or fourth-degree polynomials, while a eustatic sea level curve would have to have one or two turning points in it, and thus would most probably be a third-degree curve. As explained in the paper, it was proposed that the net relative displacement at a site was the algebraic sum of two such polynomials. There is, however, a snag. The stepwise regression analysis performed by the computer minimises the residual errors between the observed data and the sum of the two polynomials which are generated. Mathematically the computer may adjust the two polynomials so that their sum satisfies the criterion for minimum error, but individually, when taken as having physical significance in the field, the equations may be absurd. The answer which gives the best mathematical fit is also probably the correct physical solution, but it is not logically necessary that it be so. One has to check to see if the physical meaning of the solution is absurd or not. If not, then it is probably good.

Hague It seems odd to have to ask "Does it look sensible?". Surely your sort of study ought to give answers in precise terms.

Flemming Mathematics gives a precise answer if all the initial data are known, and if logical procedures are followed. The trouble in the earth sciences is that one is always losing data through erosion and decay and geological change. Many of the facts which are needed to reconstruct the past have been destroyed. From a mathematical point of view one is then faced with trying to solve n equations with $n + 1$ unknown factors, which strictly speaking is impossible. However, by making assumptions about the type of equations which may occur in the solution, and so on, one can reduce the uncertainty and get a solution which is mathematically precise. However, the computer does not know what is geologically possible or reasonable, and if some of your assumptions have implications which are geologically unsound, then the final answer may be totally wrong. There are unlikely to be two possible mathematical solutions close together, and thus the answer from the computer will either be good or absurd. It is unlikely to be just vaguely wrong. Thus the test of absurdity is a reasonable way of arriving at a very reliable answer.

Hague Can you not get this by drawing by eye?

Flemming I could not have drawn the contours by eye, nor could I have separated the tectonic and sea level/time curve. There are four variables—geographical co-ordinates (x and y), sea level, and time—and we have nearly 300 sets of observations. The human mind is simply not capable of drawing contours through 300 points in four dimensions.

Davidson We have found some quarries on the coast of North Africa which had been cut down to sea level, with a rock-cut wall left as protection from the sea and drainage channels through the wall to keep the workings dry. What was the probable height of these workings above sea level?

Flemming I have assumed that it was easier to quarry downwards than to knock the wall further back into the cliff. They would have quarried as close as possible to sea level, say to 10 cm above sea level in a fairly sheltered place.

Blackman At Koyunbaba in Western Turkey, just north of Myndus, there are quarries where the sea now just laps on to the shelf at the water's edge (Bean & Cook, 1955, 130). Sea level must have changed slightly since these were worked.

Flemming At Apollonia one can show that the original sea level must have been at a certain level to allow boats into the harbour, and this leaves the quarries absolutely at water level.

Blackman In many cases one can work out minimum and maximum change in sea level at a particular site, using indices like the depth of water in rock-cut channels and the relationship of features like quarries to present sea level. The main problem is to date the features. I hope to discuss this in a later paper (pp. 115–38).

Wallace A somewhat different pattern of quarrying has been practised on the South Coast of England, where there are tides and rougher seas to contend with. It might be termed tidal quarrying, in that at high tide boats are taken right to the working face, which is worked down to low tide level. The stone is loaded directly into the boats, which are by then aground on the quarry floor, which is left flat and clear of obstructions. The boats are then floated off again on the rising tide. But to give shelter and prevent bumping on the bottom during the awkward period when they were only partially afloat, it was a common practice to leave deliberate breakwaters of unquarried natural rock. There is one large and several smaller examples of such semi-natural breakwaters in the Bembridge stone at Whitecliff Bay in the Isle of Wight, where such tidal quarrying was practised down to the last war, and there are also examples on the Dorset coast.

Flemming Exposure comes into this a lot. As Throckmorton said, one needs to have a basic knowledge of seamanship. Everything depends on the exposure of the site, and the dominant direction of the wind and waves. A quay or harbour wall in an exposed position must have been a metre or more above the water, whereas at Marzamemi in southern Sicily the modern fishing quay slopes right down to the water.

Green How did you calculate a depth datum for this work? Presumably secondary ports may be some way from your sites. Did you level from these to the submerged sites?

Flemming The datum used was the sea surface itself. We just measured the change of the site relative to the sea.

Green Did you take tidal changes into account? What was the maximum tide range?

Flemming About 10 cm; but you can get a rise in sea level of up to a metre with strong onshore winds. I have to admit that while looking for marks on the shore of these sites I only visited them for a day or so and I have no measurement of the tide. I cannot be more accurate than 10 cm. At Elaphonisos they measured the tide and checked it every hour for the first two days and then every day and then once a week. The tidal change was negligible.

Green We found the same thing at Cape Andreas: a close correlation with tidal predictions from secondary ports. But this did vary with the wind.

Flemming Ten years ago we thought it very clever to be able to measure relative sea level change to an accuracy of ± 1 m. In that context the tidal range in the Mediterranean was not important. Now, however, we are able to observe to about 25 cm on average, and 10 cm in a few cases, so that the tide, even in the Mediterranean, is a limiting factor.

Sea level changes around South-West England

by

A. B. HAWKINS

SUMMARY

The methods of obtaining sea level data are described, including sample location and dating. The importance of the accumulating height of peat deposits and the relationship of the height to H.W.S.T., as well as consolidation and regional stability, are discussed.

The changes in the coastline around South-West England are shown in a series of four diagrams, for sea levels between −250 and −70 ft. (−76.2 and −21.3 m) O.D., covering the period approximately 11,500 to 8000 B.P. Although the upper peat band has been dated in nine coastal localities, nothing younger than 2400 B.P. has been recorded. It is during this period with no peat evidence that Godwin proposed the Romano-British Transgression. The archaeological evidence supporting this theory is presented, attention drawn to the inconsistencies and an alternative explanation put forward in the light of present knowledge.

Although the land may have accreted for several feet since the Roman period, this need not indicate an equivalent eustatic rise, but instead could indicate the consolidation of the underlying peat or the attainment of equilibrium of the accreting level with that of H.W.S.T.

Evidence of modern changes in level comes from tide-gauge records, which, if correctly interpreted, suggest that the sea level during the twentieth century is rising faster than would be expected from the curve presented.

INTRODUCTION

THE AIM OF scientists studying eustatic changes is the production of an accurate graph to show the height of sea level relative to time. If one accepts the presence of datable horizons, the major problem consists in distinguishing the tectonic and isostatic effects, the extent of consolidation and the relationship of the accumulating environment to sea level. The first requirement, therefore, is to obtain a datable sample from a known depth and position in the stratigraphic sequence. For palynological dating, the sample must contain sufficient pollen grains for a pollen count (150 Arboreal Pollen grains: Faegri & Iversen, 1964, 124), ideally in an organic band, but sufficient may be obtained in a fine-grained deposit. For a radiometric date, most laboratories require about 20 grams of peat and wood or 50 grams of shell. Thus it is usually samples from organic bands or shell horizons which are used for dating. For the twentieth century, the study of tide-gauge records has been used by some authors (e.g. Valentin, 1953; Rossiter, 1967) to extrapolate what the overall present sea level changes may be.

The actual samples may be obtained from the intertidal zone, from the sea bed or, more frequently, from deep trenches or bore-holes. The early recorders, such as Horner (1816), referred to what is known as "submerged forest beds". These have been described

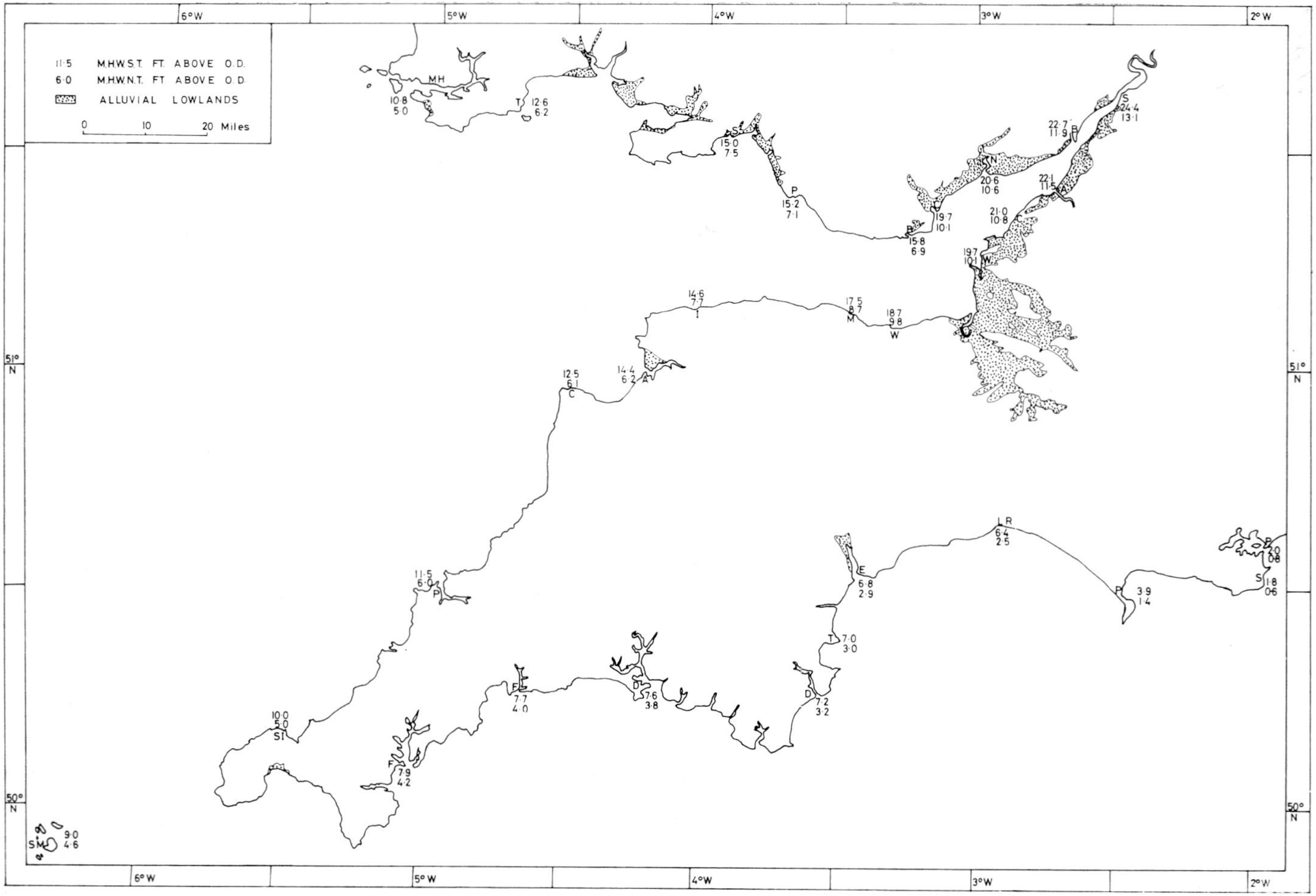

Figure 1. The level of M.H.W.S.T. and M.H.W.N.T. at sites around South-West England.

by various authorities from many localities, but their true extent may still not be fully recognized. On coastlines where modern erosion is attacking Holocene sediments, organic bands are frequently exposed. There is obviously a greater opportunity to locate and examine intertidal organic bands in regions of high tidal range. As regards S.W. Britain, there is a larger area exposed in the Severn Estuary, where the mean spring tidal range at Avonmouth is 40.3 ft. (12.3 m), than on the south coast, where, at Portland, the range is only 6.2 ft. (1.9 m). This is further accentuated during equinoctial spring tides, with a range of up to 47 ft. (14.4 m) at Avonmouth and of only 8.2 ft. (2.8 m) at Portland, allowing inspection to −20.8 ft. (−6.3 m) O.D. and −3 ft. (−0.9 m) O.D. respectively. As a result, it has been possible to record a submerged forest at −18 ft. (−5.5 m) O.D., or 40 ft. (12.2 m) below M.H.W.S., at Severn Beach.

Although there is an increase in the study of marine geology, and consequently in the coring of the sea bed, as yet few organic bands have been reported. Fortunately, a Bristol University cruise sampled six organic bands in Torbay (Clarke, 1970, 309); see Figure 2.

Most dated samples, however, are from bore-holes into the infill deposits of buried valleys. These valleys can be very deep (Codrington, 1898; Anderson, 1968; Durance, 1969; Hawkins, 1971*b*). Although there are many buried valleys in S.W. Britain, the only ones with dated horizons are in the Severn Estuary–Bristol Channel. Before a chronology, devised on the basis of evidence from the Severn Estuary–Bristol Channel region, may be accepted for the south coast, it is necessary first to establish that there has been stability between the two areas.

The extent to which S.W. Britain has been affected by isostatic uplift or tilting is not yet established. ApSimon & Donovan (1956, 134) state: "As far as we know, the Bristol region was not affected by depression and recovery due to loading by Pleistocene ice sheets, nor is there evidence of recent tectonic movement". However, the recent work by Hawkins & Kellaway (1971) suggesting the advance of the Bristol Channel Ice into inland Somerset during the Gipping, and the papers by Bowen (1970) and John & Ellis-Gruffydd (1970) indicating that Late Weichselian ice spread across South Wales, imply that although the areas were marginal, some glacio-isostatic effects would undoubtedly have been felt in the area. Although it is probable that the last ice sheet had left the area before 15,000 years B.P., some of the isostatic effects may still have persisted into the Holocene.

Various authors (including Wright, 1937, and Godwin, 1943) have suggested tilting of southern England during the Quaternary; however, it was Churchill (1965) who first gave prominence to this. He suggested a relative uplift/depression of over 40 ft. (12.2 m) between N.W. England and the Thames Estuary, and 20 ft. (6.1 m) between the Bristol Channel and the Thames Estuary. Hawkins (1971*a*), using published data, supported the hypothesis, but in that paper did not make sufficient allowance for consolidation. The dated peat samples resting on rock or gravel at Freshwater West, Westward Ho! and Margam would have suffered little lowering due to consolidation, compared with those in the alluvial sequence of the Somerset Levels and the Thames Estuary. The evidence still indicates, however, a tilting, isostatic recovery or local downwarping of 5–10 ft. (1.5–3.0 m) between S.W. Wales and the Thames Estuary during the last 6,000 years.

It is necessary also to consider possible tectonic effects, and the inconsistencies that

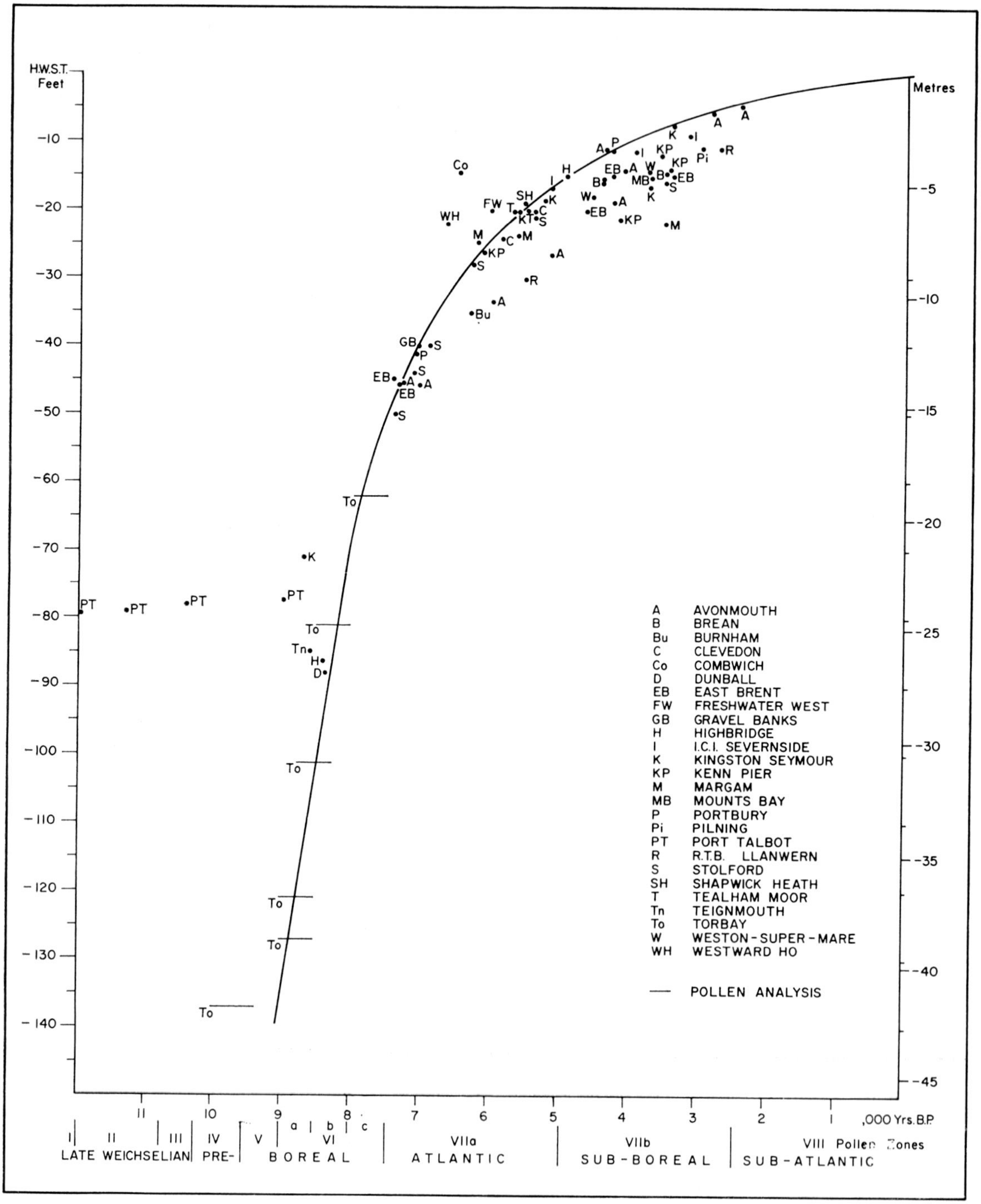

Figure 2. Height/age sea level curve around South-West England during the last 9,000 years.

these cause in the sea level data. C. Thomas (personal communication) has suggested that the Roman remains on the Scilly Islands indicate a submergence of approximately 20 ft. (6.1 m) since Roman times. It will be suggested later that there has been a rise in sea level of approximately $1\frac{1}{2}$ ft. (0.5 m) since that period; consequently there is a major inconsistency between the evidence from the mainland and that from the Isles of Scilly. Although no reports give actual vertical displacements, the occurrence of at least one earthquake off Land's End is recorded. Borlase (1758, 55) records that "a violent shock of an Earthquake was felt in the Western parts of Cornwall" on 15 July 1757, and that in the island of St. Mary "the shock was violent". How many other earthquakes have occurred during the Holocene and how great has been their cumulative displacement is not known. It is, however, imprudent to suggest that the south-west of Britain is an area of no isostatic or tectonic disturbance.

Hawkins (1971*a*) has drawn attention to the importance of the tidal ranges in the Bristol Channel–Severn Estuary and their effect on peat formation. In Figure 1 the height of M.H.W.S.T. and M.H.W.N.T. (from the Admiralty Tide Tables) has been given for sites around S.W. England. This stresses the difference not only between the various areas in the Bristol Channel–Severn Estuary but also between these areas and the south coast. In a coastal environment, both salt-marsh and freshwater peats are related to M.H.W.S.T. and M.H.W.N.T. They are unable to form much above M.H.W.S.T. because the alluvium on which they accumulate will not have accreted above that level. However, the salt-marsh vegetation does not extend seaward of the M.H.W.N.T. level, and freshwater peat is not liable to accumulate much below this level inland of any coastal barrier. The actual height of the freshwater peat accumulation around S.W. England is difficult to establish at present, as most alluvial levels are now drained and the consequent consolidation of peaty deposits makes an establishment of their height of accumulation impossible to assess (note Kaye & Barghoorn, 1964; Sharpe, 1960).

Because of the relationship between peat accumulation, the M.H.W.S.T.–M.H.W.N.T. levels and the varying height of these around S.W. England, it has been decided to take M.H.W.S.T. as the datum for the sea level curve rather than the arbitrary Ordnance Datum. The curve (Fig. 2) has been drawn through (a) the lowest points where dated horizons closely overlie bedrock or gravel, and (b) the points representing the age at the base of the peat band. Frequently, the date of the top of the peat band falls much below the suggested curve, probably owing both to consolidation and to the fact that it formed at a height less than that of M.H.W.S.T. This is shown by many points, but the following will serve as examples. At Kenn Pier, the base of the 3 ft. 7 ins. (1.1 m) peat band has been dated 6100 ± 120 B.P. (I.G.S. 14/39), a point through which the curve has been drawn, while the top, dated 4145 ± 100 B.P. (I.G.S. 14/38), falls 12 ft. (3.7 m) below the curve. At Avonmouth, the base of a 1 ft. 4 ins. (0.4 m) peat band has been dated 4960 ± 140 B.P. (GX 1203), a point which lies on the line, while the top of the band, dated 4110 ± 120 B.P. (GX 1202: Skempton and Smotrych, personal communication), is seen to lie 4 ft. 6 ins. (1.4 m) below the curve. The points representing Combwich, Westward Ho! and Freshwater West, like that of the lower band at Kingston Seymour, probably represent peat forming above contemporary sea level conditions, a situation similar to that at Port Talbot (Godwin and Willis, 1964, 124).

The points presented in Figure 2 incorporate published dates, notably Radiocarbon dates. The author would also like to acknowledge some of the Avonmouth dates from

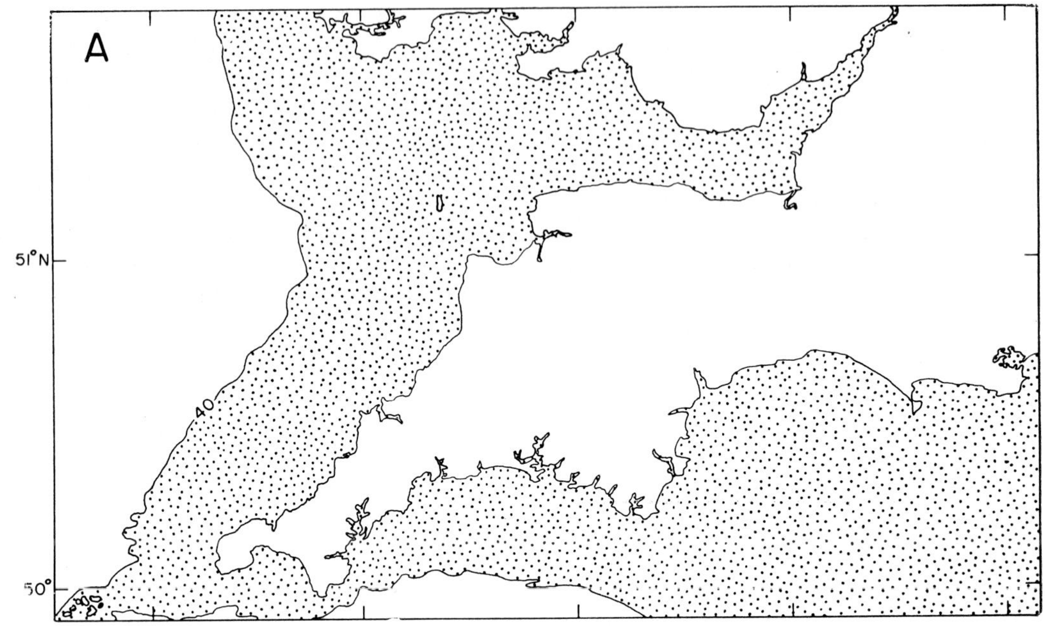
A
51°N
50°
40

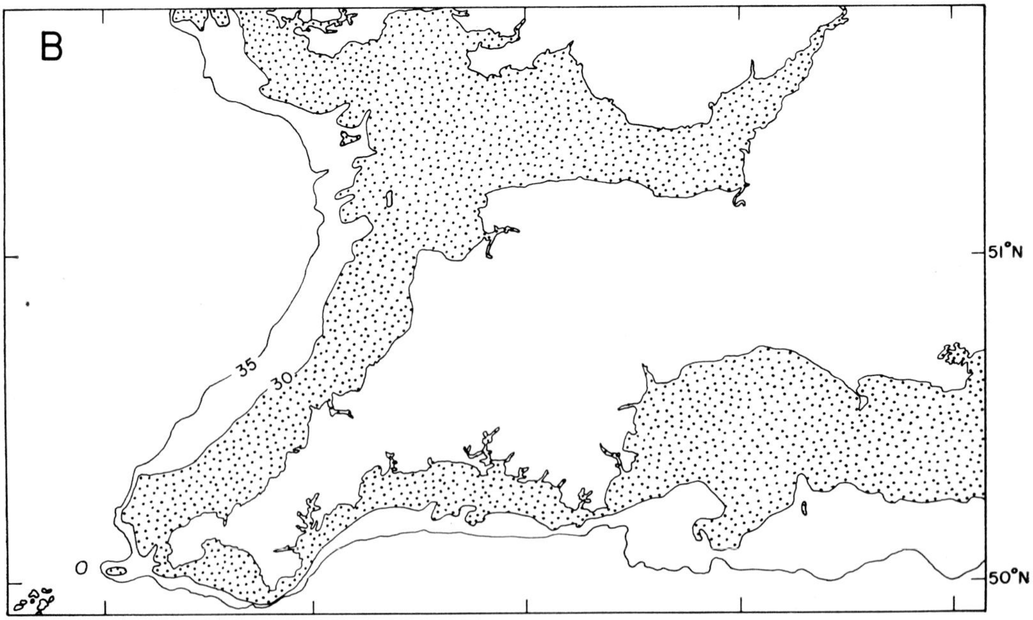
B
51°N
50°N
35
30
0

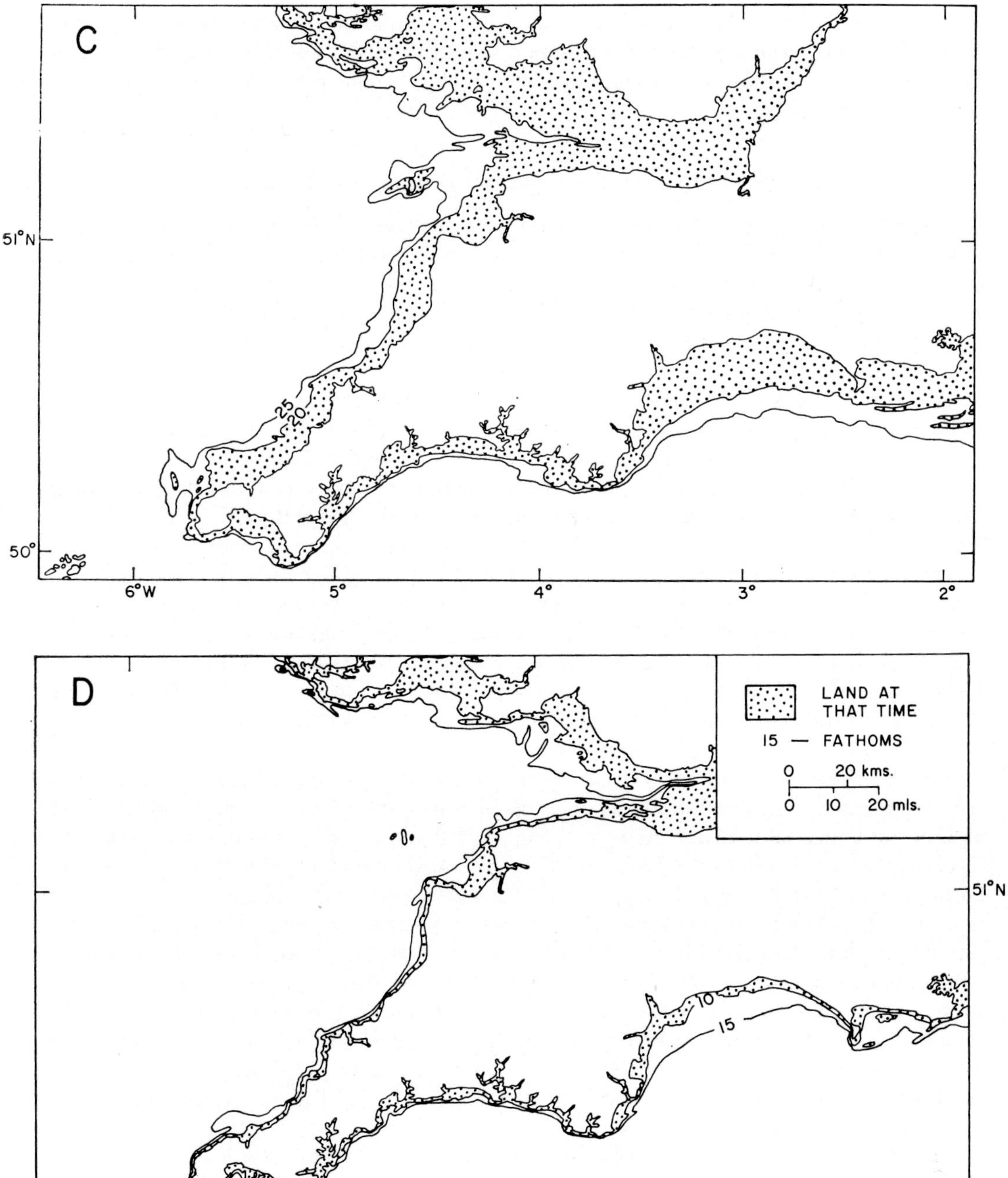

Figure 3. The changing coastline around South-West England between about 11,500 and 8000 years B.P., assuming no thick superficial cover. Taken from Admiralty Charts.

Skempton (1970, 390) and Skempton and Smotrych (personal communication); some of the dates for Brean and East Brent obtained by the Mobil Oil Company (Evans and Gee, personal communication) and the date at Highbridge from Whittaker (personal communication).

THE SEA LEVEL RISE—LATE WEICHSELIAN TO ROMAN

It has been accepted by most authors that the sea level during the Late Weichselian Glaciation was −420 ft. (128 m) O.D. or lower. About 14,000 years B.P. the temperature began to rise rapidly from a July average of approximately 9°C to a July average of about 17°C about 12,500 years B.P. (Coope, Morgan & Osborne, 1971, 94, 96). During Zone III, however, the temperature deteriorated to about 10°C, before rising again to 16°C approximately 9000 years B.P.

To what extent this very marked change of temperature affected the sea level changes during the overall rise is not known. Coope and others (1971, 96) suggest that the rise in temperature above 10°C during Zone II lasted only about 2,000 years. The natural retardation of cause and response on sea level change may have resulted in there being little eustatic effect. The papers on eustatic level which deal with this period do not comment on this, or give any indication on their graph of any sea level oscillation coinciding with the climatic amelioration in Zone II. Thus, whilst the author is conscious of the problem, for the present he will assume the sea level rise to have been steady since the withdrawal of the ice in the Late Weichselian. On the basis of the new temperature graph (by Coope and others) it would seem improbable that the submerged cliff at Plymouth with a base at 22 fathoms below L.W.S.T. (Cooper, 1948), referred to by Hawkins (1971*a*), is in fact similar in date to that described by Pinot (1968, 197) or Saint-Requier and Guilcher (1969, 84).

Figure 3 shows approximately the changing shape and position of the coastline around S.W. England. The information has been taken from hydrographic charts and the lines assume no appreciable sediment cover. Figure 3(A) shows the coastline when the sea level was about −250 ft. (−76.2 m) O.D., probably about 11,000–11,500 years B.P. (Milliman & Emery, 1968, 1121). At this time it would have been possible for early man to walk out to Lundy and the Scilly Islands. By approximately 10,000–10,500 years B.P. the sea level had risen to about −190 ft. (−57.9 m) O.D., and the coastline would have appeared similar to that shown in Figure 3(B). At this stage early man could still have walked to Lundy, but the Scilly Islands would have been separated from the mainland. As the sea transgressed, the coastline by about 9000 years B.P. would have appeared as in Figure 3(C), with a height at approximately −130 ft. (−39.6 m) O.D. At this time, the Bristol Channel valley had become a ria and Lundy had become separated from the mainland.

By 8000 B.P. the sea had transgressed up to about −70 ft. (−21.3 m) O.D. and the coastline resembled that of today, except in the Bristol Channel–Severn Estuary region (Fig. 3(D)). It was at about this time that most of the present drowned valleys became submerged. For instance, the rock surface beneath the present Somerset Levels, which descends to −83 ft. (−25.3 m) O.D. (Hawkins, 1971*b*, 303), would have been inundated by marine water between 8500 and 8000 B.P. The lowest peat so far recorded occurs at −68 ft. (−20.7 m) O.D. and is dated 8360 ± 145 B.P. (I −4,315), indicating that the land surface at that time was 88 ft. (26.8 m) below the present H.W.S.T. level, and also that the transgression had not yet inundated the area, except possibly the deep valleys.

The rise in sea level during the last 8,000 years has been discussed by many authors; the more important graphs have been recently summarized by Mörner (1971, 700). In view of the dates plotted in Figure 2, it is impossible to accept that the eustatic rise was higher than today during the Climatic Optimum, as suggested by Fairbridge (1961), Mörner (1969), etc. If their hypothesis is correct, then the peats which have beeu dated between 5000 and 3000 years B.P. must have formed below M.H.W.N.T. However, on the basis of peat stratigraphy and pollen analysis, Godwin and Willis (1959, 68; 1961, 60) date the change from estuarine clay deposition to peat accumulation, now about 20 ft. (6.1 m) below M.H.W.S.T., at about 5500 years B.P. In fact, it is known that many thick peat bands accumulated at this time, which could imply a slight lowering of the sea level. This, however, would then pose difficulties with regard to the waterlogged conditions that are presumed to have been prevalent at the time when the Neolithic Trackways were being built. If the sea level had been lower than indicated in Figure 2, the interior lands would probably have drained and the trackways would have been unnecessary. Since there is no positive evidence for a rise or fall of sea level associated with the Climatic Optimum, it is considered more appropriate to continue with a smooth curve. There is therefore possibly room for argument about the sea level during the Neolithic Period. This, however, is relatively insignificant compared with the projected sudden rise during the Roman occupation of Britain, suggested by Godwin (1943) and Cunliffe (1966).

THE ROMANO-BRITISH TRANSGRESSION

In recent years the Romano-British Transgression, first proposed by Professor H. Godwin in 1943, has become accepted, and consequently an established part of the history of sea level change in Somerset. The present author, however, does not accept the existence of a sudden marine transgression during the Roman occupation of Britain. It is proposed to consider this under three headings:

(a) relevant published literature;
(b) inconsistencies;
(c) an alternative hypothesis.

(*a*) *Relevant Published Literature*

Although Roman remains have been recovered from the low alluvial lands of Somerset since at least 1670, it was not until the paper by Godwin (1943) that the hypothesis of a Romano-British Transgression was first introduced. Prior to 1943 the main references were by

(1) De la Beche (1839, 422), who recorded "the remains of Roman potteries having been found at the depth of 12 ft. below silt, 300 yards from Basin Bridge . . ." and said "we might almost be led to infer that this difference of level was in a great measure effected since the occupation of Britain by the Romans . . .";

(2) Stradling (1849, 55), who set out "to prove that the turbaries of Huntspill, Chilton Polden, Edington, Catcott and Shapwick were occupied by Romans, at least through the summer months . . .". Reference is made to the mounds in the Burtle area "containing several hundred loads of the fragments of Roman pottery" and (p. 56) to his finding, probably at Chedzoy, on a slight rise "at a depth of about 18 inches, a square platform formed of clay, around which were several pieces of Roman ware. . . . I was soon convinced I was standing on what was once a Roman pottery". At the Nidons, again above the alluvial levels, kilns and moulds were found 1 foot beneath the surface;

(3) Phelps (1853, 103), who records "at Highbridge, in 1804. At the depth of 7 ft. in the alluvial deposits, the workmen came to a stratum of inundated peat, lying beneath it, and on it a heap of Roman pottery fragments, with pieces of small bricks . . .";

(4) Haverfield (1906, 352), who quotes a letter from Paschal to Aubrey in 1670: " 'several hundreds of casting-moulds of fine clay' were found 3 or 4 ft. deep, in low ground, on a site not easy to identify, but probably near Bawdrip, on the south side of the Polden Hills." He also refers to a find in 1801, a quarter-mile north of Chilton, on or near the Nidons, as well as the finds by Stradling between Chilton Polden and Edington Burtle. He concludes by saying (p. 354) "In sum, we have proof that in Roman days man really dwelt on the edge of the marsh that skirts the Polden Hills. The occupation may have been confined to the third and fourth centuries";

(5) Bulleid (1914, 142), who, on summarizing the available information on the pottery moulds, concludes ". . . it may be assumed that a very considerable industry was carried on in this out of the way district of Somerset during the latter part of the Roman occupation of Britain, and that the trade was flourishing in 230 A.D.".

During the early 1940s, the digging of the Huntspill Cut, a 5-mile-long east-west drainage channel, originally 23 ft. (7.0 m) deep in places, gave an opportunity for the stratigraphy of this part of the alluvial lowland to be examined. Besides an engineering report, the only account of this was by Godwin (1943) in a general paper on "Coastal Peat Beds of the British Isles and North Sea". Godwin (p. 220) gives a "schematic diagram" from the coast to Shapwick Heath, 10 miles inland. On this he indicates Romano-British remains under the coastal clay belt, approximately 9 ft. (2.7 m) beneath the present land surface. Using this information and the artefacts previously found at a depth of 12 ft. (3.7 m) at Bason Bridge and 7 ft. (2.1 m) at Highbridge, Godwin suggested a transgression of the sea postdating the accumulation of the main peat band seen at Highbridge and Huntspill. He goes on (p. 219) "Thus the onset of the second transgression seems clearly dated". As regards the end of the transgression, Godwin states ". . . at Combwich on the mouth of the Parrett, what appears to be the same upper clay, at a height of 21 ft. (6.4 m) O.D., has a Romano-British occupation at or close beneath its surface. There would thus seem to be grounds for thinking that the transgression began and ended within this restricted period". Thus the previous records of Romano-British remains were placed by Godwin into a new context: he suggested a land surface which was inundated and suffered a considerable deposition of estuarine clay within the short period of the Roman occupation of Britain.

In 1948, Godwin again referred to the transgression, stating (p. 279) "... in Romano-British times there took place a substantial marine transgression in which was laid down the tidal belt of clay land on which Bridgwater, Huntspill and Highbridge now stand".

Two papers by Godwin in 1955 refer to the Romano-British Transgression. In the paper on Meare Pool he writes (1955*a*, 162) "Meanwhile at the seaward end of the Somerset Levels about 250 A.D. the effects became apparent of a substantial marine transgression which brought marine and brackish water clays far into the valleys. The seaward edges of the raised bogs were deeply eroded, and for a distance of 2 or 3 miles overlaid by thick clay deposits reaching nowadays to about +20 ft. (6.1 m) O.D. These clay surfaces themselves were occupied within the Romano-British period. With this marine transgression, presumed to have been caused by eustatic rise in sea level, our stratigraphic evidence for the post glacial evolution of the Levels ends". In the same paper (p. 163) he records a Samian cup found at Highbridge Brickworks in 1911, 26 ft. (7.9 m) below the surface, and he describes and shows diagrammatically (p. 164) the Roman clay penetrating up the Axe Valley through the Panborough Gap into Godney Moor. It was in this paper that Godwin introduced the term "Roman Clay". In the same year Avery, (1955, 7) reproduced Godwin's "schematic profile" of 1943, and remarked that "During Romano-British times, a further marine transgression destroyed some of the peat and led to the deposition of a coastal belt of grey clay about 5 miles wide".

Some change in emphasis could be deduced from a paper in 1958 by Godwin, Suggate and Willis, in which is stated (p. 1519) "Our results differ significantly from those reported last year by Shepard and Suess, particularly in indicating that the level of the oceans attained that of the present day about 5,500 years ago rather than in the present millennium". However, in the Croonian Lecture in 1961 Godwin again refers to the Romano-British Transgression, stating (p. 315) "... after completion of the eustatic rise about 3500 B.C. [that is, 5450 B.P.], the clay surfaces were covered by raised bogs which grew up during the Neolithic, Bronze and Iron Ages ... until the Romano-British period, during which further marine transgression occurred, eroding the bog margins and bringing them under a coastal belt of clay. Thus between 3500 B.C. and the first centuries A.D. these low-lying coastal areas can have suffered no substantial marine invasion". In the same paper he produces a "schematic representation of the main freshwater and marine layers in the post-glacial deposits of the Somerset Levels' and later in the caption makes the statement "whilst the Somerset coastal peat bogs escaped marine transgression between 3500 B.C. and Roman time ...". In this diagram, Godwin indicates the peat surface at Tealham Moor at approximately the same height as that of the coastal clay belt, and the erosion channels in the peat not passing through the peat into the lower clay as shown in the 1943 diagram (p. 220).

The next paper to stress the Romano-British Transgression is that by Cunliffe (1966) on "The Somerset Levels in the Roman Period", in which he summarizes much of the material available in Somerset and the Caldicot Levels. After considering some of the published evidence, he indicates (p. 72) that "The inundation of the Somerset Levels and the south Welsh coast could have been caused by an overall rise in sea level of 10–20 ft.", and concludes: "To summarize: The alluvial levels of North Somerset were deposited in the late Roman to post-Roman period as the result of a gradual rise in sea level, beginning in the third century".

Cunliffe records the finds by

(1) Brown (1958, 121) of a Roman sherd at Lawrence Weston (Avonmouth), but no depth of the actual find is recorded;

(2) Miles (personal communication) of a Roman surface 7 ft. (2.1 m) below the ground level at Highbridge Brick Pit;

(3) Nash and Smith (1961, 43) of a Roman floor at Highbridge, $5\frac{1}{2}$ ft. (1.7 m) below the surface (but Cunliffe does not mention that this is in an area with a rise in the normal ground level of $1\frac{1}{2}$ ft. (0.5 m), and that hence the floor is really 4 ft. (1.2 m) below the average land surface of the area);

(4) Phelps (1853, 103) of peat at 7 ft. (2.1 m) at Highbridge;

(5) De la Beche (1839, 422) of Roman remains at 12 ft. (3.7 m) at Bason Bridge.

Cunliffe's reference (p. 69) to the Huntspill attributes to Dewar (1949*a*, 201) and Godwin (1943, 219) the evidence that the "Roman ground surface, on top of a peat layer, lay beneath 9 ft. of alluvial clay . . .". Dewar in this paper does not record any depth, but states that the "Roman deposits had been sealed over by water-borne clay"; he does, however, in another paper (1949*b*, 162) suggest a depth of approximately 9 ft. (2.7 m). Further, Godwin does not mention a depth, but his diagram, if taken as accurate, implies a covering of about 9 ft. (2.7 m). On the basis of these records, Cunliffe concludes (p. 69): "It is therefore clear that at some period the Roman ground-surface suffered a severe and lengthy inundation".

For the South Wales coast Cunliffe quotes Barnett (1961, 12), who records potsherds and the bones of domestic animals found at Uskmouth beneath about 14 ft. (4.3 m) of clay. Using the same reference, Cunliffe further states (p. 70) ". . . and at Goldcliff and Redwick pottery of the same date was recovered from similar positions, though less satisfactorily sealed". Since Cunliffe's paper, Boon (1967, 121) has recorded pottery and ox bones at Magor Pill, nearly 10 ft. (3.1 m) below the present land surface.

As has been demonstrated, the term Romano-British Transgression has become accepted and the term "Roman Clay" is frequently applied to the upper clay of the coastal region. Numerous papers could be cited, but it will suffice here to quote from two official memoirs. The transgression is accepted without question by Findlay (1965, 17) in the Mendip District Soil Memoir, while Green and Welch (1965, 121), besides mentioning the term Romano-British, use the expression 'Roman Clay' nine times on one page.

(*b*) *Inconsistencies*

The major difficulty arises with Godwin's section (1943, Fig. 12) and the indication which it gives that the Romano-British remains occur on peat, 9 ft. (2.7 m) below the present land surface. The section was drawn "based on borings by the Somerset Rivers Catchment Board, by the author and Dr. A. R. Chapman, and on field observations by W. Abery". A copy of the bore-hole diagram from the (now) Somerset River Authority. confirms that the general thickness of clay overlying the peat is 7–10 ft. (2.1–3.1 m) between Witchey Bridge and Woolavington Causeway. To the west, the peat lenses out, but a thinner band reappears at the same height and extends as far west as Puriton Drove. The difficulty arises in knowing whether or not the Romano-British remains are really found on the main peat band, as shown by Godwin (1943, 220), or as shown differently in his diagram (1961, 315), or, in fact, on peat hummocks above the general level of the horizon.

On 11 April 1971, the author inspected the banks of the Huntspill Cut near Woolavington Causeway at a time of unusually low water. Three Romano-British pottery hoards were found within 400 yards east of the Causeway at ST 346436, 347436 and 348436. The pottery hoards were situated on irregular peat hummocks rising as much as 3 ft. (0.9 m) above the water level (Fig. 4). Laterally there was an abrupt change to blue-grey estuarine clay, while vertically the base of the peat was not located. The peat hummocks thus closely resemble the ones indicated by Godwin between Puriton Drove and Woolavington Causeway. The bases of the hoards (i.e., the upper surface of the peat) are between $3\frac{1}{2}$ (1.1 m) and 4 ft. (2.2 m) below ground level, while the tops of the mounds are within $1\frac{1}{2}$ ft. (0.5 m) of the surface. Apart from Godwin's 1943 diagram, there are no records of Romano-British remains where the stratigraphic relationship is recorded. In view of the finds near Woolavington Causeway, the author wonders whether those recorded by Godwin were similarly located, having in fact no connection with the main peat band but resting on higher residual hummocks. Support for this view has

Figure 4. Peat on which lies Romano-British material, 3–4 feet (0.9–1.2 m) below ground level near Woolavington Causeway on the Huntspill Cut.

been obtained from Mr. Kelting, Chief Engineer to the Somerset River Authority (personal communication), who recalls several hoards being found between Gold Corner (Witchey Bridge) and Woolavington Causeway, with their tops about 1 ft. (0.3 m) below the surface of the Levels and their bases 3–4 ft. (0.9–1.2 m) below ground level. Kelting does not recall any hoards west of Woolavington Causeway, as recorded by Godwin. In the latter case, however, Dewar (1949*b*, 162) has described a countersunk-handled jar from between Woolavington and Puriton Drove and suggested that "the vessel was either released from one of the dumps of working debris or, alternatively, washed out of one of the deep erosion channels cutting across the line of the river near the site of the find."

In his 1943 paper (p. 219) Godwin also suggested that the Romano-British Transgression "began and ended within this restricted period" because "at Combwich . . . what appears to be the same upper clay, at a height of 21 ft. O.D., has a Romano-British occupation at or close beneath its surface". Unfortunately, Godwin does not give the evidence on which he compares the clays at Combwich and Huntspill. With estuarine clays in various states of desiccation, oxidization and consolidation it would be unlikely that the clays were not of the same origin, but to deduce a transgression of 7–10 ft. (2.1–3.1 m) in a period of about 150 years from the similarity of two clay deposits is a rather dubious procedure.

The importance of the tidal regime of the Bristol Channel–Severn Estuary was not fully appreciated by Godwin and others (1958, 1519), when they concluded that the present sea level was reached about 5,500 years ago rather than in the present millennium. Dating the base of the peat band at Tealham Moor, which occurs now at approximately Ordnance Datum, simply provides a date for the change from the deposition of estuarine clay to the accumulation of peat. In a tidal estuary, with Mean High Water Springs at about +20 ft. (6.1 m) O.D., a change in the character of the deposits at Ordnance Datum cannot be taken to indicate the end of the main eustatic rise, because it is probable that the main depositional change would have occurred with a land surface at about Mean High Water Springs. It would appear that in a brief description of the general eustatic rise the particular tidal problems of the Bristol Channel–Severn Estuary were ignored, and consequently an erroneous conclusion was reached.

As regards Cunliffe's summary (1966) of the information available on the Roman period in the Somerset Levels and on the South Wales coast, there are three inconsistencies that require attention. Cunliffe (p. 70) records Romano-British pottery at Redwick and Goldcliff, found in similar positions to that found beneath 14 ft. (4.3 m) of estuarine clay at Uskmouth, and quotes Barnett (1961) as the reference. Although Barnett draws attention to the fact that the finds occurred beneath "where the ground rises slightly", Cunliffe does not indicate that the 14 ft. (4.3 m) depth of overlying estuarine clay may therefore not be typical of the area. Further, Barnett (p. 12) actually speaks of "hundreds of Roman potsherds . . . and other objects on the foreshore at Cold Harbour Pill, Redwick", thus indicating that the discovery was made on the foreshore, and hence in no way implying any depth or stratigraphic relationship. With regard to Goldcliff, Barnett states (p. 13): ". . . but it was clear that they had come from the alluvium beneath a thin buried beach and about 18 ins. below the present surface of the flats". Although Cunliffe (p. 70) bases his comments on the paper by Barnett, there is a lack of consistency between the two authors.

Cunliffe makes no mention of the very significant find of a Samian cup 26 ft. (7.9 m) below the surface at Highbridge (Godwin 1955*a*, 163). Neither he nor Godwin explain the inconsistency of this with their other conclusion, that the ground surface in early Roman times was at the level of the Romano-British remains. Cunliffe also states (p. 73): "More than 100 square miles of inhabited land was inundated, giving rise to a massive movement of population and an apparent re-orientation of the economy". To a geologist, an inhabited area of the type implied by Cunliffe would suggest a land surface over which man could move easily. Cunliffe refers to the work done by the North Somerset Archaeological Research Group, but does not draw attention to the shallow depth of the Romano-British finds in the Clevedon area (6–24 inches; 0.2–0.6 m) and the inconsistency of this with the story proposed by himself and Godwin for the main area of the Somerset Levels.

If we accept the Romano-British Transgression, then it is necessary to put forward an explanation for its non-existence elsewhere in the world. Other authors provide no evidence of a sudden transgression in the third century A.D.: Shepard (1963), Milliman and Emery (1968), Hails and Hoyt (1969), Guilcher (1969), Neumann (1969), Redfield (1967).

The present author, before undertaking this more detailed survey, had accepted the existence of the transgression and attempted to explain it by regional subsidence (1969), or by breakthrough of a coastal barrier or a more rapid phase in the easterly tilting and an increase in the tidal regime (1971*a*). After his more detailed consideration, however, an alternative hypothesis is now proposed to explain the evidence more satisfactorily.

(*c*) *An Alternative Hypothesis*

During the last two years, seven dates have been obtained for the upper peat bands in the alluvial succession to the east of the Severn Estuary. These dates can be added to that already published (Godwin & Willis, 1964, 128) of 2660 ± 110 B.P. for the top of a peat band, 9 ft. (2.7 m) below present surface at Llanvern.

I.C.I. Severnside	7½ ft. (2.3 m) down	3100 ± 100 B.P.
Pilning	10 ft. (3.1 m) down	2910 ± 95 B.P.
Avonmouth	12 ft. (3.7 m) down	4105 ± 100 B.P.
Portbury	10 ft. (3.1 m) down	4240 ± 105 B.P.
Kingston Seymour	7 ft. (2.1 m) down	3350 ± 120 B.P.
Kenn Pier	7 ft. (2.1 m) down	3510 ± 100 B.P.
Weston-super-Mare	14 ft. (4.3 m) down	3675 ± 100 B.P.

In each case, the top of the peat band did not show any indications of erosion or desiccation and there was no apparent stratigraphical break above the peat band. If Cunliffe is correct in suggesting that the Romans moved freely over and cultivated the Levels prior to the Romano-British Transgression, then there should be evidence of a soil horizon, since it seems improbable that the Romans would have cultivated a mud-flat. Mr. Kelting (personal communication) has confirmed that in the many miles of drainage channels dug in the Levels since 1938 (when he became chief engineer to the Somerset River Authority) he has never seen any indication of a desiccated layer or a soil horizon. Geologically, it seems probable that the estuarine flats would have

Figure 5. The Somerset Levels in the Roman Period may have been similar to the tidal-flat landscape in the foreground. Photo: G. Evans.

continued to accrete slowly and become colonized by vegetation as their level reached the M.H.W.S.T. level. It is envisaged that during Roman times the Levels were in the transition stage between true mud-flat and grass saltings (Fig. 5). These areas would be very wet in winter due to the spring tide inundations and greater effective precipitation, and would in all probability have been totally inhospitable. In summer, however, with lower tides and precipitation and greater evaporation, the Levels, apart from the tidal pills, would have been areas of relatively free passage. The present author doubts whether even in summer any cultivation of the estuarine alluvium would have taken place, but it is probable that the sandy, drier "islands" of the Burtle Beds would have been ideal for cultivation.

For many years the North Somerset Archaeological Research Group has been recording Romano-British remains from the North Somerset Levels. Lilly and Usher (1972, 37) state that "Over the area as a whole the Roman occupation horizon lies within 6–22 ins. (0.2–0.6 m) of the present surface. It therefore appears from the evidence found in North Somerset that the depth of the Roman occupation in this area is different from that reported by numerous authors in the Levels south of the Mendip Hills". It is remarkable that in the North Somerset region none of the thirteen finds has been recorded below 2 ft. (0.6 m), while to the south material had rarely, until recently, been recorded above 2 ft. (0.6 m).

Increasing evidence is now appearing of Roman remains within 2–4 ft. (0.6–1.2 m) of the present surface. Mrs. Langdon (personal communication) has recorded nineteen pottery finds similar to those already described (p. 79) along the Huntspill between Woolavington Causeway and Gold Corner. With the construction of the M5 Motorway, Langdon, Nash and others have found many examples of Roman occupation, all within about 3 ft. (0.9 m) of the land surface. It is hoped that these finds will be fully reported in the future.

In view of the increasing evidence of finds near the surface, the present author wonders whether the recorders in the past have been partly selective in their reporting. It is possible that the odd piece of pottery found in a trench at a depth of 1–2 ft. (0.3–0.6 m) will not be reported to an archaeologist, but anything found at a depth in excess of 5 ft. (1.5 m) will be notified to the experts. Much material may have been lost in the past because the area was not so carefully watched as it is today. Consequently, past reports probably only recorded the big and unusual, the significance of the shallow finds not being appreciated.

It is suggested, therefore, that the Romans occupied the Levels during the summer for two reasons. First, the sandy regions known as the Burtle Beds would have produced good, friable, quickly-warming soils, and hence were probably cultivated in summer. It is probable that the alluvial levels were a mud-flat over which *Salicornia* was spreading as the early colonising plant. If more vegetation had been present it is surprising that no evidence in the form of plant roots can be found, and there is no observed increase in the carbonaceous content of the deposits. Secondly, we have abundant remains to indicate the importance of the area for pottery manufacture. Bulleid (1914) recorded many pottery mounds on the edge of the peat lands, and their abundance along the Huntspill Cut has been noted above. Their origin is probably due to the existence of a malleable, silty clay in close proximity to the fuel of the peat lands and the sands of the Burtle Beds.

With the unbroken geological sequence and the abundant recent finds at shallow depth, it is suggested that the ground surface in Roman times was probably about 1–3 ft. (0.3–0.9 m) below the present ground surface. This does not, however, explain the occurrence of Roman remains found between 5 ft. (1.5 m) and 15 ft. (4.6 m) below the surface, still less the Samian cup found 26 ft. (7.9 m) down at Highbridge. On present information it is possible to divide these remains into two groups: first, those found on the top of peat layers; and second, the odd deep finds.

Earlier in the paper it has been stated that owing to consolidation the dates of the tops of peat bands now fall below the suggested sea level curve. Thus any Roman occupation on a peat band will appear deeper than its original accumulation horizon, owing to the greater consolidation of the peat band (note p. 71). Phelps (1853, 103) recorded Roman fragments at Highbridge at a depth of 7 ft. (2.1 m) on an indurated peat, and Mrs. Langdon (personal communication) records remains at a similar depth at the East Huntspill Sluice, resting on about 4–5 ft. (1.2–1.5 m) of compacted peat. It is suggested that the deeper finds represent the discarded remains of the Roman period. In a region of tidal pills it is natural that man would throw his rubbish into the "ditches" rather than leave it scattered over the mud-flats. In the literature there is some evidence to support this: Barnett (1961, 12) records that "The potsherds and bones were grouped closely together . . . embedded in the glutinous estuarine clay. . . . The excavation was extended beyond immediate requirements, but there was no trace of any structural remains or any further material". Further, he writes that "Only the obvious can be stated with any certainty: that at Uskmouth has been found a rubbish pit into which someone threw bits of broken pottery and the remains of hearty meals in the 2nd century A.D.". Nash (personal communication) has observed details of the occurrence of Roman pottery at the Bristol Road Brick Pit, Highbridge. Here, in 1957, a 7-foot (2.1 m) section of pit was visible and he was able to observe six channels in a face 310 ft. (94.5 m) long. The channels varied in size from 7 ft. (2.1 m) across and 2 ft. (0.6 m) deep to 15 ft. (4.6 m) across and 4 ft. (1.2 m) deep. The Romano-British material occurred rarely on the ground surface between the pills, but in relative abundance in the bottom of the channels. Dewar (1949*b*, 162) also made reference to this when he said "the vessel was either released from one of the dumps of working debris or, alternatively, washed out of one of the deep erosion channels cutting across the line of the river near the site of the find". The suggestion of preservation within tidal pills or old river-courses also satisfactorily explains the Samian cup at a depth of 26 ft. (7.9 m), which was referred to by Godwin (1955*a*, 163).

Thus the author envisages a land surface 1–3 ft. (0.3–0.6 m) below the present. The area was a mud-flat on which vegetation was beginning to establish itself, initially probably on the upper marsh and tidal pill levées. Consequently, it is anticipated that the Roman remains will occur chiefly in the inland part of the coastal clay belt, where the clay transgressed on to the peat bands (now lower than the clay owing to consolidation and possibly peat extraction). The Romans used the mud-flats as a route to the drier sandy "hills" and a place for pottery manufacture, but all this would have been restricted mainly to the summer months.

THE POST-ROMAN PERIOD

Little is known about the area during the "Dark Ages", but by A.D. 1100 the lands in the Redwick area were being protected by sea walls. Cole (1912, 6) records that in 1312 the sea wall at Henbury was in a state of damage, while Williams (1970) has summarised the evidence for the draining of the Somerset Levels. Thus, although the date when the sea defences were constructed is not known, it is probable that the region had some protection by the end of the fourteenth century. Occasionally, however, the area was still inundated: for example, during January 1606 over a hundred square miles of land was flooded, resulting in the loss of over two thousand people and many cattle (North, 1955, 74). At both Kingston Seymour and Redwick the flood waters were about 5 ft. (1.5 m) high, as recorded by plaques in the churches. Other floods have been recorded by Cole (1912) and Richardson (1887). The floods do not necessarily imply a rise in sea level, but were probably associated with exceptional weather conditions during equinoctial tides.

The continual accretion of the Levels outside the sea walls is clearly demonstrated in the Severn Estuary region. At present the unprotected marshes of St George's Wharf are inundated by about fifteen to twenty-five tides a year. The height of this area is now about 2 ft. (0.6 m) greater than that of the land behind the sea walls, and it is suggested that this extra height has accumulated since the construction of the walls. Again, this does not imply a rise in sea level of 2 ft. (0.6 m) since that time, but an attempt by the sea to gain equilibrium and to accrete to the maximum height of H.W.S.T. during the equinoctial periods.

From a study of tide-gauge records dating between 1916 and 1962, Gordon and Suthons (1963, 5) have suggested an average sea level rise at Newlyn of 0.81 ft. (0.2 m) per century, while over the northern hemisphere as a whole the rise is approximately 0.5 ft. (0.2 m) per century. If these tide-gauge assessments, which are similar to those by Rossiter (1967, 259), are correct, then the eustatic rise at present is greater than would be deduced from the sea level curve, or they imply that we are now in a period of more rapid sea level rise. Since, however, the length of time over which tide-gauge records can be studied is small, and the implications of all the data are not yet understood, this must await further study.

ACKNOWLEDGEMENTS

The author would like to thank Professor C. Thomas, Professor Skempton and Mr. Smotrych, Dr. Whittaker and Dr. Evans and Mr. Gee for allowing him to include unpublished data, and Mrs. Langdon and Mr. Nash for helpful discussions about their unpublished work. The help of Miss S. Pritchard, who has read the script and prepared the reference list, and of Mr. P. J. Fowler, who has discussed the archaeological references, is very much appreciated.

REFERENCES

Anderson, J. G. C. 1968 The Concealed Rock Surface and Overlying Deposits of the Severn Valley and Estuary from Upton to Neath. *Proc. S. Wales Inst. Engrs*, **83**, 27–44.

ApSimon, A. M. & Donovan, D. T. 1956 Marine Pleistocene Deposits in the Vale of Gordano, Somerset. *Proc. Univ. Bristol Spel. Soc.* **7**, 130–6.

Avery, B. W. 1955 *The Soils of the Glastonbury District of Somerset*, Mem. Soil Surv. Gt. Br., Sheet 296, 131 pp. London.

Barnett, C. 1961 A Find of Roman Pottery at Uskmouth. *The Monmouthshire Antiquary. Proc. Monm. and Caerleon Antiq. Assoc.* **1**, 12–13.

Boon, G. C. 1967 Roman Pottery from the base of the alluvium at Magor. *The Monmouth Antiquary. Proc. Monm. and Caerleon Antiq. Assoc.* **2**, 121–7.

Borlase, W. 1758 *The Natural History of Cornwall*, 326 pp. Oxford.

Bowen, D. Q. 1970 *The Glaciations of Wales and Adjoining Regions*, ed. Colin A. Lewis, 378 pp. London.

Brown, J. Clevedon 1958 The Roman Settlement at Lawrence Weston—The Alleged Road and the '1850' Pavement. *Proc. Univ. Bristol Spel. Soc.* **8**, 119–23.

Bulleid, A. 1914 Romano-British Potteries in Mid-Somerset. *Proc. Soc. Antiq. London*, **26**, 137–54.

Churchill, D. M. 1965 The Displacement of Deposits Formed at Sea Level 6,500 Years Ago in Southern Britain. *Quaternaria*, **7**, 239–49.

Clarke, R. H. 1970 Quaternary Sediments off South-East Devon. *Q. Jl. geol. Soc. Lond.* **125**, Part 3, 277–318.

Codrington, T. 1898 On Some Submerged Rock Valleys in South Wales, Devon and Cornwall. *Q. Jl. geol. Soc. Lond.* **54**, 251–78.

Cole, S. D. 1912 *The Sea Walls of the Severn*. Bristol. Printed for Private Circulation.

Coope, G. R., Morgan, A. & Osborne, P. J. 1971 Fossil Coleoptera as indicators of climatic fluctuations during the Last Glaciation in Britain. *Palaeogeography, Palaeoclimatology, Palaeoecology*, **10**, 87–101.

Cooper, L. H. M. 1948 A Submerged Ancient Cliff near Plymouth. *Nature, Lond.* **161**, 280.

Cunliffe, B. W. 1966 The Somerset Levels in the Roman Period, *in* Thomas, C. (ed.) *Rural Settlement in Roman Britain* (C.B.A. Research Report 7), 68–73.

De la Beche, H. T. 1839 *Report on the Geology of Cornwall, Devon and West Somerset*. Mem. Geol. Surv. U.K., 648 pp.

Dewar, H. S. L. 1949*a* The Pottery Mounds of the Brue Valley. *Somerset and Dorset Notes and Queries*, **25**, 201–2.

Dewar, H. S. L. 1949*b* Roman Countersunk-Handled Jar from Huntspill. *Proc. Somerset Arch. and Nat. Hist. Soc.* **94**, 161–4.

Durance, E. M. 1969 The Buried Channels of the Exe. *Geol. Mag.* **106**, 174–89.

Faegri, K. and Iversen, J. 1964 *Textbook of Pollen Analysis*, 237 pp. Copenhagen.

Fairbridge, R. W. 1961 Eustatic changes in Sea Level. *Physics Chem. Earth*, **4**, 99–185.

Findlay, D. C. 1965 *The Soils of the Mendip District of Somerset*, Mem. Soil Surv. Gt. Br., Sheet 280, 204 pp. London.

Godwin, H. 1943 Coastal Peat Beds of the British Isles and North Sea. *J. Ecol.* **31**, 199–247.

Godwin, H. 1948 Studies of the Post-Glacial History of British Vegetation. X. Correlation between Climate, Forest Composition, Prehistoric Agriculture and Peat Stratigraphy in Sub-Boreal and Sub-Atlantic Peats in the Somerset Levels. *Phil. Trans. R. Soc.*, B **233** 275–86.

Godwin, H. 1955*a* Studies of the Post-Glacial History of British Vegetation. XIII. The Meare Pool Region of the Somerset Levels. *Phil. Trans. R. Soc.*, B **239**, 161–90.

Godwin, H. 1955*b* Botanical and Geological History of the Somerset Levels. *Advmt Sci., Lond.* **12**, 319–22.

Godwin, H. 1961 Radiocarbon Dating and Quaternary History in Britain. *Proc. R. Soc.*, B **153**, 287–320.

Godwin, H., Suggate, R. P. & Willis, E. H. 1958 Radiocarbon Dating of the Eustatic Rise in Ocean-Level. *Nature, Lond.* **181**, 1518–19.

Godwin, H. & Willis, E. H. 1959 Cambridge University Natural Radiocarbon Measurements. *Am. J. Sci. Radiocarbon Suppl.* **1**, 63–75.

Godwin, H. & Willis, E. H. 1961 Camb. Univ. Nat. Rad. *Am. J. Sci. Radiocarbon Suppl.* **3**, 60–76.

Godwin, H. & Willis, E. H. 1964 Camb. Univ. Nat. Rad. *Am. J. Sci. Radiocarbon Suppl.* **6**, 116–37.

Gordon, D. L. & Suthons, C. T. 1963. Mean Sea Level in the British Isles. *Admiralty Marine Science Pub.* **7**, 1–8.

Green, G. W. & Welch, F. B. A. 1965. *Geology of the County around Wells and Cheddar*, Mem. Geol. Surv. U.K. 280, 225 pp.

Guilcher, A. 1969 Pleistocene and Holocene Sea Level Changes. *Earth Sci. Rev.* **5**, 69–97.

Hails, J. R. & Hoyt, J. H. 1969 An Appraisal of the Evolution of the Lower Atlantic Coastal Plain of Georgia, U.S.A. *Trans. Inst. Brit. Geogr.* **46**, 53–68.

Haverfield, F. 1906 *A History of the County of Somerset*, Vol. I (The Victorian History of the Counties of England) 537 pp.

Hawkins, A. B. 1969 Post-Glacial Sea Level Changes in the Bristol Channel (Abstract). *Proc. Ussher Soc.* **2**, 86–7.

Hawkins, A. B. 1971*a* The Late Weichselian and Flandrian Transgression of South West Britain. *Quaternaria*, **14**, 115–30.

Hawkins, A. B. 1971*b* New Work on the Quaternary of the Severn Estuary. *Proc. geol. Soc.* No. 1664, 303–4.

Hawkins, A. B. & Kellaway, G. A. 1971. Field Meeting at Bristol and Bath with Special Reference, to New Evidence of Glaciation. *Proc. Geol. Ass.* **82**, 267–92.

Horner, L. 1816 Sketch of the Geology of the South Western Part of Somerset. *Trans. Geol. Soc. U.K.* **3**, 339–84.

John, B. S. & Ellis-Gruffydd, I. D. 1970 Weichselian Stratigraphy and Radiocarbon Dating in South Wales. *Geologie Mijnb.* **49** (4), 285–96.

Kaye, C. A. & Barghoorn, E. S. 1964 Later Quaternary Sea Level Change and Crustal Rise at Boston, Massachusetts with Notes on the Autocomposition of Peat. *Bull. Geol. Soc. Am.* **75**, 63–80.

Lilly, D. & Usher, G. 1972 Romano-British Sites on the North Somerset Levels. *Proc. Univ. Bristol Spel. Soc.*, **13**, 37–40.
Milliman, J. D. & Emery, K. O. 1968 Sea Levels during the Past 35,000 years. *Science, N.Y.* **162**, 1121–23.
Mörner, N. A. 1969 The Late Quaternary History of the Kattegat Sea. *Sver. geol. Unders.*, Ser. C NR 640, Ārsbok 63, NR 3.
Mörner, N. A. 1971 The Holocene Eustatic Sea Level Problem. *Geologie Mijnb.* **50**, 699–702.
Nash, S. G. & Smith, V. C. R. 1961 A Roman Structure at Highbridge. *Somerset and Dorset Notes and Queries*, **28**, 43–4.
Neumann, A. C. 1969 Quaternary Sea-Level Data from Bermuda. *Résumés des Communications. VIII Congrès Inqua, Paris*, 228–9.
North, F. J. 1955 *The Evolution of the Bristol Channel*, 2nd Edit, 102 pp. Nat. Mus. Wales, Cardiff.
Phelps, W. 1853 On the Formation of Peat Bogs and Turbaries. *Proc. Somerset Arch. and Nat. Hist. Soc.* **4**, 91–107.
Pinot, J. P. 1968 Littoraux Wurmiens Submergés a L'Ouest de Belle-Ile. *Bull. Ass. Étude Quat.* **3**, 197–216.
Redfield, A. C. 1967 Post-Glacial Changes in Sea Level in the Western North Atlantic. *Science, N.Y.* **157**, 687–91.
Richardson, C. 1887 The Severn Tunnel. *Proc. Bristol Nat. Soc.* **5**, 49–81.
Rossiter, J. R. 1967 An Analysis of the Annual Sea Level Variations in Europe Waters. *Geophys. J. R. Astron. Soc.* **12**, 259–99.
Saint-Requier, A. & Guilcher, A. 1969 Un grés coquillier de facies littoral, immergé a −34 m. en Baie D'Audiane (Finistère) est daté de 15,000 ans avant l'actuel. *C. r. Acad. Sci., Paris*, **268**, 1915–16.
Sharpe, C. F. S. 1960 *Landslides and Related Phenomena*, 137 pp. Paterson, New Jersey.
Shepard, F. P. 1963 Thirty Five Thousand Years of Sea Level, *in* Clements, T. (ed.) *Essays in Marine Geology in Honor of K. O. Emery*, 1–10. 201 pp. Los Angeles, Calif.
Skempton, A. W. 1970 The Consolidation of Clays by Gravitational Compaction. *Q. Jl. geol. Soc. Lond.* **125**, 373–412.
Stradling, W. 1849 The Turbaries between Glaston and the Sea. *Proc. Somerset Arch. and Nat. Hist. Soc.* **1**, 48–62.
Valentin, H. 1953 Present Vertical Movements of the British Isles. *Geog. J.* **119**, 299–305.
Williams, M. 1970 *The Draining of the Somerset Levels*, 288 pp. Cambridge.
Wright, W. B. 1937 *The Quaternary Ice Age*, 478 pp. London.

Discussion

Peel If one accepts the view that there was a minor interruption in the general Post-Glacial eustatic recovery, in the sense of a break in the steady progress of rising sea level giving this Romano-British transgression, what kind of physical cause do you think this break might be attributed to? In terms of one's normal picture of progressive change and climatic balance it is not easy to visualise a cause.

Hawkins I cannot find anything in the literature to substantiate a cause, such as ice surges or ice recessions, which could have resulted in this remarkable break. I should be delighted to know if anyone has found outside England evidence for a Romano-British Transgression.

Flemming I agree that it is highly unlikely. There is plenty of documentary evidence of fluctuation in rise of sea levels and there have certainly been fluctuations, due to climatic variation. There is no evidence for a rise of more than 1–2m in the last 5,000 years, and it is probably about $\frac{1}{2}$m.

Hawkins I did not go into all the minor oscillations; there were probably some slight ones. There is a widespread consistent peat band just above Ordnance Datum which may indicate a slight lowering or still-stand about 5,000 years ago, but our information is as yet too indefinite to postulate this.

Hague In the Western Mediterranean how early were the sites which had consistent sea level? How relevant is this to the melting of the ice?

Flemming Sites which were occupied 2,000 years ago in the western Mediterranean are almost all in correct relation to present sea leavel. The most dramatic period of ice melting occurred between 18,000 and 5,000 years ago. Minor climatic fluctuations have on the whole been played down more and more in recent years. While between ten and thirty years ago people were quite happy to think of 10–20 foot oscillations, this is not now generally accepted.

Hawkins Sea level is estimated to be rising at present at $\frac{1}{2}$ ft. per century; this is probably associated with a slight world recession of the ice-caps.

Recent coastal sedimentation: a review

by

GRAHAM EVANS

THE FLAT LOWLANDS which border many coastlines of the world are regions which both today and throughout the past have proved attractive to man for sites of his settlements: he has been attracted by the flatness and the proximity to the sea and therefore the relative ease of movement and the possibility of the use of both land and water transport. Consequently, it is useful for the archaeologist to have some understanding of the evolution of coastal lowlands if he is fully to realize the importance of this environment and its likely changes during the period that they have been colonized by man. Also, an understanding of this environment will help him to decide where he might expect to find the remains of ancient civilizations and also what is the likelihood of their preservation.

Over the past twenty-five years a vast quantity of information has been collected on the evolution of modern coastlines, the processes involved in their development and the resulting physiographic forms. The present paper reviews some of the general principles of coastal evolution and discusses their relevance for archaeologists.

The greatest single suppliers of sediment to the coastline are undoubtedly rivers: vast quantities of sediment are carried to the sea each year by the major rivers of the world (see Table 1 [after Smith, 1966]).

TABLE 1

Name	Area of subaerial deltaic plain	Average water discharge	Average sediment discharge
Mississippi (U.S.A.)	28,489.89 km²	17,301.5648 m³/s	525,196,245 t*
Nile (Egypt)	16,057.938 km²	2,831.68 m³/s	6,096,300 t
Niger (Nigeria)	19,424.925 km²	6,090.112 m³/s	25,401,250 t
Mekong (South Vietnam)	51,799.80 km²	11,326.72 m³/s	81,284,000 t
Ganges–Brahmaputra (India–Pakistan)	90,749.65 km²	38,510.848 m³/s	711,235,000 t
Danube (Bulgaria)	816,846.85 km²	6,173.0624 m³/s	101,605,000 t

* t= metric ton = 1000 kg

Generally speaking, erosion of cliffs is of minor importance in supplying sediment to a coastline (Shepard, 1963). Locally, however, where soft deposits form the coastline, coastal erosion may be important and indeed dominate as the source of sediment supply. Such areas have, under the vigorous attack of the waves, been characterized by relatively rapid recession, and the sediment so produced has been carried by waves and currents to other sites along-shore to build up new coastal lands. A good example of such rapid erosion is provided by the south-east coast of Yorkshire and the north coast of Norfolk in the east of England: in the former case a series of soft glacial boulder clays and outwash sands has receded approximately 120m between 1852 and 1952 and approximately 100 million m^3 of material has been carried away over that period (see review in Valentin, 1954); in the latter case the coastline is receding by several meters per year (Steers, 1964) and vast quantities of sediment are being lost locally.

Considerable quantities of sediment may be supplied to the coastline from the erosion and reworking of the immediately adjacent sea floor. This material may be earlier deposited land-derived sediments or in some seas may be chemically or biochemically produced detritus produced within the sea: in tropical seas large amounts of calcareous material are thus produced by organisms, and this is moved slowly landwards to build up coastal accumulation and to form dry land.

Occasionally wind may transport large volumes of sand to a coastline from arid interiors; on reaching the coast this sand will be incorporated in the coastal sediments and will be transported alongshore by wave-generated and other currents to build out coastal plains. Such a situation is seen on the south-west coast of the Persian Gulf on the coasts of Saudi Arabia and Qatar. This is an unusual case, however, as the necessary combination of abundant sand supply and oblique or offshore winds is not often found.

Many large rivers accumulate vast deltaic areas at their mouths. In other cases, where the drainage pattern is not concentrated to a single outfall by tectonic processes, smaller rivers may not join to form a single river but may flow separately to the coast; the detritus is spread over a wide front, if wave conditions are particularly violent, or in other cases forms a series of small overlapping deltas. The vastness of deltaic plains is not always appreciated, but they form some of the largest areas of flat coastal land in the world (see Table 1). These large deltas can only accumulate where large amounts of sediment are supplied to the coast and this, in turn, is only so where large drainage basins debouch on to the coast. Large drainage systems do not occur haphazardly over the earth's surface; they do so because of the presence of regional depressions or of areas of adjacent uplift which concentrate the flow and consequently the sediment supply to particular locations. If one follows this line of argument, it would appear that the major downwarp must precede the sedimentation; the truth of this statement is readily observed if one looks at the geological setting of many of the world's largest deltas and considers the geological history of the surrounding areas.

When the drainage basin pattern is such that a large single delta is constructed, a broadly simple pattern of deposits is developed (Fig. 1). The coarser material is moved along the river channels. During periods of high river flow the river water escapes from its course and floods the adjacent floodplains: it deposits sand and other finer materials along, and in the immediate vicinity of, its banks to form raised banks or levées and deposits the finer material over the wide floodplains to form valuable agricultural land.

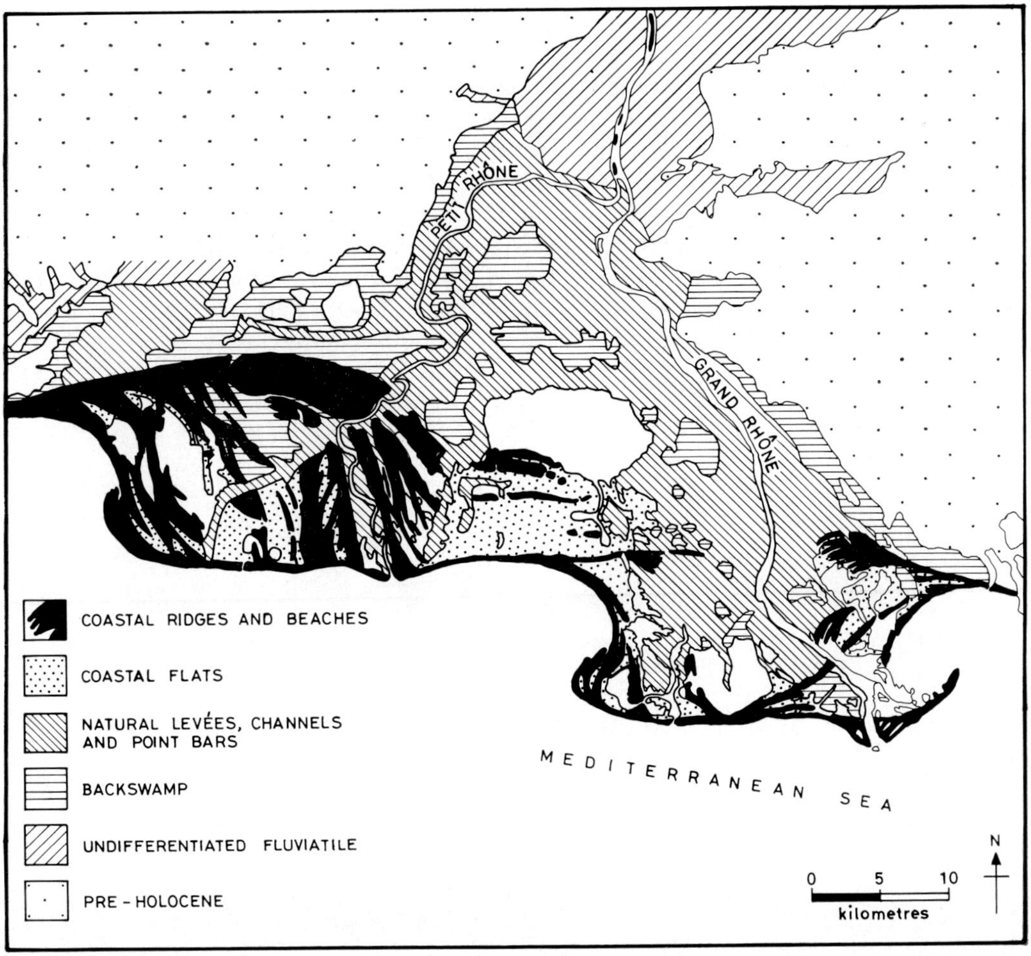

Figure 1. The subaerial environments of deposition of the Rhône delta, France, after van Andel and Curray (1960), taken from original sources.

Occasionally the levées are breached, particularly on sharp bends, and spreads of coarser material—crevasse splays—are poured into the low-lying floodplain areas to form extensions of the relatively higher and better drained land of the levées. Unless interfered with by man, the resulting alluvial plain consists of a wide marshland or swampland, or in arid areas scrub-covered salt-flats, with many shallow lakes and slightly higher, better drained ridges bordering the present-day or abandoned stream courses (see for general reviews Russell, 1936; Kruit, 1955; Kolb & van Lopik, 1958; Gould, 1970). On reaching the sea the coarser-grained sediment is deposited in bars around the river mouths. There the sand and possibly the gravel is pushed laterally by waves, often to form spits or spit-like accumulations, and moves alongshore to build out a series of beach or dune ridges and thus creates new land. It is noticeable in most modern deltas that much of the sand supplied by the rivers is piled up close to the coast, and that sand (except the very fine grades) hardly escapes seawards to any extent. Silt and clay and fine sand, in contrast to the coarser sand, travels in suspension in river water and spreads out in a sheet of fresh, sediment-laden water over the adjacent sea, settling out as this water moves offshore. Some material obviously settles in shallow water, but this is soon remobilized and is transported to less exposed environments. The pattern of dispersal of this silt and clay is dominated by local oceanographic conditions such as ocean, tidal and local wind-generated currents. Sediments usually spread laterally parallel to the coast as well as seawards; for example, muddy waters have spread for long distances to the east and west of the river mouth of the Mississippi. Some of this fine-grained material, after moving laterally, finally moves shoreward from the river mouth to accumulate in shallow bays and intertidal flats. The resulting sediment pattern consists of sands nearshore with increasing amounts of silt and clay offshore, but with a complex of

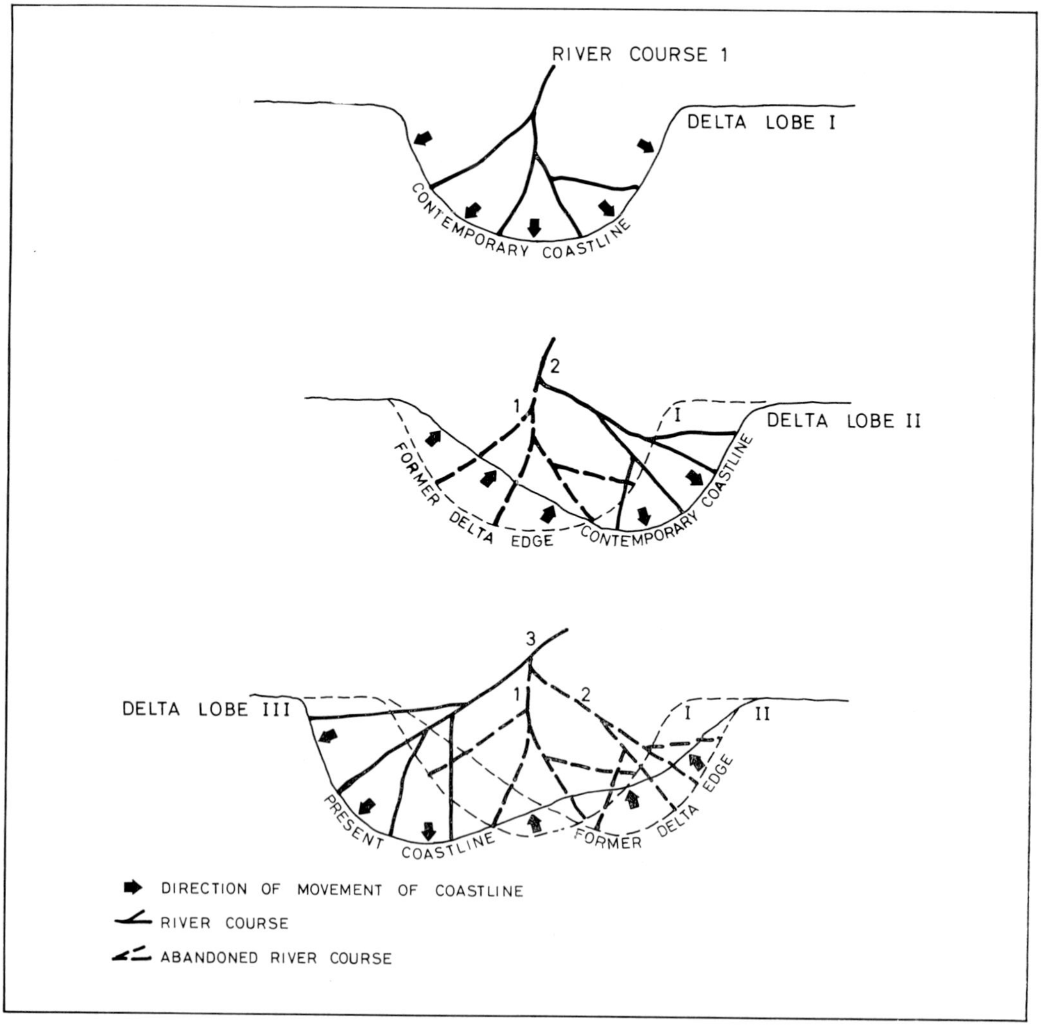

Figure 2. Schematic figure showing the sequence of changes on a delta.

muddy and sandy sediments between the various distributary mouths; the sediments build up areas which become colonized by plants to form swamps or marshes.

With continued supply of sediment an extensive deltaic plain can be built which progrades on to the adjacent continental shelf; its form will be dependent upon the type and volume of sediment transported by the river and the strength of local oceanographic agents such as waves, tides and currents. The resulting pile of sediments will show a general increase upwards in grain size.

River mouths in deltaic regions are notoriously unstable in their location. The river or its distributaries are continually attempting to reach the sea by shorter routes, so that as soon as it has extended itself in one direction it will break through its confining levées to start to build a new deltaic plain, often partly overlapping the earlier one (Fig. 2). Once the river has established its new course, the sequence already described will again develop. The cessation of the fresh water flow with its sediment supply will lead to the establishment of marine conditions over the area of abandoned distributary courses, and reworking of the surface by waves will ensue: this is the so-called "destructional deltaic phase" (Fig. 2). The wave action will destroy the old land surface around the mouths of the distributaries and over the adjacent delta, and with them any settlements developed by man. The coarser material produced by this erosion will be concentrated by wave action and will be pushed landwards and alongshore, whilst the finer material will be dispersed offshore. Such a sequence of events has led to destruction of large areas of land. Man may precipitate such changes: part of the coastline of the Nile delta is undergoing rapid erosion owing to the trapping of river sediment by the Aswan dam.

In cases where there are large quantities of fine sediment in the river load, the abandonment of a channel system will lead to depression of the land surface beneath the waves by compaction of the underlying sediment. In this case, although the destruction is still evident, there is a possibility that the rate of subsidence, due to compaction, will be sufficiently fast to allow some of the former plain to be preserved, with only part of its upper levels destroyed by the waves. In such a situation it is possible that some old sites, or remnants of them, may be preserved. Considerable compaction is thought to have occurred during the evolution of the Mississippi delta, and there individual segments of the delta, or delta lobes, have been drowned and trimmed by erosive marine processes, they still, however, retained some of their features (Fig. 3; Russell, 1936; Fisk & McFarlan, 1955; Kolb & van Lopik, 1958; Kolb & van Lopik, 1966; Gould, 1970). Such muddy deltas are therefore more likely to yield evidence of their earlier occupants than the deltas such as the Rhône (Fig. 4) and Seyhan (Fig. 5) where the sediment contains less muddy material and compaction is not evident, and where destruction by waves of surface levels of the outer parts of the successively abandoned delta lobes is more complete (Kruit, 1955; van Straaten, 1959; Oomkens, 1970). However, even in such deltas as the Mississippi occupational remains will be fragmentary and many of the earlier sites will now lie under the nearshore shallow waters. They will usually be overlain by a thin cover of reworked sandy sediments, and may therefore not be obvious from sea floor examinations and only be revealed by shallow geophysical exploration. Further shifts of the mouths and courses of the distributaries can, in some cases, bring them back to their original sites, and in this case a much thicker layer of sediment will cover the old delta lobe and hide both the physiographic feature and any archaeological sites from the eyes of man.

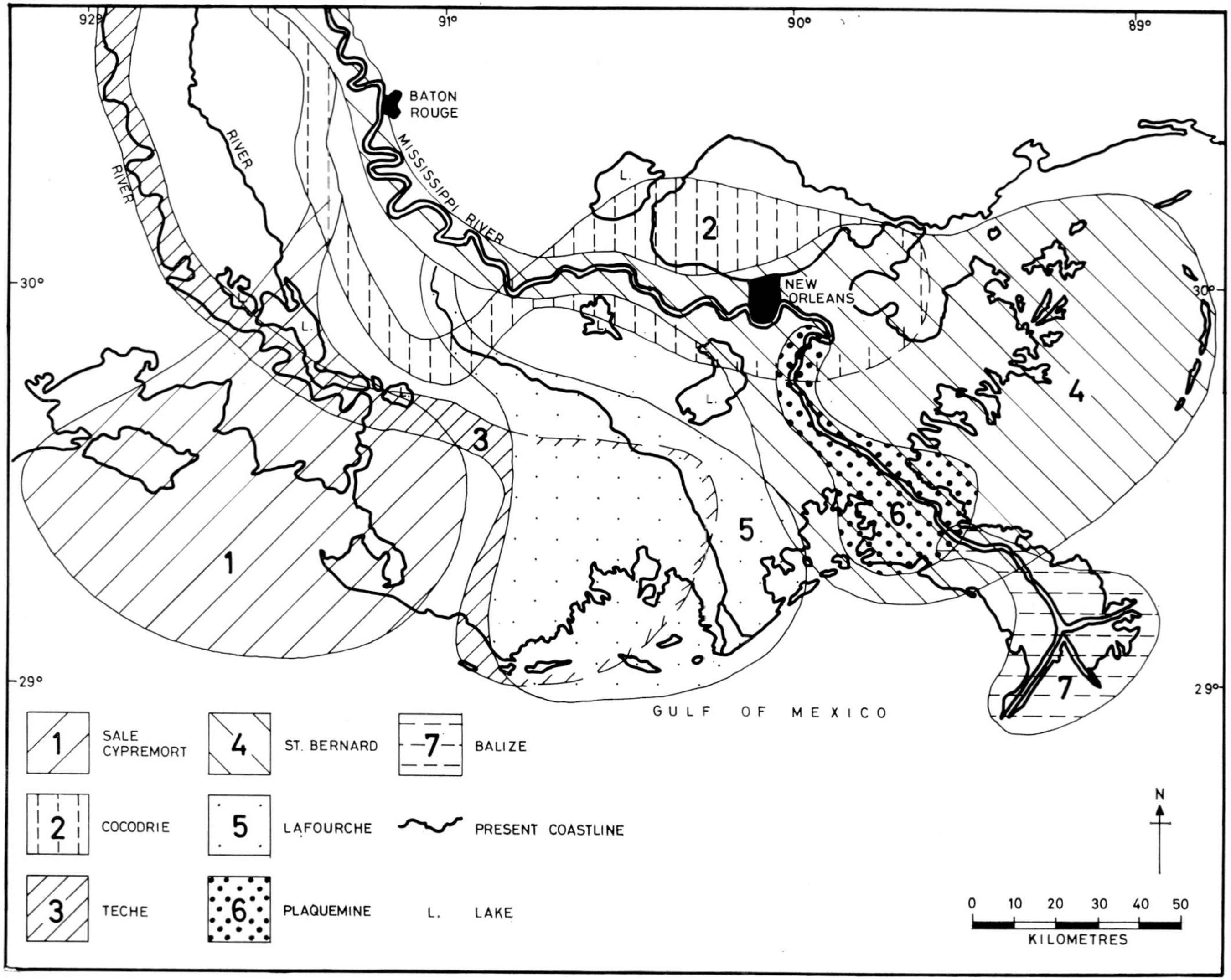

Figure 3. The various delta lobes of the Mississippi, U.S.A., after Gould (1970), taken from original sources of Kolb and van Lopik (1958).

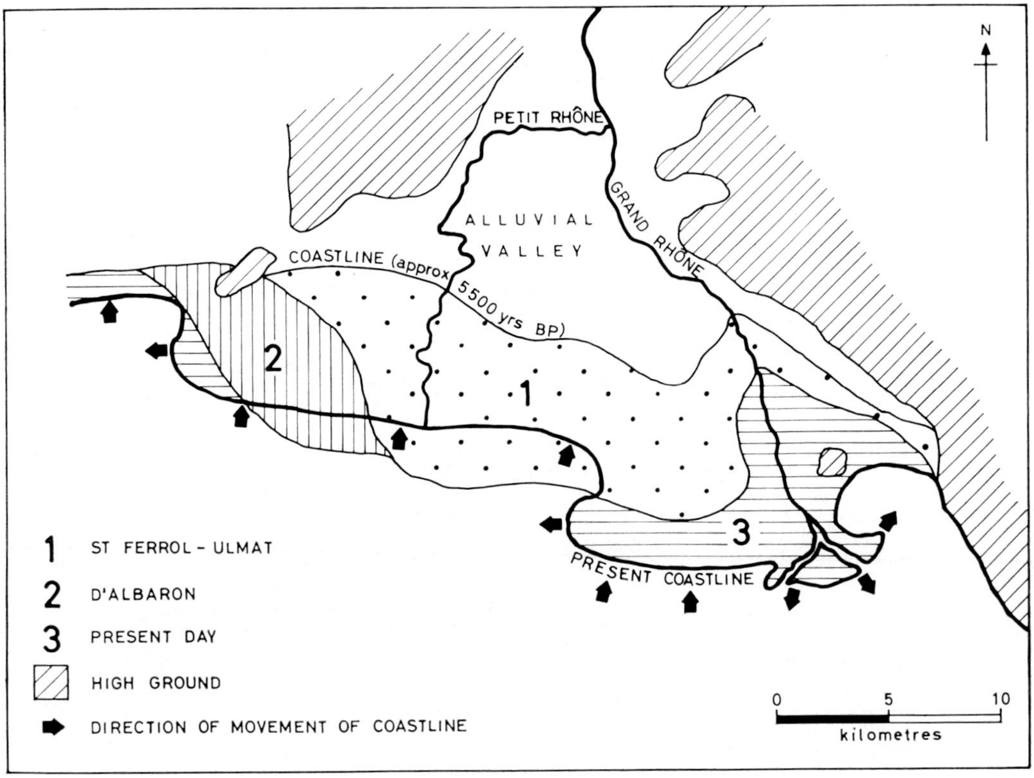

Figure 4. The various delta lobes of the Rhône, after Scruton (1960), taken from original sources of Kruit (1955) and van Straaten (1959).

A further complication arises on deltaic plains, and indeed in all coastal environments, due to the changing level of the sea during the last 20,000 years. Because of the rapid rise of sea level from approximately 20,000 to 7,000 years B.P. and the slower rise from about 7,000 to 3,000 years B.P., the coastlines were usually moving landwards even in deltaic regions, where there is abundant sediment supply. However, in some cases the rate of supply of sediment by the rivers was sufficient to arrest this landward movement: in such areas the coastline remained static in its position or moved landwards only slowly; the coastal barrier of beaches and dunes, and the fluvial plain which lay to landward of these, built up concomitantly with the rise of sea level and maintained their relative surface levels at approximately the same height above the contemporary sea surface. Under such conditions thick piles of coastal plain and fluvial deposits accumulated successively above one another at the same site in some locations; such a condition existed on the Rhône delta during the early and middle Holocene. As a result of such a balanced condition, sites of human settlement on coastal plains would be buried by many tens of metres of sediment and would be hidden, to be revealed only if large and costly excavations were undertaken. This situation may best be emphasized by reference to the Rhône where, for example, a river plain settlement of approximately 10,000 B.P. would

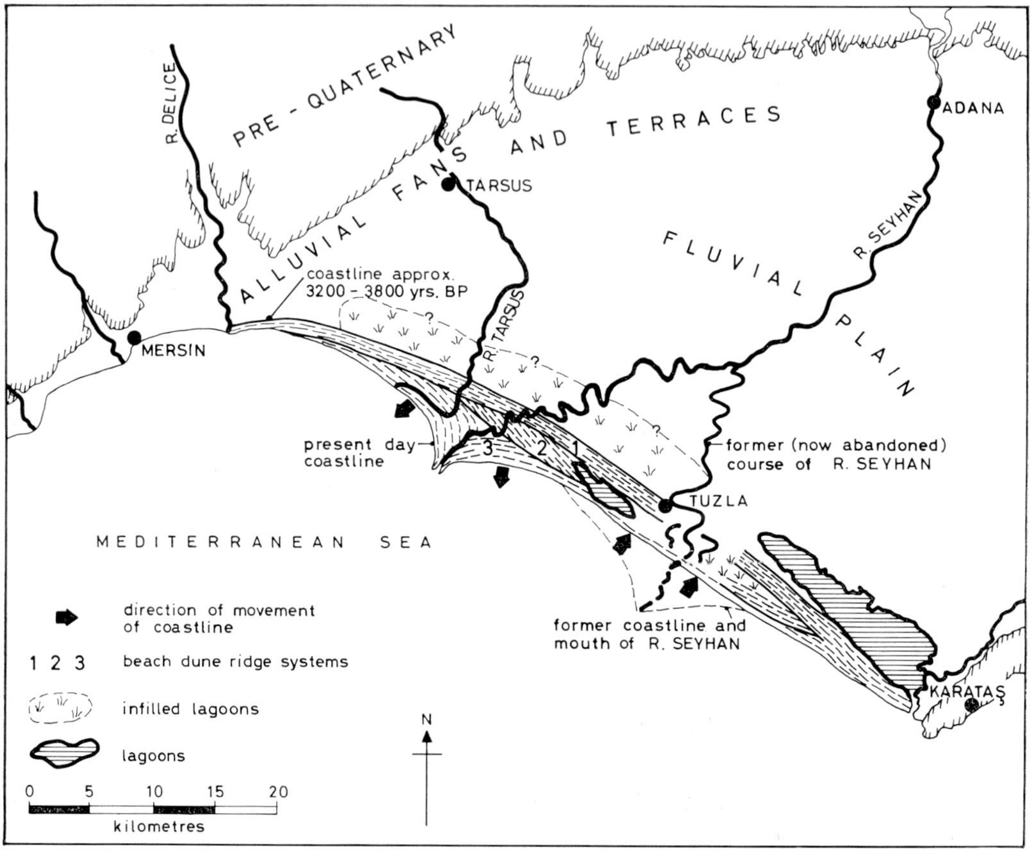

Figure 5. The Seyhan delta, Turkey.

now be overlain by approximately 30 m of fluvial and coastal plain sediment (Lagaaij & Kopstein, 1964; Oomkens, 1970).

The effect of growth of deltas on the prosperity of coastal towns dependent upon water-borne traffic has been well recorded in the literature. Many famous cities have found themselves stranded because of this natural process: for example, the two cities of Miletus and Ephesus in western Turkey were both once thriving ports, but the seaward progradation of the Little Maeander and Great Maeander deltas has led to their present landlocked state. The outgrowth of the land was particularly marked on this west Turkish coast as the rivers flow into long narrow inlets and therefore there was no loss of sediment alongshore; instead sedimentation was concentrated in a small area (see review in Russell, 1954; Eisma, 1962).

Many rivers on reaching the sea pass into large coastal indentations or estuaries, usually oriented approximately at right angles to the coastline; these are particularly strikingly developed in seas with considerable tidal ranges. Estuaries are usually bordered by mud-flats and marshes identical to those of the intertidal flats in other locations (see below), and usually have very unstable low-water channels which are a maze of shallow channels and intervening banks. Whereas the marshes and mud-flats bordering the estuaries are usually fairly stable areas, the lower channel and bank areas are very unstable and are constantly changing their position (Inglis & Kestner, 1958; Price & Kendrick, 1963). This constant movement leads to erosion and deposition, often rapidly alternating in any one part of an estuary (Fig. 6); thus there is a constant redistribution of material and the record of the history of the estuary at any one locality is usually very fragmentary (Oomkens & Terwindt, 1960).

Many of the estuaries show a long-scale deterioration; they have gradually become shallower and less extensive, and small towns on the lower river courses which were once in communication with the sea are no longer accessible to ships. In some cases this is undoubtedly due partly to the deposition of river-borne sediment, supplemented in part by wave-transported material moving alongshore; but in many cases, in estuaries bordering seas with large tidal ranges, this is largely due to the constant ingress of sediment derived from the adjacent sea floors. In such seas the high-velocity tidal currents, often aided by wave action, are eroding the sea floor and transporting vast quantities of sand and mud; this is carried into areas of lower energy in deep water offshore, where it settles, and also into sheltered embayments, lagoons or estuaries, where it is also laid down, together with material derived directly from the land and carried to the coast by rivers. There is therefore a vast quantity of material being transported by the advancing tidal currents into estuaries around Britain, Holland, Germany, etc. Much of this material is flushed out by the retreating tide, aided by river water. The landward movement of sediments in estuaries is accentuated by the fact that many estuaries have well-stratified flow conditions: salt water moves landwards along the bottom and fresh water moves seawards above it; such an arrangement causes net landward motion of water near the floor of the estuary channel, and as most of the sand is carried in this part of the water column it also means net landward movement of this coarser sediment (Inglis & Allen, 1957; Price & Kendrick, 1963; Terwindt, de Jong & van der Wilk, 1963; Kulm & Byrne, 1966).

In many cases it would appear that a natural infilling process has been taking place. This is possibly due to the fact that during the final rise of the sea from its low levels of the last glaciation many of the lower parts of the river courses were drowned, and in some cases they were not in equilibrium with the amount of water flowing in and out with each tide; they were too large and consequently have been infilled. Man was unfortunate in colonizing these estuaries in a period when, although particular sites appeared favourable, the estuaries had in fact not reached equilibrium with present-day sea-level conditions. The estuaries have thus continued to decline and in so doing have adversely affected many old ports. It is unlikely that such a process would completely infill an estuary, but it certainly will reduce the estuary's size and depth to some form of equilibrium. Consequently many old harbours and riverine towns have been cut off from their means of livelihood by this natural process. In order to maintain channels for ships to enter and leave harbour, vast quantities of sediment are now dredged from many of our large ports each year.

In other areas of the world, where rivers are more widely spaced or where sediment is produced either by erosion of the coasts or by landward transportation from the offshore zone, wide coastal plains formed of beach dune complexes and other physiographic forms may be produced. For example, a coastal plain, made up largely of sub-parallel

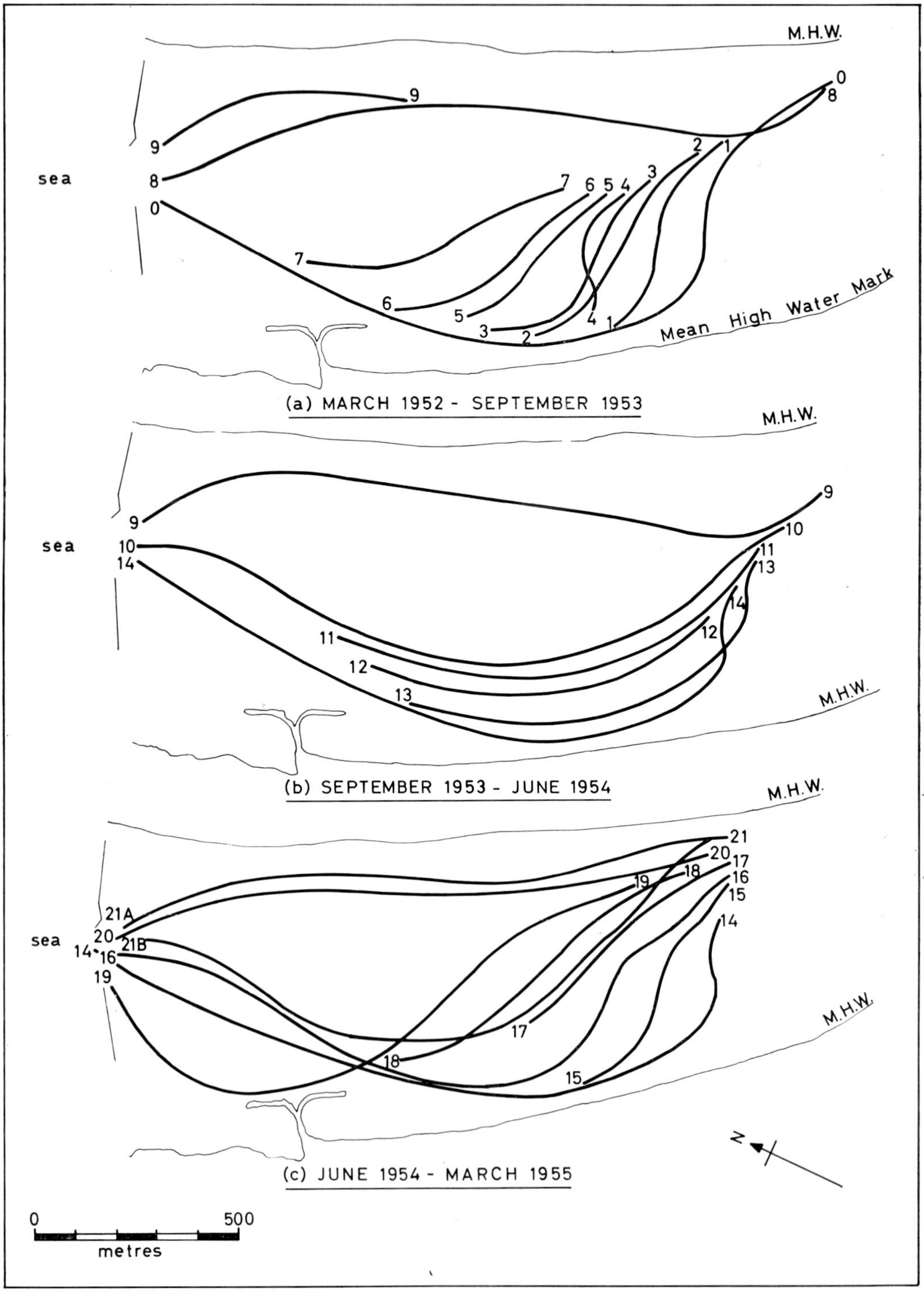

Figure 6. Successive positions of the low-water channel of the Wyre estuary at Burn Naze, England, after Inglis and Kestner (1958).

Figure 7. A coastal plain composed mainly of beach and low dune ridges on the Pacific coast of Mexico.

sandy beach ridges and with a width of 15 km (Fig. 7), runs for several hundred kilometres along the west coast of Mexico (Curray & Moore, 1964).

In most coastal areas of the world the dominant agent of sediment movement is wave action and wave-induced currents (Johnson, 1956; Shepard, 1963; Silvester, 1959; Inman & Frautschy, 1966); near deltas and in estuaries this is complicated by fluvial currents, and in tidal seas by strong tidal currents. Waves are generated by wind at sea, often many thousands of kilometres from the points where they ultimately reach the coast and break. The orbital motion of the water particles in waves is transmitted down to the sea floor, and where the water is shallow enough sediment will be moved. It has been shown that in shallow water the result of wave action is to keep coarser material close to the shoreline and to cause seaward dispersion of fine material (Inman & Frautschy, 1966). When waves reach water which varies in depth from 1.3 to 1.6 times their wave height, they break and cause a system of sediment movement which varies from being onshore to being offshore according to the character of the waves; the excess water piled up inside the breaker zone will often move alongshore, carrying sediment with it, and will escape seawards as a series of narrow belts of sediment-laden water—rip currents.

The sediment lost to seaward in this way will again move landward under the action of waves, or in other directions under the action of currents.

Seasonal changes will shift material from the offshore to the nearshore zone. Usually sand moves onshore in summer and offshore in winter, but this is sometimes not so clearly marked where there is not a great difference in the wave characteristics of the two seasons. However, the winter season is usually one in which many beaches are almost bare of sand, and only the underlying rock or gravel remain, together with any rigid human constructions. Once material has escaped seawards past the breaker zone, owing perhaps to a very violent storm, it can be moved back to the beach only very slowly; it often comes under the influence of other processes and is therefore carried away from a particular site before its return has been accomplished. The net result of these processes is to pile sand and gravel up against the coastline to form beach complexes. The escape seawards of the coarser grades of the sediment (i.e., sand and gravel) is strictly limited, although under very special circumstances it must be very great (Inman & Frautschy, 1966).

Also, waves approaching a coastline at an angle produce a longshore component to this sediment movement which is commonly known as littoral drift; consequently vast volumes of sandy and sometimes gravelly sediment are moving along many coastlines in the zone between where the waves break and the high-water mark. The direction of movement of material can change over a long period with changes in the direction of wave approach, depending upon long-term climatic changes and changing wind patterns over the adjacent seas. The magnitude of the amount of material moving parallel to the shore in this way is brought home very forcibly to man when its flow is interrupted by the construction of harbours and dredged channels. These act as wonderful traps for the sediment in transit and they soon become filled unless continuously dredged by man. For example, it has been estimated that 300,000 m^3 of sediment are transported alongshore each year by this process at Newport, California, U.S.A. (Inman & Frautschy, 1966).

The infilling and decline of many harbours is thus almost an inevitable consequence of their construction, and no special catastrophic explanation of this infilling is necessary. In most cases it is simply that natural processes have proved to be too great in magnitude for man to be able to combat them, particularly in earlier times when large-scale excavation or dredging techniques were not available.

The material piled up to form beaches may be further transported by wind; it moves inland to form the wide belts of dunes which so commonly border sandy beaches. Such dune belts are common in northern Europe, particularly on the west coasts of England, Holland and France; perhaps one of the most impressive dune ridges is that found on the coast of Landes, France (Fig. 8); it is approximately 250 km long and 5 km wide, and in places attains heights of 113 m. Similar dune belts are known elsewhere, particularly in Oregon on the west coast of the U.S.A. (Cooper, 1958). The volume of sand locked up in these dunes is truly immense. One of their most striking features is their great thickness, when compared with that of the adjacent beaches. These dune sands are receiving supplies from the adjacent beaches and nearshore zones, and in many areas are moving inland, burying coastal marshes, infilling lagoons and overriding continental deposits, burying trees, etc. For example, it has been estimated that over 200,000 m^3 of sand are driven inland each year on a 56-km length of beach in California, and over 1,000,000 m^3 on Vizcaino Bay, Baja California, Mexico (Inman & Frautschy, 1966). Many cases are known of dune sands burying human settlements, for example, medieval churches on the west coast of Britain (Steers, 1964); the site of Side on the south Turkish coast was once covered (until man re-excavated it) with such dune sands.

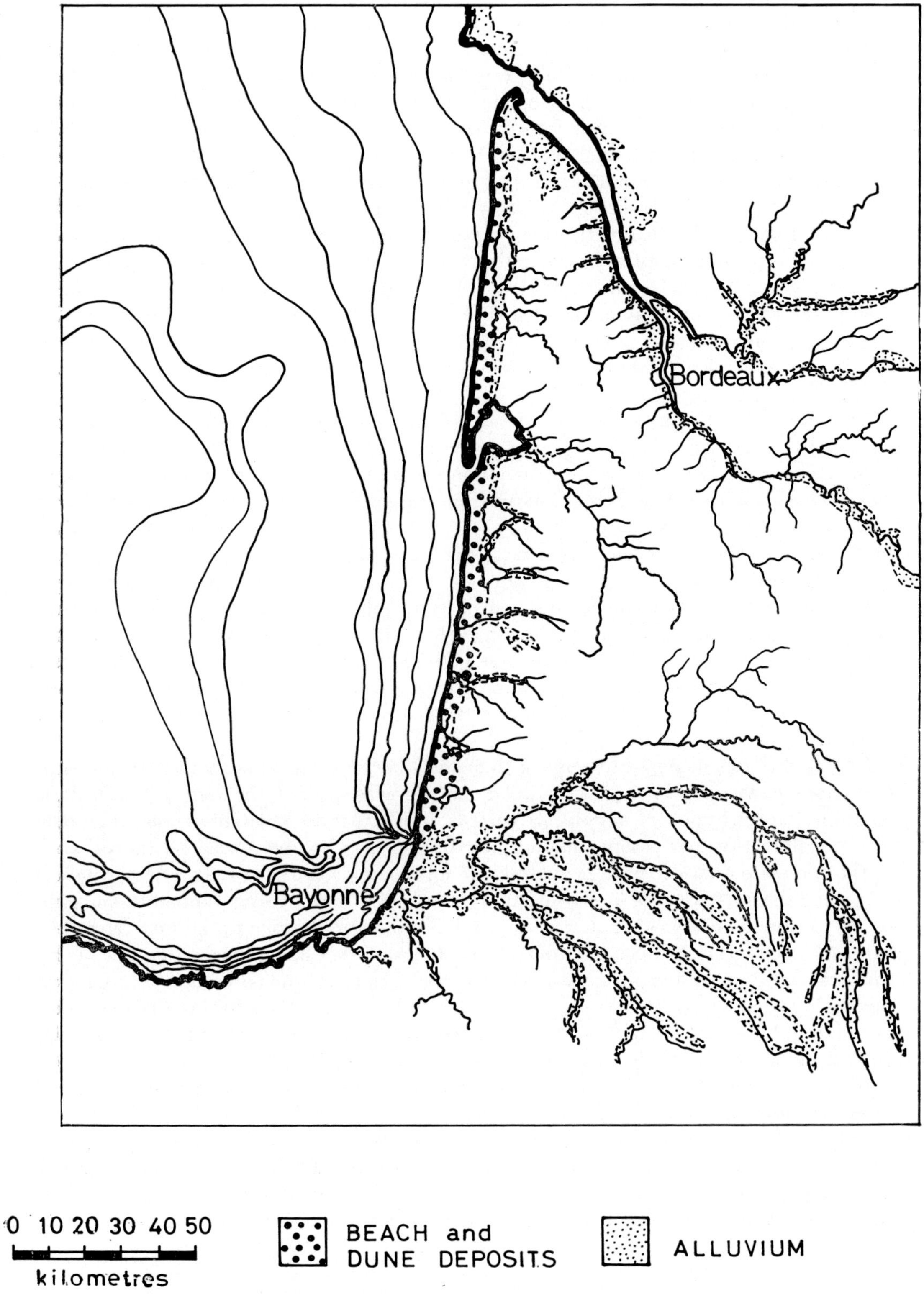

Figure 8. The distribution of the Holocene dunes on the coast of Landes, France.

These sands are thus the product of an aeolian transgression. They often contain considerable displaced marine faunal remains from the adjacent beaches and sea floor; usually, however, these remains will be fragmentary, but occasionally whole skeletons will be displaced into the dunes. Also, shore-living animals, birds, etc., will carry whole or slightly broken organic debris into dunes. A microfauna, at least as good as that of the adjacent beaches and nearshore zones, may be present; it is usually abraded, but so is that of the nearshore and beach deposits. In many areas a terrestrial fauna may be mixed with this, but in desert or arid areas the latter may be very limited.

Dune sands interbedded with other marine deposits and with continental deposits could easily be interpreted as a product of a marine transgression, when in reality they are the result of an aeolian transgression. The sea may therefore have been many kilometres away from and many metres below the site where the dune sand, perhaps containing marine organisms, is found; thus considerable caution is necessary in drawing conclusions from the position of sandy deposits containing marine organisms in coastal areas.

In areas where the dune sands are derived from beaches and nearshore zones characterized by sands rich in, or completely composed of, calcium carbonate (produced either biochemically or chemically), they may become lithified. This is usually brought about by calcium carbonate being leached from the dune sands by downward-percolating rainwater and then being precipitated at lower levels. Ridges of such cemented aeolian sand—aeolianite—have been reported from many areas of the world including the Mediterranean coasts where, for example in Israel, they are known as kurkar ridges (Emery & Neev, 1960). Changes in sea level lead to drowning of these aeolian accumulations and there are many examples of ancient drowned dune-sand ridges reported from the shallow parts of the continental shelves (Emery & Bentor, 1960). Obviously the presence of large amounts of calcium carbonate and its cementing action makes the preservation of these ridges much more likely, because of their greater resistance to erosion.

Just as the sites of deposition move their location on deltaic plains and erosion thus becomes the dominant process, a similar pattern of events can be seen in beach-dune coastlines. Interruption of supply of material to a coastline inevitably leads to erosion or re-alignment of that coast. Such an interruption may be due to natural causes, such as the complete removal, back to bedrock, of an eroding mass of soft sediment which is supplying the coastal plain, or the cessation of supply of river-borne sediment to a coast, owing to climatic changes; or it may be, and is increasingly, due to the interference of man, who artificially protects eroding areas of coastline with sea walls, thus depleting the local supply of sediment, or dams rivers for irrigation purposes and thus cuts off the supply of river-borne sediment; the latter situation has occurred on the west coast of the U.S.A., where the damming of many streams has prevented floods from carrying large volumes of sand to the beaches, and a slow but continuous shrinkage of beaches is predicted (Norris, 1964). Also, the construction of dams by Romans around the Mediterranean in areas such as the coast of Libya must have led to a cessation of sediment supply to the coast until the dams filled and then overflowed or were abandoned (Vita-Finzi, 1969). On the other hand, the extensive clearing of trees from upland areas or overgrazing has undoubtedly led to the increase of sediment supply to coastal areas; the latter, however, may have been substantial for only a short period of time and then have levelled off when the readily transportable material had been carried to the sea (see discussion in Eisma, 1962).

Climatic changes resulting in changes of wave approach and therefore of the direction of littoral drift have led to the truncation of earlier beach-dune coastal plains and the deposition of a new coastal plain with different alignments on the central west coast of Mexico (Curray, Emmel and Crampton, 1969). In this locality, at approximately 3600 B.P., the littoral drift changed from being dominantly to the north to being dominantly southwards, only to change again to northwards about 1500 B.P. Each of these changes can be clearly seen by a study of the trend of beach ridges on the broad coastal plain.

In many seas, as in the North Sea, sheltered embayments, such as the Wash on the east coast of England and the Wadden Sea on the Dutch and German coasts, are infilled by fine-grained sands, silt and clays; these have been derived from coastal erosion and from the reworking of the adjacent sea floor. These accumulations are particularly impressive in seas of high tidal range, where the high-velocity tidal currents erode the sea floor and carry the sediment into any sheltered embayment to deposit it to build up wide intertidal flats and marshes (van Straaten, 1954; Evans, 1959; 1965; Reineck, 1967). The sediments in such areas are noticeably finer than those found on the exposed coastlines, where beaches and dune are predominant. The tidal waters lay down sediment in belts of gradually decreasing grain size from low- to high-water mark: the coarser sand is found at low-water mark and this passes landwards into areas of finer sand, laminated mud-sand areas and finally fairly pure mud areas. Halophytic vegetation colonizes the inner margins of these mud-flats to form salt marshes, and these in turn would pass into swamp, fen and carr (low, poorly drained woodlands) if it were not for the fact that man is usually attracted to such areas and has drained and reclaimed such coastal marshes to form rich farmland. As more and more sand and mud is supplied to such areas, the coastline builds seawards to form wide, flat coastal plains such as those of North Holland and Germany and the wide, flat "siltlands" of the outer part of the Fenland in Norfolk and Lincolnshire (see review in Evans, 1959). In this region the natural accretion, partly aided by man, has built the coastline seawards (Fig. 9) and has allowed many square kilometres of rich farmland to be reclaimed (Darby, 1940). In such situations there are no destructive phases as found in the deltas and sandy beach-dune coastal plains, and no huge volumes of wind-blown sand as found on exposed beach-dune coastlines; as a result, remains of early settlements are likely to be free from attack and destruction by natural processes, but because of the highly desirable character of the terrain they are likely to suffer much from destruction by man.

In some parts of the world, particularly in regions marginal to large deltas, conditions can alternate from those conducive to the build-up of muddy marshes and intertidal flats (such as are found within the shelter of the Wash) to those conducive to the build-up of beaches and dunes (such as are found on the open Lincolnshire coast outside the Wash embayment). The resulting coastal plain is known as a "chenier plain" and consists of alternating strips of marsh and mud-flats and sandy beach ridges (Fig. 10), both roughly paralleling the coastline (Russell & Howe, 1935). An excellent example of this type of coastal sedimentation is seen in western Louisiana, U.S.A., between the Sabine river mouth in the west and the Vermilion Bay (a shallow bay on the western margin of the Mississippi delta) in the east. The Mississippi is the dominant supplier of sediment to this coastline. However, because of the continuously changing position of its mouth

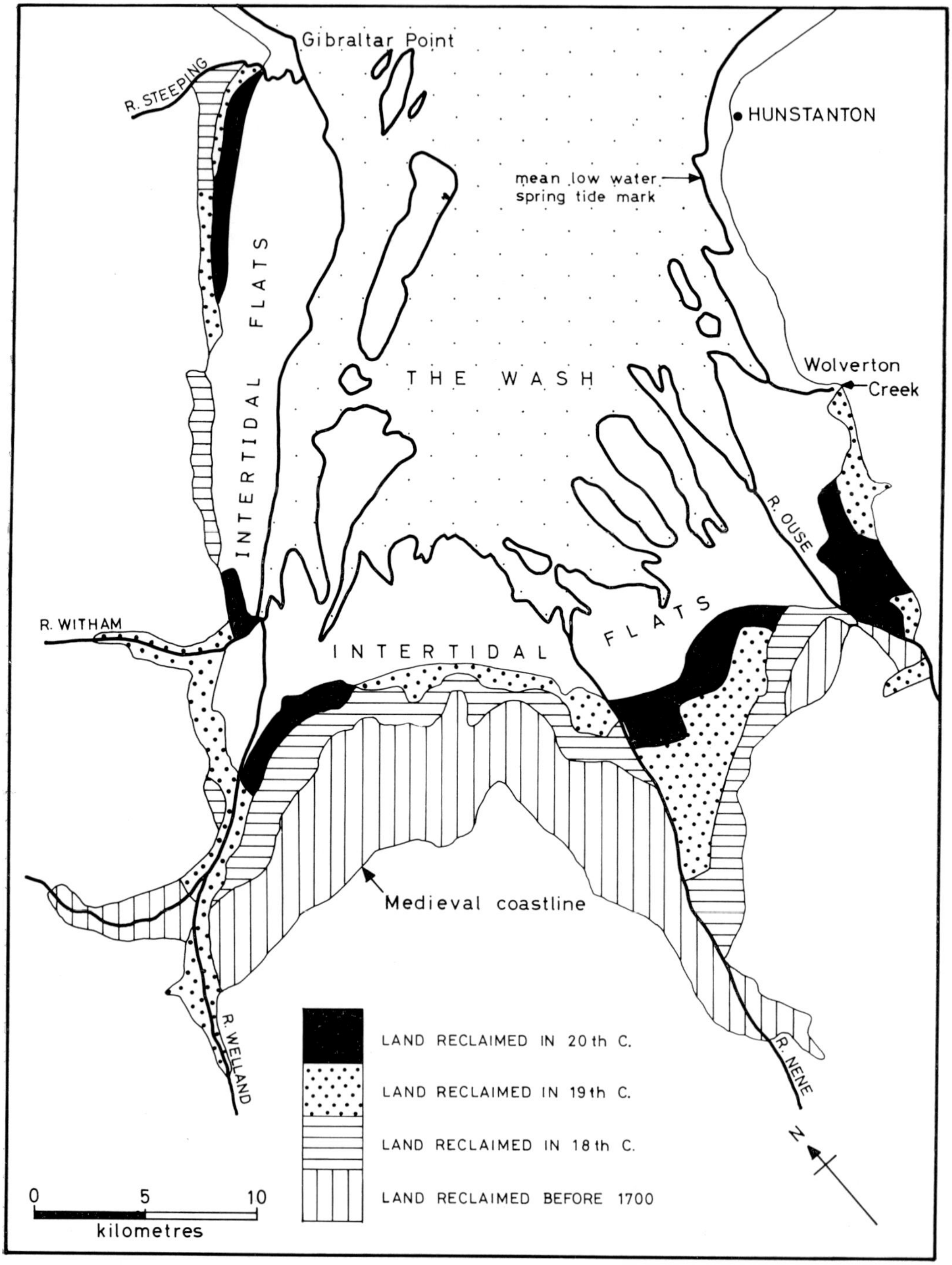

Figure 9. Land reclamation around the Wash, modified after Evans (1959) from original sources (see Evans, 1959, for details).

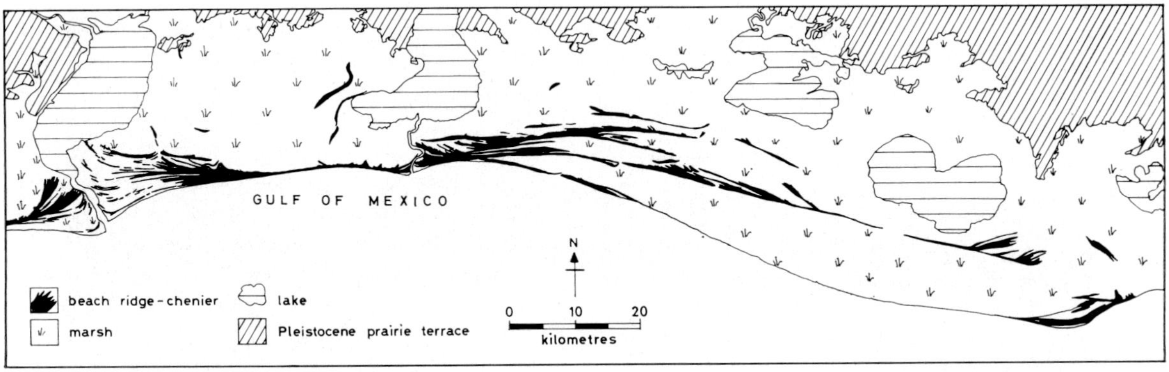

Figure 10. The physiography of the chenier plain of Western Louisiana, U.S.A., after Byrne, Le Roy and Riley (1959).

the supply of sediment to the west has been spasmodic and discontinuous (Russell & Howe, 1935; Byrne, Le Roy & Riley, 1959). When the outfall of the Mississippi has been on the western part of its deltaic plain the abundant mud in suspension has been carried westwards by the dominant current; it has accumulated along the shore to produce mud-flats which ultimately have become colonized by halophytic plants to form marshes; the whole process has led to a seaward advance of the coastline. However, when the mouth of the Mississippi has lain further to the east, the mud has been deposited in other environments of deposition marginal to deltas, and has not reached the chenier plain. Consequently erosion has been the dominant process in the nearshore zone (and sometimes on the coast) in front of the chenier plain, and the previously deposited fine-grained sediments have been reworked: the coarser sandy material (often almost entirely composed of shelly debris) has been thrown up by the waves to form beach ridges—the cheniers—which parallel the coast. In some cases these have been driven landward over the landward marsh, to expose the deposits of the latter on their seaward sides. Renewal of supply of fine-grained sediment has repeatedly led to the initiation of deposition of fine-grained mud-flats and marsh in front of these ridges, and the coast has once again prograded seawards. Some evidence has been brought forward recently to refute the simple explanation of the alternating conditions found during the development of the chenier plain, the cyclicity in progradation of the chenier plain being attributed to mere fluctuations in local sediment supply and hydraulic conditions (Otvos, 1969). Repetition of these processes over the last several thousand years has led to the construction of a plain covering a considerable area (Fig. 10) between the margins of the Mississippi delta and the western border of the state of Louisiana.

Many coastlines, particularly those bordering large deltas or other abundant sources of sediment, are fringed by coastal lagoons. For example, more than one half of the east coast of the United States, south of New York, and of the Gulf of Mexico coast is occupied by coastal lagoons; similar coasts are found throughout the Mediterranean and in many other parts of the world (Shepard & Moore, 1955; Phleger, 1969; Evans & Bush, 1969).

These relatively sheltered bodies of water are of considerable interest to man: they have been used as harbours; their waters often support large fish populations; and they

Figure 11. A coastal lagoon with a sandy barrier island on the Pacific Coast of Mexico.

are often the sites of large salt-extraction works. They are separated from the sea by a variety of barriers, perhaps the most spectacular of which are coral reefs or sandy (or gravelly) barrier islands (Fig. 11). These barriers may often be continuous for hundreds of kilometres parallel to the coastline, and may be up to 8 km wide. They are often cut by inlets which give access to the waters of the adjacent sea and also allow fresh waters from the land to drain seawards.

Behind the islands in the lagoon sands, muds and other sediments accumulate (these may be partly supplied from the land and partly from the adjacent sea), and in some places oyster- or mussel-reefs flourish. The environmental conditions in this restricted situation are very variable; waters range from brackish to hypersaline and often show a wide range in temperature. The extreme conditions lead to depletion in the diversity but not in the amount of the normal marine fauna, and in some cases to the deposition of salts.

Studies of modern lagoonal coasts make it apparent that vast quantities of fine-grained sediments are trapped in this nearshore coastal environment. The sequence of changes and seaward progradation of the barrier islands will be similar to that already described for the beach-dune complexes, with one very important modification: this is the presence of the inlets (many of which are dominated by local tides and therefore are called tidal inlets) cutting across these features. These inlets (or channels) tend to migrate, usually in the direction of the strongest littoral drift: this leads to the destruction of parts of

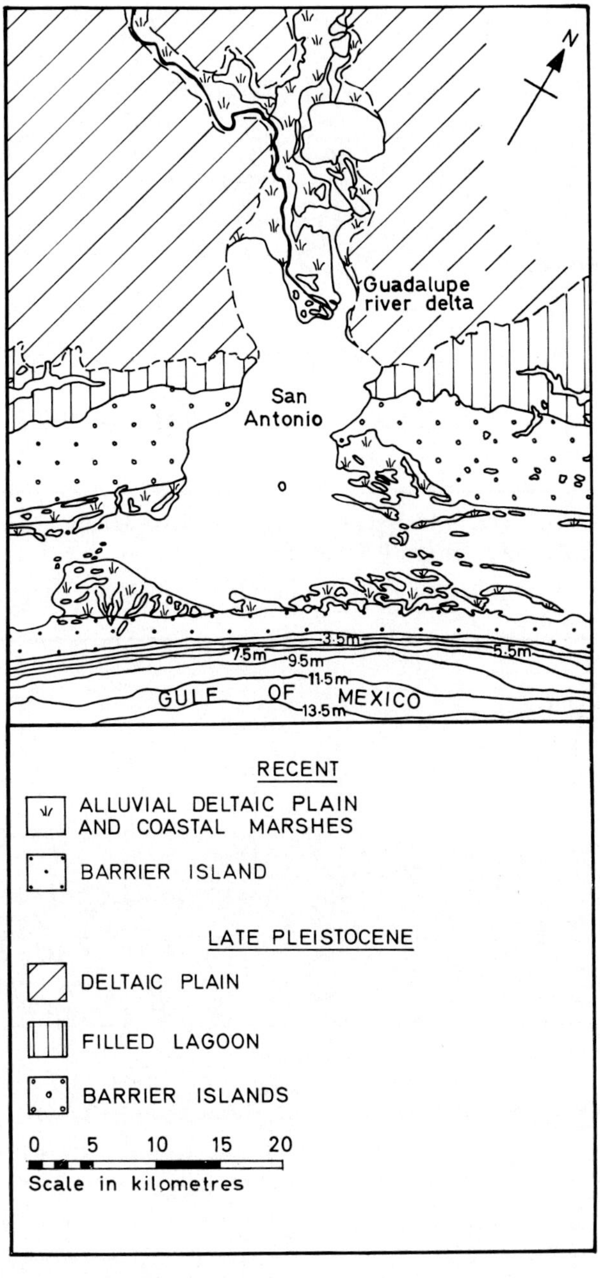

Figure 12. The coastal physiography of a lagoon and its associated barrier on the coast of Texas, U.S.A. after Leblanc and Hodgson (1959); see also Bernard and Leblanc (1965) for details of the area.

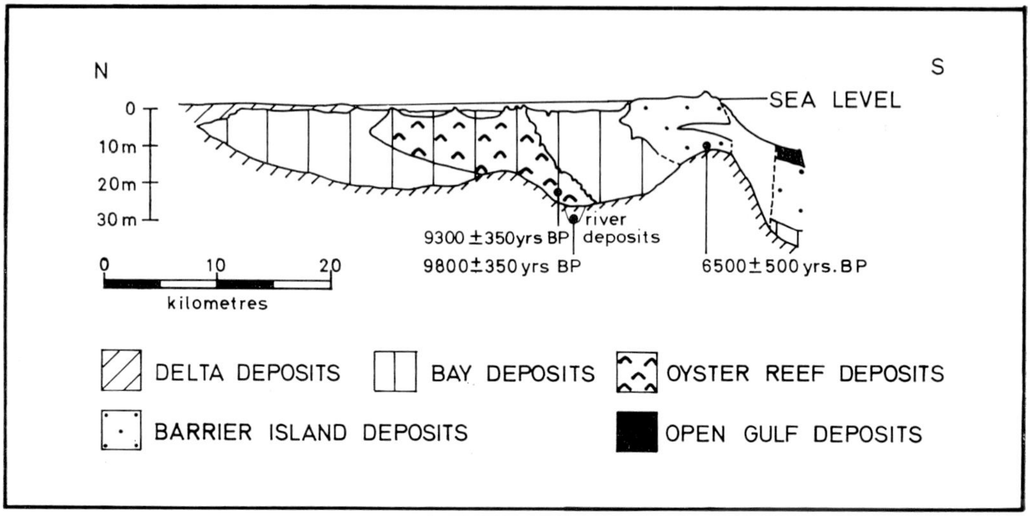

Figure 13. Cross-section of the lagoon and barrier-island deposits of San Antonio Bay, Texas, U.S.A., after Shepard (1956): an example of build-up approximately "in situ".

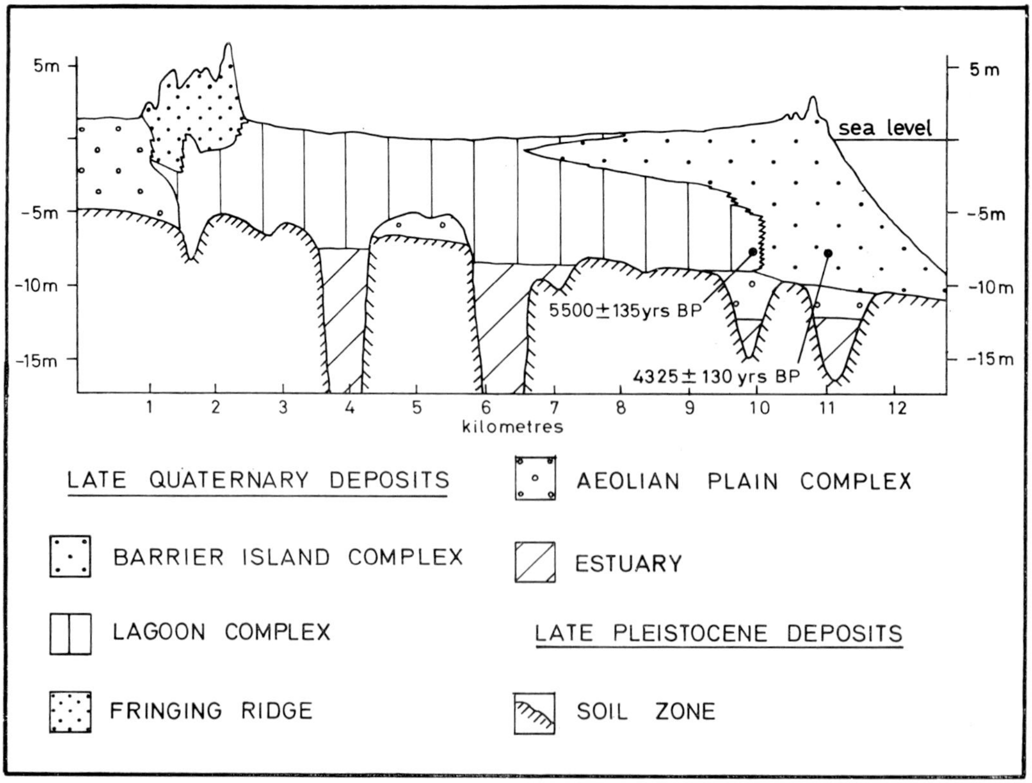

Figure 14. Cross-section of the lagoon and barrier-island deposits of Laguna Madre, Texas, U.S.A., after Fisk (1959): an example of build-up approximately "in situ".

some barriers and additions to the terminations of other barriers in an up-drift direction. Such migrations will lead to the destruction of any settlements or kitchen middens on some of the islands, and in some places these settlements may show a chronological sequence along the barrier islands. With time, the lagoons may be silted up and the intertidal flats on their landward sides will build seawards (Fig. 12). Infilling of lagoons and the seaward growth of the inner margin has led to the extension of the coastal plain (locally called the sabkha) by 4 km in 4,000 years on the Trucial Coast of Arabia (Evans, Schmidt, Bush & Nelson, 1969). Similarly, the shoreline on the inner sides of the barriers will build landward to turn the area into dry land; also dunes originally formed on the isolated barrier will advance landward over the infilled lagoon and may also, of course, aid in its infilling. Such a sequence of events leads to the development of wide coastal plains.

As in deltas, beach-dune complexes, intertidal flats, estuaries and chenier plains, where there has been a balance between the rate of sea-level rise and the rate of sedimentation, a barrier may have built up in approximately the same locality for the last few thousand years (Figs. 13, 14). In such a case the original barrier surface, together with any settlements, will now be buried by several tens of metres of sand or, if located in the lagoon, by tens of metres of mud (Shepard, 1956; Fisk, 1959; Phleger, 1965).

Conclusions

This brief review of coastal sedimentation has, it is hoped, stressed the complexity of the phenomenon. Rarely is one area the site of uninterrupted deposition for long periods; phases of erosion are very characteristic of such coastlines and sometimes much of the results of coastal sedimentation will be destroyed. Consequently most coastal lowlands have only a fraction of their history preserved. The persistence of coastal processes and their effects have been stressed. However, it should be noted that, although this is true for a long time-period, generally the processes act in a spasmodic way: rivers, when in flood, supply far more sediment to a delta in a few days than they do for the remainder of the year; storms, often lasting for only a few days, can have effects on sandy coastlines which will take years to reverse; short periods of stormy weather, in the adjacent shallow seas, probably produce much more sediment for deposition on sheltered intertidal flats and estuaries than do normal conditions acting all the year, and the movement of tidal inlets leading into lagoons can occur quickly owing to exceptional meteorological conditions.

Similarly, changes in surface level due to compaction and/or tectonic sinking have led to sinking of large areas and their accompanying remains of human settlements (if these exist) to lower, often inaccessible, levels. The rise of sea level has led to further complications: with a constant or slowly rising sea level and an abundant supply of sediment, the coasts will prograde seawards; where the rise of sea level and the supply of sediment has been approximately balanced, the coastline has remained stationary in position, merely building up its surface in phase with the rise of sea level, i.e., the environment is repeated vertically (in such cases the original beach and dunes and the river plains now lie tens of metres below the surface and they and their record are concealed); finally, if the sediment supply has been limited and the rate of sea level rise has been rapid, the coastline will move rapidly shorewards and earlier forms will be covered by water. Archaeologists involved in the study of man's activities and remains in the coastal lowlands should bear in mind the complexities of the histories of these regions in drawing conclusions about the former inhabitants of these regions and their various activities.

ACKNOWLEDGMENTS

The writer would like to record his thanks to Miss M. Pugh for help in preparing the manuscript and figures, and Mrs. R. Evans for drafting the figures; and to the following for permission to use illustrations (Figs. 1, 3, 4, 6, 10, 12, 13, 14): Tj. H. van Andel, C. R. Kolb, J. R. van Lopik, The American Association of Petroleum Geologists (Fig. 4), F. J. Kestner and the Council of the Institution of Civil Engineers, D. O. Le Roy, C. M. Riley, R. Leblanc, W. Hodgson, F. P. Shepard, and Esso Production Research Company (Fig. 14).

REFERENCES

Bernard, H. A. & Leblanc, R. J. 1965 Résumé of the Quaternary geology of the northwestern Gulf of Mexico Province, *in* Wright, H. E. and Frey, D. G. (ed.) *The Quarternary of the United States* [Review vol. for VIII Congr. Intern. Ass. Quat. Res.], Pt. 1, 137–85. Princeton.

Byrne, J. V., Le Roy, D. O. & Riley, C. M. 1959 The Chenier plain and its stratigraphy, South West Louisiana. *Trans. Gulf-Cst Ass. geol. Socs*, **9**, 237–59.

Cooper, W. S. 1958. Coastal Sand dunes of Oregon and Washington. *Mem. geol. Soc. Am.* **76**, 169 pp.

Curray, J. R., Emmel, F. J. & Crampton, P. J. 1969 Holocene history of a strand plain lagoonal coast, Nayarit, Mexico, *in* Ayala Castañares, A. & Phleger, F. B. (ed.) *Lagunas Costeras: un Simposio* [Mem. Simp. Intern. Lagunas Costeras (UNAM-UNESCO, Nov. 28–30, 1967)] 63–100. Mexico D. F.

Curray, J. R. & Moore D. G. 1964 Holocene regressive littoral sand, Costa de Nayarit, Mexico, *in* van Straaten, L.M.J.U. (ed.) *Deltaic and Shallow Marine deposits*, 76–82. Amsterdam.

Darby, H. C., 1940 *The Drainage of the Fens*, 314 pp. Cambridge.

Eisma, D. 1962 Beach Ridges near Selçuk, Turkey. *Tijdschr. K. ned. aardrijksk. Genoot.*, Tweede Reeks, LXXIX (9) No. 3, 234–46.

Emery, K. O. & Bentor, Y. K. 1960 The Contentinental Shelf of Israel. *Bull. geol. Surv. Israel*, **26**, 25–41.

Emery, K. O. & Neev, D. 1960 Mediterranean beaches of Israel. *Bull. geol. Surv. Israel*, **26**, 1–24

Evans, G. 1959 The development of the coastline of the Wash, England, *in* Russell, R. J. (ed.) *Proc. 2nd coastal Geogr. Conf., Louisiana State Univ., Coastal Studies Inst*, 265–84.

Evans, G. 1965 Intertidal flat sediments and their environment of deposition in the Wash. *Q. Jl geol. Soc. Lond.* **121**, 209–45.

Evans, G. & Bush, P. 1969 Some Oceanographical and Sedimentological Observations in a Persian Gulf Lagoon, *in* Ayala Castañares, A. & Phleger, F. B. (ed.) *Lagunas Costeras: un Simposio* [Mem. Simp. Intern. Lagunas Costeras (UNAM-UNESCO, Nov. 28–30, 1967)] 155–70. Mexico D.F.

Evans, G., Schmidt, V., Bush, P. & Nelson, H. 1969 Stratigraphy and geologic history of the Sabkha, Abu Dhabi, Persian Gulf. *Sedimentology*, **12**, 145–59.

Fisk, H. N. 1959 Padre Island and Laguna Madre flats, coastal south Texas, *in* Russell, R. J. (ed.) *Proc. 2nd coastal Geogr. Conf., Louisiana State Univ., Coastal Studies Inst*, 103–51.

Fisk, H. N., & McFarlan, E., Jr. 1955 Late Quaternary deltaic deposits of the Mississippi river, *in* Poldervaart, A. (ed.) *Crust of the Earth: a Symposium* [*Spec. Pap. geol. Soc. Am.* **62**], 279–302.

Gould, H. R., 1970 The Mississippi delta complex, *in* Morgan, J. P. (ed.) *Deltaic Sedimentation Modern and Ancient* [*Spec. Publs Soc. econ. Palaeont. Miner., Tulsa*, **15**] 3–30.

Inglis, C. C. & Allen, F. H. 1957 The regimen of the Thames estuary as affected by currents, salinity and river flow. *Proc. Instn Civ. Engrs*, **7**, 827–78.

Inglis, C. C. & Kestner, F. J. T. 1958 The long term effects of training walls, reclamation and dredging in estuaries. *Proc. Instn Civ. Engrs*, **9**, 193–216.

Inman, D. L. & Frautschy, J. D. 1966 Littoral processes and the development of shorelines, in *Coastal Engineering* [Santa Barbara Speciality Conference 1965, Am. Soc. civ. Engrs], 511–36.

Johnson, J. W. 1956 Dynamics of Nearshore Sediment movement. *Bull. Am. Ass. Petrol. Geol.* **40** No. 9, 2211–32.

Kolb, C. R. & van Lopik, J. R. 1958 *Geology of Mississippi river deltaic plain, south eastern Louisiana*, 2 vols. Tech. Rep. U. S. Army Corps, Engrs. WatWays Expt. Station, 3–483 & 3–484.

Kolb, C. R. & van Lopik, J. R. 1966 Depositional Environments of the Mississippi River Deltaic plain—South Eastern Louisiana, *in* Shirley, M. L. & Ragsdale, J. A. (ed.) *Deltas in their geologic framework*, 17–61. Houston Geol. Soc.

Kruit, C. 1955 Sediments of the Rhône delta. Grain size and micro-fauna. *Verh. K. ned. geol.-mijnb. Genoot.*, Geol. ser. **15**, 357–514.

Kulm, L. D. & Byrne, J. V. 1966 Sedimentary response to hydrography in an Oregon estuary. *Mar. Geol.* **4**, 85–118.

Lagaaij, R. & Kopstein, F. P. H. W. 1964 Typical features of a fluvio-marine offlap sequence, *in* van Straaten, L. M. J. U. (ed.) *Deltaic and Shallow Marine deposits*, 216–26. Amsterdam.

Leblanc, R. J. & Hodgson, W. D. 1959 Origin and development of the Texas Shoreline, *in* Russell, R. J. (ed.) *Proc. 2nd Coastal Geog. Conf., Louisiana State Univ., Coastal Studies Inst*, 57–102.

Norris, R. M. 1964 Dams and beach sand supply in Southern California, *in* Miller, R. L. (ed.) *Papers in Marine Geology* [Shepard Commemorative Vol.] 154–71. New York.

Oomkens, E. 1970 Depositional sequences and sand distribution in the Postglacial Rhône delta, *in* Morgan, J. P. (ed.) *Deltaic Sedimentation Modern and Ancient* [*Spec. Publs. Soc. econ. Palaeont. Miner., Tulsa*, **15**] 198–212.

Oomkens, E. & Terwindt, J. H. J. 1960 Inshore estuarine sediments in the Haringvliet, Netherlands. *Geologie Mijnb.* **39**, 701–10.

Otvos, E. G., Jr, 1969 A sub-Recent beach ridge complex in South-eastern Louisiana *Bull. geol. Soc. Am.* **80**, 2353–58.

Phleger, F. B. 1965 Sedimentology of Guerrero Negro lagoon, Baja California, Mexico. *Colston Pap.* **17**, 205–37.

Phleger, F. B. 1969 Some general features of coastal lagoons, *in* Ayala Castañares, A. & Phleger, F. B. (ed.) *Lagunas Costeras: un Simposio* [Mem. Simp. Intern. Lagunas Costeras (UNAM-UNESCO, Nov. 28–30, 1967)] 5–26. Mexico D.F.

Price, W. A. & Kendrick, M. P. 1963 Field and Model investigations into the reasons for siltation in the Mersey estuary. *Proc. Instn Civ. Engrs*, **24**, 473–517.

Reineck, H. E. 1967 Layered sediments of tidal flats, beaches and shelf bottoms of the North Sea, *in* Lauff, G. H. (ed.) *Estuaries* [*Publs. Am. Ass. Advmt Sci.*, **83**] 191–206.

Russell, R. J. 1936 Physiography of the lower Mississippi river delta, *in* Report on the Geology of Plaquemines and St. Bernard Parishes *Louisiana Dept. Bull. Conserv. Geol.* **8**, 3–199.

Russell, R. J. 1954 Alluvial Morphology of Anatolian Rivers. *Ann. Ass. Am. Geogr.* **44**, 363–91.

Russell, R. J. & Howe, H. V. 1935 Cheniers of South Western Louisiana. *Geog. Rev.* **25**, 449–61.

Scruton, P. C. 1960 Delta building and deltaic sequence, *in* Shepard, F. P., Phleger, F. B. & van Andel, Tj. H. (ed.) *Recent Sediments, Northwest Gulf of Mexico* [*Spec. Publs Am. Ass. Petrol. Geol., Tulsa*] 82–102.

Shepard, F. P. 1956 Late Pleistocene and Recent history of the Central Texas Coast. *J. Geol.* **64**, 56–69.

Shepard, F. P. 1963 *Submarine Geology*, 2nd Edit., 557 pp. New York.

Shepard, F. P. & Moore, D. G. 1955 Central Texas Coast Sedimentation: characteristics of sedimentary environments, recent history and diagenesis. *Bull. Am. Ass. Petrol. Geol.* **39**, 1463–1593.

Silvester, R. 1959 Engineering aspects of coastal sediment movement. *J. WatWays Harb. Div. Am. Soc. civ. Engrs*, *WW***3**, 11–39.

Smith, A. E. 1966 Modern deltas: comparison maps, *in* Shirley, M. L. & Ragsdale, J. A. (ed.) *Deltas in their geologic framework*, 233–51. Houston Geol. Soc.

Steers, J. A. 1964 *The Coastline of England and Wales*, 2nd Edit., 644 pp. Cambridge.

Terwindt, J. H. J., de Jong, J. D. & van der Wilk, E. 1963 Sediment movement and sediment properties in the tidal area of the lower Rhine (Rotterdam Waterway). *Verh. K. ned. geol.-mijnb. Genoot.*, Geol. ser., deel 21–2 [Trans. Jubilee Convention, Pt. 2], 243–58.

van Andel, Tj. H. & Curray, J. R. 1960 Regional aspects of modern sedimentation in Northern Gulf of Mexico and similar basins and paleogeographic significance, *in* Shepard, F. P., Phleger, F. B. & van Andel, Tj. H. (ed.) *Recent sediments, Northwest Gulf of Mexico* [*Spec. Publs Am. Ass. Petrol. Geol., Tulsa*] 345–64.

van Straaten, L. M. J. U. 1954 Composition and Structure of Recent Marine sediments in the Netherlands. *Leid. geol. Meded.* **19**, 1–110.

van Straaten, L. M. J. U. 1959 Littoral and Submarine morphology of the Rhône delta, *in* Russell, R. J. (ed.) *Proc. 2nd coastal Geogr. Conf., Louisiana State Univ., Coastal Studies Inst*, 233–64.

Valentin, H. 1954 Der Landverlust in Holdernes, Ostengland, von 1852 bis 1952. *Die Erde, Berlin*, **6**, 296–315.

Vita-Finzi, C. 1969 *The Mediterranean Valleys*, 140 pp. Cambridge.

Discussion

Wallace Is there any evidence to suggest where the sand of the Biscay coast was coming from? Out of the sea, obviously, but where did it originally come from?
Evans Most of the sand must initially have been derived from the land. It was carried, at times of lower sea levels, to the outer parts of the continental shelf and spread along the contemporary shoreline by wave action. Many of the features which we see today on the present-day coastline must have existed out on the continental shelf. With the rise of sea level these old coastal features were drowned, and much of the sand was moved shorewards by wave action to form the present-day coastal accumulations. Undoubtedly some sand is being carried to the sea by the rivers which reach this coast today, but probably most of the sand is trapped in the large estuary downstream of Bordeaux. The point that should be stressed is that it is difficult for sand to escape seawards; it tends to be trapped in the estuaries and in the nearshore zone.

Wallace There is a situation in Pagham Harbour where the sand is being pushed landwards in great quantities from the sea. Some of it is being manufactured in the shingle beach due to collision and disintegration of flint shingle. It would be interesting to determine exactly how much is being manufactured.
Evans This situation is typical of the North Sea and the seas around North-western Europe. Sand is moving into the estuaries. This causes great concern and necessitates large amounts of dredging in some estuaries, for example the Thames and Mersey. The problem is, therefore, to keep sand, derived from the sea, out of the estuaries. The actual amount of sand formed by the breakdown of flint shingle is probably very small.

Flemming Work by A. H. Stride of the National Institute of Oceanography has revealed movement of the sand deposited on the continental shelf, although this is caused by both current and wave action. Some of this sand may be moving towards the French coast.
Evans Yes, sand is moving landwards in some French estuaries. I do not, however, know the details for the estuaries in the Bay of Biscay.
Flemming It is quite difficult for the sand to get away from the continents; unless it goes into the deep water in Biscay or off Norway it comes back on to someone else's beach.

Davidson In your later example from the Norfolk coast you described how the waves produce a littoral drift away from the river mouth, yet in your earlier slide of the Seyhan delta it appeared that the sediment movement was caused by vortex entrainment causing currents towards the river. The same appeared to be the case in the Mississippi. What are your comments on this?
Evans Vortexing is probably not very important in the transportation of sand. The most important agents of transportation of sandy sediments around the river mouths are the wave-induced currents. The rivers carry the sand and drop it in shallow water once they meet the sea. This sand is then remobilised by wave action and swept back

landwards to the flanks of the river mouth, to build up the beach and ultimately to cause the forward-building of the delta.

The dominant agents of sand transport on coastlines are wave-induced currents. The direction of transportation depends upon the angle of approach of the waves, which is itself dependent upon the direction from which the strongest and most persistent winds come.

Davidson In general, are currents induced by the flow of the river?

Evans Yes, but they are of small importance as agents of sand transport, compared with currents produced by wave action. The other most important currents in the sea are those produced by wind action, and in tidal seas by tidal currents. Generally speaking, rivers dump all their coarse (sandy) sediment once they meet the opposition of the sea. However, light (fresh) river-water will spread offshore as a surface film, but this water will carry fine-grained material (mud) seawards for short distances only; then it becomes entrained in the wind-induced coastal currents.

McKee I gained the impression from your paper of some continuous machine, but on the coast which I know the prime cause of sea silting is the last gale that has occurred. Next year may well reverse the situation.

Evans There is a great return to the doctrine of catastrophism. Most people would accept that much more work is expended and much more dramatic changes are produced by intermittent storms or such violent events than during the intervening periods. I have presented a rather over-simplified story. Although I have spoken about long-term changes, these probably occur in a series of sudden short-lived episodes, with long periods of inactivity or slow activity in between. We usually, however, merely see the long-term end-product. It is exactly the same situation as that described by Flemming, where he discusses long-term changes, which have in fact probably been produced by a series of isolated rapid movements or changes separated by intervening quiescent periods. Many of the features seen on coastlines have been produced by violent meteorological conditions; this is particularly so where hurricanes or typhoons are common. Dr. D. R. Stoddart has shown that very dramatic effects are produced in the Caribbean by such events.

Frost What is your view of the possibility that offshore reefs along the Levant Coast rose or subsided in a different way from the mainland opposite? The north-flowing current carries Nile sand, and particles are deposited on these reefs as well as on the south side of capes. It has been suggested that the reefs are sinking under the weight of this sand (as well as being lowered by erosion, etc.).

Evans I have no personal experience of the area in question. But I think it very unlikely that the reefs—which are really submerged coastal barrier sands which have been drowned by the rising sea and have since been colonized by calcareous algae—would behave very differently from the adjacent land area. However, there is still very little published information on the marine geology of this area.

Blackman You mentioned the dune sands at Side on the south coast of Turkey. They are now, in fact, encroaching again on the area of recent archaeological excavations along the southern part of the east wall of the ancient city.

Evans That is very interesting.

Evidence of sea level change in ancient harbours and coastal installations

by

D. J. BLACKMAN

CERTAIN FEATURES of ancient harbours and other coastal installations may provide evidence of changes in relative sea level since the time when these features were installed. Critical evaluation is, however, necessary.

MOORING-STONES

Pierced stones projecting from the quay-face are a common feature in ancient harbours. A set of such stones is well preserved at *Teos* on the south side of the Çeşme peninsula in Western Turkey. The harbour is protected from the south by a mole 200 m long, resting on a spit of land and now partly under sand, with a quay along its inner (north) side and a wall, probably an extension of the Hellenistic city wall, along its outer (south) side (Fig. 1; compare Flemming, above, Fig. 29. General plans of site: Béquignon & Laumonier, 1925, Pl. VII; Bean, 1966, 141 Fig. 26). The quay may be of the third century B.C., like the wall, or perhaps later.

Set in the face of the quay is a long series of mooring-stones, wedge-shaped in order to take the lateral strain (Fig. 2); some of them have lost their front projection. A stetch of 87 m of the quay is preserved, with the mooring-stones mostly at intervals of 3.4–3.5 m. Sea level has changed; this is an obvious point, clear even where the top of the mooring-stone is slightly out of position (Fig. 3). The mooring-stones are mostly not fully clear of the water, and the bottom edges of the holes now lie very close to the waterline. This can be seen very clearly in the detached south-west stretch of quay, which is set at a curiously different angle (Fig. 4); the relation between the two quays remains to be worked out. The course below that containing the mooring-stones projects up to 30 cm at the west end of the main quay, but the projecting step narrows eastwards to nothing; this course is now submerged, and barely traceable above the mud. In the south-west quay the course below projects 40–50 cm. There must have been a course of blocks above the course containing the mooring-stones, though few traces of it are now visible. It is obvious that the mooring-stones must once have been completely out of the water; the problem is: how high out of the water were they originally? Hamilton (1842, II, 15–16) argued that there can have been little change in sea level; Bean (1966, 142), who follows Schäfer and Schläger (1962) in assuming a eustatic rise of sea level by over 5 feet since antiquity, accepts that the rings must have stood well above the waterline.

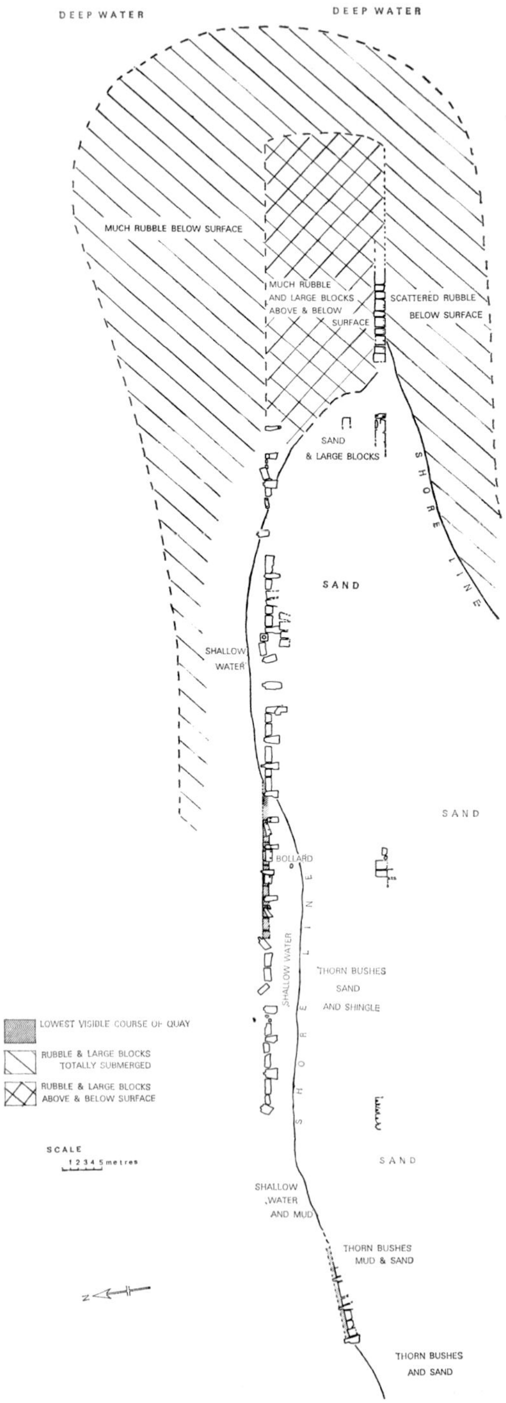

Figure 1. Teos: plan of mole.

At *Leptis Magna* mooring-stones are set into the quay-walls all round the harbour. The eastern side of the harbour is of most interest in this connection. At the south-eastern corner of the harbour, close to the watering station, are some mooring-stones

Figure 2. Teos: mooring-stone from the rear (south).

Figure 3. Teos: main quay, looking west.

Figure 4. Teos: south-west quay, looking west.

Figure 5. Leptis Magna: east mole, looking south. In the foreground, a temple; beyond, a line of warehouses at the back of the upper quay; on the right, the lower quay and the sand-filled harbour basin.

with horizontal holes, very badly worn and broken away. They are irregularly spaced and appear in a course 60 cm high, with their undersides now 1.20 m above sea level. They may be of earlier date than the rest (Bartoccini & Zanelli, 1958, 113 & Pl. LV).

At the back of the broad, high upper quay on the western side of the east mole is a line of warehouses (Fig. 5); below and in front of this, the lower quay level is a constant 1.30 m above sea level; there are mooring-stones in the back wall of the lower quay, which is the front face of the upper quay (Fig. 6). The upper quay surface, which rises towards the harbour entrance, has a series of broad, shallow steps towards its outer edge and is connected with the lower quay by a narrow flight of steps after every third mooring-stone, at intervals of *c.* 11 m (Bartoccini & Zanelli, 1958, 114–5, Pls. LIII & LVII). These stones are on average 1.20 m wide and project about 70 cm, like drawers (Fig. 7). They have a vertical semicircular hole through them. Their underside is about 90 cm above the surface of the lower quay, that is, about 2.20 m above water level.

A section was published by von Gerkan (1933, 40 Fig. 5 = 1959, 142 Fig. 1) of the quay on the east mole at Leptis, based on his own assumption of a 2.50 m rise in sea level since antiquity, which is quite unacceptable (Fig. 8.3). As can be seen from his illustration, it would involve the curious situation of ships having to moor well away from the edge of the lower quay and, one presumes, men having to flounder across the mud from ship to quay. The evidence at Leptis seems to point to a very small relative change in sea level. The crucial question is the height above water level at which the quay surface was built. The rise seems to be not more than 10–20 cm since the date of construction.

The other section from Leptis shown by von Gerkan is of vertically-pierced mooring-stones projecting from the lip of the single-step quay on the northern shore of the harbour (Fig. 8.2; compare Fig. 9). Von Gerkan noted that here the rub-marks were all along the outer edge of the mooring-stones, and quite deeply scored. In other words, he concluded, the mooring-ropes came away from the wall at a steep angle. These mooring-stones formed the main piece of evidence for his theory that sea level was 2.50 m lower in antiquity. Even if one disagrees with his conclusions, one must agree that rub-marks are certainly worth looking for on the outer and inner edges of mooring-stones and on the edge of quays.

Figure 6. Leptis Magna: east mole, upper and lower quays, looking north.

Figure 7. Leptis Magna: east mole, lower quay and mooring-stones, looking north.

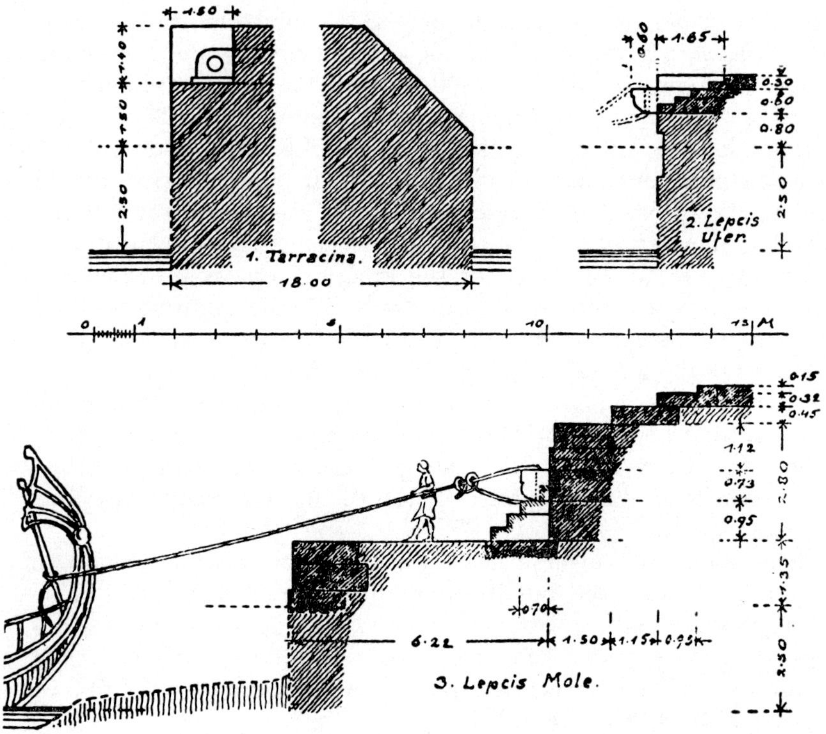

Figure 8. Sections of Roman harbour walls, at Leptis Magna and Terracina, by von Gerkan (1933, 40 Fig. 5 = 1959, 142 Fig. 1). Courtesy Koldewey-Cesellschaft.

Figure 9. Leptis Magna: mooring-stone in quay on north side of harbour.

Figure 10. Leptis Magna: rub-marks on outer edge of upper quay, east mole.

The third section given by von Gerkan (Fig. 8.1) illustrates the mooring-stones on the mole at *Terracina*, a site which I do not know at first hand. Here the mooring-stones are, according to von Gerkan, now 1.50 m above the water level and 1.40 m below the upper surface of the mole, with ramps leading up on either side of each mooring-stone to the upper surface; de la Blanchère (1881, 335 & Pl. XI) describes and illustrates the mooring-stones, but does not make clear their relationship to present water level. If von Gerkan's theory were correct, this would mean that the mooring-stones were originally 4 m above the surface of the water, which seems implausibly high.

Plausible evidence of the angle of the mooring-rope is provided by the Torlonia relief, which shows a merchant ship moored with the gunwale nearly level with the quay surface and the gang-plank therefore nearly horizontal, and the mooring-stone *below* the level of the gunwale (Meiggs, 1960, Pl. XX; Testaguzza, 1970, 171 & 230–1). Such a relationship seems very plausible, since it facilitates loading and unloading; there is no reason to have mooring-stones very high. They are more likely to have been at a height at which mooring and making fast could be carried out by men working from small boats (one must remember that in the Mediterranean they were dealing with minimal tide ranges).

The actual method of making fast the rope to the mooring-stone is not absolutely clear on the Torlonia relief, but it seems to be directly attached. This, if it was the standard method, would cause severe wear to the ropes, since the edges of mooring-stones are often sharp; one wonders whether in some cases metal rings or slings of rope or wicker may have been used, passed through the holes of the mooring-stones, but there is no direct evidence of this.

One of the most interesting puzzles at Leptis, which Bartoccini mentions and illustrates (1958, 116 & Pl. LVIII 2), but does not explain adequately, is a series of deep rub-marks along the edges of the steps of the upper quay at one point on the east side of the harbour (Fig. 10). Presumably goods must have been hauled up from the lower to the upper quay with ropes made fast on the upper quay, but the columns here look rather insecure. Bartoccini's explanation, that the ships' mooring-ropes caused the rubbing, seems very unlikely.

There was probably a similar arrangement of mooring-stones in the back wall of a quay at ancient *Cnidus* (Tekir). Here there is a series of mooring-stones set in an ancient wall surmounted by a modern field boundary-wall, well back from the likely edge of the ancient harbour and facing the modern isthmus. If the generally accepted theory is correct, that the two harbours were originally joined by a canal, these stones must have been very close to the canal, but much remains to be elucidated about the ancient outline of this area. The stones are set into the wall in what appears to be a situation like that at Leptis Magna, at the back of a working quay, which could have lined the canal. I have no accurate measurement of the height of these stones above water level, but my estimate is 3 m. A few mooring-stones are preserved in the embankment wall at the west corner of the southern (commercial) harbour (Love, 1967, 147 Fig. 14). There is no working quay below these stones, unless it is under water and buried beneath shingle and fallen blocks, which here reach almost to the surface. The stones are 75 cm clear of the water and look conveniently placed in their present position for use from the water at its present level. Furthermore, there is a quay nearby with its surface 1.40 m above present water level.

Another famous set of mooring-stones is preserved around the Trajanic harbour at *Ostia* (Calza, 1925, 55–7 & Fig. 1; Meiggs, 1960, 162–3; Testaguzza, 1970, 166, 170, compare 104). There were 24 along the south side and over 100 in all. This is a good

Figure 11. Naupactus: mooring-stone in seaward castle wall.

Figure 12. Naupactus: another mooring-stone.

Figure 13. Cnidus: rock-cut quay on south-west side of south harbour, looking west.

Figure 15. Anthedon: platform on north mole, looking north. One of the bedding-slots is visible.

solid Roman quay of brick and mortar, and the stones are all of travertine. It would be interesting to know what the present water level is in relation to these remains, but the site has been for a long time inaccessible; the available photos were taken when the harbour was drained and therefore give us no clear indication. It appears that the water level is now at about the top of the mooring-stones, but that the water level is kept artificially high. This is an interesting point which needs to be checked further.

At *Naupactus* on the north side of the Corinthian Gulf several mooring-stones project from the base of the castle wall on the seaward side. Their present relationship to water level seems very suitable, but it is not certain that they are *in situ*; they are in a curiously exposed position (Figs. 11–12).

Recent excavation of a quay of the late Roman port of *Sarepta* in the Lebanon has revealed one stone mooring-ring (Pritchard, 1971). This is now about 1 m above sea level (Pritchard, personal communication).

QUAYS

The important questions for our purposes are the present height of the quay surface above sea level, and our estimate of the likely original height. On the south-west side of the great south harbour at *Cnidus* is a rock-cut quay, and the rock surface slopes down slightly towards the water (which would help with drainage) and is on average 1.40 m above water level (Fig. 13; compare Love, 1967, 147 Fig. 13, but there are no clear traces of "cuttings for slips"). Can we be sure that we have the original surface?

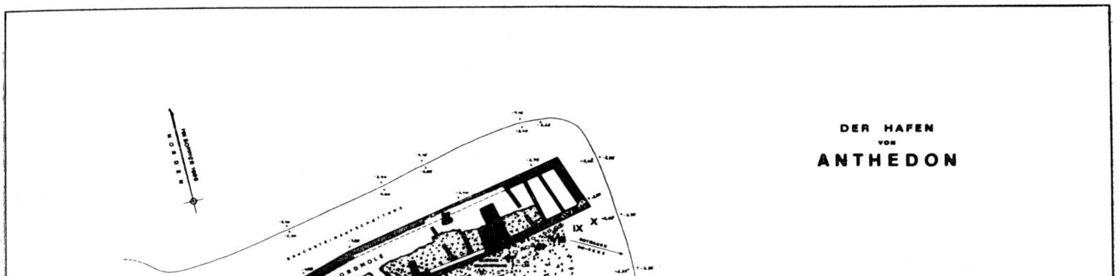

Figure 14. Anthedon: plan of harbour.

Here at Cnidus I think we can, and the height above the water looks about right. There seems to be very little change at all in sea level, for the Cnidians were not going to build a quay more than 6 feet above water level. On the other hand, the northern

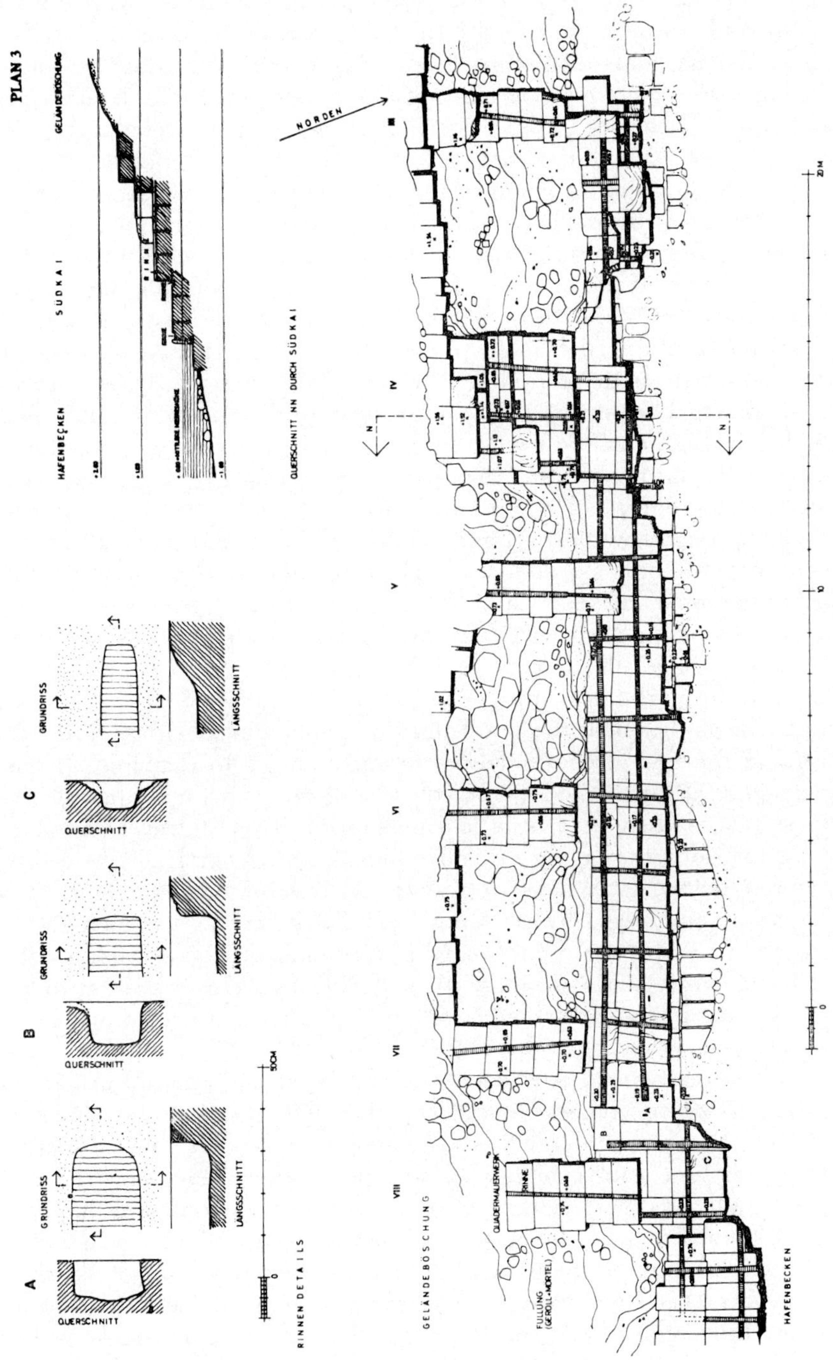

Figure 16. Anthedon: plan and section of south quay.

breakwater at the entrance to the great harbour is now just awash and was presumably built to break surface. The problem there is whether any of the topmost blocks have been washed or carted away. The breakwater on the southern side of the entrance looks just about right. Such breakwaters are difficult to date: they could go back to the fourth century B.C., but could also, in their final form, be several centuries later.

Anthedon is a small harbour-town on the north coast of Boeotia, whose harbour-works in their surviving form date from late antiquity or possibly the middle ages (Fig. 14; Schläger, Blackman & Schäfer, 1967; 1968). The harbour is protected along its north side by a mole; the inner side of this mole is lined with ashlar and may have served as a quay. The important question is whether the surviving upper surface is the original upper surface. Most of the mole consists of compartments of rubble, with narrow cross-walls of ashlar, and offers no certain evidence; but at one point there is an ashlar platform across the width of the mole (Schläger, Blackman & Schäfer, 1967, 17 Fig. 5; 1968, 47–8 & Figs. 27–8). The platform is only 5 m wide, which is surprisingly narrow. There is no certain indication, such as the presence of bollards, that we have the original surface of the platform; on the contrary, there are signs that there was once at least one more course above. The present surface is on average 0.44 m above water level, and is awash at high tide in an onshore wind; cut into its upper surface are two slots which probably once held mortar for bedding the course above (Fig. 15); there may have been more than one course above, but one seems more likely. This would mean a surface about 0.90 m above present water level and would indicate at most a small relative rise in sea level since the date of construction. A wall seems to have run out originally along the outer edge of the mole and this would have prevented waves from washing over the quay. All the builders had to ensure was that the quay surface remained out of the water at all times, at a site where the tide range is up to half a metre (much more than is usual in Greece, owing to the proximity of the Euripus Strait).

At the outer end of the mole there are lines of ashlar blocks submerged by up to 2.55 m, continuing the line of the mole and at right angles to that line. It has been argued by Hafemann (1965, 80 [684]) that these indicate a major change in sea level here, since these blocks must have been laid in the dry. This, however, seems a quite unwarranted assumption: the laying of ashlar blocks and, from Hellenistic times on, the use of concrete below water level were perfectly feasible with the aid of caissons. Arguments based on submerged walls are only valid if it can be convincingly demonstrated that these walls belonged originally to dry-land structures. Hafemann was partly misled by the mistaken assumption that the blocks were linked by timber tie-beams, whose use in harbour-works would probably have been restricted to construction above the surface.

At the back of the harbour at Anthedon is a rather curious quay (Figs. 16–17). In the upper surface of the surviving courses along its outer edge run some shallow slots still partially filled with mortar, intended as a bedding for the course above. Clearly, then, the quay was at least one course higher at each point where slots survive. What we cannot do is to assume a flat surface for the quay from back to front, and simply project the level of the highest course at the back as far as the front wall, at a height of 1.55 m or more. We must bear in mind the possibility that the quay was stepped like the upper quay at Leptis. Clearly the front edge of the quay stood clear of the water, but it could have been by anything from 2 to 5 feet, though 2 to 3 feet seems most likely. It seems most plausible to project the course which now lies 1.20 m above the surface, and allow for the possibility of a step down to 0.70 m by the edge.

At *Bodrum* the submerged structure in the harbour west of the castle is clearly the west mole of the Secret Harbour of the tyrants of Halicarnassus (Fig. 18; Frost, 1963,

Figure 17. Anthedon: south quay, looking west.

Figure 18. Halicarnassus (Bodrum): the submerged west mole of the Secret Harbour.

Figure 19. Teos: main quay, looking east; on the right, the base of a bollard still *in situ*.

Figure 20. Chersonesus: the east mole, looking south.

146–9 & Pl. VIII; Flemming, above, Fig. 42A). The remains form a long bank, with the substructure of a tower at its outer end. The most curious and as yet unexplained feature is a long channel within the bank towards its outer (west) side. One may probably assume at least a small change in sea level, on the ground that the base of the tower must have been built out of the water; this, however, seems to me not absolutely certain: it appears always to be assumed, if one finds the footings of a sea-wall, that they must have been originally laid out of the water, but this seems a hazardous assumption. It is even less certain that the present level of the top of the bank was originally out of the water; it could be that the upper courses have been robbed, and that the ashlar blocks now to be seen $\frac{1}{2}$ m under water were foundations laid originally just under the surface. The area needs further study, since interpretation is difficult when the purpose of the structure is not yet understood.

The situation with *Teos* quay is not very clear. One must assume that there was at least one more course along the outer edge of the quay. Apart from anything else, it would be needed to secure the mooring-stones in the course below. A surviving bollard (Fig. 19) shows that it is most unlikely that there was originally more than one course (the bollard has been badly broken and worn, but its base would hardly have been set more than three courses down). At Teos the mooring-stones themselves provide a clearer indication of a relative change, but a small one, in sea level.

At *Leptis*, as we have seen, the lower quay surface is now 1.30 m above water level; the water level is likely to have been somewhat lower originally, but not much. At *Chersonesus* on the north coast of Crete the Roman concrete quay has its upper surface now just awash (Fig. 20). Sea level must have been at least one metre lower originally (see below, pp. 133–4).

SLIPWAYS

A model now in the Nautical Museum in Piraeus (Figs. 21–22) provides a plausible reconstruction of a group of covered slipways or "shipsheds", used in antiquity to

Figure 21. Model of ancient shipsheds in Piraeus, front view (Nautical Museum, Piraeus).

Figure 22. Model of ancient shipsheds in Piraeus, side view (Nautical Museum, Piraeus).

Figure 23. Ancient shipsheds in Zea harbour, Piraeus: plan of 1885 excavations (Dragatsis & Dörpfeld, 1885, Pl. 2).

preserve warships by drawing them out of the water when not in service (for full discussion, with bibliography, see Blackman, 1968). A group of ten such shipsheds were excavated in Pashalimani (the ancient harbour of *Zea*) in 1885—an early example of the sort of rescue excavation which is now only too familiar (Dragatsis & Dörpfeld, 1885). The excavators were given one day to clear the central part of these shipsheds before work was resumed on the new embankment. As can be seen from the plan, the excavators made one complete longitudinal section down part of one slip, carefully avoiding the trees along the existing embankment (Fig. 23). Part of the top ends of these shipsheds is preserved in the basement of a block of flats, and a further part to the south lies under the front garden of an elegant old house now threatened with demolition. The slips have a clear width of just under 6 m and a gradient of just over 6°.

The key question is: what is now and what was originally the water level in the bottom end of the slip? On this point there is a discrepancy between the published plan and sections. The plan (correctly) shows the columns at the lower end of the shipsheds continuing on into the water; the longitudinal sections, on the other hand (Fig. 24), show the slip stopping at the water level (Dragatsis & Dörpfeld, 1885, Pls. 2–3; Blackman, 1968, 181–2 & Pl. 29). Although in fact the bed of the slip is not preserved at this level, it is obvious that such a reconstruction is impossible. How far would the slips have continued into the water? Only deep enough for ships to be able to float into the lower end, and no more: say 1 m. The warship would have entered the slip stern first, for obvious reasons; its stern swung up, which would help in this operation. It is usually almost impossible to determine the original lower end of the slip. This is the case in Pashalimani; if one assumes that the slips did not originally go much further than indicated by the plan of the 1885 excavations, then there is no evidence here of sea level change. The present dry length, 37 m on average, appears close to the original, or slightly less.

Figure 25 shows the plan and section of a group of possible shipsheds in the neighbouring and smaller harbour of *Munychia* (von Alten, 1881, 14 Figs. 7–8). If these are shipsheds for small craft, then there has been a change in relative sea level since antiquity, for at the time of construction the upper end of the slips must have been out of the water, in order to bring the hulls of the warships out into the dry (one possibility does, however, need to be borne in mind: that timber runners were laid over the rock originally, thus raising the level of the floor of the slip).

Another well-preserved group of shipsheds was discovered at *Oeniadae*, a harbour-city on the north side of the entrance to the Corinthian Gulf, by the open sea in antiquity, but now well inland, because of the alluvial deposits of the river Achelous (Sears, 1904; Lehmann-Hartleben, 1923, 115–18). These five shipsheds were cut into the rock and roofed singly (Fig. 26). The bed of the slips was cut to fit the ship's hull more closely, being 3.25 m wide at the lowest level. The slips also curved up at the top end. The clear width of the sheds is just over 6 m, very similar to that of the Zea sheds; the length of the slips is given as 47 m. The published plan and section are very vague about the lower ends of the slips, and the relative level of ground water is not given. Further investigation of these slips is highly desirable. The indications are that present ground water level is 1.5–2 m above the likely ancient sea level.

Also rock-cut are a pair of shipsheds at the foot of the hill north of the temple at *Sunium*, south-east of Athens. The slips are very steep (15° 50′) and shorter and narrower

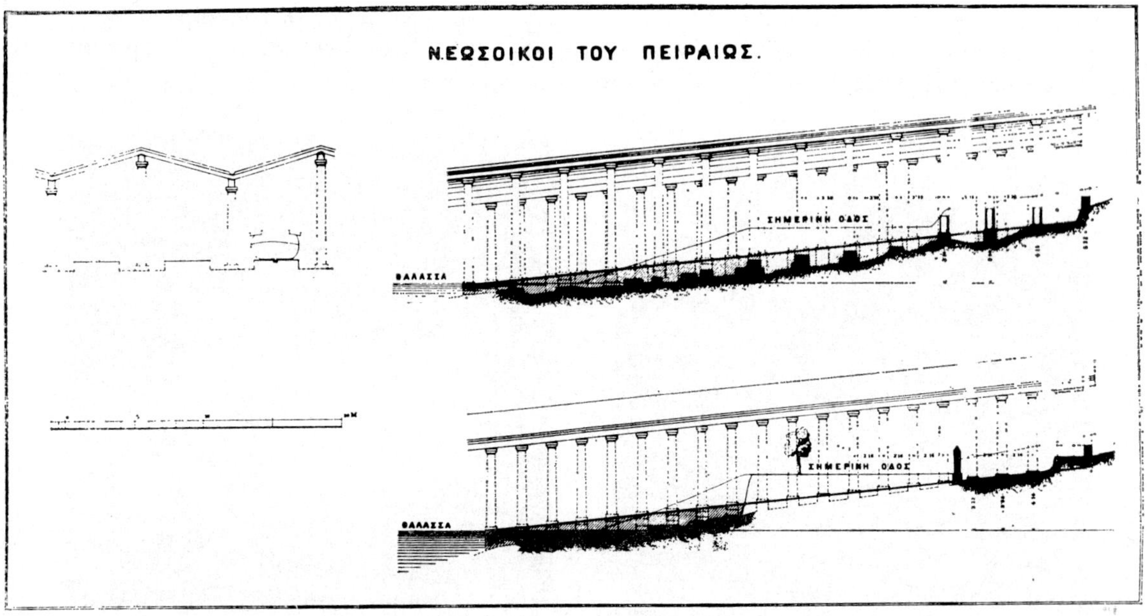

Figure 24. Ancient shipsheds in Zea harbour, Piraeus: sections (Dragatsis & Dörpfeld, 1885, Pl. 3).

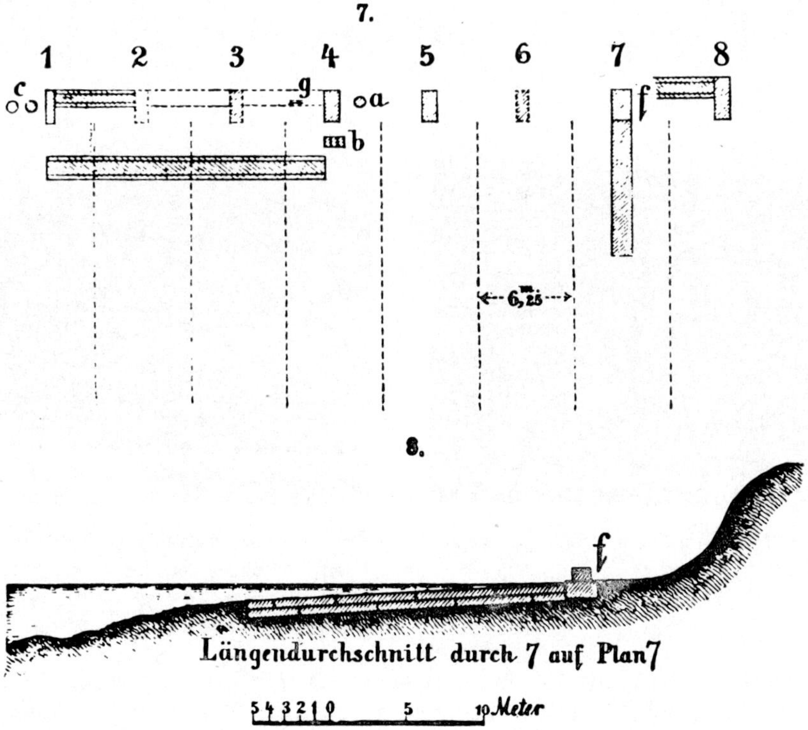

Figure 25. Remains in Munychia harbour, Piraeus, possibly of shipsheds: plan and section (von Alten, 1881, 14 Figs. 7–8).

than those previously mentioned (Kenny, 1947). The dry length of the slips is now 18 m, and they can be traced a further 3 m into the water. The reasons for the steepness are probably that the slips face the prevailing north-west wind, and that the builders,

Figure 26. Oeniadae: the rock-cut shipsheds, from the north-west.

Figure 27. Sunium: the eastern slip, from above.

Figure 28. H. Theodoroi: rock-cut tank, looking east.

Figure 29. Mahdia: the rock-cut harbour basin, looking south-east. The shadows along the edge of the east quay indicate the positions of broken-away bitts.

probably working hurriedly in the emergency of 413/2 B.C., wanted to keep to a minimum the horizontal length in order to save themselves much excavation of rock, since the hillside rises steeply. Again the key point for our purposes is the relationship of water level to the lower end of the slips. Unfortunately, these slips are full of fallen rubble (Fig. 27); it would be most interesting to clear this away. The slips would only have taken ships smaller then triremes, operating as guard-ships from this strategic point.

A very important group was found by Flemming on the south shore of the west island in the port of *Apollonia*, below Cyrene (Taylor, 1965, 170–3 & Figs. 69–70; Blackman, 1968, 183–4 & Pl. 30). The ten slips were rock-cut and later structures have been built over them, especially at the lower end. The slips are now completely flooded. Present sea level is obviously very different from the original. Flemming plausibly suggests an original depth of 80 cm at the lower end (2 m less than now), which would be a sufficient depth to float the ships in, and an original dry length of 28 m (Taylor, 1965, 177–8). Any less depth at the foot would have allowed into the slips only very small ships which would not have needed the greater dry length; any greater depth at the foot would have left too short a dry length of slip (e.g. a depth at the lower end of 1.5 m would give a dry length of only 18 m). Some problems still remain, however: in some ways these slips are similar to those in Piraeus—they are of similar clear width (6 m), similar length (just under 40 m) and have an even gentler gradient (4°)—but with an apparent maximum dry length of 28 m they cannot have held triremes. Or is it possible that the slips were longer than shown, but have been badly damaged since?

The important recent survey of the harbour area of *Aegina* has confirmed my earlier suggestion (1968, 186n) that there was a group of shipsheds at the north end of the military harbour, where a row of parallel walls, 6.5–6.6 m apart, run off inwards at right angles to the harbour wall (Knoblauch, 1969, 112 & Fig. 14). There were at least six shipsheds. The tops of the side walls are now just awash; rubble fills the actual sheds almost completely, so that the depth of the actual slips has not yet been established. This is an important task for the future.

Another rock-cut slip has recently been found just east of *Siteia* in eastern Crete (Davaras, 1967). It is 30 m long, 5.50 m wide, and has a gradient of 15° 30′. The published section shows the rock breaking away at sea level; thus it is impossible to determine the position of the original lower end. The date of this slip is not clear.

An installation which has some similar features is the *diolkos*, a paved runway along which warships could be drawn on trolleys over land, e.g. across an isthmus. The most notable example is that built across the isthmus of Corinth in the late seventh or early sixth century B.C. (Verdelis, 1956; 1958). In order for warships to be able to get on to the runway, there must have been sufficient depth of water at the lower end of the slips at either end for a ship to be able to float in and on to the trolley. Again, the problem may well be to define the original lower end of the slip, but it is possible that there was a submerged, roughly flat shelf, at least at the west end, whose depth (not recorded) it would be interesting to establish (Verdelis, 1956, 54).

DOCKS, TANKS AND CHANNELS

Other installations which may provide valuable evidence are those where we can be sure that their floors or entrance-channels must have contained a certain depth of water, in order for them to operate: notably docks, fish-tanks and various types of entrance-channel. The crucial question here is: can we be sure that we have the original floor? One can only be reasonably certain when the floor is paved or rock-cut. At *H. Theodoroi* on the north coast of Crete, just east of Heraklion, there are considerable traces of quarrying of the rock along the shore, and a small rock-cut tank *c.* 10 m wide and at least 12 m long (Marinatos, 1926; Frost, 1963, 107–9; Hafemann, 1965, 69 [673]; Fig. 28). This could have been a dock, used as a loading-point for small barges or lighters, probably to transport quarried material. What is not certain is the depth of its bottom below present water level: it is reported to be 1.80 m. Frost argues for much greater submergence of the site, in which case the cutting could not have been a dock. The question needs full investigation, preferably with a clearance of the "dock", whose date is not certain.

At *Motya* in western Sicily the entrance-channel to the "Cothon" has a tufa-paved bottom partly preserved, 1.78 m on average below the surface of the quays and 1.45 m below present mud and winter water level, summer water level being somewhat lower. The construction appears to date from the late sixth century and to have gone out of use at about the end of the fifth century (Isserlin, 1969; 1971). We know from other evidence at the site, notably the causeway, that there has been at least a small relative rise in sea level since antiquity. The importance of this evidence is that it gives us an indication of the maximum possible change since the time of construction. One may assume that there must have been at least a 1 m depth of water in the entrance-channel, if boats were to float through. If the slot along the centre of the channel was intended to take the keel of a vessel entering the channel, then the depth will not have been much greater, either. It would appear that only smaller boats could use the channel, since it is only 5.38 m wide at the narrowest section. The actual "Cothon" appears now not to have had a rock bottom, as was once thought. Isserlin (personal communication) believes that the evidence of the causeway indicates a relative rise of nearer 1 m than 50 cm, and is

Figure 30. Mahdia: the east quay, looking south. The edge of the quay is jagged where bitts have broken away.

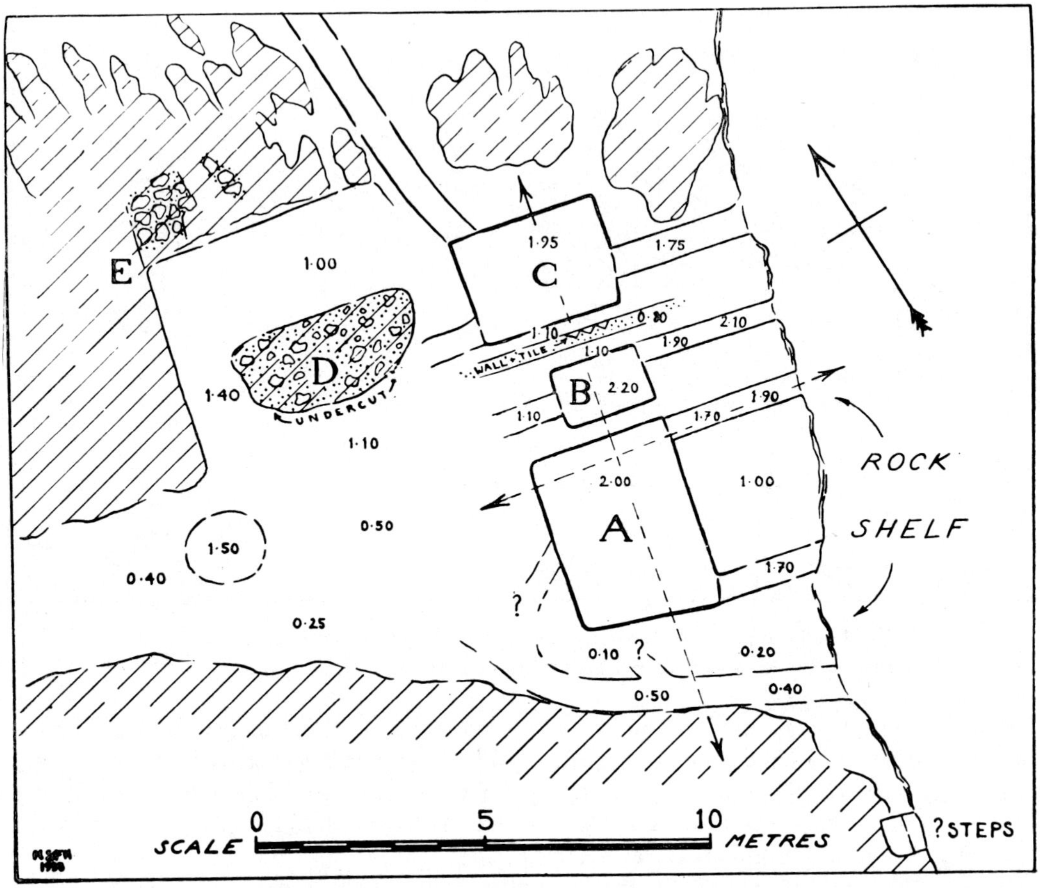

Figure 31. Chersonesus: plan of the fish-tanks (Leatham & Hood, 1958–9, 271 Fig. 4). Courtesy S. Hood & British School at Athens.

prepared to accept a depth of as little as 50 cm over the channel paving; this would involve ships having to be dragged up the channel, unless there were lock-gates to assist.

The rock-cut harbour at *Mahdia* in Tunisia is a fascinating site, which deserves closer study (Fig. 29; Yorke, 1966, 14 & Map 6; 1967, 24). One would like to know the depth of the bedrock within the harbour and in the entrance channel. I see no reason why this could not be a very early harbour indeed—why not Phoenician in origin? All around the lip of the quays which line the basin are bitts cut obliquely through the rock (Fig. 30). In many cases this has led eventually to the breaking away of the lip. The quays are now at a plausible height above the water, but one feels they may have been a little higher originally; certainly not lower.

At *Chersonesus* the evidence of the fish-tanks (Figs. 31–32) indicates that sea level was at least 1 m lower when they were built, and the evidence of the concrete quay confirms this; it is also clear from the fish-tanks that sea level cannot have been much lower at that time (Leatham & Hood, 1958–9, 264–6, 267–8, 270–2). Hafemann (1965, 69–70 [673–4], 78–9 [682–3]) argues that the quay and fish-tank must therefore have

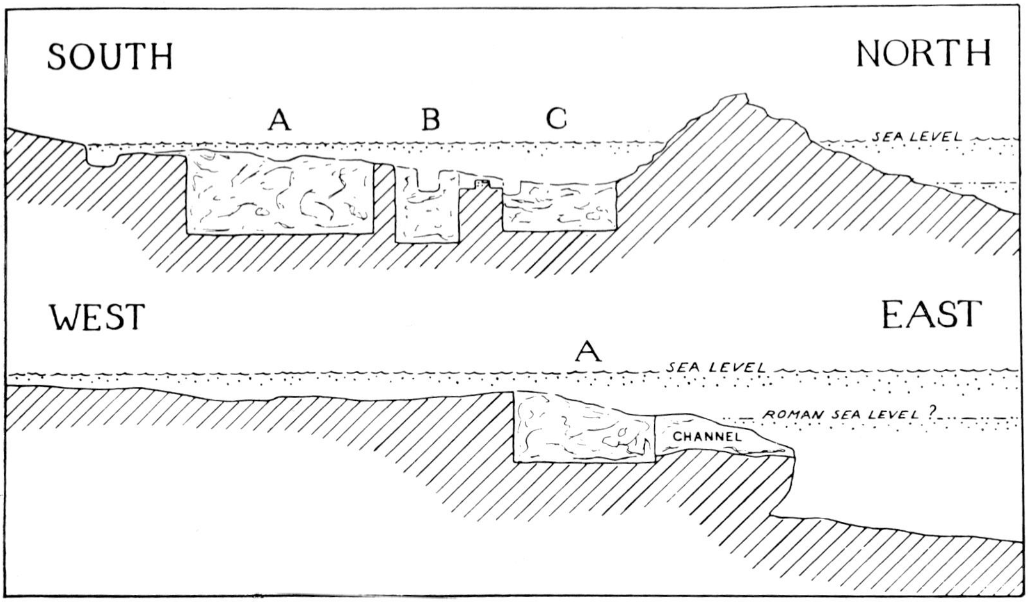

Figure 32. Chersonesus: sections of the fish-tanks (Leatham & Hood, 1958–9, 272 Fig. 4*a*). Courtesy S. Hood & British School at Athens.

been of different date, since the quay when it was built must have been 1.50–2 m above sea level, while its surface is now just awash. This seems unnecessarily high, but a small difference in date is possible, large enough in Crete for significant earth movements. Among other good examples of fish-tanks are those at Mochlos (Leatham & Hood, 1958–9, 274–5) and Apollonia (Taylor, 1965, 176–7 & Pl. 26).

Figure 33. Cosa: cuttings for sluice-gate in the Tagliata.

Figure 35. Piraeus: the "Tomb of Themistocles".

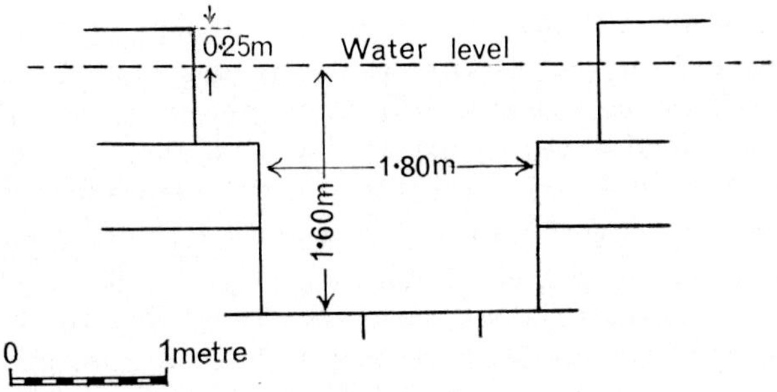

Figure 34. Mytilene: section of channel across east mole.

Fish-tanks provide very important evidence, since if well preserved they can tell us the maximum and minimum possible change in sea level since the time of construction (though dating them may be difficult, as with all rock-cut features). The water level must originally have been sufficiently high for water to run in and out through the entrance-channels, to provide free circulation of water, and yet not so high that the tanks were totally submerged. One must always allow, however, for the side walls to have been built up artificially.

A similarly close dating-bracket can be provided by sluice-gates, flushing-tanks and channels. One can be sure that there was a certain depth of water in the tanks and channels, and that the water would not have washed over the top of the gates or walls. The rock-cuttings in the wall of the Tagliata at *Cosa*, north of Rome, were clearly for a sluice-gate, and the top of these cuttings is likely to have been clear of the water (Fig. 33; Brown, 1951, 95 Figs. 96–8). Conversely, the bed of the channel must have been well submerged. At *Sidon* the flushing-tanks would only have operated effectively if water could lap over the rock into them; it is likely that water would not have been allowed to wash in too freely (Poidebard & Lauffray, 1951, 58, 66–71, 87–8; Frost, 1963, 92–3).

In the north harbour at *Mytilene* the main east mole has a series of short channels across it at intervals of about 38 m (Fig. 34; Koldewey, 1890, 7 & Pl. III.2; Lehmann-Hartleben, 1923, 104–5; Poidebard & Lauffray, 1951, 22, 42). The channels are lined with ashlar and are on average 1.80 m wide, with their bottoms 1.60–1.80 m below modern water level; the top surface of the mole (not certainly original) is now about 0.25 m above water level. Similar channels survive in the west mole. There may have been a slight relative rise in water level, but if the accepted interpretation of these channels is correct—that they were flushing-channels through the mole to maintain currents of water through the harbour to prevent silting—then there must have been at least 50–60 cm of water passing through the channels, so that sea level cannot have changed by more than 1 m.

OTHER FEATURES

Other archaeological features provide obvious evidence for a relative rise in sea level, notably land structures which are now submerged: for example, causeways (e.g. at Clazomenae and Motya); houses and public buildings (e.g. at Elaphonisos, Halieis, Antiparos and Kenchreai, where there have been at least two occasions of rapid submersion, clearly caused by earthquakes); tombs (e.g. at Elaphonisos, Antiparos, Piraeus [Fig. 35] and Matala); well-heads, cisterns and water-pipes (e.g. at Antiparos [Morrison, 1968] and Cosa [McCann & Lewis, 1970]); and vine-trenches (e.g. at Antiparos). Other features provide less certain evidence: for example, quarry-working (can we be sure at what level above the surface this stopped?) and steps (can we be sure whether or not they originally went down into the water, and if so, how far?). Similarly, certain walls may have been sea-washed: for example, at Myndus in Caria and Thoricus in Attica. With these land structures one can often show that there has been relative submersion, but since one can rarely prove how high the feature was above water level originally, one can rarely define the amount of change in sea level. This can only be done with certain features that have been discussed above, where a maximum and minimum change can be defined.

Flemming has shown how much use the geomorphologist can make of archaeological evidence for sea level change. It is for the archaeologist to be aware of the value and limitations of such evidence and to supply data to the geomorphologist, who in return can aid the archaeologist's understanding of coastal sites.

ACKNOWLEDGEMENTS

I am grateful to Dr. B. S. J. Isserlin for providing information about Motya (he stresses that the views expressed are not final); and to Prof. J. B. Pritchard for information about Sarepta.

REFERENCES

Bartoccini, R. & Zanelli, A. 1958 *Il Porto romano di Leptis Magna* [Bollettino del Centro di Studi per la Storia dell'Architettura, 13, Suppl.], 222 pp. Rome.

Bean, G. E. 1966 *Aegean Turkey: an archaeological guide*, 288 pp. London.

Béquignon, Y. & Laumonier, A. 1925 Fouilles de Teos (1924). *BCH*, **49**, 281–321.

Blackman, D. J. 1968 The Shipsheds, *in* Morrison, J. S. & Williams, R. T., *Greek Oared Ships*, 181–6. Cambridge.

Brown, F. E. 1951 Cosa, I: History and Topography. *Memoirs of the American Academy in Rome*, **20**, 89–96.

Calza, G. 1925 Ricognizioni topographiche nel Porto di Traiano. *NSc* (6th S) **1**, 54–80.

Davaras, K. 1967 Eis neosoikos para ten Seteian. *ArchEph* 1967, 84–90.

de la Blanchère, M. R. 1881 Le port de Terracine. *MélRome*, **1**, 322–48.

Dragatsis, I.Ch. & Dörpfeld, W. 1885 Ekthesis peri ton en Peiraiei anaskaphon. *Praktika* 1885, 63–8.

Frost, H. 1963 *Under the Mediterranean*, 278 pp. London.

Hafemann, D. 1965 Die Niveauveränderungen an den Küsten Kretas seit dem Altertum. *AbhdlAkadMainz, math.-nat.Kl.* 1965, No. 12. 84 pp. [609–88].

Hamilton, W. J. 1842 *Researches in Asia Minor, Pontus and Armenia*, 2 vols, 544 + 508 pp. London.

Isserlin, B. S. J. 1969 Phoenicians in Sicily. *ILN*, Oct. 18, 1969, 26–7.

Isserlin, B. S. J. 1971 New light on the "cothon" at Motya. *Antiquity*, **45**, 178–86.

Kenny, E. J. A. 1947 The Ancient Docks on the Promontory of Sunion. *BSA*, **42**, 194–200.

Knoblauch, P. 1969 Neuere Untersuchungen an den Häfen von Aegina. *BonnJbb*, **169**, 104–16.

Koldewey, R. 1890 *Die antiken Bauwerke der Insel Lesbos*, 91 pp. Berlin.

Leatham, J. & Hood, S. 1958–9 Submarine exploration in Crete, 1955. *BSA*, **53–54**, 263–80.

Lehmann–Hartleben, K. 1923 *Die antiken Hafenanlagen des Mittelmeeres*, 304 pp. [*Klio*, Beiheft 14]. Leipzig. Reprinted 1963, Aalen.

Love, I. C. 1967 Knidos: Excavations in 1967. *TürkArkDerg*, **16**.2, 133–47.

Marinatos, Sp. 1926 Anaskaphai Nirou Khani Kritis. *Praktika* 1926, 141–7.

McCann, A. M. & Lewis, J. D. 1970 The Ancient Port of Cosa. *Archaeology*, **23** No. 3 (June 1970) 200–11.

Meiggs, R. 1960 *Roman Ostia*, 598 pp. Oxford.

Morrison, I. A. 1968 Relative Sea Level Changes in the Saliagos Area since Neolithic Times, *in* Evans, J. D. & Renfrew, C. *Excavations at Saliagos*, 92–8 (Appendix I). London.

Poidebard, A. & Lauffray, J. 1951 *Sidon. Aménagements antiques du port de Saida*, 103 pp. Beyrouth.

Pritchard, J. B. 1971 The Phoenician city of Sarepta. *Archaeology*, **24** No. 1 (Jan. 1971) 61–3.

Schäfer, J. & Schläger, H. 1962 Zur Seeseite von Kyme in der Aeolis. *Archäologischer Anzeiger*, 1962. 1, 40–57.

Schläger, H., Blackman, D. J. & Schäfer, J. 1967 Un port de la basse époque romaine en Grèce centrale. *Archeologia*, No. 17 (July–August 1967), 12–17.

Schläger, H., Blackman, D. J. & Schäfer, J. 1968 Der Hafen von Anthedon. *Archäologischer Anzeiger*, 1968. 1, 21–98.

Sears, J. M. 1904 Oeniadae, VI: The Ship-sheds. *AJA*, **8**, 227–37.

Taylor, J. du Plat 1965 *Marine Archaeology*, 208 pp. London.

Testaguzza, O. 1970 *Portus*, 249 pp. Rome.

Verdelis, N. M. 1956 Der Diolkos am Isthmus von Korinth. *AthMitt*, **71**, 51–9.

Verdelis, N. M. 1958 Die Ausgrabungen des Diolkos während der Jahre 1957/59. *AthMitt*, **73**, 140–5.

von Alten, G. 1881 Die Befestigungen der Hafenstadt Athens, *in* Milchhöfer, A. (ed.) *Karten von Attika: Erläuternder Text*, Vol. I.

von Gerkan, A. 1933 Meereshöhen und Hafenanlagen im Altertum, in *Wilhelm Dörpfeld, Festschrift zum 80. Geburtstag*, 37–42. Published by the Koldewey–Gesellschaft. [Reprinted in Boehringer, E. (ed.) *Von Antiker Architektur und Topographie: Gesammelte Aufsätze von Armin von Gerkan*, 139–42. Stuttgart, 1959].

Yorke, R. A. 1966 *Cambridge Expedition to Sabratha*, 1966, 31 pp. Privately circulated.

Yorke, R. A. 1967 Les ports engloutis de Tripolitaine et de Tunisie, *Archeologia*, No. 17 (July–August 1967), 18–24.

Discussion

Marsden On the question of laying blocks under water, am I right that Vitruvius actually described how to build under water within a coffer-dam?

Blackman Yes, he does (V.12).

Marsden What is Vitruvius' date?

Blackman He was writing in the time of Augustus (late first century B.C.), but for much of his work he drew on Hellenistic technical handbooks written several centuries earlier, and we know that such handbooks were written on harbour construction. Thus a reference in Vitruvius provides only a very imprecise *terminus ante quem* for the techniques he describes.

Marsden At the ancient port of Rome, now under Rome airport, a number of boats were discovered sunk in the harbour, and also stretches of quayside have been uncovered. From this one can get some clue as to the original depth of the harbour bottom and the original level of water in the harbour.

Blackman That is a good point.

Marsden An excavation against a harbour basin wall should reveal traces of a coffer-dam construction, if such had been used.

Blackman This is certainly something which we should look for: one thinks at once of the coffer-dam found at Cosa around the well-house and the traces of another found around a pier there. This might also be a partial explanation of the vertical recesses in the inner face of the concrete mole at Chersonesus.

Blackman Reference to excavation raises what seems to me a serious point of principle: should we get involved in excavating one or two ancient harbours when far more, like Pompeiopolis in Cilicia, are being demolished or built over without ever having been recorded? Should we not rather concentrate on "rescue survey"—planning all visible remains at as many sites as possible?

Green At Kyrenia there is a mooring-post 3 m above the road, which is itself 2 m above the waterline.

Blackman That is in effect a two-step quay, which is slightly different.

Kapitän At Brucolo Augusta (Province of Syracuse, Sicily) there are bitts 15 m above sea level; but that is too high to have any precise bearing on sea level.

Green Could the ships not have moored broadside on for unloading, and then moved to a standard fore-and-aft mooring afterwards?

Blackman This could have happened, one assumes; but the few illustrations which we have indicate fore-and-aft mooring as the norm, and the close positioning of the mooring-stones in quay-faces implies the same. At Ostia there are also numbered columns marking the berths, from which one can deduce the intensity of use of quays.

Throckmorton It seems possible that certain quays were used for sideways unloading, after which ships would move to fore-and-aft moorings at other quays.

Blackman As regards mooring-stones in lower quay faces, were these intended to be worked both from the quay surface and from small boats, or only from boats? This is an important point, if one tries to deduce the height of the original surface of a quay from the level of mooring-stones. Again, the possibility does I think need to be considered that loops of rope or wicker were used to avoid the direct chafing of the ropes on the abrasive stone of the mooring-stones, or that timber spars were inserted into the holes like cleats, and the mooring-ropes made fast to these.
Lewis A possible alternative here might be that long horizontal lines passed through one mooring-stone after another, where the holes are horizontal, and that ships made fast to these.

Hague Since the mooring-stones had to take considerable strain, they must have been embedded deeply in the quay, secured by the weight of courses above.
Blackman Yes, there must always have been at least one course above. Further methods of securing them were possible: e.g. at Teos, they are wedge-shaped in plan, and some of them have a step down towards the rear of the underside, which fits over the rear edge of the stringer course below.

An underwater archaeological survey of Cape Andreas, Cyprus, 1969–70: a preliminary report

by

JEREMY N. GREEN

SUMMARY

The Research Laboratory for Archaeology, Oxford, conducted in the summers of 1969 and 1970 an underwater archaeological survey of the seabed, down to a depth of 50 m, around Cape Andreas in Cyprus. A total area of about 1 sq. km was systematically searched, using the diver swimline technique. A detailed hydrographic survey of the whole area was carried out and the coastline and islands surveyed. The survey of the material located was carried out using both conventional techniques (tape trilateration and theodolite/tape methods) and simple photogrammetric techniques (photomosaic, reference-frame triangulation, cube and cross-rod plan drawing). The various techniques were compared; the simple photogrammetric techniques were found to be a highly efficient method of recording, and the theodolite/tape system the best method of surveying the control points for the photogrammetry. A total of 10 pottery sites were located; four are thought to be wrecks, the remainder possibly spillage or jettison. Two foul ground anchor sites were located, one containing 30 anchors in an area of about 3,500 sq. m. Three unusual lines of stone anchors were also recorded. The total number of anchors recorded was about 200 : 50 iron, 10 lead and the rest stone. Twelve iron Y-shaped anchors were recorded.

INTRODUCTION

THE Research Laboratory for Archaeology, Oxford, carried out two underwater archaeological expeditions during the summers of 1969 and 1970 at Cape Andreas, the north-east cape of Cyprus (see Figs. 1 & 2). The object of these expeditions was to search for and record underwater material of archaeological interest. It was hoped that deep-water wrecks similar to the Kyrenia Wreck (Green, Hall & Katzev 1967) would be located. In spite of the fact that only one deep-water wreck was located, the two seasons' work has led to the discovery of an immense amount of material, and a thorough study has been made of the techniques involved in locating and recording underwater material. A preliminary report of the 1969 season has been made (Green, 1969; 1970) and a detailed report of the two seasons' work is in preparation. It should be emphasized that this is a preliminary report and therefore some of the conclusions may need to be amended later.

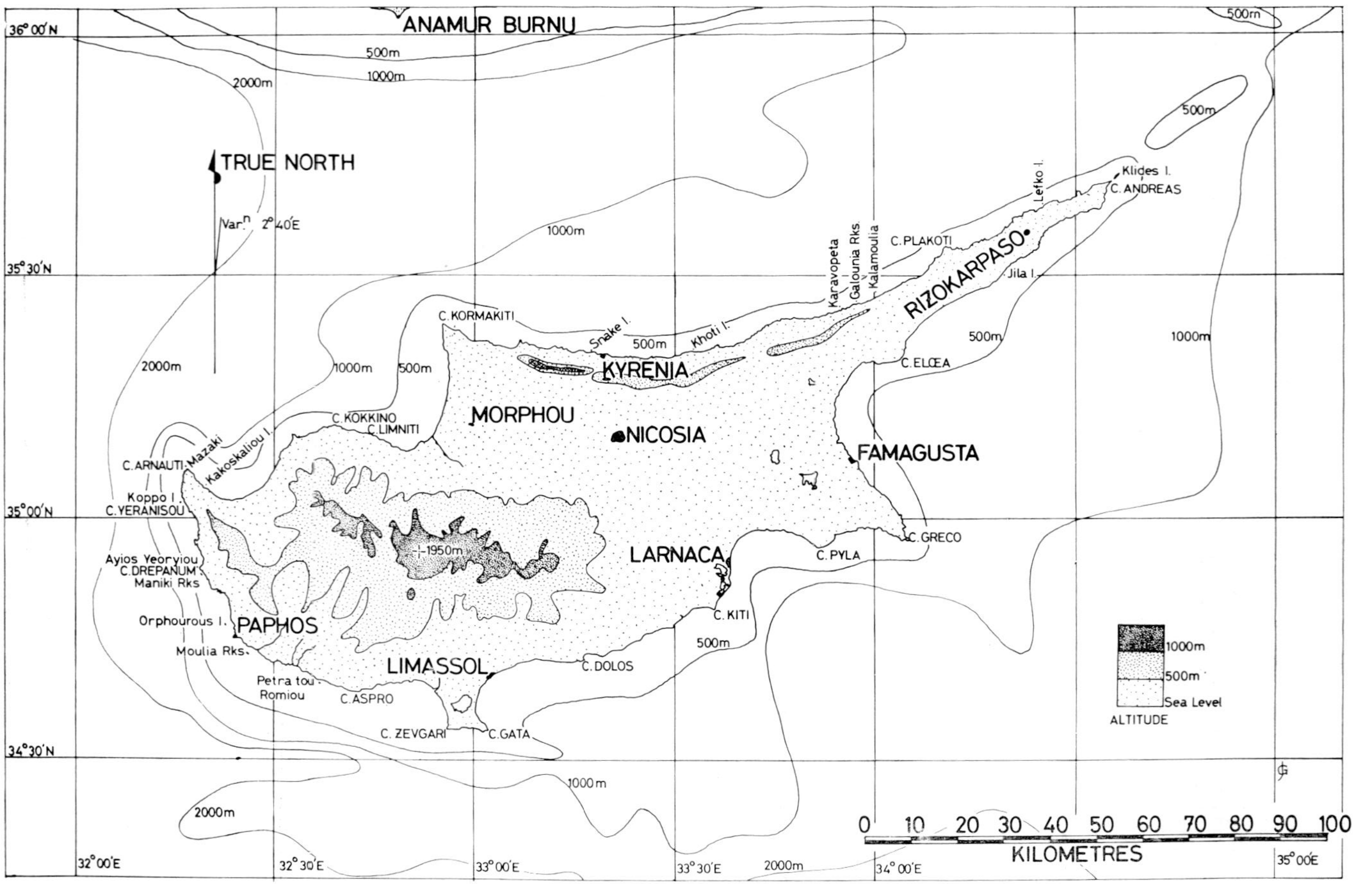

Figure 1. Map of Cyprus, showing altitude and depth contours in metres.

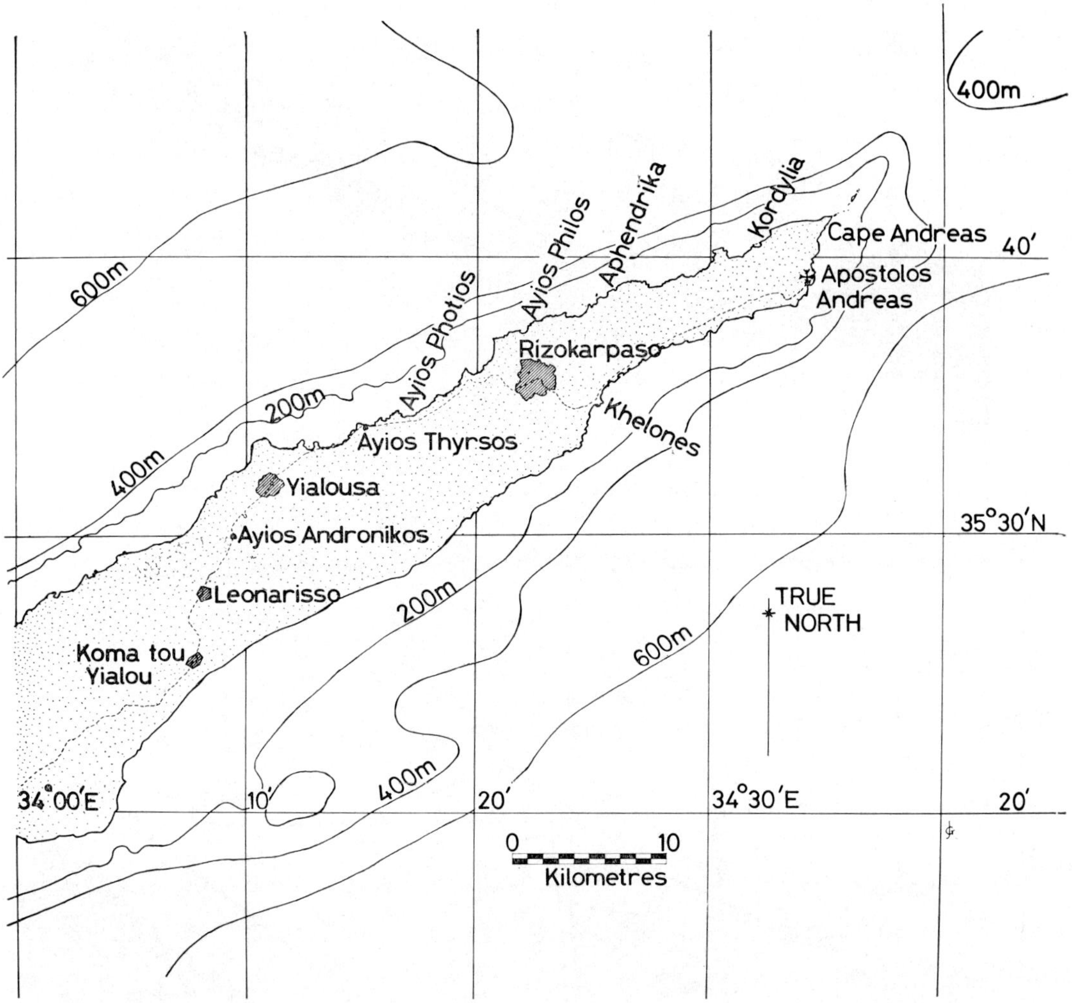

Figure 2. Map of the Karpaso Peninsula, showing main towns and survey sites.

THE SEARCH METHOD

The basis of our search method was the swimline, invented by Lt. Cmdr J. Grattan, and originally described by Wignall (1968). Three types of swimlines were used: these were developed to deal with the varying conditions experienced in the area. For the swimline diving, the maximum depth limit was 50 m, and the maximum distance that could be swum in the given diving time was 300 m, when working with the current. The area covered by the swimlines is shown in Figure 3. Figure 4 shows a basic swimline for four divers.

The three types of swimlines were as follows:

System A. (Working with the current, and covering distances less than 300 m). The

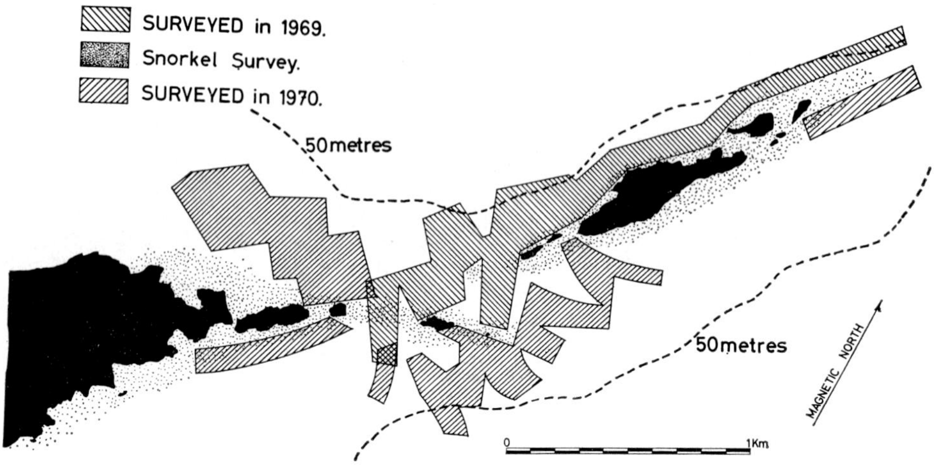

Figure 3. Areas covered by swimline surveys, 1969 and 1970.

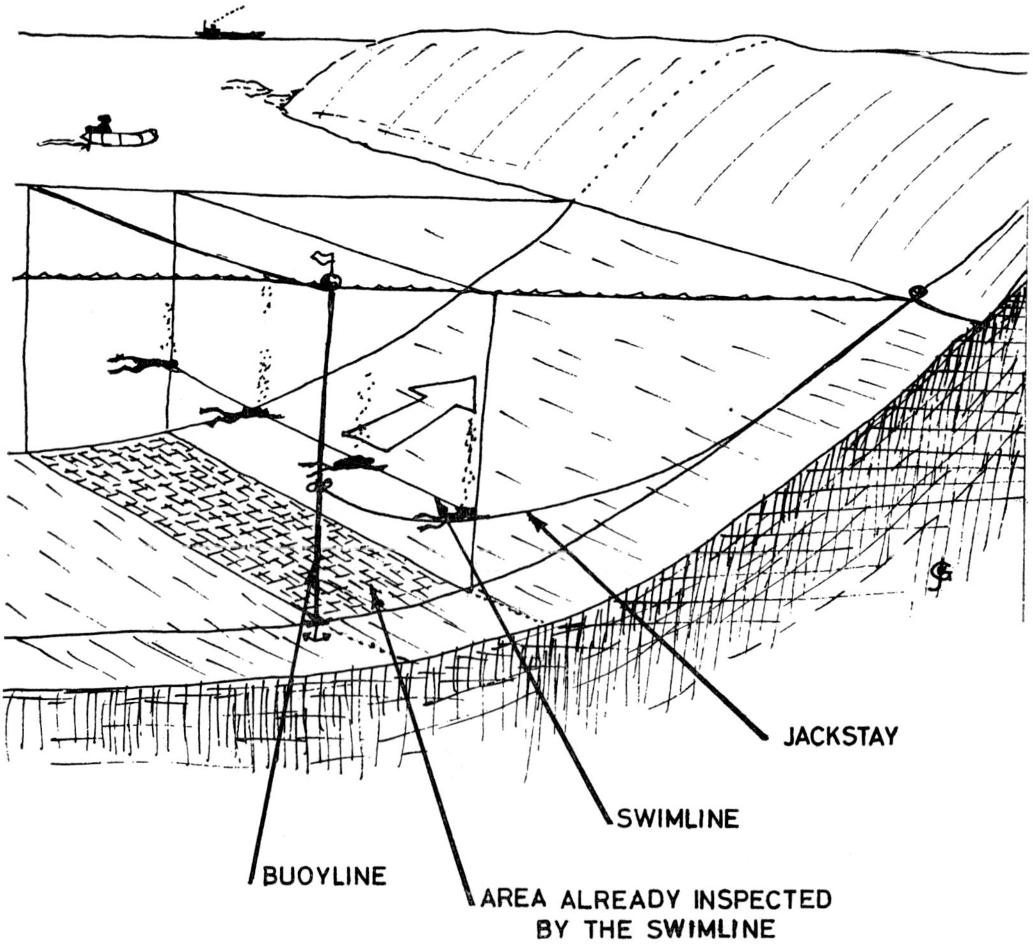

Figure 4. The arrangement of a four-man swimline.

jackstay was laid to the shore and the swimline team searched in the morning on one side of the jackstay and in the afternoon on the other side. This system was used in 1969 on the north side of the islands.

System B. (Working with the current, and covering distances greater than 300 m). The jackstay was laid to the shore and the swimline team searched the deep-water end, up to the time limit, covering generally about one-third of the jackstay. The point reached was marked and in the afternoon, after a six-hour interval, the jackstay was picked up and the mark relocated. As the swimline was then working in shallower water, which gave a longer diving time, the rest of the jackstay could then be searched. This system was used on the western end of the north side during 1970.

System C. (Working against the current). In this situation the jackstay system was discarded; a buoy was used to mark the starting position of the swimline in the shallow water. The divers at the ends of the swimline carried buoys, and as the swimline swam with the current the buoys were surveyed alternately (with sextants) by the survey-boat. This system was used on the south side of the islands in 1970.

Three safety factors on the Standard British Navy Diving Tables were always used, with no decompression stop. This was in view of the fact that no recompression chamber was available on site.

The marking of the finds on the swimlines was found to be difficult. Buoys were not practical. Eventually we found that the recording of the time of discovery of a find on the swimline enabled the approximate position to be plotted on the large-scale chart.

The shallow-water areas (less than 10 m) were searched with snorkel swimlines and also by individual free snorkelers.

HYDROGRAPHIC SURVEYING

(*a*) *Echo-sounder Survey*

An important part of our survey work at Cape Andreas was the completion of an echo-sounder survey of the area around the Cape (Fig. 5). This was carried out because the sounding information on the Admiralty Chart of the area (No. 796) was inadequate to determine accurately the position of the 50-m contour. A Ferrograph 500 Echo Sounder was used, which gave an accurate paper trace recording of the seabed. Initially, in 1969, straight line runs were made, with land survey-stations used to locate the start and finish of the runs. From our experience in 1970 we concluded that this is perhaps the worst way to locate the position of a boat. The correct method is to use sextants to locate several positions on the runs which are correlated with the paper trace and plotted on the chart. The standard text on this type of work is the *Admiralty Manual of Hydrographic Surveying* (Vol. 2: Sounding). This survey took several days to complete but it was very helpful in the planning of the swimline work.

(*b*) *Position-fixing at Sea*

In 1969 we underestimated the importance of position-fixing at sea. Having no previous experience of hydrographic work we decided to use land survey-stations to locate position at sea. This proved to be highly inefficient, since the communication problems led to a great deal of frustration and confusion in the survey-boat, and also the landing of survey-parties was time-consuming.

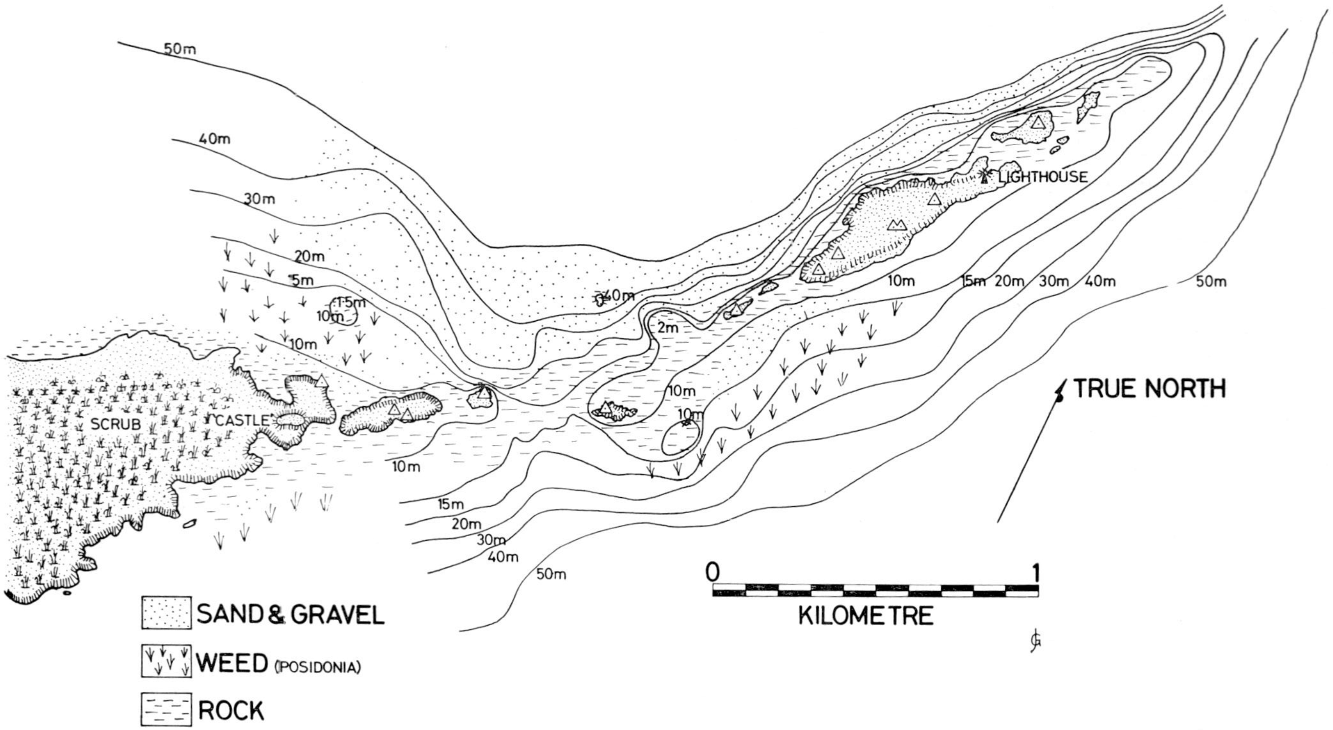

Figure 5. Hydrographic chart of Cape Andreas.

Land transits were very inaccurate in the area, since there are no back features to sight on. Sextants were found to be the best system, both for convenience and accuracy. Beacons were set up on survey-stations on the mainland and islands, which were used for sighting on. A day's training period was set aside to accustom the operators to the instruments and their operation in small boats. Plastic sextants manufactured by Ebbco were used, since in a rubber boat there is a danger of valuable sounding sextants being flooded with seawater. It was found that these instruments could be read to ± 5 minutes of an arc, if the zero error was regularly checked. In order to ensure accurate sextant work, before the survey-boat was taken out, the survey area was examined on the map to determine the best cuts. Positions located with the sextants were transferred to the master chart in the normal way with a station pointer.

The relocation of an unmarked position from two sextant angles proved quite difficult and required experienced operators. It was found that if one of the sextant operators steered the boat on the arc of the circle of one fix, the other operator could first determine if the boat was travelling in the correct direction on the circle, and then, when this was established, he could indicate the point where his sextant angle was correct. In one case, using this method, a submerged buoy was relocated to within 1 m at a distance of 200 m from the shore.

(*c*) *Land Surveying*

As there were no large-scale maps of the area available, a 1 : 10,000 map was constructed in Oxford from aerial photographs supplied by the Department of Lands and Surveys, Cyprus. In 1969 a survey of the area was carried out to check the accuracy of the map. Survey-stations were established on the mainland and the islands and were accurately surveyed by tacheometry. Owing to the large distances between islands 2 and 3 and islands 3 and 4, which exceeded the 120 m tacheometry range of the theodolite, tacheometry between those islands was impossible. In these cases triangulation was used to locate the positions of these particular stations.

In 1970 a survey of the coastline was made by triangulation with two theodolites. In both surveys, considerable difficulty was experienced in trying to triangulate accurately. This was because of the unusual nature of the area. The Cape and Islands enclose a long narrow area; therefore any base line set up at right angles to the major axis of the area covers only about 10% of the distance required to be surveyed along the axis. The map made from the aerial photographs suffers from similar distortions, since the matching of adjacent photographs has to be done over very small distances. Work is being carried out on the material in an attempt to check the accuracy of the original map: this will be published in the final report.

The permanent survey-stations used in 1969 served in 1970 as a ready-made network for the beacons used in the sextant work. These stations can be used by any future expeditions to the area, for survey work or relocation of the sites.

UNDERWATER SURVEYING

Three types of underwater surveying, excluding photogrammetry, were used on the sites located:

1. three-tape trilateration;

2. distance/angle measurement, using an underwater theodolite;
3. distance/angle measurement, using a compass.

These methods were used to plot the extent of the sites and to locate the control-points used in the photogrammetry. Any underwater surveying technique should satisfy two contrasting requirements: speed and accuracy. Generally, as time is limited, accuracy is sacrificed for speed, and thus method 3 is perhaps the most widely used.

Three-tape trilateration is rather slow and requires considerable swimming around with long tapes, but has a plan accuracy of about ±0.5%. Because of the good visibility at Cape Andreas (40 m) an underwater theodolite was constructed for the 1970 season, costing about £7 (see Fig. 6). This consisted of two parts: a heavy iron tripod with a flat iron base, and a simple cross-wire sighting-tube theodolite. The tripod serves as a permanent station, generally established in the centre of the site. The base of the theodolite can be accurately levelled, and horizontal and vertical angles recorded. The operator measures the two angles and the distance from the position indicated by the diver holding the far end of the tape. With this type of theodolite, the operator can measure horizontal angles to ±0.5° and vertical angles to ±1.0°. The plan accuracy of the theodolite/tape system is about ±1%—slightly lower than the three-tape trilateration system. However, the difficulty of setting up a trilateration system, recording the measurements, and handling the tapes (which requires three divers), is in strong contrast with the theodolite, where ease of handling and measurement, together with the simplicity of plotting the plan and extracting elevations, make it a highly efficient instrument. The theodolite/tape system which we used was about twice as fast as the trilateration system from start to finish of a survey.

PHOTOGRAMMETRY

The photogrammetry techniques used to record the archaeological material have been described elsewhere (Green & others, 1971) and will be described briefly here. Three systems were used:

1. photomosaics for large wreck-sites;
2. small site plan work using a grid-frame;
3. phototriangulation for plotting several small site plans on to an overall plan.

The photomosaic proved to be a highly effective method of recording large sites (3,000 sq. m); a vast amount of information is recorded and the overall photograph shows the site in a manner that is otherwise impossible. For technical reasons the accuracy is low (about ±5% over distances of 20 m). However, the techniques used provide facilities for accurate analysis with a stereo-plotting instrument.

The small site plan work utilized vertical photographs of a cuboid grid-frame. This system was used to record 150 stone anchors and 50 iron anchors in 1970. A stone anchor can be recorded in a few minutes with an accuracy of ±1%. Small areas of pottery that are unsuitable for mosaic work can also be recorded by this technique, with an accuracy of about ±5%. An area of 20 sq. m can be recorded in about 20 minutes.

Phototriangulation was used to plot the position and orientation of small areas of pottery recorded with grid-frames. Some care and planning is required with this system, since the various plans tend to be constructed on different planes. Position is not likely

Figure 6. Theodolite in use on Site 17.

to be more accurate than ±10% on an undulating site, but on a flat area it can be more accurate (±2%).

We found these simple techniques indispensable for recording the vast quantity of material. Photogrammetry provides a permanent record of a site which can be analysed later at leisure; the important point is to take as many photographs as necessary to cover the sites adequately. An interesting illustration of the application is given by a photograph taken in 1967 on site 19 during the Cyprus Archaeological Survey Expedition (C.A.U.S.E.) (see Bass & Katzev, 1968; Katzev, 1968). The photograph showed sherds of two stemless cups or kylikes and three amphora sherds; three years later, in 1970, we carried out a photogrammetric coverage of this site. During the analysis work and drawing of the site in England, some months later, the three amphora sherds were located but the kylikes proved to have been looted.

HYDROGRAPHY AND GEOLOGY

An investigation of the currents and tides was carried out in 1970. It was noted that in 1969 the current generally set clockwise round the Cape; this current was quite variable, on some days being exceptionally strong and on other days almost slack. On rare occasions the current set in an anti-clockwise direction. Since it was important to be able to predict this direction for the swimline work, measurements were made of the current strength with a log-ship. Tidal measurements and wind direction and speed were also recorded to see if these correlated in any way. At present these results are inconclusive and further analysis is being carried out; the maximum recorded current was 28.9 m per minute.

A geological and geomorphological study of the area was carried out partially to record evidence for recent sea level changes. From the study no evidence was found for sea level changes in recent geological time.

THE FINDS

A vast quantity of material was located using the swimline technique; this material has been divided into three categories:

1. pottery sites, including material that may possibly be jettison;
2. anchor sites—areas where anchors are closely associated;
3. individual anchors, including anchors from anchorages.

1. Pottery Sites

A total of ten pottery sites were located; some sites are little more than objects from spillage or jettison (sites 1, 14 and 18). Sites 12 and 16, 10 and 14, and 17 and 24 have material that appears to be interrelated and it is difficult to decide whether the sites represent separate or associated events. In view of the large amount of material, the less interesting sites will be mentioned only briefly. Any conclusion must be considered tentative as the full analysis in not complete.

Site 19 was first located by C.A.U.S.E., 1967; it lies approximately 50 m west of a 1.5 m reef, which lies 200 m due north of the "Castle". The site consists of two separate areas of heavily concreted sherds (Figs. 7 & 8). The material has been swept down the smooth west side of the reef and collected behind a large rock and in a shallow depression near the base of the reef (depth 15 m). It is possible that further material is buried in the sand at the base of the reef.

As was mentioned above, in 1967 fragments of two kylikes were found, which indicated a date in the fourth century B.C. (Bass & Katzev, 1968) The *seventeen* fragments of handles indicate that the main cargo was large looped-handle amphorae, and the sherds indicate that these amphorae were biconical with pointed feet. A single handle from a smaller type of amphora can also be seen. The amount of material is small for a whole

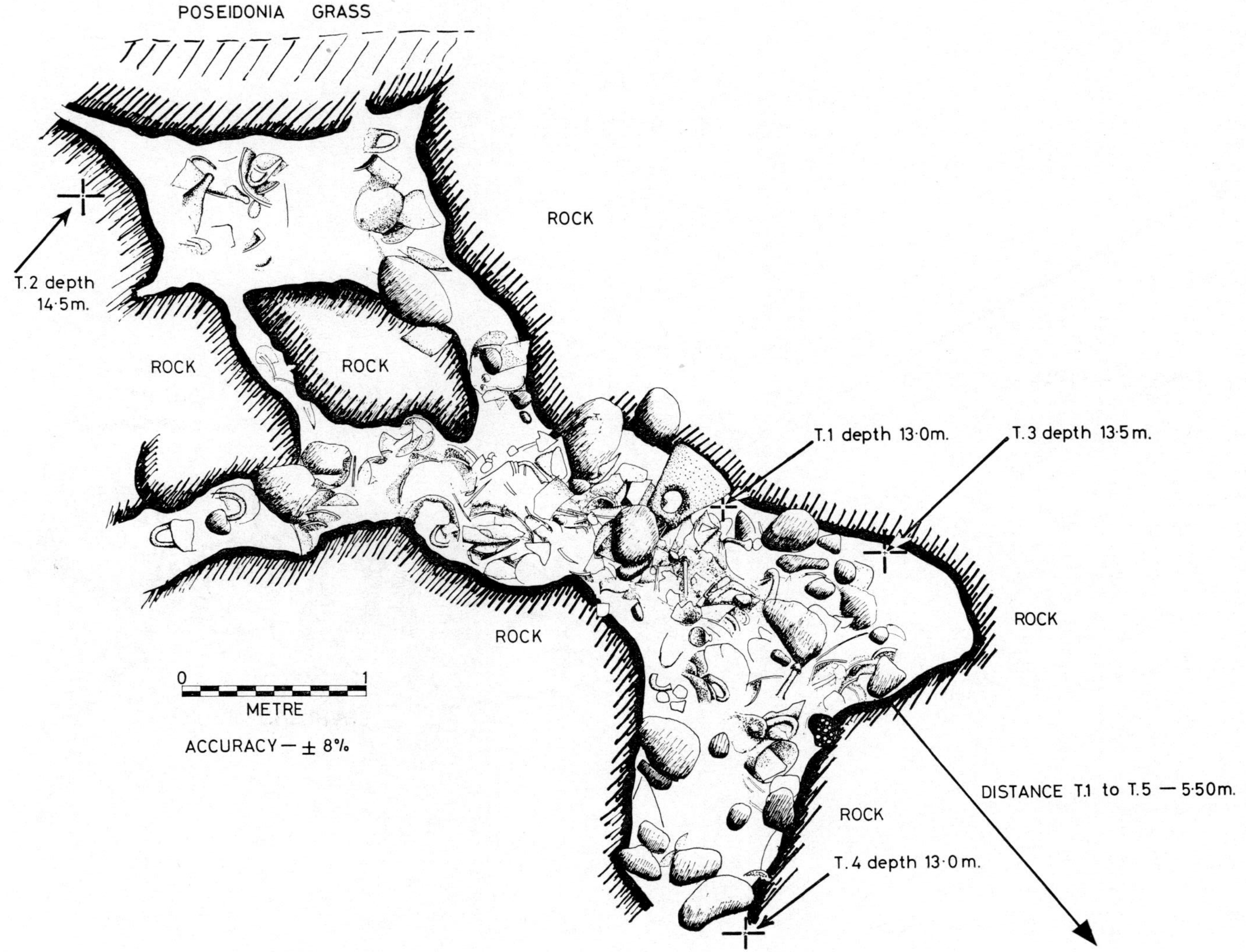

Figure 7. Site 19A.

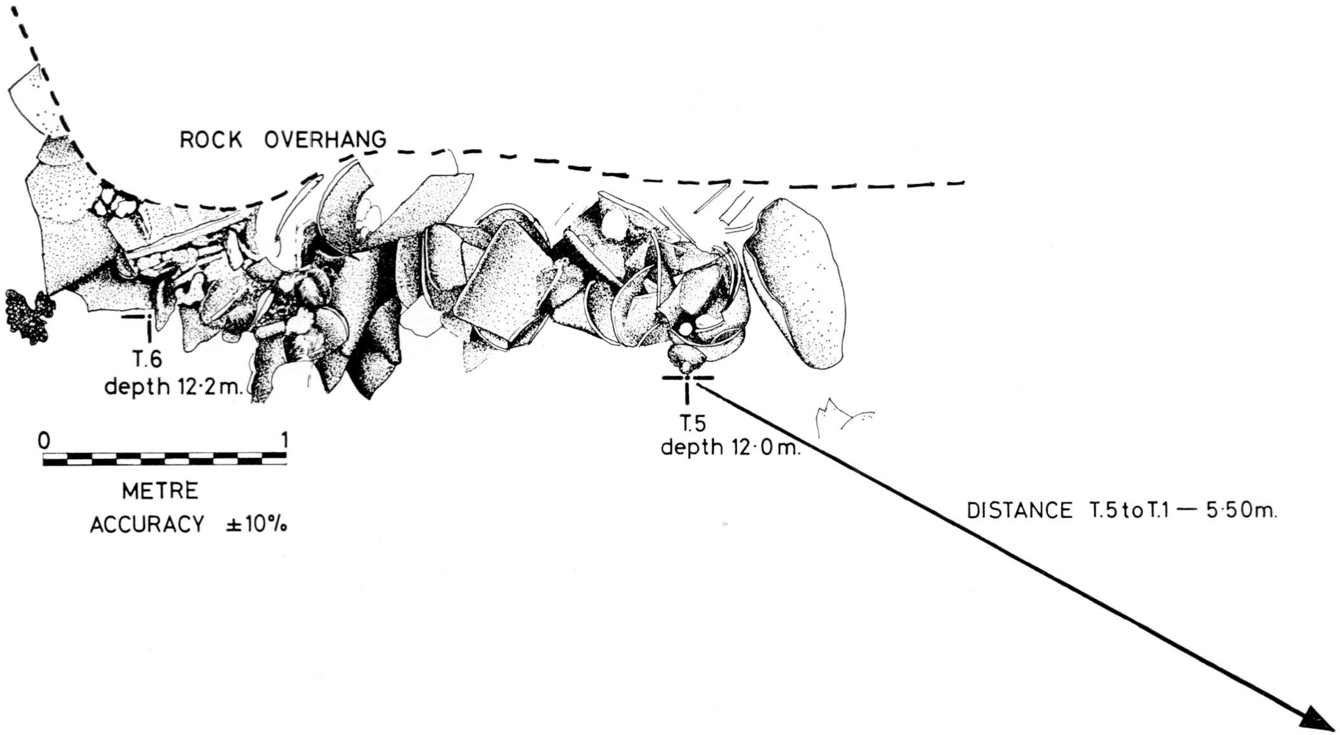

Figure 8. Site 19B.

ship's cargo, but the possibility of buried material makes this argument inconclusive. The stone anchor (No. 040; Fig. 31A) may be associated with the pottery, although it lies on top of the material.

Site 12, on the north side of the island No. 4, was located in 1969 and is clearly a wreck site. It consists of an area approximately 20 m × 15 m containing a large number of heavily concreted Corinthian-style roof-tiles and cover-tiles (Fig. 9). Figure 10 shows a photomosaic of the site and Figure 11 shows a plan of the distribution of the sherds. No antefixes or amphora sherds have been identified, which makes the dating of the site difficult. Several metal artifacts were found: a section of what appears to be a bronze box (Green 1969, Fig. 22), several small bronze artifacts of unknown purpose, and a joining piece of a Roman-type lead anchor (no stock). A large iron anchor and the ring, stock and part of the shank of a second (see Fig. 29) were found at 23.2 m and 30 m respectively from Tag 1. They lie in line slightly to the west of the main axis of the wreck at depths of 20 and 23 m as indicated in Figure 11 (T7 and T8), pointing directly towards the centre of the wreck, indicating that they are possibly associated with this site.

Site 16, a few metres to the south of islands Nos. 4 and 5, consists of a scattered collection of concreted sherds of amphorae and tiles, together with a small concentration of small bowls and plates, many of which were intact (Fig. 12.).

The tile sherds to the west of Tag 3 may represent material that has been washed over from the tile wreck, Site 12. It will be difficult to establish whether the two sites are associated and why such a large number (*c.* 25) of fine ware pottery objects should be concentrated, relatively undamaged, in such a small area. Several tile and cover-tile sherds scattered in this material further confuse the issue of association with Site 12.

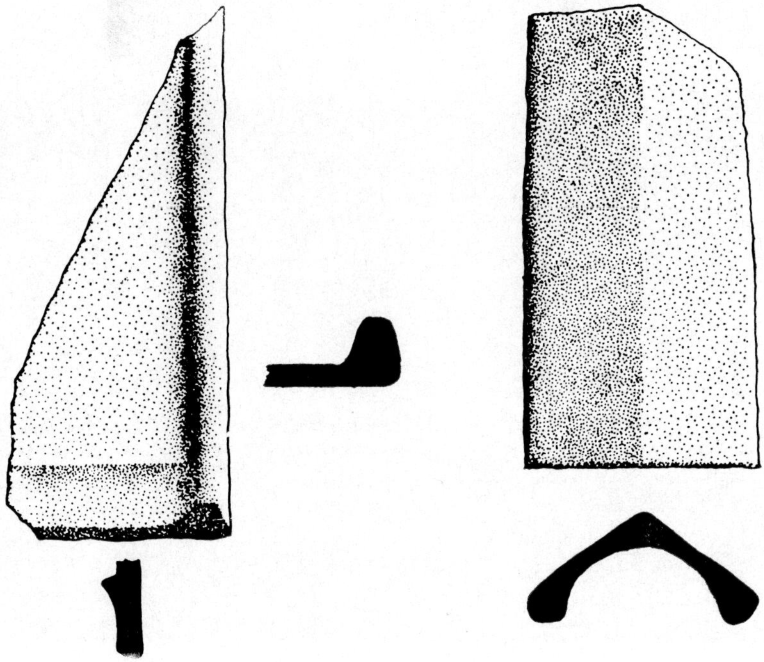

Figure 9. Tile fragments from Site 12. Scale 1 : 4.

Figure 10. Photomosaic of Site 12.

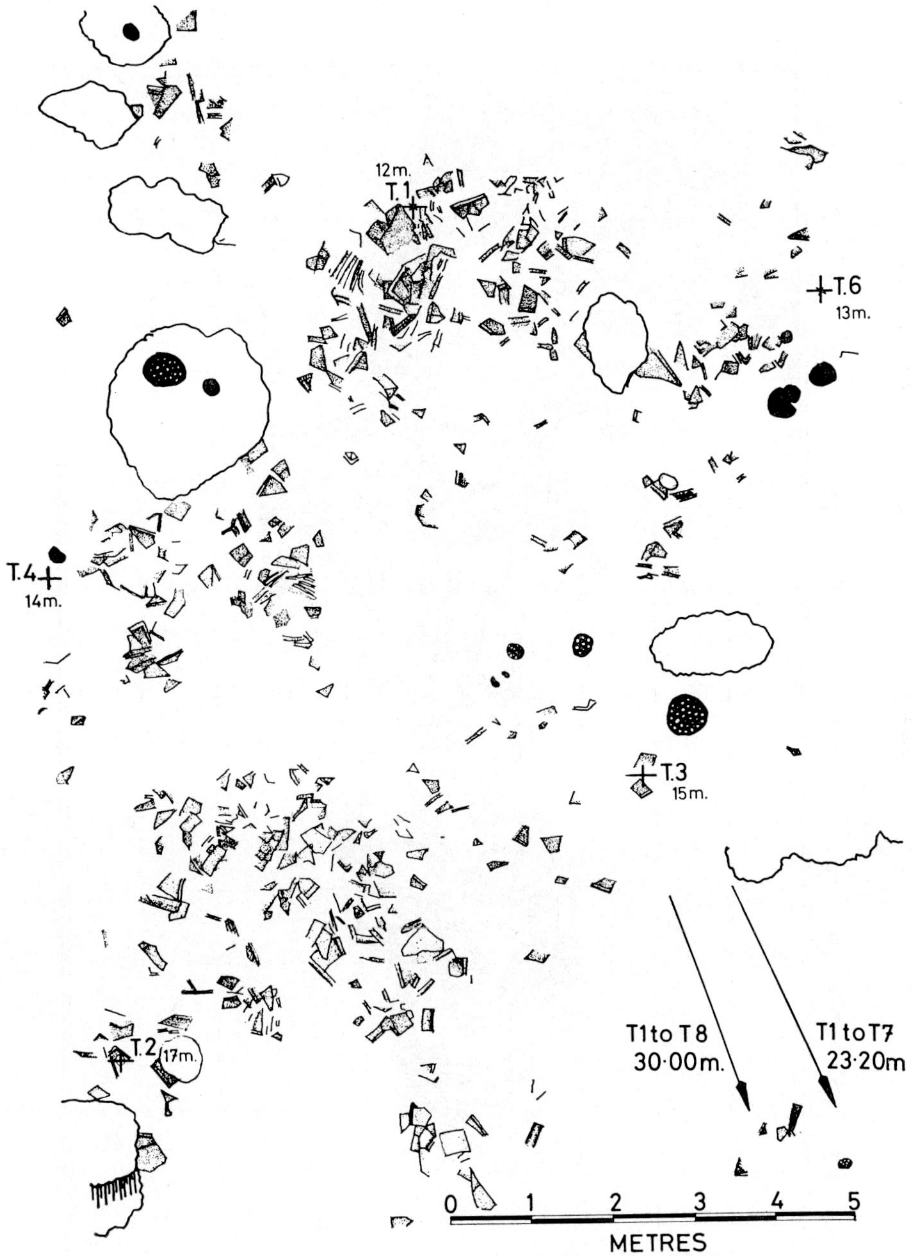

Figure 11. Site 12: plan drawn from photomosaic.

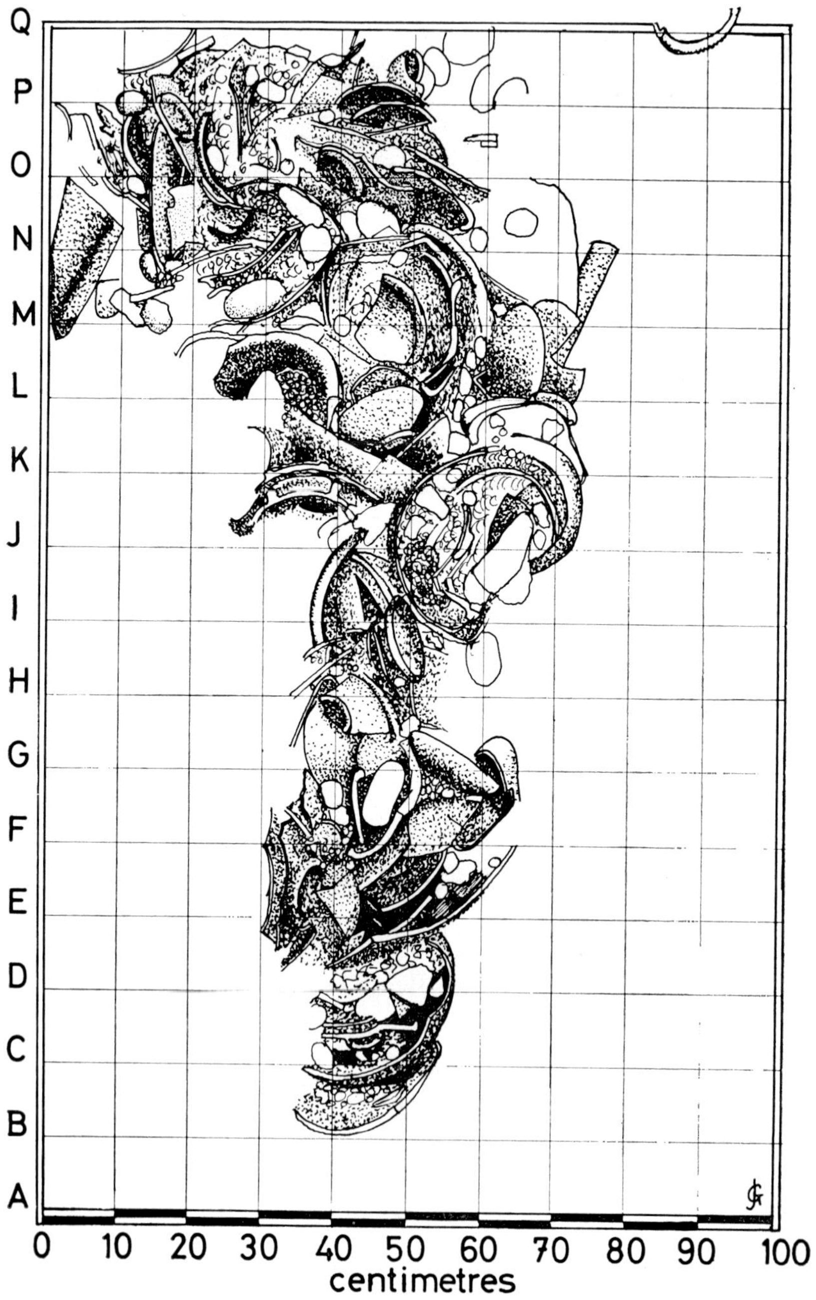

Figure 12. Site 16, Tag 3.

One of the sherds collected from the area around Tag 3 has sigillata decoration (Fig. 13) which suggests a fourth-century B.C. date. Several types of domestic pottery can be identified around Tag 3: plates, two types of bowls and a part of a lekanis or mortar. Many other types were noticed deeply imbedded in the concretion in this area, but cannot be identified from the photogrammetric coverage. Several glass fragments were found associated with an amphora and a fragment of a clear glass dish from around Tag 3 (Green, 1969, Fig. 10).

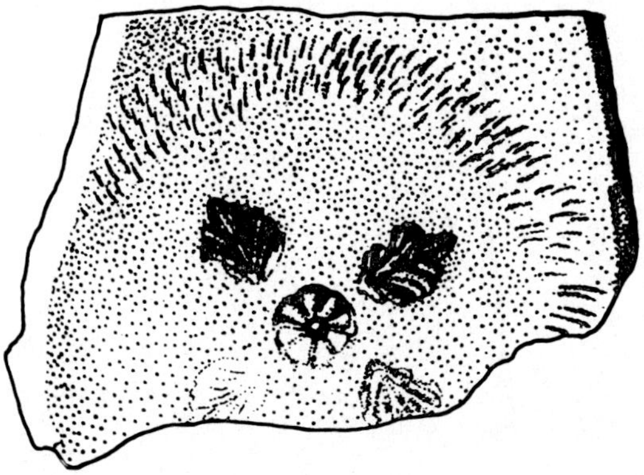

Figure 13. Sigillata decoration on bowl removed from Site 16, Tag 3 area (not to scale).

It was found that much of the rock face was in fact concretion, which when chipped proved to be a crust. This crust could be removed, revealing loose sherds and whole pottery objects. It is quite likely that there is far more material than is superficially visible, buried under these layers of concretion. A similar situation was noted on Site 17. *Site 28* was located a week before the end of 1970 expedition. The superficial material lying at a depth of 20 m is Corinthian-style roof-tiles and cover-tiles (Fig. 14). The regular stacking indicates that the site is intact and represents the surface layer of cargo of a ship buried in a soft sand seabed. Two areas of tiles can be seen, as shown in Figure 15. The larger area consists of about 60 roof-tiles arranged in four rows, together with 8 cover-tiles; a further layer can be identified underneath these. The smaller area consists of about 15 tiles. The stacking arrangement is interesting because the orientation of the smaller pile (approximately E/W) is duplicated by a line of tiles lying on the same axis and orientation in the main area; presumably this is the axis of the ship. The tiles are slightly trapezoidal (see Fig. 14) and this suggests that they were intended for part of a conical-section roof.

Probe, magnetometer and metal detector surveys similar to the Kyrenia Wreck survey (Green, Hall & Katzev, 1967) and the *Santa Maria de la Rosa* survey (Green & Martin, 1970) were carried out over the site. The probe survey (Fig. 16) shows the extent of the buried material up to a depth of 1 m. The axis of the ship inferred from the orientation of the tiles is verified by the survey. It is interesting that the visible material lies at the north end of the site and not in the centre. The magnetometer survey (Fig. 17) indicates that there are no obviously large iron objects. A typical reading is obtained from

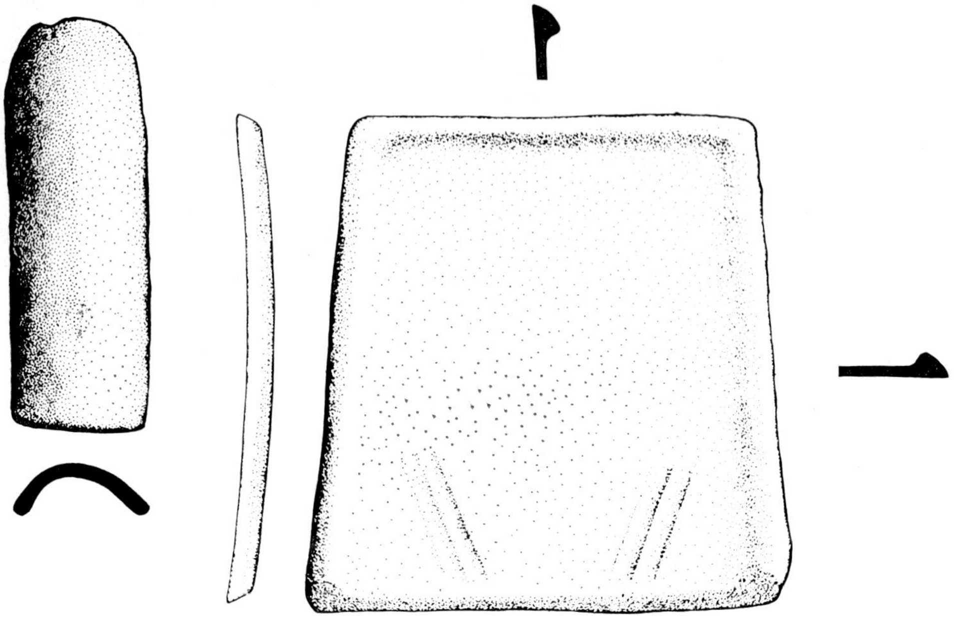

Figure 14. Tiles from Site 28. Scale 1 : 5.7.

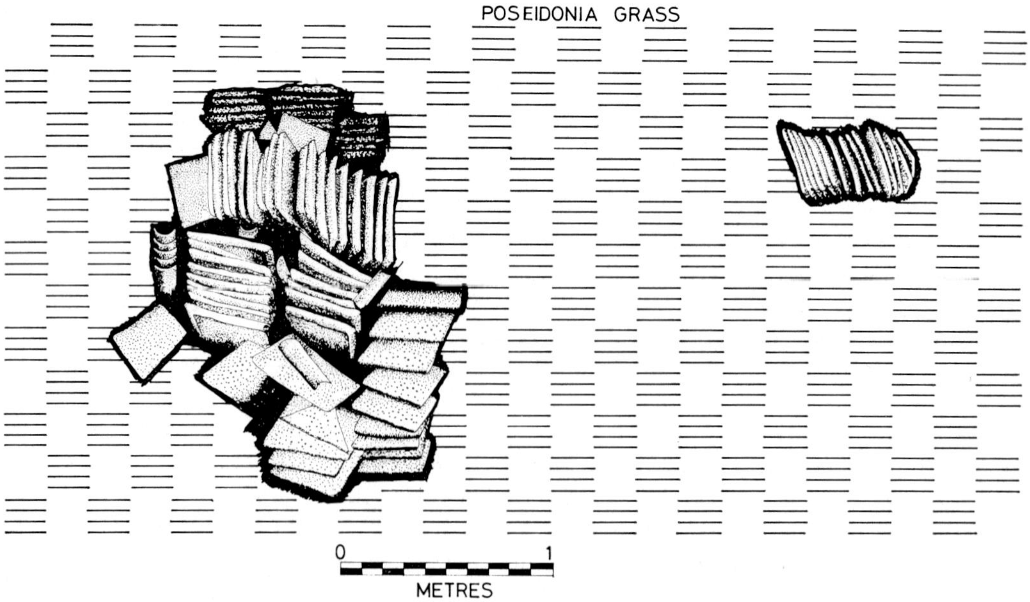

Figure 15. Site 28.

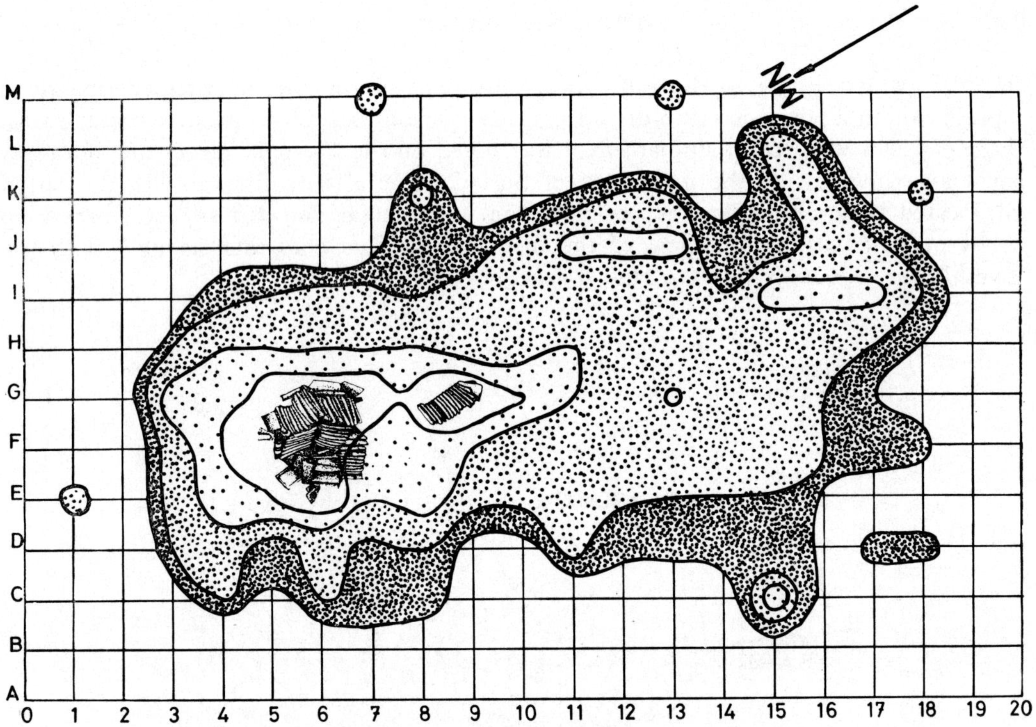

Figure 16. Probe survey of Site 28. The three shades of stippling indicate depth constants of 0–25, 25–50, 50–75 and 75–100 cm.

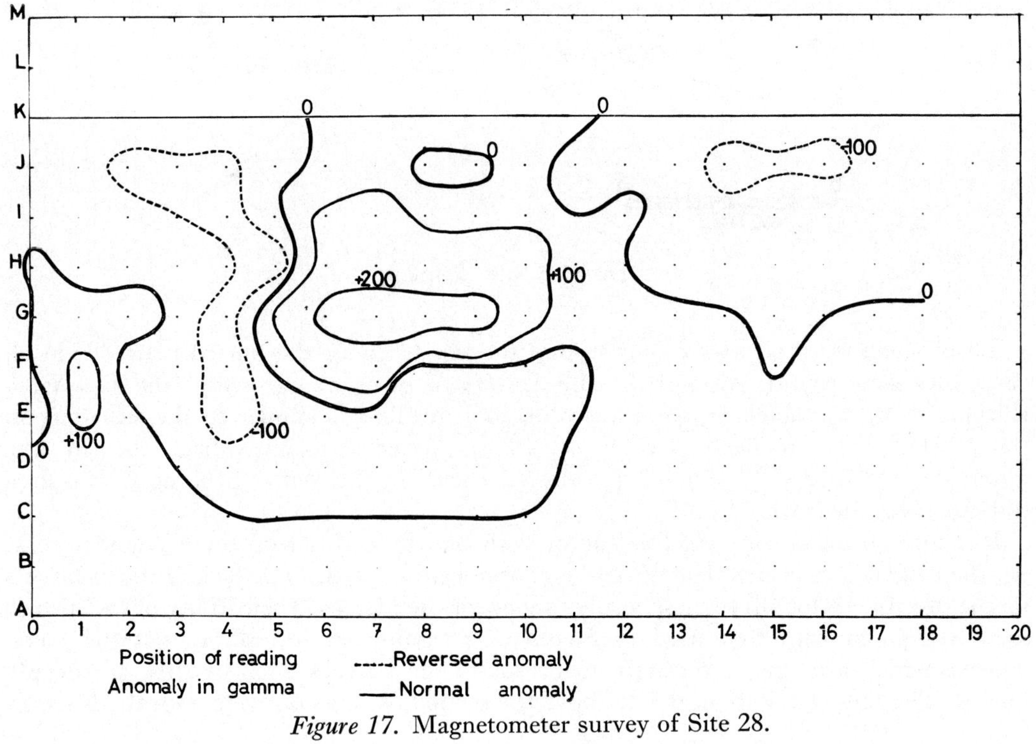

Figure 17. Magnetometer survey of Site 28.

the tiles, which owing to the random arrangement of the thermoremanent magnetic dipoles exhibit a pure susceptibility effect; this was confirmed by a positive reading with the metal detector, and a similar effect was noted on the Kyrenia Wreck amphorae. A small anomaly outside the main area of buried material corresponds with the target E1 located by probing, and is possibly iron. The metal detector survey showed no metal present within the range of the instrument. This contrasts strongly with the Kyrenia Wreck survey (Green, Hall & Katzev, 1967).

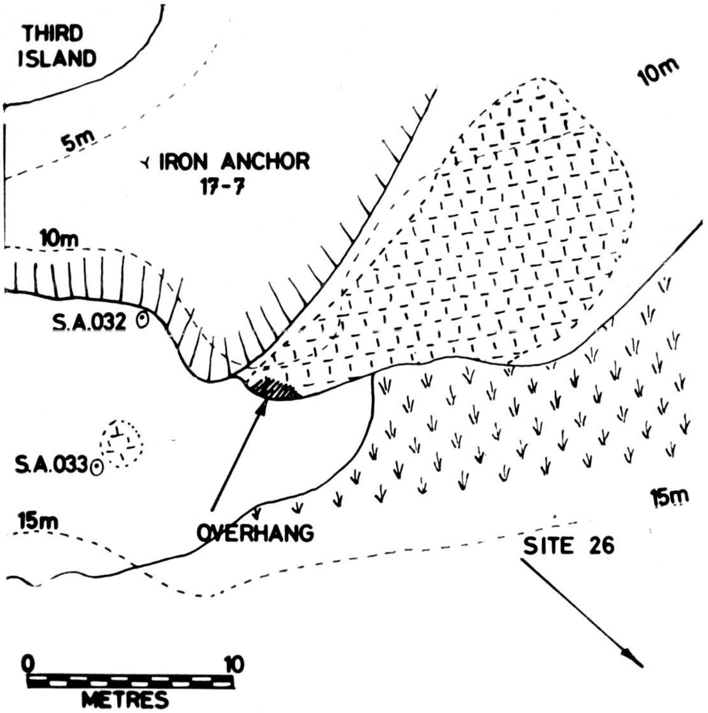

Figure 18. Site 17: plan.

Three small test-holes were dug around the site to check the buried material; in all cases tiles were found. Around the site *Poseidonia* grass was growing; the *Poseidonia* rhizome *matte* was thick, in some cases up to 1 m. This is similar to the situation on the Mortar Wreck in Malta (see Frost, 1969). About 50 m away from the site was *intermatte* or "sandpool" about 2 m below the level of the *matte*; probing in this area did not reveal bedrock.

It is interesting to compare this survey with that carried out on the Kyrenia Wreck. All the evidence indicates that the site is more deeply buried. The lack of metal targets on the metal detector survey, especially in view of the increased sensitivity of the instrument compared with that used in Kyrenia, is significant, indicating that the metal objects, which are almost certainly to be found on a wreck such as this, are deeply buried. The tiles stand about 0.5 m above the seabed, which contrasts with the Kyrenia

Wreck where the amphorae stood at about 1 m. In view of the fact that the Kyrenia Wreck is about 500 years older than the Cape Andreas wreck, it is likely that the sedimentation rate at Cape Andreas is greater than that at Kyrenia, which indicates that the wood of the Cape Andreas ship may be well preserved. (For a further discussion of the significance of this wreck see Green, 1971).

Sites 17 and 24 lie around the north side of the second island; Site 24 was located by C.A.U.S.E. in 1967 and was further investigated in 1969 (see Green, 1969, Figs. 11 & 13). However, in 1970 we were quite surprised to find that the thick concretion layer covering the site had been broken through, and a number of whole amphorae lying underneath had been exposed (Figs. 18, 19 & 20). It is likely that several whole amphorae have been removed, judging by the number of freshly broken sherds (Fig. 19). Around the whole of the two sites numerous amphora sherds of similar type can be seen. In some cases these were closely associated with the terracotta sarcophagi of Site 24. The amphorae (Figs. 21 & 22) were common in early Byzantine Cyprus and the smaller (Fig. 21) closely resembles the amphora of the Kornos Cave near Lapethus found by Catling and Dikigoropoulos (1970) and also the smaller of the two types of amphora found by Bass (1962) on the early Byzantine wreck at Yassı Ada. One example of a third type (Fig. 23) was found, but this is thought to be medieval or modern.

Site 10 was located in 1969; it lies to the north of the rocks between the third and fourth islands. It is one of the most difficult sites to analyse, as the material is spread out over a large rocky area, 50 m × 20 m. A variety of amphora sherds of different types and periods have been noted and recorded (Green, 1969, Figs. 7 & 8). At present a large-scale mosaic is being constructed of the site, in order to try to produce a detailed plan. The initial impression is that this site represents spillage or jettison from several periods, and not several wrecks.

Site 1 consists of several looped handles and flat amphora bases concreted to the rocks around the south-west corner of the first island. In view of the small number of amphorae, this site can only represent jettison or spillage.

Site 18 consists of looped handles and pointed feet of amphorae scattered over an area of 300 sq. m. It is situated to the north of the small group of rocks off the south side of the Cape. This area is used as shelter for fishing boats (and indeed our own survey-boat) when the north-easterly Tramoundana blows. In view of the considerable amount of pottery (and beer bottles) in the area it is likely that this has been used as a lee shore by ships since antiquity. The site therefore probably represents jettison of damaged amphorae from a ship sheltering and waiting for favourable winds.

Site 14 lies on the south side of the rocks mentioned with reference to Site 10. The site consists of a few tiles (Figs. 24–25) and amphorae, possibly jettison or spillage.

It is surprising that out of the ten sites described, five consist mainly of looped-handle amphorae and four of tiles. Sites 12 and 28 are clearly complete wrecks of ships carrying tiles as a cargo. After leaving Cape Andreas we were shown material from another possible wreck-site outside our search area, which again contained looped handles. The examples of this type of amphora outnumber the sum of all the other types found and recorded. This is perhaps a reflection of the fact that this type of amphora has been

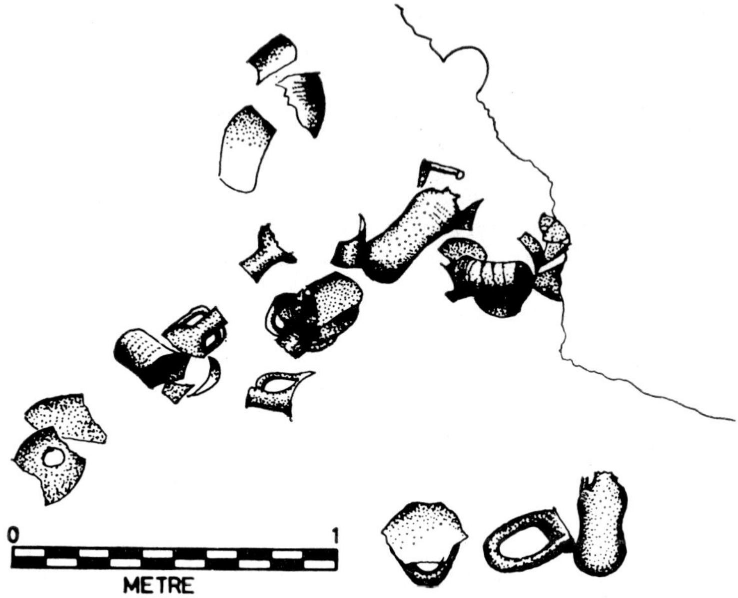

Figure 19. Site 17, detail from plan: the overhang.

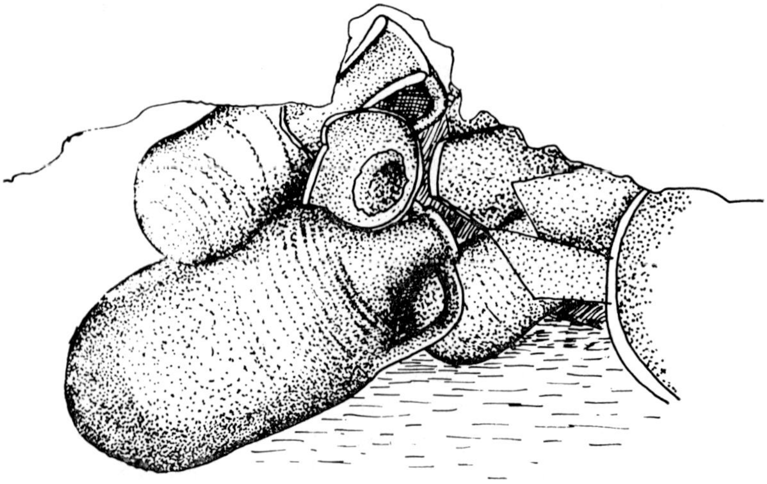

Figure 20. Site 17: view into the overhang.

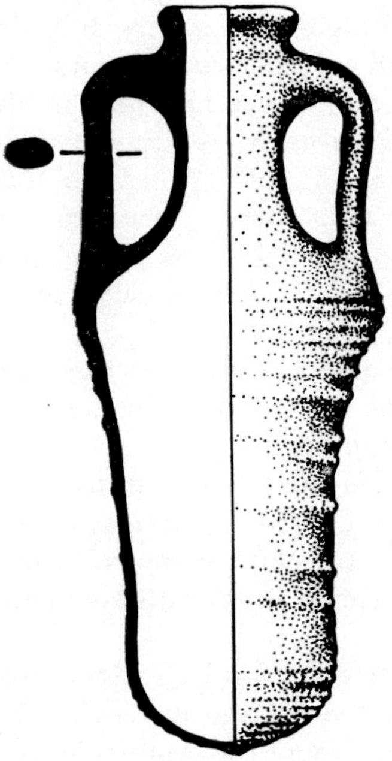

21

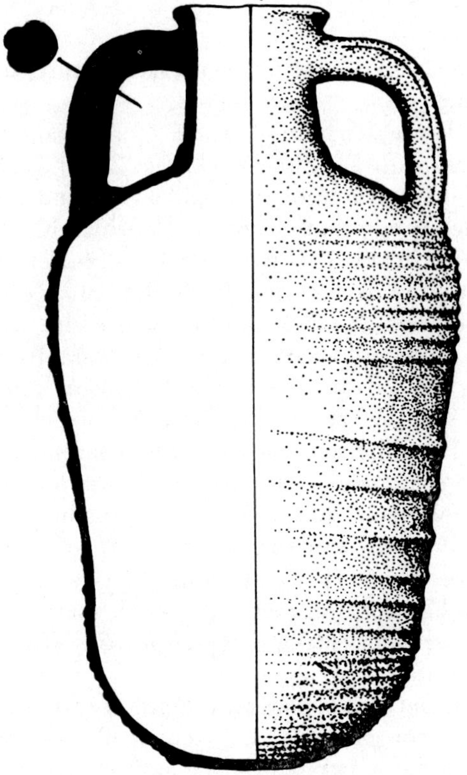

22

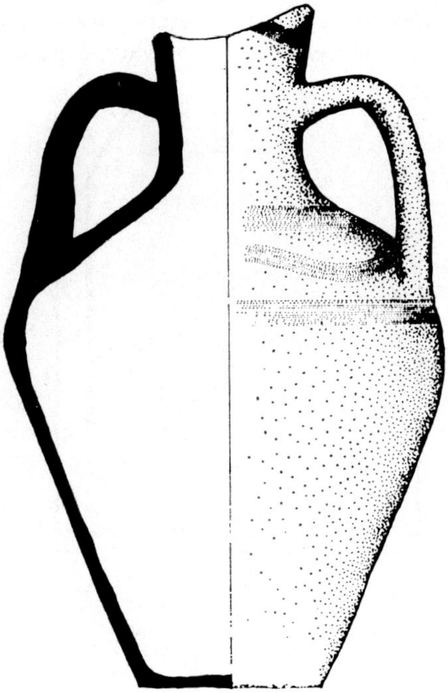

23

Figures 21, 22, 23. Amphorae from Site 17. Scale 1 : 4.

noted as of local Cypriot manufacture, and the style covered a considerable period of time.

Three separate styles of Corinthian-style tiles and cover-tiles have been recorded from sites 12 (Fig. 9), 14 (Fig. 25) and 28 (Fig. 14). The dating of tiles is very difficult, as it is uncommon in a land site to find complete examples in a datable context, and also the styles often covered a considerable time period. Two tile wrecks have previously been recorded (Frost, 1963*a*, 214–21): the Frioul Wreck, near Marseille, which is reported as carrying Gallo–Roman tiles with a similar stacking arrangement to that found on Site 28; the other wreck-site, in the Ceramic Gulf (W. Turkey), was recorded as carrying Laconian-style tiles dating from the Byzantine period. There was no evidence on any of the sites at Cape Andreas that the tiles were associated with a galley area, as was the case on the Byzantine wreck at Yassı Ada (Bass, 1962).

If we are recording a random sample of wrecks, then the evidence indicates that tiles were an important cargo and that looped-handle amphorae were a common form of amphorae. Table 1 shows the possible date and cargoes of the sites.

What is surprising is the lack of late Byzantine, Ottoman and early medieval material, especially in view of the importance of Cyprus at the time of the Crusades. This may reflect the better sailing techniques of the period, or the decline in the use of amphorae in favour of sacks for carrying dry cargo; the latter would make this type of wreck rather difficult to find.

A detailed report on the pottery from the sites has been deferred until the expedition archaeologist (Mr. D. Robinson) has completed a full analysis of the material. The material illustrated by the author here is only a small proportion of the total recovered and has been used purely to illustrate the pottery sites.

The fact that we were recording all the material located meant that in some cases rather anomalous finds were made. The medieval or modern amphora on Site 17

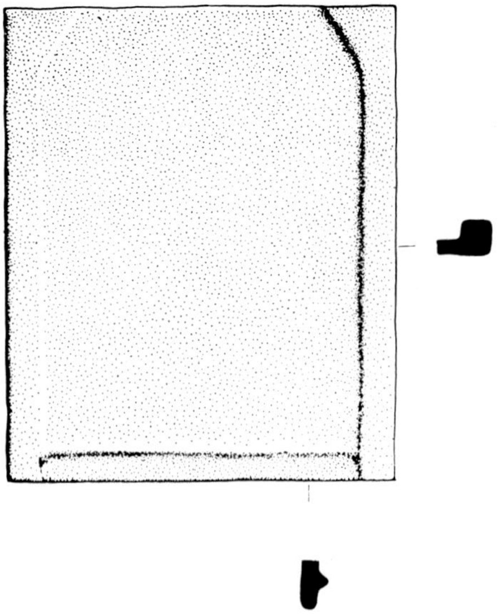

Figure 24. Tile from Site 14. Scale 1 : 8.

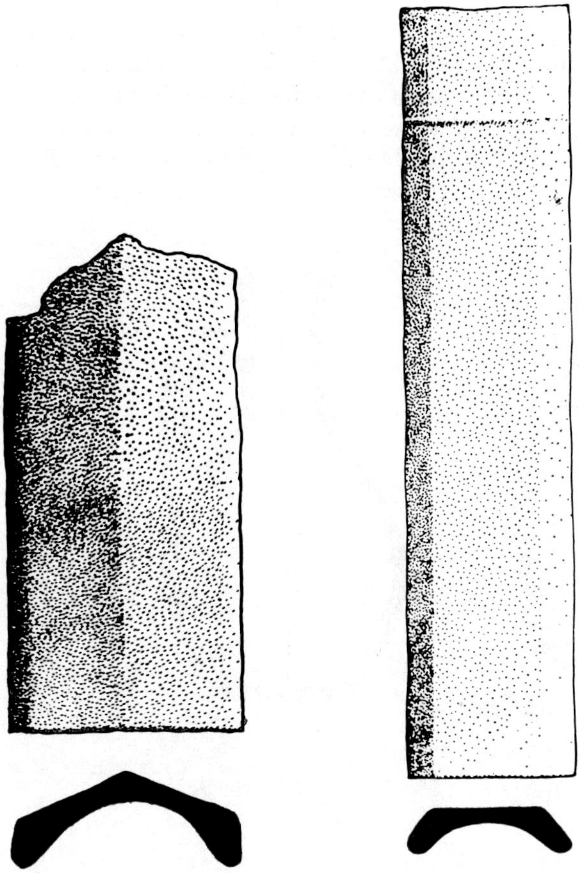

Figure 25. Cover-tiles from Site 14. Scale 1 : 4.

TABLE 1
The Pottery Sites

Site No.	Possible date (approx.)	Material	Type of site
1	400 B.C.	Looped-handle amphorae	Jettison
10	?	Amphorae (looped-handle and others), mortaria	?
12	?	Tiles	Wreck
14	?	Tiles and amphorae	Jettison
16	400 B.C.	Small bowls, tiles and amphorae	?
17 & 24	A.D. 700–800	Amphorae and sarcophagi	Wreck
18	?	Looped-handle amphorae	Jettison
19	?	Looped-handle amphorae	Wreck
28	Perhaps A.D. 200	Tiles	Wreck

(Fig. 23) is an example of this; a similar type of find was the two small jugs and cup (Fig. 26) from another site. This illustrates the fact that on this type of survey material can be recovered from almost any time period. It would be most useful to have a record of the styles of amphorae and pottery vessels that have been made in Cyprus or in the Eastern Mediterranean, from medieval to modern times, to help with classification of this material.

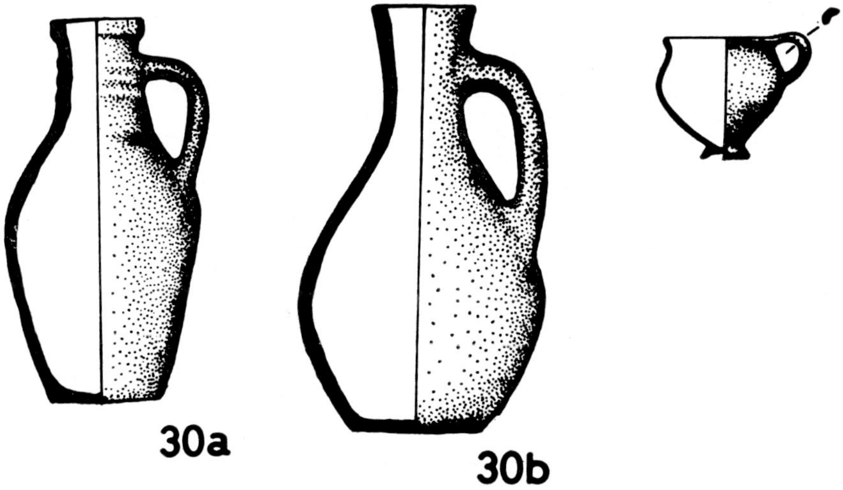

Figure 26. Two jugs and a cup. Scale 1 : 4.

2. Anchor Sites

Four anchor sites were recorded on the north side of the Cape Andreas. Two of the sites (23 and 26) were areas containing a large number of different types of anchors. The other two sites consisted of a number of stone anchors arranged in a line, and a further example of this type was recorded at Akrotiri.

Sites 23 and 26 were located at the point where the gently upward-sloping sand seabed changes to a steep rock cliff face. It will be noted from Figures 2 and 5 that the seabed to the north of the Cape is very deep. A ship attempting to anchor in the deep water would encounter a fine sand seabed which would be a particularly bad holding ground. Presumably the anchors on Sites 23 and 26 are from ships that have dragged their anchors in the sand, up to the point where they fouled. Many of the anchors were still firmly lodged in the crevices at the base of this cliff face, and the others, although not necessarily fouled, may have had their cables chafed through on the rock face.

In the area along the whole of the line to the north of the islands, at the point at which the rock formations emerge from the sand seabed, individual anchors were found. This area is a good holding ground, and is the first that ships dragging from the north would encounter. Such sites have been described by Dumas (1962, Chap. 1) as "forced moorings". However, owing to the high cliff faces at Sites 23 and 26, these particular forced moorings are also foul ground.

Figure 27 shows a plan of Site 23; the site has a total of 28 anchors: 18 iron, 8 lead and 2 stone. Some of the iron anchors (prefixed 23) are illustrated in Figure 29; one of the stone anchors (039) is illustrated in Figure 31A. Figure 28 shows a reconstruction of the lead-stocked anchor 23-17; the drawing was made on the assumption that the position of the two lead parts concreted to the rock indicated their original positions on the wooden shank.[1] A metal detector survey around this anchor (the shaded area around 17 on Fig. 27) was carried out in an attempt to locate concreted metal flukes, but no evidence of flukes was found.

Three examples of lines of stone anchors were located (Fig. 30): Sites A and B are at Cape Andreas; the third site (C) was located by an expedition member (B. Richards) at Akrotiri. The anchors were drawn from a photogrammetric coverage, and the sites

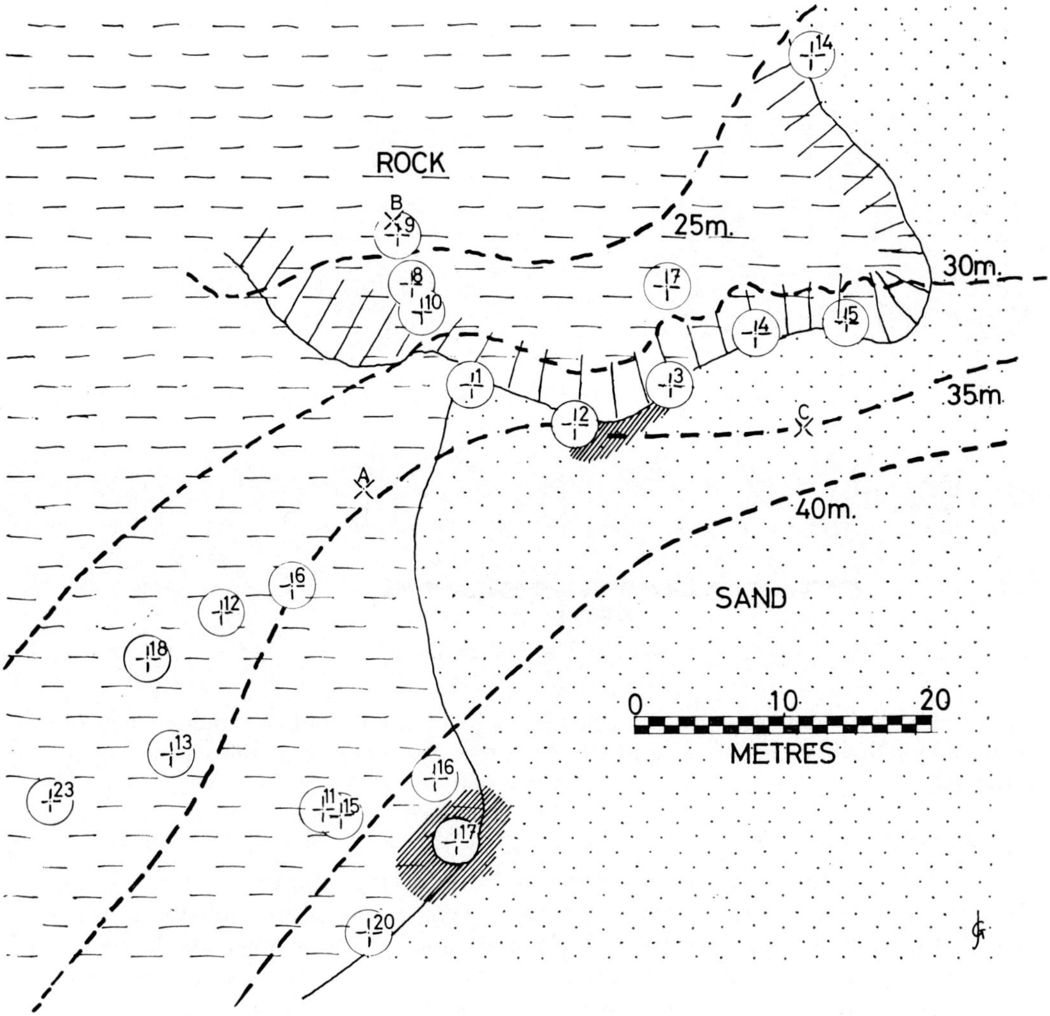

Figure 27. Site 23.

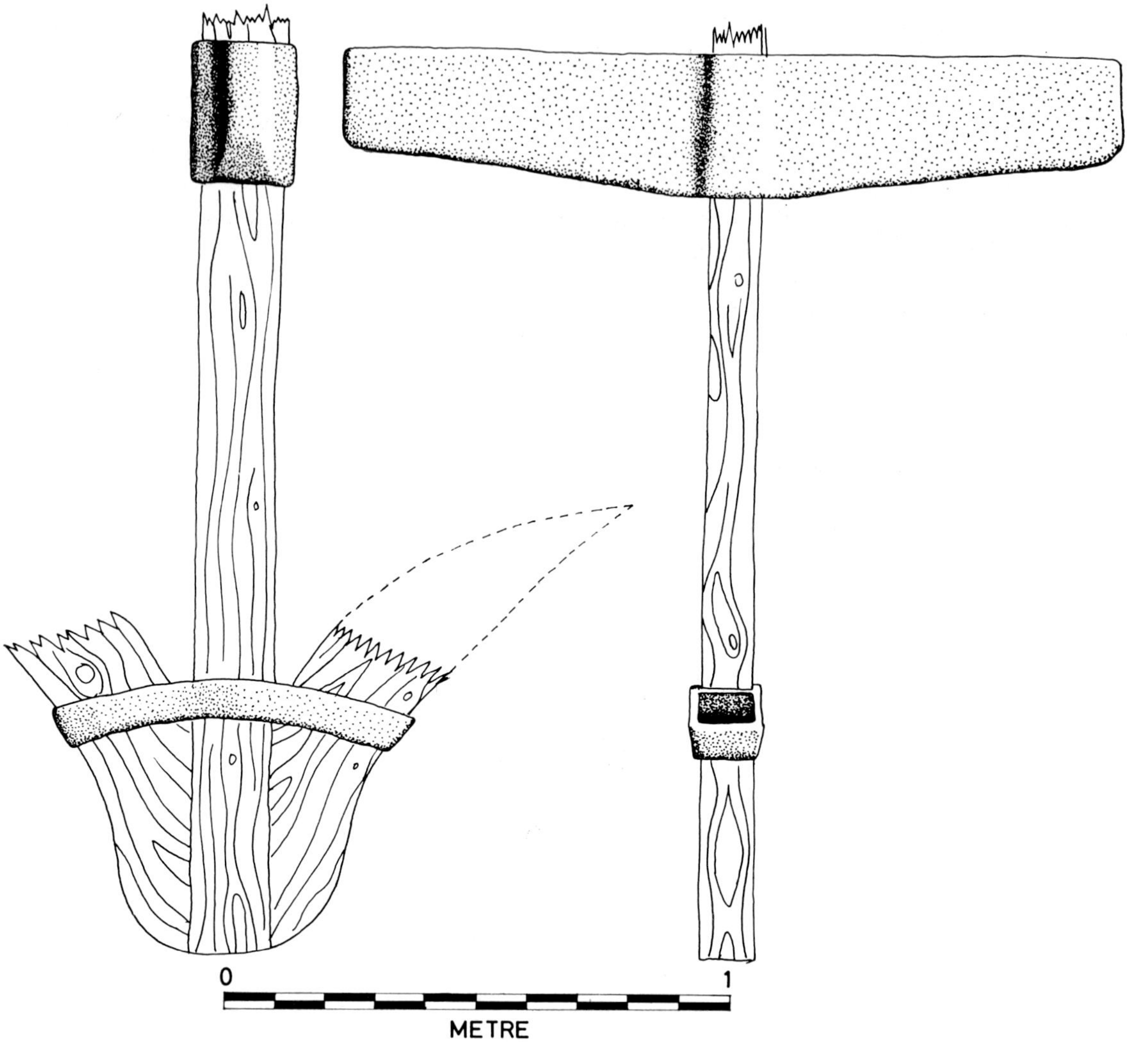

Figure 28. Lead-stocked anchor.

surveyed with theodolite, tapes and compass. The orientation of the anchors is indicated in the upper half of the plans, and the extent of the sites (at a different scale) in the lower half.

3(a) Iron Anchors

A selection of the iron anchors recorded by cube photogrammetry is shown in Figure 29. The positions of a total of about 50 anchors were recorded, but only about half were recorded photogrammetrically owing to lack of time. The drawings should be treated with caution. Iron in seawater forms a concretion around its outside; this tends to exaggerate the thickness of the objects, although the overall shape and size remains reasonably representative. Two stages of the formation can be seen in Figure 29. Anchor

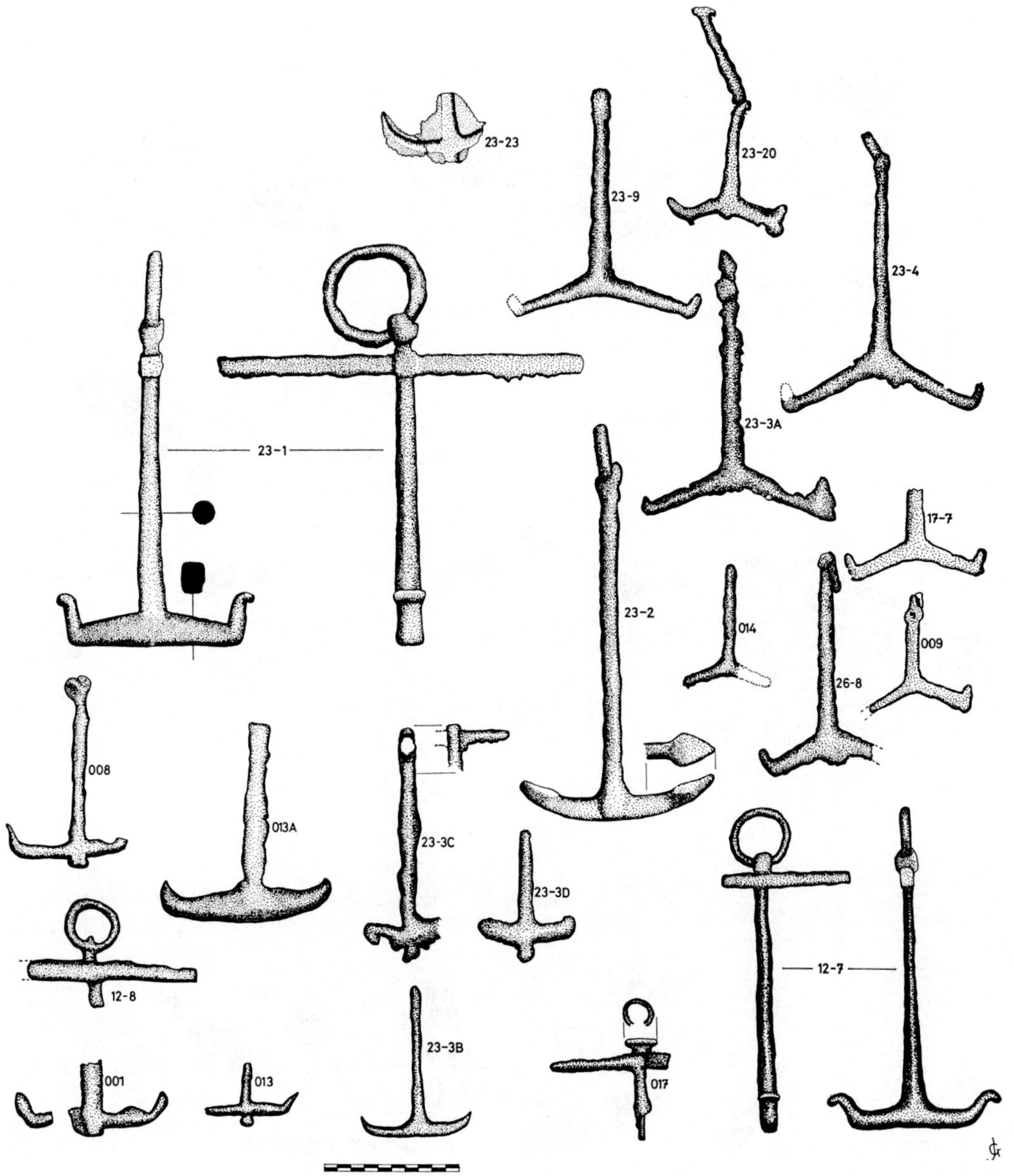

Figure 29. Iron anchors. Scale 1 m long.

23-23 shows a broken-open concretion in an advanced stage of decomposition; all the iron has disappeared, leaving an iron oxide mould of the original shape. These iron moulds can be used to cast a replica of the original object (see Katzev & van Doorninck, 1966). Anchor 017 shows a less advanced stage, where the iron is still intact but a concretion has formed around it (note the shank projecting from the concretion).

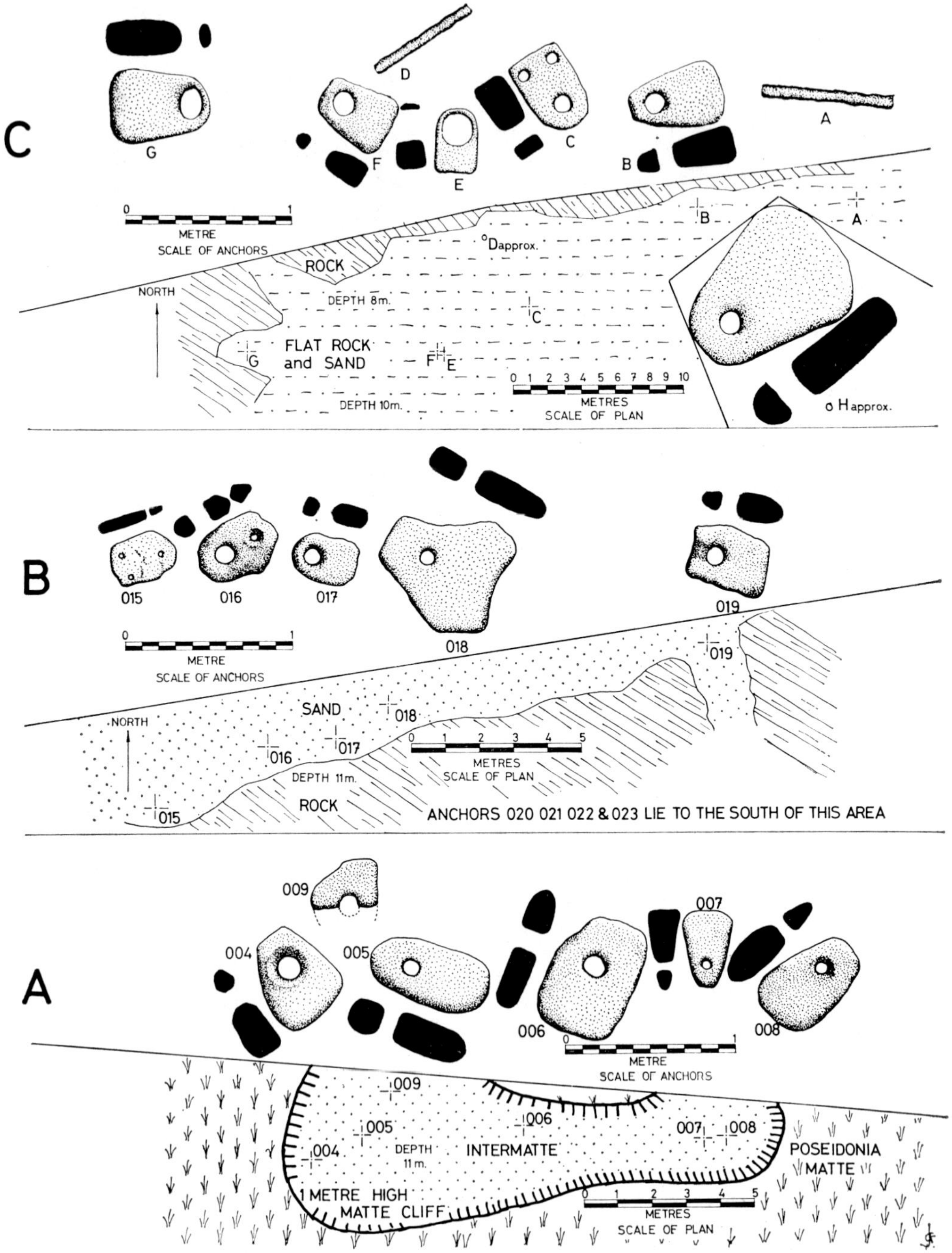

Figure 30. Stone anchor sites: A, B & C.

The shanks of the anchors appear in general to be large in relation to the arms. Tinniswood (1945, 84) quotes Mainwaring that for seventeenth-century English anchors the shank is approximately equal to the width of the arms. Anchor 23-2 (Fig. 29) and 26-1 (not illustrated) have the same proportions, although much larger and with somewhat less curved arms, as the anchor from Bulberry Camp, Dorset, and the anchor from Pompeii, reported by Frost (1963*b*, 18–19).

Out of a total of 50 iron anchors recorded, 12 examples (eight illustrated) of "Y"-shaped anchors were found. Other examples of this type have been noted (*Plemmyrion Report*,1969) and Kapitän is reported as giving a late Byzantine or early medieval date for this type. In view of the large numbers recorded here it would seem that they were more widely used than previously thought, and it is surprising that more have not been recorded elsewhere.

3(b) Stone Anchors

A selection of stone anchors recorded by the 1970 expedition is shown in Figure 31. Four other sites apart from Cape Andreas were investigated to see if there was any difference in anchor types at different sites. This work was carried out by D. M. Squire and R. Marsh. The sites–Ayios Philos (Philon), Ayios Photios, Aphendrika (Ourania) and Khelones–are all sheltered anchorages with wells nearby. The anchor numbers relating to the various sites are indicated in Figure 31.

The weights of all the anchors were calculated from their volumes, using a value of specific gravity of 2.7, as all the anchors were of limestone. The weight histograms for Cape Andreas and Ayios Philos show a striking difference in the number of small stone anchors (Fig. 32). The reason for this is indicated by Frost's suggestion that small stone anchors are used by small fishing- and sponging-boats. Since Cape Andreas is a good fishing- and sponging-ground, and the Ayios Philos area is not, it may be assumed that the reason for the weight discrepancy is related to this occupation. Many of the small stone anchors were recorded in shallow water, close to the islands where normally boats would have no reason to anchor. Local fishing-boats can be seen at the present day, working in these areas with ground nets and long lines, although they no longer use stone anchors, preferring the engine to control drifting.

Stone anchors can be dated as far back as the Bronze Age and are still used at the present day in some parts of the Eastern Mediterranean. The stone anchors recorded here are presumably a representative cross-section; the problem arises, however, as to the mode of operation of stone anchors in the Bronze Age. Examples of Late Bronze Age anchors from Cyprus (Catling & Nikolaou, 1967; Frost, 1970) have weights ranging between 80 and 130 kg in air (with one example of 500 kg). Bass (1967) records that the Late Bronze Age ship excavated at Cape Gelidonya loaded a ton of metal cargo in Cyprus. A ship of this size (10 m) is liable to encounter a variety of seabeds; in fact it is thought to have come from Syria via Cyprus and almost certainly made its first landfall in Cyprus at Cape Andreas. The medium-size anchors, if they were carried by such a ship, would if used individually on lines almost certainly drag on a sand bottom in a strong wind. It should be noted that the weight of these anchors when placed in water would be reduced by one-third due to Archimedes' Principle. A composite anchor with wooden stakes will behave in the same way as a conventional anchor, and the introduction of lead stocks and chain was used as an early means of keeping anchors horizontal on the sea

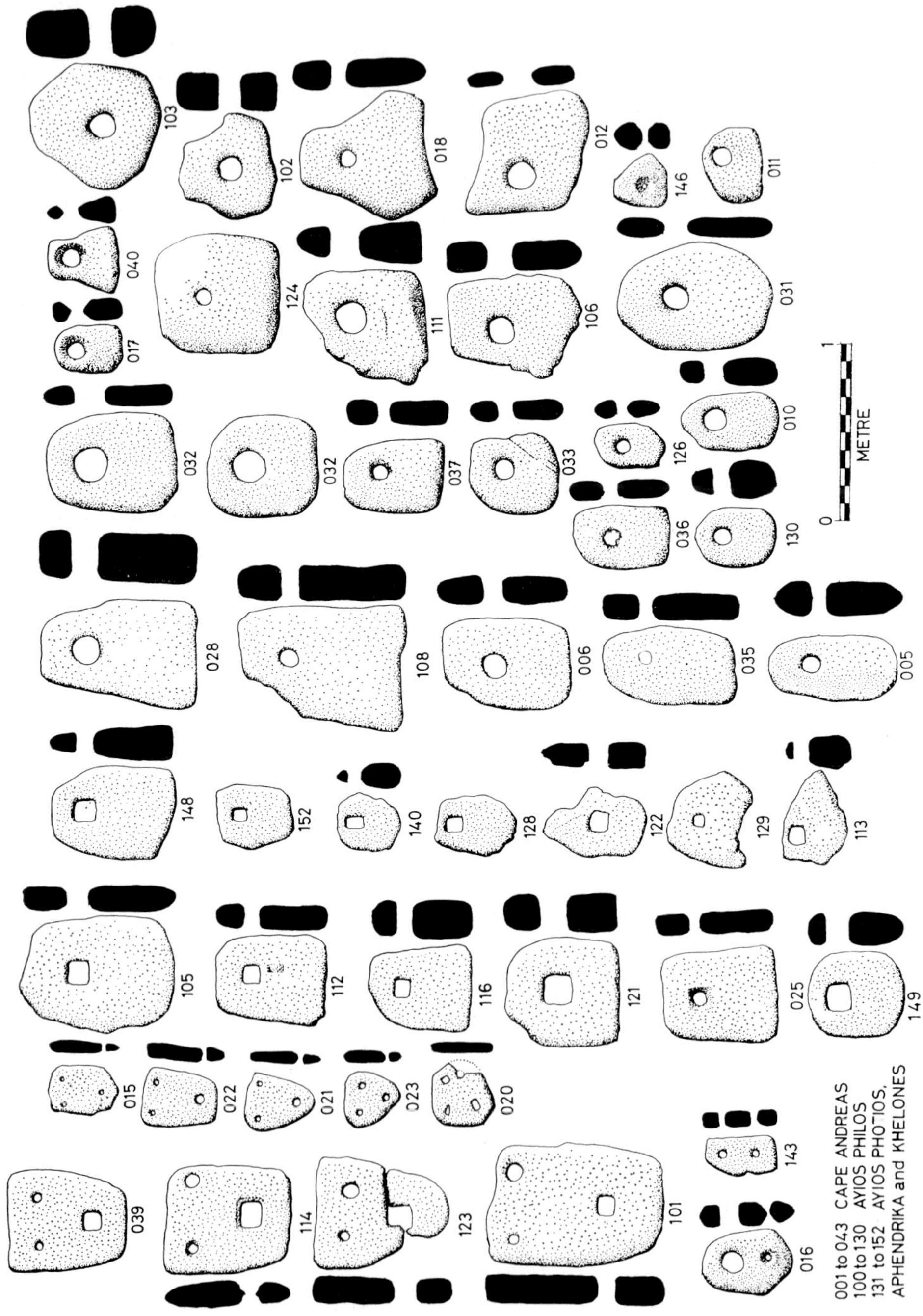

Figure 31A. Stone anchors.

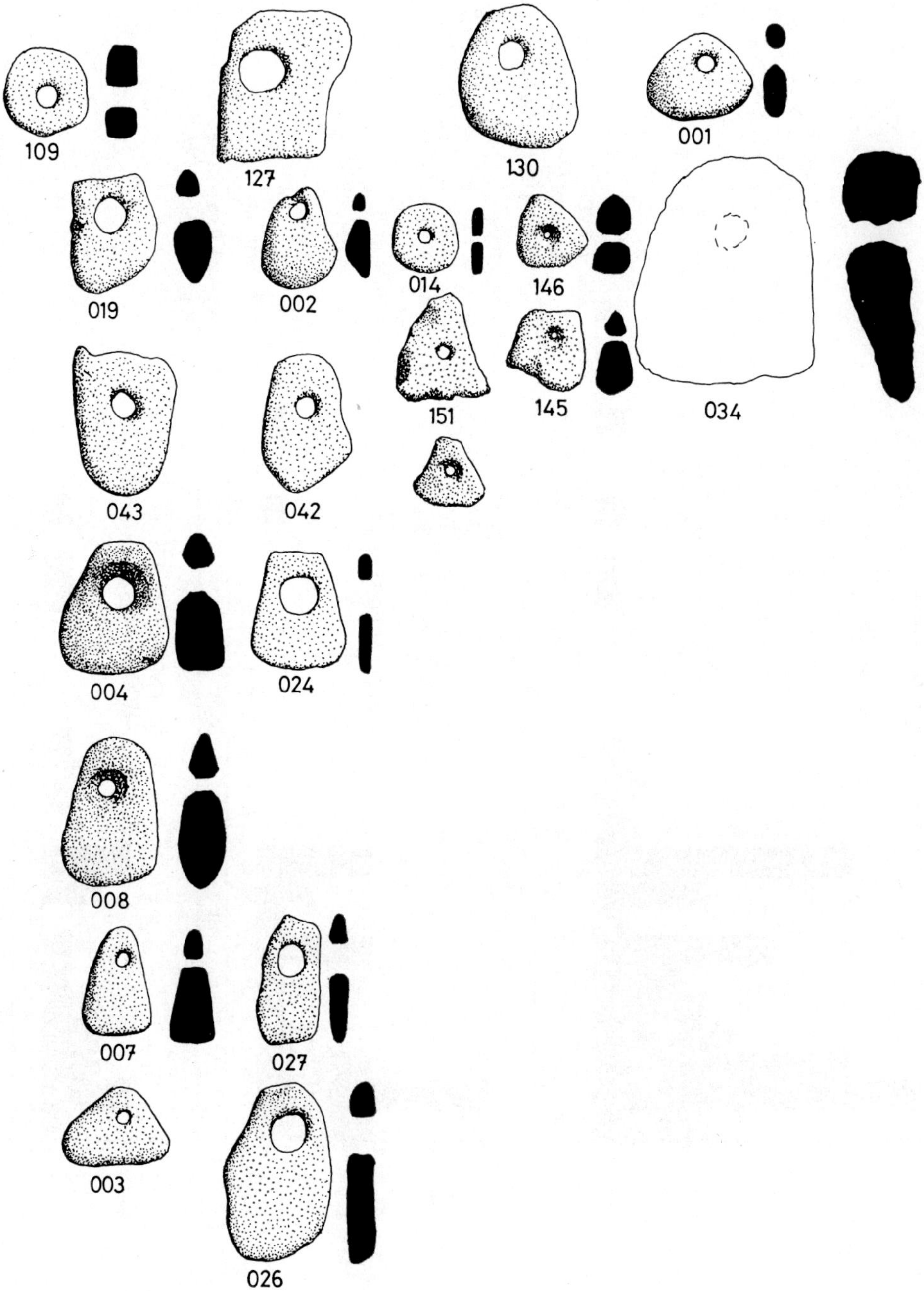

Figure 31B. Stone anchors. Scale as Fig. 31A.

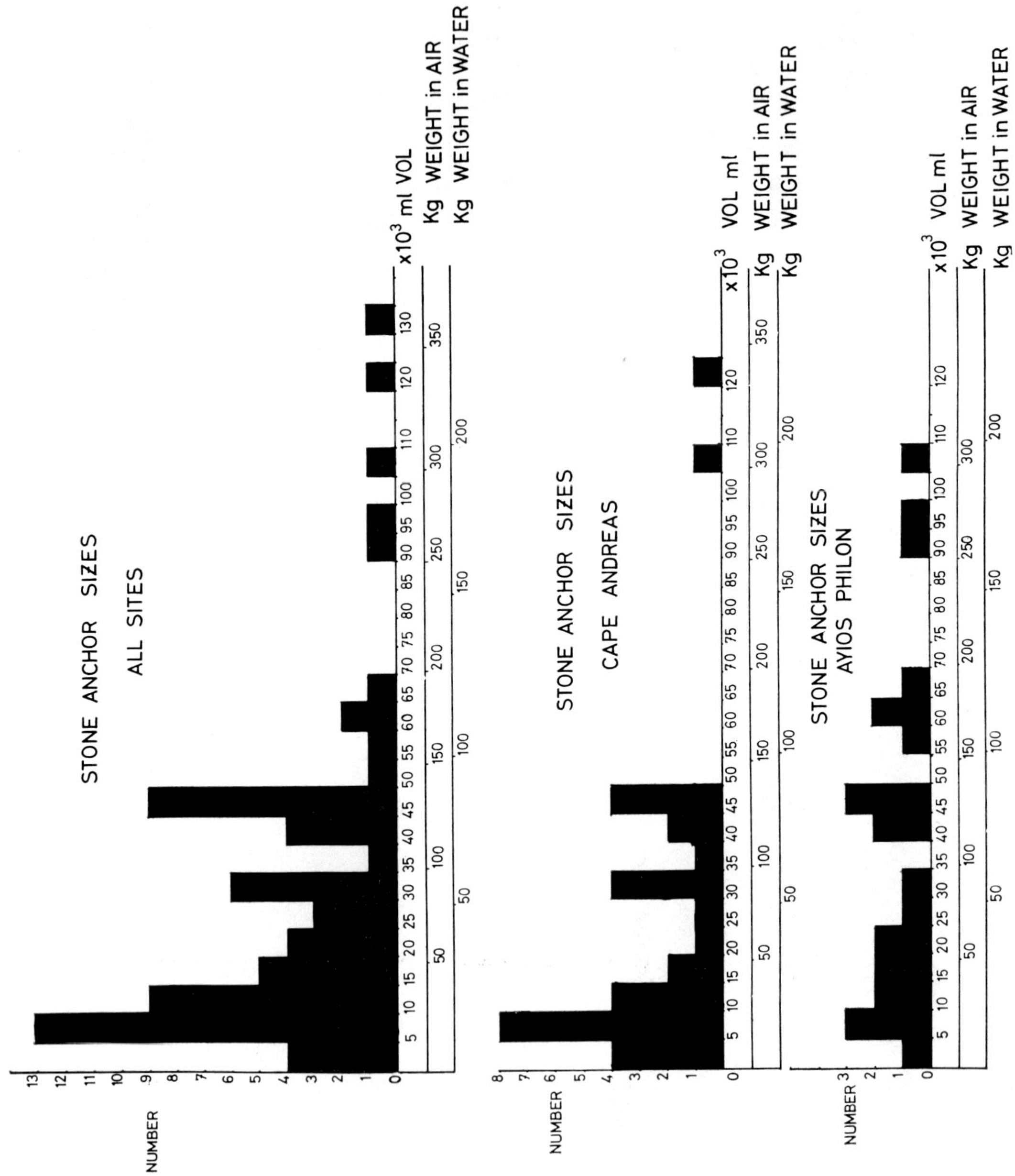

Figure 32. Stone anchor sizes—by sites.

bed. Although there was not the technology to make chain in the Bronze Age, it is quite feasible to make a rope behave in the same way as chain, by weighting it at intervals with stones.

It is a well-established modern seafaring principle that the anchor plays no part in the holding of a ship (except in violent storms) and it is the chain that plays the major role. It is suggested here that the lines of stone anchors represent the remains of an alternative anchoring technique to the use of several single anchors on single lines, and one which would be expected to be more efficient. It is possible that the system used was a composite stone anchor on one end with a number of single-holed anchors attached to the rope at intervals. This question may be partially resolved by conducting tests of the holding power of anchors used in the two different systems, for various-sized ships in different sea states.

The fact that such a large number of isolated stone anchors are recorded in relation to lines of stone anchors may be partially explained by the fact that the "anchors" were lightly attached to the main cable. If an individual anchor fouled, the attachment line could be broken, thus preserving the rest of the anchors.

It may be noted that a large proportion of square-holed anchors was recorded at Ayios Philos (12) compared with Cape Andreas (2) (see Fig. 32). The reason may be that Ayios Philos is an anchorage or that the site and the anchors relate to a certain time period. Catling and Nikolaou (1967) have questioned the function or purpose of these square holes on composite anchors, and it would seem that the same questions apply to the single-square-holed anchors.

The analysis of anchor weights against types of bottom (Fig. 33) shows no particular indication that particular weights relate to particular types of bottom, except that rock bottoms tend to have the lighter types of anchors.

An analysis of chippings made from the stone anchors is being carried out and will be published in the full report.

CONCLUSIONS

The work at Cape Andreas has shown that, with limited finances and personnel, an archaeological search and survey expedition can expect to record a considerable amount of useful information. The survey must be carried out systematically with techniques that are adequate to record the information. Experience in this field is very important: for example, in 1969, with little or no experience, we filled one textbook with data and took about 360 photographs. In 1970 we filled five textbooks with data and took a total of 3,000 photographs.

In the clear water of the Mediterranean relatively sophisticated underwater surveying techniques can be used: photogrammetry and theodolites. These systems can only be effective if careful thought and planning go into the preparation of the work. It is also essential to be able not only rapidly to locate position underwater but also, and more important, to locate position on the surface, for efficient survey work.

The two seasons' work at Cape Andreas has been a unique opportunity to train relatively inexperienced divers to carry out this sort of work. The work has allowed a study of a wide variety of techniques and subjects, and has resulted in a clear understanding of the problems involved. The material located has provided a considerable

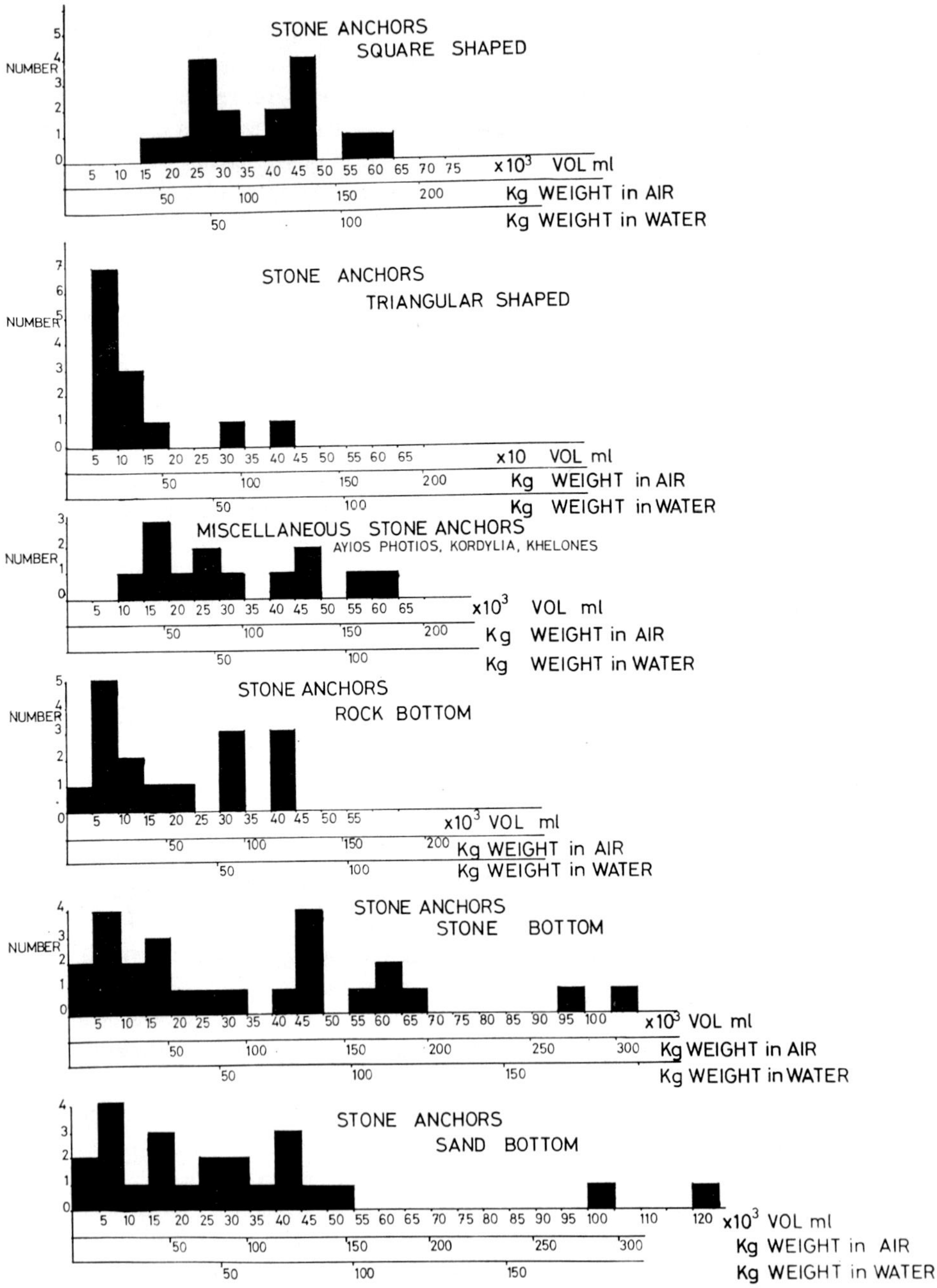

Figure 33. Stone anchor sizes—by shapes and bottoms.

field of study in some quite unexpected topics. It is hoped that this work will provoke further study in the field and constructive criticism and discussion of the material and methods.

ACKNOWLEDGEMENTS

The writer would like to thank Dr. E. T. Hall and the Research Laboratory for Archaeology, Oxford, for allowing the writer to do this work, also Dr. V. Karageorghis and the Department of Antiquities, Cyprus, for generously granting permission to carry out the work. The writer particularly wishes to thank all the expedition members of the 1969 and 1970 seasons, especially Miss S. Klep (chief diver), Miss F. Jarman, Miss M. Stanbury and Miss A. Corben; also Mr. D. Robinson (archaeologist), Mr. S. Whittaker (surveyor), Mr. B. Richards, Mr. P. Baker, Mr. D. Squire and Mr. J. Chetham (photographers), and Mr. P. Sutor (geologist). He would like to thank all the local Cypriot people who so generously helped and assisted us in our difficulties, particularly Mr. Chrisostomos Athenasi (our faithful boatman), Mr. N. Charalambos (Customs Officer) and Mr. A. Cariolou; and he would like to acknowledge the help and assistance of the British Near East Land Forces and the Ministry of Defence, particularly Maj. Gen. M. W. Holm, Col. T. M. Braithwaite and Lt. Col. (retd.) R. J. Dickenson. The financial assistance was granted by the following organizations: the Royal Society, the British Academy, the Royal Geographical Society, the Society of Antiquaries, the Ministry of Technology, Dr. E. T. Hall, Oxford University, Decca Navigator Co. Ltd. (Cmdr. W. J. M. Roberts), Mobel Marine Co. Ltd. (Mr. J. Brookes), Mrs. M. Bennett (St. Hilda's College), the Institute of Electronic and Radio Engineers, Seismograph Service Ltd., Hunting Surveys Ltd. and the Rubery Owen Trust.

The writer would like to thank Dr. H. Catling, Dr. M. Katzev, Dr. A. Parker, Dr. J. Hayes, Miss J. du Plat Taylor and Miss V. Grace for advice and help on archaeological matters.

NOTE

1. The orientation of this stock has since been questioned by Kapitän, who suggests that in fact our orientation for this stock is upside-down.

REFERENCES

Bass, G. F. 1962 Underwater Excavations at Yassı Ada: a Byzantine Shipwreck. *Arch. Anz. 1962*, 537–64.

Bass, G. F. 1967 Cape Gelidonya: a Bronze Age Shipwreck. *Trans. Am. Phil. Soc.* (*N.S.*) **57** Part 8. 177 pp.

Bass, G. F. & Katzev, M. L. 1968 New Tools for Underwater Archaeology. *Archaeology*, **21** No. 3, 164–73.

Catling, H. W. & Dikigoropoulos, A. I. 1970 The Kornos Cave: an Early Byzantine Site in Cyprus. *Levant*, **2**, 37–62.

Catling, H. W. & Nikolaou, K. 1967 Composite Anchors in Late Bronze Age Cyprus. *Antiquity*, **42**, 225–9.

Denham, H. M. 1964 *The Eastern Mediterranean*, 186 pp. London.

Dumas, F. 1962 *Deep-Water Archaeology*, 71 pp. London.

Frost, H. 1963*a* *Under the Mediterranean*, 278 pp. London.

Frost, H. 1963*b* From Rope to Chain: On the Development of the Anchor in the Mediterranean. *Mariner's Mirror*, **49**, 1–20.

Frost, H. 1969 *The Mortar Wreck in Mellieha Bay*, 38 pp. London. (Gollcher Foundation, National Museum of Malta, Archaeological Series, No. 1).

Frost, H. 1970 Bronze-Age Stone-Anchors from the Eastern Mediterranean. *Mariner's Mirror*, **56,** 377–94.

Green, J. N. 1969 *Cape Andreas Expedition Report, 1969*, Research Laboratory for Archaeology, Oxford, publication.

Green, J. N. 1970 Cape Andreas: an Underwater Survey. *Underwater Association Report 1970* (In publication).

Green, J. N. 1971 Cape Andreas: Survey of a Tile Wreck. *Prospez. Archeol.* **6,** 61–4.

Green, J. N., Hall, E. T. & Katzev, M. L. 1967 Survey of a Greek Shipwreck off Kyrenia, Cyprus. *Archaeometry*, **10**, 47–56.

Green, J. N. & Martin, C. 1970 Metal Detector Survey of the Armada Ship "Santa Maria de la Rosa". *Prospez. Archeol.*, **5**, 95–100.

Green, J. N., Baker, P. E., Richards, B. & Squire, D. M. 1971 Simple Underwater Photogrammetric Techniques. *Archaeometry*, **13** (2), 221–32.

Katzev, M. L. 1968 The Search Below. *Expedition*, **10** No. 3, 11–14.

Katzev, M. L. & van Doorninck, F. 1966 Replicas of Iron Tools from a Byzantine Shipwreck. *Stud. Conserv.*, **11** No. 3, 133–42.

Tinniswood, J. T. 1945 Anchors and Accessories, 1340–1640. *Mariner's Mirror*, **31**, 84–105.

Wignall, S. 1968 *The Spanish Armada Salvage Expedition*, 128 pp. Privately published.

Admiralty Manual of Hydrographic Surveying, Vols. 1 & 2, 1965. Admiralty Hydrographic Department, London.

Mediterranean Pilot, Vol. 5, 1961. Admiralty Hydrographic Department, London.

Plemmyrion Report 1969 The Plemmyrion (Sicily) Expedition. *Oxford Univ. Exp. Club Bull.* **17**, 25–52.

Discussion

McKee With regard to your illustration of four or five stone anchors in a straight line, and the possible significance of this, this arrangement was in fact our own basic mooring plan for last year's work on the *Mary Rose*. Each of the four moorings consisted of five 1–cwt. concrete blocks attached to a wire hawser through iron rings.

Green One of the things that suggested this idea to us was that we used one of the stone anchors which we had located as an anchor for a buoy. In a reasonable breeze it dragged. This could not really be called a control test because we had quite a taut line on it. We went down with another stone anchor and tied it to the line ahead of the end anchor so that the working was done by the first anchor and the end anchor held fast.

McKee The idea is that blocks 1 and 2 lift, as "springs" to absorb the strain. We have seen this done: it is a well-known mooring arrangement.

Shallow-water instrumental searching

by

D. A. FREY

IN ORDER to evaluate instrumental techniques for discovering shallow-water shipwrecks, a pilot project has been carried out at Porto Longo harbour, near Methone, at the south-west tip of the Peloponnese. The primary searching instruments were an EG&G mud-penetrating sonar system and an ELSEC proton magnetometer. Both instruments were found to be only moderately successful in locating known shipwrecks known to be in the harbour. In the case of sonar, the cargo, or lack of it, was a key determining factor, while the success of the proton magnetometer depended on the presence of magnetic materials.

Porto Longo was chosen by Throckmorton because of its position on classical trade routes from Italy to the eastern shores of the Mediterranean. The harbour, a seemingly well protected anchorage (Fig. 1), is subject to sudden winds which will drive ships on to the western shore if their anchors do not hold in the soft mud which makes up the harbour bottom. The small size of the harbour, approximately 300 metres wide and one kilometre long, and the fact that it is almost completely surrounded by land, make it ideally suited for simple and accurate positioning of survey crafts. This is a key factor in underwater survey, since it avoids needless repetition of data runs and assures the possibility of immediately returning to an arbitrary anomaly at a later date without additional searching. It also allows for cross-referencing of targets found separately by sonar, magnetometers or divers.

In the sonar survey, Dr. Edgerton chose to make short east/west runs using range poles at approximately 10 m intervals along the shore. This technique proved acceptable in most cases, although some difficulty was experienced in reproducing longer runs, particularly at the harbour mouth where range poles on only one side could be used. In the afternoon, the prevailing southerly winds also made it difficult to stay on course. The raw sonar data obtained presented cross-sectional representations of the harbour bottom and sub-bottom with a penetration of between 5 m and 10 m into the harbour mud. For marking anomalies, tagged rocks painted white were dropped on to the harbour bottom each time that a suspected anomaly was crossed. Simultaneously a mark was made on the sonar profile and the tag letters were recorded. Repeated "bombing" of likely targets produced a clear pattern on the bottom which made it quite simple subsequently to instruct divers where to dig exploratory trenches. Unfortunately some of the most promising targets were piles of ballast rock with no traces of shipwreck in the vicinity. Since in more recent times Porto Longo had been a popular rendezvous for

Figure 1. Porto Longo harbour. Courtesy National Geographic Society.

smugglers, Throckmorton concluded that these ballast piles were probably dropped by ships taking on cargo in the harbour. Significant exceptions were the well-preserved wrecks of the *Congo* (about 1890) and the *Heraclea* (1941). The *Congo* produced a very sharp signal with extended parabolic edges (indicating reflecting from the side as well as the top of the target). These rather strong reflections can be explained on the basis of the gaseous sludge and mud which remain from the cargo of raisins carried by the Congo when she was shipwrecked. The weaker signals from the *Heraclea* are attributed to the organic remains of her cargo of wheat. It should be pointed out that the reflection of acoustic signals is primarily dependent on changes in density, such as occur at the sea/mud or sea/bedrock interfaces on the bottom. It is much easier to detect hard targets lying in the mud than it is to see waterlogged wood. Certainly the interpretation of sonar records depends greatly on the surrounding geology. In the case of Porto Longo the bedrock is often covered by only a few metres of mud, and in these regions it is difficult to distinguish between bedrock outcrops and possible anomalies.

For the magnetometer survey, Dr Hall chose to make the longer north/south runs against the prevailing winds. This was primarily dictated by the fact that the magnetometer "fish" must be streamed about 100 feet (30 m) behind the survey craft in order not to pick up radio interference from the engines. In order to keep the survey craft *Blue Bonito* on course, a shore observer first aligned the cross-hairs of a transit telescope along the desired course, established by bench-marks painted at each end of the port. Using a walkie-talkie radio, he was then able to direct the craft along this course with considerable accuracy. The bow of the *Blue Bonito* rarely strayed more than a few feet off course and this was always followed by a quick correction. The magnetometer fish, streaming 100 feet behind the boat, should have undergone considerably smaller variations and indeed this was verified when trial runs were repeated and data were found to be identical. Thirty-three such runs were made at an approximate spacing of 10 m. Interpretation of the resultant data was greatly hampered by the fact that *Porto Longo* contains substantial deposits of magnetite and haematite which produced strong variations in the background signals in the harbour. Subsequent to the survey a magnetic contour map, drawn up by D. Krotser, simplified the interpretation somewhat, because the natural magnetic anomalies are generally broader and less intense that those due to iron or steel objects. This magnetic map suggests at least six targets. Of these two are known shipwrecks (one is the *Congo*) and two more are in an area where other modern shipwrecks have been reported. The remaining two targets were examined at the time of the survey and both turned out to be unidentifiable modern steel structures, perhaps remnants of the last war. On the other hand, there were at least half a dozen other known shipwrecks which did not show up on the magnetic map and there are an equal number of suspect anomalies in other locations on the magnetic map which are probably only natural in origin, but this can only be determined by diver inspection.

In conclusion, it should be stressed that the success of either a sonar or magnetometer search depends greatly on the type of wreck being searched for and the natural environment in which one is searching. In Porto Longo both systems failed to detect a majority of the wrecks previously known or discovered by divers and the survey can therefore be considered only a qualified success.

On the other hand, one must take into account the fact that the harbour apparently does not contain a well preserved amphora wreck buried deep in the mud. There was, therefore, no spectacular find, otherwise undetectable by divers, which would have made the sonar an unqualified success. Similarly, the magnetometer survey, as has been mentioned, was greatly hampered by the natural anomalies in the harbour, and a number of significant targets, such as anchors, may have gone undetected because of this background.

Discussion

Hall Is the *Columbine* there or not? I feel sure she isn't.
Throckmorton But we have Public Record Office documents and court martial records of the ship, all saying that she is there.
Hall I have no doubt that we should have found her with all that she had aboard, if she is in the area which we searched, but there was no trace of her, so she can't be there.

The search for King Henry VIII's "Mary Rose"

by

ALEXANDER McKEE

SUMMARY

Part I: Prospection

Historical research: the ship, the sinking, the salvage attempts; the pioneer divers who worked on the wreck in the nineteenth century; discovery of a chart position of that period. Seabed search without instruments, followed by scientific prospection: examination of the site by proton magnetometer, sidescan sonar and sub-mud profilers. Construction of a three-dimensional sonar map of a completely buried wreck.

Part II: Excavation

The digging of a trial trench which finally proved the existence of the site and led to tentative conclusions regarding what had been shown by the sonar graphs: a dense layer of dead weed trapped in the upper, decaying interface of the wreckage. Proof of the theory of the "wreck as artifact collector"; discovery of identifiable species of teredo in plank (evidence of a different biological environment in late Tudor times); recovery of a wrought-iron gun constructed by a hitherto unknown method.

PART I: PROSPECTION

OPERATIONAL BACKGROUND

THE SUCCESSFUL search for what proved to be a completely buried wreck, and the subsequent trial excavation, was a result of Project "Solent Ships", which I planned during the winter of 1964–5 and began during 1965 with the help of a small group of fellow members of Southsea Branch of the British Sub-Aqua Club. The hard core of the team consisted of those who had carried out the Hayling Bay "Church Rocks" surveys from 1960 to 1964, and had consequently gained some archaeological experience. I now thought that it was time to investigate the many historic wrecks known to lie in the Solent Area, particularly those in the naval anchorage at Spithead, off Portsmouth. At that time, little was known about the forms which such wrecks would take in British waters, and therefore the main intention was a search for general knowledge. Consequently, among the many targets listed were the *Royal George* (sunk 1782) and the *Boyne* (sunk 1795), both line-of-battle ships from a relatively well-known period. The ships themselves were not interesting, but what had happened to them (particularly the results of explosive demolition) might well be of importance. These two wrecks were put at the top of the list, because it was thought that they would be easy to find and also because any site damage resulting from our inexperience of wreck investigation would be of no significance. Conversely, the *Mary Rose* (sunk 1545) was well down the list, partly because no accurate position for her was known, partly because we felt that we needed to build up experience before dealing with her. The number of divers taking part rarely exceeded five at any one time, and operations were usually carried out from one small boat lacking instrumentation.

HISTORICAL BACKGROUND

The *Mary Rose* was built at Portsmouth as a carrack of 500–600 tons during 1509–10. Very little is known about this type of ship, whereas from 1700 onwards constructors' plans and models are plentiful. Additionally, the *Mary Rose* is a "key" vessel of the period, being the first English warship to carry complete batteries of siege artillery as main armament on complete gundecks. The period 1400–1600 was one of very rapid development both in shipbuilding and in armament, but information is fragmentary and the period as a whole has been termed a "gap" in nautical knowledge.

In 1536 the *Mary Rose* was rebuilt to 700 tons, with a listed crew of 200 mariners, 185 soldiers and 30 gunners (compared with an earlier list of 100 mariners, 200 soldiers and 20 gunners). She capsized accidentally during the action against the French off Portsmouth on 19 July 1545, while acting as the vice-flagship of Sir George Carew. There were some 20 to 40 survivors. Both Carew and the captain, Roger Grenville, were drowned. Losses were estimated variously as between 400 and 700, and it is possible that she was carrying a greater number of soldiers than usual, the action being fought within close view of Southsea Castle, from where King Henry VIII and Lady Carew witnessed the tragedy.

Immediate attempts were made to right the ship and then lift her by stages into the shallows, one of the hulks used for this purpose being the *Jesus of Lubeck*, subsequently lost by Hawkins at San Juan de Ulua. But all that happened was that her foremast broke under the strain; probably she had already filled deeply with mud and embedded herself. Intermittent operations to recover some of her artillery went on until 1549.

The wreck was discovered by the pioneer divers of the nineteenth century, and the position then lost again. Consequently, one of my main lines of enquiry was into the operations of these divers, and eventually the true story emerged for the first time, thoroughly documented (McKee, 1968). But in 1965 I was not aware that the accepted stories of the development of diving gear and the use of it in the discovery of the *Mary Rose* were substantially inaccurate.

PRELIMINARY PROSPECTION

In 1965 I had accurate positions for both the *Royal George* and the *Boyne*, but for the *Mary Rose* only areas, various and conflicting. There were two quite wild areas given for the sinking, which I ignored: "off Brading/St. Helens" (Oppenheim, 1896; Portsmouth Dockyard Museum catalogue, 1919) and "the mouth of Portsmouth Harbour" (Laird Clowes). The latter was probably misreading Hall's and Holinshed's "in the middest of the haven". The only firm contemporary clues were:

(*a*) A large panorama (5 feet 9 inches × 1 foot 7 inches) of the battle of 19 July, known as the "Cowdray Engraving" and copied from a contemporary painting subsequently lost by fire at Cowdray House, Sussex (Basire, 1778). This shows the *Mary Rose* sunk off Southsea Castle, her foremast and mainmast visible above the water, heeled 40 degrees to port. A line taken out from Southsea Castle through the wreck passes very near to the wreck of the *Royal George*, but the *Mary Rose* appears to be much closer to Southsea.

(*b*) A statement by an eye-witness (Monson, Vol. II, 1902) that "Part of the ribs of this ship I have seen with my own eyes; there perished in her 400 persons". Monson was born in 1569, and if we allow him to have seen the wreck between 1580 and 1590 at the earliest, then the capsize must have occurred in a much shallower area than that of the *Royal George*, which lies in about 75 feet at average low water.

This contemporary statement, therefore, confirmed the area indicated by the contemporary painting. But how accurate was that painting, known to us only through a copied engraving?

There was a third indication, a much more precise one, which, although not contemporary with the period of the sinking, appeared to be based on documentation contemporary with the discovery of the wreck in the nineteenth century. This clue was provided by Sir Robert Davis (1962), when he wrote of the *Mary Rose*:

> "The wreck was abandoned and forgotten until, during the *Royal George* operations, divers came accidentally upon the remains of the ship sunk 237 years earlier, lying but a short distance away".

This implied (although it did not expressly state) that the "operations" were those of Colonel James Pasley's Royal Engineer divers (1839–43), and that the two ships must lie close together. If so, the *Royal George* would lead me to the *Mary Rose*.

I personally led the dive which discovered the wreck mound of the *Royal George* (7 June 1965)—an immense mound with much shingle and some concreted ironwork still protruding, sited on a fairly firm seabed which still held up to plain view the anchorage jetsam of centuries. Pre-arranged sweep searches were then carried out in the north-east arc from the mound, in excellent visibility and with negative results: firm soil but no sign of any other wreck.

I therefore moved the whole search some half a mile to the north-east, into much shallower water, meanwhile studying carefully the course which the *Mary Rose* was most likely to have taken in the context of the battle situation on 19 July. The indicated area of probability showed an exceptionally soft seabed and, although it was an anchorage, there was an almost complete absence of anchorage artifacts. A small test "dig" suggested that not only artifacts, but even a complete ship might disappear in such soil, and, moreover, without any large central ship-mound forming to mark the site. This uncomfortable appreciation made me decide to call off the search until I could obtain sonar instruments.

HISTORIC PROSPECTION

The year of certain knowledge was 1966. In May, a visit to the Admiralty Hydrographic Department uncovered a large-scale chart (Sheringham, 1841) on which the wreck of the *Mary Rose* was precisely marked. In November, a visit to the Public Record Office turned up the complete and final evidence regarding the nineteenth-century divers, notably the files WO/44/281 and WO/44/613. Pasley had not discovered the *Mary Rose*; Siebe had not invented the diving helmet and dress. The actual inventors of the diving helmet, Anthony and John Deane, had found the *Mary Rose*, by chance. While working on the *Royal George* in 1836 (three years before Pasley came to Spithead) they had been called away to clear the fouled lines of some Gosport fishermen. The "fastener", although not much of it showed above the mud, was later declared by a Board of Ordnance committee to be undoubtedly the *Mary Rose*. John Deane worked the wreck for two seasons—1836 and 1840—removing some guns and artifacts, blowing a crater amidships with six 13-inch bomb-shells, and finally removing a small amount of timber, which he sold by auction. That timber was then in excellent condition and souvenirs made from it are still well preserved.

PRIMITIVE PROSPECTION

The true site of the wreck was some 200 yards from my nearest search position of 1965, based purely on theoretical deduction, and the seabed was just as soft. I did not expect a main hull-mound, but we all expected scour. Modern local wrecks produce disturbance patterns on the surrounding seabed with the eddies created through the action of the fast tidal streams; this phenomenon probably aids the burial process. On clay seabeds the basic pattern might remain long after all surface traces of the hull had vanished, and as the primary product of scour is a depression—the exact opposite of the conventional ship-mound—I regarded the discovery of such a feature as an important clue which might be obtained merely by visual search.

With Margot Varese, a diver-archaeologist then at London University, I made runs across the site from opposite directions and on courses bound to pass over the invisible hull on the broadside (its south-east heading being known from the Cowdray Engraving). On both occasions we passed over a deep depression and on the last dive a visibility of 8 feet enabled me to report with confidence:

> "A real rise of seabed to a marked crest, coupled with a depth reduction of an indicated 5 or 6 feet within a short distance. The crest curved round and then led away S. or S.E."

The dive was cut short at that point, as Miss Varese's demand-valve ceased to supply her with air and we had to make an emergency ascent from about 45 feet. Without instruments we could not tell whether the hull lay under the depression or to the side outlined by that curiously narrow, crested mound; our knowledge of scour patterns indicated that either explanation was possible.

SCIENTIFIC PROSPECTION AND MAPPING

A Wardle & Davenport proton magnetometer was tried out on two occasions in 1966. It obtained a "contact" and I found a metal cable near the buoyed position, but was unable to ascertain whether it was an uncharted seabed cable or a discarded ship's cable, as visibility on the bottom was only a few inches and the surface wind was gusting to Force 7 and 8 ("Full Gale"). There was a calm sea next time, and some disturbance of the needle over a part of the site. Much later I found part of a wire hawser actually lying on the site, and therefore it is not clear whether the magnetometer detected the cable or the *Mary Rose*, or both. Tests on known modern wrecks established that the instrument ignored small metal items and reacted only to the main mass of the hulls. Readings were not affected by bad weather.

After a long wait we obtained the first sub-mud profiler—an EG&G "boomer". This had its generator swamped and put out of action by a mighty wave which swept us from cabin to stern as we came out of harbour. In any case, sonar instruments lose efficiency in such conditions, from wave noise and also from any seabed noise such as a torrent of shingle during a spring tide. But in October 1967 EG&G were able to

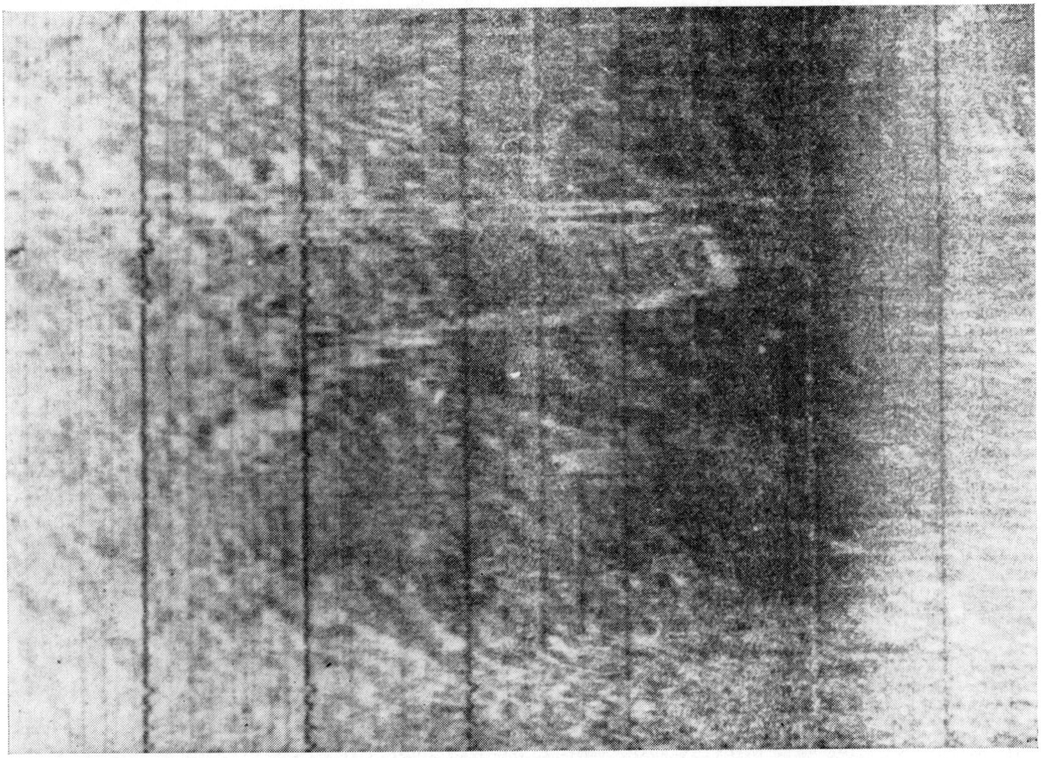

Figure 1. Photographic enlargement of detail from sidescan sonar graph, showing the anomaly. When interpreted, this reads (from top to bottom): counter-mound; scoured depression; port side mound. The starboard side mound did not show on the scanner, although it can be picked out faintly on "pinger" graphs.

let us use briefly the ideal combination of sonar instruments: a dual-channel side-scanner for mapping the surface patterns and disturbances of the seabed, and a linked "pinger" which gave simultaneous sub-mud profiles. In effect, the sidescan sketches the surface contours of the sandwich, while the "pinger" records the layers of which it is composed—and anomalies in them. While a diver may be able to see only a few feet on either side of his course, the scanner can be set to ranges of up to 1,000 feet on each side. Similarly, while the diver can physically probe into the seabed for a few feet only, the "pinger" may reach depths of up to 75 feet or more.

Commercial considerations allowed only 15 minutes out of the four days to be devoted to the survey of the *Mary Rose* site, but this proved adequate. Although the hydrophone hose of the "pinger" had been damaged, sea conditions were perfect. We crossed the bows of the *Mary Rose* and then turned for a run right over the wreck. The crossing provided the best sidescan picture (Fig. 1), but the direct run allowed the "pinger" to register as well, if it would—and it did. Both instruments registered an anomaly simultaneously. Robert Henderson, the sidescan operator, interpreted his graphs as follows:

> "There was a consistency in the bottom, but here was an anomaly affecting everything. Nothing similar to it in the area. Shown by both "pinger" and scanner—therefore a disturbance in the area. This argues for an artificial object as against, say, a rock outcrop".

John Mills interpreted his "pinger" graphs as follows:

> "Pinger" not working well, but showed (1) a mound 4–5 feet high on seabed; (2) an object 20 feet below seabed; (3) a geological layer below this at 35–40 feet below seabed. The lower layer was obviously geological because it was continuous, appearing throughout the record. The object appeared at only one point, and was therefore unique in the area examined."

Sidescan had not been used before to detect completely buried wrecks, and it was not then known that they could do so; that is, there were no precedents whatever, so far as we were aware. We concluded that what the sidescan had actually shown was not the buried object itself, but the "entry wound" made by it in the seabed originally, plus the effect of scour action around the wreck while it was still only partially buried. The recordings on graph paper produced by the instrument were in effect "pictures" of the seabed surface disturbance area, with lines of distance measurement conveniently laid across them. They were the underwater equivalent of oblique aerial cine-photographs. To produce a large-scale two-dimensional map it was only necessary to enlarge the relevant portion of the first mile-long "run". The site map so produced covered the whole of the disturbance area, not just that section of it actually occupied by the "anomaly".

But the site as a whole was not fully understood until, in July 1968, Prof. Harold Edgerton came over from Boston with two "pingers"—a 5 kc. and a 12 kc.—to carry out a detailed two-day survey. Once more we were careful to cover a large area, about a mile long and more than half a mile wide, in order to detect all possible anomalies and to obtain an effective delimitation of them.

Four sub-mud anomalies were shown. One only—a feature shaped like a flattened letter "W"—was exactly at the chart position of the *Mary Rose*. It was associated also with the mound-scour pattern previously recorded by the sidescanner, as was another anomaly which curved up under what we were to call the counter-mound and apparently consisted of disturbed clay. Neither of the two remaining anomalies had any connection with a matching anomaly on the seabed above them; one was later shown to be clay, the other was too deep to sample but also much too small to be a ship.

The basis of the third dimension to the sidescan map was the careful plotting of the best sub-mud profiles on a dozen different navigational lines. Eight of these showed the

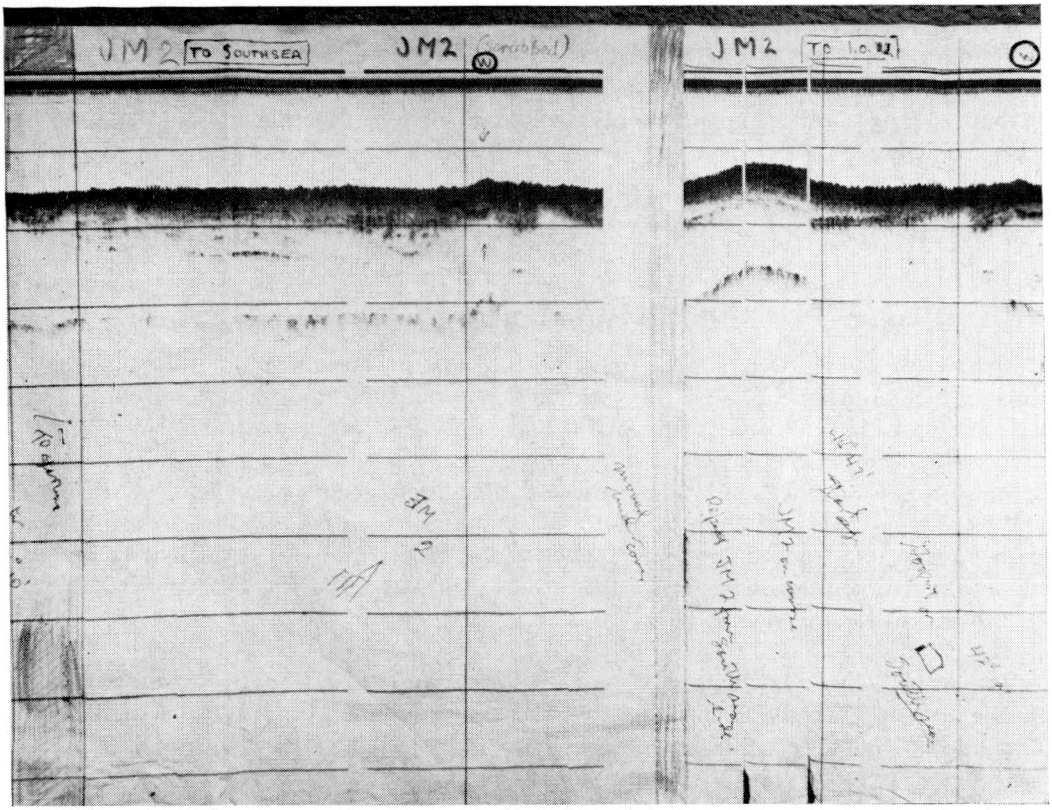

Figure 2. Photograph of parts of two "pinger" runs over the site, on navigational line JM2 in both directions. The arrows pencilled on the original graph by Prof. Edgerton point to a distinctive sub-mud anomaly underlying a marked mound-and-scour pattern, which is itself an anomaly on an otherwise almost featureless plain.

"W" feature; the remainder delimited it. Now, not only could it be seen where the "W" was in relation to the sidescan picture, but the whole disturbance area could be read at a glance and interpreted.

Only one interpretation satisfactorily explained the site—a large wreck which had been scoured far more on one side than on the other. In addition, what was not clear on the sidescan graphs became abundantly so when the "pinger" cuts were studied (Fig. 2). I could even see the areas where Miss Varese and I had crossed the site. It was plain also that the combined anomalies (seabed and sub-mud) were roughly "ship-shaped", aligned approximately south-east, and had a sub-mud length of about 170 feet. Shape, dimensions and alignment, as well as the chart position, allowed the site to be that of the wreck of the *Mary Rose*.

The least depths of the sub-mud anomaly varied sharply between 5 and 15 feet (thus producing the "W"); the profile varied between 2 and 4 feet thick; the outlines were harder and more regular than those of clay features; there was deeper penetration on either side, the "W" itself appearing to block the sonar waves. Underlying the whole site was a geological layer at the 35–40 foot level which showed a marked discontinuity or fracture. It was not clear whether the "W" was a true cross-section through the hull or merely the upper interface of the wreckage. Only excavation could determine this, or perhaps supply another explanation altogether. But we had what many land archaeologists would give a great deal to possess, a three-dimensional site map in advance of excavation.

PART II: EXCAVATION

OPERATIONAL BACKGROUND

The two prime requirements for an excavation in tidal waters are money and moorings; digging techniques come later, for without the former one can do nothing. After that come organization and planning, with actual excavation problems a long way behind (and comparatively easy to solve). The main digging tools are compressors and pumps, to suck or blow air, or to suck or blow water; they are large and heavy and require large and expensive boats and large teams to keep them running continuously. Teams from both Southsea and Southampton branches of the British Sub-Aqua Club were mainly involved, with additional assistance from the Royal Navy, the Royal Engineers, Portsmouth Fire Brigade, the Ministry of Public Building and Works and several small diving clubs.

The word "excavation" tends to be used loosely in the underwater world and often means no more than the casual collection of artifacts lying on the surface of the seabed. Genuine excavators in tideless or near-tideless waters, such as the Mediterranean or the Caribbean, usually excavate in sand soils to depths rarely exceeding 5 feet and very often considerably less. But we had to operate on a site with complicated tidal streams of roughly an "X" shape, and had to dig down through mud and clay to a depth of 12 feet.

TECHNICAL ADVANTAGES

Most of the digging tools used were more gentle than their land equivalents, with less risk of breakage. Conservation facilities locally were excellent, and often there was a conservationist in the boat for immediate treatment of objects, if necessary. Where a wet mud and clay site is concerned, the immersion of the whole site in water is a positive advantage, and it is infinitely easier than working such a site in a breathable atmosphere while subject to the full force of gravity, as those of us who had worked on the *Grace Dieu* well knew. In tidal waters correct trench alignment allows the water itself to remove the excavated soil from the site.

INTENTIONS

The prior existence of a three-dimensional sonar map gave us a complete range of choice as to where a trial trench should be laid down. It showed (and this was confirmed by probing) that the area of the sterncastle was nearest to the seabed and therefore easiest to uncover. However, apart from being fragile in itself, this "summer castle" was also likely to contain the most delicate artifacts, possibly even documents. Legal protection against plunderers had been obtained in 1968, but the site was still exposed to the ravage of ships' anchors and the 90-lb otterboards of trawls; a trench here, although tempting, was perhaps inadvisable.

I finally decided on the area of the waist just forward of amidships. This was the deepest point of burial, but also the strongest part of the ship. Furthermore, it might give us not merely the formal identification, but also information as to how much of the hull remained. Bearing in mind that the wreck was heeled over to port 40 degrees from the vertical, and that the bulwarks were lowest in the waist, I felt that their preservation or otherwise should provide a workable guide.

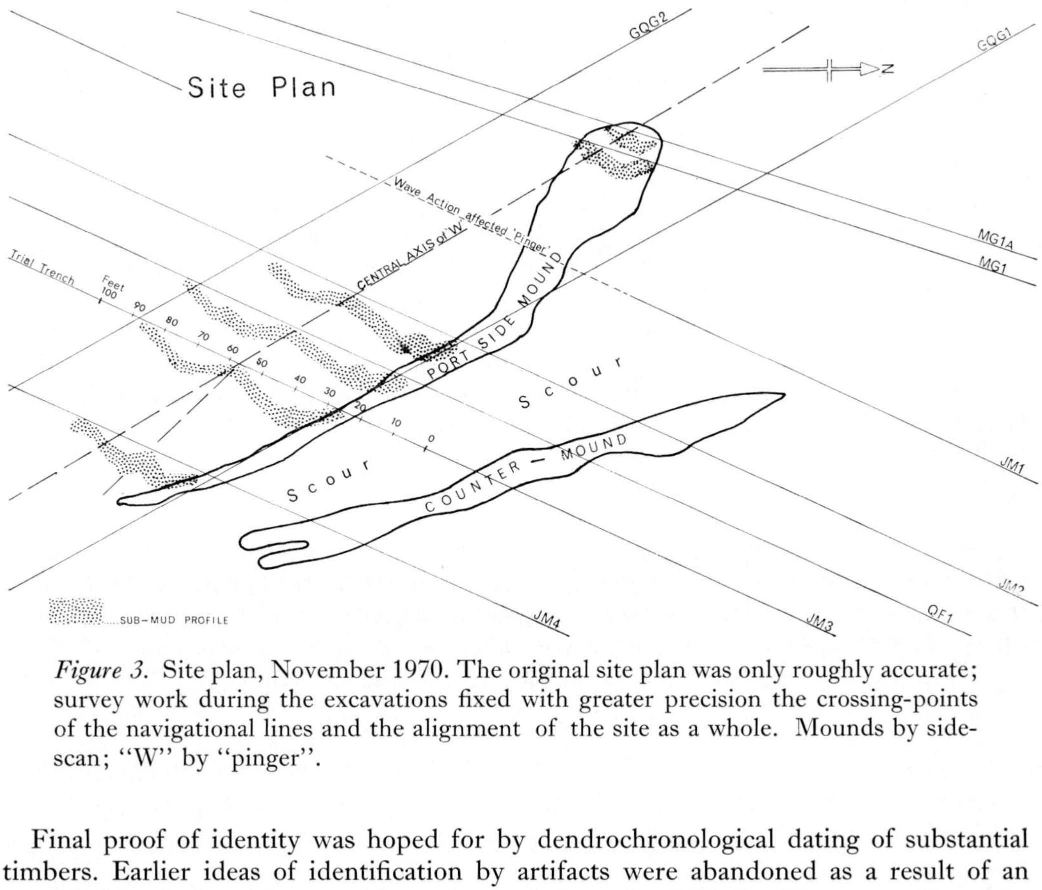

Figure 3. Site plan, November 1970. The original site plan was only roughly accurate; survey work during the excavations fixed with greater precision the crossing-points of the navigational lines and the alignment of the site as a whole. Mounds by side-scan; "W" by "pinger".

Final proof of identity was hoped for by dendrochronological dating of substantial timbers. Earlier ideas of identification by artifacts were abandoned as a result of an investigation into modern wreck scour carried out by Maurice Young, a shipwright who led the Southampton contingent of the team. He was able to demonstrate a typical form of wreck scour, and to show that the scour pits so formed very quickly became artifact collectors and stratification mixers. In due course our own trench acted in the same way, collecting a wide assortment of seabed transit material, both natural and artificial, as well as driftweed.

The trench was to be aligned exactly on transit JM3, crossing the hull at a slight angle from port side to starboard and overlapping both sides (Fig. 3). This alignment gave certain navigational advantages, on both surface and seabed, and also allowed excavated soil to be deposited by the tidal streams clear of the trench.

RESULTS

Two seasons of part-time excavation on a shoe-string budget in tidal waters and British weather conditions resulted in a trial trench 90 feet long, 4 feet deep, 15 to 25 feet wide, and with shafts 7, 8, 10 and 12 feet deep dug down to "contacts". About 1,000 cubic yards of mud and clay were removed.

Recent overburden

The first five feet consisted of extremely light sediments, which nevertheless contained certain organic elements and were extremely cohesive. The first winter produced only slight fill and some rounding-off of the fairly straight sides of the trench, as expected. As also expected, the missing anchorage artifacts were found in, rather than on, this topsoil. It was studded in depth, like a cake with raisins, with the seamen's pipes, chipped or broken crockery, old shoes, old bones, boiler clinker, modern stanchions and iron concretions, so markedly absent from the seabed. Among the very few artifacts lying on the surface were polythene bags, plastic cups, two plastic light-fittings, one broom in good condition, one lavatory seat, one egg and one tarpaulin. The bulk of these were in the trench, apart from one length of unexposed 35 mm film found wrapped round one of our sub-surface buoys. That date of deposition was only one factor in determining an object's depth in the stratification was proved by an intact cup protruding from the wall of the trench about 18 inches below the seabed, of Woolworth type (*c.* 1930). The major factor was probably rate of sinkage, which clearly was based on the mass : weight ratio.

We formed the opinion that approximately the first five feet of the topsoil were new seabed laid down after Deane and Edwards left the site in 1840; that the rate of sedimentation was unusually rapid; and that it was due to a new factor appearing shortly after that time—the passage over the site in large numbers every day of paddle- and screw-propelled vessels, which stir up the sediments of the shallows over Spitsand. This latter fact has been repeatedly observed over a period of five years.

Stiff clay layer

At about the 5–6 foot level a quite different soil was encountered. Possibly it is "blue clay"; certainly it has all the characteristics of slightly damp plasticine. It will not flow up an air-lift, but has first to be broken up either by hand or by entrenching tool and then "fed" to the lift. All items discovered so far which are definitely from, or likely to be from, the *Mary Rose* were found in this layer, at a minimum depth of 7 feet below original seabed level. In the boundary area between 5 and 7 feet were found objects indicating a "mix": e.g., part of a lantern of *c.* 1700 was found tucked just underneath one side of a large plank, inclined at a slight angle between the 7 and 8 foot levels and almost certainly from the *Mary Rose*. Around this plank also was a suspicious concentration of iron concretions or hollow concretions where the iron had entirely disappeared, leaving a mould. This was off the starboard side, where one would expect a scour pit to have existed at one time.

Dense decayed weed concentration

Some 10 feet further on from the plank, probes had obtained a firm contact at a depth of 12 feet beneath the mud. When the shaft being driven down to this had reached the 7 foot level, I was carrying out a routine inspection when I noticed in the dangerously near-vertical side a band of darker strata, angled downwards from about the 5 foot level, which was producing minute puffs of sediment at short intervals. This was probably methane gas, as the samples which I took in the near darkness proved to consist of a compacted mass of decaying laminarian holdfasts attached to pieces of glass, small shingle, etc., and therefore likely to have been driftweed originally, before burial. As the shaft was driven further downwards the weed band continued, and a piece of very old timber was found in it at the 10 foot level, two feet short of the contact, which we have still to uncover.

The presence of driftweed on the site required no explanation: our trench filled up very quickly with recently dead weed, and in the shafts these layers, although not yet compact, built up to a height of 3 feet almost immediately and had to be cleaned out before work began. But it is not only trenches which collect dead driftweed; any obstruction on the seabed will do this, and modern wrecks tend to fill up with it. A good example which I was exploring at the time, as a holiday from excavation direction, was the wreck of the German submarine *U.B.-21*; although one hatch was open, the mass of weed inside deterred me from trying to enter.

I concluded, therefore, that this weed layer, "locked in" 5 feet below the seabed, could only have formed in and around the upper parts of the wreck of the *Mary Rose* at a time when at least part of the upper (i.e., starboard) side was still above the seabed and in a state of decay and collapse.

This environmental analysis appeared to be borne out by expert examination (by Mr. W. O. B. Majer of the Society for Nautical Research) of deeply-buried recovered timbers likely to be from this wreck; three out of the four structural items were definitely from parts of ship well above the waterline—from the bulwarks or higher. The fourth piece (the one inside the weed) was too fragmentary to be identifiable. The state of decay of all three, together with clear evidence of attack by either gribble or teredo, or both combined, showed that they had been exposed to water for some time, and that a very long time ago.

Tentative, but still reasonable, was the linked supposition that the weed layer was in fact the peculiar "W"-shaped feature recorded by the "pinger". It occurred on the starboard side at the same depth beneath the mud (5 feet) and inclined downwards at much the same angle. It was visibly a mass of decaying matter and gaseous mud, which would blank off the "pinger"'s penetration, and the graphs did show mostly white under the "W", with deeper penetration indicated on either side. This suggested a quite new reconstruction of the collapse-sequence, with two of the inclined, parallel arms of the "W" being perhaps two part-collapsed, superimposed decks of a wreck heeled over at a steep angle. Unlike earlier attempts to postulate a collapse by opening-out (suggested by Peter Throckmorton's Methone wreck studies), this indeed fitted all known facts, particularly the optimistic appreciation that a strongly-built ship like the *Mary Rose* would be unlikely to open out to anything like the same degree as a brig or schooner.

If these appreciations are accurate, then the "W" feature is not the *Mary Rose* at all, but merely an interface of organic matter, with the bulk of the surviving hull underneath it.

The biological tale told by the timbers

In 1969 part of a light (elmwood?) plank was recovered; it had been attacked by gribble (*Limnoria lignorum*) only. It had been secured by iron nails which had completely disappeared. In 1970 four timbers were recovered. One was an (oak?) plank about 10 feet long which had been fastened with 1½-inch diameter (oak?) trenails; it had been attacked by gribble and, massively, by teredo. Sufficient remained of one specimen for X-ray examination by Mr. P. Board of the Central Electricity Research Laboratories, Leatherhead, who identified it as *Nototeredo norvagica*, which has world-wide distribution in fully maritime conditions; other tunnels may have been made by *Teredo navalis*. Another large timber was a stag-horn or cleat (of oak?) which originally would have been some 3–4 feet long; this had been attacked by gribble only. Mr. Majer associates it on the basis of size with the foremast rather than the mainmast, and the shaft from which it came was indeed much nearer to the presumed position of the foremast. It had been secured by 1½-inch trenails and, as with the plank, one sample was still in place. Both the small pieces had been attacked by teredo: a fashion-piece, or capping-piece for a castle (found in the presumed area of the bowcastle), and the unidentifiable piece found in the middle of the dead-weed band.

The eastern Solent is virtually free of teredo at present, and those which do exist in the area are generally not of the size attained by the identified specimen in the large plank. According to the biologists, this argues for a different, notably warmer, sea environment at some time in the past, possibly in Tudor times. For arriving at a conclusion as to when that might have been, Admiral Monson's statement, that he had seen parts of the ribs of the ship with his own eyes, is crucial. There could have been no massive teredo infestation then, or otherwise, in that depth of water, the remains of the upper hull would not have reached anywhere near the surface of the sea. It appears, therefore, that the infestation must have begun at some time after 1580 at the very earliest. We do not know precisely when it ceased, but it is likely to have been before 1711, the date of the sinking at Spithead of the *Edgar*, which was still standing two gundecks high above the seabed in 1843, when it was found by Colonel Pasley's divers. Five years' submersion is required before timber is sufficiently broken down to allow teredo spat to settle; but after that, another five years would probably see the collapse of all exposed portions of the hull (but not, of course, of the buried parts below the mud, where teredo cannot live). We conclude that the *Mary Rose* had at least 35 years, and possibly much longer, in which to work herself well down into the clay.

The technological story told by the gun

As far back as 1966 I had proclaimed that we were looking for a "big Tudor battleship headed south-east". The sonar had shown us both large size and a south-east alignment. Towards the end of the 1970 season the recovery of the barrel of an antique wrought-iron breech-loading gun gave us both "Tudor" and "battleship". When this was combined with a very good chart position, there could be no further doubt.

The gun was recovered from a 12 foot deep shaft driven down through the port side mound amidships. One at least of Deane's explosions had occurred in this area (he reported recovering part of the mainmast), and the gun bore clear signs of having been temporarily uncovered, and its concretion cleaned, by low explosives. The chamber was missing and only a few fragments of the wooden bed remained attached. The barrel itself was just under 8 feet long and had a bore of $3\frac{3}{4}$ inches; in the muzzle end was a blockage caused by clay, whereas the breech end was blocked by a $3\frac{1}{2}$-inch diameter pig-iron shot in mint condition, with hemp wadding in place and some of the powder charge still adhering.

At first this gun appeared to be an almost perfect partner to the $3\frac{3}{4}$-inch bore built-up gun, already on display at Southsea Castle, which had been recovered by John Deane from the *Mary Rose* in 1840. Like most of the wrought-iron guns which he had raised, this had so deteriorated that the interior details of the hoop-and-stave "built-up" method of construction were visible to the naked eye. It had been a shock, when we had got our gun safely on deck, to see at one point, where a triple-ring was exposed, grey metal which looked new for about ten minutes before it rusted over, instead of a badly decayed structure. With the aid of the Ministry of Public Building and Works, the time which elapsed between our gun breaking surface at Spithead and arriving at the conservation laboratory at Southsea Castle Museum (which specializes in artillery) was 3 hours and 10 minutes. We look forward with interest to Mr. C. O'Shea's report (in preparation) on the successful conservation of this gun.

We had already, for timber, obtained the use of the best possible radiograph techniques, as recently developed by the Leatherhead laboratories, for internal examination of the plank with its teredo tunnels. In the case of the gun barrel, local X-ray methods did not produce adequate pictures and therefore Mr. O'Shea had the barrel examined by the gamma-ray method in Portsmouth Dockyard. The resulting high-definition pictures were startling. Not only did they show the unexpectedly complicated construction of the reinforcing rings, but they also revealed a single seam along the barrel from muzzle to breech. There were no staves at all. Instead of being a normal "built-up" gun, this barrel had been made out of a single sheet of wrought iron, rolled into a cylinder and then rough-welded. At the present time, we know neither of any existing example nor of any written records of this type of construction, which appears to be intermediate between "built-up" and "cast", and it may be that we have contributed new evidence of the development of Tudor gun-making techniques.

What other surprises there may be in the wreck we cannot surmise. But the objective for the current season is to establish how much of the hull is still intact, and we do not underestimate the magnitude of the underwater excavation task involved.

POSTSCRIPT

Within three weeks of the Symposium taking place, two successful operations were carried out at Spithead (on 17 April and 1 May 1971), and I personally could not only say with Admiral Monson "Part of the ribs of this ship I have seen with my own eyes", but had been able to dig around them with my hands and establish that, apart from the upper few inches, they were untouched by marine borers, the only marks being those of the Tudor shipwrights. We have now surveyed a long stretch of one side of the bow-castle main frames and a shorter uncovered section of the much lighter castling itself. At this point, the side of the wreck appears to be intact to about the level of the lower storey of the forecastle. Whereas amidships there were clear traces of Deane's gun-powder explosions, there are no signs here of any disturbance of the structure. The survey was carried out by Commander Alan Baldwin, R.N., with myself as Director of Excavations, Mrs. Margaret Rule being Site Secretary.

REFERENCES

Anthony, Anthony 1546 *The fyrst rolle Declaryng the Nombre of the Kyng's Majestie's own shyppes with each Shyppe and Shyppe's Naem with theyr tunnage and Nombre of men also the Ordenaunce, Artillary and Municions and habilliments for Warre, for the Armyng and Deffence of every of the sayd shyppes against theyr enemys uppon the See*, Pepysian Library, Magdalene College, Cambridge.

Basire, James 1778 *The Encampment of the English Forces near Portsmouth: together with a view of the English and French Fleets at the commencement of the action between them on the XIXth of July MDXLV: engraved from the original painting at Cowdry in Sussex, the seat of the Right Honourable Anthony Browne, Lord Viscount Montague.*

Clowes, G. S. Laird 1932 *Sailing Ships*, 95 pp. London.

Daniel, F. *Histoire de la Milice de France: Memoirs of Sieur Martin du Bellay*, MSS. Paris.

Davis, Sir Robert H. 1962 *Deep Diving and Submarine Operations*, 7th edit., 693 pp. London.

Hall, Edward 1548 *Chronicle.*

Holinshed, Raphael 1577 *Chronicles.*

Maclean, Sir John (ed.) 1857 *The Life and Times of Sir Peter Carewe, from the original Manuscript.* London.

McKee, A. 1968 *History Under the Sea*, 342 pp. London.

Monson 1902 *The Naval Tracts of Sir William Monson*, ed. M. Oppenheim, Vol. II (*Publ. Navy Records Society*, Vol. 23), 395 pp. London.

Oppenheim, M. 1896 *A History of the Administration of the Royal Navy*, 411 pp. London.

Public Record Office. WO/44/281: Account of the Ordnance recovered from the wreck of the *Mary Rose* lost off Spithead in 1545, from *Ordnance Board Correspondence, South-West District*, 1841, Jan-March. WO/44/613: Report by Col. C. W. Pasley, R.E., concerning diving apparatus used on the wreck of the *Royal George*, 1839—Deane's, Bethell's, Siebe's.

Sheringham, W. L., Captain R.N. 1841 *Survey of Portsmouth and Spithead*, Admiralty Hydrographic Department.

State Papers 1907 C.S.P. (Foreign and Domestic) Henry VIII, Vol. XX, Part I (1545).

Discussion

Lawrence Is the "weed" on the surface of the wreck likely to remain gaseous for hundreds of years?
McKee I don't really know. The ship was sunk in 1545 and it seems that there was no teredo much before 1600, which gives about 50 years of slow collapse. How long after that she would remain a weed-collecting obstruction, is a matter for conjecture. We are not certain that the "W"-shaped layer shown by sonar is decaying weed, but Throckmorton's examples of sonar picking up ships with cargoes of raisins and wheat, also in decay, is some corroboration.
Wallace On the survival of weed, I am informed that they have found seaweed on the gravel beds to the east of Chichester which must be at least half a million years old.

Richards Was the gun found on the site?
McKee Yes, on the port side, amidships, 12 feet down.

Davidson Have you taken any core-samples down into the wreck?
McKee We went to Southampton University in the hope of obtaining sediment samples, but they did not have a corer that would go to 15 feet, the depth of this ship, but only to 6–8 feet. For locating wood, we have used probes.
Throckmorton The Woods Hole staff have designed a large core-sampler for Helike. We estimate that it will cost £100 to build in Athens.

McKeone What evidence is there that this gun was in fact welded? And does the seam of the gun run parallel to the axis of the gun?
McKee Yes.

Kennedy Surely there must be a reason for sedimentation. I should have thought this was due to changes in agriculture, leading to increased run-off from the land, increase in deposition of clay, silt, earth, etc. This may be an important factor in dating the total deposition.
McKee I had not thought of this. But as far as the *Mary Rose* is concerned, the site is virtually unique in the Solent area. The upper 5 feet of sediment consist of very light material, which does not support artifacts, whereas the *Royal George* site in deeper water is firmer and does hold them.
Lewis Did they dredge anywhere near your site?
McKee No. It is basically clay and mud, not a commercial dredging area, and not near a navigational channel. The Channel ferry does not go past, but only the Isle of Wight ferries for half of each tide.
Lewis Could it have been a dump site?
McKee No. The *Royal George* is used as a dump site by trawlermen, but not the *Mary Rose.*

Lawrence Is there any evidence consisting in reports of ships losing their anchors in that region of the wreck area?
McKee No. They would not report that sort of thing to us, but only to their owners. We have not found any anchors, but only the one uncharted cable which was probably part of a ship's cable.
Croome I don't quite follow your comments about the Isle of Wight ferry boat and its relation with the sedimentation and the weed.
McKee Sedimentation is quite different from the weed. The Isle of Wight boats do stir up the sediments, locally. But there is a movement of weed throughout the whole area; the Solent is a big circulation pattern for weed.
Green You have double tides in this area. Do you have any explanation of why you have this counter-mound on just one side, and what form does this take? A counter-mound on one side only is difficult to explain when you have currents moving both ways.
McKee I have no rational, detailed explanation of the mechanism. One would have to try with models. The *Lusitania* produced the same pattern.
Green Presumably there is a continuous running current around the *Lusitania*.
McKee Whatever there is, it has produced an almost identical pattern to the *Mary Rose*, where you have a minor and major scour-pit. I cannot explain exactly why this should be so. There are four currents at the *Mary Rose* site, in an "X" shape.
Green North Sea oil-rigs have the same scouring effects. They have trouble with scour-pits.
McKee All obstructions tend to cause scour, but the patterns are not always the same. The normal scour is a pit all round the obstruction. The best local example is the wreck of a World War I freighter on the Princessa Shoal off the Isle of Wight, on a clay bottom, which is called the "Norman Castle wreck", because the scour-pit all round it resembles a moat, and the upperworks of the ship the castle. A few years ago, the upperworks were above seabed level, but now they are level with it, after about 50 years in all. Eventually this wreck will disappear completely under the clay. We think that scour helps a wreck to dig in, but all we know of the mechanism is that it is an eddy.
Throckmorton I support McKee. The same phenomenon of wreck-mounds is seen in the Atlantic, especially on the east coast of the U.S.A. We have seen a similar pattern yesterday on the Austrian brig and in Porto Longo.

Martin How do you know that the 10-foot plank came from the upperworks?
McKee We took the opinion of Mr. W. O. B. Majer, of the Society for Nautical Research, who thought it could have come from as high as the castling. One of our divers, a professional shipwright, thought it might have been from near the bulwarks. On both views, it was well above the waterline.
Lyon Is it likely that the gun and bits of wood you found are actually parts of debris, and not the bottom of the ship?
McKee In our nightmares, we see something like the *Grace Dieu* with just the bottom of the hull left. But we think the *Mary Rose* must be better preserved, because she sank heeled 40 degrees to port; and if you have most of the port side intact, then you

can reconstruct the starboard side. The gun came from under the port side mound, where we were widening our trench in order to dig down to 15 feet. Unfortunately, there is clear evidence from the corrosion and biological records that this gun came from the crater made by Deane's gunpowder, which we also know was amidships. That is, it came from a disturbance area. So we shall not approach that point again except with a new trench along the line of the port side, which will define the disturbance area before approaching Deane's crater.

Wignall What is the thickness of the metal of the gun, excluding the bands?

McKee This information is not yet available, but we do know that we have lost, on average, the outer quarter-inch by corrosion.

Sherborne I am not an archaeologist but a medieval historian. You made reference in general terms to fighting decks from the fourteenth century onwards and to the forecastle of this ship. It happens that I have been investigating the fighting complements of ships of the later fourteenth century; some of the chaps you would find there would have been longbowmen.

McKee I attempted to make a model last year of the *Mary Rose* from the Anthony Roll picture and found features which could only be arrow-slits. I agree that most of the soldiers in the bowcastle must have been bowmen. But I think there were men-at-arms, too, because there were also rows of holes in the side of the castle which were not right for guns or bowmen. I think they must have been sally-ports for pikemen and billmen engaged in boarding another ship.

Sherborne In the fourteenth century the number of archers and the number of men-at-arms was commonly identical and they were really only soldiers transferred to the sea.

McKee Some naval historians say that guns were installed to sink other ships. The *Bismarck* is an example of the fact that to sink a battleship you have to hit it below the waterline. I think the *Mary Rose* represented rather land-siege techniques transferred to naval warfare. You had long-range guns to put in counter-battery fire to overwhelm the enemy's artillery, then you brought up heavy battering-pieces for a day or so, to make as large a breach as you could manage in the time (these cannon firing solid shot would be more effective for the purpose than modern field guns firing explosive). Once you have battered your breach in the wall you bring up your bowmen to give short-range covering fire to the forward rush of the men-at-arms, the billmen and so on. It is not just guns, but a weapons system. It is this system which I believe ships like the *Mary Rose* were designed to carry at sea.

Naish Longbows were found by divers in the hold of the *Mary Rose.*

McKee Deane found eight longbows in the *Mary Rose.* Archery experts say that these were not finished, and were therefore from the stores. The vital point about them, I understand, is that they are the only fully-authenticated English longbows in existence.

Naish Deane got right down to the bottom of the ship and brought up cannon-balls, bows and a lot of other objects; he might have destroyed far more than you realise.

The Royal Engineers blew up three ships with tons of explosives: the *Royal George*, the *Boyne* and one other. I suspect they blew up the *Mary Rose* too.

McKee The usually accepted story is that the *Mary Rose* was near to the *Royal George* and therefore must have been destroyed too. But this story is not true; the *Mary Rose* is half a mile from the *Royal George* and whatever exploded in the *Royal George* would have had no effect on the *Mary Rose*. The story that the Royal Engineers found the *Mary Rose* is also not true. Deane found the *Mary Rose*, at a time when he was working on the *Royal George*. I found out the true story some years ago, when I discovered an Ordnance Board file on the *Mary Rose* gun salvage in the Public Records Office. This actually included Deane's indent for explosives—six 13-inch bomb-shells filled with gunpowder. These bomb-shells were hollow cannon-balls with 2-inch thick walls and a fuse-hole, so they were suitable for underwater demolition. But you had to fit a long pipe to the fuse-hole, which projected above the surface; thus necessarily your boat was directly over the explosion. Deane certainly made a crater amidships, but for these reasons I do not think the damage was very great.

Wignall With reference to the guns in the ballast of the *Jesus of Lubeck*, she was identical in build to ships of the period of the *Mary Rose*. In her ballast she had several of these old guns which John Hawkins had not wanted to use because they were so obsolete. Could your gun have been ballast?

McKee I agree that the *Jesus of Lubeck* was of the same period as the *Mary Rose*; indeed, she was one of the two ships used in the attempted salvage of the *Mary Rose* in 1545. But our gun was loaded.

Naish But so was the one at the National Maritime Museum.

McKee All the guns raised by Deane in 1836 and 1840 were loaded, so they are unlikely to have been ballast. And you have only to look at the picture of the *Mary Rose* to see which are the bronze guns and which are the iron guns.

Rule The gun recovered last year was not only loaded, but also primed and ready to fire.

Reasons for preservation and methods of conservation

by

DAVID LEIGH

1. INTRODUCTION

SOME TIME AGO G. Thomson (1966) wrote of Conservation Science as being no further advanced than a "kitchen art". It is clear that he was referring to the art of stabilizing and restoring objects merely by *recipe*, an art with little deeper understanding of the chemical and physical processes involved, and even less of those processes of decay which artefacts undergo in the course of time. The situation is to some extent now remedied, and a growing body of scientific knowledge underpins the empirical practice of conservation. However, while this is true for the treatment of most museum materials and of archaeological finds from land excavations, it is sadly not so true of material recovered from the sea. In this case neither the processes of conservation nor those of decay are even partially understood, and indeed the kitchen art of conservation is more often than not totally neglected. There are a number of reasons for this. First, marine archaeology is a relatively new study, whose techniques, including that of conservation, are still at an early stage. Secondly, it is usually undertaken by groups of people who have little or no knowledge of the principles and practice of modern conservation methods. Most importantly, the condition of materials being excavated from the seabed is presenting a quite new range of problems with which conservators are totally unfamiliar.

2. PRESERVATION

As in medicine an understanding of what causes an illness is a pre-requisite of diagnosis and treatment, so, in a similar way, an understanding of the causes of decay and corrosion is needed before it is possible to diagnose and to suggest a suitable treatment for submerged remains. However, that which fails to decay must surely be preserved, and it is perhaps of even more relevance to the marine archaeologist to know why artefacts are *preserved* in the sea and in what condition he can expect to find them. Unfortunately there is very little evidence or previous research on this topic, and we are forced to rely on our own observation of what is excavated as it is found. We have to study the partially decayed wood, the sometimes totally corroded lead, the stable but abraded pottery and the strangest of concretions found round vanished iron objects (Fig. 1), and ask why they survived and what known and as yet unknown ways of marine life and chemistry were responsible for producing these results.

To begin answering these questions it is necessary to examine the effects on man-made objects of an environment of the utmost complexity, namely the sea. We have to consider its salinity, its mineral content, its floral and faunal life, its movements and temperature changes, etc., and we must be able to relate these factors not only to each other but also

Figure 1. Three concretions formed round iron objects. Scales 1 : 1.

to position on the earth, to time and to the properties of artefacts deposited on the seabed by accident or war. It is perhaps not surprising that in the face of these complexities we find ourselves almost alone in our study; *almost*, because there is one group of people who have already had to face some of these problems: the corrosion scientists. They help to design and choose materials for ships and harbour works and it is to them that we can turn for help.

Taking first the corrosion of metals, we see just how complex the biological, electrical and chemical reactions are. In its simplest form the corrosion of a metal in an electrolyte such as the sea can be thought of as a straightforward electrochemical mechanism.

Two parts of the same metal object become respectively anode and cathode in an electrolytic cell, and there is then a flow of electrons causing the metal at the anode to undergo oxidation, or corrosion. Millions of these cells may form over the surface of the object, and in a short time corrosion takes place freely and on a massive scale. This electrochemical reaction will continue until a stage of equilibrium is reached when the cells become polarized by a build-up of hydrogen at the metal surface. Alternatively, depending on such factors as the oxygen content and the pH (acidity) of the water, the metal may continue to corrode.

At this stage it is necessary to consider the role of bacteria in either destroying this equilibrium, in enabling the corrosion to continue, or even in promoting the corrosion at an accelerated rate. It is thought that various bacteria are responsible for depolarization of the cells, the bacteria using up the hydrogen and so enabling the reaction to continue (Uhlig, 1963, 83). It has also been assumed that this activity (cathodic depolarization) was solely associated with a group of anaerobic bacteria, the sulphate-reducers, which use the hydrogen to reduce sulphates to sulphides and to hydrogen sulphide. Although Iverson (1968) and others have now cast doubt on this assumption and suggested that other mechanisms may be involved, it remains clear that these bacteria (mainly *Desulfovibrio*) do play a very large part in the electrochemical corrosion of archaeological metal in the sea. Simply by producing hydrogen sulphide they convert iron, for example, to black iron sulphide, and when this reaction is combined with the electro-chemical reaction, a combination of ferrous hydroxides and sulphides is produced which is the major component of the corrosion found on much of the iron recovered from the sea. Ferrous hydroxide becomes the familiar reddish-brown rust, and ferrous sulphide is the black material that often produces evil-smelling hydrogen sulphide when it is first removed. This latter phenomenon is due to the presence of quantities of ferric chloride, formed by reaction with salt, which hydrolyse to liberate hydrochloric acid; this in its turn reacts with the sulphide to evolve hydrogen sulphide gas (Hodges, 1970). Sulphate-reducing bacteria are often found in association with submerged wrecks, and a sulphide-rich environment is indeed characteristic of many underwater sites.

A further complication is that those very reactions with which the bacteria so readily assist are responsible for an increase in the pH that upsets the equilibrium between dissolved calcium carbonate and dissolved carbon dioxide in the sea. The result of this is the precipitation of insoluble calcium carbonate and, by a related mechanism, of magnesium hydroxide. Here again is what may be part of an explanation for the formation of the mysterious concretions round metal objects; for it is likely that they consist largely not only of sulphides and hydroxides, but also of calcium carbonate and magnesium hydroxide. A visual examination of these concretions often shows that shells and numerous forms of dead animal and plant life became attached to and embedded in this matrix material. In addition sands and pebbles are accreted and so a very solid mass grows up as the metal corrodes; thus what is left is a naturally formed solid mould of an object that no longer exists. This need not always happen, however. Whilst at times the object itself disappears without trace, at other times a thinner concretion forms round an apparently intact object, and so it is often difficult to know in advance exactly what a concretion will contain. It would appear that when concretions do form they grow at a considerable rate, the whole process taking perhaps only twenty years. This is a subjective judgment, however, based on a few random experiments, and is in need of further investigation. It is clear also that these interdependent processes are subject to immense variation, as can be seen in the great differences between concretions, in their colour, texture and density. For instance, concretions found in northern waters tend to look much rustier and are less dense than those found in the Mediterranean.

A further indication that bacteria are partly responsible for the formation of concretions, is that many marine bacteria have a marked tendency to settle on solid surfaces (Zobell, 1946). These surfaces provide something of a foothold for the bacteria; they may themselves provide a good food supply and they serve to still the molecular action of the water in contact with them, thus keeping readily available the exoenzymes and the partially digested food that enable bacteria to function. Such surfaces are of course to be found on the remains of a wreck, and so we should not be surprised to find intense bacteriological activity at our sites.

There are further complications, however, for in addition to the great variety in marine surroundings that can affect the type of metal corrosion, there must also be considered the variations in the composition of the metal itself. It is by no means yet understood how these differences affect corrosion properties, but it has been suggested, for instance, that the phosphorous content of iron is important (Eriksen and Thegel, 1966). By making the iron more porous it is thought to enable corrosive solutions to penetrate more deeply. The carbon content of iron is also thought to be of some significance. Generally speaking, cast iron, with its higher carbon content, survives much better than wrought iron, the former often retaining its original shape, even though heavily corroded; the reason for this is that its higher content of graphite cannot corrode, but must remain as a rigid though fragile skeleton of graphite flakes within a matrix of iron corrosion products (Rogers, 1968, 84).

The effects of different conditions and compositions on other metals is equally problematical. Sometimes copper-based alloys and silver survive remarkably well; often not at all. Both can survive owing to cathodic protection. In this case, the electrochemically baser metal nearby, usually iron, corrodes in favour of the nobler metal and in this way protects it. On the other hand, silver can corrode entirely beneath a crust of silver sulphide, in a similar way to iron.

These few examples of the corrosion of metals serve to show how complex are the processes of decay and preservation in the sea.

The decay of wood must be equally complex. Exposed wood rarely survives. In the first place it is physically destroyed by the sea, especially where the wreck is quite shallow so that waves and currents can batter it to pieces in a short time. Upstanding timbers are eaten away by marine borers, in particular two groups of marine invertebrates, the ship-worm and the wood-gribble. The ship-worm (*Teredo*) is in fact a mollusc, related to the oyster and clam, whose average size is six to eight inches in length and half-an-inch in diameter; the holes it bores are of comparable size. A closely related group, the stone-borers (*Pholadidae*), can also attack rocks and stones such as the marble which was a not infrequent cargo of Mediterranean ships. It is important to remember that the work of the ship-worm may not always be obvious, for the interior of the wood can be completely riddled while externally it appears unchanged. This is because the young ship-worm makes a barely-visible hole when it first enters the wood, but grows to maturity and to greater proportions inside it. The wood-gribble, on the other hand, tends to confine itself to the surface, where its activities are more obvious.

Both of these creatures ingest wood, thereby destroying its cellulose content, and with the help of bacteria a large variety of marine fungi do the same; thus it is often only a short time before submerged wood is eaten and rotted away.

There is room for a close study of the way in which ships break up and the order in which timbers decay, for the exact shape of a broken ship can be very important to the marine excavator. Throckmorton (1965) has traced the stages in the destruction of an actual wooden vessel sunk in quiet waters on a muddy bottom.

There are many instances of wood having survived in an extraordinarily good condition for considerable periods, often for several millennia. Although dark brown and spongy on the surface, it often still white and hard towards the centre, suggesting that the destructive processes have been arrested at an early stage. It would seem that surviving timbers are invariably those that have been buried in mud or sand or beneath a heavy cargo. One of the reasons why the *Wasa* survived was that the low salt-content of the water did not favour the teredo (Barkman, 1965). In other cases we cannot be sure whether the simple act of burial is the sole cause of preservation. It has been suggested that the marine borers will only attack wood that has already to some extent been broken down by microorganisms and that they may even live on the fungi themselves. (Galler, 1969). As there seem to be neither microorganisms nor live marine borers at the centre of waterlogged archaeological wood, it may be that a study of such remains could cast some light on the relationship.

Clearly the study of the marine corrosion and decay of various materials in many different surroundings is extremely complicated and cannot be undertaken without the combined efforts of scientists from many disciplines. As an aid to this study I should like to suggest that the controlled collection of archaeological material from different marine environments could be extremely useful not only to the marine archaeologists and conservators, but also to oceanographers and corrosion scientists who can gain samples of known date that display the results of marine processes over known and very long periods, much longer than can be simulated in the laboratory. The information collected in this way could be supplemented by the results of controlled experiments in the deliberate submergence of modern disused boats and of typical archaeological materials.

3. CONSERVATION

Turning now to the kitchen art of conservation, we have first to go to the kitchen-garden where some of our ingredients are to be found, for it is on the seabed itself that conservation begins. It must be understood from the outset that the marine archaeologist in excavating a wreck is usually disturbing a delicate biochemical equilibrium, and unless great care is taken his destruction of this equilibrium can lead to disastrous consequences. Metal objects, when they do survive, will have reached a balance with their corrosion products and both the metal and the corrosion will have reached a balance with the sea. Wood, where it survives, will have decayed only up to a point and will have reached a water-content balance with the sea. To remove such materials into a different environment, such as air, can result in the original decay—physical, chemical and biological—picking up where it left off or, as is more usual, continuing at an even greater rate.

The main danger on the seabed during excavation is of physical damage. Wood, in particular, is likely to have a very soft surface that demands the utmost care in handling, even down to such elementary precautions as the removal of fins by the diver when swimming near it. In raising it to the surface every care must be taken not to abrade it by rough handling or by wear with ropes; for larger timbers, the only solution may be the use of a cradle in which the wood can be raised and transported and at a later stage lowered into a preservative bath. Such a cradle must be inert to sea-water and to polyethylene glycol, if that be the preservative, and it must be neither so heavy as to add appreciably to the weight of the wood (which of course becomes much greater as it emerges from the water) nor so light as to float in such a way that the cradle is turned upside-down.

It need hardly be said that wood must be kept wet. Yet so often a valiant attempt is made with only thin polythene sheeting, and the wood immediately dries out. A single sheet of thin polythene is permeable to water vapour to a surprising degree, and only several sheets of heavy-grade polythene, well sealed, can be really effective. Further, for temporary storage a fungicide must be added, preferably sprayed on in a very dilute solution. There are a number on the market but one of the most readily available and perhaps the safest fungicide is "Dowicide 100". This should not be relied upon, however, for over very long periods of storage renewed rotting may eventually take place, and for this reason the aim should always be to carry out full conservation *as soon as possible*.

If waterlogged wood is allowed to dry out, the evaporation of water from its degraded cellulose and lignin cells will cause the remaining cell walls to be collapsed by surface tension effects. As this happens the wood distorts, warps, cracks and powders beyond recognition. The aim in all treatments is to remove the water without producing these damaging effects and to replace it with some strengthening and consolidating material. One method is to replace the water with a liquid of low surface tension, such as ether, and to allow that to evaporate. It is an expensive and dangerous method, though it has been used successfully in the treatment of small objects. It is followed by impregnation with a suitable resin.

At present the almost universal treatment for waterlogged wood is the relatively slow and laborious process of replacing the water with polyethylene glycol, a synthetic water-soluble wax. It is an expensive chemical, and so also is the plant needed to use it. This normally takes the form of either a large heated immersion-bath with facilities for re-circulation of the solution (e.g. Christensen, 1970), or a series of sprays that operate at predetermined intervals (e.g. Barkman, 1965). Large timbers can take from a few months to over five years to treat and are in need of constant attention throughout the process. Despite the cost and time involved, the method has been used very successfully and with a high degree of reliability. The water slowly diffuses out of the wood and evaporates harmlessly to be simultaneously replaced by the wax which becomes solid at ordinary temperatures. Economies can be made by spreading the capital cost over a number of projects (i.e. by using the same tanks or sprays and by re-using the chemical), and provided that there is a steady supply of wood, large preserving centres can be run on a relatively economical basis. Failing such a centre or a generous benefactor, the best way to conserve waterlogged wood is to leave it on the sea-floor, untouched.

Mention should perhaps be made of a material that is now undergoing tests and that may one day supersede polyethylene glycol. The material is a de-watering agent having the trade name of Ferromede, and its application to the treatment of waterlogged wood was first investigated by O'Shea (1971). Its exact composition is not known, but it works simply by removing the water from the wood in such a way that the cell walls do not collapse. Wet wood is immersed in the liquid for a number of weeks, after which it is removed and allowed to drain, and is then impregnated under vacuum with a consolidant of one's choosing. No complicated heating, pumping or spraying devices are called for, nor any control of specific gravity. I should emphasize that its use is still at the experimental stage, but if it succeeds it does offer considerable hope for a much cheaper and easier method of treating wet wood. It should also be valuable in the treatment of waterlogged leather.[1]

When concreted metal objects are recovered from the sea, it is a natural temptation to chisel away the outer crust in order to examine as quickly as possible the objects within. This is a temptation that must be firmly resisted, unless it is first known of what metal the object is made and what its condition is. Bronze and copper objects appear to survive reasonably well, often intact beneath their encrustation, so that their careful removal can cause no harm provided that the objects are immediately washed in fresh running water.

Concretions of iron objects, on the other hand, can contain anything from sound iron to nothing at all, and extreme caution is called for before attempting to open such concretions. Ideally, as a first stage, all concretions should be subjected to examination by X-radiography. A white image at the centre will suggest solid metal, whereas a black image will suggest a void. Obviously, few marine excavators are likely to have X-ray apparatus readily to hand, but a small magnetic compass might serve to give just as good an answer. Only if the presence of solid iron is confirmed should any attempt be made to open the concretion, and even then the opening should be followed by washing in fresh running water. Unless this is done, the ferric chloride that is formed will turn into hydrochloric acid that will in turn attack the sulphide and the iron. This may not happen, but if it does the results can be quickly seen and are often dramatic. Ferric chloride is itself a serious source of instability. To begin with, it will cause cracks to open up, and then the whole outer surface may fall away. Under the peeling layer the corrosion processes continue, and after a few years the object crumbles to a pile of rusty powder. Under adverse conditions rusting can take place at such a rate that great heat is generated, and the object can disintegrate with explosive violence. Unfortunately we do not yet know enough about the corrosion processes to be able to distinguish relatively stable iron from unstable. Having removed the iron and washed it one should now take the greatest care in handling it, especially if it is thought to be cast, since it may in reality be no more than a mass of graphite held together by rust.

If solid iron is present, the task is then to stabilize it. There are at least two possible approaches. One is reduction by electrolysis, a method which, while best carried

[1] Since this paper was read McKerell & Roger's (1971) experiments with Ferromede have suggested that it may not always be successful. The exact procedures are not mentioned, but the findings give reason for caution when using the chemical for the treatment of birch or oak. The use of Ferromede for the treatment of leather has not yet been called into question. See now also McKerrell & Oddy, 1972, and for details of a more recent and tested process, especially suitable for oak heartwood, McKerrell, Roger & Varsanyi, 1972.

Figure 2. Stages in taking a cast from a concretion: (a) the concretion as found; (b) its two halves after slicing; (c) the finished cast—a round-headed nail.

out under laboratory conditions by experts, can be performed in roughly-made apparatus by the archaeologist himself. The other is reduction by heating or annealing in a furnace in the presence of hydrogen or carbon monoxide, a process fraught with dangers and never to be attempted outside carefully controlled laboratory conditions.

One important disadvantage of the annealing techniques of reduction is that the high temperatures used result in a change in the microstructure of the metal, and this can severely prejudice any metallographic examination that may have to be made subsequently. This is typical of the difficulties that have to be met during all conservation treatments, for there is no material excavated that cannot now or in the future be made to reveal something of possible archaeological significance by scientific techniques. Microscopic study, for instance, can now lead to the identification of woods and of textile fibres and other organic remains, to the elucidation of the manufacturing techniques of metal artefacts, and to the identification of minerals in pottery and perhaps conclusions about its origins. A multitude of analytical techniques enable nearly all materials to be identified by their composition. With the accumulation of this sort of data each subsequent analysis becomes of increasing significance to the archaeologist, and it is therefore in his interest to ensure that his finds are so conserved as not to alter them physically or chemically in any way. From this point of view, then, furnace reduction of iron is not to be generally recommended. However, it should be said that in the right hands, and provided that a technical examination is made beforehand, it can be of value and has been used most successfully on the ironwork from the warship *Wasa* (Barkman, 1965).

Electrolysis is a simple treatment, requiring only a vessel of sufficient size, steel electrodes, a rectifier and a transformer and an electrolyte of 5 % sodium carbonate. The object is made the cathode and a current is passed for a period of anything from two weeks upwards. The larger the object the bigger the vessel needed, the higher the total current and the longer the period of reduction required (for details see Plenderleith & Werner, 1971).

If it is suspected or established that a concretion is hollow, it will be obvious that the destruction of the outer crust would mean the loss of a potentially useful natural mould. From such moulds Katsev and van Doorninck (1966) have shown that casts can be taken in a synthetic material and replicas of the original objects produced. Casts so made can be accurate in every detail, though the nature of this technique demands that they be in some pliable material such as rubber (Fig. 2). However, there is no reason why solid casts should not in turn be made of the rubber casts, or a solid-setting material used in the first place in cases where the concretion can be sacrificed in order to remove the cast.

The stabilization of bronze is now a relatively simple matter, made easier by the use of benzotriazole, an organic chemical that complexes with copper and its corrosion products (Madsen, 1967). It can be used either as a short-term stabilizer by impregnating it into the wrapping material used on site, or in the laboratory to provide stability for many years.

Other metals, if they survive, can often be treated by adaptations of established techniques. Silver objects that survive only as silver sulphide encrustations, for instance, can be treated as moulds for casting, in the same way as iron concretions.

4. CONCLUSION

I have tried to make clear first the problems in understanding the processes of marine decay, and secondly the care that needs to be taken in prescribing conservation techniques. First-aid treatments that the archaeologist and his assistants can carry out on site do exist, but they are only short-term remedies. Long-lasting cures and the safe treatment of unstable and fragile material demand the expert advice of a conservator. The marine archaeologist may be fortunate in having a resident conservator. If not, then he will have to rely on the services of local museums who may or may not be willing to help. Therefore, before he embarks on any excavation that may result in the removal of artefacts from the sea, it is in the interest of the archaeologist to ensure that there will be adequate facilities and staff to treat his material in a relatively short time. Long delays can only result in the deterioration of finds. If there is no chance of early expert assistance, then the best course might well be not to excavate. This is cold comfort, but until there are available more conservation facilities and conservators this solution must remain one of the most important methods of conservation.

REFERENCES

Barkman, L. 1965 *The Preservation of the Wasa* (Wasastudier 5), 19 pp., Stockholm.

Christensen, B. B. 1970 Developments in the treatment of waterlogged wood in the National Museum of Denmark during the years 1962–69. *Reprints of the Contributions to the New York Conference of Conservation of Stone and Wooden Objects, 1970,* Vol. 2 ("Conservation of Wooden Objects"), 27–44. International Institute for Conservation, London.

Dowman, E. A. 1970 *Conservation in Field Archaeology*, 170 pp. London.

Eriksen, E. & Thegel, S. 1966 *Conservation of Iron Recovered from the Sea*, 135 pp. Copenhagen.

Galler, S. R. 1969 Boring and Fouling, *in* Myers, J. J. (ed.) *Handbook of Ocean and Underwater Engineering*, Section 7 ("Materials and Testing"), 12–19. New York.

Hodges, H. W. M. 1970 Treatment of iron recovered from the sea. *C.N.A. Newsletter*, **4**, 48–50.

Iverson, W. P. 1968 Mechanisms of microbial corrosion, *in* Walters, A. H. & Elphick, J. J. (ed.) *Biodeterioration of Materials: microbiological and allied aspects*, 740 pp. Elsevier.

Katsev, M. L. & van Doorninck, F. H. Jr. 1966 Replicas of iron tools from a Byzantine shipwreck. *Stud. Conserv.* **11**, No. 3, 133–41.

Madsen, H. Brinch 1967 A preliminary note on the use of benzotriazole for stabilising bronze objects. *Stud.Conserv.* **12**, No. 4, 163–7.

McKerrell, H. & Roger, E. 1971 Some problems and experimental evaluation of conserved waterlogged oak. Duplicated notes, Int. Inst. Conservation, U.K. Group, London.

McKerrell, H. & Oddy, W. A. 1972 The Conservation of waterlogged wood using dewatering fluids: an evaluation. *Museums J.* **71**, No. 4, 165–7.

McKerrell, H., Roger, E. & Varsanyi, A. 1972 The acetone/rosin method for conservation of waterlogged wood. *Stud. Conserv.* **17**, No. 3, 111–25.

Oddy, W. A. & Hughes, M. J. 1970 The stabilisation of "active" bronze and iron antiquities by the use of sodium sesquicarbonate. *Stud.Conserv.* **15**, No. 3, 183–9.

Oddy, W. A. & Van Geersdaele, P. C. 1972 The Recovery of the Graveney Boat. *Stud. Conserv.* **17**, No. 1, 30–8.

O'Shea, C. 1971 The use of dewatering fluids in the conservation of waterlogged wood and leather. *Museums J.* **71**, No. 2, 71–2.

Plenderleith, H. J. & Werner, A. E. A. 1971 *The Conservation of Antiquities and Works of Art*, 394 pp. London.

Rees-Jones, S. G. 1972 Some aspects of the conservation of iron objects from the sea. *Stud. Conserv.* **17**, No. 1, 39–43.

Rogers, T. H. 1968 *Marine Corrosion*, 307 pp. London.

Thomson, G. 1966 Conservation science—the next stage. *Museums J.* **65**, No. 3, 266–70.

Throckmorton, P. 1965 Wrecks at Methone. *Mariner's Mirror*, **51**, 305–20.

Uhlig, H. H. 1963 *Corrosion and Corrosion Control*, 371 pp. New York.

Zobell, C. E., 1946 *Marine Microbiology: a Monograph on Hydrobacteriology*, 240 pp. Waltham.

Discussion

Throckmorton How does Ferromede work?
Leigh This organic chemical simply eliminates water from the cells of the wood and causes it to sink to the bottom of the vessel where it can be drained off. When the wood is removed the Ferromede evaporates harmlessly. Full details will be found in O'Shea's article (1971). There is no doubt that it is cheaper than polyethylene glycol, but the total cost of the Ferromede and a suitable consolidant may almost equal it. On the other hand, processing would not be so expensive.
Throckmorton Perhaps you wouldn't need a consolidant.
Leigh That is a possibility, but although the wood remained solid it would become very light and brittle.

Anon. How does one use benzotriazole for bronze, and what is its visible effect on the metal?
Leigh There is no visible effect, as it does not change colours or remove corrosion or patina. However, I would refer you to the article by Madsen (1967). It is commonly used as a solution in methylated spirit and impregnated under vacuum. One is always hesitant to recommend easy techniques that can be used blindly, but I do feel that benzotriazole is safe to use at least until the bronze can be taken to a laboratory.
Richards When one is dealing with ferrous and non-ferrous metals, for what period of time should they be immersed?
Leigh If you are referring to electrolytic treatment, this will partly depend on the size of the object. Really large objects may need six months or a year, but it is not easy to predict. One should always refer to Plenderleith and Werner's book (1971).

Green How would Ferromede deal with large timbers?
Leigh It certainly works with small timbers, but it has not yet been tried on large timbers. This for the moment is its major drawback.

Throckmorton When Miss Taylor, George Bass and I worked at Gelidonya, we asked Dr. Plenderleith what should be done with heavily concreted material. His advice was, in short, "Hit it with a hammer". I remember that at the time I was bitterly disappointed that there was no magic way of delicately removing concretion but only this, and that I felt quite angry at Dr. Plenderleith for not understanding the problem. I owe him a large apology, because subsequent experience shows that he was dead right. It seems that the concretion undergoes a chemical change if allowed to dry out, and becomes much harder. At Pelagos, in 1970, when we worked on a twelfth-century A.D. ship, with a cargo of Graffito Ware, we found that the only plates which could be cleaned of their concretion were those that were kept wet, and then cleaned by hand with dental tools. Most of the surviving plates in good condition were saved because I cleaned them while hanging on the decompression stop. Some 500–600 others, which were allowed to dry in the sun, uncleaned, are now, I understand, impossible to clean manually, without destroying the glaze. The same applies to copper and bronze: objects can be cleaned manually so long as they are never allowed to dry. It also seems that bronze disease attacks very rapidly if bronze is not cleaned of this concretion. In countries where material is going to be locked up in a museum store, it seems desirable to clean everything at once.

Leigh I agree, but you must be sure that the metal is copper or bronze.

Throckmorton If it is iron under the concretion it will keep for ever.

Leigh Only if the iron has disappeared. But what experience have we with solid iron?

Wignall We have experienced a great deal of difficulty with artifacts on the west coast of Ireland. We learned that there were no conservation facilities anywhere in Eire. We tried Peterson's system of using caustic soda buff with a mass of zinc, and the result was disastrous. We sought the advice of Stephen Rees-Jones of Belfast University, who was treating the *Girona* artifacts with vacuum impregnation, and we built two vacuum-chambers. Rees-Jones wanted six months' leaching in distilled water, but for lack of money we had to use fresh water. We took silver nitrate tests every few days until no salt was left. The iron shot was put into a vacuum-chamber, and in 10% solution of phosphoric acid. Shot which we did not treat disintegrated. Shot which had the vacuum treatment has shown no signs of disintegration, except for a ball sent to the British Steel Corporation for analysis. Scientists drilled two small holes, and the ball started to disintegrate within a fortnight; therefore phosphoric acid had not got into the centre of the ball. Any advice on wood and metal conservation beyond what we received from Rees-Jones would be most welcome.[1]

Leigh Clearly these are the right lines to work on, but unfortunately any sort of soaking can be a long process.

Wignall Vacuum impregnation is very quick. I should like to raise another query from our work on the *Santa Maria de la Rosa*. Her iron shot was very badly disintegrated, having lost density and weight. Samples were analysed by the Royal Armaments Research and Development Establishment, who for comparison also analysed samples of shot supplied by us from the *Gran Grifon*. Although the two ships sank only a few days apart, there is a remarkable difference in the quality of the shot. That from the *Gran Grifon* was in far better condition: it looked like steel and not iron; it could cut plate glass, and withstood a compression test of 6 tons. The *Santa Maria* was loaded on the coast of Spain, while the *Gran Grifon* may have loaded her shot in Rostock. But I still do not understand why one lot of shot has deteriorated badly and the other has not, when both have been under the sea for over 380 years.

Leigh I do not know, but there could be a number of reasons. For instance, sulphur or phosphorus surrounding the shot might affect it.

Fenwick I am not speaking as a conservationist. However, the sodium sesquicarbonate method for stabilizing iron should be mentioned (Oddy & Hughes, 1970). It is a cheap and straightforward method which could be used in the field. In the British Museum sodium sesquicarbonate is being used on some completely corroded ironwork which has encrustations on it which we dare not remove.

[1] See now, for a full description of these techniques, Rees-Jones, 1972.

Leigh Sodium sesquicarbonate can be very useful. I had not mentioned it, but it can often be used for stabilizing iron in the way benzotriazole is used for bronze.

Richards Is there any danger in handling badly corroded lead objects? Persons removing any encrustation must beware of lead poisoning.
Leigh Certainly there is that danger. The only badly corroded lead I have seen was on Throckmorton's wreck off Taranto. It was little more than black mud with some lead inside it, the black mud being lead sulphide; but we had no poisoning trouble then.
Swiny We did have trouble on the Kyrenia ship with the vast amount of lead sheathing. It is believed that Miss Talbot, the conservator, and myself suffered mild lead poisoning. We found that we had more trouble when we were working with polyethylene glycol and then with the lead. A substance within PEG is also used in ladies' hand creams to pass the cream into the skin. One must be very careful to wear rubber gloves or to wash one's hands very well. The same applies when one is working with PEG and then with "Dowicide A".
Richards Lead objects which have been found must be left for the conservation experts in a museum to clean up and remove the encrustation. Bad removal of encrustation destroyed seals at Kyrenia.
Leigh Whenever one removes encrustation from old iron one runs the risk of removing the outer $\frac{1}{4}$-inch of the metal also. But this loss is almost inevitable, as that layer has already corroded away.
Fenwick It is possible to do something about preserving designs on the badly corroded surface of lead. Some years ago I worked under Organ's direction on the treatment of leaden bullae in the British Museum (Organ, R. M. The Consolidation of Fragile Metallic Objects, *in* Thomson, G. 1963 *Recent Advances in Conservation*, 131). Many were in a terrible state. We experimented with methods of recovering the impressions which existed only in the powdery lead carbonate surface layer. By cathodically reducing the bullae at a very low current density it was possible to consolidate this outer layer, but the long-term conservation prospects are rather poor. We tried various things, including mounting the bullae in acrylic pellets, to keep the air from them. This worked rather well, but we had to control the pressure carefully because of the low melting-point of lead.

Green Would you comment on the storing of material recovered from the sea? Would you store it in the sea or in fresh water? In general, things left in the air without drying will corrode. Would a simple solution be to store things in sea-water or will you get deterioration?
Leigh If you are talking of wood the answer seems to be no. Fresh or sea-water alone will not do, in the long term at least. Over shorter periods, of up to say six months, fresh water with fungicide should be perfectly safe. It is of no use, however, to store wood on the seabed, though perhaps if the wood were re-placed beneath the sand it might survive. This needs investigation.
Green A good idea would be to seal wood in polythene bags—possibly also leaving it under the sand for protection.
Leigh As for metal objects, simple storage in fresh water cannot be a complete answer because there is a high oxygen-content in fresh water, which is why distilled water is

to be preferred. Even distilled water absorbs oxygen from the air and therefore becomes a corrosive medium. Boiled water would be better than fresh, and deep water better than shallow.

Swiny One must keep material away from light, and cover containers. Light breeds organisms.

Wignall Is there any treatment for large ferrous objects too large to put in a bath? We inadvisably raised two anchors in 1968. We thought we had just to ring University College, Dublin, and they would come and take them away; these two anchors are just rotting away in Dublin on the quayside.

Swiny The only temporary measure is to leave material in fresh running water.

Bax Is it possible for the deterioration of wreck to be determined by the oxygen-content of the water? Some water on the sea-floor appears to be nearly stagnant, and it seems possible that this will affect the rate at which iron deteriorates.

Leigh I think it would.

Fenwick We were certainly depressed at the prospect of conserving the Graveney Boat. It is oak in the worst condition from that point of view, being well-preserved in appearance but structurally very weak. However, after a recent trip to the *Wasa*, Andrew Oddy of the British Museum Research Laboratory, who is in charge of the conservation of the boat, seems more optimistic. Apparently, after running into difficulties with PEG there, they had to think again and do a series of controlled tests. I gather that they are now using a different grade—PEG 1500 I think—and use very weak solutions over a long initial period to get penetration. At the moment certainly there is no alternative to PEG for the Graveney Boat.[1]

McKee Gerry Munday brought up a gun of about 1800 in Bracklesham Bay—a dead area, with very little oxygen. This gun had been coated in mud, and when cleaned, was perfect. The mud seal had provided temporary protection on the seabed.

Leigh An oxygen-free mud is the ideal surrounding for many of the bacteria, but in this particular case there was clearly some other protective action.

Frost I remember a paper published in the 1950s on the "teneur d'oxygène dans le fond marin", which showed that the amount of oxygen did not decrease in direct proportion to the depth of burial below the seabed.[2] It would seem important to continue such tests and make comparative studies of the chemical conditions on different wrecks. It has, for instance, been observed that certain objects embedded in *Poseidonia mattes* are exceptionally well preserved; I have heard it described as "tannery conditions". Are there any recent studies on this?

Leigh Not to my knowledge.

Frost Is this not where we should start? You should tell us to bring back samples to study, and tell us how they should be taken.

Leigh I agree. That is the first vital step. But the next problem is: to whom should we send the samples?

Throckmorton I am working as consultant on man-made junk in the sea for the Sea Probe Project. Sea Probe is a large ship with a thing like an oil-derrick in its middle, from which a pipe hangs to the bottom. The working-head has grabs, televisions and

[1] Oddy & Van Geersdaele, 1972.

[2] Brouardel, J. & Vernet, J. Variations en mer de la teneur en oxygène dissous au proche voisinage des sédiments. *Bull. Inst. Océanographique de Monaco*, **3**, 27 January 1958.

so forth, which can be controlled by water-jets. This is the most advanced deep-sea salvage-vehicle ever built. It can lift perhaps 200 tons, from perhaps 20,000 feet. Ocean Science and Engineering, of Long Beach, California, the designers of Sea Probe, have a simple television and grab-sled which has been used for recovery of crashed aircraft in California. It is interesting that they have found, within a few miles of each other, World War II aircraft that were completely corroded to junk, and identical aircraft of the same type and the same date, which were in good condition. When the two-man submersible *Alvin* sank in the Atlantic a couple of years ago, in very deep water, and was recovered about 9 months later, the sandwiches that the crew had stored on board before the boat slipped off her sling and dived without them, were still edible. So it seems certain that conditions change, and that no place on the sea bottom is necessarily chemically similar to any other place.

Swiny I have just received an encouraging report from Prof. Katsev on the conservation of the Kyrenia ship. From October 1969 to June 1970 selected samples from the Kyrenia ship were immersed in solutions of PEG in a programme of experiments that varied these factors: the molecular weight of PEG (1,000 to 4,000), the concentration of the solution (30 to 100 %), temperature of solution (20 to 80°C), and the time of immersion (6 weeks to 6 months). The first results were discouraging. After treatment with PEG 1500, with a concentration increasing to 30 %, and upon drying, the wood failed to retain dimensional stability. Miss Talbot, the conservator, began to increase the concentration markedly and thereby obtained more encouraging results. By June she had also found that by using PEG 4000, the successful treatment for all the Kyrenia timbers could be assured (see Appendix).

Kennedy As a conservator I feel that the basic reason why most treatments fail is that they are not carried out for long enough, for example the leaching process. The time factor is vital. Sometimes two years or more is necessary, and the size of the object is not necessarily the governing factor. There is no substitute for the presence on the site of a conservator with experience *outside* the laboratory; there are few who are able to make the essential assessments and to adapt techniques to the "non-laboratory" situation.

Throckmorton There is no doubt that the general principle is "It is only all right to raise material if you know how to conserve it". Everyone must make proper arrangements for conservation before starting operations. Only when conservation facilities are actually available should one lift anything out of the water.

APPENDIX

Comments by Miss Frances Talbot on the Kyrenia ship conservation

With an estimated 3.5 m^3 of predominantly pine to treat the task is not so formidable as that of the warship *Wasa*, 900 m^3 of hardwood, oak.

All the numbered pieces of the hull are being drawn on a 1 : 1 scale, both as a guide to the success of the treatment in maintaining the dimensions of the ship, and so that a lot of the preparatory work of the reconstruction can be done on paper.

The conversion of soft waterlogged timbers to hard sound wood involves immersing the wood in a thermostatically controlled solution of polyethylene glycol by adding

PEG and controlling the evaporation rate. The rise in concentration must be at a rate that will not overstress the wood, since too fast a penetration can cause as much warping as undertreating the wood. The rate of increase and the length of the treatment depends on the ability of the wood to assimilate the consolidant, and the percentage of consolidant necessary to prevent shrinkage during the final stages of the treatment is variable.

Summary of our treatment:

Immersion %	30	for	1 week
Increasing %	30–45	over	10 weeks
Rest			1 week
Increasing %	45–60	over	5 weeks
Rest			1 week
Increasing %	60–75	over	3 weeks
Rest			1 week
Increasing %	75–90	over	2 weeks
Total treatment			24 weeks, i.e. 6 months

TEMPERATURE KEPT CONSTANTLY AT 60°C

Removal from treatment-tank, air drying in a high RH, and cleaning up of the surface excess, with hot air, and hot sponges (almost dry, well-squeezed of water).

This is a rather lengthy process, but the equipment required is minimal, and not over-expensive to install. And hopefully, if the treatment with PEG fails at any stage it is easily stopped and reversed.

Halieis at Porto Cheli

by

M. H. JAMESON

ON THE south side of the Saronic Gulf, across from Athens and Attica, stretches the hilly peninsula of the Argolid, the Argolic "Akte" of antiquity. The southern tip of the peninsula, well defined below a line of schist and limestone mountains, consists of an area of low conglomerate hills, much indented by the sea, which in fact has cut off a number of islands, of which one of the largest is Spetsai. From at least the eighth century B.C. to around 300 B.C. this area had as its center the town of Halieis, which lay on the south, that is, the seaward side of an excellent natural harbor, on the north side of which the village of Porto Cheli is now located. The southern and eastern sides of the harbor have been subject to a marked rise in sea level, so that the edge of the classical town is now submerged to a depth of over 2 m. The sea has, in effect, been excavating the margins of Halieis. Changes in sea level for the south-east Peloponnese have been discussed by N. C. Flemming (1968) with specific reference to the site of Halieis.

The University of Pennsylvania began the excavation of Halieis in 1962 and continued since 1965 and 1966, with an interruption only in 1969 (Jameson, 1969). The 1965 season saw the first attempts to examine and record the northern submerged portions of the city. Swimmers using mask and snorkel located most of the visible remains, and measured them by triangulation and with the help of surveyors on land. The results left a conspicuous gap in the middle, of some 150 m (Ervin, 1967). In addition, a reef at the north-eastern point of the classical city walls was cleared by hand and proved to be the foundations of a calidarium of a late Roman establishment, built on the foundations of a large circular tower and gate of the classical period, which can be seen in an aerial photograph taken by a camera suspended from a balloon (Jameson, 1969, Pl. 90).

A precise date for this late Roman construction has yet to be found, but activity as late as the sixth century A.D. further west in the submerged area suggests that up to that time the water did not yet threaten a bath-house along the shore.

In 1967 and 1968 work was resumed on the submerged remains in the town site, by which time Indiana University had joined Pennsylvania in the study of the area. To solve the puzzle of the gap in the middle of our plan we probed systematically under the mud by means of metal-tipped surveyors' poles along lines fixed at measured intervals. We were able to determine the presence of a second tower to the west of the bath and the gate, a first tower having been clearly visible in 1965 (see Fig. 1). Further west the walls turned slightly away from shore and seemed to end in a larger tower. At the same time Julian and Eunice Whittlesey were trying out their balloon-borne camera for shallow-water photography. Their pictures detected a larger circular tower, constructed of

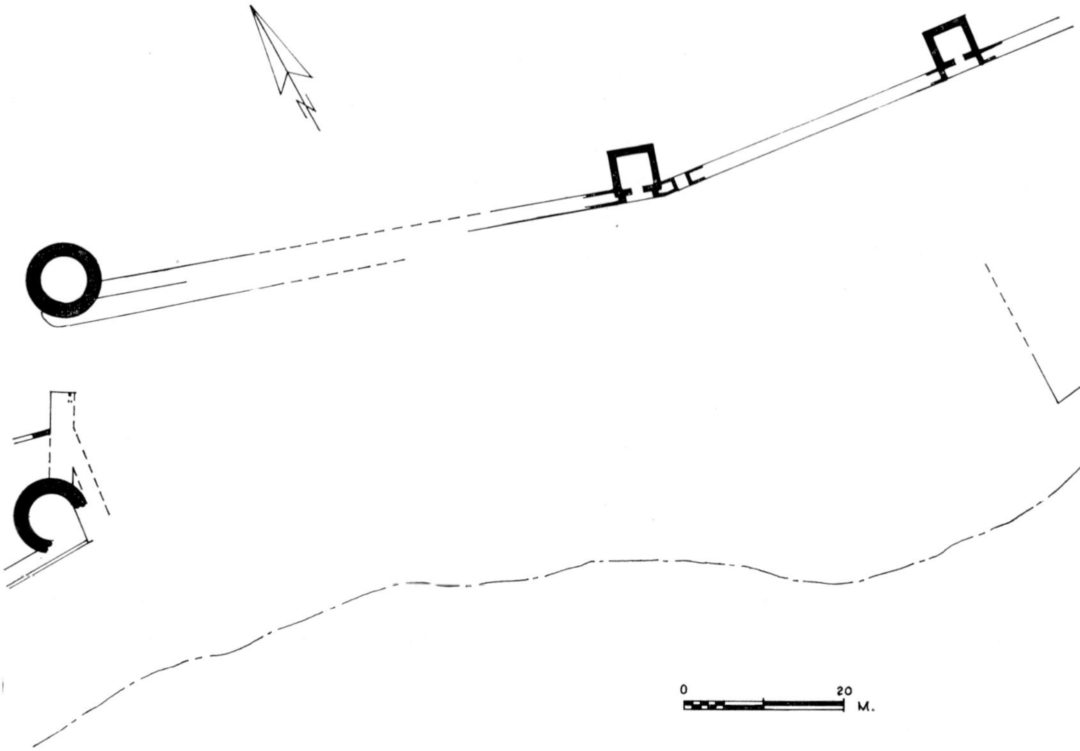

Figure 1. Plan of the enclosed harbor at Halieis after the excavations of 1968.

headers and stretchers, 20 m south (that is, inshore) from the last construction found by probing. Figure 2 shows the southern tower (below and to the left of the white control line from the balloon) and the first blocks of the north tower as they are being cleared. In Figure 3, the circumference of the north tower has been cleared and we can see the beginning of the city wall tied into, and so contemporary with, the tower.

At this point something should be said of the techniques which we were using. A tethered balloon of 3 m diameter, filled with hydrogen, suspended a camera (Graflex in 1967–68, Hasselblad in 1970), which was balanced on a very sensitive gimbal. Shutter release and film advance (after 1967) were activated by radio controls. The great advantage of balloon-borne photography is that it permits a perspective of remains in shallow water, both before and after excavation, which is not available to the swimmer or diver. Unknown remains have been detected and much more accurate and detailed surveying and recording have been done. But for good results the water must be calm and clear, and this at Porto Cheli means working as near dawn as possible, which has the added advantage of allowing a night's interval after disturbance by archaeologists and before they begin the new day's work. Even so, wind conditions are often a problem (see Jameson, 1969, 332–3; Whittlesey, 1969).

In 1967 excavation consisted mostly of clearing superficial mud and rubble with a stream of water from a pump mounted on a boat through an adjustable high-pressure

Figure 2. The south tower (bottom) revealed by balloon photograph, 1967. Excavation of the north tower is in progress.

nozzle (manufactured by Galeazzi of La Spezia). The method proved too violent and indiscriminate, and it caused serious clouding in the shallow, muddy and virtually currentless waters. An air-lift is not practical at these depths. In 1968 a portable dredging system, used by prospectors panning for gold, was tried at Halieis, as well as at Kenchreai by Dr. Joseph Shaw, and was very effective with the pump mounted either on a boat or on a platform. A tube or pipe joins at an angle the hose carrying the stream of water from the pump. Suction along this second tube draws whatever is fed into it or simply clears the water in the diver's vicinity. In our efforts in 1968, discharge was too close to

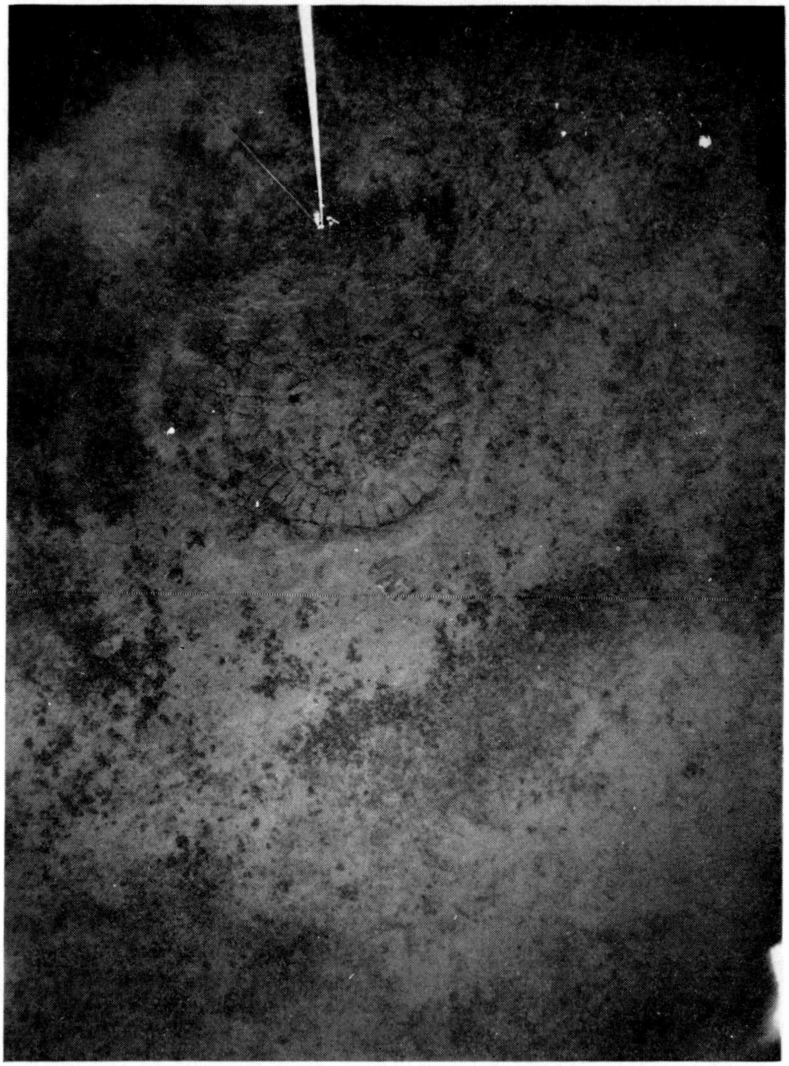

Figure 3. The north tower after excavation.

the working area and visibility was often poor. In 1970 a system of metal irrigation pipes carried the discharge far enough away not to interfere seriously (two dredges with pipes can be seen in Figure 7). Divers can excavate by hand or with small picks and knives, and can record as they excavate. Accurate excavation is possible, but it is evident that analysis of stratigraphy depends on examination of finds after excavation rather than on the color of soil or its feel during excavation.

We can now return to the problem of the two circular towers. Excavation showed that the inshore half of the space between them was occupied by a heavy foundation ending in a number of cuttings at its tip (Fig. 4). But it ends neatly, and the northern half of the space (some 7 m) is devoid of structures, so that there is no reason to suspect robbing.

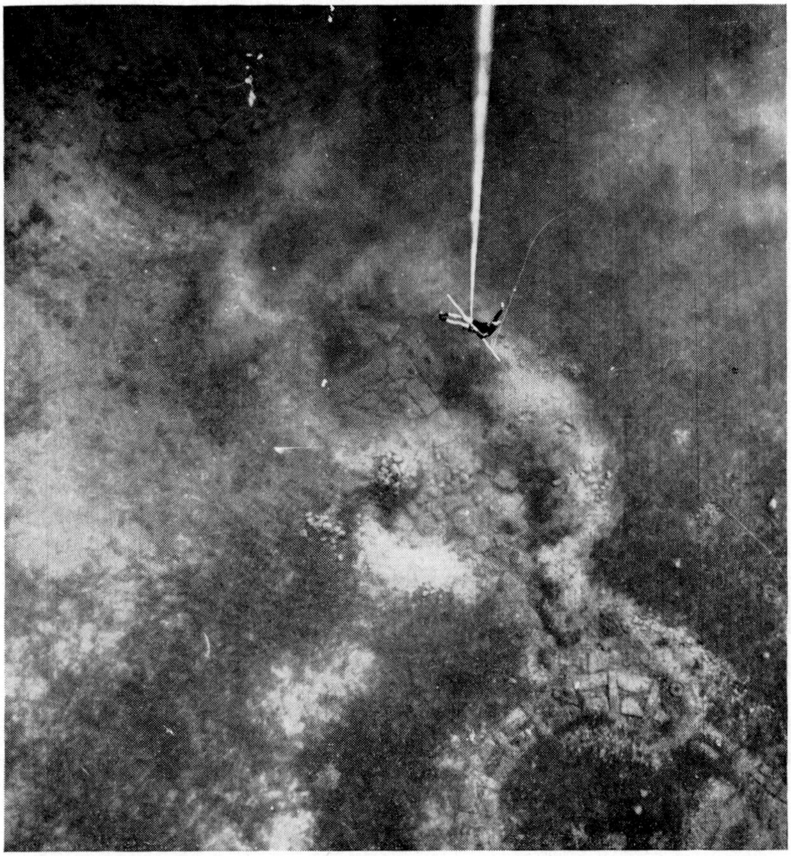

Figure 4. Foundations constricting the passage between the two towers, with cuttings for boom.

An area within the walls to the east (roughly 100 m east–west by 50 m north–south) was trenched extensively, and in contrast to all other areas within the walls, whether or not submerged, yielded no evidence of construction of any date. We believe the explanation is that we have here a constricted entrance to a small enclosed harbor. The cuttings we explain as intended for a boom to close the harbor entrance (see reconstruction in Jameson, 1969, 336). A retaining wall projecting at right angles, on the outside, would have served to prevent silting of the entrance and protect the embankment below the city walls.

It s perhaps worth noting that one of the few historical events reported in the town's life was the capture of Halieis in the fifth century B.C. by a Spartan with a merchant ship filled with troops (Herodotus, VII. 137). Did he slip innocently into the enclosed harbor through this passage, perhaps before the construction of the boom? The fortifications along the sea resemble those of the first half of the fourth century B.C. on the town's acropolis, and their latest form may be of that date.

In 1967 heavy foundations were pointed out to us on the north-east side of the bay, well outside of the town walls. A balloon photograph confirmed the existence of extensive

Figure 5. Shrine and stoa in the north-east of Porto Cheli harbor.

remains lying 10–40 m offshore at an average depth of 1.5 m (Jameson, 1969, Pl. 92 and Fig. 8, p. 339). This past season (1970) our attention was concentrated on this area. Two of the improved dredge systems were used, with a pump and compressor mounted on a platform offshore, devised and constructed of scaffolding and boards by our mechanic, Alfred Kann. Empty oil barrels were used to change its position as needed (see the bottom of Fig. 5).

The first step was the establishment of a grid system, tied to the system for the town site and the detailed Greek maps of the area. Though it proved impractical to read markers on shore from the sea they were indispensable for final mapping. Next, the superficial vegetation, mud and rubble was removed from the walls of three sizable structures on the north side of the complex (Fig. 6). The largest building, 7.50 by 29 m, in the center, has only the lowest line of foundations preserved (Fig. 5). They are in rather rough work on three sides, but consist of handsome ashlar blocks on the long, west side. Thus, the building had the shape of a stoa, with a colonnade facing west. However, immediately to the west, that is, towards the ancient shoreline, lies another long building (4.50 by 28 m) with a slightly different orientation. It lies so close to the colonnade of the stoa (as little as 1.50 m away) that it can not have been contemporary with it. Finds from its floor level show that it was used as early as the second quarter of the seventh century B.C. and was probably destroyed near the middle of the fifth

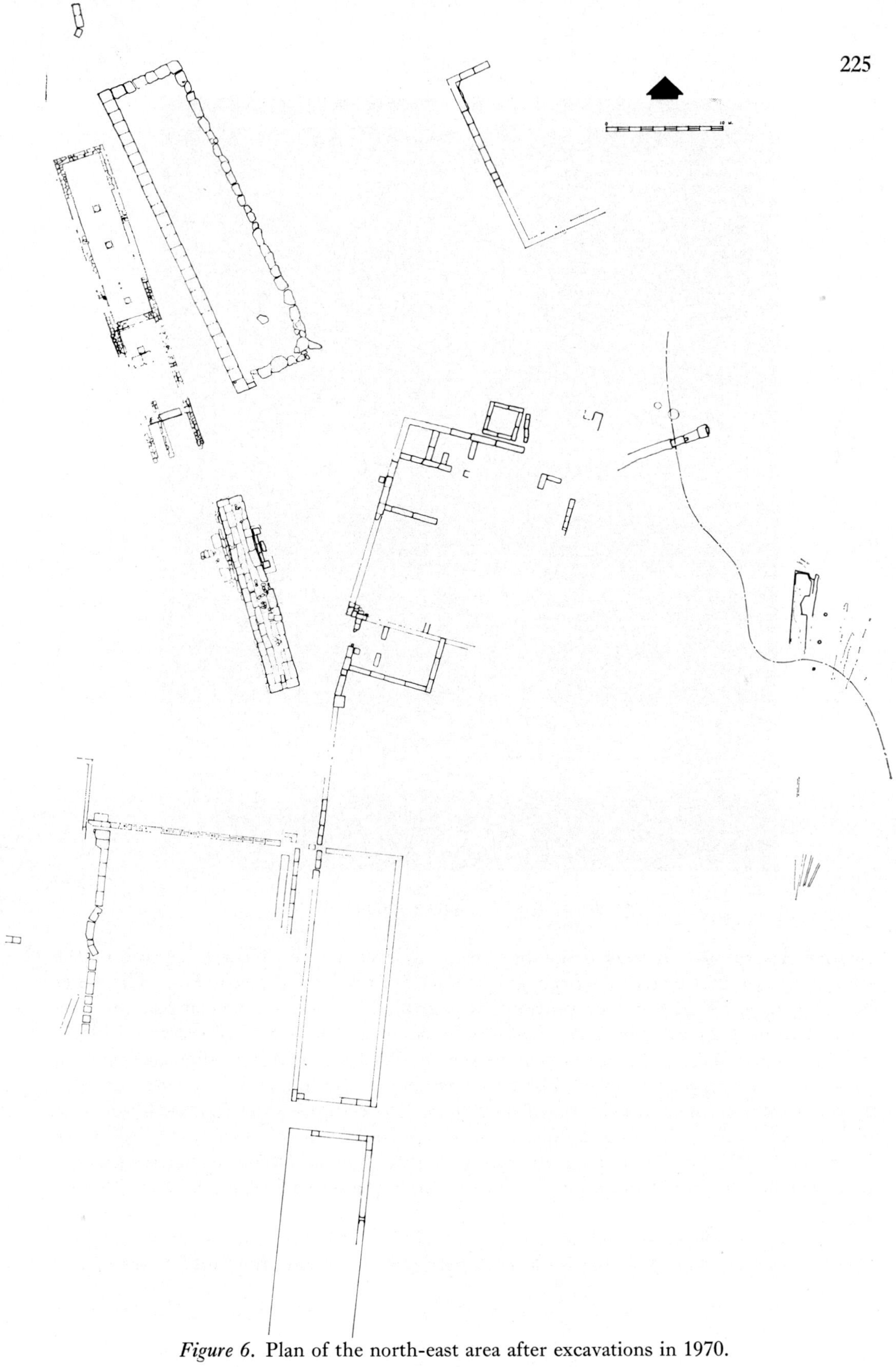

Figure 6. Plan of the north-east area after excavations in 1970.

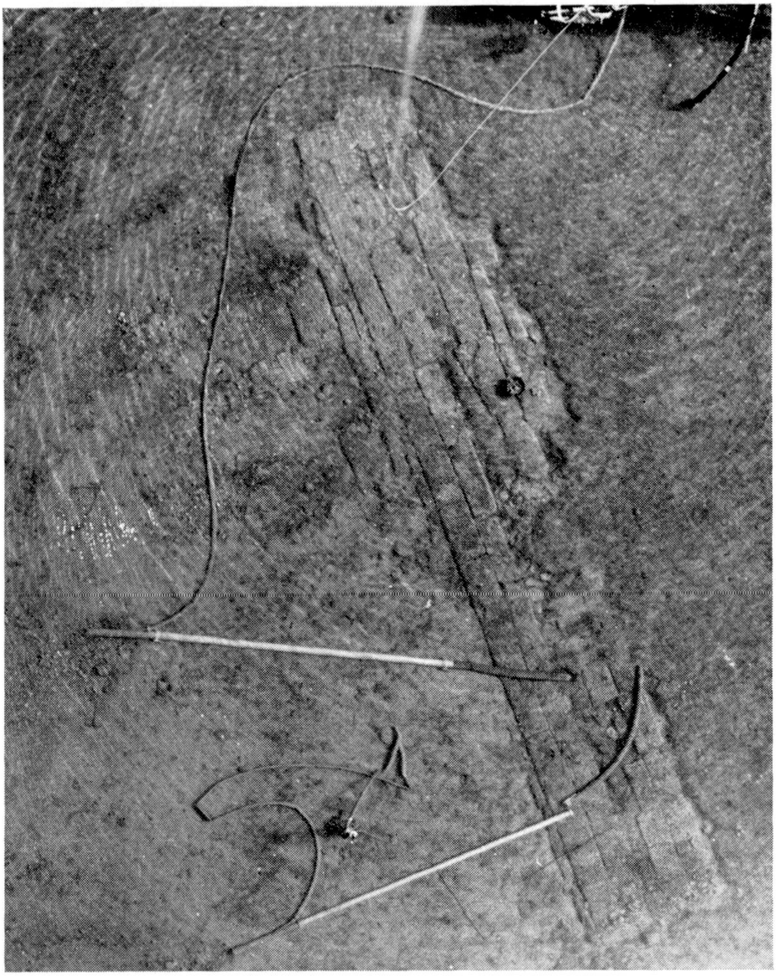

Figure 7. Base of monumental altar.

century. Its ruins were then smoothed over—it is at a level lower than that of the stoa—to serve as a terrace in front of the stoa built after its destruction. The older building shows its age by its proportions. It is divided into two main chambers, the first entered from the south through a porch or *pronaos*, and over a large threshold block. To the rear of this chamber are two heavy rectangular bases with a smaller base behind, presumably to support a pillar. The rear chamber is the longer (15 m) and has four bases for columns at somewhat irregular intervals; the columns show signs of fluting and give an indication of the original floor level in the room. The construction of the walls is unique for Halieis, but not uncommon in early archaic architecture: flattish slabs of limestone laid to provide an even face on the inner and outer faces of the walls, though irregular within.

So far systematic excavation has been confined to the back part of the front chamber, the *sekos* of the shrine, for that is clearly what we have. There, the fluted bases of two marble *perirrhanteria* or lustral basins were found on either side of the square bases. On the west side of the trench were numerous fragments of one or more marble statues. Restoration of the fragments is under way; at present we seem to have the upper half of a nude male figure, about two-thirds life-size, no later in style than the first half of the fifth century B.C.; a badly damaged face looks later in date, but none of the numerous finds from the floor of the building are of later date. They include a great quantity of miniature votive cups, Corinthian pottery and Attic (both black- and red-figure), much metal (including a hoard of 18 Aeginetan silver coins of the sixth century), bone and wood.

The male figure in marble could well be the cult-statue of Apollo, whose shrine is mentioned in a treaty between Halieis and Athens of 424/3 B.C. (*SEG*, XIV, 8; *IG* I^3 75) and whose head appears on fourth-century coins of the town. The archaic shrine looks south to a long, monumental altar, 3 by 17.50 m, which had two bases on either side near its north end, perhaps for a canopy or baldachin (Fig. 7). Similar altars with bases are known at Perachora and at the Aphaia temple on Aigina (Plommer and Salviat, 1966; Furtwängler, 1906, 70, Fig. 17; 72, Fig. 19; 74, Fig. 22). They have been restored as being for a symmetrical canopy over the whole altar, but our better preserved foundations suggest that only a partial canopy is needed.

To the east of the altar lies a complex of buildings divided into small, roughly square rooms, suggestive of a hostel or bath. To the south of the altar, at a distance of 12 m, is the starting-line of a race-track, 16 m wide (Fig. 8). Rectangular slabs of limestone, without foundation, show the characteristic pair of parallel grooves for the feet of the runner, separated by square cuttings for upright posts into six individual lanes. The race-course is relatively narrow when compared with the fourth-century courses at Olympia (20 lanes) and Epidauros (10 lanes). Two lines of wall run along either side of the track, which, we must suppose, terminates in another starting-line a stade (i.e. some 180 m) to the south. The structure to the east may have served as foundation for wooden bleachers or for mounded earth for spectators. On the west side, the inner line of wall takes the form of a slightly curved recess from 5.5 to 10 m from the northern end, before resuming its straight course to the south. One may compare traces of a similar (and unexplained) curved construction on the south side of the track at Epidauros (Kavvadias, 1902, 91). About a meter east of the curve, on the edge of the track itself, excavation uncovered the top half of a black-glazed Laconian stirrup-crater, and between the crater and the recess other fragments of black-glazed and black-figure pottery, notably a large piece showing a gigantic bird and a running man, of the middle or third quarter of the sixth century. From the level of this pottery in relation to the starting-line and the line of blocks to the west it seems to belong to fill used in the construction of the race-course which, in its existing form, would be later than the middle or third quarter of the sixth century, but as yet it can not be said how much later. Brief tests to the west of the race-course have shown the presence of other walls. At the south end of the stadium, the end which faced the city gate, we may also expect other structures.

We find ourselves in the midst of a large sanctuary complex of the archaic and classical periods. Most of what we have examined so far was already visible to some degree, but the starting-line and in fact the whole stadium was a complete surprise and was discovered by the discharge of the dredge. It is a warning that all the unrevealing eastern side of the harbor may conceal buildings under a coating of mud. Valuable as balloon

Figure 8. Starting-line of race-track.

photography has proved in our work, it cannot penetrate mud and must be combined with excavation.

In general, it may be suggested that the simple but useful techniques we have worked out may be applicable to a large and hitherto little-developed branch of archaeology, the study of settlements that have been inundated since antiquity. The alarming rise in the value of coastal land around the Mediterranean may drive archaeology into public water, whether we like it or not. To judge from our experiences at Halieis, there could be worse fates for the archaeologist.

ACKNOWLEDGEMENTS

We have to thank the National Endowment for the Humanities for financial support in 1967 and 1970 and the Ford Foundation for its support of students of archaeology in 1968 and 1970.

REFERENCES

Ervin, M. 1967 News Letter from Greece. *AJA* **71**, Pl. 88, Fig. 15.

Flemming, N. C. 1968 Holocene Earth Movements and Eustatic Sea Level Change in the Peloponnese. *Nature, Lond.* **217**, 1031–2 (Note: the age for Lorenzon, Site No. 5, must be corrected from first millennium to *c.* 200 B.P. on the basis of radiocarbon dates).

Furtwängler, A. 1906 *Aegina, Das Heiligtum der Aphaia*, vol. I, 504pp. München.

Jameson, M. H. 1969 Excavations at Porto Cheli and Vicinity, Preliminary Report, I: Halieis, 1962–8. *Hesperia* **38**, 311–42. (This is the fullest account of work up to 1968; for 1970, see reports forthcoming in *Archaeological Reports*, *Archaiologikon Deltion: Chronika*, and *BCH*).

Kavvadias, P. 1902 Anaskaphai en Epidhavro: To Stadhion. *Praktika* 1902, 78–92.

Plommer, (W.) H. and Salviat, F. 1966 The Altar of Hera Akraia at Perachora. *BSA* **61**, 207–15.

Whittlesey, Julian Hill 1969 Tethered Balloon for Archaeological Photos. *Photogrammetric Engineering*, Feb. 1970, 181–6.

POSTSCRIPT

by M. H. Jameson

A further season of excavation in 1971 has shown that the full length of the stadium is 167.40 m. The identification of the shrine as that of Apollo has been confirmed by the discovery of the god's name on one of three large, iron temple keys of the early fifth century; what was taken to be a long rear chamber is now seen to have been divided by a cross-wall. In general, the prognosis for stratigraphic excavation is more optimistic as the result of further experience.

The marble statue now appears to be archaizing and of late Hellenistic date, indicating a rather surprising return to the ruined shrine long after the abandonment of both town and sanctuary.

Discussion

Tayless What is the cost of setting up the balloon and equipment?
Saxon This was done privately by Mr. Whittlesey; the cost is considerable. Much depends on the arrangements made with the suppliers of hydrogen.
Lewis It is probable that the complete rig—cameras, balloon and radio equipment—cost $3–4,000.
Blackman The possibility of rapid descent must be quite a problem.
Saxon The camera never actually crashed. If the balloon began to descend rapidly, then we moved fast to catch the camera before it hit the ground.

Baker Did you or Prof. Jameson try to make up mosaics?
Saxon This was possible but not usually necessary. The balloon coverage was sufficient. Some mosaics were made when we could not get sufficient height.
Baker It would be relatively easy to do so from your balloon coverage, even if there were gaps in the coverage.
Saxon We found that high altitude aerial shots were sufficient; on the whole a higher picture was preferable.

Wignall Did you have any problems with the balloon rotating on the cord?
Lewis A gimbal on the balloon-suspended camera allows it to hold orientation and level. The camera does not revolve since it is held in place by the offset tethering from the gimballed frame of the camera.

Hague Have the data on the shrine site been established by normal archaeological methods? Did you get a cross-section to correlate the two buildings properly, or did you come to the conclusion later?
Saxon We started with the assumption that the two buildings were not contemporary. They had been built one in front of the other, and the problem was: which came first? Our criteria were architectural and historical.
Hague Could the relationship not be established from the relative depths of the buildings? And was there a deliberate filling?
Saxon The buildings were at different absolute depths. There was deliberate in-filling to alter the lower (and probably earlier) building but not the upper (and probably later) one.
Blackman In any case, how valuable a section would one get, with the two buildings located side by side, founded on bedrock and with very little deposit over and around them?
Hague How many courses of the walls survived?
Saxon One course about 40 cm high remained in the larger, more recent structure, and two to four courses 5 cm high remained in most areas of the earlier building.

McKee Why did you use a balloon rather than an aircraft?
Saxon The balloon was more versatile and was readily available.
Blackman In many countries, for example Greece and Turkey, it can be very difficult to get aircraft permits, quite apart from the cost.
Green Might not radio-controlled aircraft be a cheaper method?
Saxon What we really wanted was many photographs of one area from slightly different positions. The balloon is ideal for this—it will float along and is more easily aimed than an aircraft.

Cosa: an early Roman harbour

by

J. D. LEWIS

1. HISTORY

THE FORTIFIED COLONY town of Cosa was founded by the Romans in 273 B.C. on the coast of Tuscany 138 km north-west of Rome. Although the site is overshadowed by the larger mountain peninsula of Argentario, the hill of Ansedonia, upon which Cosa was built, had two distinct advantages. First, the location provided a small and thus defensible oval hill-top; and second, a sheltered cove existed to the east, affording protection for a harbour from the predominantly south-western winds. An additional benefit was the existence to the east of the Ansedonia hill of a lagoon which extended east for 20 km, parallel to the sea and separated from it by low sand-dunes. A portion of the lagoon, known as Lago di Burano, now reduced in size by modern drainage projects, still exists. To the west of Ansedonia another sand-dune connects Ansedonia to the Argentario peninsula, behind which a large shallow lagoon almost makes an island of the town of Orbetello, 7 km from Cosa.

Cosa was founded during the final struggle between the Romans and the Etruscan states. Vulci lay only 27 km to the east and Telamon just 20 km to the north. Although nothing of Etruscan origin has been found at Cosa, the nearby necropolis of the sixth to third centuries B.C. at Orbetello attests to the Etruscan dominance of the area. Excavations have been carried out at Cosa by the American Academy in Rome since 1948 (Brown, 1951).

Strabo mentions Cosa in his coastal itinerary, as do Vergil and Pliny, each attaching Etruscan significance to it. Even the name has an Etruscan origin, but Cosa was a Latin colony strategically placed between the Etruscan cities and their access to the sea. The cove at the base of the cliffs and the lagoon provided a natural harbour, perhaps the best between Gaeta to the south and La Spezia to the north for ships coasting their way to Marseille, Spanish ports and the island of Sardinia and Corsica (Fig. 1). The dolphin on the coinage of Cosa reflects the strong influence of maritime orientation, both commercial and naval. The harbour can therefore provide us with a transitional example in the study of Roman port construction and an early, perhaps the earliest, use of natural formations of the coast combined with the most available construction materials for improving upon nature.

The following discussion centres primarily around the engineering aspect of this early Roman port, to determine the level of skill of her engineers. Archaeological evidence will be used merely to substantiate the chronology of events and to place the harbour in the proper context with relation to earlier and later harbour-works.

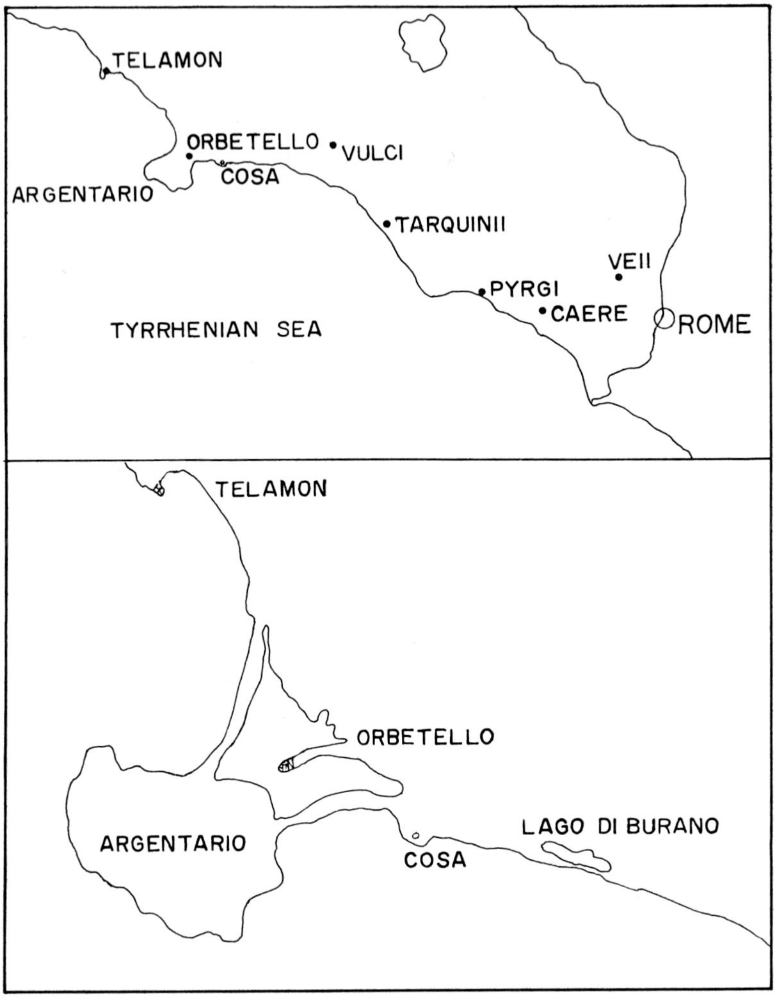

Figure 1. The coast of Tuscany and Cosa.

2. VISIBLE REMAINS

To the casual observer, there is little remaining to identify a once prosperous port, for shifting sand and changes in topography have erased the maritime features of the harbour. A number of the telltale marks do remain: the most obvious is the tufa-and-mortar piers still standing, but eroded to half their original size. The three closest to the shore are rectangular, measuring 10.6 m × 6.8 m, and extend seaward on a slightly offset line (Fig. 2). An additional two stand in the centre of the harbour with no apparent connection joining them to the others. One is just awash, while the furthest is submerged. The tufa is a grey-purplish variety, the nearest source being from the vicinity of Vulci, and they are similar in construction to those found at other coastal port towns. Their foundation is local limestone rock, and the alignment suggests their

Figure 2. Piers 1 and 2 extending seaward; Pier 4 visible beyond, just awash. Note the original left edge of Pier 1, indicating the erosion that has taken place.

use as a protective shield for a portion of the harbour, as well as piers for a loading and unloading dock. The upper courses, most likely a later repair, contain hundreds of potsherds, mostly of amphora and tile mixed with small pieces of limestone rock.

The second most obvious feature is the large amount of quarrying that has cut into the limestone cliff adjacent to the harbour. Here, immediately at hand, was the source of the huge quantities of rock required for the construction of the harbour. The principal use for the limestone rock was in the construction of an enormous breakwater, now completely submerged and partially covered by sand, silt and seaweed (Fig. 3). When the water is clear, the outline of the harbour breakwater is visible from the cliffs above the harbour. If one swims over the area of the harbour with mask and snorkel, a main

Figure 3. Aerial photograph of the harbour, revealing the outline of the main breakwater and the rock island "breakwater extensions", which form an enclosed harbour.

breakwater can be identified extending directly east from the cliff, while several islands of unconnected rock piles extend further east and then turn to the north, joining the beach. This enclosed area is large enough for several commercial ships of up to 30 m in length. The protection afforded the ships from the south and south-west is excellent and the staggered arrangement of the rock islands provides for a scouring current to keep the silt and sand from settling in the harbour.

Finally, a first visit to the area would reveal two unusual constructions in the limestone cliff itself. At the extreme end, where the cliff meets the water, a narrow cut paralleling the cliff face leads through a tunnel and into a canal that continues back toward the inner lagoon. Along its course it is joined in a large trapezoidal basin with a cave emerging from the cliff wall. The seaward end of this cave is 260 m to the south-west and has a triple entrance formation facing the south, north and south-east. The first of these two cuttings, known as the Tagliata, is completely man-made, while the second, the Spacco della Regina, was originally a natural geological cleft in the hillside. The course of the latter was broadened, deepened to sea level and cleared in order to connect the water outside the silt-free rock entrance to the sandy beach area of the harbour. The purpose and arrangement of these de-silting devices will be discussed in Section 8.

Before discussing the details of the Cosa harbour, one should mention evidence of an inner land-locked harbour which was joined to the outer harbour by a channel. As was mentioned in the first section, a long narrow lagoon extended from the base of the Ansedonia hill for 20 km to the east behind a sand-dune ridge. Traces of the not yet completely drained Lago di Burano can be seen directly under the hill. Ruins visible within the enclosed lagoon include a cistern on the side of the hill and stone piers leading down to the silted lagoon. Huge blocks of limestone rock form retaining-walls of polygonal construction along the east and west sides. Rubble constructions along the west face of the hill appear to be terraced retaining-walls. Finally, the remains of an early Roman Imperial villa extend from the shore inland just beside the harbour itself.

3. THE OUTER HARBOUR BREAKWATER

The outer harbour was protected on the west by the natural limestone cliffs which rise to heights of 30 m at the water's edge. The Ansedonia peninsula provided both a protection for the small harbour and a problem for the harbour engineers. For while the hill blocked the prevailing south-westerly winds, the protected zone would be shallow, a depository for sand flowing with the waves as the sand-laden seas reached the calm waters behind the hill. Here sand would quickly settle to the bottom (Fig. 4). If the harbour were to have an extended lifetime, not only would shoaling be troublesome, but, what was more difficult, the breakwater structure required for extending eastward the protection for the harbour would further increase the likelihood of silting. Thus the ancient harbour engineers must have studied the land and underwater topography very carefully, to analyse the direction from which the sand-bearing waves arrived and the various possible layouts for a breakwater. The arrangement would have to minimize silting, while ensuring that the breakwater would not be destroyed during the first storm.

There were thus two distinct problems to be solved: the orientation and the size of the structure to protect the ships in the harbour; and a method of preventing the harbour

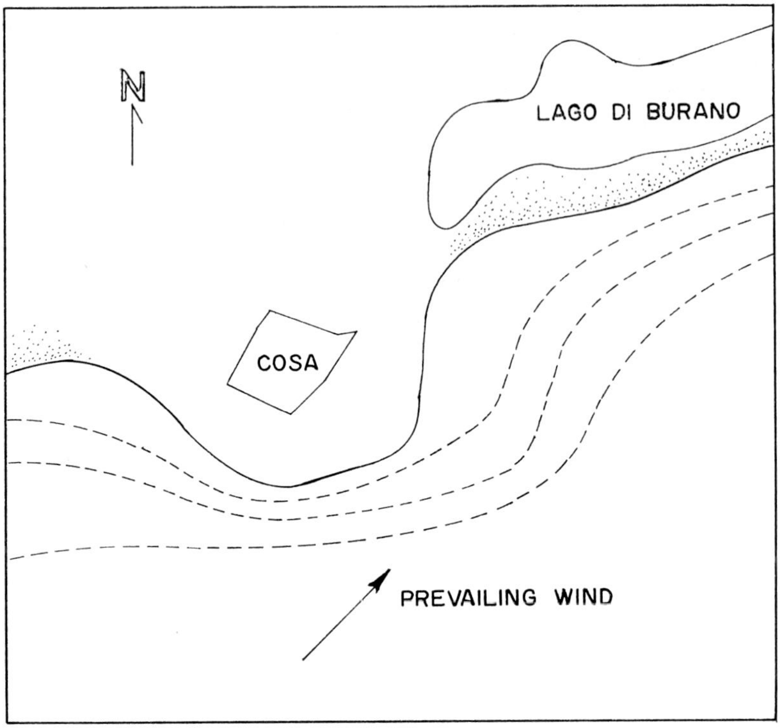

Figure 4. Shoaling of the sand (indicated by dotted lines) east of the Ansedonia hill.

from silting up. The two are interrelated, for the engineer could build a massive breakwater, but would most assuredly find his harbour useless almost immediately as a result of sand filling the area behind the breakwater.

The breakwater chosen was a broad rock pile that extended further to the east the natural protection afforded by the Ansedonia hill. It was built to absorb the massive destructive power of the predominantly south-westerly waves. The conflict between size and silting was solved by using loosely packed huge blocks of limestone rock spread over a broad area. The waves breaking over and through the rock would provide some current or flow into the harbour, thus reducing silting. To increase further the circulation of the water and provide a scouring action, the main breakwater only extended out to 110 m from the cliff face.

Discontinuous piers, or islands of rock, referred to as "breakwater extensions", continue east for an additional 100 m (Fig. 5). Their spacing clearly suggests that they were constructed with the primary purpose of breaking the crushing force of the seas, without affecting the flow of water in and out of the enclosed harbour. This staggered arrangement blocks the waves but keeps the harbour clear of sand through the constant action of the water flowing around these islands of rocks and into the harbour. These rock breakwater extensions are no doubt the fore-runners of the discontinuous configuration of the piers at Pozzuoli, Baia and Anzio.

The breakwater extensions continue in a semicircular line, interrupted once for the harbour entrance and anchoring finally to the shore to the north. The waves thus have

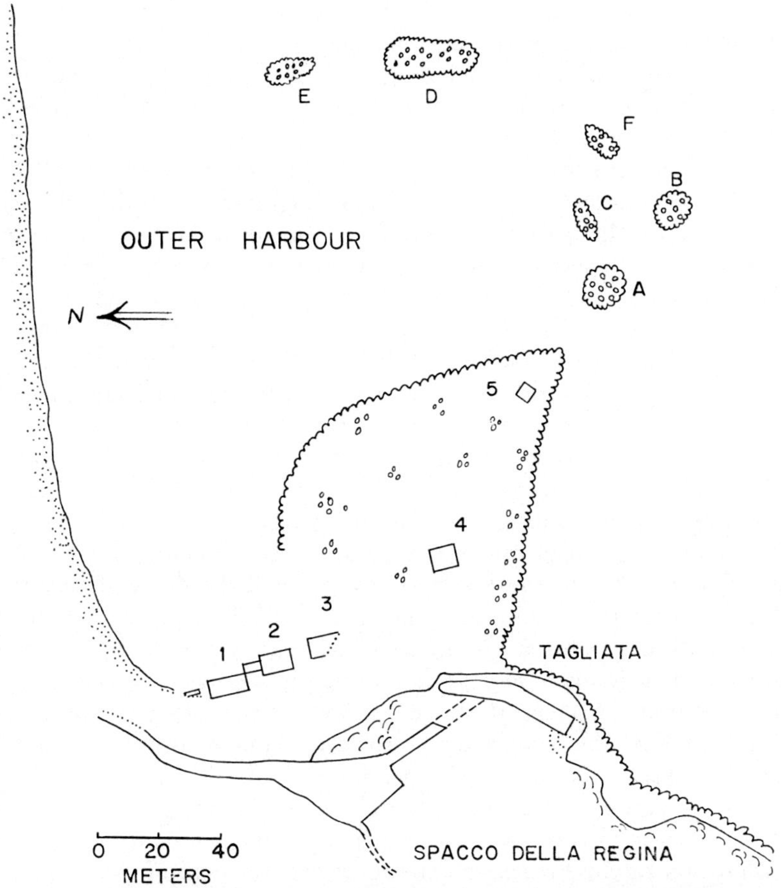

Figure 5. The outer harbour breakwater, with Piers 1–5 indicated and Breakwater Extensions A–F identified. The harbour entrance is between Breakwater Extensions D and F.

a path through the harbour to act as a de-silting current. The circulation of water through the harbour has been used at other ports. The scouring action of a swiftly flowing river, if directed through the harbour, can keep silt-laden water from precipitating its load to the bottom of the harbour. This method, however, is a dangerous approach, as the very waters used for de-silting are sediment-laden, especially during spring. The port of Marseille, said to have been in use during the sixth century B.C., successfully used a river flow to prevent silting. The ancient engineers at Cosa would certainly have known of the classic method of preventing silting: that of providing the harbour with two entrances to enable currents to flow through the harbour. Lehmann–Hartleben (1923) lists three examples of harbours that allowed currents to sweep through the enclosed areas: Syracuse, Halicarnassus and Mytilene. With no appreciable tide in the Mediterranean, controlling the currents through the harbour required a thorough knowledge of prevailing winds and resulting currents in order to establish the proper orientation of the breakwaters and the harbour entrances, or the result would be an early abandonment of the harbour. The arrangement of the main breakwater and the breakwater extensions was a considered engineering solution to enhance the safety of the ships within the harbour as well as to reduce the silting effects behind the breakwaters.

The engineer must have also known that if the breakwater were built parallel to the wave front, the wave would strike the breakwater along its full length at the same instant. To solve this problem, the breakwater would be angled toward or away from the wave front, thus extending the period that the wave strikes the breakwater. It is easy to see that this planning was carried out by the engineers at Cosa, for the breakwater forms an angle to the wave front breaking upon it on a stormy day. Merely angling the breakwater was not sufficient, for the shape and size of the structure could be designed either to reflect or absorb the force of the wave. In some harbour designs the wave can be reflected directly back to intercept the next wave. This solution would be difficult at Cosa as there must be deep water just to the front of the breakwater, and the breakwater itself must be built with a strong vertical front; the latter requires clamped worked blocks and a prepared underwater foundation. Waves can also be reflected upwards, allowing the water to fall back on the structure. The difficulty in this design is the resultant destruction of the breakwater from the force of the descending waves. Erosion of the sand underneath the breakwater takes place, which requires that the breakwater be built up periodically. This no doubt took place at Cosa, where there is evidence that additional rock and even discarded building materials have been added to the original rock breakwater to keep it above sea level. Then later, perhaps, the series of piers was constructed on the breakwater for the same reason, as well as to act as marks to warn ships of submerged portions of the breakwater.

At Cosa the east–west line of the main breakwater facing the prevailing winds presents an angle of 45 degrees to the oncoming waves arriving from the south-west (Fig. 6). Thus only a portion of the breakwater is under the full load of the wave at one time. This design feature alone would not nullify the destructive power of the wave; the breakwater would also have to be built to absorb the force of the waves over a broad base. The resistance of rocks to the forward progress of the waves would depend upon the size and shape of the rocks, as well as the distance over which the wave's power would be dissipated. The engineers at Cosa had at their disposal limestone from the cliffs that extended down to the harbour on the west. The specific density of limestone, 167–71 lb/ft^3, compares favourably with that of granite, 165–75 lb/ft^3. The forces required to overturn the denser rock are much greater than for less dense materials. The rough, angular quarrystone used in the Cosa breakwater was also important, for a rock with flat or plane surfaces is easily displaced, while a round, rough surface absorbs the wave, breaking it up and reducing the force for the next rocks to contend with. It is true that connecting clamped rectangular blocks increase the strength of a breakwater, but they are by no means as lasting as randomly-shaped natural rocks which are locked together because of their shapes and sizes (*Shore Protection, Planning and Design*, 1966, 345). Again the Cosa engineers, whether by chance or knowledge, hit upon the proper combination, for the large limestone rocks used in the main breakwater weigh over 2,000 Kg with medium and smaller rocks wedged between the larger rocks, cemented together by the natural concretion of sand and shell to form a conglomerate with the

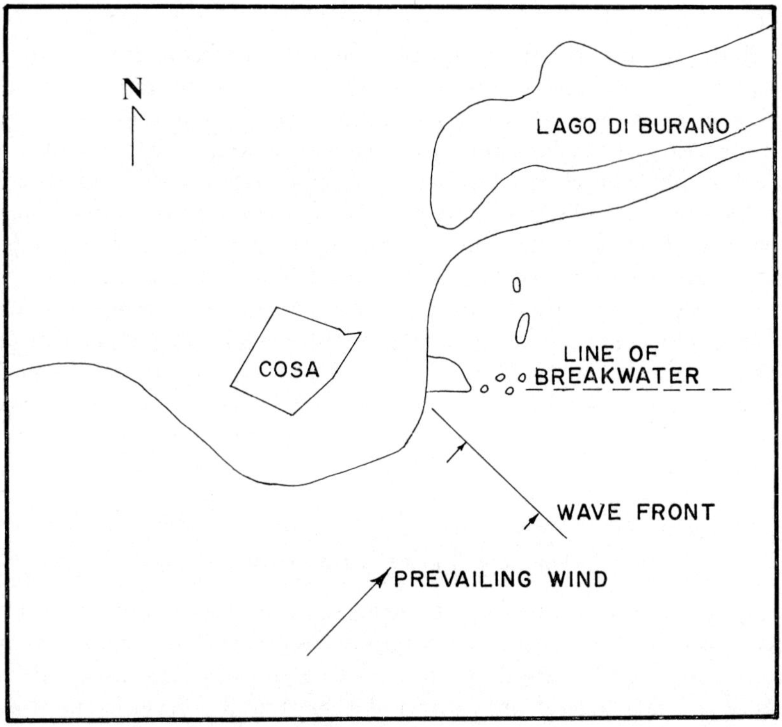

Figure 6. The wave front and the line of the breakwater, meeting at an angle of 45°; this reduces the load on the breakwater.

bonding strength of hydraulic cement. Year after year the breakwater became stronger and stronger as the bond between the rocks increased with the addition of broken pottery as an aggregate in the concretions.

The breakwater is three metres below present sea level, the result no doubt of several actions. First and foremost must be the effect of building the breakwater on a sand base rather than on a more solid base of bedrock. Although the exact depth of the bedrock has not been established, a series of probes into the sand along the east side of the main breakwater disclosed the presence of rock which could be penetrated to lower depths. In a number of cases the prober descended more than 2 m within a distance of 10 m from the breakwater. The most likely conclusion is that these obstructions represent scattered stone from the main breakwater rather than bedrock.

The erosion of the sand from under the breakwater must have taken place, caused by tons of water cascading over the breakwater and washing the sand from under the rock as it drained back into the sea. No doubt an accompanying scattering of the top layers has also taken place without the necessary replenishment since the harbour fell into disuse. Thus the present submerged state of the breakwater is a result of the action of the seas eroding and spreading the rocks of the breakwater. The distinct line of the breakwater on the south and east sides leaves little doubt that this is the original shape of the main breakwater, no doubt somewhat extended by the constant reshaping of the rock and the necessity for renewal of the upper surfaces following a stormy winter.

Two additional factors must be considered in explaining why the breakwater is now submerged. Both are acts of nature and both are of indeterminate extent: the first of these is a possible sea level change and the second is marine borings combined with the abrasive action of sand. Sea level change is the subject of Section 4. A considerable amount of destruction of the limestone rock by marine animals is evident in the breakwater. These borings, where there has been protection from additional abrasion by the sand, can be measured to depths of 0.01 m. The total amount of destruction by marine borings must have been considerable over the past 2,000 years. Abrasion, helped by marine borings, could easily account for 0.50 m of height in a 4–5 m rock breakwater. The evidence is clear, for although the rocks were quarried along the adjacent cliffs in blocks with edges generally at right angles, the present rocks are completely worn to an oval shape. Similar rocks along the shore, not exposed to boring and abrasion, still retain their angular proportions. Thus it must be concluded that a reduction in breakwater height has in some measure been due to the combined effects of animal borings and sand abrasion.

4. SEA LEVEL CHANGES

The topography of the Tuscan coast during ancient times must have been similar to that which we see today, with few exceptions. Reduction in size of rivers and lakes and the absence of large forests that once covered the hillsides are good examples of changes. There are also several indications at Cosa that sea level in ancient times was lower than today. Although the amount indicated varies, the direction is consistently toward a lower sea level.

In the Tagliata the rock cuttings along the side of the wall just south of the modern foot-bridge that leads into the entrance of the Spacco della Regina are at the height of

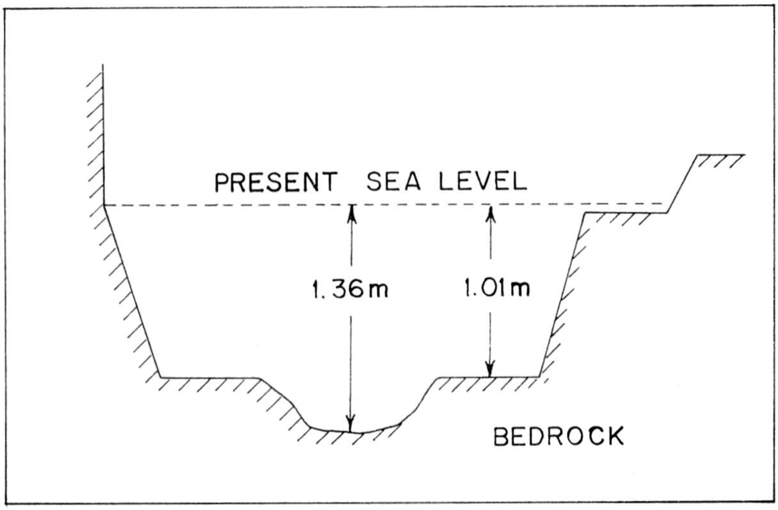

Figure 7. Profile of sluice canal, 25 m west of Pier 1.

present sea level. These vertical grooves, located on opposite sides of the channel, were no doubt used for vertical sliding boards which would have served as sluice-gates to control the flow of water. As the top of each groove is now flush with the present water level, it is difficult to see how such a sluice-gate could function with the water at its present level. In order to control effectively the water flow, the water level would have had to have been below the present level; between 0.5 and 1 m lower would have been sufficient. The grooves were found to extend over 1 m down the wall under the present sand fill.

A further indication of a sea level variation was obtained in a test-trench dug across the sluice canal to obtain a profile for study. The maximum depth was found to be 1.36 m below present sea level (Fig. 7). Again it would appear that a sea level between 0.5 and 1 m lower is probable.

It is generally agreed that there has been a change in the sea level within recorded history. This contention has been supported by the examination of old shorelines and Carbon^{14} dating of plant and animal remains, which suggest that eustatic changes of sea level have taken place. For example, Bloch (1963, 89) shows that the overall rise in sea level over the past 6,000 years has been about 3 m. The figures for the height of sea level at various periods of interest are extracted:

237 B.C.	0.9 m below present S.L.
137 B.C.	0.7 m below present S.L.
37 B.C.	0.3 m below present S.L.
A.D. 63	Equal to present S.L.
A.D. 500	1.7 m above present S.L.
A.D. 1500	0.5 m above present S.L.
A.D. 1970	Present S.L.

Thus although the oscillation of the sea level has been no greater than 3 m during the last 4,000 years, the present level is 0.7–0.9 m higher than it was during the third and second centuries B.C. There is no evidence at Cosa of land subsidence or emergence due to geological instability such as that found in the region of Naples.

A further confirming indication of the variations of sea level can be seen in the construction of the piers leading out into the harbour. In order not to block the flow of water behind the piers, diagonal "through-holes" were constructed to increase the flow of water in and out of the area behind the piers. The level of these "through-holes" coincides with the sea level changes extracted from Bloch, if the assigned date of their construction is the latter part of the first century B.C. Specifically, Pier 2 was constructed to ensure the flow of water, with a "through-hole" as a de-silting device. The cut which is presently about 0.5 m below sea level allows for the flow of water in and out of the confined basin to the west of the piers. A sea level appreciably lower than the present level would not permit the desired flow.

A tufa-and-mortar foundation enclosing a freshwater well within the inner harbour was studied for sea level data. The upper surface of the foundation is 0.10 m above present sea level. For better protection of the freshwater spring, a height of 0.5–1 m would be more suitable. This corresponds to the Carbon^{14} dating assigned to wooden construction forms found buried in the mud and sand around the platform, that of the first century B.C. Thus, on the basis of Bloch's variations, the top of the platform would have been 0.5–0.7 m above the ancient sea level. There is an interesting sidelight which gives further evidence that sea level at the time of construction of the well enclosure was somewhat lower—the overflow drain from the well. The drain spills the water down to a lower tufa-and-mortar platform where a pantile was used to prevent erosion of the soft tufa and mortar. The present distance of 0.62 m down to the pantile would seem to indicate that the platform was at least that high above sea level.

If we consider the outer harbour again, there are indications that the sea level was lower than it is today. The exact amount depends upon the date assigned to the construction of the breakwater. The evidence does not support a change in sea level of more than 1 m, and thus cannot account for the entire present water depth over the breakwater.

Position on breakwater	*Depth of water over breakwater*
Near Tagliati shore	3.0 m
Vicinity of Pier 4	2.8 m
Vicinity of Pier 5	3.3 m
Extreme east end	2.7 m
Highest point	1.5 m

It is apparent that a sea level change of less than 1 m would not account for the depth of more than 3 m, plus perhaps an additional 1 m that the breakwater would have stood above sea level. The explanation must lie in the factors mentioned in the preceding discussion: erosion by the sand; the spreading and tumbling of the breakwater rocks; and finally, a considerable amount of marine animal destruction eating away the limestone rock over the past 2,000 years.

5. THE BREAKWATER EXTENSIONS REVEAL THE HARBOUR PLAN

Until 1968 the limits of the outer harbour breakwater could only be guessed at. Several feet of sand covered all but the highest portions of even the main breakwater. The existence of additional rock islands extending the main breakwater to the east was only revealed after a violent storm cleared the ancient harbour floor of a layer of sand $\frac{1}{2}$ m thick. This was a surprise, for after initial dives in the harbour in 1965 it was apparent that either Cosa was a harbour with a simple one-arm breakwater, or there was a great deal more hidden from our view. What emerged in 1968 proved that Cosa was indeed a completely enclosed protected harbour of the classical type. From the cliff's edge the main breakwater extended 110 m east, then turned toward shore, due north, for some 70 m and again turned back toward the west and tied again to the cliff. The breakwater extensions continue the protection for the harbour to the east in a staggered pattern in order to block the waves no matter from what direction they attempt to enter the harbour. The series of four to the east of the main breakwater extends the breakwater an additional 100 m. The rocks that form these extensions are distinctly "placed" in a round pattern with, except for the eastern two, clearly defined boundaries. The limestone boulders are of a smaller size than those used in the main breakwater, with perhaps only a few 2,000 Kg stones being used.

A large, almost rectangular breakwater extension limits the harbour's eastern side, with at least one additional extension between it and the shore. Since the initial discovery of the breakwater extensions in 1968, the question of the method of their construction had not been clearly understood. Several suggestions had been offered, including the scuttling of rock-filled hulls over the desired position; the possibility existed that it was actually a continuous breakwater which had been scattered and destroyed over 2,000 years of wave action. This latter solution had to be discarded when, at the end of the 1968 season, excavations at the extremities of the breakwater extensions proved that there was no rock connection joining them under the sand. The most likely explanation of the construction of these breakwater extensions was that the rocks were transported underwater between two barges and dropped in place in the desired location. Excavations in 1969 failed to reveal any trace of wood under the rocks.

As a result of the underwater work accomplished during 1969, it is now quite certain that the entire encircling breakwater system has been located and surveyed. The 1969 programme included a requirement to study the construction of the breakwater system by cutting a trench under water into a breakwater extension. The purpose was to determine, if possible, how the breakwater was constructed, identify a foundation, and measure the thickness of the rock piles. As there was 2.7 m of water over the breakwater extension selected, new data for sea level determinations would be obtained. Finally, datable materials within the breakwater extension, or under it, would provide a possible date for its construction.

Breakwater Extension D was selected for the excavation (Fig. 8). It is tear-drop in shape, 33 m long and 14 m wide at its northern end. The depth to the present sand bottom is 4 m; thus, the rocks stand some 1.3 m above the present sand level. A portion of the trench overlapped the sand while the other portion lay within the breakwater itself. Rocks weighing 200–300 Kg were detached from the breakwater and lifted by means of air-bags to positions clear of the trench. When rocks had been cleared from the trench to the level of the sand, an air-lift was used to dig down and under the rocks to determine the foundation and the depth of the rock pile. Amphora sherds, tile and pottery were heavily encrusted between the rock. The strongly cemented conglomerate made considerable effort necessary to free the rock with the use of large crowbars. A layer of gravel, small stones, and a heavy concentration of pottery and amphora sherds lay in a layer at a depth of 1.1–1.6 m below the sand level. This level was just one of the many found during the season that indicated the existence of an ancient harbour floor. Below 2 m fewer sherds were found, until almost sterile hard-packed sand was encountered at 2.5 m. Deep probes penetrating down an additional 4 m with the use of a water-jet prober failed to find a foundation under the rock. The conclusion reached was that no foundation exists within 5 m of the sand level. An additional trench location was selected and again the same gravel mixed with sherds was found. Again at a depth of 2 m there was sterile sand, with no trace of a foundation under the rock. It appears most likely that the rock breakwater extensions, approximately 4 m thick, were laid on a sand foundation.

6. ANCIENT HARBOUR FLOOR

Portions of the ancient harbour floor were first uncovered during the 1968 season by air-lifting of sand at the end of the main breakwater and Breakwater Extensions

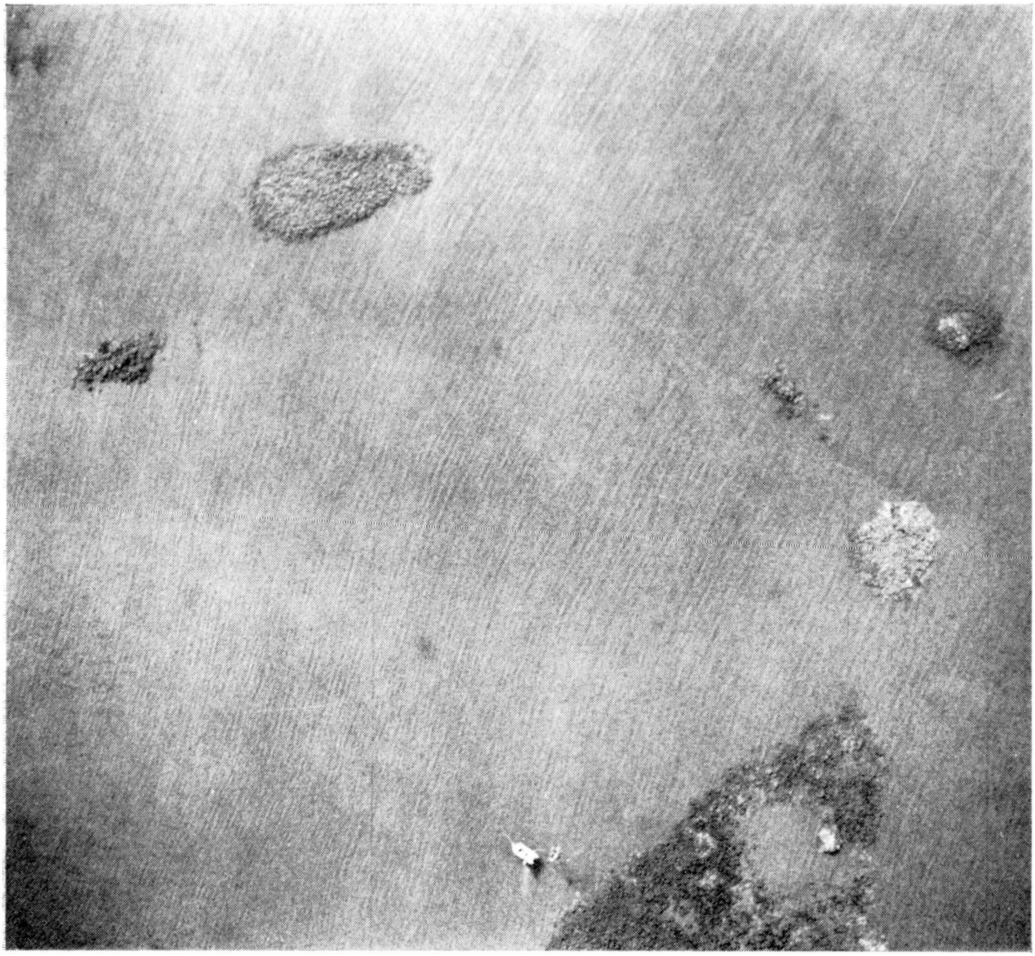

Figure 8. Aerial photograph of Breakwater Extensions A–D (Breakwater Extension F does not show up through 4.5 m of water).

A, B and C. Potsherds and other debris were found at approximately 1.5 m below the sand level. Characteristic harbour floor materials such as smooth pebbles and worn pottery, and common construction materials such as bricks, tile, and tufa were also encountered. The detailed stratification of the harbour floor down to these materials could not be reconstructed owing to the continuously cascading sand that refilled the trench almost as fast as it was excavated. It is impossible to cut a trench under water with anywhere approaching vertical sides; sand slides down into the excavation and forms an inverted-cone-shaped recess with only a point at the bottom momentarily visible for inspection. Some means of controlled excavation would have to be devised if information about the true harbour floor and stratification were to be obtained. To verify the existence and depth of the ancient floor, several methods were studied for use during the 1969 season.

Acoustic survey: Recent work with sonic devices by several individuals and institutions has suggested the possibility of obtaining a sub-bottom profile system that could measure the depth of the sand that has been deposited over the ancient harbour floor. Bedrock depths would also be measurable. Although surveys of this type have been successful in mud-filled harbours, there are no satisfactory results available from working through the medium of sand, especially at the shallow-water depths found at Cosa. The difficulty is the reverberations of echo information on the recorder just at the depth readings between zero and 5 m, which are the critical depths of interest at Cosa. The obvious solution, of reducing the power of the sonic signal to preclude this "bounce", would result in no penetration of the sand level.

Core sampling: A second possibility for determining depth information under the sand was by the use of underwater core sampling equipment. Several systems are on the market for such work; however, the expense appears to be prohibitive.

Jet Prober: When it appeared that the desired results could not be achieved either by acoustic survey or by core sampling, a simple water-jet prober was designed, built and tested by the author during the spring of 1969. The Jet Prober uses water under pressure directed through a nozzle and into the sand. The force of the water "digs" the nozzle and accompanying pipe into the sand. The $\frac{3}{4}$-inch pipe is marked every $\frac{1}{2}$ m and can be read at the point when the nozzle strikes objects under the sand, indicating the depth of sand fill over these objects. The water pressure is provided by a portable gasoline-driven pump at 30–40 lb/in^2 pressure through a $1\frac{1}{2}$-inch fire-hose to the pipe and nozzle. The maximum depth that the Jet Prober could penetrate, without becoming wedged or buried, was 3.5 m. A more powerful water-pump would be required for deeper probes. The Jet Prober was used extensively under water in the outer harbour, with the pump operating on the Zodiac working boat while the pipe and nozzle were directed by a diver under water. A second diver stood by to record the readings.

During the jet probing of the breakwater extensions, discussed in a previous section, an ancient floor was "felt" as the Jet Prober nozzle passed through a rock, pebble and sherd layer. This was first noted at a depth of 1.3–1.8 m between Breakwater Extensions D and F. Again between Breakwater Extensions B and C, at depths of 1.5 and 1.7 m, some obstructions were "felt" as the Jet Prober passed through this layer. The same indications occurred at locations between Breakwater Extensions A and C, A and B, and also B and C. Further indications of the ancient floor were noted when the Jet Prober was used along a line east and west at a distance of 20 m north of Breakwater Extension C. In addition to the trenches dug during the 1968 season, two trenches dug in 1969 along the sides of Breakwater Extension D indicated a sherd-and-gravel level at depths of 1.5 m below the present sand level. Also mixed with the sherds were mud, grass and decayed vegetation. These results had been anticipated from data gained during the 1968 season and, as a result, a harbour stratification system was designed by the author to allow air-lifting in a controlled environment without being continually obstructed by the sand sliding into the excavation. The backfill of sand was controlled by use of a caisson, similar to that used in tunnel and bridge construction in rivers, but in this case the caisson was used in a vertical position. The caisson was constructed of sheet steel to form two cylinders which were fabricated 1 m high and 1.27 and 1.3 m in diameter respectively, the larger diameter fitting over the smaller, which was held in place by bolts. Each caisson weighed approximately 36 Kg. The area to the north of

Breakwater Extension C was selected for the first controlled air-lift test to verify the existence of a layer which might be the ancient floor level. The area, in the centre of the harbour, was first examined by jet probing on a line 20 m north of Breakwater Extension C and parallel to it. The results of the probe indicated that a layer of material existed below the sand through which the Jet Prober could penetrate. After penetrating the layer the Jet Prober passed freely into a sand medium without further obstruction, indicating a layer of debris "floating" in the sand which could represent an ancient harbour floor. A position 26 m directly north of the east end of Breakwater Extension C appeared to be the most promising for the trial underwater excavation.

The two sections of the caisson were moved by towing and floating behind the Zodiac boat to the desired location. The standard air-lift was modified with a flexible hose secured to the end of the air-lift pipe to enable the diver working cramped inside of the caisson to direct the nozzle to the desired position for sand removal. As the sand was evacuated from the caisson, the caisson sank into the sand. At a depth of 1 m, the second caisson was bolted to the top of the first, giving a combined height of 2 m. The system functioned perfectly, allowing a controlled excavation and thus an opportunity to examine the stratification of the sand in the harbour. The walls of the caisson prevented the sand from sliding back into the excavation and permitted the ocean floor to be examined and photographed in detail without haste (Figs. 9, 10).

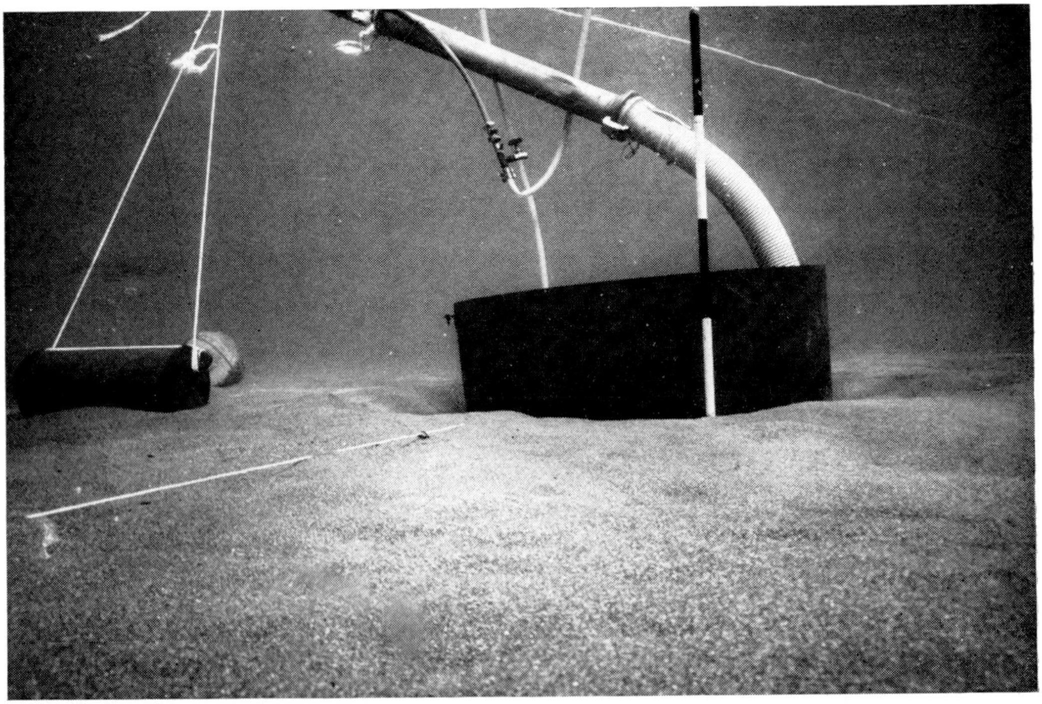

Figure 9. The caisson sinks into the sand as the excavation continues within the caisson. The depth is now 1.5 m below the sand level.

Caisson One, as this excavation was known, was set up in 4.1 m of water, and lowered to a depth of 2.2 m below the sand level. The following chart indicates the stratification found in Caisson One. The depths are from the present sand level; to obtain sea level readings add 4.1 m to the figures.

Levels in meters	*Material found*
0–0.75	Sterile sand down to this depth.
0.75–1.15	Characteristic colour changed to darkish-grey sediment consisting of mud and rotted vegetation and some gravel. The first two levels merge together without an abrupt change of material.
1.15–1.25	Zone in which the first sherds appear.
1.25–1.40	Level in which small- to medium-size stones, gravel and some sherds were encountered.
1.40–1.50	Pebbles and small stones with sherds.
1.50–1.90	Blackish sand with many pottery sherds, including an amphora neck and tile. At 1.55 m, two amphorae without handles and neck were found with a piece of window-glass and a tufa brick.
1.90–	Below this depth only sterile hard black sand was found. The deepest probe was to 2.2 m.

The reconstruction of ancient ports is made difficult by the tons of sand that obscure the outline of the harbour-works. Where modern construction has extended the port's life into modern times, a further obstruction is often created. Cosa has a portion of both of these problems, for sand has blanketed the entire area behind the Ansedonia hill, and modern road and drainage construction prohibits the exact delineation of the original configuration of either the northern boundary of the harbour or a possible entrance for an inner harbour. The sand layer in the centre of the harbour has been penetrated by probes, and by a round incision into the sand. The result is confirmed photographic evidence of the ancient harbour floor: of material no doubt jettisoned

Figure 10. A diver directs the nozzle of the air-lift in a controlled excavation within the caisson

before the harbour was covered by sand in the following winter storm. The area of the first controlled excavation (1.32 sq. m) uncovered two broken amphorae, green window-glass and a tufa brick. What wealth of information must lie under the sand throughout the additional 25,000 sq. m of the outer harbour?

7. THE OUTER HARBOUR ENTRANCE

An important objective of the 1969 season was the determination of the location of the entrance from the sea into the outer harbour between the breakwater extensions. The 1968 survey information, including five days of selected air-lifting at the extremities of the breakwater extensions, indicated that the most logical location for an entrance, and one free of visible obstructions, was the opening, some 50 m wide, between Breakwater Extension D and Breakwater Extension C (Fig. 5). However, these conclusions from the 1968 season had to be modified somewhat when an additional breakwater extension, now known as Breakwater Extension F, was found at the beginning of the 1969 season, rising only 0.5 m above the sand floor. Not only was it necessary to re-define the harbour entrance, but two unknowns still required resolution before the true orientation, depth and width of the harbour entrance could be delineated with certainty. Knowledge of the thickness of the sand layer covering the ancient harbour floor would be required in order to define the true depth of the harbour entrance, and the extent to which the rock of the breakwater extensions had spilled over into the entrance passage would complicate width estimates.

There was no way to know, without excavating the entire entrance channel, if there was in fact a clear passage between the breakwater extensions for ships to pass through. This fact was vividly illustrated during the 1969 season, for at the close of the 1968 season the entire extent of the breakwater system had been surveyed. The chart of the harbour indicated the extent of the breakwater system known at that time. The width of the harbour entrance was 50 m, as measured between Breakwater Extensions C and D. The area east of Breakwater Extension C had been thoroughly searched both under water with an underwater search board and by numerous surface reconnaissances in the area. It was therefore with surprise and some consternation that Breakwater Extension F was discovered some 18 m east of Breakwater Extension C, protruding only 0.5 m above the present sand level (Fig. 5). Obviously, a natural excavation of the harbour had occurred during the winter months when stormy seas and ensuing currents had swept the sand from the top of this new breakwater extension. In fact, throughout the harbour a cover of 0.5 m of sand had been removed. Ancient walls and even the ribs of an ancient hull were now exposed as a result of the winter storms (Fig. 11). Carbon[14] dating indicates the ship's age to be less than 500 years. Thus, there was no way of telling if additional rock breakwaters obstructed the area selected as the "logical" entrance to the outer harbour. The Jet Prober was the technique devised for "feeling" under the

Figure 11. Walls of the Roman villa and the outline of a ship are visible after a winter storm which removed 0.5 m of sand from the harbour (the grid at the stern is 3 × 3 m square).

sand, for if there were additional obstructions within the harbour entrance, the Jet Prober would strike them while penetrating the present sand floor. The data obtained from a survey of the harbour entrance would also provide information to determine how far the rock of the breakwater extensions, now buried under sand, had spread into the channel. This information was important, for it would further narrow the usable width of the harbour entrance.

A Jet Prober survey directly across the harbour entrance was initiated from Breakwater Extension D toward Breakwater Extension F by laying a plastic line, marked at every metre, from the southern extremity of Breakwater Extension D, terminating at the northernmost visible portion of Breakwater Extension F (Fig. 12). A profile was constructed from the data obtained and shows a section across the area of the harbour

Figure 12. The Jet Prober in action along a line between Breakwater Extensions D and F, to verify the harbour entrance.

entrance (Fig. 13). Probes, 43 in all, were made at 1 m intervals between Breakwater Extension D and Breakwater Extension F. Throughout the survey, a noticeable layer of firmer material was frequently "felt" under the sand as the prober penetrated down to its maximum length of 3.5 m. This layer caused the Jet Prober to hesitate momentarily as it "glanced off" small objects buried in the sand. These obstructions in the path of the Jet Prober could be "felt" by the diver as vibrations of the Jet Prober pipe. The depth at which this layer was most noticeable was between 1.3 and 1.8 m under the sand, which again confirmed the existence of a layer of debris 1.5 m under the sand, previously suggested as identifying the ancient harbour floor. Having observed these layers in air-lifting operations on several occasions, the diver did not find it difficult to visualize the material that momentarily obstructed the path of the Jet Prober nozzle. At a point 15.5 m from Breakwater Extension D towards Breakwater Extension F there was a noticeable "soft" spot where the prober pipe descended with almost no resistance. Sand and material rising with the stream of water in the Jet Prober hole turned grey to brown in colour, suggesting either a decayed layer of vegetation or a rotted ship's hull buried beneath the sand. The investigation of this area will have to await further work in the harbour using the controlled excavation methods described in the section on the harbour floor (6, above).

The readings show clearly that there is a definite "deep channel" in the center of the assumed harbour entrance. Along the sides of the entrance, rock has tumbled or spread out toward the centre of the channel from the foundations of the breakwater extensions. From Breakwater Extension D the rock extends horizontally under the sand an additional 4 m. This spread or extension of the rocks under the sand from Breakwater Extensions D and F further narrows the harbour entrance to 33 m, a width clear of obstructions down to 1.5 m below the present sand level—still ample room for medium-sized ships to enter safely and depart from Cosa harbour without difficulty. Through this opening ships could pass without excessive manœuvring, either under

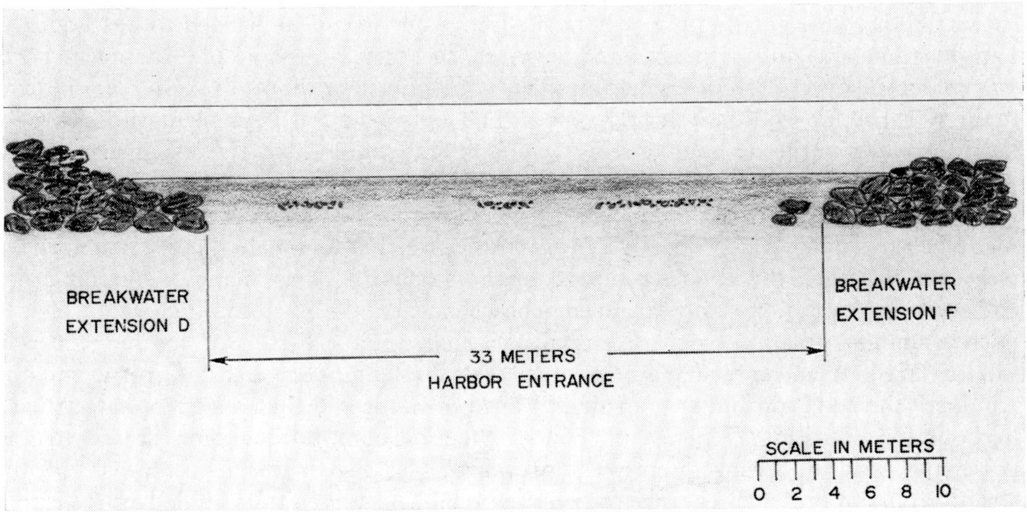

Figure 13. Section across the harbour entrance, looking E.S.E., obtained from the Jet Prober survey.

sail if the wind was favourable, or, if necessary, by the use of oars. Ships could also easily be warped into the harbour, using the breakwater extensions to secure the necessary lines, or by the use of a kedge anchor carried into the harbour by the ship's tender. The total depth of the water in the entrance passage, taking into consideration both the present sand depth over the harbour floor and the depth of the water above the present sand level, is 6 m. Sea level conditions and changes are discussed above (Section 4).

The orientation of the harbour entrance, east-south-east by west-north-west, would provide ships both clearance from the Ansedonia hill and also a comfortable distance from the beach to the north. Once within the shelter of the harbour there appears to have been no obstacle to obtaining a safe anchorage for unloading or docking along the piers. Ships entering the harbour would be relatively safe after passing Breakwater Extensions F, C, and A, and could, if necessary, anchor behind the main breakwater for more protection from strong southerly and south-westerly winds. Ships leaving the harbour, a heading of east-south-east, would normally find it easy going, as the prevailing winds during the summer are from the west and south-west. With such winds, ships could even conceivably depart under sail with a wind almost astern. From the detailed survey, and additional probes completed during the 1969 season, it is concluded that the outer harbour had a single harbour entrance, as described above, which satisfied the requirements for medium-sized merchant ships and warships in both entering and departing from the Cosa harbour.

8. DE-SILTING DETAILS

Two important areas for discussion have been left to the end: the designed use of the elaborately cut Tagliata and Spacco della Regina as de-silting devices; and in Section 9, evidence for the existence of an inner harbour.

Details of the two sluice systems can be traced in Figure 3; both have their ocean termini in areas with relatively sand-free rock bottom, the Spacco to a much greater extent. Both converge at a point where silt-free water would be needed to flush out the harbour. The ancient engineers must have realized that the usable life of ancient ports was reduced by the troublesome problem of silting; without dredging equipment modern harbours would suffer the same. The only solution in ancient times was to keep the water in the harbour moving, which in turn would keep the silt in suspension. Ancient harbour engineers constructed their harbours to take advantage of the natural resources available to them, such as rivers which were sometimes diverted through man-made settling-tanks before the water was introduced into the harbour. When rivers were not available, the engineer turned to the sea itself for assistance. Obtaining and collecting sea water at a higher mean elevation than the surrounding sea level is a fairly common practice where a significant tidal range exists. But in the relatively tideless Mediterranean that method is useless. The engineers therefore turned to the wind and the resulting waves to provide a head of water and thus a current through the harbour for de-silting. When a portion of their harbour bordered on the sea facing prevailing winds and consequently the prevailing seas also, it was a simple task to construct ramps over which the waves could sweep. The waves thus spilled water into a collecting-basin at an elevation higher than sea level. The level depended upon the height of the waves created by the prevailing wind.

Sluice-gates held the water in the basin until the desired water level was reached, at which time the sluice-gates were opened into the enclosed harbour. The result was a flow of water through the harbour, and its entrance, and out to sea. An example of this de-silting arrangement is still apparent in the ruins at the ancient seaport of Sidon, where ramps, basin and sluice-gates have been surveyed (Poidebard & Lauffray, 1951, Pl. II).

At Cosa the identical ingredients are available in a slightly different arrangement. Silt-free water is obtained from a portion of the nearby shoreline which is relatively rocky. The entrances to these sluices face in several directions, to allow the sea's swells to force the water directly into the openings and through a system of sluices cut into the rock, which are equipped with sluice-gates, used to control the water flow. Finally, a basin was provided at the harbour end of both sluices, to collect the water to a desired height above sea level. Although the exact exit of the basin into the harbour is still unknown, the possibility of its use as a de-silting device for keeping the harbour free of silt cannot be dismissed.

A counter-explanation of the purpose of the Tagliata and the Spacco della Regina has been offered by Rodenwaldt and Lehmann (1962), who after examining these cuts in the limestone cliff suggested their use as part of a melioration system. The purpose was simply to drain the Lago di Burano by conducting water from the lagoon to the sea. The reasons given for drying up the lagoon were to rid the area of a stagnant malaria-breeding source and to gain land for cultivation from the swampland of the lagoon. That such engineering skill existed is clearly illustrated by the extensive irrigation schemes of the Etruscans and later the Romans. The existence of miles of such drainage-tunnels has been verified and mapped at Veii (Ward-Perkins, 1962, 394–5). Whether or not the Etruscans realized the source of the breeding-ground of the mosquito or whether the purpose, if not to obtain usable land, was to rid the area of marshy and unhealthy odours, has not yet been verified by archaeological evidence. The introduction and circulation of salt water into the freshwater lagoon would in itself have reduced stagnation and unhealthy odours. This latter possibility must be considered, for there was a general rise in the sea level during this period, making drainage all but impossible.

To support further the suggestion of a circulating saltwater system, an additional canal was discovered further east along the lagoon, connecting the Lago di Burano with the sea. The opening at the seaward end was constructed in the water of tufa and mortar, and provides a means of blocking the waves at the entrance to prevent damage to the canal leading back through the sand-dune. The circulation of salt water would result simply from the wind forcing water through the east canal while salt water flowed in through the Tagliata and Spacco. The flow would be reversed for winds in the opposite direction.

The evidence to explain the use of these man-made canals is not yet available to us. No doubt the answer lies hidden under tons of dirt now used as a parking and camping facility at the harbour site. Whether they are de-silting or drainage devices, one must conclude that the engineering skill was exceptional and worthy of continued search for the archaeological evidence with which to solve the riddle.

9. AN INNER HARBOUR

The existence at Cosa of an inner land-locked harbour for smaller ships with shallow draught, such as warships, must be considered a distinct possibility. The necessary requirements are at hand: a well protected outer harbour with a location for a ship-channel leading through the sand-dune with one side, the cliff, well defined; and an inland lagoon of sufficient proportions to handle at least a dozen warships which could be drawn up along the shore.

The archaeological evidence to support the existence of an inner harbour is not conclusive; however, several clues do suggest the possibility. Retaining-walls of large limestone rock, forming a polygonal wall several courses high, are visible on both sides of the silted-in lagoon just below the Ansedonia hill. Both polygonal walls have been traced toward the seaward entrance; on the east, the wall disappears under modern construction 150 m from the sea, while on the west, the wall has been traced to a point 90 m from the sea, where it joins the bedrock of the western side of the outer harbour. Projecting the east wall to the shore, a twin line of additional polygonal wall was excavated leading into the sea; its west side, however, does not line up with the west polygonal wall. The distance between these inward-facing beach walls is only 5 m, suggesting a drainage-canal rather than an inner harbour entrance.

To identify further an entrance to the inner harbour, excavations were carried out along the beach. To the north of and in line with the piers, a further tufa-and-mortar structure was discovered leading toward the inner harbour. This structure was identified as a retaining-wall by its shape and size. The distance for which this wall could be traced inland was limited by a modern parking-lot; however, it is possible that this represents one side of an entrance-channel leading to the inner harbour.

Further evidence within the inner harbour is the existence of a freshwater storage-cistern on the hillside overlooking the harbour and a freshwater spring just at the base of the hill directly under the cistern. Enclosing the spring to protect the source of fresh water from the swampy lagoon is a foundation surrounding the well (Fig. 14). The materials are tufa and mortar, and when it was discovered in 1968, wooden pilings and boards were still in place. The boards were used as forms within which the foundation was constructed. Vertical pilings secured the boards in place, while an additional line of vertical boards had been driven along the southern side, forming a coffer-dam. This arrangement was necessary to divert the flow of water around the foundation while it was under construction. To prevent seepage through the porous sand, additional lower foundations were enclosed with wood and poured after the main foundation was completed. The condition of the wood indicates that the foundation was built in swampy mud and sand rather than open water, as the boards are not worn, nor are the oak pilings rubbed free of their bark. Although the wood is waterlogged, no marine borings are evidenced; this suggests that the lagoon was free of salt water, or that the wood was buried in sand and mud soon after being installed. Carbon^{14} dating has provided two dates for determination of the time of construction. Wood samples from the foundation forms produced Carbon^{14} dates as follows:

Sample	*Type of wood*	*Date*
PC–69–W22a	Board, Red Oak	131 ± 45 B.C.
PC–68–10a	Wood Piling I, Oak (Genus *quercus*)	25 ± 85 B.C.

Figure 14. Aerial photograph of the tufa-and-mortar well foundation. Ancient wood was left in place after being used as a form during construction.

Datable material within the inner harbour verifies habitation in the vicinity of the harbour from the second century B.C. Especially common are amphorae of Dressel Type I, with a large number of SES stamps on the lips. From a negative point of view, no shipsheds, landing-quays, or foundations for storehouses have yet been uncovered.

It is difficult to determine which was built first: the polygonal retaining-walls or the foundation surrounding the well. Although the limestone blocks rest upon the well foundation, and the architectural structure of the well foundation is not normal in the polygonal wall, it is possible that the wall might have been broken in order to facilitate the construction of the well foundation. Roofing-tiles and tufa voussoirs, together with many large and medium wooden members, suggest that the well was covered to form a well-house. A settling- and storage-tank adjacent to the well is fed through a channel at the bottom of the well, reinforced by cut limestone blocks.

Two square stone piers just south of the well foundation appear to have carried a superstructure, most likely a later construction for an aqueduct crossing the lagoon to the cistern of the Early Imperial villa, located on the sand-dune just opposite the outer harbour. Sections of a lead pipe as well as a lead sieve were found in the well, no doubt components of water-conducting devices.

To determine the existence of further remains under the mud and sand of the inner lagoon, both resistivity and magnetometer surveys were conducted. Both proved futile, as the high moisture content and the magnetic nature of the sand-filled lagoon made interpretation all but impossible. Additional work within the inner lagoon is planned, using earth-moving equipment to uncover structures and linked steel coffer-dam pilings to provide an enclosure within which to work.

10. CONCLUSIONS

Not even the usual fishing-boats, nestled together for protection behind the crumbled ruins, mark the location of the once flourishing port of Cosa. The reconstruction of the ancient port clearly indicates its transitional pattern between the wholly natural anchorages of the early Etruscans and the elaborate man-made harbours of the Romans. As to the effectiveness of the massive main breakwater and the staggered breakwater extensions there can be little doubt, for datable pottery commencing during the second century B.C. and continuing through the second century A.D. attest to its constant use for a period of some 400 years.

Considerable work will be required to enlarge upon our knowledge of the finer features of the harbour. The Italian Government has declared the area an archaeological zone, thus preserving the ruins for future examination by both spade and aqualung. Clearly Cosa deserves a special place in the evolution of harbours, for it represents perhaps the earliest Roman harbour construction and illustrates what could be accomplished prior to the revolutionary discovery of hydraulic cement.

11. ACKNOWLEDGEMENTS

The work at the port of Cosa has been carried out as part of the American Academy in Rome's excavations at Cosa, with funds provided by the National Endowment for the Humanities and the University of Missouri. Photographs are by A. M. McCann and the author, drawings by the author and aerial photographs by Mr. and Mrs. Julian Whittlesey.

REFERENCES

Bloch, M. R. 1963 The Social Influence of Salt. *Scientific American*, **209** (July 1963), 89–98.

Brown, F. E. 1951 Cosa, I: History and Topography. *Memoirs of the American Academy in Rome*, **20**, 89–96.

Lehmann–Hartleben, K. 1923 *Die antiken Hafenanlagen des Mittelmeeres*, 304 pp. [*Klio*, Beiheft 14]. Leipzig.

McCann, A. M. & Lewis, J. D. 1970 The Ancient Port of Cosa. *Archaeology*, **23** No. 3 (June 1970), 200–11.

Mori, A. 1963 Problemi dell'Insediamento Umano e della Vita Marittima nell'Antica Etruria Centrale. *Boll. Soc. geogr. ital.* (Ser. 9) **4**, 343–55.

Poidebard, A. & Lauffray, J. 1951 *Sidon. Aménagements Antiques du Port de Saida*. 103 pp. Beirut.

Rodenwaldt, E. & Lehmann, H. 1962 Die Antiken Emissare von Cosa-Ansedonia. *SB Heidelberg, math.-nat. Kl.*, 1962, 3–31.

Scullard, H. H. 1967 *The Etruscan Cities and Rome*, 61, 68, 104. 320 pp. Cornell & London.

Shore Protection, Planning and Design 1966, U.S. Army Corps Engrs Coastal Engineering Research Center: Technical Report No. 4, 3rd Edit. U.S. Govt. Printing Office, Washington D.C. 341–357.

Ward-Perkins, J. 1962 Etruscan Towns, Roman Roads and Medieval Villages: The Historical Geography of Southern Etruria. *Geogr. J.* **128**, 389–405.

Discussion

Blackman What do you think was the width of the entrance channel to the inner harbour?
Lewis A close estimate would be 20 m.

Parker What were the earliest and latest datable finds from the outer harbour?
Lewis The earliest finds are amphorae of the second century B.C. (the Sestius stamp variety), and the entire area is covered with sherds of the second century A.D.

Hagie I was very struck by the extraordinary width of the breakwater. Did it simply rest on sand?
Lewis The breakwater is some 70 m wide, the result perhaps of some scattering of the rock. It was built on sand rather than bedrock, and this must account in part for its depth of submergence now. We could not find bedrock.
Blackman This does introduce a further unknown factor in any estimate of sea level change. One had tended to regard massive breakwaters as fairly stable, except for spread from the upper surface and sides. It is not very impressive to find such a vital breakwater apparently floating on sand.

Hague Have you taken a series of spot levels along the actual bottom of the sluice channel, to determine its fall? This would help to establish its purpose.
Lewis No, not yet.

Linder The proportions between the width of the breakwater and the apparently small size of the harbour look very awkward. Have you considered the possibility that perhaps this whole construction which you called a breakwater could have earlier served some other purpose?
Lewis There are two points here: first, there is no doubt that the shoreline now is very different from what it was in antiquity. Perhaps the harbour was a lot bigger than now appears. The shoreline must have moved out as a result of the construction of the walls connected with the villa. Second, the breakwater has certainly spread somewhat, as a result of winter storms.

The harbour installations of Roman Britain

by

JOHN FRYER

SUMMARY

In contrast to what is known of the road system of Roman Britain our knowledge of the ports of that period is somewhat limited. Some harbour installations—including wharves, quays, jetties, moles, and lighthouses—have been located, largely in the course of modern building construction, but doubtless many more await discovery.

Many military and civil settlements are located in such a position at the junction of land and sea routes—that there can be little doubt that they were a part of the system of river and coastal communications. The harbours at Brough-on-Humber and Old Winteringham—terminals of the Roman ferry across the River Humber—have been located, but as yet no harbour installations have been found. The seaport town of Caister-by-Yarmouth, the harbour of which lies in the West Caister Marshes to the south of the site, once stood just inside the entrance to a wide, extensive estuary, in a position to give a short sea-crossing to the mouth of the River Rhine. There are many other sites which are similarly positioned, for the most part on rivers, at or near the head of tidal limits, or on navigable arms of the sea. The erosive processes of water action have in some cases—notably along the east coast—removed all trace of harbour installations; gravel extractors have accounted for others, such as Fordwich and Fingringhoe, the ports for Canterbury and Colchester. But many more were silted up—as at Chester, Caerhûn, Caerleon, Reculver and Dover—and these may well provide some information of a substantial nature. The excavations at Dover, the Portus Dubris, are a good example of this. While other sites to be reviewed have yielded only isolated features, the work at Dover resulted in the recovery of a considerable portion of the plan of the port, and yielded detailed information on the installations thus discovered and the techniques involved in their construction.

It would appear that the search for information about the ports and harbours of Roman Britain will, in the future, be in the hands of the "land archaeologists" and that there is no major site, with the possible exception of Walton Castle, at which the techniques of underwater exploration utilized in the Mediterranean may be employed.

IN CONTRAST TO what is known of the road system of Roman Britain, our knowledge of the ports of that period is somewhat limited. Some harbour installations—including wharves, jetties, quays, moles and lighthouses—have been located, largely in the course of modern building construction, but many more doubtless await discovery. It is the aim of this paper to present an account, based upon already published work, of the installations that have been located, to draw the reader's attention to a few of the many sites which, by nature of their position in relation to land and sea routes, may in the future yield further information on such works, and finally to complement in some way S. E. Rigold's recent paper on the port of Dover (Rigold, 1969).

A considerable portion of the plan of Portus Dubris has been recovered (Rigold, 1969, Fig. 1), together with detailed information on the harbour installations which have been observed or excavated, and the techniques involved in their construction. A full bibliography of the quays, jetty, mole, pharoi, the inner basin and the harbour settlement appears in Rigold's paper. As he says, "the early harbour installations were on a scale without known parallel in the province and (were) consistent with the view that at that period Dover was not merely a base, but was second only to Boulogne in the organization of the Classis Britannica".

Little can be said of the river-frontage of Londinium. The port installations that doubtless lined the River Thames along this strand now lie beneath Upper and Lower Thames Streets, at a level somewhat below Ordnance Datum. The only feature in this area which may have formed a part of these works is a wall which was located, in 1911, in Lower Thames Street, near the foot of Fish Street Hill. This lay at a depth of 7.1 m below ground level—approximately 1 m below O.D. Based on a foundation of substantial timbers, secured by pointed piles, this wall survived to a height of 0.91 m and was 3.05 m wide; among the sandstones, ragstones, chalk and tiles (in a bonding course) which were used in its construction were some apparently re-used stones. While it seems likely that this was once a river wall, possibly serving as a quay, its function must remain uncertain owing to a lack of adequately recorded data on the date of its construction and on its relationship to Ordnance Datum (Grimes, 1968, 56–64; Merrifield, 1965, 285).

It seems that none of the supply-bases of the invasion and later periods, such as Richborough, Fishbourne, Fingringhoe-Wick, Hamworthy, Sea Mills and South Shields, has as yet yielded any evidence for the presence of harbour installations, although all lay on what was navigable water. Similarly, the legionary fortresses at Colchester, Gloucester, Lincoln, Wroxeter, Inchtuthil, Chester, York and Caerleon, and, of course, the *coloniae* which succeeded some of them, were all situated on navigable rivers; of these, harbour installations have been located at Gloucester, Lincoln, Chester, York and Caerleon (cf. Vitruvius, V. xii. 2). However, secure dating evidence and data on the level of the structures in relation to Ordnance Datum are all too frequently lacking.

At Gloucester (Fig. 1), building excavations in 1937 revealed the foreshore of a former creek of the River Severn, some 90 m north-west of the *colonia* wall (in the area bordered by Quay Street and Upper Quay Street). This creek lay off the main course of the river and would afford some protection from its tidal bore and from the spate of its flow. Following the line of the foreshore, a continuous line of "rough" oak piles, 10.1 to 12.7 cm square and spaced at 1.83 m intervals (centre to centre), was traced over a length of 30.5 m; these were ranged at "varying depths". While neither timber nor hurdling was seen to be associated with the piles, there can be little doubt that they acted as a reinforcing agent for the earthen bank of the creek and may, therefore, have been an integral part of a landing stage (Green, 1942, 47–9; but see Knowles, 1937 & 1938). Sherds of pottery found close by, above the waterline, were attributable to the first century A.D. The line of this creek must have run past the northern termination of a harbour wall, or quay. This was located in the nineteenth century and was found to run in a line parallel to the river, but some 45 m to the east of it (Clarke, J., 1850; Fullbrook-Leggatt, 1933, 94–5; *Gents. Mag.*, 1846 & 1854). This wall was constructed of massive blocks of stone, "well squared and jointed", which derive from the Forest of Dean; these rested upon a large number of piles—6.1 m below ground level, perhaps a

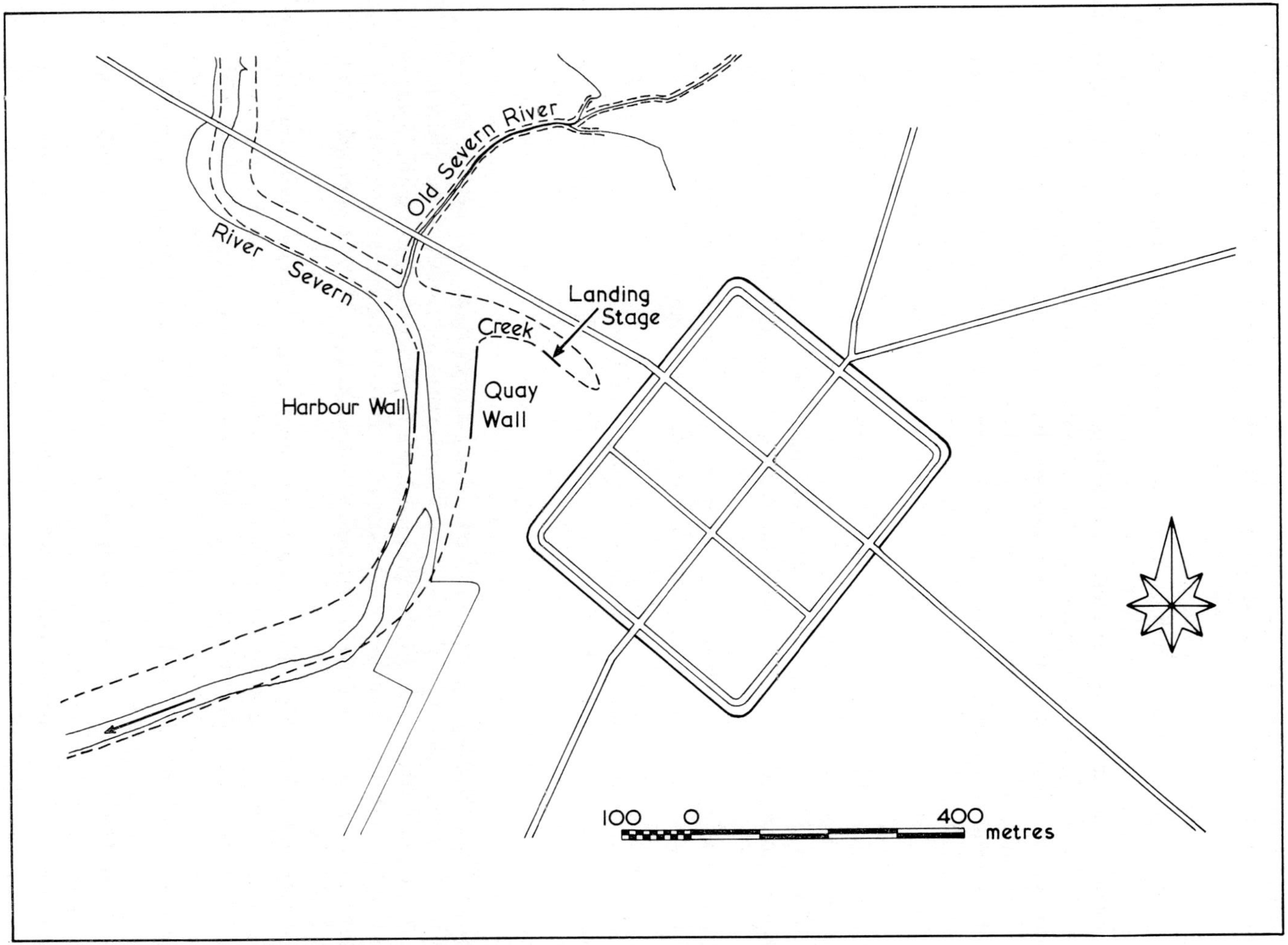

Figure 1. Plan of the legionary fortress, and *colonia*, at Gloucester, after nineteenth-century accounts and map. The approximate course of the River Severn in the first century A.D., designated by the broken lines, is here seen in relation to the nineteenth-century channel of that river. The siting of the harbour wall is uncertain, although its alignment is known.

little more than 3 m above O.D. The feature appeared to represent a continuous frontage, probably some 140 m in length, along the east bank of the river. The wall may be assigned to the Roman period on style of construction, but other dating evidence appears to be lacking.

Another nineteenth-century account tells of a second "massive" wall (Bellows, 1877). This was said to have run, at a depth of 2.5 m below the low-water mark of the river, in a line parallel to the harbour wall referred to above, from a point west of the north end of the Prison to the site of the gasworks. At the time of its discovery it was regarded as "certainly Roman", but, despite the fact that a fibula is reported to have been found when part of it was demolished, it does not seem prudent to attribute a date to it without more proof of age; however, a second-century date does seem likely.

Outside the south-east corner of the extended *colonia* at Lincoln, 91 m north of the present channel of the River Witham—beneath the junction of St. Rumbold Street and Broadgate—a substantially constructed wall, resting on rubble foundations 0.91 m deep, survived to a height of 38 cm; it has been traced over a length of 6.1 m, running in an east-west direction (Thompson, 1955). At its western end it turned north (under St. Rumbold Street). To the north it continued as a solid platform, while to the south much pottery of Flavian date has been collected from the surface of clean sand and gravel, 4.8 m below ground level; this has been taken to represent the old bed of the river. There is some evidence that the wall had been subjected to water action. It seems almost certain, therefore, that this wall was once part of a quay, situated, as Thompson has indicated, at a point well suited for traffic to the west and along the Lincolnshire Car Dyke.

This section of canal, together with the Cambridgeshire Car Dyke and in association with existing river systems, was apparently constructed to provide water communications between the area around Cambridge and Lincoln and York. Excavation of the Car Dyke at Cottenham, Cambridgeshire, has indicated a construction date soon after the middle of the first-century A.D. (Clark, 1949; Clark, R. R. 1960, 122; R.C.H.M., *Peterborough*, 1969, 40–3). Near Peterborough, on the east side of a large S-shaped meander of the River Nene, the termination of a Roman road, which passes just south of the settlement area centred on Grid Reference TL 136971, reaches a large depression near the river; it has been suggested that this may prove to be the site of a wharf or another type of harbour installation, designed to serve the river transport system (R.C.H.M., *Peterborough*, 1969, 22 & 39 No. 251).

The harbour at Chester (Fig. 2) was situated just outside the West Gate of the fortress, which itself lies within a loop of the Dee, a river which was tidal and navigable to Chester. The course of this river, like many others, has been subjected to considerable change since Roman times. At high tide, at least, a sheet of navigable water once stretched westward from just below the medieval city wall well out into the Roodee (Thompson, 1965, 47). A short distance south of the south-west corner of the Roman fortress the entrance, some 108 m wide, of what has been regarded as a creek, has been located. There is good reason to think that this was in fact the entrance to an arm of the Dee, which ran between the fortress and Castle Rock (Watkin, 1886, 102–3), and that the river may have been divided by two or more islands, now represented by the names Roodee (alternatively Roodeye) and Little Roodee, to the south-west of the fortress.

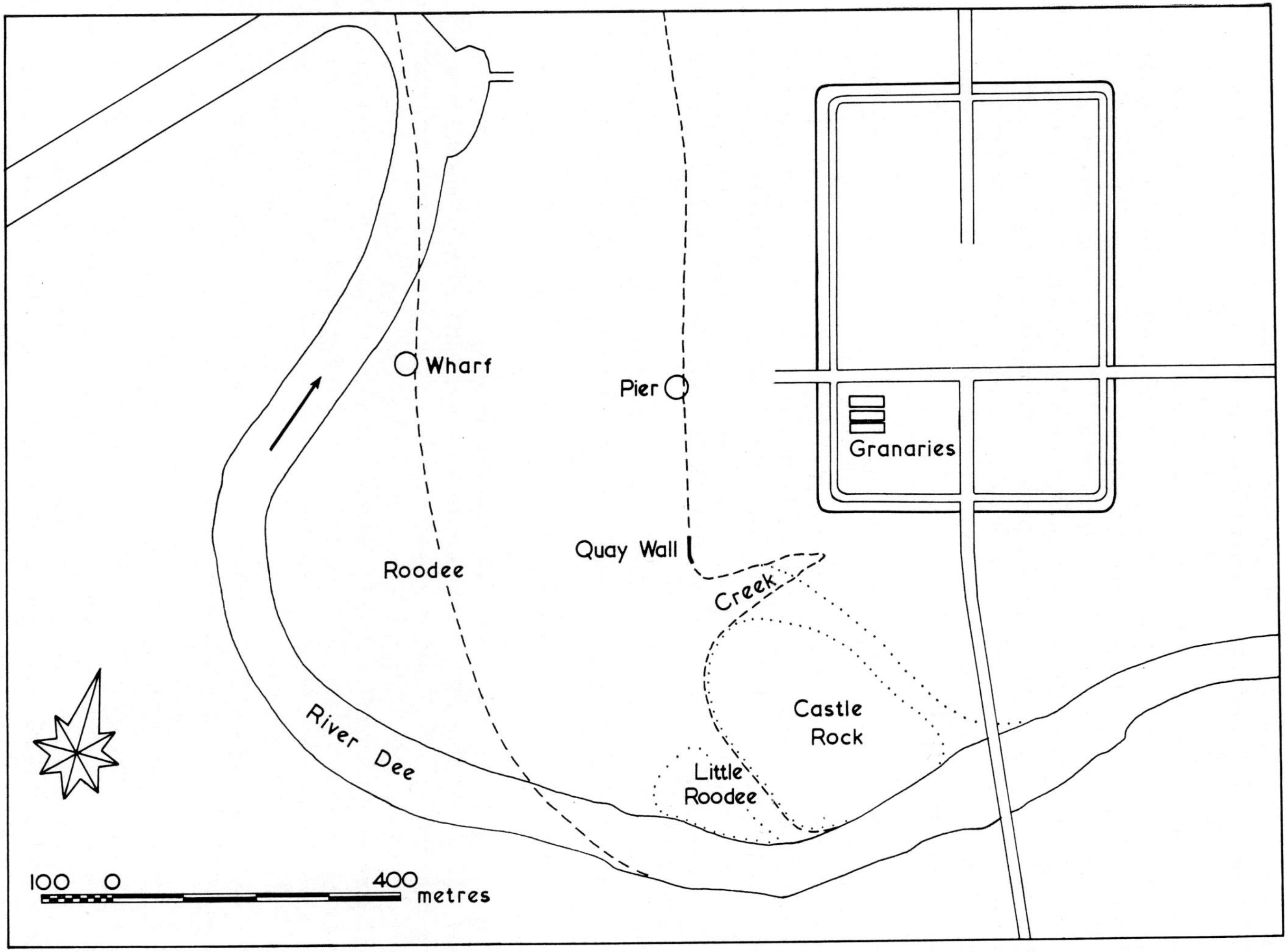

Figure 2. Plan of the legionary fortress at Chester. The first-century channel of the River Dee, as reconstructed by F. H. Thompson (1965, Figs. 2 & 4), is represented by the broken lines. The dotted lines mark the possible course of the arm of the river which may have run between Castle Rock and the fortress, and also the outline of one of the two or more islands in the channel, the existence of which is indicated by the names Roodee and Little Roodee.

Just north of the entrance to the "creek", at the foot of the medieval city wall, opposite Nun's Road, a wall 30 m in length of substantial masonry stands to a height of 2.74 m above and 4.57 m below ground level (Shrubsole, 1887). Attached at an angle of 90° to groyne walls, it may have been constructed for a dual purpose—to revet the bank at the foot of which it lies and to protect the entrance to the channel to the south; it seems reasonable to suggest that it also served as a quay (Thompson, 1965, 47 & Pl. 31). The "immense" blocks are held together by weight alone; some appear to have been undercut by the action of water and sand (Shrubsole, 1887). The masonry appears to be Roman in style, but dating evidence here, as in too many other instances, is lacking.

To the north of this quay, just below the medieval Watergate, sewerage excavations in 1874 revealed the remains of a "pier of oaken piles blackened with age" (Watkin, 1886, 114). This feature may be Roman or medieval in date; no Roman material was found associated with the timbers, although some debris of that period was found in the immediate vicinity.

Due west of this "pier", on the Roodee some 46 m east of the present channel of the Dee, excavations for a gasholder in the late nineteenth century revealed the remains of what may have been a Roman wharf. "In a bed of river gravel, covered by 20 ft. (6.1 m) of silt, logs of wood, oak piles, two human skulls, a layer of concrete" were found to be associated with pottery and coins of the first and early second centuries as well as a pig of Flintshire lead, dated by its inscription to A.D. 74 (Watkin, 1886, 163; Tylecote, 1962, 84–5, Table 34, No. 34). It is tempting to assign this wharf, if it is such, to the period of the construction of the fortress.

It is interesting to note that North Wales slate was used at Chester and that Chester sandstone was employed in the construction of the fort walls of Segontium, Caernarvon (Nash-Williams, 1954, 8 nn. 1–3 and s.v.). Two milestones have been found at Rhiwiau-uchaf Farm, 11 km west of the fort at Caerhûn (Sedgley, 1969, 14 Nos. 51–2; Collingwood & Wright, 1965, 709, Nos. 2265, 2266; on Caerhûn, see below p. 269). One is Hadrianic; the other is dated to 198–209, in the joint rule of Septimius Severus and Caracalla. The stone is thought to have come from Cefn-y-fedw, a few kilometres north of Llangollen. Sedgley (1969) has suggested that the crude milestones were probably transported to Chester, most likely along the Dee, where they were then inscribed and finished before being taken to Caerhûn by road or, as seems more likely, by sea. Incidentally, the granaries of the fortress at Chester were situated just inside the West Gate, at a point convenient of access from the harbour. It is by reference to evidence such as this that it is possible to reconstruct to some extent a picture of the sort of commodities which were transported through the ports of Roman Britain. Some of the voyages were never completed: the inscription on a memorial stone found at Chester tells of an *optio* who perished in a shipwreck (Collingwood & Wright, 1965, 181, No. 544).

For some 3 km above Chester the Dee was rocky and shallow, but the 16 km stretch from Heronbridge to the works depot at Holt was navigable. It seems that cargoes were shipped downriver to Heronbridge, where the Dee flows near to Watling Street, and that they were thence transported along that road to the fortress. The remains of what has been interpreted as a small dock, some 6.7 m wide, have been found at Heronbridge (Hartley and Kaine, 1954; Thompson, 1965, 62 Fig. 14). About the year 130 A.D., a natural hollow which runs through the site from west to east, at an angle of 90° to the river, was apparently artificially deepened and revetted with masonry on both sides.

Strip-buildings to the north may have functioned as storehouses. As the depot at Holt was established towards the end of the first century A.D., it seems reasonable to suggest that riverside installations of that time once existed at Heronbridge and may yet await discovery.

Resting above the confluence of the Rivers Ouse and Foss, York (Fig. 3) has yielded evidence for wharves lining the banks of the latter river, which appears to have been somewhat wider in Roman times than at present and to have been tidal and navigable (R.C.H.M., *York*, 1962, xxxi, 64–5).

On the site of the Telephone Exchange (SE 60595180) and built into what was once the steep west bank of the River Foss, was a large platform of great gritstone blocks, with associated walling, 1.52 m thick, of the same material (Fig. 3A: feature A; R.C.H.M., *York*, 1962, Monument 52, p. 64a & Figs. 52–3). Above this, a massively built stone platform of rectangular plan, 7.0 m × 6.1 m, may have had some functional connection with the waterfront, possibly as the base for a crane. Below the platform and in front of it, on the river bed, a double row of wooden piles, the remains, possibly, of a revetment or of the substructure of a wharf, have been traced over a length of over 12 m. North of the whole feature, a cobbled area 3.0–4.6 m wide ran along the top of the river bank; to the west lay a scatter of Roman pottery. It is quite likely that the structure is Roman in date, if only on structural grounds.

In 1829, during the excavations for a well, south of the present bank of the Foss (but on its east bank in Roman times), a "wall of Roman bricks" was found "resting on gravel and supporting a jetty formed of beams and posts", located at a depth of 9 m below ground level (Fig. 3A: feature B; R.C.H.M., *York*, 1962, Monument 53, p. 64b).

On the same side of the river, some 150 m to the south, two rows of rough stone columns, 0.91 m high and 30–45 cm square, were taken to be, at the time of their discovery in 1938, "clearly meant to support a platform, probably a wharf" (Fig. 3A: feature C; R.C.H.M., *York*, 1962, Monument 54, p. 65a; *JRS*, **29**, 1939, 204). Samian pottery, said to be Antonine in date, was recovered from the mud of the river bank.

It is of interest to recall the discovery at York of an altar dedicated to the mother goddess of Africa, Italy and Gaul by one M. Minucius Audens, *gubernator* of the Sixth Legion (Collingwood & Wright, 1965, 219, No. 653). As a river-pilot he would have been responsible for the navigation of army supply-boats up the difficult course of the Rivers Humber and Ouse.

Caerleon, legionary fortress of Second Legion, lay, like Chester on the Dee, on the inside of a loop of the River Usk, within its tidal reaches (Fig. 3B). To the south-west of the fortress the timber buildings of a supply-base of the invasion period have been located. From the fortress itself an extension of the *via principalis* ran down to wharves bordering the Usk, the north bank of which lay, in the Roman period, some 228 m within its present bend (Boon, 1964). At the termination of the road the remains have been found of a massive quay set into the bank of the river. This was excavated over a length of 15.2 m and was found to be running in a direction 25° south of east. A timber stage, supported by oak posts, was built in front of a revetment wall, 1.52 m thick. The posts were arranged in two rows, one set against the wall and the other approximately 2.28 m out from it. The posts in each row were spaced at 1.22 m intervals; they were held together laterally by horizontal ties and were braced from front to back by struts, fixed at an angle of 45°. The corner of the quay was protected by a groin of planks. The wall

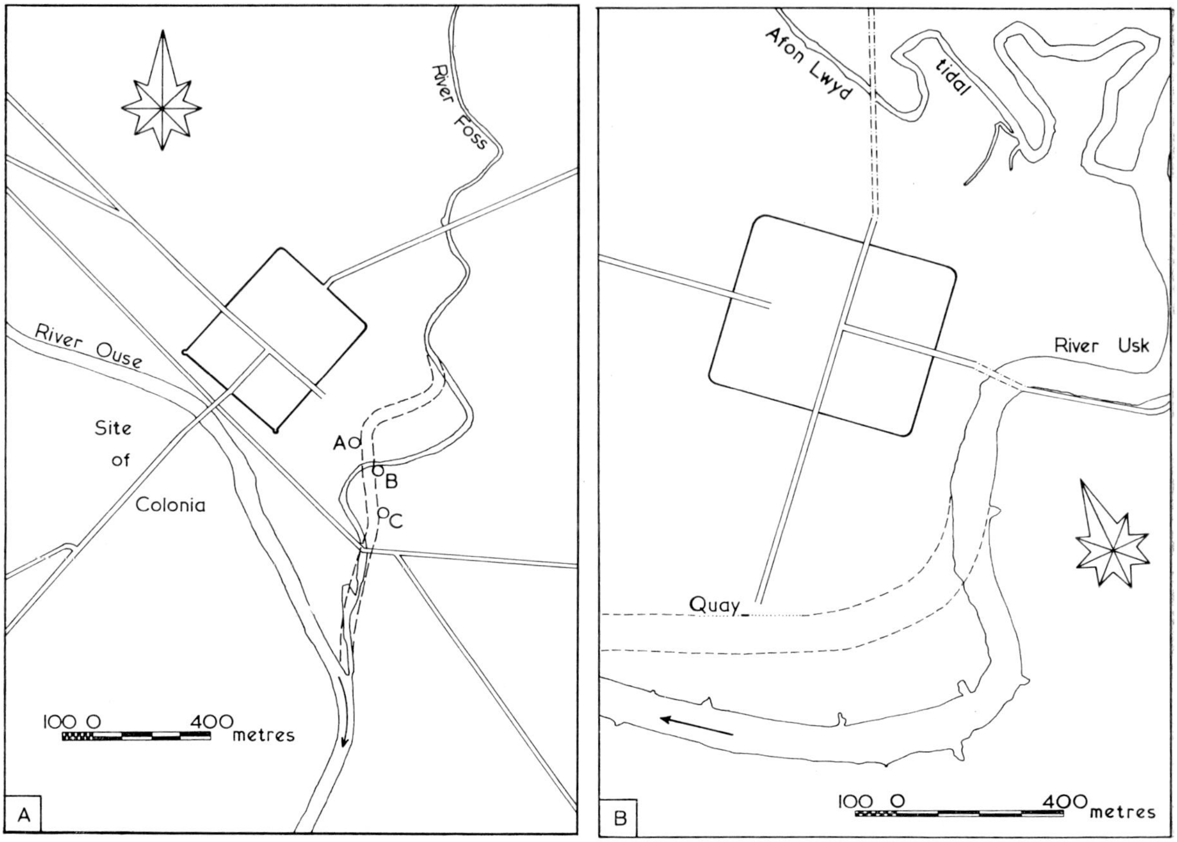

Figure 3. A: Plan of the legionary fortress and the *colonia* at York, illustrating the relationship between them and the harbour installations which lined the River Foss, the first-century A.D. course of which is shown by the broken lines. After R.C.H.M., *York*, 1962, Fig. 52 & Map.

B: Plan of the legionary fortress at Caerleon, showing the location of the quay on the north bank of the first-century A.D. channel of the River Usk. Partly based on Nash-Williams, 1940, Map B.

was of two periods, of the early to middle and the late third century. To the rear of the quay the mud-flat was metalled with ballast of Presili slate. Boon (1964) has calculated that at high water there would be sufficient water alongside this installation to accommodate vessels of up to 1.67 m draught. It is to be expected that other harbour features await excavation around this section of the river-frontage as far upstream as the bridge.

The distribution of auxiliary forts around the coastline of Wales can be regarded as a good example of a communications system based partly on water transport. Harbour installations have been found at Caerleon and Chester, as we have seen, and the auxiliary forts at Cardiff, Neath, Loughor, Carmarthen, Pennal, Caernarvon and Caerhûn are all situated on navigable rivers, at or near the head of tidal waters.

The fort at Caerhûn lies on the west bank of the River Conway, 6.4 km south of its mouth at Conway, and within its tidal reaches (R.C.A.M., *Caern.* 1, 1956, 34b). Although the Roman road which runs along the north coast of Wales crosses the river downstream of Caerhûn, it would seem that the river was still navigable up to the fort, at least at high water. It has been suggested that the bank of the river was lined with quays or wharves. But the Conwy River is short in comparison to its fall from the mountains and is as a result liable to a heavy flood spate. It is probable that a dock was constructed a short distance downriver from the fort to combat this danger. Some 338.5 m north of the fort a sunken channel, 82.35 m long and 9.15 m wide, leads to the river. It is flanked to the south by a stone platform, 68.58 m long by 12.2 m wide and at a height of 0.91 to 1.52 m above the base of the depression. The sides seem to have been revetted with large boulders. Trial excavation in 1929 suggested, but did not prove, a Roman date for the feature (Reynolds, 1930, 100–01).

Many military and civilian settlements are located in such a position, at the junction of land and sea routes, that there can be little doubt that they were a part of the system of river and coastal communications. The harbours at Brough-on-Humber and Old Winteringham, terminals of the Roman ferry across the River Humber, which occupy such a postiion, have been located, but as yet no installations have been reported (Wacher, 1969; Stead, forthcoming).

In East Anglia, the estuaries and marshlands which lie to the west of Yarmouth are the site of a large, open estuary which ran far inland in Roman times (Green & Hutchinson, 1960; Steers, 1964, 376–80). It was on the north bank of this estuary, just inside its mouth, and in a position to give a short sea-crossing to the mouth of the Rhine, that the seaport town at Caister-by-Yarmouth was founded in the first part of the second century A.D. (Clarke, R. R., 1960, 119). To the south its harbour, the outline of which is probably represented by the configuration of the 15 m contour, is now covered by the West Caister marshes, from which, in the last century, iron anchors and planking, said to be derived from a boat, are reported to have been recovered (Clowes, 1837). The nodular flint of which the town walls and the exterior walls of the buildings are constructed derives from the Norwich and/or North Walsham areas. It was almost certainly transported to Caister by way of the Rivers Yare and/or Bure. An extensive timber platform, probably a wharf, has been found on the north bank of the River Yare, just below its confluence with the River Wensum, at a depth of 3.66 m below marsh level, 2.44–2.74 m below O.D. (Clarke, R.R., 1962). Associated with the structure was a thick spread of building debris and sherds, including Gallo-Belgic wares of the mid-first to mid-second centuries A.D. It has been thought that the cantonal capital of Venta Icenorum at Caister-St.-Edmunds, south of Norwich, was served by a port on the south bank of the River Yare, somewhere in the vicinity of Kirby Bedon (downstream from the feature described above). While it does seem likely that the two places were connected by road, there appears to be no other evidence to support the theory, other than that Venta was almost certainly served by a port somewhere on the south bank of the Yare (Margary, 1967, 270).

All the forts of the Litus Saxonicum and the late Roman forts at Cardiff, Caernarvon and Caer Gybi (Holyhead) were originally situated on estuaries or arms of the sea (White, 1961, 33–40; Nash-Williams, 1969, 174 and s.v.). The Saxon Shore fort at Burgh Castle, across the estuary from Caister-by-Yarmouth, has provided some evidence for the presence there of a quay (Green, 1961; M.o.W., 1967). The fort lies on a shelf of ground some 9 m above the east bank of the River Waveney at its opening into Breydon Water—formerly part of the great estuary referred to above (p. 269). At the foot of this shelf, beneath a stratum of water-deposited clay, 45–61 cm thick, Harrod's excavations in 1850 and 1855 revealed masses of broken mortar which contained large quantities of flint and tiles. In one of a series of trenches which ran in a line along the foot of the shelf, a wall 1.52 m wide (and 1.22 m below marsh level) rested upon a number of decayed oak piles which extended outwards 3.35 m from the inner (eastern) face of the wall. To the south, Harrod found that clay, chalk lumps and mortar had been rammed, to a depth of 45 cm, in between piles set 30 cms apart; the piles themselves had been driven into "black mud" (Morris & Hawkes, 1949). This piling was also 3.35 m wide. Elsewhere layers of flints rested upon apparently puddled clay, 1.83 m deep. A thin spread of gravel was traced in three, although not consecutive, trenches. The area to the west of the feature was very wet. The evidence as a whole seems to point strongly to the conclusion that this was the foundation of one or more harbour installations—probably a substantial quay—associated with the Saxon Shore fort. It has been suggested that a "naval dockyard", a base for a squadron of the Classis Britannica, lay a little way to the south of the fort in what was once a sheltered creek, now Belton Fen (Green and Hutchinson, 1960, 138).

While the erosive processes of water action have destroyed some sites, such as Walton Castle, others, for example Fingringhoe-Wick and Fordwich, have succumbed to gravel extractors.

Fordwich lies at the head of the navigable waters of the River Stour, on its north bank, nearly 5 km east of Canterbury, to which it is linked by the road that passes by the settlement at Fordwich. Rescue excavations have revealed the remains of what may have been a Roman wharf. A considerable number of large stakes and a heavy oak beam were located, lying at the edge of the alluvium—alluvium which was thought to represent the former shoreline of a creek of the River Stour (Jenkins, 1949, *a* & *b*). The trees from which these timbers are derived were felled in about the middle of the third century A.D., a date which agrees with that of the stratified levels to the north, which show occupation in the second and third centuries, and possibly into the fourth century A.D. Without further adequately recorded data it is not possible to reach any conclusion other than that the presence and position of the timbers seem to indicate a functional connection with the waterfront, perhaps in the form of a revetment for the bank of the creek or of a substructure for wharfage.

The river frontage at Bitterne was probably given wharves by Flavian times, but Roach Smith's description of the finding of a "very substantial wooden pile framework", which had been partially excavated some years before he wrote his paper, cannot be regarded as reliable evidence. Although such a structure is to be expected in such a position, there appears to be no evidence regarding the level of the feature in relation to that of the River Itchen nor concerning the date of the wharf, if it is such (Smith, 1883; Cotton & Gathercole, 1958, 14, 139–40).

At the head of the most easterly inlet of Chichester Harbour lies Fishbourne, a site that has seen the establishment of a supply-base, a harbour settlement and a palace. Excavations conducted by B. Cunliffe have located an area of made-up ground, approximately triangular in shape, with its base lying along the south side of the palace, and its apex some 64 m to the south, towards the harbour (Cunliffe, 1968, 34–5; 1970). The make-up consisted of 0.9–1.2 m of tipped gravel, silt and clay; it consolidated the ground in such a way that a "new steeper shoreline was created closer to deeper water" (Cunliffe, 1968). It has been suggested that this feature may be ornamental in function; but this need not necessarily preclude its use as a quay.

Basing his theories on an estimate that in the first century A.D. sea level was some 3–6 m below the present, H. Wallace has suggested that the waters bounding this feature were in the form and nature of a freshwater basin to which access was gained by one or more locks (Wallace, 1969). But there is as yet no published evidence that these waters were not marine; nor have the banks and "very massive stone foundations", which, he claims, may have been part of the system of locks, been dated by archaeological methods. Indeed, the entire theory depends on the supposition that sea level in the first–second centuries A.D. was considerably lower than now.

At Dover, alongside the Stembrook quay and jetty, the floor of the Roman River Dour lay between 3 and 9 cm below O.D.; for a distance of 16 m in advance of the quay, it was apparently no deeper than 0.73 m below O.D. (Rahtz, 1958, 112–17; Rigold, 1969, 83). The surface of the jetty lay at a height of 1.4 m, and that of the quay at 1.8 m, above O.D. These installations may have been given superstructures, but the level of the strata of occupation of the harbour settlement dictate that normal high water springs must have been below 2 m above O.D. If the high tide at springs rose to a height not far short of the surface of the jetty, there would have been sufficient water alongside this installation to accommodate vessels of up to approximately 1.3 m draught (cf. Caerleon). In other words, mean high water at springs in the first and second centuries A.D. at Dover can have been only slightly lower than modern high water, which varies between 1.85 and 3.05 m above O.D. If one allows for coastal variation, mean high water in Chichester Harbour cannot have been more than 1 m below the present level. Thus there seems to be no reason to doubt that vessels could have sailed right up to the harbour at Fishbourne without the aid of locks.

Cunliffe has also reported the finding of a deep-water channel at Fishbourne, constructed in *c.* A.D. 75; this was revetted on its northern side with timber and stonework (Cunliffe, 1970).

Such are the sites that have yielded evidence on harbour installations. There are approximately one hundred others which, by nature of their position in relation to land and sea routes, may in the future provide more data. But the work will, it seems, be in the hands of the "land archaeologist", for there appears to be no major site, with the possible exception of Walton Castle, at which the techniques of underwater exploration used in the Mediterranean may be employed.

REFERENCES

Bellows, J. 1877 *Proceedings of the Cotteswold Naturalists' Field Club*, **6**, 179.
Boon, G. C. 1964 Report summarized in *JRS*, **54**, 152–3.
Clark, J. G. D. 1949 Excavations on the Cambridgeshire Car Dyke, 1947. *Antiquaries' J.* **29**, 145–63.
Clarke, J. 1850 *The Architectural History of Gloucester*, 105pp. *Gloucester.*
Clarke, R. R. 1960 *East Anglia*, 240 pp. London.

Clarke, R. R. 1962 Report summarized in *JRS*, **52**, 176.
Clowes, T. 1837 Roman Antiquities found at Caister, Norfolk. *Gentlemen's Magazine*, N.S., **8**, 518–21.
Collingwood, R. G. & Wright, R. P. 1965 *Roman Inscriptions of Britain*, Vol. 1, 790 pp. Oxford.
Cotton, M. A. & Gathercole, P. W. 1958 *Excavations at Clausentum, Southampton, 1951–1954*, 169 pp. (Min. of Works Archaeological Reports, No. 2). H.M.S.O., London.
Cunliffe, B. 1968 Excavations at Fishbourne, 1967: Seventh and Final Preliminary Report. *Antiquaries' J.* **48**, 32–40.
Cunliffe, B. 1970 Report summarized in *Britannia*, **1**, 303.
Fullbrook-Leggatt, L. E. W. O. 1933 Glevum. *Trans. Bristol & Gloucestershire Archaeological Soc.* **55**, 55–104.
Green, C. 1942 *Glevum* and the Second Legion. *JRS*, **32**, 39–52.
Green, C. & Hutchinson, J. N. 1960 Archaeological Evidence, *in* Lambert, J. M. & others, *The Making of the Broads* (Royal Geogr. Soc. Research Series, No. 3) Part III, 113–46.
Green, C. 1961 Report summarized in *JRS*, **51**, 183.
Grimes, W. F. 1968 *The Excavation of Roman and mediaeval London*, 261 pp. London.
Hartley, B. R. & Kaine, K. F. 1954 Heronbridge Excavations—Roman Dock and Buildings. *Chester and North Wales Architectural, Archaeological & Historical Society Journal*, N.S., **41**, 15–37.
Jenkins, F. 1949*a* Recent Excavation in the Canterbury District: Sturry. *Archaeologia Cantiana* **62**, 145–6.
Jenkins, F. 1949*b* Report summarized in *JRS*, **39**, 111–12.
Knowles, W. H. 1937 Notes: Roman Research Committee, Gloucester. *Trans. Bristol & Gloucestershire Archaeological Soc.* **59**, 337–8.
Knowles, W. H. 1938 Roman Research Committee: Report on finds during 1938–9 . . . *Trans. Bristol & Gloucestershire Archaeological Soc.* **60**, 165–8.
Margary, I. D. 1967 *Roman Roads in Britain*, 546 pp. London.
Merrifield, R. 1965 *The Roman City of London*, 344 pp. London.
Morris, A. J. & Hawkes, C. F. C. 1949 The Fort of the Saxon Shore at Burgh Castle, Suffolk, *Arch. J.* **106**, 66–9.
Nash-Williams, V. E. 1940 *The Roman Legionary Fortress at Caerleon, Monmouthshire*, 33 pp. National Museum of Wales & University of Wales, Cardiff.
Nash-Williams, V. E. 1954 *The Roman Frontier in Wales*, 161 pp. Cardiff.
Nash-Williams, V. E. 1969 *The Roman Frontier in Wales*, 2nd Edit. by M. G. Jarrett. 206 pp.
Rahtz, P. A. 1958 Dover: Stembrook and St. Martin-le-Grand, 1956. *Archaeologia Cantiana*, **72**, 111–37.
Reynolds, P. K. Baillie 1930 Excavations on the site of the Roman Fort at Caerhûn: Fourth Interim Report. *Archaeologia Cambrensis*, **85**, 74–102.
Rigold, S. E. 1969 The Roman Haven at Dover. *Arch. J.* **126**, 78–100, with references.
Sedgley, J. P. 1969 *Roman Milestones of Britain*, University of Keele Thesis.
Shrubsole, G. W. 1887 The Traffic between Deva and the Coast of North Wales in Roman Times. *Chester Archaeological & Historic Society Journal*, N.S., **1**, 76–96.
Smith, C. Roach 1883 The Antiquary's Note-Book: Notes on Clausentum; now Bittern Manor. *The Antiquary*, **7**, 79–80.
Stead, I. M. Report forthcoming.
Steers, J. A. 1964 *The Coastline of England and Wales*, 2nd Edit., 750 pp. Cambridge.
Thompson, F. H. 1955 Report summarized in *JRS*, **45**, 131.
Thompson, F. H. 1965 *Roman Cheshire*, 122 pp. Chester.
Tylecote, R. F. 1962 *Metallurgy in Archaeology: A prehistory of metallurgy in the British Isles*, 368 pp. London.
Wacher, J. S. 1969 *Excavations at Brough-on-Humber, 1958–1961*, (Reports of the Research Committee of the Society of Antiquaries, London, No. 25) 243 pp. Leeds.
Wallace, H. 1969 Selsey and Chichester Harbour. *Committee for Nautical Archaeology, Newsletter*, **3**, 18–21.
Watkin, W. T. 1886 *Roman Cheshire*, 327 pp. Liverpool.

White, D. A. 1961 *Litus Saxonicum: The British Saxon Shore in scholarship and history*, 122 pp. Madison, Wisconsin.

Gents. Mag. 1846 Roman Antiquities at Gloucester. *Gentlemen's Magazine*, N.S., **26**, 517.

Gents. Mag. 1854 (Clarke, J.) The Diggings at Gloucester. *Gentlemen's Magazine*, N.S., 6–7 **41**, 486–7.

M.o.W. 1967 *Guide to Burgh Castle*, Ministry of Public Buildings and Works.

Ordnance Survey 1956 *Map of Roman Britain*, 3rd Edition.

R.C.A.M., *Caern.* 1 1956 *An inventory of the ancient monuments in Caernarvonshire*, Vol. 1: *The East*, 215 pp. Royal Commission on Ancient and Historical Monuments, Wales and Monmouth.

R.C.H.M., *York* 1962 *An inventory of the historical monuments in the City of York*, Vol. 1: *Eburacum: Roman York*, 168 pp. Royal Commission on Historical Monuments, England.

R.C.H.M., *Peterborough* 1969 *Peterborough New Town: A survey of the antiquities in the areas of development*, 87 pp. Royal Commission on Historical Monuments, England.

Discussion

Hawkins Is there any relationship between modern surface currents and Roman ports around Britain? For instance, were the Romans influenced by the water velocity? You mentioned several Roman ports in southern England; are any changes in sea level indicated by these? I am interested because I am committed in print to the suggestion that there is a tidal change in the Severn estuary in the post-Roman period.

Fryer The influence of such factors as surface current velocity upon the choice of the site of a Roman port is an unknown quantity. But Wacher's discussion of the River Humber, in relation to the Roman harbours at Old Winteringham and Brough-on-Humber, is of some relevance (Wacher, 1969, 76–81 & Figs. 31–33). These terminals of the Roman ferry across the Humber were based on harbours which were sheltered from the main stream of the river: that at Brough in a natural inlet west of the fort, that at Old Winteringham in a now silted-up haven, east of that settlement, at Flashmire. The harbour at North Ferriby, which was apparently in use in pre-Roman times, afforded little or no protection from the river's flow, although its opposite number at South Ferriby, situated near the mouth of the River Ancholme, may have provided superior facilities. A third possible alternative site lay some 6 km upstream of Brough at Faxfleet, opposite the outfall of the River Trent, which itself is swift of flow and does not afford the shelter which is offered by the harbours which the Romans used.

The River Humber itself was not an easily navigable river, "with rough water, constantly changing shoals and banks and high current speeds", of 3–4 knots and up to 7 knots in places. To cover the 56 km to Brough and Old Winteringham from the open sea, vessels would have to come up river with the flood tide, to make the most of the current.

Which of the two harbours was more suitable for upriver traffic probably depends upon the ease with which it could be approached. But there is, as Wacher commented, apparently no way of reconstructing the configurations of the river channels of the Roman Humber.

It should be noted that the floors of the harbours at Old Winteringham and Brough are of sand and shingle, which gives foreshores on which ships could be beached more easily for repair and laying-up. The harbours at North and South Ferriby and Faxfleet have bottoms of mud or clay.

It does seem, then, that current flow and velocity may have played some part in the choice of the harbours at Brough and Old Winteringham. Many Roman ports and harbours, as at London, Caerleon and Chester, lie at or near the head of tidal limits; this may have been to diminish the effects of tidal range as much as possible. However, the ports at Dover and Richborough and the forts of the Litus Saxonicum do not seem to conform to this rule.

As to tidal change in the Severn estuary, I would refer you to the results of G. C. Boon's excavations at Caerleon and the levels of the harbour installations at Gloucester, referred to in my paper. As regards relative change of sea level, I would refer you to Wacher's report on Brough-on-Humber, Rigold's compilation of the material on Dover,

Green and Hutchinson's findings at Great Yarmouth (and to the Roman harbour installations found at Norwich and Burgh Castle, and described in my paper); and finally to the publications of Grimes and Merrifield on the river-frontage of Londinium.

Parker Where do you think the wheat came from to the West Gate of Chester? Granaries are not normally near the gates of fortresses.

Fryer There appears to be no evidence concerning the provenance of the corn which was supplied to the West Gate at Chester. A study of the distribution patterns of certain commodities, such as lead ingots, or imported artifacts, may throw some light on trading routes. Mendip lead may have been exported through Bitterne (Cotton & Gathercole, 1958).

Apart from Chester, three of the six granaries at Inchtuthil are situated in close proximity to gates.

King's Lynn and east coast trade in the Middle Ages

by

HELEN CLARKE

1. INTRODUCTION

IN 1963 AN ARCHITECTURAL, archaeological and documentary investigation of the medieval port of King's Lynn, Norfolk, was begun by the King's Lynn Archaeological Survey in response to plans for the rapid expansion of the town and redevelopment of its historic core. The aim of the Survey was to record all buildings of historic interest within the town centre, to assemble documentary references to the history of the town in the Middle Ages and to carry out rescue excavations on sites temporarily vacant because of the rebuilding programme. The areas available for excavation were naturally limited by circumstances, but were selected as far as possible to represent the different areas and periods of the town's development (Fig. 1). Excavation continued on a number of sites from June 1963 until 1969 and the final report is now in preparation (Clarke & Carter); a volume on the architecture is in the press (Parker, V., 1971) and it is hoped that publication of the documentary history of King's Lynn will follow.

The rich documentary sources for the development of the town have long been recognized and a number of histories published (Beloe, 1899; Harrod, 1874; Hillen, 1907; Richards, 1812; Taylor, 1844). There are also some more recent works (Carus-Wilson, 1962–3, 182–3; Hoskins, 1959; Smith, 1970, 57–8). The scope of this paper is not a general history of King's Lynn, but rather an illustration of how archaeological evidence drawn from excavated material may supplement and reinforce written sources.

2. THE ORIGINS OF THE TOWN

King's Lynn lies on the east bank of the River Great Ouse in low-lying land which was made habitable only by drainage. There is sparse evidence for settlement before the end of the eleventh century when, about 1095, Herbert Losinga, Bishop of Norwich, founded both the parish and priory church of St. Margaret and the Saturday Market on land adjoining the church to the north-west. These foundations lie roughly in the centre of an area bounded by two streams, the Purfleet to the north and Millfleet to the south (Fig. 1); this area appears to have remained the nucleus of the town until the middle of the following century when Bishop William of Norwich founded a town extension, the *New Land*, defined on its northern edge by the Fisher Fleet. The history of the growth of South Lynn, lying south of Millfleet and east of the River Nar (or

Figure 1. Map of King's Lynn taken from Henry Bell's *Groundplat of Kings Lyn* c. 1680. Sites mentioned in the text—A: Thoresby College; B: Marks and Spencer; C: Sedgeford Lane; D: Baker Lane; E: All Saints' Street.

Friar's Fleet) is more obscure and it is usually considered a later suburb, perhaps of thirteenth-century date. In 1966 and 1967, however, excavations on the All Saints' Street site (Fig. 1E) produced eleventh- and twelfth-century pottery which indicated very early occupation, and it may be that there was settlement in South Lynn contemporary with, if not pre-dating, Bishop Losinga's foundation farther north (Wilson & Hurst, 1968).

The growth of the town was intimately bound up with trade, especially with water-borne traffic plying up and down the east coast of England and across the North Sea. Lynn was particularly fortunate in its geographical position at a time when water transport was predominant—its connections by river with eastern and midland England were excellent and goods from Bedfordshire, Buckinghamshire, Huntingdonshire, Cambridgeshire, Rutland, Leicestershire, Northamptonshire and Warwickshire could easily reach the town. In addition, it lay sufficiently far from the coast to be removed from the danger of piracy, a factor in medieval trade.

3. DOCUMENTARY EVIDENCE OF TRADE

In her excellent survey of the medieval trade of the ports of Boston and Lynn Professor Carus-Wilson (1962–3) has described the fluctuations in prosperity of the two towns from the twelfth to the sixteenth century. Documentary evidence suggests that from the end of the twelfth and throughout the thirteenth century Lynn's main export was grain—with the associated products of ale and malt—brought by river to Lynn from the fertile, newly-drained fenland around the Wash and shipped out northwards along the east coast as far as Scotland and also across the Channel and North Sea to the Low Countries and Norway.

By the beginning of the fourteenth century corn had been supplemented by wool as an important export and Lynn was linked particularly closely to Flanders, where the weaving industry generated a great demand for the fine wool of England, particularly that grown in Lincolnshire and the east midlands. The middle of the century, however, saw a sharp decline in the amount of raw wool being exported from England, and Lynn suffered as a result. The rise of the Hanseatic merchants of North Germany and their virtual monopoly of trade with north-west Europe was a severe setback to English traders, and contacts with much of the Continent were broken. At the same time the Hundred Years War led to a decline in trade with France and a general stagnation in Lynn's export activities. At the beginning of the fifteenth century contacts with Iceland (a dependency of Norway and therefore officially banned to all but Hanse traders) appeared to give trade something of a boost, but this was soon stopped and when, in the middle of the fifteenth century, both English cloth and English merchants were forbidden the Baltic ports, the end of Lynn's contacts with northern Europe was reached.

Imports from abroad seem to have followed much the same pattern, with an increase in the thirteenth century. Fish, both cod and herring, was imported in enormous quantities and the main sources seem to have been the Baltic and Norway; timber, timber products, furs and even hawks are recorded as coming from Scandinavia, the Baltic islands and coasts, and there were particularly close relations with Norway. Flanders was an important source of fine cloth at a time when raw wool rather than woollen cloth was being exported from England; Picardy produced woad, used fo:

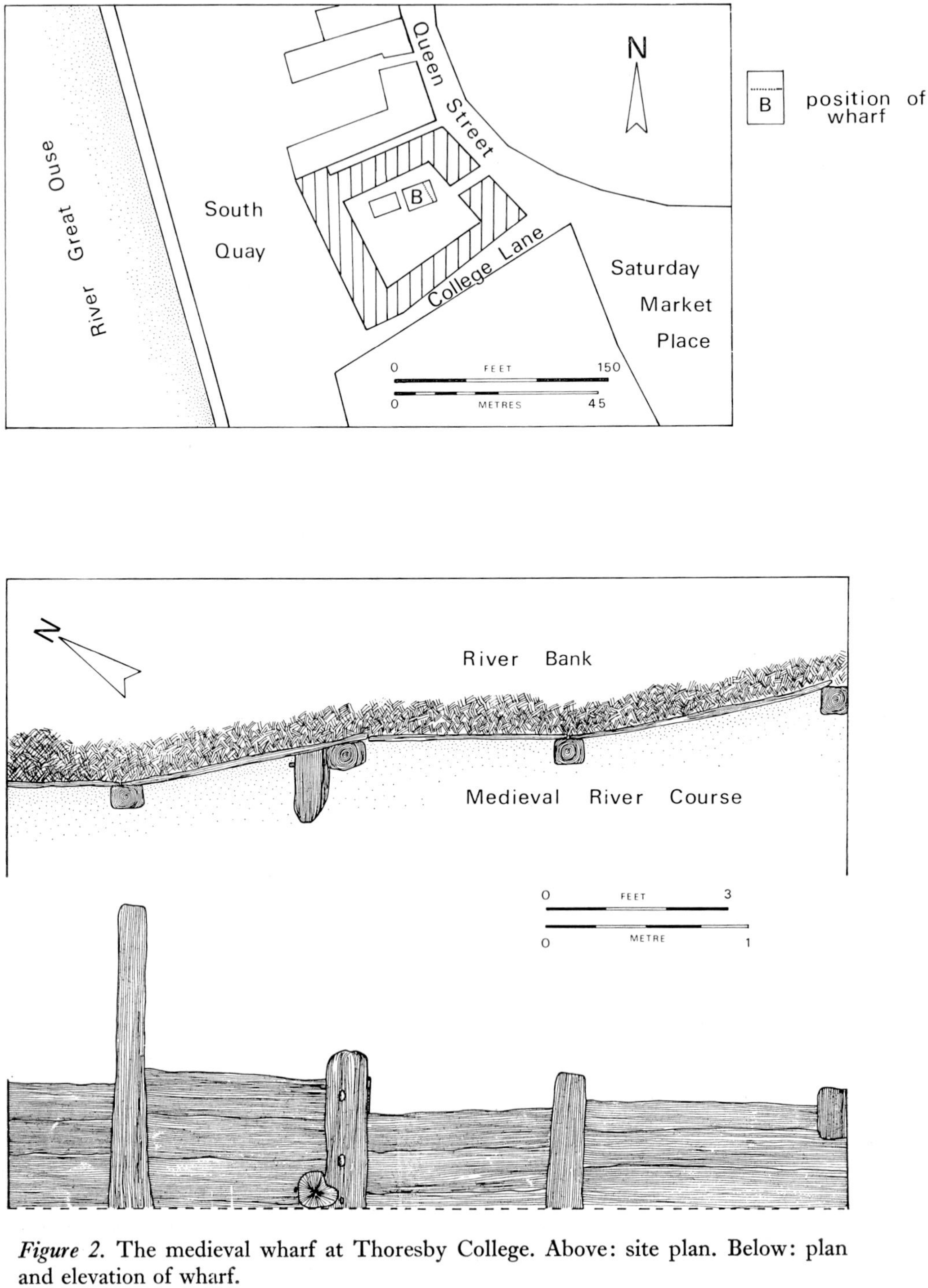

Figure 2. The medieval wharf at Thoresby College. Above: site plan. Below: plan and elevation of wharf.

dyeing; wine came in great quantity from France, particularly Gascony, and exotic goods such as fruit and olive oil came from Spain.

From the list of goods passing through Lynn in the Middle Ages one can infer a number of general trends. The volume of trade was probably at its largest in the thirteenth century when Lynn's foreign interests embraced an enormous area stretching from Iceland in the north to Spain in the south. At this period Lynn was in close contact with the fenland and immediately surrounding areas for supplies of corn for export; by the end of the century wool was more in demand and Lynn's sources of supply extended farther inland into central England and southern Lincolnshire. After the middle of the fourteenth century Lynn's foreign trade diminished and the prosperity of the port declined, although fish still remained a significant import and coastal traffic continued. We hear of herring being brought down to East Anglia from the ports of Hull, Whitby and Scarborough (Waites, 1964) and even of East Anglian ships taking part in the coal trade—in 1394–5 a "ship of Lyn" delivered coal to Whitby Abbey (Waites, 1963).

4. ARCHAEOLOGICAL EVIDENCE OF TRADE

Although Miss Carus-Wilson says (1962–3, 194–5) "[swords and helmets] would seem to be the only wares, of all those we have mentioned, which could possibly have left any trace for the archaeologist; the principal exports and imports on which the trade of the ports of the Wash depended remain invisible save in the records", enough archaeological evidence has been produced by the King's Lynn excavations to supplement, if not extend, our knowledge of its medieval trade.

The main source of information is provided by the large amounts of pottery which have been discovered on all the excavated sites; the pottery includes not only that produced by the local kilns at Grimston, some 6 miles east of King's Lynn, but also wares which are known to have been made by kilns in eastern England and abroad. Such pottery seems to have been brought to Lynn both incidentally—together with the main products which were being traded—and also, especially in the case of fine decorated table-wares (for instance, Fig. 6), deliberately for sale. It is also possible that much scrap pottery reached the port from ships discharging broken pots into the harbour, the pottery having been either intended for sale, or merely part of the ship's equipment (Herteig, 1959, 186).

Other evidence for trade may be found in the structures discovered on excavation sites and both these types of evidence will be discussed below.

Figure 1 shows the sites of the excavations of 1963–9. Those at Thoresby College (A), Sedgeford Lane (C) and Baker Lane (D) all lie within the area of Bishop Losinga's foundation and were investigated in the hope of producing material to confirm their early date. The Marks and Spencer site (B) is situated within Bishop William's *New Land*, close to the mid-thirteenth century Tuesday Market Place, and could be expected to represent the expansion of King's Lynn at the height of its prosperity. The final site (E), All Saints' Street, is in the more problematic area of South Lynn, of which so little is known from documents (p. 277–9) and where excavation might provide fresh information about the town's development.

Figure 3. Part of the Thoresby College wharf viewed from the north-west. Photo: King's Lynn Archaeological Survey.

Sites A, C and D were also positioned close to water, so that they might reveal evidence of the water-borne trade about which the documents tell us so much (p. 279). Sixteenth-century documents in particular[1] are rich in references to wharves and staithes along the Great Ouse and the fleets, and although there are only occasional references in earlier texts it is possible that those sites with well-attested sixteenth-century quays also possessed them during earlier occupation.

Thoresby College (Fig. 1A; Fig. 2) is mentioned as having a wharf at College Lane in 1557 (*Rentals & Surveys*, Bc. 7, p. 12) and in 1570–1 a new wharf and staithe were ordered to be built (*Chamberlains' Accounts*, Bc. 7). A wharf is mentioned "at Purfleet Street end on east side of Purfleet Bridge" (*Rentals & Surveys*, Bc. 7, p. 12), which appears to lie on the opposite bank to Site D, Baker Lane. Even as far upstream as Site C, Sedgeford Lane, there was a quay, "on the north side of Sedgeforth Lane to the fleet against a little lane there" (*Rentals & Surveys*, Bc. 7, p. 12). The Marks and Spencer site (B) is the only site not mentioned by the texts as having a wharf, for even All Saints' Street (Fig. 1E) seems to have been at least close to a wharf which lay

[1] *Rentals & Surveys* and *Chamberlains' Accounts* in the King's Lynn Town Hall. Quotations from the documents are taken from unpublished transcripts made by Mrs. D. M. Owen for the King's Lynn Archaeological Survey. Reference numbers refer to the catalogue system in the town archives.

"between Fyshers house and John Glovers house on east of Friar's flat" (*sic*) (*Rentals & Surveys*, Bc. 7, p. 12). At the time of settlement the site may have lain immediately beside a fleet—probably the present River Nar or Friar's Fleet. There is, therefore, plenty of evidence for the importance of the river and the fleets in the town at the end of the Middle Ages, and these could only have gained such prominence through water-borne traffic and trade.

One site, Thoresby College, produced invaluable evidence for quay construction in medieval King's Lynn (Parker, H., 1965). The College was built as a chantry college for St. Margaret's Church in the early sixteenth century by Thomas Thoresby, sometime Mayor of Lynn, who purchased the land from the Guild of Jesus (Eller, 1861, 133–40). There are no documentary references to buildings on the site before the construction of the College, but the area must always have been of economic importance, lying as it does at the junction of Queen Street, College Lane and Saturday Market Place (Fig. 2), and even in the sixteenth century having a frontage directly onto the river. According to Henry Bell's *Groundplat of Kings Lyn* of *c.* 1680 the west wing of the College still lay immediately beside the Great Ouse, but today the distance between the west face of the College and the edge of the South Quay is something over 30 yards. In the Middle Ages the site may have been used as a loading place for goods on their way to and from Saturday Market Place.

In 1964 two trenches were opened in the courtyard of the College. The more westerly trench proved to have had all its medieval layers obliterated by the construction of a

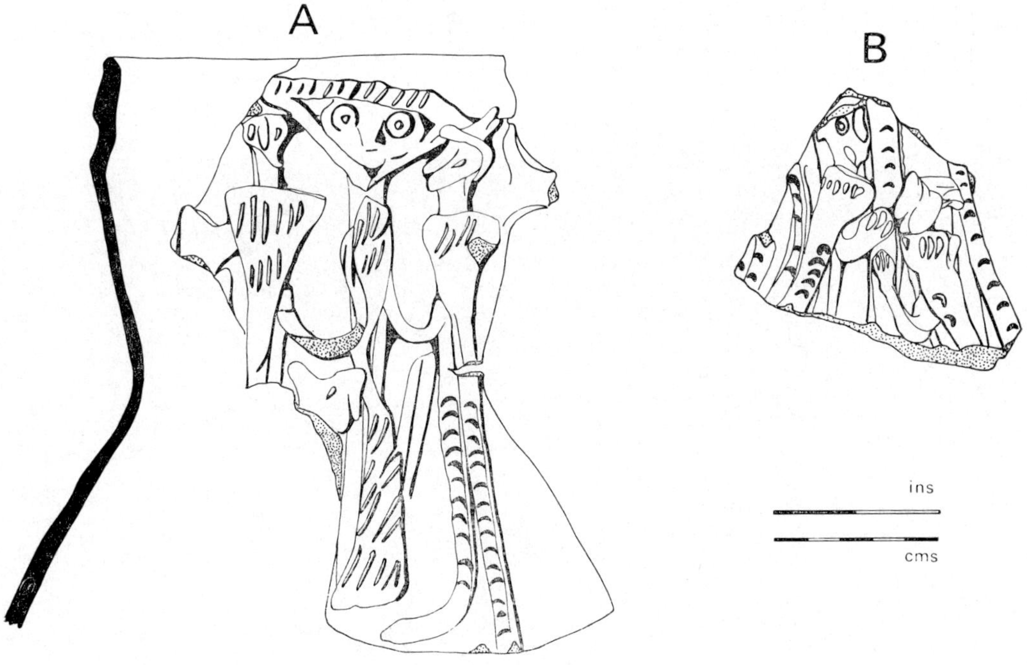

Figure 4. Fragments of Grimston ware knight jugs—A: found at Thoresby College, King's Lynn; B: found at Bryggen, Bergen.

Figure 5. Sources of pottery and stone imported into King's Lynn.

vaulted cellar in the eighteenth century, but in the eastern trench (Fig. 2B) two structures of considerable interest were discovered. One was the remains of a rectangular brick building belonging to a period earlier than the sixteenth-century College. It may have been owned by the Guild of Jesus when they had the site and it was probably a brick warehouse beside the river.

The brick building stood on unconsolidated and waterlogged earth which had led to the walls being placed on foundations considerably deeper than those normally found in medieval Lynn. Beneath the walls, about 9 feet below the present ground level and about 10 feet above Ordnance Datum, the top of a wooden post was found. This proved to be the most northerly post (Fig. 2) of a stretch of wooden sea-wall or wharf which, because of the waterlogged nature of the soil in which it lay, had been extremely well preserved (Fig. 3).

The structure consisted of upright oak posts and horizontal oak planks revetting a bank of mixed earth and silt. One post lay horizontally and at right angles to the body of the wharf and was probably an anchor beam used to tie the wall into the bank. Because of severe flooding it was impossible to excavate to the bottom of the wharf; Figure 2 shows it as excavated, the dotted line at the bottom of the drawing representing the water level (about 4 feet above O.D.) when excavation stopped.

Material which was found to the west of the wharf, that is, in the river when the wharf was in use, consisted very largely of domestic refuse which had presumably been dumped into the river. Such dumping was one of the causes of the considerable shift in the river line since the days of the wharf's construction; the present river bank lies some 60 yards to the west (Fig. 2). Finds from the medieval river bed at Thoresby College included a large quantity of pottery, which could be used for dating the wharf to the thirteenth century (Parker, H., 1965, 99–100) and also for indicating trading contacts.

The most significant single pottery find from Thoresby College is that illustrated in Figure 4A. This is part of an early fourteenth-century jug made in the local Grimston ware and elaborately decorated with a female figure flanked by knights carrying shields. Such knight jugs are known from Scarborough (Rutter, 1961, Fig. 2/8) and Nottingham (Dunning, 1955), where the Moot Hall jug illustrates the type to perfection, but the Thoresby College example differs from both of these in its fabric and style of decoration. The Scarborough and Nottingham jugs are much more plastic, and the figures of knights and horses are modelled in the round. The Thoresby College jug, on the other hand, has its decoration reduced to strips of clay applied to the surface of the vessel so that the figures stand out only in rather low relief. Fragments of true Scarborough knight jugs have been found in Lynn at other sites, and it is probable that the Thoresby College example is a local copy of one of these imported originals. It certainly suggests that fine pottery was arriving in Lynn from the east coast and midlands in the late thirteenth and early fourteenth century, probably in connection with the wool trade (p. 279).

The Thoresby College jug has one other interesting association with Lynn's trade. Figure 4B shows a single sherd of a knight jug identical in style, fabric and glaze with the Thoresby College example. It is obviously a product of the same kiln, if not the same craftsman, but it was found during the excavation of the medieval harbour at Bergen, Norway (Dunning, 1965–6, 200). Particularly close contacts between Lynn and Norway have already been mentioned (p. 279) and other finds of Grimston ware jugs have been made at Bergen (Herteig, 1959, 182, Pl. XIIIA).

The Thoresby College site, therefore, has provided two types of archaeological evidence for trade—structures and pottery. The other sites in the town, however, despite the documentary references quoted above (pp. 282–3) to their having wharves, have produced only small finds as evidence for trading connections. On all sites bones of cod, ray and herring have been found, herring being much less frequent than one might expect from its mention in documents. Whetstones also occur on all sites and are made of a micaceous schist imported from Yorkshire; lava from the Rhineland was used for grindstones and at the Marks and Spencer site mortars of Caen stone and Purbeck marble were found (Dunning, 1965–6, 208, Fig. 17).

Figure 6. A fourteenth-century Scarborough ware face jug found at All Saints' Street, King's Lynn. Photo: L. Hobson.

Pottery, however, is the most common imported object. Figure 5 shows the sources of English pottery found in Lynn. At All Saints' Street pottery of St. Neots, Stamford and Thetford types was found (Dunning, 1959) at the lowest levels and is the earliest dated pottery to be found in the town, belonging to the late eleventh and twelfth century. Stamford ware was also found at Baker Lane in early contexts and continued into the thirteenth century, after which time it died out. The disappearance of Stamford ware coincides with the arrival of Yorkshire pottery in great quantity, mainly the highly decorated table-wares such as the face jug from Scarborough shown in Figure 6, and it

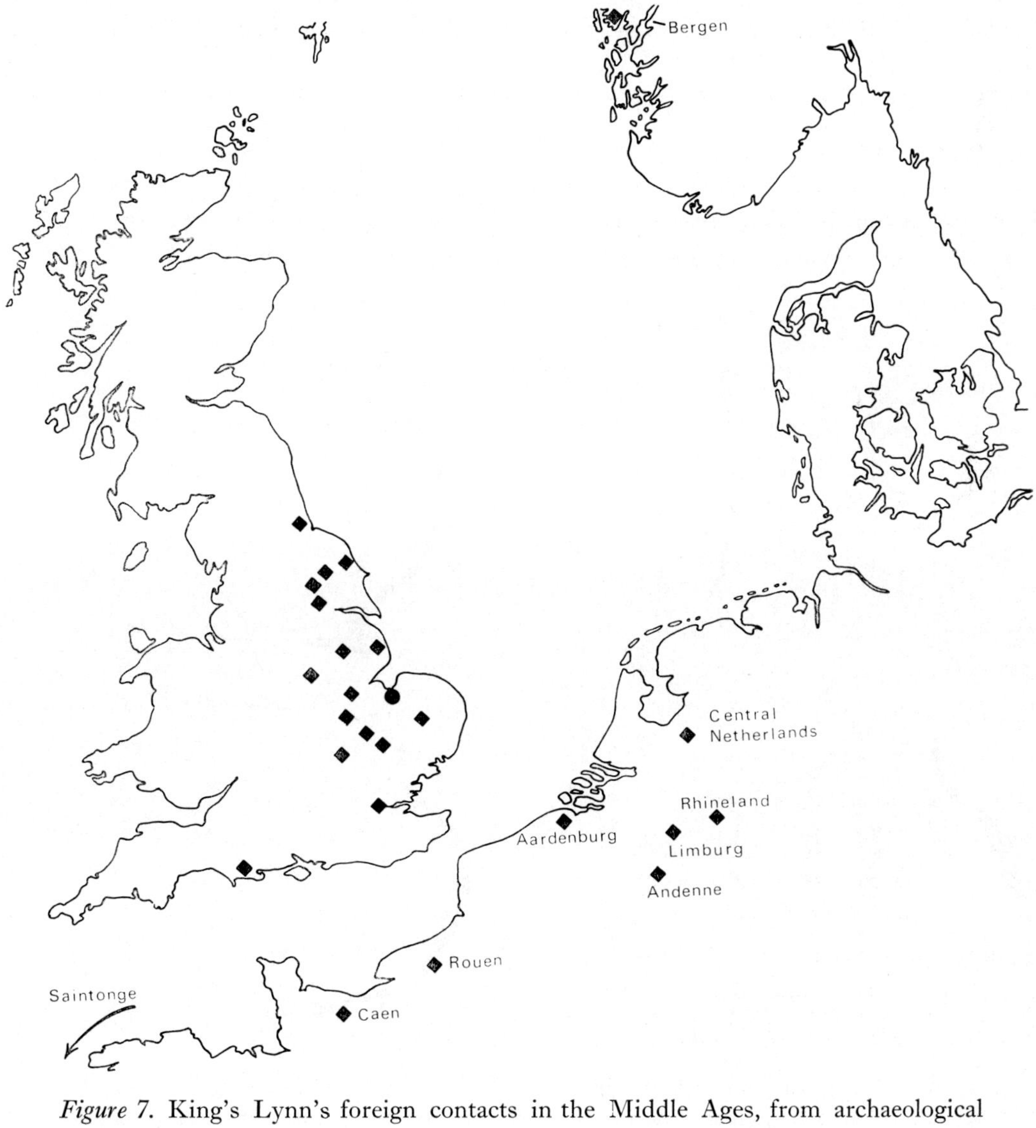

Figure 7. King's Lynn's foreign contacts in the Middle Ages, from archaeological sources.

is possible that the change in source of English imports into Lynn may be a result of the greater emphasis on wool exports from the late thirteenth century onwards (p. 279).

It is interesting to note that most of the English pottery could have reached Lynn by water—either by river or sea. Figure 5 shows clearly how closely the distribution of sources is linked to the east coast rivers.

Lynn's continental connections can be seen in Figure 7. Early imports came mainly from northern France—Rouen and Caen—which produced pottery such as that in Figure 8B (Barton, 1966); then, after the loss of Normandy early in the thirteenth century, this pottery was replaced by the fine, decorated jugs from south-western France, part of one of which is shown in Figure 8A (Barton, 1964). Both types of pottery came to England with the wine trade, but were probably also brought to be traded in their own right.

Pottery from the Low Countries arrived in Lynn from the late twelfth century until the end of the Middle Ages. Handled ladles—small globular pots with long tapering handles (Fig. 8D and Dunning, 1959; Herteig, 1959, 181–2, Pl. XIII D)—were brought from Flanders during the thirteenth century, and small globular cooking pots came from Limburg during the same period (Fig. 8C and Bruijn, 1962–3, Figs. 36 & 46). At the

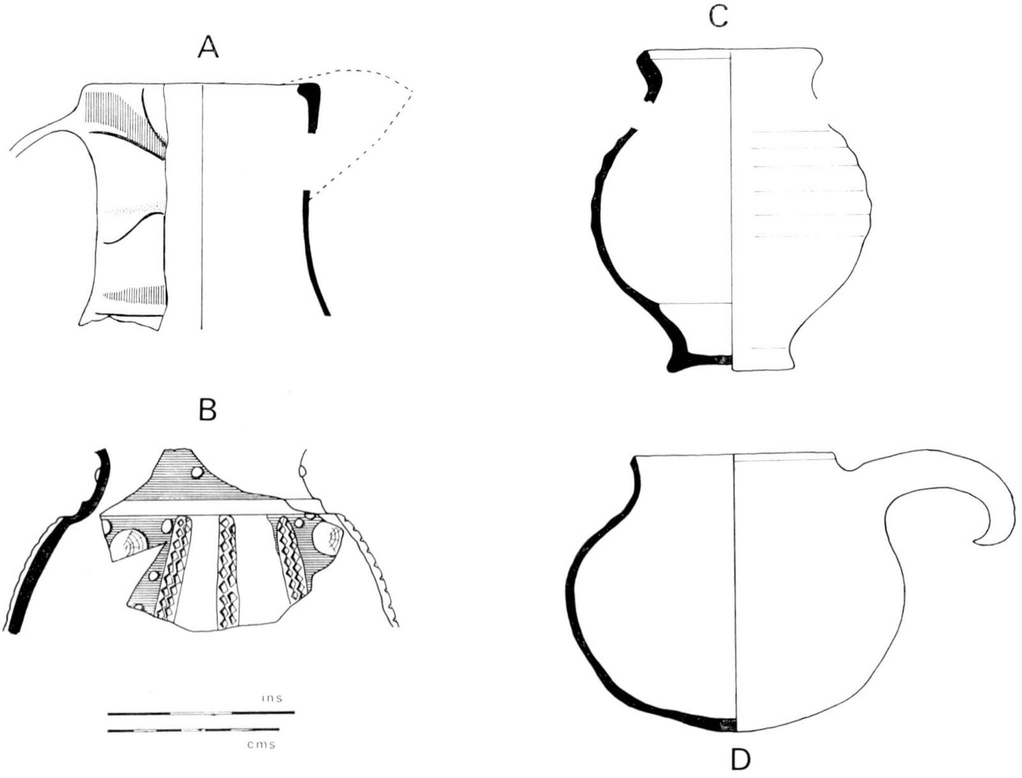

Figure 8. Imported pottery found in King's Lynn—A: polychrome jug from south-western France; B: polychrome jug from Normandy; C: globular cooking pot from Limburg; D: handled ladle from the Low Countries.

same time Lynn was exporting its own pottery; a large jug of Grimston ware has been found in Aardenburg (Trimpe Burger, 1962–3, Fig. 14; Dunning, 1965–6, 200–2, Fig. 3). Towards the end of the fourteenth century and in the fifteenth century stoneware was imported from the Rhineland; from the amount of Low Countries pottery discovered at Lynn it would appear that contacts across the North Sea remained close even though trade was becoming more and more concentrated in the hands of the Hanse merchants (p. 279) who were perhaps responsible for bringing in Rhenish stoneware and German beer. The establishment of the Hanseatic warehouse in King's Lynn in the fourteenth century is material evidence for their ascendancy, but whoever was responsible for carrying on the trade, it is apparent from the archaeological record that Lynn continued to be in contact with Europe throughout the Middle Ages.

ACKNOWLEDGEMENTS

I am most grateful to all those who have helped in the preparation of this paper, especially to Dr. A. E. Herteig for allowing me to publish the Bergen knight jug sherd and to Mrs. Jean le Patourel, Dr. G. C. Dunning and Mr. J. G. Hurst for their comments on the pottery. My colleague, Mr. A. Carter, provided unpublished information about the Baker Lane site. My deepest thanks are due to the staff of the King's Lynn Museum and to Miss A. S. Mottram, Curator of the Museum and joint secretary of the King's Lynn Archaeological Survey, for all her help, patience and encouragement during many seasons of excavation.

REFERENCES

Barton, K. J. 1964 The medieval pottery of the Saintonge. *Arch. J.* **120**, 201–14.

Barton, K. J. 1966 Medieval pottery at Rouen. *Arch. J.* **122**, 73–85.

Beloe, E. M. 1899 *Our Borough, Our Churches*, 210 pp. Cambridge.

Bruijn, A. 1962–3 Die mittelalterliche keramische Industrie in Südlimburg. *Berichten van de Rijksdienst voor het Oudheidkundig Bodemonderzoek*, **12–13**, 357–459.

Carus-Wilson, E. 1962–3 The medieval trade of the ports of the Wash. *Med. Archaeol.* **6–7**, 182–201.

Clarke, H. & Carter, A. (in preparation) *Excavations in medieval King's Lynn* (The Society for Med. Archaeol. Monograph Series).

Dunning, G. C. 1955 The decorated jug from the Moot Hall at Nottingham. *Annual Report of the Peverel Archaeological Group*, 18–23.

Dunning, G. C. 1959 Pottery of the late Anglo-Saxon period in England, *in* Anglo-Saxon Pottery: A Symposium. *Med. Archaeol.* **3**, 56–61.

Dunning, G. C. 1965–6 Medieval pottery and stone mortars imported into Aardenburg from England and France. *Berichten ROB.* **15–16**, 199–210.

Eller, G. 1861 *Memorials, Archaeological and Ecclesiastical, of the West Winch Manors*, 240 pp. King's Lynn.

Harrod, H. 1874 *Reports on the Deeds and Records of the Borough of King's Lynn*, 154 pp. King's Lynn and London.

Herteig, A. E. 1959 The excavation of "Bryggen", the old Hanseatic wharf in Bergen. *Med. Archaeol.* **3**, 177–86.

Hillen, H. J. 1907 *History of the Borough of King's Lynn*, 2 vols, 964 pp. Norwich.

Hoskins, W. G. 1959 *Local History in England*, 196 pp. London.

Parker, H. 1965 A medieval wharf in Thoresby College courtyard, King's Lynn. *Med. Archaeol.* **9**, 94–104.

Parker, V. 1971 *The Making of King's Lynn*, 226 pp. London & Chichester.

Richards, W. 1812 *The History of Lynn*, 2 vols, 1216 pp. King's Lynn.
Rutter, J. G. 1961 Pottery in the Scarborough Museum, 13th and 14th centuries. *Scarborough and District Archaeological Society, Research Report 3.*
Smith, T. P. 1970 The medieval town defences of King's Lynn. *J. Brit. Arch. Assoc.* (3rd Series) **33**, 57–88.
Taylor, W. 1844 *The Antiquities of King's Lynn*, 158 pp. King's Lynn.
Trimpe Burger, J. A. 1962–3 Ceramiek uit de bloetijd van Aardenburg. *Berichten ROB.* **12–13**, 495–550.
Waites, B. 1963 The medieval ports and trade of north-east Yorkshire, I. *Trans. Scarborough & District Archaeological Soc.* **1**, No. 6, 13–20.
Waites, B. 1964 The medieval ports and trade of north-east Yorkshire, II. *Trans. Scarborough & District Archaeological Soc.* **1**, No. 7, 12–19.
Wilson, D. M. & Hurst, D. G. 1968 Medieval Britain in 1967. *Med. Archaeol.* **12**, 184–5.

Discussion

Hague Was the horizontal tie driven in afterwards and did it break the boarding, or was allowance made for it?
Clarke It seems to have been built in simultaneously with the upright, and the plank which ran around it was cut to accommodate the tie-beam.
Hague Did you remove any of the piles?
Clarke We got one out—the tallest one which was 15 feet long.
Hague Was it finished at the end?
Clarke We couldn't get to the bottom because we were below sea level, but it did have a tenon at the bottom.
Hague Was it re-used wood?
Clarke I don't think so.
Hague I presume it must have been set as a buried sill-beam.

McKee Did the river move or did perhaps trade expand? Normally quays expanded outwards to cope with increasing trade and the demand for extra space.
Clarke It is certainly happening today. The South Quay has been rebuilt after the floods and has moved 6 feet west into the river. One of the reasons why the river moved was that people in the Middle Ages disposed of their rubbish in the river. Eventually the water was too shallow in front of the wharf, so another wall encasing the rubbish was constructed, and then the cycle started all over again. This is why the river bank of the town is built of silt and domestic rubbish.
Marsh Could you see any difference in composition between the material outside the quay and the material inside? Presumably the rubbish inside had been dumped earlier than that outside.
Clarke Material inside was dumped in the early thirteenth century and that on the outside is of the early fourteenth century.

McKeone Have you thought of getting any samples carbon-dated?
Clarke No, mainly for financial reasons.

Anon. Is there any evidence of the bank on the other side of the river being cut away?
Clarke No, but this is a very interesting point. The map of *c.* 1680 shows the river with about twice its present width, and it does seem that the far bank had been scoured. The bank has remained fairly static on the west side, whereas the east side has moved towards the west.

Lighthouses

by

D. B. HAGUE

INTRODUCTION

MOST OF WHAT has been written about lighthouses has understandably been concerned with epic stories of the erection of towers on remote rocks. For some fifteen years I have been making a study of these buildings as an archaeologist, noting the evolution in design and the modifications caused by improvements in optical apparatus or by differing needs. For a short paper, rather than over-simplify a complex story, I have chosen to discuss in some detail three or four very different types of lighthouse. These date from the Roman, medieval and renaissance periods; the last is a small group of unusual Irish examples.

1. THE LIGHTHOUSE AT LA CORUÑA

If only because it is the oldest working lighthouse in the world, the tower at La Coruña in north-west Spain (Figs. 1–2) is a worthy introduction to any talk on lighthouses, but this monument also claims our consideration on architectural and aesthetic grounds. Representations of classical lighthouses in various media present a somewhat confused picture. The most common form illustrated in mosaics and carving is that of a building of two or three storeys decreasing in width towards the top (Fig. 3); the detail is conventionalized and uninformative as regards stairs or ramps. In the case of coins, the engraver is further limited by size, and verisimilitude was inclined to suffer; the pharos of Alexandria was portrayed as having perpendicular sides and not the stepped silhouette it is known to have had (Fig. 4).

The lighthouse at La Coruña, popularly known as the "Tower of Hercules", stands about 3 km north of the town and on the end of the peninsula protecting the harbour and bay, where it also serves as a guide to El Ferrol to the north-east. Its present appearance is almost entirely that of a remarkably sensitive reconstruction which in a subtle way evokes its ancient origin. It is remarkable too in having the architect's name carved on the rock face, now covered by a little stone building. The inscription (Fig. 2) runs as follows:

MARTI / AVG · SACR / C · SEVIVS / LVPVS / ARCHITECTVS / AEMINIENSIS LVSITANVS · EX VO

Marti Aug(usto) sacr(um) G(aius) Sevius Lupus architectus Aeminiensis Lusitanus ex vo(to)

"Sacred to Mars Augustus; Gaius Sevius Lupus, architect, from Aeminium in Lusitania, in accordance with his vow (dedicated this)."

Figure 1. La Coruña: view of lighthouse.

Its present plan is cruciform, being 10.08 m square externally, with walls 2.03 m thick; it is divided into four compartments by walls 1.45 m thick. Its total height is about 53 m; no Roman work is visible externally because of the 1791 refacing, but internally it is exposed up to a height of 33 m. In this there are two stages, the lower 9.09 m and the upper 13.04 m high, each of the 12 compartments so formed being roofed with a barrel vault, intact except where broken by the wooden stairs inserted later. Several communicating doors have since been made and some original ones blocked or mutilated; a few Roman doorways are open and one window, 1.84 m high by 0.95 m, survives at the first stage.

Figure 2 includes an attempt at a restoration of the tower to its original appearance, together with drawings illustrating its subsequent evolution up to the present day. The

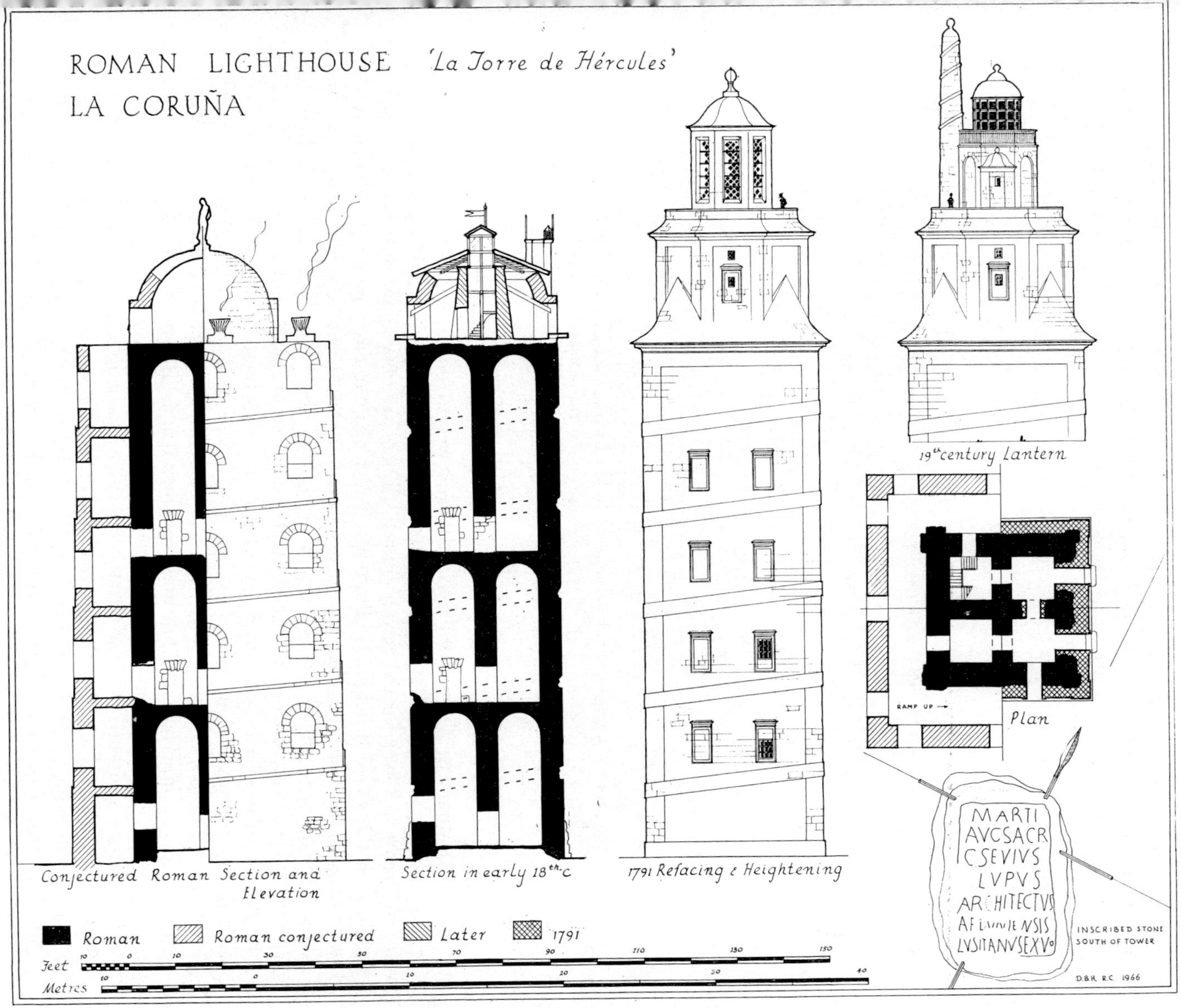

Figure 2. La Coruña: survey of lighthouse.

drawing is based on an examination and survey of the building and the study of several eighteenth-century surveys (Florez, 1765; Cornide, 1792; Servicio Historico del Ejercito) and one recent German account (Hutter, 1958), together with various analogous structures. The two main problems facing a "restorer" are the design of the ramped access to the top and the details of the top platform. The latter can only be conjectured, but the details of the former might be recovered by archaeological excavation.

Figure 3. Ostia: relief on sarcophagus.

Before dealing with these problems it will be as well to look briefly at two other Roman examples. The pharos at Dover (Fig. 5) stands to a considerable height because at times it was used as a tower for the Saxon church. (There are very slight remains of a second pharos on the western heights). Internally it is 4.22 m square, the perpendicular walls with beam-holes indicating that the floors were wooden. Externally it is octagonal, the walls decreasing in thickness in a series of shallow steps from 3.66 m at the base to about 1.05 m at the top; it has a total height of about 24 m. All but a few fragments of the Roman offsets have been smoothed off by medieval refacing, but sufficient survives to make it quite clear that these were horizontal steps, and not in the form of a spiral. From the drawings it would seem that the companion tower at Boulogne, the Tour d'Ordre, was of similar design. The main conclusion to be drawn from these two examples is that their fuel was not carried up by means of an external ramp.

Excavations at Leptis Magna (Bartoccini, 1958) have revealed many details of the Roman port layout including the pharos, and the excavators have been able to produce a restored drawing. The tower was 13.03 m square internally and 18.03 m externally, and it still survives to a height of about 21 m. The plan (Fig. 6) is divided by three parallel walls which carry barrel vaults, and around these walls is devised an internal ramped stair up which the fuel was carried. Here again the restoration of the top is conjectural, but there is evidence of slight set-backs which would have given a shallow

Figure 4. The pharos of Alexandria: mosaic in St. Mark's, Venice.

stepped silhouette similar to that at Dover and very different from the portrayals of Ostia (Figs. 3 & 7).

The tower at La Coruña is different, as there is good evidence that this building now standing is in fact only the core of a Roman building, which in its pristine state was encased in an outer shell of masonry which supported an ascending ramp. On my drawing (Fig. 2) this has been made 17.75 m square, which provides a ramp wide enough to accommodate pack animals. The existence of the ramp can be established from several sources; it is recorded (Cornide, 1792) that in order to strengthen the defences of the tower it was removed about 1470. By this time the tower had long since ceased to function as a lighthouse and was used as a look-out or stronghold in the event of attack by privateers; Drake is said to have beseiged it on one of his visits. Other good evidence is to be found in a number of undated eighteenth-century drawings which appear to have been made independently some time before the 1791 restorations. The attention paid to small structural details makes it perfectly clear that they were drawn on the site, and I have incorporated these in producing the section which is labelled

Figure 5. The Roman pharos at Dover.

"early eighteenth century". A conspicuous feature is a ragged chase or groove in spiral form embracing the building for its full height. This has clearly been caused by the rough removal of either a continuous corbel table or the springers of a continuous arch, or there is a possibility that it was the housing for stone slabs, or even heavy baulks of timber which might have formed the floor of the ramp. Were it vaulted, the Romans would most likely have employed a barrel vault, as this would exert the minimum

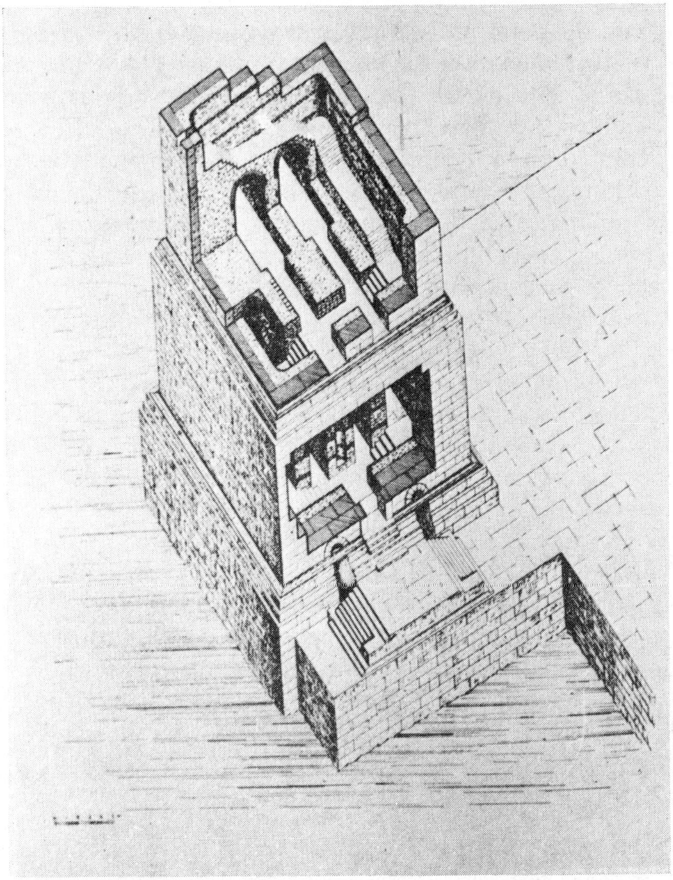

Figure 6. Leptis Magna: isometric drawing of lighthouse (Bartoccini, 1958).

Figure 7. Ostia mosaic.

horizontal thrust on the outer walls, but the narrowness of the slot is more indicative of the removal of the springers of a segmental arch. This, although not common Roman practice, would not be out of place here as all the extant original openings have heavy "flat arches". Although the paved area around the base is below floor level, it is possible that trenches excavated up to the tower might reveal either the foundations or the foundation trench marking the position of the outer shell. One of the early drawings shows ragged pieces of walling projecting from the base corners; these are far too slight and ineffective to represent angle buttresses, but they might be vestigial remains of responds of stiffening arches associated with the outer shell.

In the late seventeenth century lights were once more displayed from the tower at the request of several foreign countries (Cornide, 1792) and evidence of these is shown in the drawings, which also show the wooden stairs inserted at the time. In 1781 it was decided to make a thorough restoration and to show an effective modern light. According to an inscription in the fine vaulted room beneath the lantern, this work was done by a naval engineer, Eustaquia Giannini, who must have been a remarkably perceptive and sensitive man. Few architects of any date, even had they realised the significance of the ragged slot, would have wished to do more than fill it up and forget about it. Giannini knew that this spiral was all that was left of a vital feature of the building and, despite encasing the tower in about 0.76 m of entirely new masonry, he decided to echo the spiral in the form of a projecting string course following the same outline. He furnished all sides with four pairs of windows, although the vast majority were mere ornamental blanks, since only when they coincided with the stair were they accessible, or indeed was there any point

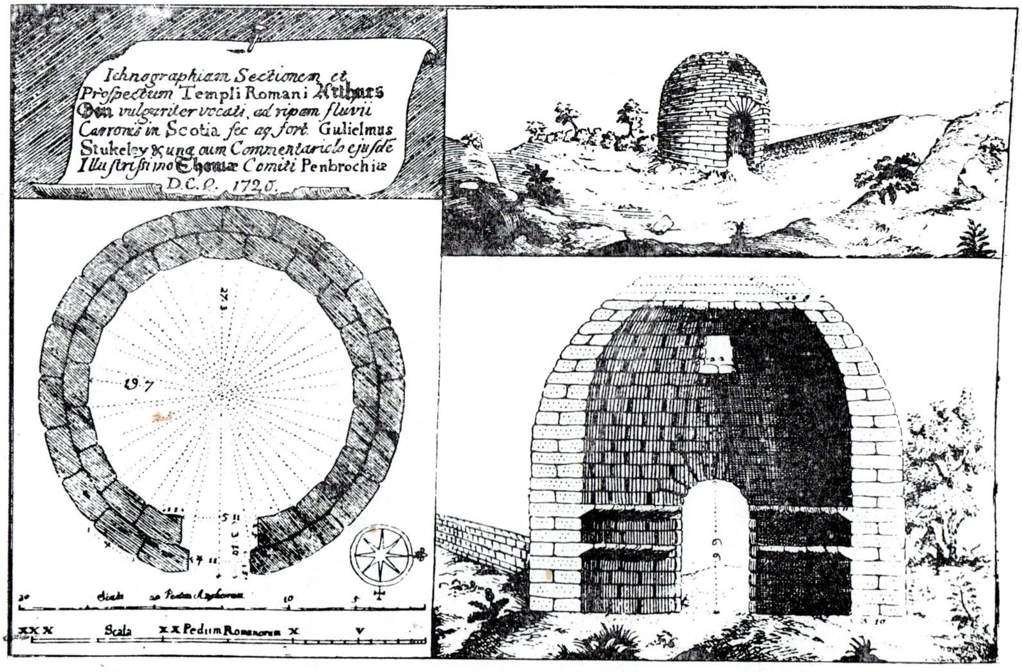

Figure 8. Arthur's O'on, Stirlingshire: Stukeley's drawings, of 1723.

Figure 9. Building on Monte Faro, Pontevedra. Photo: Alfredo G. Alén.

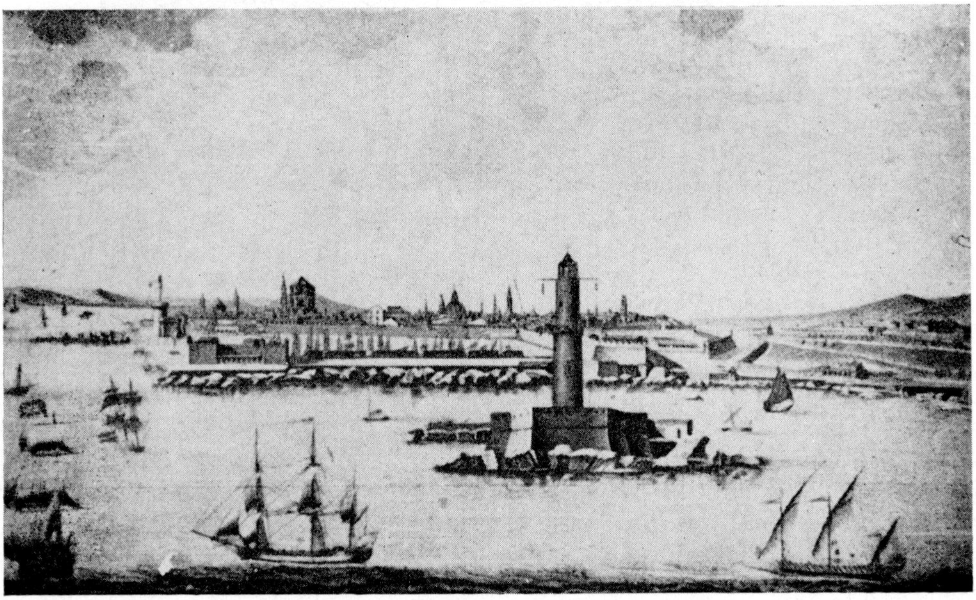

Figure 10. Livorno lighthouse in the 1600s (Vigo, 1915).

Figure 11. Torre della Meloria: view.

in admitting light. Each "window" has a moulded architrave and a "flat pediment" of the same granite as was used for the entire refacing; a projecting plinth, pilaster quoins and moulded cornice were also provided. The cornice was level with the top of the Roman fabric; above this he continued up about 6 m in an octagonal form against which the stone roof of the square tower rose and finished as a squinch. On top is an observation platform and above this the 9.25 m high lantern with eight windows 4.03 m high. In the mid-nineteenth century this was reconstructed as a service room and the present circular lantern placed on top. Even then great care was taken with the new work; the newel from below was terminated in a delightful octagonal house and a new newel giving access to the upper lantern was finished with a flourish by a 12.08 m high spiral which adds much to its distinguished silhouette.

We will now return to the reconstruction of the Roman top and my reasons for completing it in this way. The early drawings show what appears to be the lower part and springing of a dome-like structure which stops at a height of about 4.06 m, where it carries the wall-plate of a shallow-pitched conical tiled roof. On one of the drawings the apex of the roof is given central support by a small tapering newel. This is an improbable structure to support roof eaves; a simple cylindrical drum of masonry would be better. It seems obvious that this masonry was the remains of a dome, and it was desirable to find a comparable example in Roman architecture. At La Coruña the dome was about 6.07 m in diameter with two doors set diametrically opposite, with jambs deliberately thickened to counter the thrust of the dome. There are two buildings with which it may be compared. The first is Arthur's O'on (oven) at Stenhouse in Stirlingshire (Fig. 8; Steer, 1958). Unfortunately this was destroyed in 1743, but we are lucky in having two excellent measured drawings made shortly before this date. It was 5.08 m in internal diameter and about 6.08 m high; the section shows that it was partly roofed in the corbelled fashion of Mycenaean tombs or later Irish oratories, and had an arched doorway and an open eye in the centre of the dome. This little building stood near the Antonine wall, and from the votive objects found in it during demolition there are strong grounds for ascribing to it a Roman date. The other, smaller example stands on a hilltop on the Morraze peninsula about 19 km south-west of Pontevedra, also in the north-west of Spain. Its internal diameter is about 3.55 m and its height 3.04 m. It is built of carefully fitted squared masonry, with very small square windows and a lintelled doorway; the dome is slightly less than hemispherical and is set in from the outer wall face (Fig. 9). There are Roman remains on this hill, although there is no absolute proof that this structure is Roman.

With these two examples in mind and, I believe, the exercise of a little common sense, I have "completed" the dome at La Coruña. It might well have been capped with a statue, perhaps of Minerva, and the interior would have been useful as a shelter for both the fireman and fuel. The illumination would almost certainly have been by means of braziers, of which there might have been several. The fire would certainly never have been displayed from the top of the dome. The many representations of classical and later lighthouses producing vast volumes of flame and smoke, worthy of the discharge from a blast furnace, must be regarded as natural artist's licence.

2. THE FIRST ROCK LIGHTHOUSE

The Tour de Constance (Aigues Mortes), Hook Tower (Waterford) and Chale Down (Isle of Wight) are among the very few surviving medieval lighthouses, and it may seem a little perverse to select for discussion an example which no longer exists. The first rock, or wave-swept, lighthouse is usually accepted as having been the Eddystone light of 1698, or perhaps (after a little research) Cordouan in the Gironde, which although a rock light by accident antedates it by a century. Pisa is rightly famed for its twelfth-century cathedral and in particular for its leaning tower, but it is not generally known that the Pisans can also claim the distinction of having erected the world's first rock lighthouse.

Set on the River Arno, Pisa was from Roman times served from the sea via Porto Pisano, a port now lost owing to the silting up of the great bay. Like Genoa, Venice and other Italian city republics, Pisa joined in the First Crusade in the twelfth century. Pious

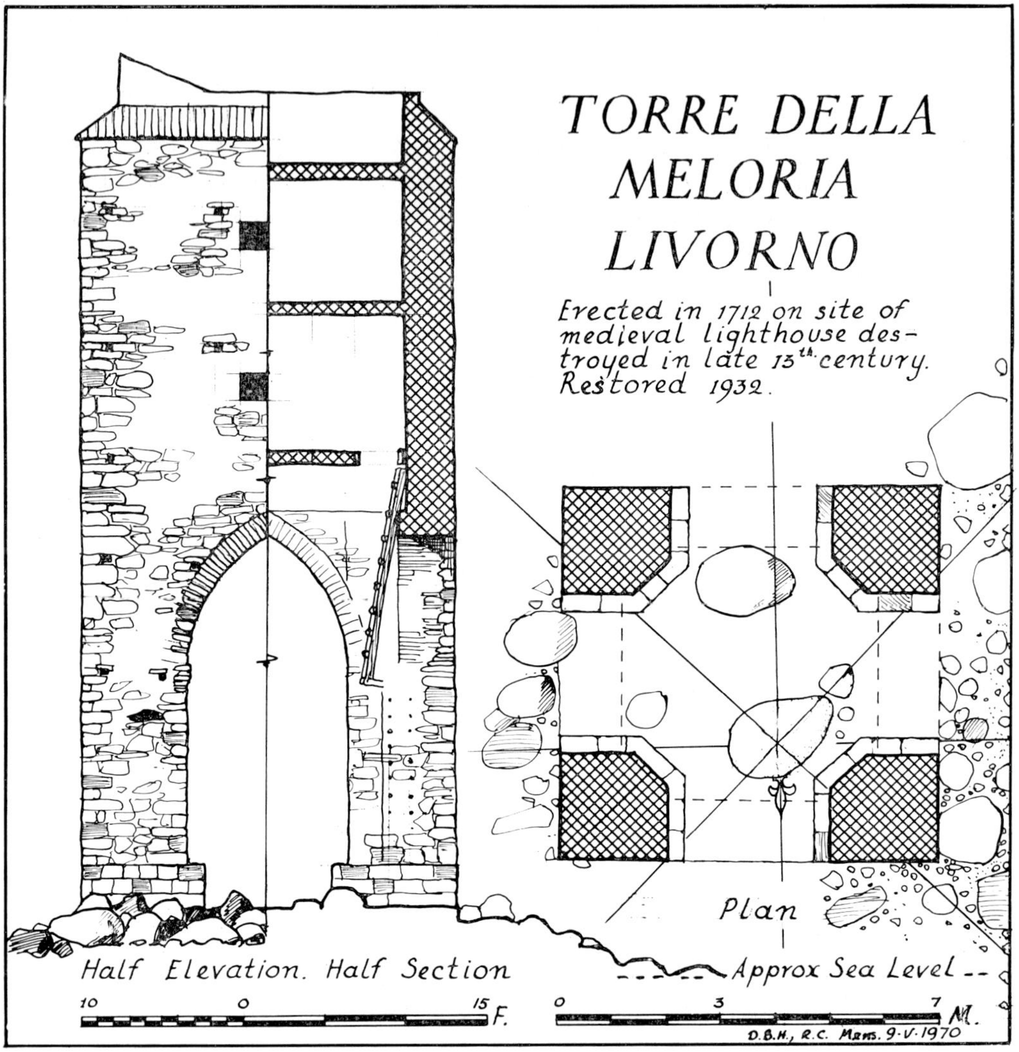

Figure 12. Torre della Meloria: survey.

as their motives may have been, it was not long before the great commercial potential of trading concessions resulted in a substantial traffic in trade with the east. Convoys of galleys returning home with valuable cargoes needed guidance, and lighthouses began to be built: one at Genoa in 1130 and one on Secche Meloria in 1157. Secche Meloria is a series of shoals varying between 5 and 8 km off shore abreast of Livorno and extending in length for about 5½ km. By this time Livorno (Leghorn) had replaced Porto Pisano, and the Meloria reef was a great hazard to shipping approaching its harbour and to any ships making for Genoa which took a course too far to the east. The Pisans erected a tower here in 1157, on the northern of two dry patches; the small southern patch about 180 m away is the site of the southernmost of the two modern lights marking the reef. This lonely medieval tower was a sitting target for enemy attacks and its keepers must

Figure 13. San Raineri, Messina: view of lighthouse.

have been brave or desperate men. It suffered many attacks during the thirteenth century; it was destroyed in 1267 by Charles of Anjou, ruler of Sicily, and after being rebuilt it was finally destroyed by the Genoese in a great sea battle fought off the reef in 1284. After this defeat the Pisans never rebuilt the tower and never challenged the authority of the Genoese; instead they built another tower on another rock just outside their own harbour.

Although we have no knowledge whatever of the appearance of the original Meloria tower, it is not unreasonable to assume that it probably resembled the new one at Livorno, about which we know a good deal, although it would have been on a more modest scale. The mosaic illustration in St. Mark's, Venice (Fig. 4), which purports to represent the pharos of Alexandria, may be regarded with more confidence as the twelfth-century artist's impression of a typical Italian lighthouse of his day. The tower

Figure 14. Genoa: view of the "Lanterna".

at Livorno continued in use until its unfortunate deliberate destruction by the Germans in the last war. It is a great credit to the Italian authorities that they have carefully rebuilt it in a most sympathetic manner; although reinforced concrete is used and exposed internally, its external appearance is exactly as it was, and they have even been able to recover and re-set in shield form some fragments of the original inscription which in Lombardic letters gives the date 1302. The ruins of the barracks, which had been built in brick around the base of the tower in the late sixteenth century by Cosimo de Medici, survive as left by the explosion. The reconstruction was possible because photographs survived, together with a considerable number of drawings and engravings, from the seventeenth century onwards (Fig. 10). Rising from a smooth spreading base or talus, the tower consists of two superimposed drums, the lower 11 m in external diameter, the upper 8.08 m. These three units give a total height of 49.05 m which, with the addition of the lantern set on top of a slender central turret, gives an overall height of 52.05 m. The top of each drum has a balcony with a crenellated parapet, and the tower is now connected to the mainland by a recent enlargement of the docks.

Despite our lack of knowledge of the original tower of Meloria, we must salute it as an outstanding achievement in the annals of marine engineering. It might well have survived natural hazards for much longer had it not been for the barbaric hand of man. In 1709 the reef was marked by an extraordinary building (Fig. 11) which served as a sea-mark, and this, despite its never having served as a lighthouse, deserves a mention in any study of rock lighthouses, as it appears to be the earliest demonstration of the principle later used in the construction of pile lighthouses. It is 6.07 m square on plan and about 15 m high; each side is pierced by a tall, pointed arch and consequently the superstructure in effect stands on four pentagonal piers through which the seas wash freely rather than battering against a solid structure. To judge from illustrations it has been little altered, although concrete floors were inserted and masonry repaired and two window openings inserted (Fig. 12). It stands on a small patch of the exposed reef which barely rises more than two or three metres above sea level.

3. LIGHTHOUSES OF THE RENAISSANCE PERIOD

Lighthouses of the renaissance period are rare, and none exists in Britain. Three continental examples are well worth considering in some detail: Messina, Genoa and Cordouan. All are on sites of medieval lights.

At Messina we are not concerned with the tower of classical origin at Capo Peloro, which stood at the north-east extremity of Sicily, but with San Raineri (Fig. 13), which stands on the middle of the curved tongue of land enclosing the harbour of Messina from the south and east. It is a massive structure of rusticated masonry, about 24 m square at the base of its battered lower stage, which is about 17 m high. Half-way up is the entrance, reached by a bridge, and it is clear from the mutilated masonry that some elaborate, and perhaps decorative, defensive works have been removed. The upper stage, about 15 m high, tapers very slightly to a flat top, 14.02 m square, which is surrounded by iron railings. On top of this is a handsome octagon 5.23 m across and about 4 m high; this now supports a slender modern turret and lantern. Its general appearance differs very little from an illustration published in 1593–4 (Braun & Hogenberg) which is likely to show it in its original form. On the sides flanking the entrance the two main floors are lit by impressive windows with externally splayed reveals and arches, but the small size or lack of windows in the lower part leave no doubt that the building was designed with defence in mind.

The tallest lighthouse in the world is the famous "Lanterna" at Genoa (Fig. 14). There was a tower there in 1130, about which nothing is known, but it was probably the one of which Antonio Colombo (the uncle of Cristoforo) was keeper in 1449. The French captured Genoa in 1507 and it was on the occasion of its recapture by the Genoese in 1512 that the tower was destroyed by bombardment. This date and the rebuilding of the tower in 1543 are recorded on a carved stone panel on the middle gallery. The light is displayed at an elevation of 117.03 m above sea level; the tower is of brick with walls 2.05 m thick at the base, where it is 9.01 m square on plan. At a height of 33 m it is reduced to 7 m square, and this stage is marked by an elaborate projecting balcony carried on a double row of corbels. On top of the second stage, which is 30 m high, similar corbels carry the upper balcony, which still retains its original turned stone balusters; above this the circular lantern is supported on a murette 3 m high. The total height of the tower above the rock on which it stands is 75.09 m. Around its base are a few undistinguished buildings, which together with a new lantern and optic and a lift are the only modifications which the tower has undergone since 1543.

Perhaps the most singular lighthouse in the world is that at Cordouan. When rebuilt by Louis de Foix on a very grandiose scale soon after 1584, the island of Cordouan measured about 150 m by 60 m, to judge from an oft-reproduced early seventeenth-century drawing (by Claude Chatillon: Fig. 15*a*). This shows not only the original

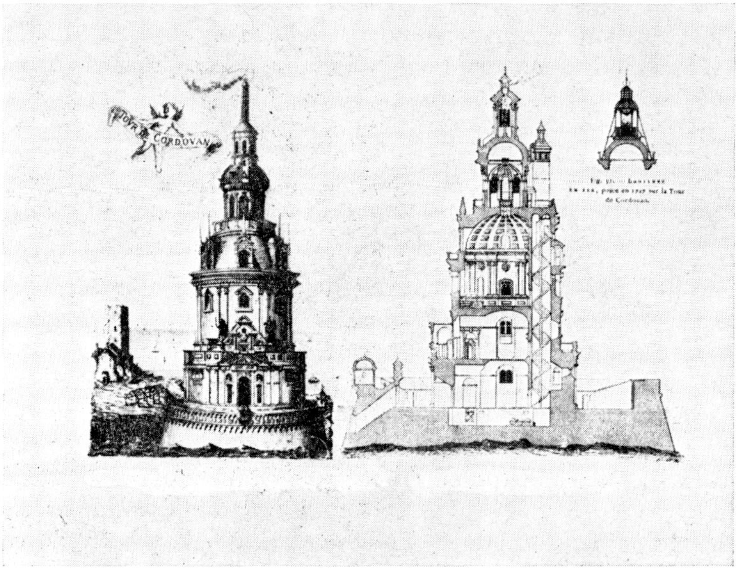

Figure 15a. Cordouan lighthouse: drawing by Claude Chatillon, 1612.
Figure 15b. Cordouan lighthouse: section, after Belidor.

medieval tower, standing to its full height, but also very clear indications of wooden sea defences erected around the base of the new tower. During the course of a few years the whole island was eroded away, thereby leaving the building as a rock tower. Fortunately this process was slow enough to enable the massive and effective circular sea wall to be built around it. This is 40 m in diameter and 2.44 m thick, and still survives with the keepers' houses and stores built against its inner side. A full architectural description of Cordouan is not a task to be undertaken lightly, and one might even be thankful that the late eighteenth-century reconstruction removed the greater part of its architectural embellishments and excesses, of obelisks, pediments, statuary and swags.

The tower is circular on plan, the external diameter at the base being 16 m, but internally the first two floors contain single apartments 6.75 m square (Fig. 15*b*). These are elaborately decorated with shallow-domed ceilings. At first-floor level, which is known

Figure 16. Cordouan: view of present-day lighthouse. Photo: René Faille, Paris.

as the King's Hall, is an external gallery. Above this is what must be the most remarkable room ever to be devised in a lighthouse. The Royal Chapel, 9.04 m in diameter, is ceiled with a richly coffered dome 11.04 m high, the walls being decorated with pilasters and swags and the floor with inlaid marble. It was originally lit by three windows and three fancy dormers, which for external effect were augmented by blind repeats; the dormers were obliterated when the tower was heightened in 1788–91. A wide newel stair led to the small domed room above the chapel, and on top of this was the cupola containing the fire. At first the fuel was wooden billets, and the smoke from it was discharged through a tall obelisk-like chimney. In 1727 coal was substituted and an ingenious iron superstructure provided which included a suspended reflector which was to prove ineffective. The reconstruction by Joseph Teulère consisted in the removal of all structure above the chapel dome, which was strengthened to carry a 29.05 m tapered tower containing an elegant spiral stair. This distinguished building (Fig. 16), apart from being the most exotic, is also the tallest rock tower in the world, and has been chosen as the site for many important optical experiments.

4. IRISH BRAZIER-LIGHTHOUSES

In Ireland there is a small number of unusual structures quite unlike lighthouses elsewhere (Fig. 17). They consist of a stone-vaulted keeper's cottage containing stone stairs leading up to a small platform on the roof on which was displayed an open fire; this could be of coal, wood or at times turf or peat. In most cases they stand on high headlands, but one example at low elevation was provided with a tower. The principal difference between these and their nearest parallels—at the North Forelands, Isle of

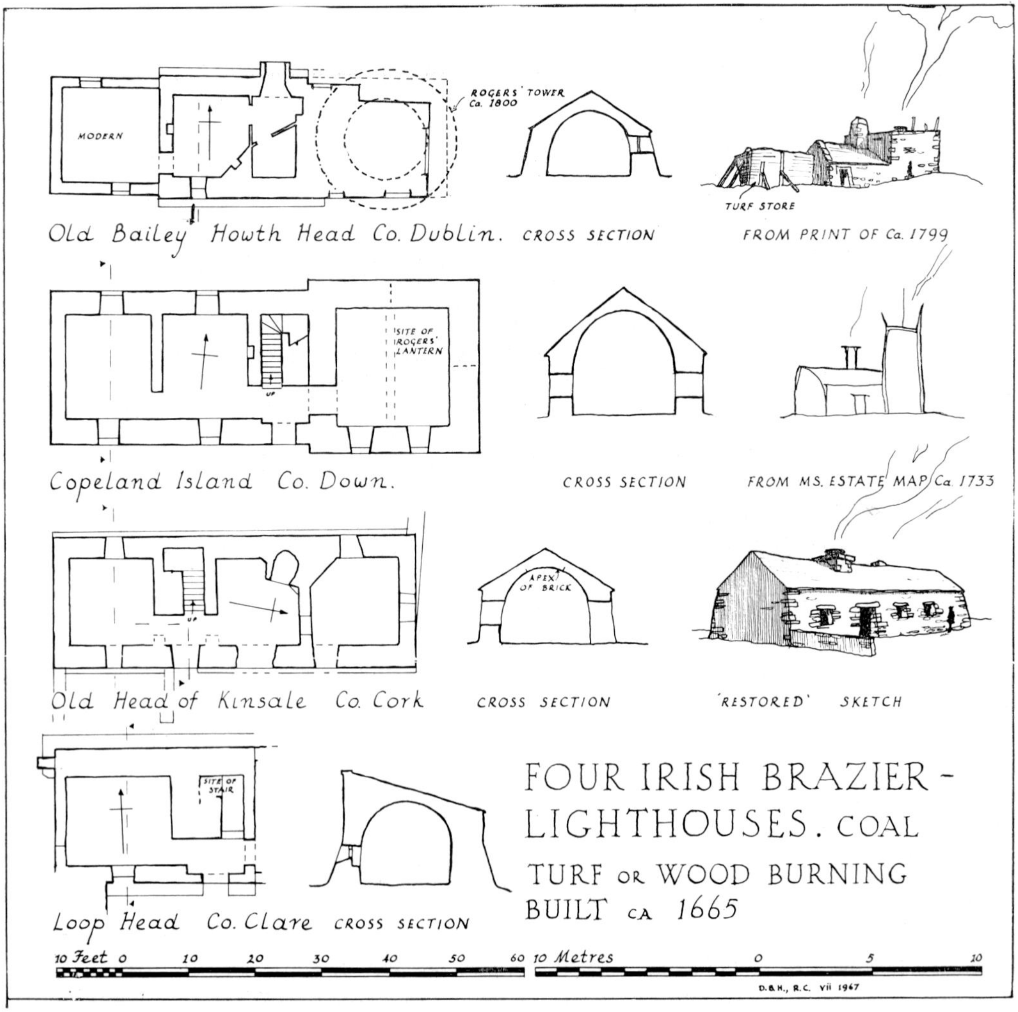

Figure 17. Irish Brazier-Lighthouses.

May or Flamborough Head, where the residential quarters are contained in the structure of the tower—is the Irish insistence on a vaulted single-storied cottage. Their vaulted roof is clearly a protection against fire, but the form springs from the ancient tradition of stone-vaulted oratories such as the famous Gallarus in Kerry (Leask, 1955). The longevity of this can be seen in such buildings as the English-built powder-magazine at Charlesfort or the famous nineteenth-century Black Church in Dublin.

The northern entrance to Dublin Bay is marked by the promontory of Howth Hill, the present Baily lighthouse being set on the low southernmost tip. Howth was one of the several sites for private lighthouses granted to Sir Robert Reading by patent in 1665, and it can be assumed that he commenced building with little delay. Here the elevation of about 120 m does not demand a tall tower, and an engraving by Francis Jukes, published in 1799 (Fig. 17), shows the station in operation. In the centre is the vaulted cottage with battered walls and chimney; on the right, very little higher than the roof, is a squat tower or platform holding the brazier; on the left is a propped-up pile of what appears to be turf or peat. Turf was used here, and the stone basin in which the fire was kindled survived in part, into the nineteenth century (Sloane, 1873), but is is clear that coal was the main fuel and its use is recorded in 1690 (Belfast P.R.O., 1690–91). Late in the eighteenth century it was decided to provide an oil lamp, and Thomas Rogers demolished the square structure and replaced it by a small round tower of similar height. In the Ballast Office in Dublin is an early nineteenth-century water-colour showing this and some enigmatic buildings. All that survives of the original building is the single-roomed vaulted cottage measuring about 5.05 m by 3.65 m; this is subdivided and provided with modern extensions to the west and on the site of the tower, the latter being echoed by a curved section of garden walling; the only hint of antiquity is the battered side-walls (Fig. 18).

Loop Head lies at the extreme end of the Shannon mouth, on the north side of the river. An application was made for a light here in 1717 (Callwell, 1863), and the result of this must be the small vaulted building now used as a store in the present compound. It has the same battered walls as the building at Howth, and is about the same size, but now has a single-pitch roof. Its stair has been removed, but it is clear that the very thick mass of masonry on its inner side must have carried the fire-platform. As the ground slopes down to the north the wall on this side is considerably thicker than the opposite one containing the entrance and a single small window. There are indications that it was a single unit; the door in its east end, now leading to a nineteenth-century building, might have led to an earlier one in that position. In 1802 Rogers built a 20 m high tower to the east, and this was removed in 1854 when the present 23 m high tower was erected by George Halpin.

The third and best-preserved example is that situated on the Old Head of Kinsale, 1 km north of the present lighthouse which is at the extreme end of the headland. The fine deep-water harbour of Kinsale was considered to be one of the very best in Ireland. After the siege of Kinsale in 1601, when the Spanish garrison was given honourable terms of surrender, the port became increasingly important. A naval dockyard was established and in the late 1660s the splendid Charlesfort was built commanding the entrance to the harbour and the main anchorage. Like Howth, Kinsale was covered by the patent granted to Reading in 1665, in which he was given the right to erect two lighthouses, one on the Old Head and a second on Barry Ogee's Castle; the latter was

Figure 18. Howth Head, Dublin: remains of old lighthouse.

engulfed by the new Charlesfort masonry buildings and the light was shown from a window in the fort. The Old Head is about 11 km south of the town and is a long sinuous headland with the extremity isolated by a narrow isthmus defended by a prehistoric or medieval earthwork on which stands a medieval tower. The original lighthouse is situated about 1 km to the south-east on high ground where the headland widens out.

The building measures 16.05 m by 5.08 m and contains three rooms, one of which must have been a store, since in addition to being exposed it is 7 km from the nearest hamlet. Externally the walls are battered, internally the crown of the vaults is in brick. The stair is badly ruined, but access to the top is possible, and here coal ash from the fire can still be found. In 1703 complaints were made that the light had not been shown for the last twenty years (Callwell, 1863). In 1714 notice was given that the light was to be "made with coals and not candles as it hitherto hath been there" (*Dublin Gazette*, 21 Sept 1714). This was presumably another example where mariners found that a change to candles or oil was not an improvement, and demanded the reinstatement of the coal brazier (as at North Forelands and Isle of May). In 1810 an inspection was made of a temporary lighthouse which had a small lantern containing "twelve lamps with cylinders, but without reflectors" (Halpin, 1810), but it is not clear from the description whether this was carried on the roof of the cottage or was an independent structure; the latter is the more likely as the roof shows no signs of alterations. Whatever its form it survived until 1814, when George Halpin built a new round tower about 17 m to the south-east

Figure 19. Old Head of Kinsale: remains of old lighthouse.

nearer the cliff edge. This had keepers' dwellings around it on a concentric plan, and the tower, now ruined, is unlikely to have been very high. This was replaced by Halpin's 30 m tower at the end of the headland in 1853. This old "cottage lighthouse" is the best example of its kind and it is to be hoped that it will be restored and preserved as an Irish Ancient Monument of considerable interest (Fig. 19).

A structure rather different from the previous three examples is the light on one of the Copeland Isles at the entrance to Belfast Lough, about 3 km north of Donaghadee. The small island now known as Old Lighthouse Isle, but originally as Cross Isle, rises to an elevation of only 27 m and consequently it has always been necessary to have a tower. Furthermore, the light being on an island, it was necessary to provide more accommodation for living quarters and stores; consequently two stories were provided, and this part, 11.09 m by 7 m, still survives intact. At the east end are the ruins of a square tower a little wider than the living quarters, with walls 1.22 m thick. In 1774 a description by Walter Harris states that the tower was 70 feet high with walls 7 feet thick (Harris & Smith, 1744), whilst in 1810 it was reported as 44 feet high (Halpin, 1810); as the extant walls are not of this thickness it is possible that Harris's "sevens" are a mistranscription of "fours". In 1796 Rogers built a turret on the north-east corner of the tower, of which remains can still be seen. Soon after 1813 it was decided to build a new lighthouse, and Halpin's 15.08 m high tower was erected to the south; the old one was used to carry a bell. In 1844 yet another lighthouse was built, this time on Mew Isle, and this 37.05 m tower is still in use. The plan of the old building presents some problems, particularly the relationship of the stone stair to the tower, which is very awkward. It is possible that there might have been an earlier tower such as that clearly shown on an estate map of 1732 (Sloane, 1732; see Fig. 17), which was completely removed in the late eighteenth century. The date is not known precisely, but Harris is probably correct in recording that in 1744 it was "built thirty years ago". This is supported by the fact that it is not shown on Price's map of Ireland of 1711.

ACKNOWLEDGMENTS

I wish first to thank Rosemary Christie for her help on all the expeditions and in later research. Very special thanks are due to Sr. Jaime Martínez García of La Coruña; also Sr. Alfredo García Alén of Pontevedra; the Italian Naval Authorities and Capt. Macchiavelli of the Hydrographic Dept., Genoa; M. René Faille; Mr. Colin MacFarlan and Mr. Michael Costeloe of the Commissioners of Irish Lights; and finally to all the keepers whose kindness and hospitality we have enjoyed.

REFERENCES

Bartoccini, Renato 1958 Il Porto Romano di Leptis Magna. *Boll. del Centro Studi per la Storia dell'Architettura*, No. 13, Suppl.

Braun, G. & Hogenberg, F. 1593–4 *Civitates Orbis Terrarum*. Cologne.

Callwell, R. 1863. MS at Commission of Irish Lights, Dublin.

Cornide, José 1792. *INVESTIGACIONES SOBRE LA FUNDACIÓN Y FÁBRICA DE LA TORRE LLAMADA DE HÉRCULES, SITUADA A LA ENTRADA DEL PUERTO DE LA CORUÑA, POR DON JOSEPH CORNIDE, VECINO DE DICHA CIUDAD, y Académico Supernumerario de la Real Academia de la Historia*. 58 p. Madrid.

Florez, P. Enrique 1765 *España Sagrada*, Tom IX. Madrid.

Gelati, Giovanni 1968 *Livorno e il suo Porto*, 22 pp. Florence.

Guillaume, Jean 1970 Le Phare de Cordouan .... *Revue de l'art*, **8**, 33–52.

Halpin, George 1810 *Report on the State of Lighthouses*. MS at Comm. Irish Lights, Dublin.

Harris, Walter & Smith, Charles 1744 *The Antient and Present State of the County of Down*. Dublin.

Hutter, Siegfried 1958 *Der Antike Leuchtturm von la Coruña*. Thesis submitted to the Technische Hochschule, München.

Lanoire, J.-Fernand 1950 *Le Phare de Cordouan*, 45 pp. Bordeaux.

Leask, Harold G. 1955 *Irish Churches and Monastic Buildings*, Vol. 1, 170 p. Dundalk.

Sloane, John 1732 *Survey of the Estate of the Honble Capt. James Ross of Portavoe in the Barony of Ards & County Down*. MS in possession of Capt. Ker of Portavoe.

Sloane, John S. 1873 *Manual for lightkeepers*, 188. Dublin.

Steer, Kenneth 1958 Arthur's O'on, a lost shrine of Roman Britain. *Arch. J.* **115**, 99–110.

Tettamancy, Gaston F. 1920 *La Torre de Hércules*, 203 pp. La Coruna.

Vigo, Pietro 1915 *Livorno* [*Italia Artistica*, No. 78], 136 pp. Bergamo.

Belfast P.R.O. *Payment & Receipt Book. Revenue & Army, Ireland.* June 1690—March 1691.

Report of the Commissioners . . . on The Condition and Management of Lights, Buoys and Beacons 1861. H.M.S.O.

Servicio Historico del Ejercito, Madrid. Two MS drawings of La Coruna.

Discussion

Parker Why do you call the Boulogne lighthouse a companion to the Dover one?
Hague Although the Tour d'Ordre is an emperor earlier it seems reasonable to assume that they are related. Nothing survives on the site at Boulogne today. It has been suggested that the Dover tower was not a lighthouse, but I do not share this view. It is perfectly possible that it was also used as a semaphore station. Lighthouses have often been built in ludicrous positions, where they are shrouded in mists, and it is not unreasonable to assume that even the Romans made mistakes.
Fryer Is it true that the only evidence for a relatively early date for the eastern pharos at Dover is the absence of the re-used material reported in that on the western heights?
Hague I rely on Romanists here. All I can say is that on the western heights two lumps of masonry core, obviously not *in situ*, have been propped up rather like a cromlech on a high point of a nineteenth-century fortress. I regard it as a sentimental gesture by a Victorian military engineer with an historical sense.
Fryer Is there not a section preserved within the fort itself?
Hague Not to my knowledge. The remains that I described are within the fort, standing on top of one of the great stone revetted bastions, and are not likely to have been moved far.
Fryer Drawings and paintings of the sea-approach to Dover, executed prior to the burial of the western pharos in 1805–06, show it as a substantial if formless mass of masonry. In 1861, building excavations brought to light a projecting layer of cemented rubble, containing two or three brick courses. The masonry incorporated re-used material, including *Classis Britannica* tiles.

The masonry is embedded into the stonework of the Redoubt and shows as a long streak of Roman flint-rubble concrete surmounted by a tile-course. Overhead, on the surface of the Redoubt, three pieces of the concrete (the "cromlech"), hewn off the foundations in 1861, have been set up to represent the stump of the pharos in the eighteenth century. R. E. M. Wheeler's detailed paper (The Roman Light-houses at Dover. *Arch. J.* **86**, 1930, 29–46) includes a photograph taken of the section exposed in 1861 and reproductions of the paintings and drawings.
Hague I have been to Dover several times, once since visiting Corunna, and I find I agree absolutely with Wheeler's interpretation.

Wignall On the north-east side of Anglesey there is a small reef or island on which there is a small tower said to be a refuge, and furnished with flint and timber. There seems little point in it being so tall, unless it was used as a lighthouse. I heard that only two people had ever been picked up from there, but I found remains of five shipwrecks on the eastern side.
Hague I understand the tower on Ynys Dulas was built as a philanthropic gesture by Col. Hughes, a local landowner, in 1824. It was to be furnished with provisions for mariners and was also intended to serve as an unlit beacon or sea-mark, as the reef was

not protected by the original light displayed from Lynas Head to the north. It is said that local fishermen took advantage of the food and provisions, and that this amenity was soon discontinued. Although quite different in appearance, there is a similar refuge on Horse Island off Ardrossan, built around 1840.

May I ask any of you who operate in the Mediterranean to record the dimensions and plan of any lighthouse structures which you may find.

Naval warfare in the El-Amarna Age

by

ELISHA LINDER

The El-Amarna Age, roughly corresponding to the first phase of the Late Bronze Age in the Eastern Mediterranean, is well known for its international diplomatic activities which helped to create a certain equilibrium between the two great powers—the Egyptian and Hittite Empires. Treaties were contracted between the rulers of Mitanni, Kassite Babylon, Hatti and Egypt, resulting in the establishment of an international organization of trade. Merchants were free to cross the borders of different states, their safety guaranteed by the mutual interest of both Empires.

Technological knowledge was exchanged through the mobility of craftsmen organized in guilds (Gordon, 1956) and a rich variety of ideas was spread beyond recognized frontiers. Maritime trade flourished with the development of commercial centers like the "free port of trade" in Ugarit, serving Mycenaean ships together with merchantmen arriving from Cyprus, Egypt and Asia Minor.

Although dissonant in such an era of international synthesis and peaceful coexistence, we nevertheless find the art of naval warfare developing and consolidating at just this period, the fourteenth century B.C. Furthermore, we shall try to show (a) that engagement at sea between ships specially constructed and manned for sea battles was introduced in the El-Amarna Age by "foreign" mariners coming to the Eastern Mediterranean shores from the west and north-west; and (b) that from the strategic point of view, the outcome of any large-scale military encounter in this part of the ancient world was henceforth largely dependent on the naval strength of the parties involved.

Thutmosis III, probably the most sea-oriented Pharaoh, introduced an innovation which opened this new chapter in the maritime history of the Eastern Mediterranean almost a century before the period under discussion.

We refer to the establishment of "supply-ports" for his armies along the Syro-Palestinian coast. The strategic importance of this was obvious. It freed the marching armies from burdensome loads, since their provisions were carried by ships directly to their overnight camping-grounds. Next we find the army itself being transported by sea, and the facilities of the harbors extended to serve the "troopships" as well as the cargo vessels. As a result, trading-posts with limited shipping facilities, after prolonged use as naval bases, were turned into flourishing centers of maritime commerce. The cities gradually became economically and politically detached from their immediate "hinterland", and depended more and more for daily existence and safety on the free passage of their ships at sea. They acquired their own ships, and some of the larger harbor cities controlled quite a sizable fleet of merchantmen.

Permanent political control by Egypt over such a string of harbor cities could only have been exercised by means of a strong navy dominating the seas. Such a navy had to possess the proper type of ships for combating hostile fleets, and had at the same time to keep open a good number of operational bases along the Syro-Palestinian coast.

Hence, we would expect a reorganization of the Egyptian armed forces with a special emphasis on naval power, and at the same time the necessary developments in shipbuilding from "troopships" and supply ships into "coastal defense" and combat vessels. This, however, was not the case. The Egyptian administrative texts of the period do not indicate such naval developments. There is no evidence for the growth of a military élite solely engaged in naval warfare. Major maritime expeditions were still commanded by treasury officials and the same officers were assigned to duty with the armed forces both at sea and on land. For example, Amenophis II, who ruled Egypt after Thutmosis III, appointed the chief stablemaster of the army's chariotry to be the "Admiral of the Fleet" (Hayes, 1962, Part 2, p. 9).

As far as shipbuilding is concerned, we do not find any evidence for the construction of new types of ships which could suit the needs of an active combat-navy. At least, nothing of the sort is mentioned in the detailed document describing the various activities at *Prw-nfr*, the principal dockyard and naval base of this period (Glanville, 1930).

When at the beginning of the El-Amarna Age the Egyptian supremacy at sea was for the first time seriously challenged, we learn of the short-comings of the Egyptian navy in protecting their Asiatic empire.

Our main source of information for the study of this chapter in Egypt's maritime history is the El-Amarna Letters. It is surprising and regrettable that this aspect of the *EA* correspondence has as yet not been thoroughly studied. In the present limited framework of our survey, we shall confine ourselves to general observations and a few examples to illustrate the gradually deteriorating situation:

Over a dozen harbor cities, which were located along the Mediterranean coast, are mentioned in the letters. With the exception of Azzati, Ascalon and Jaffa in the south, and Byblos and for a while Ṣumur in the north, all of these cities betrayed the Pharaohs by supplying food and various commodities to the enemy, while opening their harbors to alien ships. Some joined forces with the enemies of the Pharaoh and assisted in conquering the last Egyptian strongholds on the Syrian coast.

Aziru, who was at that time the chief instigator in the rebellion against Egypt, succeeded in subduing one coastal city after another, by enforcing a total blockade and cutting off all their food supply.

Ṣumur, the center of the Egyptian administration, is described as "a bird that has been put in a cage; . . . the son of Abdi-Aširta (Aziru) by land and the people of Arwada by sea, day (and) night are against it" (*EA* 105: 8–13). Byblos came under complete blockade, unable to get from Ugarit the requested wood for the king: "I cannot send my ships there, for Aziru is hostile to me, and all the regents are one with him. According to their pleasure their ships go and take what they need. . . ." (*EA* 126: 7–14).

At an earlier stage, when Tyre was still loyal to Egypt (before joining the enemy: *EA* 113) and the island was cut off from its water supply, there was no force to look after its vital interests, although the city still had her own fleet of merchantmen, which were in the king's service and were called the "king's ships" (*EA* 155).

Our last example illustrates clearly the incompetence of the local city fleets to look after their own interests in time of grave emergency.

There was only one alternative—the use of a naval force strong enough to keep the local city fleets in line, and repel external pressure from the sea.

Surprisingly enough, we hear of no naval expeditionary force in action either from the *EA* correspondence or from any other Egyptian records. It is most remarkable that in all the urgent, almost desperate demands for help from the coastal dynasts in Palestine and Syria, it was always troops and chariots and not naval support which were requested.

Literary and archaeological data on the navy of the Eighteenth Egyptian Dynasty, amply collected by Säve-Söderbergh (1946), do point to the presence of an Egyptian navy in the Mediterranean during the period under discussion; the question remains, however: was it adequate to cope with the new challenge at sea?

Let us turn to the problem of sea battles and the question of when ships were introduced as tactical weapons in military operations.

It is generally accepted (Yadin, 1963) that the first naval battle in history took place between the "Sea Peoples" and the Egyptians at the time of Ramses III, around 1189 B.C. Casson (1964), who defines a sea battle as "an encounter involving the overtaking and boarding of an enemy ship", gives a much later date. According to him it was only in the ninth century B.C., when the ram was fully introduced as an offensive weapon, that a new era in naval tactics was inaugurated.

New evidence based on recently published Ugaritic and Hittite texts requires our revision of the relatively late dating of the first naval battle in history.

In the thirteenth century the Hittites fought and conquered Alašiya (Cyprus) after Suppiluliuma's decisive sea victory over the latter's fleet. "The ships of Alašiya met me in the sea three times for battle and I smote them and set fire to them in the sea" (Güterbock, 1967). From the Ugaritic texts of the same period we also learn of a series of naval encounters in which scores of ships were involved. One text mentions a fleet of not less than 150 ships belonging to the kingdom of Ugarit, in the service of the Hittites in Asia Minor (*UT* 2062).

In another text (*RS* 20: 18) Ešuwara, the Great Minister of Alašiya, warns the king of Ugarit that 20 swift enemy ships are on their way to attack him, but have suddenly disappeared.

We are witnessing here a highly developed naval warfare which must have been the result of a long process of development both in ship construction and in combat tactics.

This leads us to the re-examination of some of the El-Amarna texts which we believe have been overlooked or misinterpreted in previous studies. When Rib-Addi of Byblos complains before the king of Egypt: "And he (Iapa-Addi) has actually seized one of my ships and has really sailed forth upon the sea in order to capture my other ships" (*EA* 113), does he not describe "an encounter involving overtaking and boarding an enemy ship"? Even more striking is the evidence from those Byblian Amarna letters which discuss naval activities.

In them a group of people appear, the *ameluti mi-ši* (*EA* 101, 105, 108, 110, 111, 126). What distinguishes the *mi-ši* people is their engagement in military operations conducted from ships against the Egyptians and their allies of their subordinate coastal cities (*EA* 111).

Who were these *mi-ši* people? We reject emphatically Lambdin's identification (1953) of the *mi-ši* in the *EA* letter with the Egyptian troops, i.e. a unit in the service of the

Egyptian king. If objectively analysed, all the texts where these people appear speak against this identification. Our contention is that they were outsiders to the Syrian coastal scene of action. They served whoever needed their support or, to be more exact, those who paid for their services. They were mercenaries with no ethnic or political affiliations to the inhabitants of the coastal cities; nor did they seem to be strongly committed or loyal to the inland rulers, whether Aziru or others.

It is suggested that they were an island people, in obvious association with the Sea Peoples, who were known as mercenaries serving in foreign lands. From a typological point of view the parallel is sound, since both the Sea Peoples (in the Egyptian service) and the *mi-ši* people were foreign mercenaries. However, the latter belong to a new type, the naval mercenaries. They specialize in naval warfare; their home is the ship which serves as their operational base and possibly also as their "engine of war".

Can we identify them? *Mi-ši* is not an ethnic but a *nomen professionale*. Assuming that *mi-ši* is an Egyptian loan-word derived from *ms*ᶜ, then the word normally means "army", "troops". However, we suggest the alternative meaning for the word, the one attested from Old Kingdom texts: "warship". *Ameluti mi-ši* could be translated "men of the warships" (Erman & Grapow, 1926–31).

Since they were a new phenomenon in the sphere of warfare, the Egyptians, when they first encountered them, must have given them a general descriptive name, which was later adopted as a loan-word by the El-Amarna scribes.

The problem remains of defining the geographical provenance of the *mi-ši* people. The definition of "island people" or Sea Peoples is too vague, since we find a number of groups appearing in the Egyptian texts under this name: Lukka, Sherdana, Shekelesh, and others. Chronologically, the Lukka (Lycians?) are among the first to be mentioned. They appear in the El-Amarna correspondence, alien to the Egyptians and committing hostile acts against Alašiya: "The people of the land of Lukki, year by year take a small city in my land", complains the king of Alašiya when reproached by Amenophis III for giving shelter to Egyptian enemies (*EA* 38).

We suggest linking the *mi-ši* people with these Western Anatolian seafarers, well known from Hittite texts through their contact with the Hittites when the latter were trying to secure trade routes to the west (Mellaart, 1968). Together with other Sea Peoples who were hostile to Egypt, they are still mentioned by Merneptah (1224–1204), and we hear of them again in an Akkadian text from Ugarit, just before the collapse of the Hittite Empire (*RS* 20, 238).

The evidence which is building up, when pieced together, leaves little room for speculation as to the growing rôle of naval warfare in the struggle for the domination of the Eastern Mediterranean coast. Nevertheless, we still face a major argument against the early dating of actual sea battles from those who see in them mere acts of piracy which are characterized by "hit and run" tactics conducted by armed men against coastal inhabitants or merchantmen at sea.

It is once again the maritime texts from Ugarit, principally those describing the organization of shipping, which aid us in clarifying the problem. Five Ugaritic texts (*UT* 83, 319, 2057, 2085, 2124), which may be classified under the heading "catalogues of ships", list the crews and captains of different types of ships in the service of the Ugaritic king. A closer analysis of these texts reveals that one category of ships, the *tk*$\underline{t}$ types was headed by captain-commanders who belonged to a growing class of naval aristocracy, counterparts of the *mariannu*, the élite chariot-warriors. Under their command appear the enlisted men from various localities. These were recruited to serve on what we believe was a type of warship manned by approximately 30 men.

To students of classical antiquity, this principle of mobilization recalls a passage in Thucydides referring to the mobilization of ships during the Trojan War: "All (on the ship) were rowers as well as warriors; this he has shown in the case of the ship of Philoctetes" (I. 10. 4).

A striking parallel to this system of manning ships, also from the Homeric age (though there cannot be any doubt as to its historicity) is recorded on a tablet from Pylos (An 12(1)) in Linear B script: "Rowers to go to Pleuron—eight from Ro-o-wa; five from Rhion; four from Po-ra-pi; six from Te-ta-ra-ne; seven from A-po-ne-we". Five different places provide 30 rowers; this could very well be the average complement of a single warship. In one of the Ugartic texts (*UT* 83) four places provide $18+x$ men to form the personnel of one ship—a number very close to that of the Pylos crew.

The comparable material in Homer's "catalogue of ships", the Ugaritic administrative texts, and the Linear B tablet suggests the use of a *navis longa* ("long ship") by the East Mediterranean seafarers, including both the Syrians and the "island people".

In conclusion we suggest the following phases in the development of naval warfare in the El-Amarna Age: first, we witness an increasing development in maritime trade and growth of commercial centers as an outcome of the political stability and relatively peaceful coexistence.

Next, seafaring peoples from the west and north-west were attracted by the rich prey of sailing merchantmen and wealthy coastal cities. They intensified their acts of piracy and raids, using mostly Alašiya (Cyprus) and the Cilician coast as their temporary base of departure. They seem to have sailed in small, swift vessels of a type known to us from Minoan and Mycenaean depictions, which do not resemble any known Egyptian or Syrian ships.

As a result of the growing menace to maritime trade and to the safety of the coastal centers of commerce, appropriate countermeasures were required: on certain occasions the units of the enemy fleets were incorporated into the existing military organizations of the various coastal states; gradually, however, the coastal cities built their own ships and trained their sailors in the new naval tactics.

When the great powers came to acknowledge the strategic importance of naval warfare it was the growing Hittite Empire, under Suppiluliuma, which first took advantage of the new development. Their vital interests, both military and economic, in the north-eastern corner of the Mediterranean were directly involved. Since the Hittites were not a maritime power and depended completely on the services of foreign fleets, they must have encouraged the coastal maritime centers in their sphere of influence in building proper navies, while at the same time enlisting the services of mercenaries from Western Anatolia.

The Egyptian Pharaohs of the El-Amarna Age, who were engaged in continuous struggle to keep their Asiatic Empire from collapsing, were too late in adapting their military prowess to the emerging naval warfare. Surprisingly, we find the Sherdana, one of the Sea Peoples, serving as mercenaries under Ramses II at the battle of Qadesh on land and not on their ships. When at last, in the famous "Sea Battle of Ramses III", Egyptians appear on "long ships", they do so, ironically enough, near the coast, repelling the Philistine invaders who arrived in sailing ships resembling the Syrian "Hippos" type.

REFERENCES

Casson, L. 1964 *Illustrated History of Ships and Boats*, 272 pp. New York.

Erman, A. & Grapow, H. 1926–31 *Wörterbuch der Aegyptischen Sprache*, 5 vols. Leipzig.

Glanville, S. R. K. 1930 Records of a Royal Dockyard of the Time of Tuthmosis III: Papyrus British Museum 10056. *AZ*, **66**, 105–21.

Gordon, C. H. 1956 Ugaritic Guilds and Homeric ΔΗΜΙΟΕΡΓΟΙ, *in* Weinberg, S. S. (ed.) *The Aegean and the Near East*, 136–43. 322 pp. New York.

Güterbock, H. G. 1967 The Hittite Conquest of Cyprus Reconsidered. *JNES*, **26**, 73–81.

Hayes, W. C. 1962 Egypt: Internal Affairs from Tuthmosis I to the Death of Amenophis III, in *Cambridge Ancient History*, Vol. II, Chap. IX. 2nd Bdit.

Lambdin, T. O. 1953 The Miši-People of the Byblian Amarna Letters. *JCS*, **7**, 75–7.

Mellaart, J. 1968 Anatolian Trade with Europe and Anatolian Geography and Cultural Provinces in the Late Bronze Age. *Anatolian Studies*, **18**, 187–202.

Säve-Söderbergh, T. 1946 *The Navy of the Eighteenth Egyptian Dynasty*, 94 pp. Uppsala and Leipzig.

Yadin, Y. 1963 *The Art of Warfare in Biblical Lands*, 484 pp. London.

EA = Knudtzon, J. A. (ed.) 1915 *Die El-Amarna-Tafeln*, 2 vols. Leipzig.

UT = Gordon, C. H. 1965 *Ugaritic Textbook*, 547 pp. Rome.

RS = Ras Shamra Texts (*Le Palais royal d'Ugarit* III & IV, ed. J. Nougayrol, 1955 & 1956, Paris; *Ugaritica* V, ed. C. F. A. Schaeffer & others, 1968, Paris).

Discussion

Tilley Do you not think that in the battle against the Sea Peoples, the ships on the Egyptian side are shown ramming their opponents?
Linder I was expecting some assistance from you to clarify the problem of the ram. It is a matter for discussion in every classical book on the subject, whether the ram was introduced by the Minoans. Marinatos in his article, which is based mainly on the study of Mycenaean and Minoan seals, believes that the part which sticks out like a ram was there just to keep the boat from striking obstacles in its way (La marine créto-mycénienne, *Bulletin de Correspondance Hellénique*, **57**, 1933, 170 ff.); but he may have changed his mind. In the depiction of the famous battle between Ramses III and the Sea Peoples, there is a very interesting phenomenon: the Egyptians were fighting from long ships which were unlike any Egyptian boats known to us, with oars. The incoming Sea Peoples were in round ships, and therefore we may have to consider this whole sea battle as something peculiar, since they did not come in warships.

Humphreys I am very doubtful about calling the Sea Peoples' ships "round" ships simply because there is no appendix in the front. The ships are symmetrical on both sides, but low in the water; not like Egyptian representations of merchant ships with high sides, e.g. the Tomb of Kenamun. They are not roundships in the sense of ships meant for carrying a lot of cargo. There may not have been much functional specialization of ship design in this period; I doubt if the terms "roundship" and "longship" are really applicable.
Linder This kind of small round boat may have been a development of the typical Syrian "roundship", but it was propelled with oars and was therefore closer to the Sea Peoples' own kind of "longships" than to the Egyptian ships.

Frost May not Bronze Age warships have been even larger? If I remember aright, the Cheops ship, which is 36 m long (built in 2650 B.C. of massive pieces of juniper wood imported by sea from Lebanon), had 18 paddles to a side—so that only 15 to a side on a warship could be a conservative estimate.
Linder I do not think that this example provides a parallel, because the Cheops ship was a big merchantman and very different from the kind of very light, swift ship we were discussing. In one text from Ugarit they are described as "ships which hide in the woods". This was only feasible with light boats pushed ashore at night, waiting for the morning to resume their combat activities.

Frost Can you identify Bronze Age harbours along your coastline?
Linder I wrote an article some years ago on the ancient harbour of Athlit, one of the most ancient Phoenician harbours known. The construction of this harbour was dated

by me to the seventh or eighth centuries B.C. I am now more than convinced that man-made harbours existed in the Late Bronze Age. On the Israeli coast the earliest evidence is still our Athlit harbour.

Frost Do you have no reef islands with rock-cut foundations or a sea wall on the weather side?

Linder The only offshore islands along the Israeli coast are near Akhzib. Others are actually part of the coast. This raises the problem of the rise of sea level. We found on them some quarries, but no traces of actual sea walls.

Frost They always over-quarried later.

Linder At Athlit a storm helped to unearth Persian constructions near the harbour site and we are now almost sure that our harbour is not later than seventh-century B.C.

Frost Braidwood has a ninth-century B.C. mole at Tabbat el Hammam. He gives stratigraphic and quarry evidence for the dating. I think it is the earliest known Phoenician built (as distinct from rock-cut) harbour structure.

Linder The stones and architectural features of this harbour are very similar to those at Athlit.

Frost Geological evidence adduced by René Wetzel corroborates this: the earlier rock-cut installations on the island opposite had been submerged by the time the mainland mole was built. Braidwood says the Bronze Age levels were missing from the seaside tell, though they were present on two related tells in the hinterland.

Linder We must all quickly look for more ancient harbours along the eastern coast of the Mediterranean.

Cook At what stage in history can one start using the word "navy"?

Linder I believe that the Late Bronze Age is definitely the period for which one can first use the word "navy", on the basis of the literary evidence concerning the organization of sailors and ships. I can distinguish in the texts the groups of ships which belong to merchants and others which appear to belong to an organization under the command of captains, part of a warrior aristocracy.

Frost van Effenterre has an interesting interpretation of the Linear B tablet which you mentioned: he claims that it is a list of ships' parts (Un navire mycénien, *in* Mollat, M. (ed.) *Sociétés et compagnies de commerce en orient et dans l'Ocean Indien* [Actes du 8ième Colloque Internat. d'Histoire Maritime, Beyrouth, 1966], 43–53. Paris, 1970).

Ships on Minoan seals

by

JOHN H. BETTS

In VIEW of the fact that Minoan civilization came to be regarded in later antiquity for the remarkable extent and richness of its sea power (e.g. Thucydides, I.4), one might imagine that ships would figure largely in its art. But, while a keen and lively interest in marine life is exhibited in the major Cretan Bronze Age arts of pottery decoration, fresco painting and gem engraving, ships are not often depicted. And when they are, they tend for the most part to be represented as cult objects or as symbols of some sort in stylized forms rather than realistic illustrations of the actual vessels in which the Minoan Cretans sailed. A hunt for informative naturalistic representations of ships of the period rewards the nautical archaeologist with only disappointing material.

A glance at Marinatos' fundamental, but sometimes mistaken and now outdated, article (1933) or at Hutchinson's brief but useful account of Minoan shipping (1962, 91 ff.) shows that a great proportion of this material is to be derived from representations of ships on engraved gems or sealstones and their ancient impressions in clay (sealings). It is the purpose of this paper to show the types and function of the sealstones on which these representations occur and to re-examine some of the problems which they raise for the nautical archaeologist. The problems are such that the paper aims to invite rather than provide solutions.

The long series of Cretan seals began shortly before 2000 B.C. with large ivory and bone seals found almost exclusively in the circular tombs of Crete's southern central plain, the Mesara, in the Early Minoan period before the construction of the first palatial buildings in Crete. These ivory and bone seals are in a wide variety of shapes: cones, rings, cylinders engraved on the ends, various asymmetrical shapes dependent on the original shape of the bone used and occasionally more elaborate natural and theriomorphic forms. Engraving in soft stones such as steatite, serpentine and soapstone soon made its appearance alongside the ivories (Xanthoudides, 1924, pls. IV, VIII, XIII–XV; Matz, 1928; *CMS* II.1).

The motifs engraved on these earliest seals are usually decorative patterns of varying degrees of complexity, but there are also some quite elaborate representations of human and animal figures, and from Platanos a single important ship, the earliest on a Minoan sealstone (Figs. 1 & 2). This piece has been frequently discussed and illustrated, usually in one of a variety of inaccurate drawings which have led to erroneous conclusions. For instance, the yard-arm shown on the drawing used by Branigan (1970, 191, Fig. 44d) or the rigging, steering oar(s?) and prow shown on the drawing reproduced by Casson (1960, pl. Ic) are by no means as clear and obvious as they show them. The yard-arm may be an unintentional scratch in the ivory, and Casson's dogmatic assertion that "the high end is the prow" is scarcely merited, although he is following the authority of Evans (*PM* II, 239 ff.) which has received wide acceptance (e.g. by Marinatos, 1933; Hutchinson, 1962; Branigan, 1970).

Figure 1.

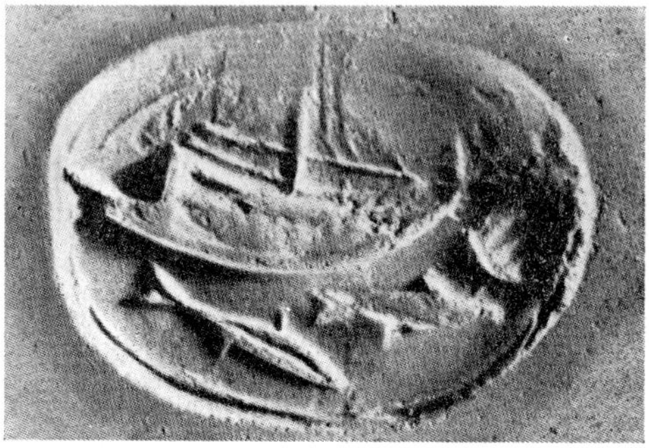

Figure 2.

"Two idiosyncrasies which distinguish Middle Minoan ships from their contemporaries in Egypt are the very high prow rising at an angle of about sixty degrees, and the low stern with keel projecting, a form persisting from the old long boat type of the earliest Bronze Age both in Crete and in the Cyclades"—so Hutchinson (1962, 95), but his insistence on high-prowed Minoan ships does not seem to be consistent with Late Minoan representations and is apparently based on only two pieces of slender evidence. First, pictures of vessels roughly incised on Early Cycladic pots of the so-called "frying-pan" type show a fish mounted on their high end; the fish, it is argued, must point forward; therefore the high end is the prow. But even if this assumption is correct, the crudely scratched boats seem very different from Minoan ships of the Middle and especially the Late Bronze Age periods, when identical sterns and prows and perhaps even higher sterns are found. Secondly, a small clay boat of the Early Minoan period from Palaikastro Siteias is cited for its high prow and "projecting keel" (Hutchinson) or "fixed rudder" (Evans). This, with only two internal benches, seems to represent an inshore rowing-boat or, as it served as a votive offering, perhaps a cult vessel like those depicted on Late Minoan gold rings or that carried as a votive offering on the Hagia Triadha sarcophagus, rather than a seagoing ship. It seems dangerous, at least, to reach any categorical conclusion as to the direction in which it was intended to sail; its only parallel, another clay votive from Mochlos, has identical prow and stern.

By contrast, the higher end of the ship on the ivory seal from Platanos (Figs. 1 & 2) shows a three-pronged arrangement paralleled in later Minoan illustrations, and in Classical ships such an arrangement is invariably seen at the ship's stern (Morrison & Williams, 1968, pls. 15 & 16d). It was apparently referred to as *aphlaston* (Homer, *Iliad* XV. 717) or its plural *aphlasta* (Herodotus, VI. 114). If the high end of the Minoan vessel is the stern, then the prow is apparently fitted with a kind of beak or ram like Classical Greek and Phoenician warships, but this is far from certain and it seems inherently unlikely that the sort of naval tactics implied by such an arrangement were in use at so early a date.

While ivory and soft stones in a wide variety of shapes were in vogue, especially in southern central Crete, a smaller three-sided prism seal of triangular section began to become popular in northern central and more especially eastern Crete (Xenaki-Sakellariou, 1958*a*). These three-sided prisms in soft stones were engraved, usually on all three sides, with a limited variety of semi-naturalistic motifs which during the course of the Middle Minoan I and II periods (*c*. 2000–1750 B.C.) tended to become more and more stylized. By the Middle Minoan III period (by *c*. 1650 B.C.) the shape was being increasingly engraved with hieroglyphic or pictographic script. Even on the earlier prisms the range of motifs was not large, and they were depicted in a schematic way that seems to indicate that they, like the repeated three-sided shape on which they occur, had some symbolic, magical or amuletic force.

A number of these prisms carry representations of ships (Fig. 3). They are single-masted, rigged with either two or three stays fore and aft. Sails are generally not depicted. The row of lines below the hull seems to represent the oars or, less probably, waves. Even if they are definitely oars, they give no clear indication of the direction in which the vessel was thought to be sailing. Some examples do not differentiate between prow

Figure 3.

Figure 4.

and stern (Kenna, 1960, 95, no. 55, pl. 3), while others show in a rudimentary way the three-pronged *aphlaston*-type arrangement at their higher end (stern?) and not at the other (Kenna, 1960, 94, no. 50, pl. 3). There is often a great deal of stylization, as in one example where exaggerated spirals curl over both prow and stern (Fig. 4). The series of three-sided prisms on which these schematic and often crudely engraved ships become a quite common motif for the first time are still disappointingly vague in the information they provide for the nautical archaeologist.

During the course of the Middle Minoan II period, after the construction of the first major palatial buildings in Crete, improvements in engraving techniques made it possible to start cutting harder semi-precious stones such as carnelian, jasper, agate, chalcedony, quartz and even rock-crystal, and a number of the later hieroglyphic or pictographic prisms are in such materials. The same technical developments also gradually produced considerable experimentation with new shapes of seal such as the "signet", the "discoid" and the rectangular cushion-shaped sealstone, usually referred to as a "fattened cylinder", which had a relatively brief vogue, mainly during the Middle Minoan III period and the earliest part of Late Minoan I (*c*. 1700–1550 B.C.). Finally, the circular "lentoid", developing from the discoid, and the almond-shaped "amygdaloid" became the main shapes in use throughout the heyday of the second palatial era down to the time of the major destruction of the last palace at Knossos (*c.* 1650–1375 B.C.). The ultimate product of the technical development begun during the Middle Minoan II period was an excellence in glyptic art scarcely surpassed in any subsequent age. A wide variety of scenes was engraved on Late Minoan sealstones with that astonishing skill and attention to detail which makes them objects which every book on Minoan art rushes to illustrate. But their very attractiveness has led to disproportionate emphasis being laid upon them; the ivories and soft stone seals and the three-sided prisms which preceded them and from which they developed are often cursorily treated, and it is also forgotten that, while these artistic triumphs were being achieved in hard stones, humbler schools of craftsmen continued to engrave less spectacular pieces in soft stones. These persisted into the post-palatial Late Minoan IIIB-C period (*c.* 1350–1150 B.C.), but need not all be relegated, as they sometimes are, to a late degenerate phase.

There are, disappointingly, no ships engraved on hard stones during the Late Minoan period. A number of boats engraved on metal rings of the period appear in cult or mythological scenes and can practically be discounted from a discussion of real seagoing craft; they are listed by Marinatos as "bateaux de culte" (1933, 223 ff.). The ship on a steatite lentoid (Fig. 5), which was quite wrongly assigned by Evans (*PM* II, 243, Fig. 139) to the Middle Minoan II period and by Kenna (1960, 102, no. 106, pl. 5) to Middle Minoan I, has now been rightly placed in the Late Minoan IIIB period, on grounds of material, shape and style, by Boardman (1970, 106, pl. 196). It does not add a great deal to our knowledge of Minoan ships. The lines of "tooth pattern" above the stays are typical of the ornamentation used to fill, or clutter, engravings of this late period, and have no connection with the vessel itself. They may represent foliage and be a late descendant of the vegetation sprays sometimes associated with ships on the earlier "talismanic" class of gems to be discussed below (Fig. 14). As Kenna suggested, "the circular marks above the thwarts may represent the heads of rowers", but the three higher dots in the sail area cannot be so explained, unless they are the start of a second line of rowers on the opposite side of the vessel, and all the dots may simply be decorative. The companion lentoid in the Ashmolean Museum (no. 1938, 959; Kenna, 1960, 103, no. 107, pl. 5) is also wrongly dated by Kenna (as are his nos. 104 and 105), but its less cluttered style may make its date somewhat earlier in the Late Minoan period than that of the other piece.

Figure 5.

There are two well-known fragmentary clay sealings from Knossos impressed by seals depicting ships. They have been discussed on a number of occasions, often on the basis of drawings in which the artist's inexpert eye has noted less or his vivid imagination reproduced more than is actually visible in the original. The first (Fig. 6) is a sealing from the Northern Entrance Passage of the palace and owes its preservation to the fire which gutted the building in the course of the Late Minoan IIIA period (*c.* 1375 B.C.). It was probably impressed by a lentoid sealstone. Only the central part of the impression remains. It shows a single-masted ship; two stays hang slackly either side the mast, apparently attached to a sail-boom or low yard-arm. A row of pendent semi-circles below the yard-arm were said by Evans (*PM* II, 244, Fig. 141b) to represent the hanging folds of furled sails, though his drawing, clearly showing them as such, is imaginative interpretation rather than complete reality. He regarded the vertically barred structure below as some sort of deck-canopy or cabin. No oars can be seen, nor is there any indication of how the prow and stern were depicted or of the direction in which the ship was sailing.

Figure 6.

Figure 7.

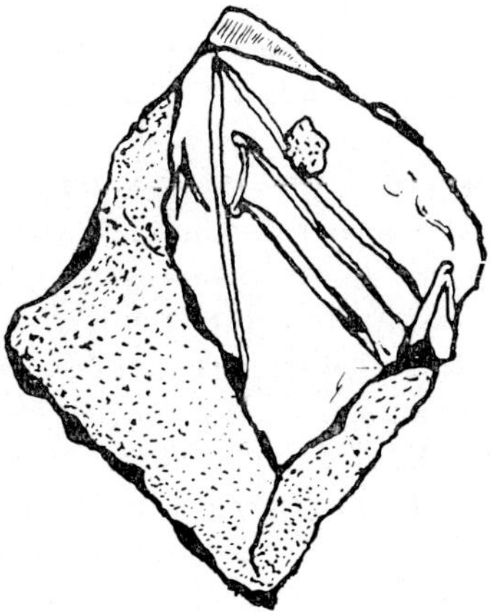

Figure 8.

The second sealing (Fig. 7) derives from a deposit of sealings from the Little Palace which owe their preservation to a conflagration usually reckoned to be somewhat later than that which destroyed the main palace. The impression was made by a large lentoid sealstone or, less probably, by the oval bezel of a metal or stone ring. The ship is again apparently single-masted, but with three instead of two stays to one side and presumably to the other, though they do not appear on the surviving portion of the sealing. Evans' drawing (*PM* II, 244, Fig. 141a) seems to imply that only two of the stays are part of the vessel's rig and that the third is a tether for the large horse which the ship appears to be transporting. His reconstruction drawing is fanciful: all three stays are part of the rigging, as on some of the Middle Minoan three-sided prism representations already referred to. The heads and shoulders of three rowers appear beneath a horizontal line which Evans regarded as part of a deck-canopy over them, but which could equally well represent a low sail-boom or yard-arm. Marinatos (1933) concluded, on the basis of an ingeniously complex but surely mistaken and irrelevant argument about the direction of Minoan writing, and perhaps because he was tempted to regard the horse as travelling forward, that the ship's prow was to the left. He therefore considered that the artist had in error made his rowers face in the wrong direction. Even if his initial argument were tenable, the sealing could still illustrate some kind of rowing manoevre such as beaching in which the rowers might reverse their normal position; beaching, after all, is an operation in which a landlubber gem-engraver would often see ships involved. The disproportionately large horse also presents problems; it has usually been regarded as being transported on the vessel: "If, as seems to be a fair inference, we may regard this as indicating the character of the cargo, we may here trace a reference to the maritime agency by which thoroughbred chariot-horses were brought to the island" (Evans, *PM* II, 244)—hence "l'arrivée du cheval en Crète" (Marinatos, 1933, 179, no. 55); but such symbolic representation and such disproportion in the elements of composition are not usual features of Minoan art. Some kind of mythological or cult scene may be depicted—a fanciful interpreter might think of transportation of the Wooden Horse!—but it seems safer to see the horse as entirely distinct from the ship. Those features of Evans' drawing which make the horse and ship parts of a single composition are illusory. The stay which becomes a rein or tether has already been dismissed. Nor is the impression created in the drawing of all four feet resting firmly on the ship's keel entirely correct; the horse's hindmost foot appears to be above the line and the missing forefeet may well have been below it. It seems that this sealing was impressed by a sealstone which had been engraved twice, first with a ship and later with a horse. Even Evans seems to have felt this to some extent when he described the horse as "superimposed on the intaglio of the vessel". Again a fanciful interpreter might suggest that, as the sealing comes from the Little Palace in the so-called period of Mycenaean dominance, a landsman mainlander, inheriting it from a nautical Cretan, had it re-engraved with a form of transport more to his taste!

A third very fragmentary sealing (Fig. 8) from Knossos, rediscovered in an *apotheke* of the Stratigraphical Museum in 1962 and published by the author of this paper (Betts, 1967, 34, no. 20), shows lines which probably represent the upper rigging of a ship with single mast and three stays.

Apart from the cult vessels on metal rings, the two late steatite seals in the Ashmolean Museum and the three sealings from Knossos so far discussed, there are apparently no other representations of ships on Late Minoan seals in naturalistic styles. But at the same time as Late Minoan naturalism in glyptic art developed out of the technical advances of the Middle Minoan period, some of the more symbolic and stylized motifs that had characterized the three-sided prisms of the Middle Minoan I–II periods persisted through Middle Minoan III and Late Minoan I, at least until the destruction of all the major sites in Crete except Knossos (*c.* 1500 B.C.). They occur on seals of the so-called "talismanic" class and include the largest concentration of ship representations in the history of Minoan glyptic art.

In addition to its incidental artistic attractiveness as jewellery, the sealstone had two main functions as the personal symbol of its wearer. The one was sphragistic: the functional use of a seal to make a mark guaranteeing a document or product as authentic; the vast number of clay sealings from the Cretan and Mainland palaces, often found in association with tablets bearing script, indicates the extent of this function. The other was amuletic, the seal being the personal symbol of the individual and so in some way his magical protector. In the case of most sealstones the two uses were not apparently distinct, and it is in general not possible to say that one served as a seal and another as an amulet; but in the case of those sealstones for which Evans coined the name "talismanic" it seems possible to make such a distinction and to say that their function must have been almost entirely magical. They are very rarely used sphragistically; clay sealings are not often found bearing impressions made by them. From their earlier and more frequent appearance in eastern Crete in Middle Minoan III, especially in the cemeteries at Mochlos and Sphoungaras, it is probable that they, like the earlier three-sided prisms, originated in eastern Crete. They seem to be almost exclusively Cretan; very few have been found on the Mainland of Greece and their manufacture does not seem to continue much after 1500 B.C. into the period when the Minoans began to use Greek Linear B. The superstition that they were made to serve was Minoan, not Greek. Their magical protective qualities seem to have derived not only from their shape and material, like the normal amulet, but also from the schematic motifs engraved on them and perhaps even from the consistent style of their engraving. Red carnelian is by far the most common material, with green jasper a distant second, and by far the most frequent shape is the amygdaloid, along with a type of three-sided prism engraved on all three or only two of its faces, faces almost exactly the same shape as the single face of the amygdaloid. Lentoids are not so common, flattened cylinders even less so. The probable east Cretan origin, the use of the three-sided prism shape for this and for no other type of seal in Crete in this late period, and the schematic rendering of a limited repertoire of motifs (some of them, like the ship, derived from the Middle Minoan I–II prisms), all suggest that the talismanic gem was in some respects the direct descendant of the prism and that both had a similar function. It was only when pictographic signs became common on the prisms that they were used sphragistically, as in the Hieroglyph Deposit of sealings at Knossos (*PM* I, 271 ff.). Certainly none of the sealings of Middle Minoan I–II from the palace at Phaistos in the Mesara appear to have been impressed by the normal type of contemporary three-sided prism (Levi, 1958; *CMS* II.5).

The distinctive technique of engraving the talismanic gem relied on simple but deft strokes of a wheel cutter for straight lines and of a tubular drill for circles and semi-circles, with little or no subsequent elaboration. The range of motifs is limited and they are, as the technique to a certain extent dictates, often very schematic and stylized: vases of various shapes are common; marine life is represented by dolphins, flying fish, squid and octopus, with circular and semi-circular drill marks skilfully used to represent suckers and tentacles; simple fronds of vegetation occur with most of the talismanic motifs from time to time. Some of the more stylized and confusing motifs are variously said to represent vegetation, the foreparts of fish, or bundles of some kind of merchandise such as flax (Kenna, 1969). Marinatos' suggestion that some of these confusing motifs were intended to represent ship's sails lacks cogency (1933, 208, Fig. 7).

There are two basic types of ship representation on talismanic gems. The first is less common but easier to interpret. Four examples are listed here for discussion, but there are numerous others:

(1) Fig. 9.
(2) *CMS* VIII, no. 106.
(3) Xenaki-Sakellariou, 1958*b*, 52, no. 341, pls. XIII & XXVIII.
(4) Erlenmeyer & Zai-Börlin, 1961, 17, no. 45, pl. 6.80.

On this type the whole of the vessel is shown in full sail. The single sail is always cross-hatched, usually with vertical and horizontal lines, perhaps intended to represent the weave of the cloth, though diagonal lines occasionally appear as well (3). The sides of the sail are often shown as inturned chevrons (1 and 2). The sail is sometimes right at the top of the mast, almost disappearing off the gem (3 and 4), while in other examples a considerable amount of the rigging is visible above it (1 and 2). Oars are either omitted

Figure 9.

completely (4) or shown as a row of diagonal lines below the hull, all pointing at the same angle (2 and 3). Pairs of lines below the hull pointing in different directions (1) might be thought to represent oars on both sides of the vessel, but they are almost certainly to be regarded as waves, for on some examples they appear in addition to the oars (Fig. 11). Prow and stern of the ship are usually identical (2 and 4); sometimes a version of the three-pronged *aphlaston* arrangement is found with a downstroke on each of the two outer prongs, forming a kind of fleur-de-lys device. When it occurs at only one end (as probably on (1), though the ends of the gem are damaged and difficult to distinguish) it is tempting to see it as the stern, but this is far from certain, as a single example (3) seems to have it at both ends!

This fleur-de-lys arrangement is a puzzling feature, and the puzzle deepens when one turns to the second, more common type of ship representation on talismanic gems. A list of selected examples of this type follows (some others are given by Kenna, 1969, pls. 12 & 13):

(5) Fig. 10; Carnegie, 1908, no. O15; *CMS* VIII, no. 139.
(6) *CMS* VII, no. 104; Walters, 1926, no. 13.
(7) Fig. 11.
(8) Fig. 12.
(9) Fig. 13.
(10) Fig. 14; *CMS* VIII, no. 55.
(11) Fig. 15; *CMS* VII, no. 227.
(12) *CMS* IV, no. 227.
(13) *CMS* VII, no. 101.
(14) *CMS* VII, no. 72; Walters, 1926, no. 12.

This type seems to represent only one end of the ship. The artist allows the other end to disappear off the end of the gem (5, 9 and 11), or marks off the edge of the illustration

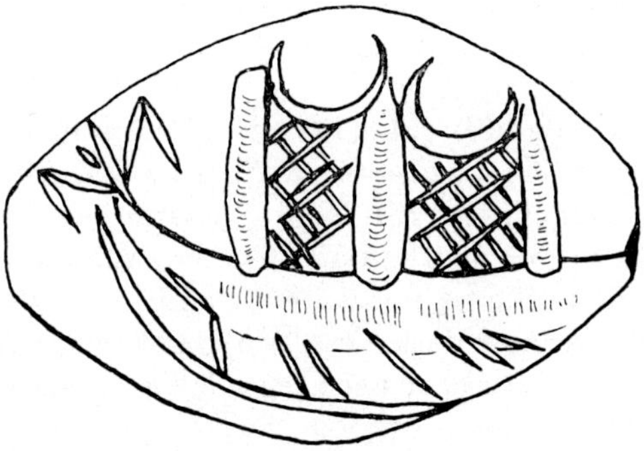

Figure 10.

Figure 11.

Figure 12.

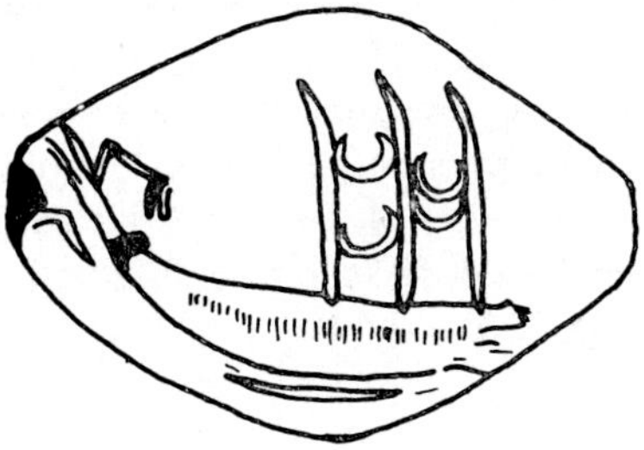

Figure 13.

Figure 14.

Figure 15.

at the unfinished end of the vessel with a single vertical line (6, 8 and 10) or with two such lines (7). At the other end the fleur-de-lys arrangement remains an almost constant feature of these representations. It is usually to the right on the gem (to the left on the impressions illustrated here) but this is not an infallible rule (11). If the cross-hatched area below the end of the vessel on one example (12) may be regarded as representing a fishing-net, then it adds some weight to the argument that this kind of illustration shows the stern of the vessel. A keel-board seems to run below the hull on some examples (5, 6 and 8–12). Some show oars (6 and 10), some both oars and waves (7 and 11), and yet others show neither (8 and 9). The superstructure on these vessels remains enigmatic. It often has three upright members (5 and 6) and these have been regarded as masts, but ships with more than one mast are not otherwise known in Minoan representations. The pair of pendent tubular-drilled semi-circles might be furled sails and the diagonal cross-hatching between the uprights, rigging. Or again, the central upright might be the mast and the two outer ones the edges of a full sail; the semi-circles would then be the top edges of the sail hanging in two loose folds from the yard-arm; but the yard-arm itself is never shown and the diagonal cross-hatching is different from the vertical/horizontal lines conventional for sails on the first type of talismanic ship representation. In any case, there are often more than two semi-circles between the uprights (9). In examples with only two uprights they are often much fatter and the semi-circles, instead of hanging between the uprights, either surmount them (7) or seem to go round them (8 and 10). Here the bulging uprights are perhaps intended to be tied-up bundles of cargo. Full circles occasionally replace semi-circles (10 and 11), and some examples (11) suggest that the superstructure may be some kind of deck-canopy. Sprays of vegetation appear on some examples (10). All these features tend to disintegrate and become even more confused, descending into an almost meaningless fantasy of straight and semi-circular cuts (13 and 14).

This survey of the types of sealstone on which representations of Minoan ships occur will leave a number of nagging problems for the nautical archaeologist, but its central thesis remains clear. Almost all the ships occur on Middle Minoan I–II three-sided prisms and on Middle Minoan III–Late Minoan I talismanic gems. Neither type had much sphragistic use. Both had an amuletic function, apparently based as much on their limited range of symbolic motifs as on their material and shape. This curious fact, along with the evidence of boat votives and "bateaux de culte", indicates that, despite Minoan Crete's reputation in later antiquity as a sea power, the ships which occur in Minoan art almost all have some kind of symbolic, semi-religious or occult significance. The illustrations tend, especially in the Late Minoan period, to be schematic and to overemphasize certain features of the ship, perhaps those which had some special magico-religious significance. More or less naturalistic representations of ships are rarely found.

THE FIGURES

Figure 1. Herakleion Museum seal no. 1079; ivory three-sided prism with one circular and two oval faces, the ship being on one of the latter; 18 × 12 mm; from Tholos B at Platanos. *PM* I, 118, Fig. 87.7; II, 239, Fig. 136a; Xanthoudides, 1924, 114, pl. XIV; Matz, 1928, 25, pl. 8.7; Marinatos, 1930, 109, Fig. 1; 1933, 175, no. 28, pl. XV; Pendlebury, 1939, 88, Fig. 12.4; Herbig, 1940, 61, Fig. 2; Zervos, 1956, pl. 211; Kenna, 1960, 26, no. 10; 32, no. 6; Casson, 1960, pl. Ic; *CMS* II.1, no. 287; Branigan, 1970, 191, Fig. 44d.

Figure 2. Impression of the same.

Figure 3. Oxford, Ashmolean Museum no. 1938, 761; impression of white steatite three-sided prism; 17 × 11 mm; from Mallia. Kenna, 1960, 94, no. 49, pl. 3; Hutchinson, 1962, 94, Fig. 15; Boardman, 1970, pl. 11.

Figure 4. Oxford, Ashmolean Museum no. 1938, 760; impression of black and white mottled steatite three-sided prism; 20 × 10 mm; provenience unknown. Kenna, 1960, 98, no. 71, pl. 4; Boardman, 1970, pl. 12.

Figure 5. Oxford, Ashmolean Museum no. 1938, 958; impression of black steatite elliptical lentoid; 20 × 16 mm; from Central Crete. *PM* II, 243, Fig. 139; Marinatos, 1933, 176, no. 40, pl. XV; Herbig, 1940, 61, Fig. 3; Kenna, 1960, 102, no. 106, pl. 5; Boardman, 1970, 106, pl. 196.

Figure 6. Herakleion Museum sealing no. 146; baked clay sealing impressed by a lentoid seal; 14 × 23 mm; from Northern Entrance Passage at Knossos. *PM* II, 244, Fig. 141b; IV, 827, Fig. 806; Marinatos, 1933, 178, no. 54, pl. XVI; Gill, 1965, 68, no. J3.

Figure 7. Herakleion Museum sealing no. 417; baked clay sealing probably impressed by a lentoid seal; 13 × 27.5 mm; from the Little Palace at Knossos. *BSA*, **11**, 1905–6, 13, Fig. 7; *PM* II, 244, Fig. 141a; IV, 827, Fig. 805; Marinatos, 1933, 179, no. 55, pl. XVI; Kenna, 1960, 58, Fig. 121; Gill, 1965, 90, no. U112.

Figure 8. Herakleion Museum sealing no. 110; fragment of baked clay sealing; 9 × 13.5 mm; from Knossos. Gill, 1965, 96; Betts, 1967, 34, no. 20.

Figure 9. Geneva, in private possession; impression of red carnelian amygdaloid; 17 × 13 mm; provenience unknown. *CMS* X, forthcoming.

Figure 10. Geneva, Musée d'Art et d'Histoire no. 20475; drawing from impression of rock-crystal amygdaloid; 22 × 15 mm; formerly in the Southesk Collection and then in the Kenna Collection; provenience unknown. Carnegie, 1908, no. O15, pl. 16; Marinatos, 1933, 178, no. 51, pl. XVI; *CMS* VIII, no. 139; Betts, 1968, 149, no. 8, pl. 61, Fig. 6.

Figure 11. Herakleion Museum seal no. 643; drawing from impression of orange-red carnelian amygdaloid; 17 × 12 mm; provenience unknown. Xanthoudides, 1907, 184, no. 164, pl. 8; Marinatos, 1933, 177, no. 45, pl. XVI; Betts, 1968, 149, no. 3, pl. 61, Fig. 5.

Figure 12. Geneva, in private possession; impression of red carnelian three-sided prism with amygdaloid-shaped faces, engraved on two of them; 20 × 13 mm; provenience unknown. *CMS* X, forthcoming.

Figure 13. Herakleion Museum seal no. 613; drawing from impression of orange-red carnelian amygdaloid; 16 × 11 mm; from Knossos. Xanthoudides, 1907, 182, no. 149, pl. 8; Marinatos, 1933, 177, no. 46, pl. XVI; Betts, 1968, 149, no. 2, pl. 61, Fig. 4.

Figure 14. Stafford, in private possession; impression of red carnelian amygdaloid; 14.8 × 12.2 mm; formerly in the Dawkins Collection; provenience unknown. *CMS* VIII, no. 55.

Figure 15. Cambridge, Fitzwilliam Museum no. GR.58.1901; drawing from impression of red carnelian amygdaloid; 18 × 15 mm; from Palaikastro Siteias. Betts, 1968, 150, no. 9, pl. 61, Fig. 7; *CMS* VII, no. 227.

REFERENCES

Betts, J. H. 1967 Some Unpublished Knossos Sealings and Sealstones. *BSA*, **62**, 27–45.
Betts, J. H. 1968 Trees in the Wind on Cretan Sealings. *AJA*, **72**, 149–50.
Boardman, J. 1970 *Greek Gems and Finger Rings*, 458 pp. London.
Branigan, K. 1970 *The Foundations of Palatial Crete*, 232 pp. London.
Carnegie, H. 1908 *Catalogue of the Collection of Ancient Gems in the Southesk Collection*, Vol. I, 226 pp. London.
Casson, L. 1960 *The Ancient Mariners*, 286 pp. London & New York.
Erlenmeyer, H. & Zai-Börlin, H. 1961 Von minoischen Siegeln. *Antike Kunst*, **4**, 9–20.
Gill, M. A. V. 1965 The Knossos Sealings: Provenance and Identity. *BSA*, **60**, 58–98.
Herbig, H. 1940 Philister und Dorier. *Jahrbuch des deutschen archäologischen Instituts*, **55**, 58–89.
Higgins, R. A. 1967 *Minoan and Mycenaean Art*, 216 pp. London.
Hutchinson, R. W. 1962 *Prehistoric Crete*, 373 pp. Harmondsworth.
Kenna, V. E. G. 1960 *Cretan Seals*, 163 pp. Oxford.
Kenna, V. E. G. 1969 *The Talismanic Stone in the Late Minoan Age*, (Studies in Mediterranean Archaeology, 24), 39 pp. Lund.
Levi, D. 1958 L'Archivo di Cretule a Festòs. *ASAtene*, **35–36** (N.S. **19–20**), 7–192.
Marinatos, Sp. 1930 Ai Thalassographikai Parastaseis tes Kretomykenaïkes Epoches. *ArchEph*, 1930, 108–26.
Marinatos, Sp. 1933 La Marine Créto-mycénienne. *BCH*, **57**, 170–235.
Matz, F. 1928 *Die frühkretischen Siegel*, 277 pp. Berlin and Leipzig.
Morrison, J. S. & Williams, R. T. 1968 *Greek Oared Ships, 900–322 B.C.*, 336 pp. Cambridge.
Pendlebury, J. D. S. 1939 *The Archaeology of Crete*, 400 pp. London. (Reprinted 1963).
Walters, H. B. 1926 *Catalogue of the Engraved Gems in the British Museum*, 419 pp. London.
Xanthoudides, St. A. 1907 Ek Kretes. *ArchEph*, 1907, 141–86.
Xanthoudides, St. A. 1924 *The Vaulted Tombs of Mesara*, 142 pp. Liverpool. Reprinted 1971.
Xenaki-Sakellariou, A. 1958*a* Sur le Cachet prismatique minoen, *in* Grumach, E. (ed.) *Minoica: Festschrift zum 80. Geburtstag von Johannes Sundwall*, 451–60. Berlin.
Xenaki-Sakellariou, A. 1958*b* *Les Cachets minoens de la Collection Giamalakis*, (Études Crétoises, X), 95 pp. Paris.
Zervos, Chr. 1956 *L'Art de la Crète Néolithique et Minoenne*, 524 pp. Paris.

CMS = Biesantz, H., Matz, F. & Pini, I. (ed.) *Corpus der minoischen und mykenischen Siegel*, Berlin:
II. 1 Platon, N. 1969 *Iraklion, archäologisches Museum: die Siegel der Vorpalastzeit*, 606 pp.
II. 5 Pini, I. 1970 *Iraklion, archäologisches Museum: die Siegelabdrücke von Phästos*, 289 pp.
IV Kenna, V. E. G. & Sakellarakis, J. A. 1969 *Iraklion: Sammlung Metaxas*, 425 pp.
VII Kenna, V. E. G. 1967 *Die englischen Museen*, Vol. II, 336 pp.
VIII Kenna, V. E. G. 1966 *Die englischen Privatsammlungen*, 223 pp.
X Betts, J. H. (forthcoming) *Die schweizer Sammlungen*.
PM = Evans, A. 1921–35 *The Palace of Minos*, Vols. I–IV. London. (Reprinted 1964).

Discussion

Hague Is the fleur-de-lys arrangement a grappling-iron?
Betts This would be an interesting sidelight on Minoan "naval warfare", but I think it most improbable. I imagine that the ships represented on seals are merchantmen rather than warships; in fact they may be no more than ritual vessels of some kind.
Humphreys What you find on Geometric and Classical Greek ship representations is the stern-post coming up and curving over, the end often being decorated. Quite often one seems to find the gunwale and waling-pieces projecting behind the stern-post. There was presumably some functional point in this, perhaps to make a stronger joint, and one may very well have something like this happening in Minoan ships. Sometimes one finds the whole arrangement coming together at the same point, rather than the stern-post projecting. Also one sometimes finds in Classical ships a post (*stylis*) with streamers coming from it, and on the vase of Odysseus and the Sirens in the British Museum (E440) there is a cloth hanging over the stern. The Minoan fleur-de-lys might be a stern-post with streamers, and these might have some religious significance.
Betts This is roughly what I suspected.

Humphreys One additional point: I liked your point about the character of Minoan representations of boats, but some of the talismanic seal scenes do look quite dramatic.
Betts Higgins (1967, 52) describes the engraving on talismanic gems as being in "a hasty, scratched style". I do not entirely agree. The motifs, it is true, tend to disintegrate and become highly schematic and stylized, but the technique can in skilled hands produce some fine and, as you suggest, almost dramatic representations.
Humphreys Some look as though they deliberately represent a ship in danger; being talismanic, the seals might have been supposed to protect people from shipwreck.

Naish A combination of rudders on either quarter and the decoration over the stern-post may together be responsible for the fleur-de-lys pattern.
Humphreys Yes. Some seals show two rudder-oars, as well as oars, slanting in a different direction.
Betts Such an arrangement is illustrated here (Fig. 5).
Johnstone A ninth-century A.D. Byzantine manuscript of St. Gregory of Nazianzus shows perfectly a Byzantine ship which has a triple ornament on the stern. Is that deliberate archaism by the Byzantine architect, or could they have known Minoan seals?
Humphreys Ancient sealstones continued to be used as amulets by Cretan peasants up to modern times, but it is not very likely.
Throckmorton Similar things survive in the Aegean today. Perhaps the three timbers were the stern-post carried up, or wales carried up, and perhaps they served a function such as acting to put the galley's head up to the wind, or making her steer better with the wind forward.

Humphreys Would that have had enough effect on a big boat?
Throckmorton One wonders. I am only making a suggestion.

Frost I am very interested in your remarks about the ships being votive. One begins to suspect that the Minoans did not have a fleet—let alone a thalassocracy! The anchor with an octopus in bas-relief (Herakleion Museum; *PM* IV, 650ff., Fig. 635) looks votive; otherwise insufficient anchors have been found either at sea or on land. On land one cannot hope for the large dated groups like those found in Levantine Bronze Age temples because the Minoans only seem to have had domestic shrines. I am very keen to get more anchors from Crete and I hope that archaeologists will check through their collections for them.

Humphreys Is there a possibility that the superstructure on those representations which look like three-masted ships might have been some light kind of cabin?
Betts On one example in particular I showed what looks like a kind of cabin or similar deck structure (Fig. 15).
Naish Indian rock-paintings from Elephante Island near Bombay show something similar.
Johnstone Surely these are much later and a result of Chinese influence?
Naish I believe so.
Frost If the ships on talismanic seals are votive and taken from a non-Minoan source, such as Egyptian votive boats, then the trellis between the uprights might be the deck-cabin, which had an awning thrown over it. The drapery of the awning was perhaps represented by the semi-circles.
Kennedy I think all satisfactory explanations assume that the representations show either deck-cabins or cargo. They would have to be light and the uprights might be shoved into the hull to keep deck cargo from sideways movement. I like the idea of some sort of lattice and canvas deck-cabin with perhaps a sagging canvas top.
Bailey It seems to me possible that the central vertical groove represents the mast and the flanking grooves the edges of the sail; the semi-circles above, which connect the outer grooves with the central one, could either be the spar holding the sail or the stays supporting the spar. The criss-cross panels would thus be the sail, but, if the weave of the cloth was intended, one might expect the lines to be horizontal and vertical.

Higgs Is it necessary for the ship to have a bow and a stern? Could there not have been ships with both ends the same? The seals seem to indicate this. If this were the case, we should not be surprised to see seals showing only half the ship.
Betts Yes. Where both bow and stern are shown they sometimes appear to be identical (my 2–4 above).
Kennedy The stern seems to be the most important part, perhaps of "votive" significance. Hence this is the part depicted in preference to the bow, where there was not enough room on the seal to engrave the whole vessel. I suggest that the so-called fleur-de-lys surmounting the stern-post may be an attempt to illustrate the attachment of a sprig of olive or other ritually significant foliage.

The Kyrenia shipwreck: A fourth-century B.C. *Greek merchant ship*

by

HELENA WYLDE SWINY and MICHAEL L. KATZEV

A GREEK MERCHANT SHIP wrecked off the north coast of Cyprus had been found in the early 1960s by Mr. Andreas Cariolou, a prominent member of the town of Kyrenia, as he was searching for sponges. In the autumn of 1967 a small team of underwater archaeologists who had been working with Dr. George Bass on a fourth-century A.D. shipwreck off the island of Yassı Ada near Bodrum, Turkey, came to Cyprus. The group, led by Prof. Michael Katzev, planned to undertake a survey to locate ancient shipwrecks off the Cypriot coast. Mr. Cariolou took them to the spot less than one mile to the north-east of Kyrenia harbour, half a mile off shore. They saw, as he had, a mound of eighty amphoras (Fig. 1), lying at a depth of 90 feet, on a mud-sand bottom overgrown with Poseidon grass.

During the next few weeks Katzev and his group carried out a preliminary survey with a proton magnetometer and a metal detector. This was supplemented by a probe survey with metal rods, to determine if much more of the cargo and perhaps the hull itself lay hidden under the sand. The metal detector located nine metal concentrations; the magnetometer identified two as ferrous, and the probe extended the dimensions of the amphora cargo to approximately 10 by 19 metres, compared with the dimensions of 3 by 5 metres of the visible mound. Since these results were most encouraging and a sand-mud bottom is ideal for wood preservation, Katzev applied for permission to excavate from the Director of the Department of Antiquities, and returned to the United States to organize funding for a full-scale expedition.

In the early summer of 1968 an international team of student archaeologists, divers, a doctor, and various technicians arrived in Kyrenia.

A flat-decked wooden barge called Alasia (26 ft. by 53 ft.) was moored over the wreck site to accommodate the large amount of necessary equipment. On board was also placed a one-man recompression chamber, to be replaced by a four-man chamber in the 1969 season. In the event of a case of the "bends" the diver could be treated immediately *in situ*.

Equipment was lowered over the side and placed on the sea floor beside the wreck. Included was a plexiglass hemisphere, 6 feet in diameter, called the "telephone booth", which was filled with air from the height of a diver's waist up, and could accommodate several people at one time. Divers could enter and discuss excavation problems over a two-way telephone communication system to the barge above. Also it was a worth-while safety device, for if a diver's breathing equipment failed while on the bottom, the "telephone booth" was within easy swimming distance from the extremities of the wreck area.

A series of grid frames, each three metres square and made of plastic irrigation pipe, was centred and placed over the axis of the ship. These were to provide orientation for the divers and serve as the base for the photogrammetric plotting of the amphoras.

Figure 1. The original amphora mound. Photo: Michael Katzev.

The grid was made of plastic so that it would be non-corrosive and could be left in place over the winter between seasons. Also it allowed the use of a metal detector throughout the excavation without interference.

The initial amphora mound grew and by the end of the second season over 400 had been plotted and lifted. The amphoras had been placed shoulder to shoulder in rows within the hull. Many, of course, were broken by the impact of the ship hitting the bottom and the subsequent decomposition of the hull. More, too, were broken when the cargo was lifted, as they had become firmly cemented together. Stowage extended well into the stern and up to the bow, where there had been little disturbance. The concentration, however, was amidships.

There were eleven different types. The most common is Rhodian and has been identified by Miss Virginia Grace as dating to the last third of the fourth century B.C. They were originally to contain liquid: this is confirmed by the fact that they were coated inside with a thick layer of bitumen or resin. Thirty-four of the 343 Rhodian jars bear stamps impressed on their handles. The most frequent is a circular stamp with API, but the letters were also found within a rectangle. Other combinations of letters were noted, but their exact meaning is not clear.

Figure 2. Grinding stone from above. Photo: John Veltri.

Concentrations of a different shape, from the island of Samos, were located in the bow and stern areas, indicating a different consignment. A stamp consisting of an omicron impressed within a circle was found on some of them. A slender, very delicate type may come from Paros, while the provenance of others is still unknown.

As the excavation and removal of the amphoras progressed, a new and unexpected cargo began to appear. Buried beneath, and in some cases holding the amphoras, grinding stones of a hopper design were laden in two or three rows along the axis of the ship. Two blocks made up each mill (Fig. 2). Grist would be poured into the V-shaped bin of the upper block and would fall through a narrow slot on to the upper surface of the block below. A wooden bar placed across the notched rim of the upper block would facilitate grinding by two people. They would move it from side to side across the corrugated surface of the lower member. The results in experimenting with grain were very poor, and they may not have been used for making bread flour.

The 29 blocks, made of a grey volcanic stone, had a variety of single Greek letters cut into one face. The idea that these might define matching pairs had to be dismissed, as there were often uneven numbers of one letter. Thus probably the letters are mason's marks, put on at the quarry.

Their disparity in size, odd number and various states of finish (only a few had notches to receive the wooden bar) make the purpose of the blocks on board unclear. Katzev has suggested (1970*b*,8) that they were remnants of an earlier cargo, now serving essentially as ballast.

Figure 3. Black-glazed pitcher. Photo: John Veltri.

Grinding stones of this hopper design are known throughout the Greek world: from Palestine, the Greek islands and mainland, and even as far west as southern Italy. Never, however, has such a large number been found together.

Another trade item of interest began to appear as excavation went deeper. Substantial quantities of almonds were found in the bow area, heaped upon the interior of the hull.

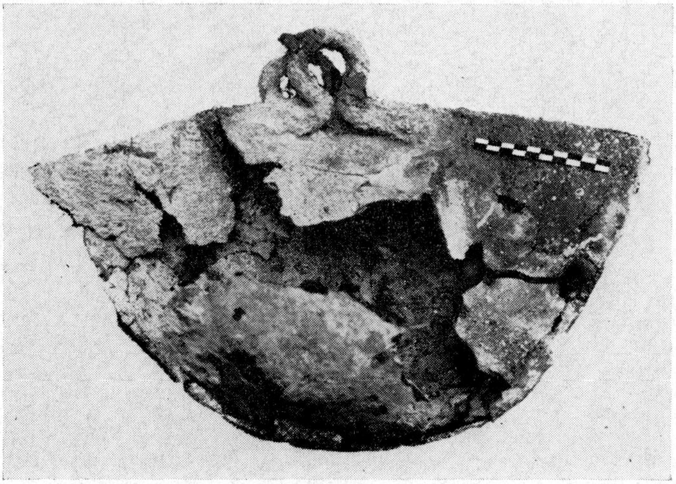

Figure 4. Bronze cauldron. Photo: Susan W. Katzev.

Figure 5. Black-glazed kantharos. Photo: John Veltri.

The total of more than 9,000 almonds discovered in this manner would indicate that the commodity was being transported in sacks made of some perishable material.

Though the spillage was considerable, coarse and fine pottery was concentrated in two areas, one towards the bow and the other more to the stern. The finds from these areas,

Figure 6. Hull after removal of the amphora cargo. Bow in foreground. Photo: John Veltri.

which may be storage spaces or living quarters, give insight into the equipment available to the crew. Several small pitchers (Fig. 3), fragments of a pottery sieve, an assortment of broken cooking pots, casserole lids, a pottery ladle, a mortar and a bronze cauldron (Fig. 4) were used for food preparation. Fish must have supplemented the diet, as over 300 lead weights once attached to a net were found in the bow.

Utensils for eating included: thirteen black-glazed echinus bowls, various flat black-glazed dishes, four small salt dishes, four kantharoi or drinking cups (Fig. 5), four gutti or oil jars, and fragments of four wooden spoons. The recurrence of the number four may indicate the size of the crew. The base and fragmentary profile of a lathe-turned wooden bowl shows that wooden utensils may have occurred more frequently aboard ancient ships than was previously realized. It was surprising to find only one small lamp fragment. An unexpected refinement was a black-glazed "ink-well" found adhering to a concretion of iron that lay just off the stern. This concretion, which weighs 1,400 pounds, was raised to the surface and will be cut open in the near future.

A trial trench cut at the very end of the 1968 season gave a tantalising glimpse of the hull, and confirmed expectations that it was well preserved. Once the amphora and grinding stone cargoes had been removed, and a 3 m-wide trench had been cut around the area that had been cleared the year before, the excavators could get an idea of exactly how much of the hull was preserved.

The outline measured 4.8 by 11.7 m, the bow facing to the north (Fig. 6). On examining the hull itself and reconsidering the amphora plans, one was able to tell what had happened to the ship once she hit the bottom. She must have come down on her keel, and listed to port; this would explain the neatly stacked rows of amphoras on this side. Upon impact or at a subsequent date she broke her back, the keel being out of its original alignment, as it was found resting at right angles to the sea bed. The break occurred at the port garboard strake, which split. A portion of the starboard side collapsed outwards and lay at a short distance to the east of the keel. It must have done so not at once but over the years that the ship lay on the bottom. As will be noted from the photograph (Fig. 6), it is much smaller than the port side and has suffered considerably from decomposition and teredo worm. Also the spillage of amphoras to starboard is negligible, indicating that they had had some time to settle and concrete together prior to the break.

A layer of ceiling planking lying across the frames formed a platform on which to place the cargo (Fig. 7). On the port side it was made up of six boards in the stern and midships area, tapering to five towards the bow. The weight of the cargo had crushed the planking, making both widths and thicknesses very difficult to calculate. The ceiling planking extended across the beam of the ship to a stringer, the only one found. It was bordered near the keel by an L-shaped piece of wood which supported short boards that traversed the keel and could be easily removed to get to the bilges.

The keel was made in three sections, the bow segment being composite, and has considerable vertical curvature towards its extremities. It is seen to extend some distance beyond the preserved hull in the stern, and has a total length of 11.65 m. The point of juncture with the stern-post is visible at the extremity, and a fragment of the knee was found 1.5 m forward (Fig. 8). There is also evidence for the stem-post. The dimensions of the keel varied considerably, but an average width would be 12 cm and height 20 cm. Rabbets 4 cm in width were cut to seat the garboard strakes, which were joined by mortises and tenons, the latter being held in place by two dowels.

THE KYRENIA SHIP

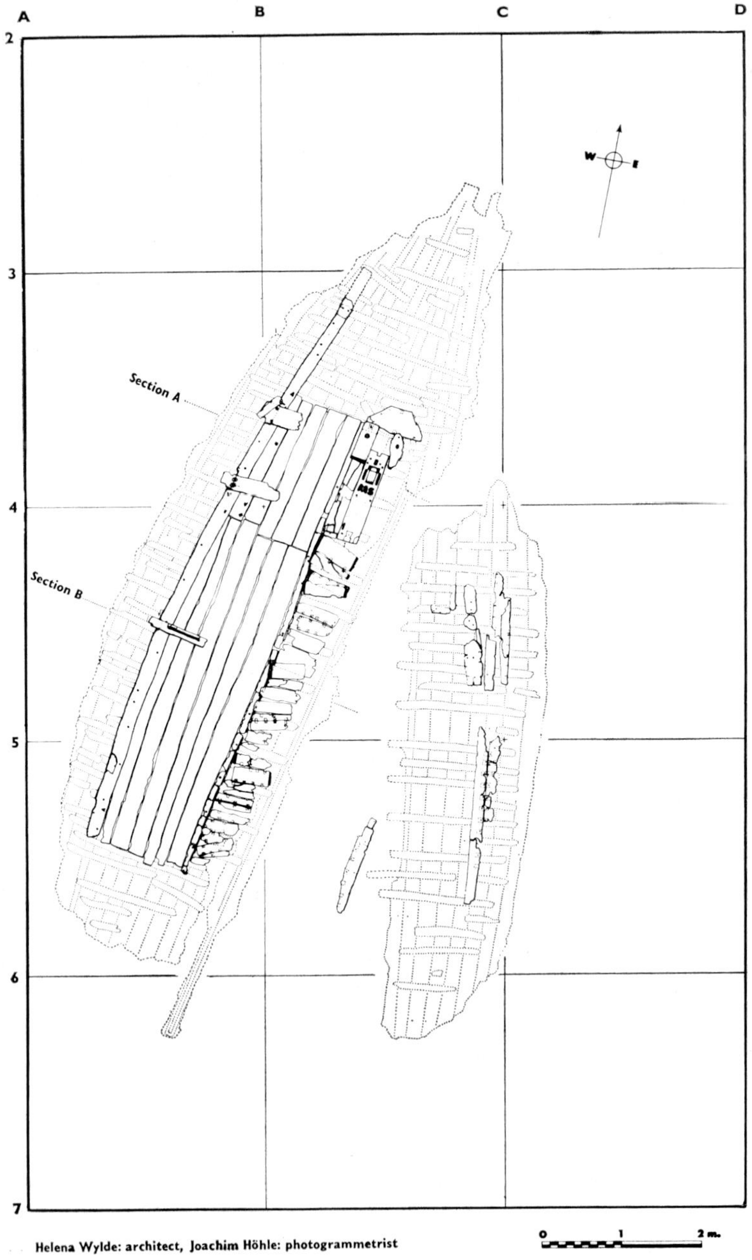

Figure 7. Preliminary plan of inner ceiling planking.

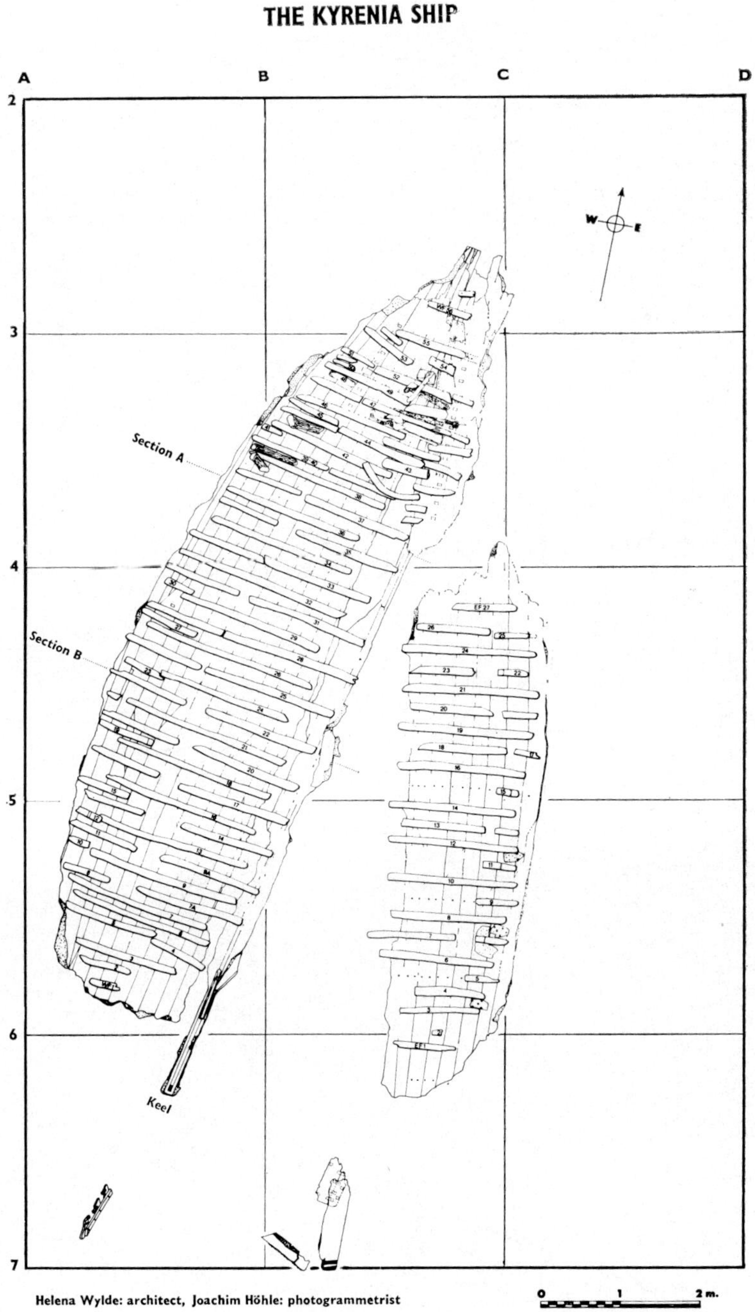

Figure 8. Preliminary plan of outer hull.

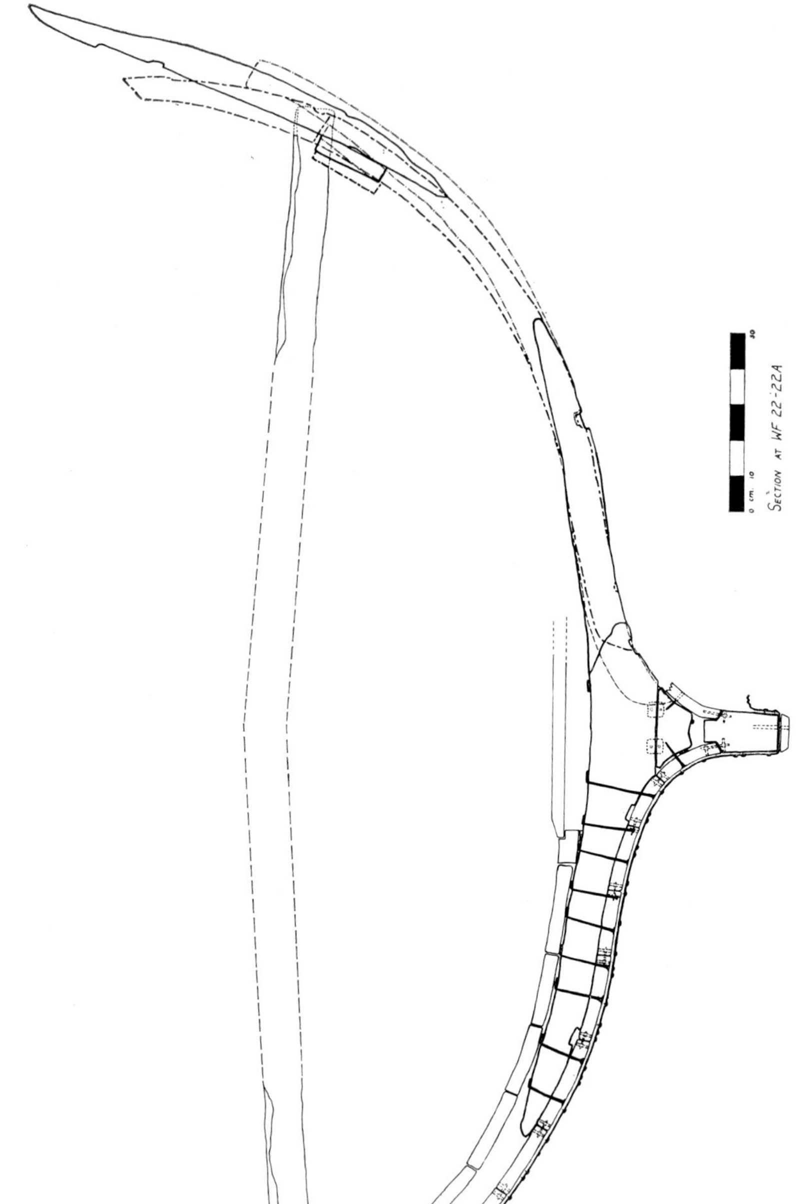

Figure 9. Tentative midships section (Section B).

South of the keel two rather complex pieces were found. They are conjectured to be part of the steering mechanism (see Fig. 8).

The hull was carvel-built, the strakes being held together by mortises and tenons, set on average at intervals of 12.3 cm from centre to centre. Mortise and tenoning used as a technique from the fifth century B.C. to the seventh century A.D. is documented by ancient ship excavations in the Mediterranean: by Dr. David Owen at Messina, Italy, and Dr. George Bass at Yassı Ada, Turkey. There were nine strakes between the keel and the first wale (Fig. 9). The width of these strakes varies from 14 cm to 27 cm and they have a thickness of *c.* 4 cm. Two wales, measuring 8 cm and 6.5 cm respectively in thickness, remain on the port side, while a badly damaged first wale forms the farthest extent of the starboard side. One strake separates the two wales, and there is tentative evidence that two more strakes extended above the second wale.

The frames, numbering over 50, were set on an average of 10–15 cm apart from edge to edge. Their normal height throughout their preserved lengths was 8–10 cm, but over the keel a height of 18 cm was not unusual. The half-frames alternated with floors and futtocks, the former commencing at either the garboard or second strake. Though all the frames have been flattened by the uneven distribution of the cargo on the seabed and softening of the waterlogged wood, both the curvature up to the waterline and the counter-curve down to the keel have been retained.

The vessel is of shell-construction. The keel was laid first and the outer planking was then assembled and joined to it. The frames were then laid within the hull and fixed into position by copper nails driven in from the outside and clenched over the inner surface of the frames. There is evidence also that the dowels were put in from the inside and these often lie under the frame. No proof has yet been found of score marks on strakes for placement of frames, as found by Bass on the fourth-century A.D. wreck at Yassı Ada.

One of the most exciting finds as far as our knowledge of ancient shipwrightry is concerned was the mast-step complex (Fig. 10). The step itself is a piece of wood 1.20 m long and is cut with a complicated series of notches and grooves. What appear to be two additional half-rounded bracing members lie forward. Though its method of use has not been fully determined, the relative lightness of the pieces of wood involved, and their placement so far forward (one-third from the bow) has led Prof. Lionel Casson (personal correspondence with Katzev) to comment that he believes that the ship may have had a fore-and-aft rig, rather than a square sail. Prof. Casson (1956; 1960) has produced pictorial evidence of fore-and-aft rigging used by the Greeks at least as early as the second century B.C.

The ship was made predominantly of pine, as analysed by Dr. Kukachka of the Forest Service of the U.S. Department of Agriculture. Frames were of pine, except for a few which were of beech. The strakes were of the Sula group of pine, as was a thin second layer of planking in the bow. The tenons were of oak (live oak group), but the dowels were also of pine. An analysis has not yet been received on the keel, but it also appears to be of a pine group.

During the 1968 season small pieces of lead were found scattered amongst the amphoras. These formed part of a lead sheathing that encased the entire hull and the keel. Its purpose was to try to protect the hull from teredo attack. The lead was put on in large sheets that were scored with diagonal lines to indicate where to place thousands of copper tacks. Internal lead patching was also found, a method still used today, and

Figure 10. Hull after removal of ceiling planking, showing the mast-step complex. Photo: Robin Piercy.

two large rolled sheets of lead stored on board must have been for repairs. A wooden mallet possibly used for flattening the lead was found in the bow area (Fig. 11).

The technique of protecting a vessel with lead was well known to the Romans. Now with the Kyrenia ship, and the finding of similar fragments of lead with copper tacks by Dr. David Owen on a late fifth-century B.C. shipwreck in the Straits of Messina, the technique can be dated over 300 years earlier (Owen, 1970, 28, and in conversation. See also Blackman, 1972).

Figure 11. Wooden mallet. Photo: Susan W. Katzev.

Though none of the actual rigging of the ship remained, a few objects may aid in further conjecture. A beech-wood block was found fallen between the two sides of the hull (Figs. 12–13). Belaying-pins were wedged firmly between frames near the mast-step. Scattered throughout the stern area were over one hundred flat lead rings which may have been used for brail lines. Amidships and resting directly on the hull were ten lathe-turned double wooden knobs, resembling toggles. That they may also have served in the ship's rigging is a strong possibility. Similar ones were also found by Dr. Owen, but his interpretation is that they were fishing-net floats.

One of the aims of the Kyrenia Ship Excavation was to raise the hull, preserve it, and reconstruct it as found lying on the sea bottom, so that it might be displayed out of the water for the first time in 2,200 years. It had been proposed to leave the lifting for a third season, but the hull was now totally exposed and it was September. How would it survive another winter without the protection of its cargoes? Would re-covering it with plastic sheeting and sand, as we had done after the 1968 season, do more harm than good? Would the knowledge of the existence of the hull of a Greek merchant ship in this area bring many curious divers to have a look during the winter months? The decision was to go ahead and lift in the second season, in the hope that the weather would hold.

Figure 12. Wooden pulley-block. Photo: Otis Imboden.

Raising the quantity of wood that faced the expedition was not an easy task. Though the wood was well preserved, and from outer appearances looked solid, a sectional view showed that it was riddled with worm holes and was exceedingly fragile. The U.S. Forest Service's report came back, stating that the wood had almost a complete lack of cellulose and in appearance was on a par with Pleistocene buried woods.

Thus it was impossible to raise the hull in one piece. The broken-away portion of the starboard side, as it was small and had little curvature, was used for experimentation. A saw driven by compressed air was used to cut the lead sheathing and hull into manageable one-metre sections. A thin metal palette of galvanised iron with saw-toothed edge was eased under each piece; then both were carefully moved into a rigid steel frame equipped with flexible bands which adapted to the curvature of the hull. The frame was moved to the edge of the excavation area to await balloon-lifting to the surface.

Though handled with great care, the wood was so soft that the strakes settled within the trays, and the sections lost their contours. It was also clear that the timbers would have to be dismantled after, if not before conservation, for proper reconstruction. Thus such a system would not work for the far more complex port side. The decision was made to take the hull apart piece by piece, as had been done most successfully by Danish archaeologists on five Viking ships within the Roskilde Fjörd. After several days of labeling to ensure correct reassemblage, the ribs were removed and placed in rigid metal trays, designed to take their greatest length. Next the mast-stop complex and keel were lifted, followed by the outer planking which was cut into manageable lengths.

Once the trays were transported within the castle the wood was washed and catalogued. The frames were traced at once on draughting film for fear that they might lose more of their curvature now that they were freed from the strakes, and later during the conservation treatment. All the wood was then placed in fresh water in a large concrete tank built within a closed gallery of Kyrenia castle. Here the salts are slowly leached out as the wood awaits conservation treatment.

The amphoras and some of the small pottery finds had given a tentative date for the use of ship in the last third of the fourth century B.C. Of the five bronze coins found, two, though very badly corroded, could be deciphered. One dated to the reign of Antigonos Monophthalmos (316–301 B.C.), the other to his son Demetrios Poliorketes (306–294 B.C.). A Carbon^{14} date for the planking of the hull was 389 ± 44 B.C. (i.e., the date when the tree was felled). The almonds, however, yielded a date of 288 ± 62 (University Museum analysis). This difference could give the ship a considerable age before she sank.

Analysis of the finds and details of the hull itself gives one a remarkable insight into the ports of call of the Kyrenia ship prior to her sinking.

The assortment of amphoras may indicate stops at the islands of Samos and Rhodes. The volcanic rock of the grinding stones has its closest parallel on the island of Kos, but this does not eliminate the sources on the Cycladic islands of Melos and Thera.

It is interesting to consider the ancient sites of Laurion and Thoriko, well known for their silver and lead mines during the Classical period. Here would be the ideal source of the abundant amounts of lead necessary for lead-sheathing a ship. Grinding stones of a hopper variety, made from grey volcanic rock, have also been found at Laurion, used to crush the ore prior to refining and smelting (Communication with Dr. R. Cooke, who had been working with Dr. Kornofagos on the site).

Did the ship stop on Cyprus? Evidence that she may have been leaving the island when she went down is provided by the cargo of almonds. In antiquity Cyprus was known for her almonds.

From this excavation and the one by Dr. Owen on the fifth-century B.C. Messina wreck, it is now clear that Mediterranean trading ships in the Classical and Hellenistic periods normally carried mixed cargoes over long distances. The Messina cargo consisted not only of 12 different types of amphoras, but of a shipment of loaf-shaped lead ingots, and scrap bronze, etc.

Figure 13. Wooden pulley-block, dismantled. Photo: Otis Imboden.

As Dr. Owen states (1970, 28) "It is likely that these merchantmen picked up and discharged cargoes as they sailed. Remains of a cargo, therefore, are nearly as good as a written itinerary of a ship's route . . . . We now know that ships were constructed in a well-known technique which hardly varied from one end of the Mediterranean to the other. Even the crew's equipment was similarly uniform. It is only through underwater excavation that this type of information can continue to be made available."

REFERENCES

Bass, G. F. & Katzev, M. L. 1968 New Tools for Underwater Archaeology. *Archaeology*, **21** No. 3, 164–73.

Blackman, D. J. 1972 Further early evidence of hull sheathing. *Int. Jl Nautical Archaeology*, **1**, 117–19.

Casson, L. 1956 Fore-and-Aft Sails in the Ancient World. *Mariner's Mirror*, **42**, 3–5.

Casson, L. 1960 The Sprit-Rig in the Ancient World. *Mariner's Mirror*, **46**, 241.

Green, J. N., Hall, E. T. & Katzev, M. L. 1967 Survey of a Greek Shipwreck off Kyrenia, Cyprus. *Archaeometry*, **10**, 47–56.

Katzev, M. L. 1968 Survey of the Cyprus coast for submerged wrecks. *Underwater Association Report 1968*, 13–15.

Katzev, M. L. 1969 The Kyrenia Shipwreck. *Expedition*, **11** No. 2 (Winter 1969), 55–9.

Katzev, M. L. 1970*a* Resurrecting the oldest known Greek ship. *Natn. geogr. Mag.* **137** (June 1970) 840–57.

Katzev, M. L. 1970*b* Kyrenia 1969: A Greek ship is raised. *Expedition*, **12** No. 4 (Summer 1970), 6–14.

Katzev, Susan W. & Katzev, M. L. 1968 The search below. *Expedition*, **10** No. 3 (Spring 1968), 11–14.

Owen, D. I. 1970 Picking up the pieces: the salvage excavation of a looted 5th century B.C. shipwreck in the Straits of Messina. *Expedition*, **13** No. 1 (Fall 1970), 24–9.

Owen, D. I. 1971 Excavating a classical shipwreck. *Archaeology*, **24** No. 2, 118–29.

Discussion

Blackman The lead sheathing is very interesting. It appears that there was also lead sheathing on the Messina wreck. In addition, the Russians in 1964–5 worked on a wreck lying in shallow water off the west coast of the Crimea; it is a Greek merchant ship, probably wrecked in the late fourth century B.C. when sailing with a cargo of wine, probably from the south to north coasts of the Black Sea; this ship too had lead sheathing (Blackman, 1972). The Russian report talked about "bronze" nails, not copper. Could the nails in fact be bronze or copper?
Swiny The analyses that were done by Cyprus Mines Corporation show that our clench nails were of copper, because no tin was found. What remains of the nails is the copper cores; the tin could have been leached out during corrosion. The analyses showed no tin in either the corrosion product or the remaining copper. The tacks holding on the lead sheathing were copper. I cannot answer for the Messina wreck's nails or tacks. They may not have been analysed at the time of Dr. Owen's publication.
Throckmorton In Roman ships copper was mostly used. Bronze nails would be very susceptible to electrolysis.
Blackman The Russian report talks of tacks for the lead up to twenty-eight centimetres long.
Swiny They must have been clench nails for holding the frames and strakes together, or for holding the garboard to the keel; or, with that thickness, perhaps they were clench nails through a wale.
Blackman Where do you think these ships were built? They belong to a period of innovation, which we now know goes back into the fifth century, and is not confined to the fourth.
Swiny The identification of where an ancient ship was built is very difficult. One might hope for a name-plate or perhaps a rare wood used in the construction which might delimit the area. Wood used on the Kyrenia ship is mainly pine, beech and oak; we did have a few branches of oleander. These trees grow all around the Mediterranean. In antiquity wood used in shipbuilding was often exported from certain ports in the Mediterranean, e.g., the famous Cedars of Lebanon. Thus, even if one could track down the area from which the wood of the ship came, one would not necessarily know the area of the shipyard where the ship was built.

This is a problem that we may never solve.
Throckmorton At Torre Sgarrata we had *Ilex*, a typically Syrian wood, used as packing between frames and planks.

Frost The Corning Museum have published a couple of papers on a method of deducing the mine of origin from a sample of manufactured lead.
Swiny The Corning Museum has had samples of the lead from the Kyrenia ship. The lead is being worked on presently elsewhere in the U.S.A. I mentioned Laurion and Thoriko because Dr. Cooke, who has been working with Dr. Kornofagos at Laurion, came to Kyrenia and looked at the lead. He was quite optimistic about being able to trace

the origin of the lead sheathing by identifying the properties of the ore and comparing them with what he had found at Laurion.

Green How much weight of lead sheathing was used on the ship?
Swiny I believe that R. Piercy has been calculating this. It is difficult to do, however, as we don't have the original thickness of the lead. A lot of what we have is corrosion products.
Kennedy Was the ship sheathed overall below the waterline, or was the sheathing just the patching of an old hull?
Swiny She was sheathed all over, including the keel, up to a point above the waterline.
Blackman The lead sheathing of the Grand Congloué wreck is estimated to have weighed 20 tons.

Wignall Did you find any indication whatsoever of wooden trenails or dowels for pinning timbers together?
Swiny A large number of dowels were used. Two, of course, held each tenon in place. Dowels were also used to hold the ceiling planking to the frames. The metal clench nails in the frames were driven through long dowels or trenails that had been inserted in pre-drilled holes. In other cases trenails alone were used, along with the metal clench nails. Square dowels were used to hold a shoe on to the keel.

All in all, the methods used were both complex and competent. We are sure that more study will discover other uses of dowelling.

Lewis How many Carbon^{14} dates did you take on the ship?
Swiny Two samples were sent to Philadelphia to the laboratory at University Museum; they are the two that I quoted. Some others were sent to England, but to my knowledge we have had no results yet.
Lewis Do they correlate fairly closely?
Swiny It depends on how you calculate the plus and minus factors within the C^{14} dates. If you take the mean dates for the hull and for the almonds, without considering the plus-minus factor, the ship could have been 80–90 years old when she sank. If, however, you take the earliest date for the almonds and the latest date for the wood of the hull (i.e., the date when the tree was cut down) the ship might have been 45 years old when she sank. Fortunately, the C^{14} date correlated quite nicely with the coins that could be identified.

Parker Until the Kyrenia ship was discovered I always thought that the stone grinders were called grain-rubbers (this is the term used by Forbes in *Ancient Technology*); but since the Kyrenia ship was discovered, all sorts of names have been given to these.

I do not believe entirely in the "sailing round the islands" story, which appears every time that an ancient ship is excavated and different kinds of jars are found. I suggest that several amphoras were collected at entrepôts in Rhodes and Delos and transported by ship from port to port.

Swiny I am glad that you raised this point, as I do not agree completely with the view that I quoted in the lecture. The occurrence of Rhodian or Samian amphoras on board a ship does not prove stops at either of these ports. There is no way of telling how many central warehouses there were in the Mediterranean, nor do we know how many times a cargo could be off-loaded by one ship and then picked up by another ship which happened to be continuing on to the importing island. These are points which are all too easily forgotten.
Taylor It was noticed that your grain-rubbers are deeper and narrower than average ones we have found on our excavations, which are therefore perhaps lighter. Might this have something to do with the milling of ore rather than flour?
Swiny The fabric of the stones had changed considerably with the amount of time that they had been under the sea. The results that we had in grinding grain (corn) gave a very poor, coarse flour, that in my opinion would not be good enough for bread. They must have been used for something that did not need to be finely ground. Stones very similar in design have been found at Thoriko and Laurion, where they were used for crushing ore. However, the "hopper" was shaped quite differently.
Did the ones that you found have notches?
Taylor Yes, but they were wide and flat, about four centimetres deep.
Cook Fourth-century ones are about that deep.
Taylor Ours was also about fourth-century in date.

Taylor In re-reading Hornell's book lately, I came across the drawing of the mast-step for lowering the mast on an Indian ship which showed two slots beside the mast, which could be supports for a pivot-bar on which the mast rotated. This appears to be close to the plan on the Kyrenia ship.
Swiny The mast-step complex has not yet been researched properly. This idea will certainly be considered.

Martin Was there evidence of ballast other than cargo?
Swiny Yes. Large numbers of river stones, approximately the size of oranges, were used. They have been identified as Cypriot, unlike the grinding stones. There was also a large amount of gravel. We have not yet been able to calculate the tonnage, as the gravel is mixed with the sand of the bottom. Certainly she was very heavily laden.

Wignall Was there any evidence of brushwood to save the cargo from smashing?
Swiny Small quantities of oleander were found under the stringer, but we are not sure of its use. There were no large quantities of brushwood or the like. The amphoras have lots of holes in them, and rub marks, and when you examine them closely you can see that some of the rub marks are not modern, i.e., they were there before the ship went down.

Green Do you have theories about the sinking of the ship?
Swiny There is some evidence for burning on the inner surface of the hull, but only what may have come from cinders blown during preparation of a meal on board. There is no evidence of a battle; no weapons were found.

There may be several explanations if the ship was old. Perhaps the teredo worms had made their way through the lead sheathing and she was quite riddled with holes prior to sinking. We did find internal lead patches, which indicate that her hull was not sound. Storms come up quite quickly on the north coast of Cyprus. Perhaps she was caught by one when she was heavily laden, and got herself broadside to the sea. If several waves broke over her, she would have filled quite quickly and gone down.

The fact that only five coins were found on board makes it seem likely that the captain made it to shore.

Frost When you got the wood up, was there anything underneath the ship?
Swiny Yes, quite a lot of pottery and small sherds. There was wood underneath which had been dowelled to the hull; in particular, two very thin planks. There were also lots of almonds and a few other pieces of assorted wood.

Humphreys Do you have any of the crew's personal pottery, which might tell you where the boat was built?
Bailey Some may be: the kantharoi are very like some from Kalymnos which are certainly Athenian. There is a guttus very much like the Kyrenia examples from the Lion Tomb at Cnidus. I should like to see the fabrics. There are several black-glazed wares which were produced locally in many areas, not all of which can as yet be recognized. I think an early third-century date is more probable than a late fourth.
Swiny The pottery is being worked on by M. Katzev.

Davies Do we know whether Kyrenia was in fact a port in antiquity?
Swiny Kyrenia was a Hellenistic settlement with an acropolis and necropolis. Much of it was where the Castle now stands, but it also is said to have extended to the landward side of the Castle and present harbour. It is not known where the Hellenistic harbour was located, but it may have been to the east of the Castle and present-day harbour.

Kennedy Can anyone say if lead sheathing was customary—do we know enough yet? Was it done when the ship was new or when it got older? I do not believe it was done when the ship was new, but rather as the last resort on an old hull, as the age of this vessel suggests.
Swiny The best time to sheath a ship would be when she was new, to try to keep the teredo worms out from the start. It would have been a technique similar to the anti-fouling methods of today. Probably the lead would have been checked quite often, and areas replaced if cracks appeared. Of the Roman shipwrecks that have been found, a good percentage were lead-sheathed. So it does not appear to be a rare phenomenon in Roman times. With the ship found in the Black Sea we see another lead-sheathed ship of the fourth century B.C. The wreck found in the Straits of Messina puts the technique back into the fifth century B.C. We need more discoveries, in different parts of the Mediterranean, to be able to say that it was a normal protective measure in that part of the world in antiquity.

The evidence provided by underwater archaeology for Roman trade in the Western Mediterranean

by

ANTHONY J. PARKER

I BEGIN WITH the chart (Fig. 1), in which I have used the information given by West (1929) to indicate the commodities which, according to Strabo, Pliny, and other writers, were exported from southern Spain (mostly to Rome) in the first centuries B.C. and A.D.; in the right-hand columns I have indicated whether or not there is archaeological evidence for the export of these goods.

One can see from this one example that archaeological evidence can never entirely supplant written records, and that underwater archaeology offers only slightly more evidence than terrestrial. Ancient authors marvelled at the richness of Spain, especially Baetica, the southern province, and at the ease with which goods could be exported (Strabo 3.2.4 ff.); but one could scarcely infer this from the underwater archaeological record, which offers only two kinds of material: first, metals; and second, food products packed in pottery amphoras.

As regards metals, underwater finds have made possible a typology of Spanish lead ingots, by Domergue (1965, with refs; 1966); indeed, one may hope for very considerable gains in the study of Spanish mining and metal export from future wreck excavations and even from surveys. (For other discussions, see Davies, 1935, 94 ff.; Wilson, 1966, 24; Benoit, 1958, 39, No. 5; Mascaró, 1971; Tchernia, 1969*a*, 482, 495–6). Excavations have, in the past, been incomplete and thus missed possible finds of heavy materials; or they have been inadequately published, so that study of ingots, and especially of the inscriptions on them, is impeded. On Figure 1 I have indicated (under "Archaeological Finds: Sea") the many lead ingots known to have come from Spain, and the copper ingots from the Planier D wreck and from Agde (Benoit, 1962, 150; Bouscaras, 1964, 269–78). I have indicated with queries iron and tin; a tin ingot from a wreck near Hyères has been published by Tchernia (1969*a*, 477), who says that the ship also carried iron objects. The date and origin of the ship are unknown; the ingot is inscribed, but there is no obvious interpretation of the marks (CVM and MN). As for the other metals and mineral products, Spain was an important source of mineral colorants (West, 1929, 53–4): these have been found at Mellieha, Malta, at the Planier C wreck, and elsewhere, but without specific evidence of Spanish origin (Frost, 1969; Tchernia, 1969*b*. But note Atkins, 1971, 56, n. 1: "the Egyptian blue of ancient times is certainly

Commodity	Historical references				Archaeological finds	
	Late Republic		Early Empire		Land	Sea
	Strabo	Other	Pliny	Other		
Timber and cork	×		×			
Pitch	×		×			
Spartum grass	×	×	×	×		
Drugs and perfumes	×	×	×	×		
Olives	×	×	×	×	?	?
Olive oil	×	×	×	×	×	×
Wine	×	×	×	×	×	×
Wheat	×		×	×		
Barley			×			
Apples			×			
Cherries			×			
Figs	×	×	×	×		
Pears			×			
Quinces				×		
Nuts			×			
Honey and wax	×		×	×		
Horses (N.W. Spain)			×	×		
Fowls			×			
Snails			×			
Muria			×		×	×
Garum	×	×	×	×	×	×
Murena				×		
Salted fish	×			×		
Gold	×	×	×	×		
Silver	×	×	×	×		
Lead	×	×	×	×	×	×
Iron			?			?
Copper	×		×	×		×
Tin			×			?
Other metals and minerals	×	×	×	×		?
Salt	×	×	×	×		
Wool	×		×	×		
Linen	×	×	×	×		
Vegetable dyes	×					
Building stone			×			

Figure 1. Exports from Southern Spain and the Balearics (Source: West, 1929, Tables).

all synthetic"; colorants may have been used for painting the ship, see Torr, 1964, 35–7).

If we turn to amphoras (and leave aside questions such as the evidence of names on anchors, e.g., T. AELI on an anchor stock in Syracuse), we can see that olive oil, wine and fish sauce are marked on the chart. (As for olives, it is uncertain whether amphoras for *olive fruit* can be identified as coming from Spain: see Beltrán, 1970, 487, n. 1071. With Callender (1965, 17), I follow Körber (1909) in reading *oleum* on the Weisenau amphora, and not *oliua* as Körber (1911). The amphora is of evidently south Spanish form, cf. Rödgen 228a & Tour Sainte Marie E; but *not*, as Callender, Dressel 7–9). For the export of oil in Dressel 20 amphoras from *c.* A.D. 1 to *c.* A.D. 260, the case has been thoroughly argued (by Callender, 1965, and Beltrán, 1970, *passim*, with refs.); for fish sauce, certain amphoras bear painted labels, identifying the contents as *garum*, *muria*, *liquamen* or *allec* (for *garum*, see now Étienne, 1970). A question I should like to raise is whether actual bones of fish can be preserved for 2,000 years in an amphora on the seabed, as has often been claimed; I have thought the bones would be destroyed by seawater. As for wine, more comments later; but in this case, as with the other amphora-borne commodities, no *actual* wine in amphoras has been discovered and identified as Spanish.

Hence amphoras are of use to the economic historian only if their *form* or *stamp* can be assigned to a place of origin, a date and a particular commodity. This involves taxonomy, and I want to discuss some principles of amphora study.

Amphoras can be classified only by finding a congruence of (1) fabric, (2) dimensions, (3) lip-form, (4) body-form, (5) handles, (6) foot, and (7) type of stamp, if any. Thus, *complete* amphoras are necessary for the initial building-up of a classification, and hence the importance of underwater finds, even unassociated. Once the initial classification has been satisfactorily arranged, fragments (as usually found in land excavations) can be attributed to a class.

A class of amphora can be said to originate from a particular area on the basis of (1) a kiln-deposit, (2) self-identifying stamps or other inscriptions, (3) intelligent reading of distribution maps, (4) stylistic, technical or physical/chemical similarity with another class, and (5) association, e.g. in a wreck, with other objects of secure provenance. Association with other amphoras is not in itself proof of common origin.

A class of amphora may be *dated* by (1) an inscription, (2) inclusion in a reliably dated and sealed context on land, and (3) association, in a wreck, with well-dated objects. Association with other amphoras provides only a relative date.

Hence, wrecks provide reliable material for amphora taxonomy and economic history only if (1) they really *are* closed deposits and not just a heap of pottery strewn on the seabed, (2) they are *properly* excavated to avoid contamination or confusion, (3) they are *completely* excavated, so as to yield all possible dating or other diagnostic material, and (4) the finds are accurately, fully and rapidly published. No wreck excavation in the western Mediterranean has yet fulfilled *all* these conditions.

IDENTIFICATION OF SPANISH AMPHORA TYPES

I take this opportunity to demonstrate some of the classes of amphora which (in the last five years) have been shown to be Spanish. I should like to draw attention to the recent

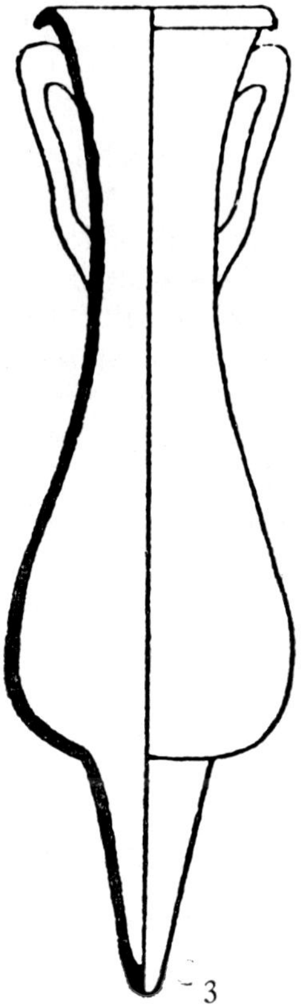

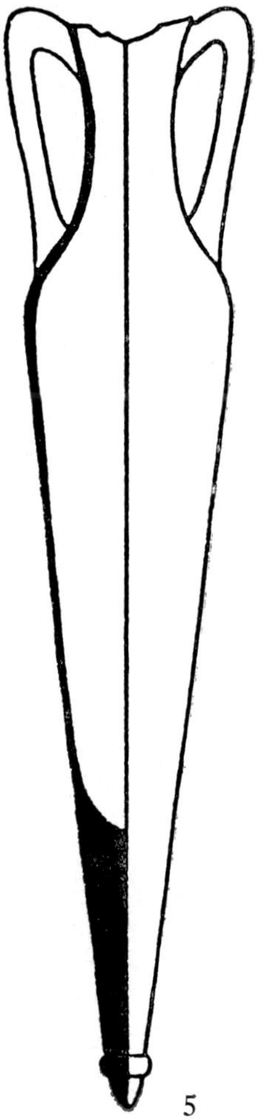

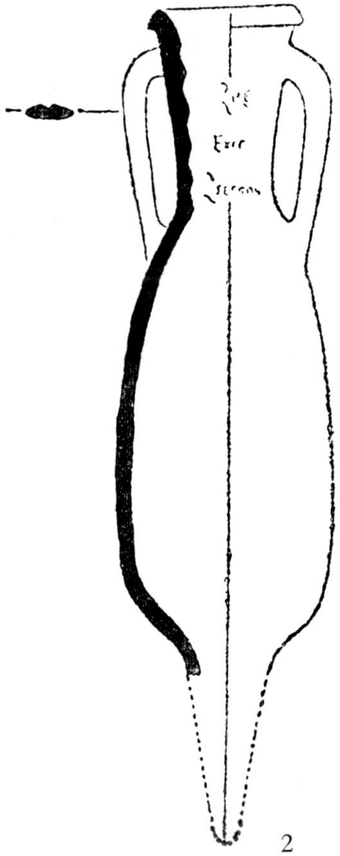

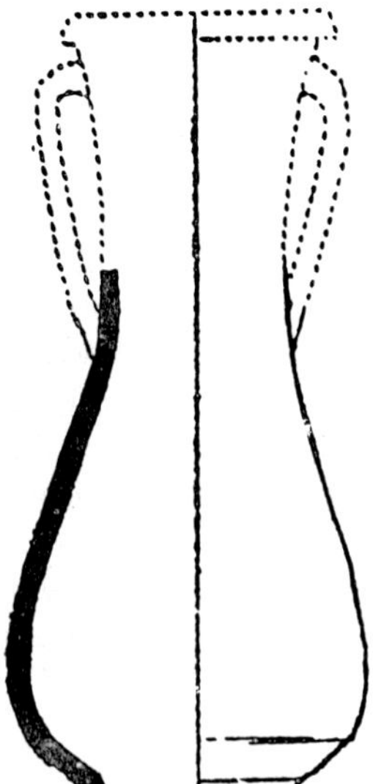

Figures 2–5. Amphoras from the Pecio Gandolfo wreck. After Pascual, 1968. Scale 1 : 10.

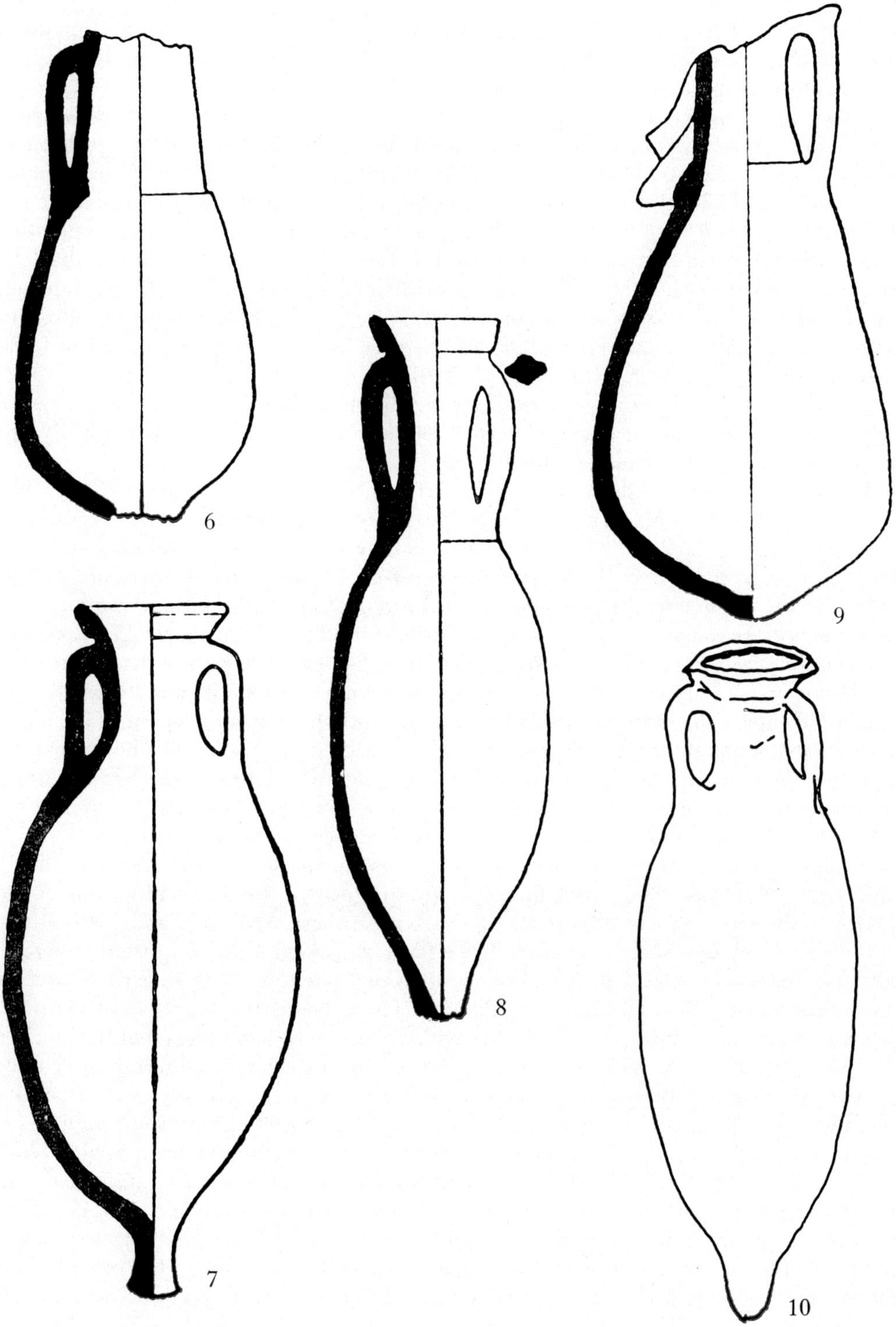

Figures 6–10. Amphoras from Spanish workshops: 6, 7, 8, Algeciras; 9, Puerto Real; 10, San Bartolomeu de Castro-Marim. *Figures 6–9* after Beltrán, 1970, Figures 167, 159, 180, 175; 10 after Leite de Vasconcelos, 1898, Figure 6. Scale 1 : 10.

book by Miguel Beltrán Lloris of Zaragoza (Beltrán, 1970), which provides, for the first time, a comprehensive and reliable account of amphoras found in the western Empire.

One of the amphoras from the wreck known as Pecio Gandolfo, prov. Almería (Fig. 2), bears a painted inscription of typical Spanish form, and, in that wreck, it was associated with others (Figs. 3–4) of a type found also in a potter's workshop at Puerto Real, near Cádiz (Fig. 9; Pascual, 1968; Jiménez, 1958; Beltrán, 1970, Fig. 175). The thin amphoras from Pecio Gandolfo (Fig. 5) appear to be Spanish too, owing to their resemblance to the tall amphoras from the Congloué B wreck; and they, in their turn, share similarities of fabric and form with amphoras which can be classed as Dressel 12, such as those from the Titan wreck (Tchernia, 1969*a*, 483–5, with refs.; Taylor, 1965, 76–93). Dressel 12 amphoras were made at Algeciras, in the Bay of Gibraltar (Fig. 8), and there too, apparently, were made amphoras (e.g. Fig. 6) which can be paralleled, for instance, in a pit in London dated before A.D. 60 (Merrifield, 1965, Pl. 120).

Also from Algeciras came sausage-shaped amphoras (Fig. 7); similar amphoras were made near Castro-Marim, in the eastern Algarve (Fig. 10); and the Puerto Real deposit included radish-shaped examples (as Fig. 11).

In the Tour Sainte Marie wreck (Corsica), published by Tchernia (1969*a*, 496–9), over 565 amphoras of six of these classes were mutually associated: three types showed great similarity of fabric, while three shared closely similar stamps. Another wreck with such a group was Lavezzi B, also in Corsica (*idem*, 495–6). Though there are still some chinks in the argument, the inescapable conclusion is that all the amphoras which I have mentioned were made in coastal areas of southern Spain and Portugal. The *contents* are not certainly known; many must have contained fish sauce, which is named in painted labels on some specimens of all these classes, but wine or even oil cannot be entirely excluded: compare an example displayed in a wine-shop at Herculaneum (Fig. 12). We now see that amphoras of different form could be made in the same workshop; what, then, was the point of the different forms, if not to contain different goods? Unfortunately, information from painted inscriptions has (till now) been imprecise (cf. Tchernia, 1967). Perhaps underwater finds will contribute more evidence on the question.

What *does* emerge from all this is the role of the army, for we can now recognize the amphoras, often mere fragments, found in frontier forts of the first century A.D. A group found at the river port of Mainz all came from southern Spain (Anon., 1901, Taf. 17, 2–7); all except two (Nos. 211 and 240) of the amphoras from Augustan Rödgen are likewise Spanish (Simon, 1961), and so are all except one (No. 8) of an early first-century A.D. group from Mainz (Baatz, 1962, Pl. 10). There could be other examples, but the point is clear: the frontier army was now settled in more or less permanent positions, and composed to a considerable extent of Roman citizens from Mediterranean countries (under Augustus, Tiberius and Caligula, 65 per cent of legionaries came from Italy: see Webster, 1969, 107–9, with ref.); it demanded a large and constant supply of its customary foodstuffs, and the fish and oil constituents were shipped from Spain. The fact that the distinctive Baetican amphoras which we have been considering disappear during the later first and early second centuries, as shown by Beltrán (1970, Fig. 240), appears to relate to the declining proportion of Italians in the army (after Hadrian, less than one per cent). The economic effects of this in Spain have still to be judged. (For other economic factors in the early Empire, see Rostovtzeff, 1957, 211–18, and Van Nostrand, 1937, 145–215).

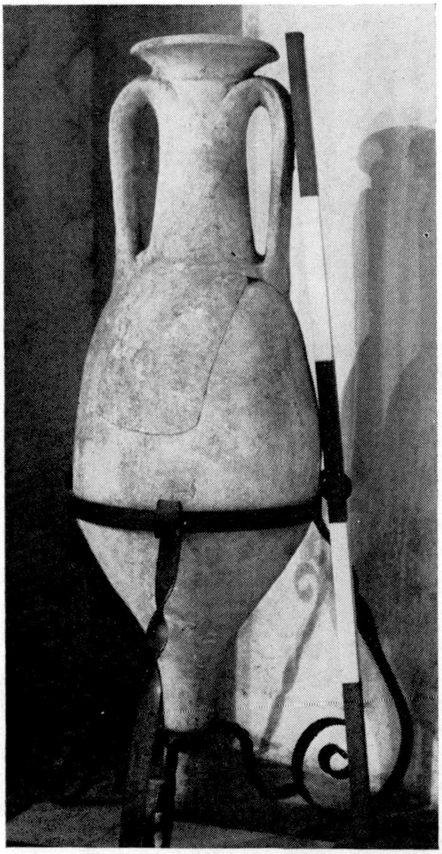

11

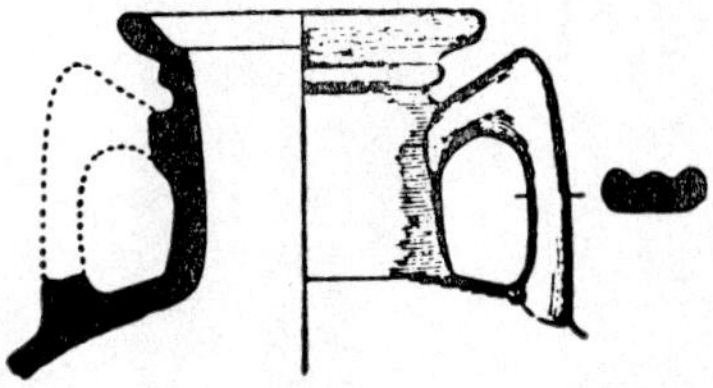

13

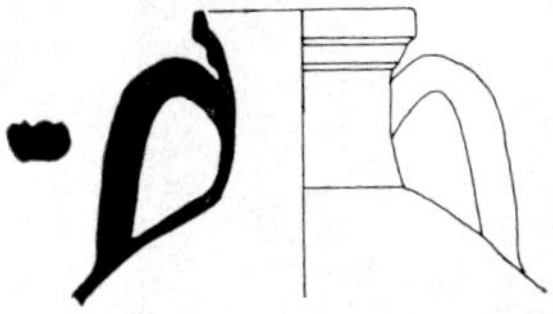

14

12

Figure 11. Radish-shaped amphora from workshop at Puerto Real. Jerez de la Frontera, Mus. Arqueológico. Scale marked in 0.20 m divisions.

Figure 12. Radish-shaped amphora in *taberna* at Herculaneum.

Figure 13. Amphora from Hod Hill. After Richmond, 1968, Figure 54, No. R3g. Scale 1 : 5.

Figure 14. Amphora from Rödgen. After Simon, 1961, No. 240. Scale 1 : 10.

15

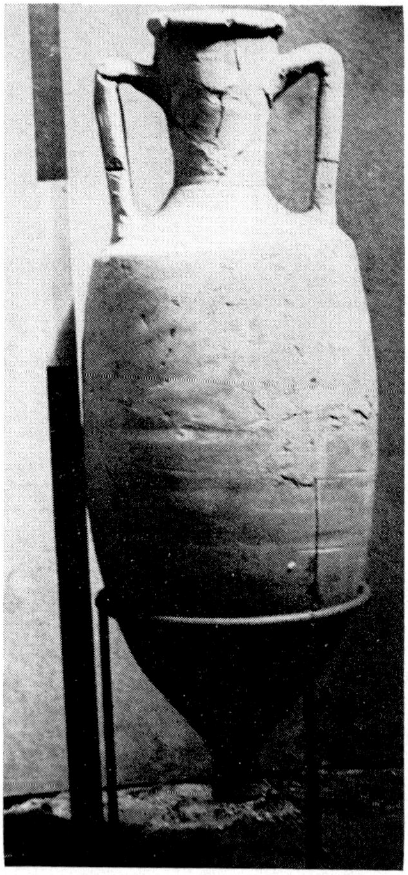

16

17

Figures 15–17. Amphoras in the Colchester and Essex Museum. Scale marked in 0.20 m divisions.

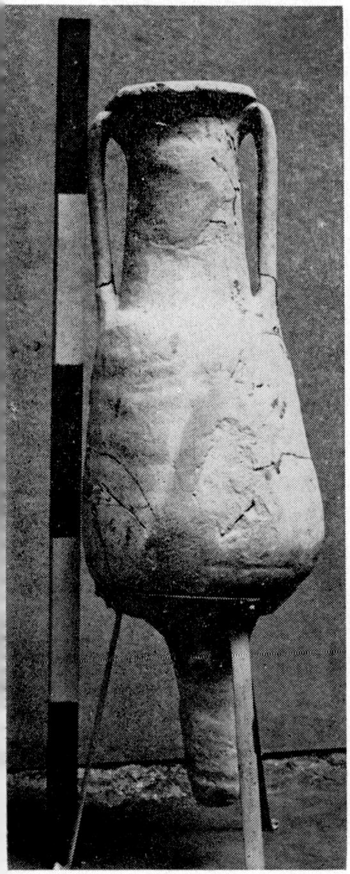

18

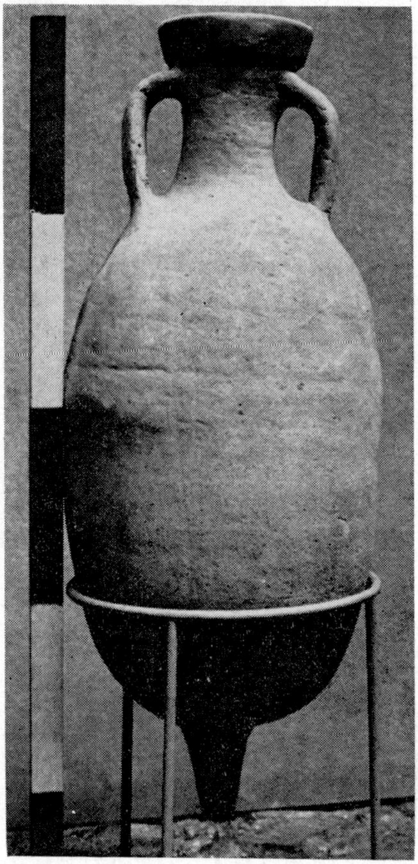

19

20

Figures 18–20. Amphoras in the Colchester and Essex Museum. Scale marked in 0.20 m divisions.

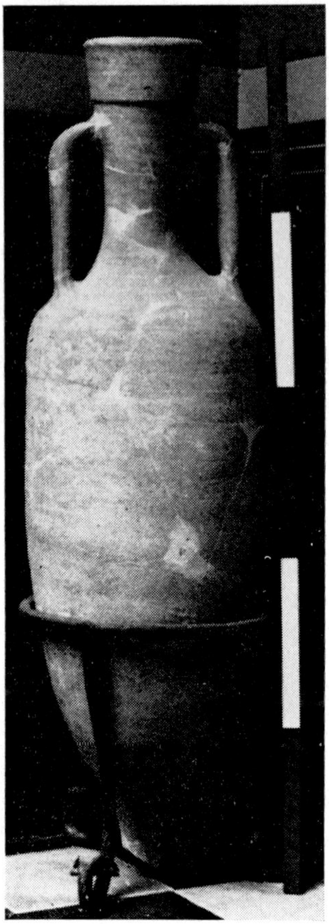

21

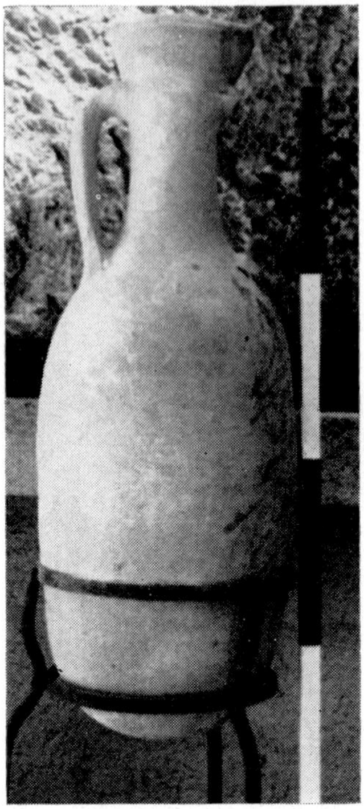

22

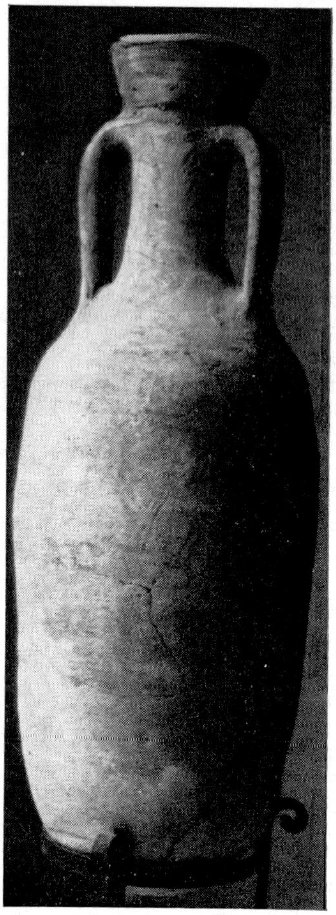

23

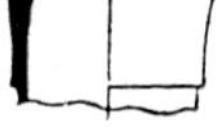

24

25

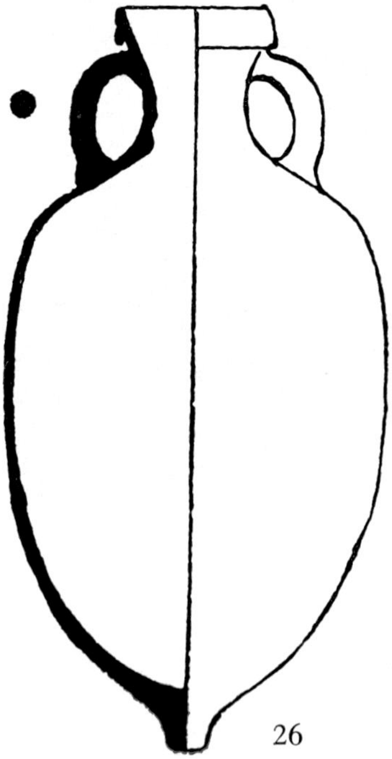

26

Figures 21–23. Catalan amphoras: 21, Barcelona, Mus. Arqueológico; 22, Jaén, Mus. Arqueológico; 23, Sevilla, Mus. Arqueológico. Scale approx. 1 : 10.

Figures 24–25. Amphoras from Vieille-Toulouse: 24, No. 273; 25, No. 7. After Fouet, 1958, Figure 5. Scale 1 : 10.

Figure 26. Amphora from Maïre. After Benoit, 1956, Figure 2.15. Scale 1 : 10.

Naturally, Spanish products do not constitute *all* the military supplies: some amphora forms are still unidentified, e.g. two at Hod Hill and Rödgen (Figs. 13–14); but a *Rhodian* amphora can be recognised at Hod Hill (R1c), as at Colchester (Fig. 15; cf. Camulodunum Form 184; Callender, 1965, 16–17; Tchernia, 1969*a*, 469–70). At Colchester we may also see pseudo-Koan amphoras (Fig. 16; Dressel 2–4; Camulodunum Form 182; Callender, 1965, 9–12). These amphoras, of several types, are probably mostly Campanian in origin, as is suggested by their common occurrence at Pompeii (cf. Grace, 1961, Figs. 60–61). *Some* of these Colchester amphoras are pre-Conquest, but on the whole the picture is one of Spanish amphoras predominating, whether in the pre-Boudiccan Colonia (Hull, 1958, 98 and Fig. 42.1), or in earlier military contexts (see Figs. 17-18). Sausage-shaped amphoras are also common (see Figs. 19–20). Pre-Roman finds of Spanish amphoras are discussed by Peacock (1971, working independently). The statistics of all this were already studied by Hawkes and Hull (1947), but their study fails to emphasize the large number of fragments of early Dressel 20 amphoras which appear at Colchester (cf. Dunnett, 1967, and report on Camulodunum excavations, in preparation). However, at Rödgen, at Holsterhausen, and elsewhere, these amphoras from the Baetis valley appear in Augustan times (Stieren, 1954, Fig. 5; Beltrán, 1970, 464 ff.).

THE CATALAN WINE AMPHORA[1]

We know from literary references that wine and oil were produced on the villa estates of Catalonia in early imperial times, and from archaeology that, close to the villa's oil- or wine-press, there often stood a kiln for the production of pottery, including amphoras (references and discussion in Beltrán, 1970, 599–602, etc.; see also Ribas, 1952). A number of these kilns have been discovered, and the common occurrence throughout Catalonia of the amphoras found in them enabled Pascual (1962) to describe this class for the first time. An example from Holsterhausen dates from the first years of the first century A.D. (Stieren, 1954, Fig. 4). It is of a type, with upright collar-lip, rather straight handles, and almost cylindrical body, which is common in Catalonia and the Ebro valley; compare Fig. 21, in Museo Arqueológico Provincial, Barcelona. Elsewhere this type is found only, to my knowledge, off Agde (Fonquerle, 1966, No. 32; cf. No. 395). Later on, as it would appear, the lip becomes trumpet-shaped, the handles are flexed, and the body often shows a double bulge, as in an example from Jaén province (Fig. 22). The date of this change is unknown: the later type appears at Herculaneum, thus before A.D. 79; and at London, thus presumably some time after A.D. 43 (Harmand, 1966, Fig. 2). There is no evidence for the survival of this class to the second century A.D., nor does it appear before the birth of Christ. There is nothing which definitely identifies the contents; many of these amphoras are lined with resin, but this is not in itself proof that they carried wine, since, for example, the Dressel 14 amphora from the Gandolfo wreck, labelled as containing fish sauce, was also so lined. (The fragment illustrated by Harmand [1966, Fig. 1], whose restoration may not be correct, was trawled up by French fishermen 25 miles south-west of Newhaven). Two wrecks are known to have existed in Catalonia, but neither has been accurately recorded (Beltrán, 1970, 329–38). And that is really all that is known of these amphoras. Their importance for economic history is that this class

[1] M. André Tchernia is preparing an article on this class of amphora for the *Archivo Español de Arqueologia*.

is the only one which was made not in the southern province (Baetica), whether on the coast or inland (in the Guadalquivir valley), but rather in Hispania Tarraconensis, the northern province. We badly need to understand their typological development better, in order to make some kind of historical narrative for the produce they contained; and we need better evidence for their contents. These amphoras appear not only on the northern frontier of the empire, but also in the south of Spain, at Jaén and at Sevilla (Fig. 23; finds from the frontier: besides the list given by Beltrán, add Augst, from a probable first-century context, Callender, 1965, Pl. III*b*).

Thus one infers that a Catalan product, probably wine, was traded with southern Spain during the first century A.D., but the development of this trade is still unclear. It remains possible that other kinds of amphora from N.E. Spain are still unidentified: compare the wreck of pseudo-Koan amphoras at Berá, partially excavated by the Tarragona Museum. Eventually I hope that more finds from the sea, and especially a Catalan wine-amphora cargo, will build up typologies and distributions, and so enable this chapter of Spain's economic history to be told.

ITALIAN AMPHORAS WITH COLLAR-LIP (DRESSEL 15)

In a ritual pit at Vieille-Toulouse, in Aquitaine, were found nearly 60 amphoras, most of the well-known Central Italian wine-amphora form Dressel 1B (Fouet, 1958; a list of *puits funéraires*: Fouet, 1970). Of two of the other amphoras in this pit, one (No. 273) has a collar-lip (see Fig. 24; Fouet, 1958, Fig. 5) and at first sight belongs to the Catalan class just discussed; in my view, however, this is an amphora of Dressel Form 15 (cf. Beltrán, 1970, 503–4), and can be identified as coming from Italy, like the other amphoras in this first-century B.C. deposit.

Amphora No. 7 at Vieille-Toulouse (Fig. 25) is a spheroidal amphora, of a kind recently published by Tchernia (1969*a*) from his partial excavation of the Planier C wreck in Marseille Bay (for earlier reports of the wreck, see Benoit, 1962, 153–4; 1967); for the type, compare Figures 26 & 36. Tchernia has argued (1969*b*) that the M. Tuccius Galeo whose name is stamped on this amphora (cf. Callender, 1965, No. 1187) is the Italian businessman who died in 47 B.C. and was a friend of Cicero (*Ad Atticum*, 11.12.4). The spheroidal form of amphora has been found among kiln waste near Brindisi, and often bears a single, Greek name like that of the Demetrius whose stamp (DEMETRI) appears on one handle of Vieille-Toulouse 7 (Sciarra, 1966; cf. Callender, 1965, No. 537).

Now, at the Planier C wreck the spheroidal amphora was associated with amphoras of form Lamboglia 2, a type first recognized at Albenga (Taylor, 1965, 53–66; Lamboglia, 1955, 262–63). As may be seen (e.g. from Squire and others, 1969, 38–9), they are common in Sicily and southern Italy, but many have been found in northern Italy also; indeed, amphoras of this form are said to have been found at a pottery in Istria, near Pula (Schörgendorfer, 1942, 93 & Taf. 44, with refs.). Thus, there is a controversy over their origin: Zevi (1967*b*, not seen by me) and Baldacci (1968) have argued for *northern* Italy; Tchernia (1969*a*, 488–9) and now Zevi (in a personal communication) support a *south* Italian source. I feel unable to opt for one side or the other, mainly because the class has not been properly defined. Baldacci notes correctly the close links between Lamboglia 2 and Dressel 6, but to my eye his sub-divisions are irrational and his definition of the whole class is

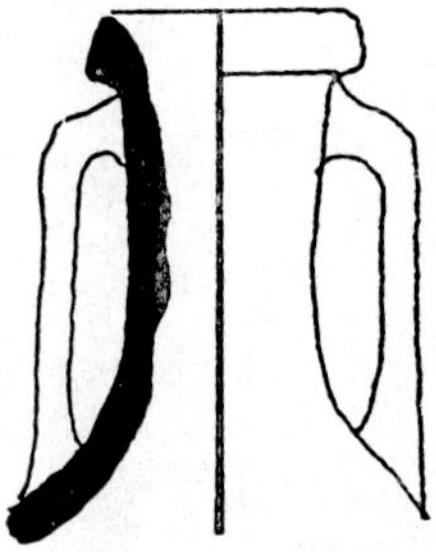

27

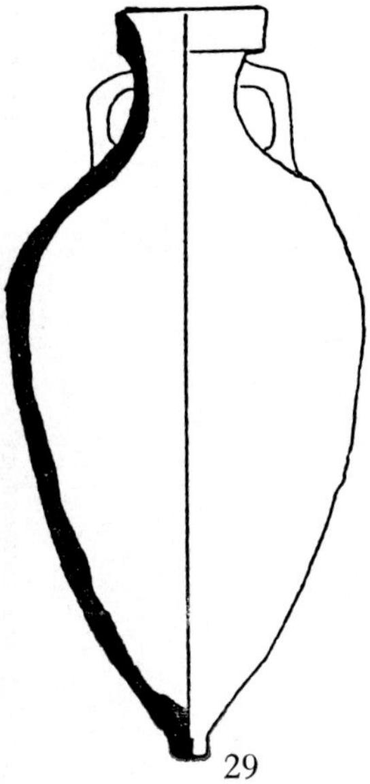

29

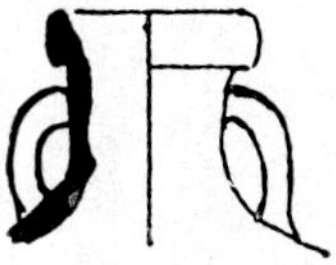

28

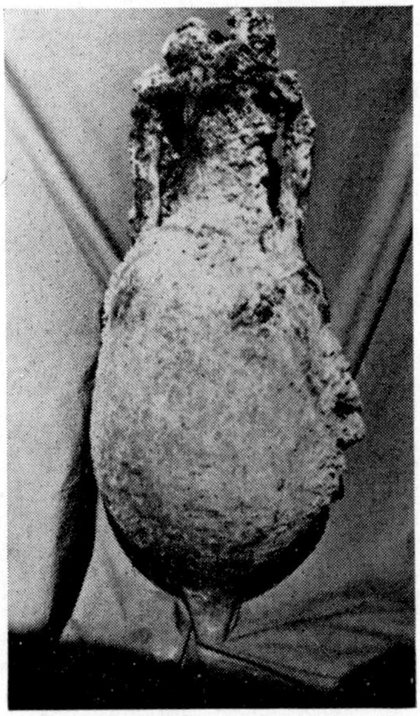

31

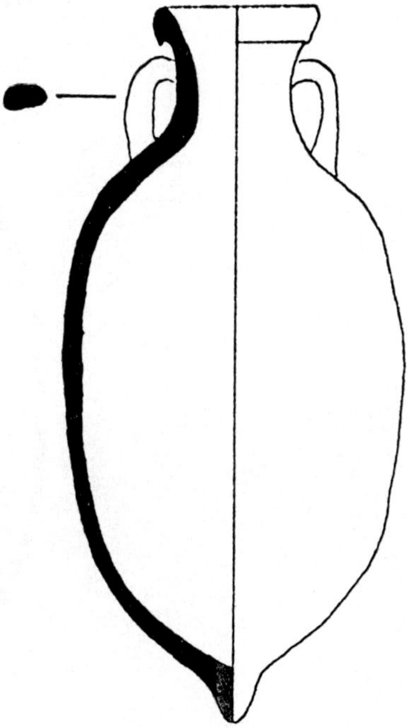

30

32

Figures 27–29. Amphoras from the Cala Pedrosa wreck. After Pascual, 1961*b*. Scale approx. 1 : 10.

Figure 30. Amphora from the wreck at Les Formigues, Palamós. Scale 1 : 10.

Figures 31–32. Amphoras from a wreck at the Tremiti Islands. Photos: Br. S. Dominic Ruegg, FSC.

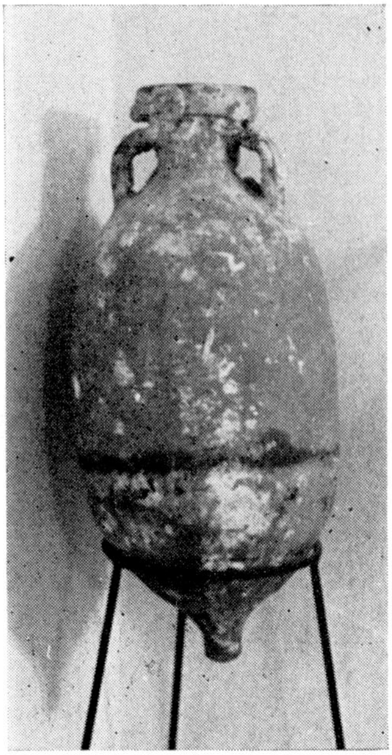

33

34

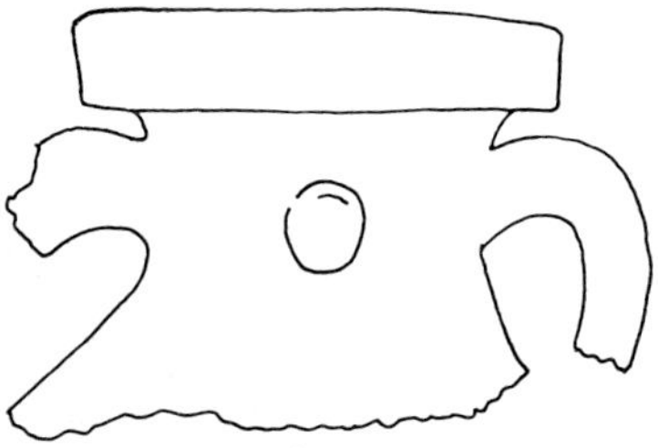

35

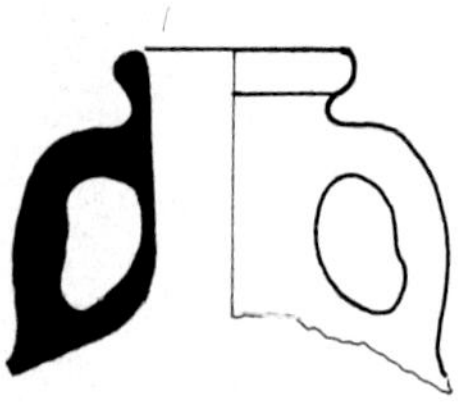

36

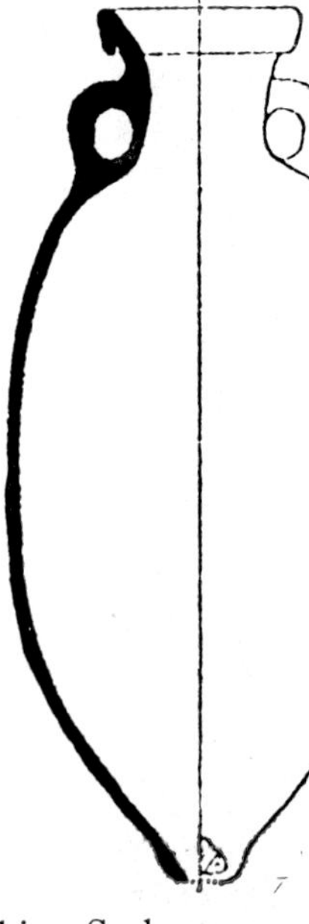

37

Figure 33. Amphora in private collection, San Antonio, Ibiza. Scale approx. 1 : 13.

Figure 34. Amphora at Zaragoza, Mus. Arqueológico. Scale marked in 0.20 m divisions.

Figure 35. Amphora from the Cerro de San Lorenzo cemetery, Melilla. After Tarradell, 1954, Pl. ix. Not to scale.

Figure 36. Amphora stamped M.TVCCI.L.F.TRO | GALEONIS, from the Planier C wreck. After Tchernia, 1969*b*, Figure 9. Scale 1 : 10.

Figure 37. Amphora from the Planier E wreck. After Benoit, 1962, Figure 20. Scale approx. 1 : 10.

vague. At all events, the first-century B.C. date of Lamboglia 2 is generally accepted: the earliest examples are of the late second century B.C., at Cala Pedrosa wreck, Catalonia (Fig. 27; Pascual, 1961*b*; Oliva, 1961) and the Athenian Agora (Grace, 1934, 208, 294–5); the latest are not much later than 50 B.C., as at Antikythera (*c.* 80–50 B.C.: Grace *in* Weinberg and others, 1965, 5–17) or Ventimiglia (Lamboglia, 1955, 263).

Many different types of amphora appear to be related to the "classic" form Lamboglia 2 of the Albenga wreck. Thus, at Azaila in Spain there are some amphoras, probably to be dated before 77 B.C., for which the closest published parallels known to me seem to be, not from Italy, whether north or south, but from Greece (compare Holwerda, 1936, No. 1090, from Chios, and Cabré, 1944, Pl. 60, No. 17; Holwerda, No. 1100, no provenance, but possibly Greek, and Cabré, No. 13.).

A Spanish shipwreck is of relevance here. At San Pedro del Pinatar, near Cartagena. amphoras of form Lamboglia 2 have been found with name-stamps which, though they are without exact parallel, are typical of Sicily or Magna Graecia (Más, 1970). This association is at least suggestive, with regard to origins.

The Lamboglia 2 amphoras from San Pedro del Pinatar appear to be an early form of the "classic" type. "Classic" specimens are common in the Adriatic: an example from Korčula has been published by Squire and others (1969, 38–9), and at least two wrecks containing amphoras of this class are known, off Čiovo Island, near Split (newspaper reports), and at Baška, Krk Island (Matajčič, 1968). The "classic" type may be seen in a wreck at the Tremiti Islands, investigated by Br. S. Dominic Ruegg in 1970 (Fig. 31; I am grateful to Br. Dominic for permission to publish these illustrations). Here we come to the *dénouement* of the argument: the Lamboglia 2 amphora is Italian, and first-century B.C., as we have seen; its companion in the same wreck (Fig. 32), however, is an amphora with tall collar-lip, just like Vieille-Toulouse No. 273! Again, the association can be no more than suggestive, but the suggestion is that here we have *another* Italian form; that the Vieille-Toulouse amphora bears only a superficial resemblance to the Catalan wine amphora, and is in fact an amphora from Italy (and perhaps northern Italy at that; cf. Baldacci, 1968, Fig. 5*a*). This association is repeated in the cargo of the Sa Nau Perduda wreck (Catalonia), to be published by R. Pascual in the memorial volume for F. Benoit (Pascual, personal communication).

In conclusion, then, we may see how land and sea finds reveal a wide diversity of Italian amphoras of the second and first centuries B.C., and thus gradually help to build a taxonomy which illustrates exports to Gaul and to Spain.

SPHEROIDS AND OVOIDS

For my final discussion, I return to the spheroidal amphora of the Planier C wreck (Fig. 36). We may now recognize its relations: from Punta Scaletta, Giannutri—published by Lamboglia (1964), but not excavated by him, and doubtless not from the mid-second century B.C. wreck. Comparable examples, of which one is illustrated here (Fig. 30), come from the wreck of Les Formigues, Palamós (Catalonia), which belongs to the mid-first century B.C. (Pascual, 1959, and Vidal, 1959, discuss the wreck; Pascual, 1961*b*, the date). Another example from Maïre (Fig. 26), was published by Benoit (1956, 28, No. 4). One in a private collection in Ibiza (Fig. 33), and another in the Provincial Archaeological Museum of Zaragoza (Fig. 34), may be compared.

Now, amphoras which are broadly similar, and which we may, for convenience, call "ovoid", can be shown to be earlier. Three from the Cala Pedrosa wreck (cf. Figs. 28–29) belong to the end of the *second* century B.C. (Pascual, 1961*b*, and Oliva, 1961), and there are other examples, e.g., from Melilla, N. Africa (Fig. 35). An ovoid amphora, of slighter profile, is apparently dated *c.* 74 B.C. in a wreck at Cap Sicié (Tchernia, 1969*a*, 483); closely similar amphoras were found in the Planier E wreck (Benoit, 1962, 156; cf. Fig. 37); while in two further wrecks, Congloué B and Titan (see above, p. 366), amphoras of this family were associated with south Spanish types.

What I am saying, then, is that ovoid or spheroid amphoras were exported from Italy during the second and first centuries B.C. These forms were imitated in Spain; and they developed in turn into the early Dressel 20 (spherical) and the sausage-shaped amphoras of Augustus' reign with which I began. Fuller documentation is still necessary for absolute certainty, but the outline of this development can now be seen; and the relevance of all this to underwater archaeology is that nearly all the amphoras which I have been discussing in this last section came from the sea. Without the evidence provided by marine finds we should probably remain ignorant of the growth of one of the largest economic factors in the Roman Empire: the export of sauce, wine and oil from Roman Spain.

APPENDIX 1—AMPHORA STUDIES AND MARINE ARCHAEOLOGY

The importance of underwater material was hardly recognized by most Roman archaeologists in the 1950s; thus, Callender's work was published in 1965 without reference to the underwater finds which had been made since it was completed in 1950. The studies of amphoras and of ancient sea-borne trade are collected and listed in Taylor (1965); other references will be found in the important reviews of Callender by Zevi (1967*a*) and Tchernia (1967). Zevi (1966) drew attention to the use which could be made of painted inscriptions for ascribing a date and an origin to a form; in their study of Late-Empire African amphoras (1969) Zevi and Tchernia developed this approach into a scientific method of study, using form and stamp together in order to arrange their material. Meanwhile, besides articles on particular sites, and his pioneer study of the Catalan amphora (1962), Pascual had contributed valuable surveys which have not received due recognition (especially 1961*a*). The recent book by M. Beltrán (1970) deals exhaustively and perceptively with many classes of amphora and shows (for the first time on a large scale) a unified system of study making full use of all available material from sea and land. See also Reusch (1970) for a recent discussion of carrot-shaped amphoras. Important work by Peacock (1971) and others has appeared since this paper was written.

APPENDIX 2—ITALIAN SPHEROIDS

An amphora of this kind was discussed by Elisa Lissi Caronna (1968), who compared a Pompeii specimen stamped L. ALLI DIONY | NICEPHORI. Note that Wilkes (1969, 502–3) cites a stamp NICEP from Dalmatia, and gives it a south Italian origin. Wilkes' list of stamps is a valuable comment on the origin of the Lamboglia 2 group and associated amphoras. On the basis of the Rome (Casilina) group and the Pompeii comparison, it appears that spheroids continued into the first century A.D., when Dressel 6 had taken over from Lamboglia 2.

ACKNOWLEDGEMENTS

I am grateful to the Directors or Curators of the following museums for permission to take photographs: Barcelona, Colchester & Essex, Jaén, Jerez de la Frontera, Sevilla and Zaragoza. Financial help has been given by the Craven and Meyerstein Funds (Oxford University) and by University College Dublin.

REFERENCES

Titles of British journals not listed in the *AJA* instructions are abbreviated as in *British Archaeological Abstracts*.

Anonymous, 1901 [Report in] *Westdeutsche Zeitschrift*, **20**, 344.

Atkins, F. B. 1971 Egyptian Blue, *in* Brodribb, A. C. C., Hands, A. R. & Walker, D. R., *Excavations at Shakenoak Farm, near Wilcote, Oxfordshire*, Part 2, 56–8. Oxford.

Baatz, D. 1962 Mogontiacum: neue Untersuchungen am römischen Legionslager in Mainz. *Röm.-germ. Kommission d. Deutschen Archäol. Inst., Limesforschungen*, 4.

Baldacci, P. 1968 Alcuni aspetti dei commerci nei territori cisalpini. *Atti del Centro Studi e Documentaz. sull'Italia romana*, **1** (1967–8), 8–50.

Beltrán Lloris, M. 1970 Las ánforas romanas en España. *Monografías arqueológicas, Anejos de Caesaraugusta*, 8.

Benoit, F. 1956 Épaves de la côte de Provence: typologie des amphores. *Gallia*, **14**, 23–34.

Benoit, F. 1958 Nouvelles épaves de Provence. *Gallia*, **16**, 5–39.

Benoit, F. 1962 Nouvelles épaves de Provence III. *Gallia*, **20**, 147–76.

Benoit, F. 1967 Archéologie sous-marine et histoire économique de la Gaule. *Archéologia* (Paris), **18** (Sept.–Oct. 1967), 20–24.

Bouscaras, A. 1964 Notes sur les recherches sous-marines d'Agde. *R.St.Lig.* **30**, 267–87.

Cabré Aguilo, J. 1944 *Cerámica de Azaila* [*Corpus vasorum Hispanorum*, Fasc. 1], 101 pp. Madrid.

Callender, M. H. 1965 *Roman Amphorae*, xxix + 323 pp. London.

Cintas, P. 1950 *Céramique punique*, xiv + 685 pp. Tunis.

Davies, O. 1935 *Roman Mines in Europe*, xii + 291 pp. Oxford.

Domergue, C. 1965 Les *Planii* et leur activité industrielle en Espagne sous la République. *Mél. Casa Velázquez*, **1**, 9–25.

Domergue, C. 1966 Les lingots de plomb romains du musée archéologique de Carthagène et du musée naval de Madrid. *Arch. Esp. Arq.* **39**, 41–72.

Dunnett, B. R. K. 1967 Excavations on North Hill, Colchester. *Archaeol. J.* **123**, 27–62.

Étienne, R. 1970 A propos du garum sociorum. *Latomus*, **29**, 297–313.

Ettlinger, E. & Simonett, C. 1952 Römische Keramik aus dem Schutthügel von Vindonissa. *Veröffentlichungen der Gesellschaft Pro Vindonissa*, **13**, Basel.

Fonquerle, D. 1966 Classification des amphores d'Agde. *L'aventure sous-marine*, **59**, 102–5.

Fouet, G. 1958 Puits funéraires d'Aquitaine. *Gallia*, **16**, 115–96.

Fouet, G. 1970 Vases gaulois de la région toulousaine. *Gallia*, **28**, 11–34.

Frost, H. 1969 *The Mortar Wreck in Mellieha Bay*, 38 pp. London.

Grace, V. 1934 Stamped amphora handles found in 1931–1932. *Hesperia* **3**, 197–310 and folding chart.

Grace, V. 1961 *Amphoras and the Ancient Wine Trade* [*Excavations of the Athenian Agora: Picture Book 6*] 32 pp. Princeton, N.J.

Harmand, L. 1966 Col d'amphore trouvé dans la Manche, in *Mélanges d'archéologie, d'épigraphie et d'histoire offerts à Jérôme Carcopino*, 477–89, Paris.

Hawkes, C. F. C. & Hull, M. R. 1947 Camulodunum. *Reports of the Research Committee of the Society of Antiqs. of London*, 14.

Holwerda, J. H. 1936 *Het Laat-Grieksche en Romeinsche Gebruiksaardewerk uit het Middellandsche-zee-gebied in het Rijksmuseum van Oudheden te Leiden*, 76 pp. s'Gravenhage.

Hull, M. R. 1958 Roman Colchester. *Reports of the Research Committee of the Society of Antiqs. of London*, 20.

Jiménez Cisneros, M. J. 1958 Beobachtungen in einen römischen Töpferbezirk bei Puerto Real. *Germania*, **36**, 469–75.

Körber, K. 1909 Die im Jahre 1908 gefundenen römischen und frühchristlichen Inschriften und Skulpturen. *M.Z.* **4**, 14–33.

Körber, K. 1911 Die in den Jahren 1909 und 1910 gefundenen römischen und frühchristlichen Inschriften und Skulpturen. *M.Z.* **6**, 121–41.

Lamboglia, N. 1955 Sulla cronologia delle anfore romane di età repubblicana. *R. St. Lig.* **21**, 241–70

Lamboglia, N. 1964 La campagna 1963 sul relitto di Punta Scaletta. *R.St.Lig.* **30**, 229–57.

Leite de Vasconcelos, J. 1898 Olaria luso-romana em San Bartolomeu de Castro-Marim. *O Arqueologo Português*, **4**, 329–36.

Lissi Caronna, E. 1968 Piccolo deposito di anfore in via Alessandro Nelli. *N. Sc.* 1968, 10–15.

Loeschke, S. 1942 Die römische und belgische Keramik aus Oberaden, *in* Albrecht, C., *Das Römerlager in Oberaden*, Heft 2, 101 ff. Dortmund.

Más García, J. 1970 La nave romana de Punta de Algas. *Notic. Arqueol. Hispan.* **13–14**, 402–7 & Pls. CX–CXIV.

Mascaró Pasarius, J. 1971 El tráfico marítimo en Mallorca en la antigüedad clásica. *Atti del III Congresso Internazionale di Archeologia Sottomarina, Barcellona 1961*, 69–86. Ist. internaz. di studi Liguri, Bordighera.

Matajčič, R. 1968 Baška, otok Krk, uvala Dubno-hidroarheološka akcija.*Arheološki Pregled*, **10** 122-4 (French synopsis, p. 255).

Merrifield, R. 1965 *The Roman City of London*, 344 pp. London.

Oliva Prat, M. 1961 Avance al estudio de los materiales arqueológicos de la Isla Pedrosa. *CRIS, Revista de la Mar*, **3**, No. 31, 23–6.

Pascual Guasch, R. 1959 El material del pecio de Palamós. *CRIS, Revista de la Mar*, **1**, No. 8, 12–13.

Pascual Guasch, R. 1961*a* Las ánforas que no figuran en la tabla de Dressel. *CRIS, Revista de la Mar*, **3**, No. 25, 4–7.

Pascual Guasch, R. 1961*b* Las ánforas del pecio del Estartit. *CRIS, Revista de la Mar*, **3**, No. 31, 14–15.

Pascual Guasch, R. 1962 Centros de producción y difusión geográfica de un tipo de ánfora. *7° Congreso Nacional de Arqueología, Barcelona, 1960*, 334–45. Zaragoza.

Pascual Guasch, R. 1968 El Pecio Gandolfo (Almería). *Pyrenae*, **4**, 141–55.

Peacock, D. P. S. 1971 Roman amphorae in pre-Roman Britain, *in* Hill, D. & Jesson, M., *The Iron Age and its Hill-Forts. Papers presented to Sir Mortimer Wheeler*, 161–88. Southampton.

Reusch, W. 1970 Kleine, spitzkonische Amphoren. *Saalburg Jahrbuch*, **27**, 54–62.

Ribas i Bertrán, M. 1952 El Poblament d'Ilduro. *Institut d'Estudis Catalans, Memòries de la Secció Històrico-Arqueològico*, 12.

Richmond, I. A. 1968 *Hod Hill*, Vol. 2, 157 pp. British Museum, London.

Robinson, H. S. 1959 *Pottery of the Roman Period. Chronology* [*The Athenian Agora*, Vol. 5], xiv + 149 pp. Princeton, N.J.

Rostovtzeff, M. 1957 *Social and Economic History of the Roman Empire*, 2nd edit., revised by P. M. Fraser, 847 pp. Oxford.

Schörgendorfer, A. 1942 Die römerzeitliche Keramik der Ostalpenländer. *Sonderschriften der Zweigstelle Wien des archäolog. Inst. des Deutschen Reiches*, 13.

Sciarra, B. 1966 Alcuni bolli anforari brindisini. *Epigraphica*, **28**, 122–34.

Simon, H. G. 1961 Die Funde aus dem Bereich des Lagers in Rödgen. *Saalburg Jahrbuch*, **19**, 59–79.

Squire, D. M. and others 1969 The Oxford University Plemmyrion Expedition, 1968. *Bull. Oxf. Univ. Explor. Club*, **17**, pp. v and 25–52.

Stieren, A. 1954 Das neue römische Lager in Westfalen. *Germania*, **32**, 165–70.

Tarradell, M. 1954 La necrópolis del Cerro de San Lorenzo, Melilla. *1° Congreso Arq. de Marruecos español, Tetuán, 1953*. Tetuán.

Taylor, J. du Plat (ed.) 1965 *Marine Archaeology*, 208 pp. London.

Tchernia, A. 1967 Les amphores romaines et l'histoire économique. *J. Sav.* 1967, 216–34.

Tchernia, A. 1969*a* Informations archéologiques. Direction des recherches archéologiques sous-marines. *Gallia*, **27**, 465–99.

Tchernia, A. 1969*b* Les fouilles sous-marines de Planier (Bouches-du-Rhône). *C.R.A.I.* 1969, 292–309.

Torr, C. 1964 *Ancient Ships*, reprint of 1st edit., 1894, with introd. by A. Podlecki, xvi + 222 pp. Chicago.

Van Nostrand, J. J. 1937 Roman Spain, *in* Frank, T. (ed.) *An Economic Survey of Ancient Rome*, vol. III, 119–224. Baltimore.

Vidal Solá, C. 1959 El Pecio de Palamós. *CRIS, Revista de la Mar*, **1**, No. 10, 5–9.

Vuillemot, G. 1965 *Reconnaissances aux échelles puniques d'Oranie*, 453 pp. Autun.

Webster, G. 1969 *The Roman Imperial Army*, 330 pp. London.

Weinberg, Gladys D. and others 1965 The Antikythera Shipwreck reconsidered. *Trans. Am. Philos. Soc.*, N.S. **55**, Pt. 3.

West, L. C. 1929 *Imperial Roman Spain: the Objects of Trade*, 92 pp. Oxford.

Wilkes, J. J. 1969 *Dalmatia*, xxvii + 572 pp. London.

Wilson, A. J. N. 1966 *Emigration from Italy in the Republican Age of Rome*, xvi + 208 pp. Manchester.

Zevi, F. 1966 Appunti sulle anfore romane. *Arch. Cl.* **18**, 208–47.

Zevi, F. 1967*a* [Review-discussion of Callender, 1965]. *J.R.S.* **57**, 234–8.

Zevi, F. 1967*b* Anfore istriane ad Ostia. *Atti e Memorie della Soc. Istriana di archeol. e storia patria*, N.S. **15**, 21–31.

Zevi, F. & Tchernia, A. 1969 Amphores de Byzacène au Bas-Empire. *Antiquités Africaines*, **3**, 173–214.

Discussion

Humphreys Could you tell us more about the re-use of amphoras, if any? Are inscriptions on amphoras a reliable guide to the contents at the time of shipwreck?
Parker The only good example of re-use, other than smashing them up, breaking holes in them, etc., is the spheroidal amphora in the Maïre wreck, which was filled with lime—and this seems most unlikely to have been the original contents. The amphora bore a stamp which had been erased. I expect you would do something like this if you were re-using an amphora in normal trade.

There are painted inscriptions from Pompeii or Rome with a second inscription in different ink, but the known examples were found long ago, and the publications may not be reliable. I do not see why we should not find more.

We are much more dependent on argument from these things in the west than are archaeologists working in the eastern Mediterranean.

Hague In view of the number of amphoras there must be, how many kiln sites have been properly excavated, and how many marks have been identified with actual sites?
Parker Four or five in Catalonia, but without proper details. In the Guadalquivir valley a large number of kilns have been found, and one can tie down the exact village or estate whose name appears on the handles. There are one or two known from the coastal area of south-west Spain, and more could probably be found there. On the whole, this is not nearly as many as one would like, but it is another aspect of what I call archaeo-politics: it is often easier to study museum material than to get funds or permission to dig.

Swiny How many of the amphoras have a resin coating inside? Has the coating of yours been analysed and identified as resin, or could they have been coated with bitumen? The coating of the Kyrenia amphoras has been identified as bitumen.
Parker As far as I can make out, reports of bitumen coating come from American, and reports of resin coating come from French and Spanish archaeologists.
Frost My samples, collected from many classical wrecks over some ten years, were analysed by the Government Chemist. All turned out to be rosin, not resin. He asked me at the time to check on the modern use of resin products—for example, for lining gourds in Cyprus; but I was unable to gather sufficient detail about it. Apparently Cypriot resin, for making rosin, was particularly sought after in antiquity.
Swiny It is not always resin in the gourds, but sometimes bitumen.
Frost I asked the conservationist in Nicosia, but he was not sure.
Parker I am not certain what the lining of the amphoras is. As far as I know, it is not usual to find a lining in oil amphoras; but this does not mean that an amphora with no lining is necessarily an oil amphora, since the lining often disappears.

Throckmorton Resin, coal tar and bitumen are all products which would have been used in ships, and they would have been carried in containers such as amphoras, in the Mediterranean in antiquity.

Will wine jars work if you do not coat them inside?

Parker I think not.

POSTSCRIPT—ANALYSIS OF AMPHORA LININGS

The British Museum Research Laboratory is, at the moment, investigating the black resinous substances which were used for various purposes in antiquity. The nomenclature of these materials has become very confused, but essentially "bitumen" is the material found in association with crude oil (although modern terminology tends to use the term "asphalt" to describe the solid and semi-solid products of oil-wells); "wood tar" is the material derived from the destructive distillation of wood, which can then be further distilled to give a residue called "wood pitch"; and "resinous materials" is the term used to describe sticky substances which are exuded by certain species of tree. On distillation of the "resin" from pine trees, the solid residue obtained is usually known as "rosin".

Samples of the black linings of about 15 amphoras, ranging in date from the third century B.C. to the first century A.D., have been examined. The amphoras were found on several different Mediterranean wreck sites. The samples were dissolved in chloroform and examined by paper chromatography, the resulting chromatograms being compared with those given by standard samples of rosin, wood tar and bitumen. The results indicated that, with one possible exception, all the samples which were examined are similar to rosin, although a definite identification was not possible by this technique. On the basis of these tests, it would seem likely that the main materials used to line the amphoras were "resins of vegetable origin" and not either wood tar or bitumen, although Pliny states that wood pitch was used. Further work using infra-red absorption analysis is in progress and should enable more specific identifications to be made.

W. A. Oddy
J. C. Bateman

Greco-Roman anchors and the evidence for the one-armed wooden anchor in antiquity

by

GERHARD KAPITÄN

Greco-Roman anchors, like certain modern anchors, usually consisted of a shank with two arms and a stock that keeps the anchor in the required position in which one arm grips the bottom (Fig. 1). This was recognized definitely only some forty years ago, when two perfectly preserved Roman anchors were discovered in Lake Nemi (Ucelli, 1950, 234ff): one of wood with a fixed lead stock, the other of iron with a movable stock similar to that of the admiralty anchor invented in the nineteenth century by Capt. Rodger.

Before the Nemi finds the archaeological evidence on anchors had been very sparse. Besides the remains of a few iron anchors, there were some lead stocks or halves of them that had been found in the Mediterranean by sponge divers. For a long time these lead stocks were almost always interpreted wrongly by scholars. As a curiosity I might mention, for instance, one attempt to explain how half of a lead stock, which obviously had been cut in two parts, perhaps to facilitate its salvaging, could have been used as an anchor (*Bulletin*, 1880). At the end of the last century, the famous marine archaeologist Cecil Torr (1894, 71 & Pl. 8) thought that the two lead stocks in the British Museum were parts of one and the same anchor. The smaller, in his opinion, was the stock, and the two halves of the larger piece would have formed the arms. Even in the late 1920s, Friedrich Moll (1929), in a study of fourteen lead anchor stocks in European museums, still took them for the arms. The first and for a long time the only archaeologist who, against the authoritative opinions of the experts, suggested the explanation of these pieces of lead as anchor stocks was Dr. L. Magon (1894) in his article on a stock decorated with four astragals from Carry-le-Rouet near Marseille.

In the last twenty years archaeological research under water has vastly extended and deepened our knowledge of ancient anchors. For stone anchors of prehistoric origin I refer to Miss Frost's paper in this volume (below, 397–409) and to her recent article (1970). We have learned that the lead stocks had predecessors made of stone which have a simple notch in the centre instead of the sophisticated box with which the lead stock is provided. The first underwater finds of stone stocks were reported by F. Braemer and J. Marcadé (1953, 151–2 & Fig. 12). Three main types of lead stocks can be distinguished, according to the fastening device in the box: first, the common type with a lead cross-bar; second, a type with a wooden core that crossed the shank; third, a type

Figure 1. Reconstructed wooden anchor of the common type with fixed lead stock and assembly-piece, in anchorage position on the sea floor.

without any bar at all. The last must be the earliest; we have examples that go back at least to the sixth century B.C., for a stock of this type was found in an Etruscan wreck at Antibes (Benoit, 1958, 30–31 & Fig. 36). The type with the wooden core showed clearly that the lead had been cast directly on the wood. How this was achieved was demonstrated by F. Benoit, whose name is closely connected with the first studies in classification of ancient anchors (see especially Benoit, 1952, 266ff; 1955, 117ff & 122, Fig. 6; 1961, 170ff).

Besides stocks of solid lead, divers have found on ancient anchorages numerous longish lead pieces almost trapezoidal in cross-section; strikingly often these are found in pairs. From a study of their peculiarities in shape, such as protruding nails, lateral indentations, projections at one end, covering flange-shaped parts, the mixture of the metal with stones or precast lead pieces, etc., which obviously all could serve to fix the lead in place, it appears that these lead pieces must have been cast in wooden cases. A pair of these leads connected by a bar, found in the entrance of the Great Harbour of Syracuse, demonstrates beyond any doubt that the shape of the wooden case which surrounded the lead would correspond perfectly to that of an anchor stock (Kapitän, 1968*a*; for a more detailed study see Kapitän, 1967). Confirmation of the explanation of these leads as cores of wooden stocks came recently with the discovery of two pairs of such leads in the Greek wreck off Kyrenia, Cyprus, dated *c.* 300 B.C. (Swiny & Katzev, above 339–59, and bibliography there). They were found in the extreme bow area of the ship, where one would expect to meet with the anchors. This find also confirms the tentative conclusions that had been drawn (Kapitän, 1968*b*) about the period in which lead-filled wooden anchor stocks may have been used (see now also, 1971, 126).

A further new discovery was that the detachable stock with which the Roman iron anchor from Nemi was equipped had a predecessor of lead employed on wooden anchors (Benoit, 1955, 122ff). Detachable lead stocks were in use already in Hellenistic times and most probably are not a Roman but a Greek invention.[1] From such wooden anchors with detachable stocks must have come the inspiration for the Roman iron anchor. The earliest form of the ancient iron anchor, with straight arms in a V-shaped position with respect to the shank, is a precise replica of the wooden anchor: for example, the iron anchor from a wreck at Isla Pedrosa near Estartit in Spain, dating to 150–100 B.C. (Foerster, 1969). Iron anchors with detachable stocks lasted through the whole Imperial era. What changed was mainly the shape of the arms and their angle to the shank. Several types can be distinguished.[2] In late Roman and early Byzantine times the arms were set to form a right angle to the shank. A few such anchors still have a detachable stock with rectangular cross-section: as examples I cite an anchor found near Haifa and now in the National Maritime Museum, Haifa (Inv. No. 613, 6; see Kapitän, forthcoming); also a specimen found off the Spanish coast (Martin Avila & Saludes, 1966, 159–60, Pl. II*b*). Much more common, however, are stocks of round section. Iron anchors with a round stock hole in the shaft are known from several finds: a dated group of 11 anchors of this type comes from the seventh-century A.D. wreck at Yassı Ada, Turkey (information by courtesy of F. H. van Doorninck, whose dissertation (1967) dealt with this wreck).

More than a thousand pieces or parts of ancient wooden and iron anchors are now in European museums.[3] Particularly rich typologically are the anchor collections in Sicily.[4] Here I have had the opportunity over a period of more than ten years to study several hundred finds. The large variety of forms not only allowed me to elaborate a classification of this material,[5] but also enabled me to look into some special problems. Favoured by

[1] This is an inference from the fact that these stocks were found preponderantly in the waters of Magna Graecia. Several specimens are provided with figures, or inscriptions in relief, or both, of the same type as those known from fixed lead stocks, a few of which are dated. Very common as symbols of good luck are representations of astragals, the use of which in games of fortune was widespread among the Hellenistic Greeks in Southern Italy (Rohlfs, 1963).

[2] As far as I know, a detailed classification of ancient iron anchors has not yet been worked out. In a preliminary typology I have listed four main types and at least five transitional forms.

[3] The total number of anchors and parts of anchors actually found in the Mediterranean is much greater, since several thousand lead stocks and other lead parts of anchors were found by private individuals. Usually these have been melted down. According to detailed information which I have received from divers, far more than a thousand pieces have been lost through looting in Sicily alone.

[4] The largest collections of ancient anchors are those of the National Museums at Syracuse and Palermo, with a total at this time of about 400 pieces. The former was founded by Piero Gargallo di Castel Lentini, the latter is the work of Prof. Vincenzo Tusa (see Tusa, 1961; 1971, 270ff; and his papers at the Fourth Congress, Nice 1970, and at this Symposium, below 411–37). Also important in Sicily are the collections in the Museo Eoliano at Lipari and in the Antiquario of Naxos near Taormina. Several anchor finds are kept in the museums at Messina, Trapani and Ragusa and in the collection at Ustica, Terrasini (Sig. V. E. Orlando) and that of the Circolo Pescatori Subacquei "Mares" at Catania, now transferred to the Greek Theatre.

[5] During the winter of 1961–2 I prepared a first draft of a study on the typology of ancient anchors (in German); this has not been published, but a copy is kept in the library of the Soprintendenza alle Antichità at Syracuse. A summary of my findings was the subject of my paper at the Second International Conference on Underwater Archaeology at Toronto, 1955, the proceedings of which unfortunately have never been published. I have now prepared an article on "Ancient Wood Anchors", to be published in *Mariner's Mirror* it deals with the classification of this anchor group, which I can only summarize here. I regret that a paper by Miss F. Pallarés (1971) was for a long time inaccessible to me because of the long delay in the publication of the proceedings of that congress. Only after having completed this paper did I learn of certain interesting data which it contains.

some chance discoveries of interesting artifacts which were made recently in Sicily and Southern Italy, I was able to explain certain details, for instance the significance of the box-shaped lead brackets of which as yet only a few examples have been found. It turns out now, from the examination of a well-preserved anchor find at Isola Lunga near Marsala (Kapitän, in press), that they are reinforcements for the upper part of wooden anchor shanks, close to or just over the aperture for the rope or a detachable stock. They are repair-pieces attached when the wood had developed dangerous fissures.

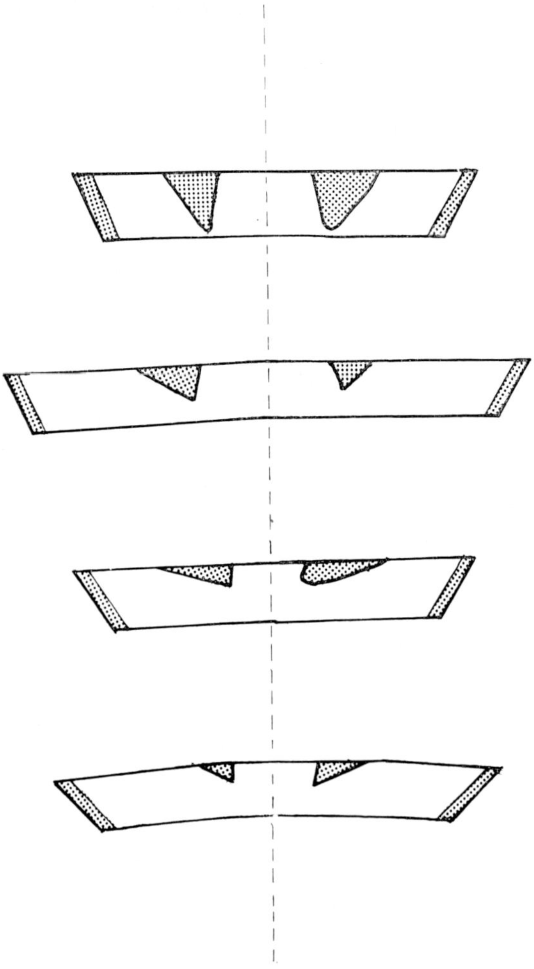

Figure 2. Sections of four assembly-pieces in the anchor collection at Syracuse (SIR A 41, 106, 98, 44). Scale 1 : 10.

A rather interesting discovery has come now from a lead piece of unusual form. It is an example of the so-called assembly-piece or "piece with three holes", the function of which as a device to secure arms to shank was first described by F. Benoit (1952, 268–9). Though by no means all ancient wooden anchors had such a piece—the wooden

Nemi anchor, for instance, had none—it is clear that they were very commonly used. Indeed, a group of four wooden anchors so equipped was identified together with some iron anchors in a second-century B.C. Roman wreck at Punta Scaletta, Giannutri (Lamboglia, 1964, 252ff & Pl. II).

The assembly-pieces, it is thought, probably added weight to the anchor in this part. We know now that they were used on anchors of different types; they have been found together with fixed lead stocks of the type with a cast cross-bar as well as the type with a wooden core, and also with detachable lead stocks. In addition, from the form of the assembly-piece we can determine the shape of the wood of arms and shank in this portion, because the lead was cast over the junction. Again, they enable us to observe that the

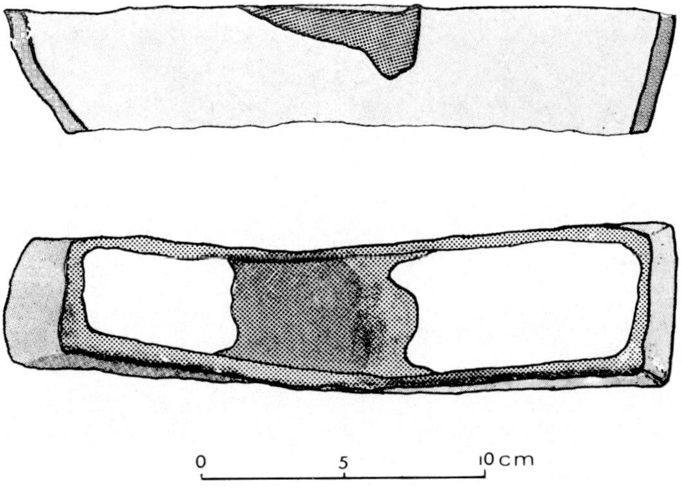

Figure 3. The assembly-piece of a one-armed anchor from Brindisi: section and view of the bottom side.

position of the arms with respect to the shank varied considerably, from an arrowhead-shaped arrangement to a form with the arms spread wide (Fig. 2). I think that this is connected with the employment of differently shaped anchors on different kinds of sea bottom. Lastly, and certainly not unimportant, the assembly-pieces with three holes confirm that the anchors had two arms.

Now a small undamaged assembly-piece *with two holes only* was found recently in the harbour entrance of Brindisi, near the Pedagne Islands, unfortunately without the related stock.[6] From the shape of the openings in this lead (Fig. 3) the conclusion is inescapable that it must have covered the junction between a shank and one arm of an anchor. With the shank in a vertical position the piece would not sit at right angles to it, but would slope somewhat, and this makes it theoretically possible to have a second arm joined to the shank on the opposite side below where the lead fitted (Fig. 4*a*). But this is very unlikely—why cast lead on the junction between only one arm and the shank, if there

[6] I am much indebted to Sig. Zongoli, librarian at Brindisi and a skilled diver, who discovered this piece and kindly allowed me to examine and publish it. The length of the lead is 24 cm. It is now kept in the Museo Archeologico "Francesco Ribezzo" at Brindisi. A short note on this find has been published (Kapitän, 1971). See postscript, p. 394.

were two arms? The answer is that this piece was indeed the fitting for an anchor that had only one arm. This interpretation is supported by the following consideration: if the lead is held in a horizontal position, as it was when cast in a simple open mould, the silhouette of a one-armed anchor can be traced precisely in the counterbalanced position in which such an anchor would have been placed in the mould (Fig. 4*b*).

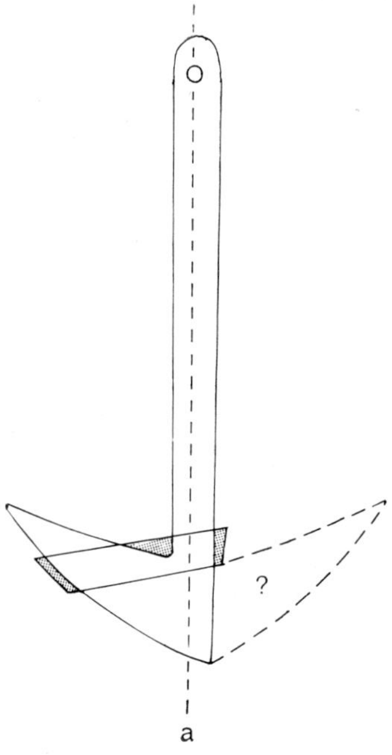

Figure 4. Reconstructions of the anchor equipped with the two-hole assembly-piece from Brindisi (see the text).

That this anchor was used in the classical period need not be questioned; the lead proves this sufficiently. What we have to do is, first, to explain how it worked, and then to ask whether there is perhaps more evidence for anchors of this kind and for their particular function.

To answer the first question presents no problem, since the one-armed anchor and its functional principle are well known. This anchor type is still used by native people in Indo-China. Among the ethnological material on primitive anchors published by van Nouhuys (1951, Figs. 14–22) we find several examples, and models of such anchors are on view in museums, e.g. in the Science Museum in London (Ucelli, 1950, 241, Fig. 274). From these illustrations we can see how these anchors were made. The device which ensures that the anchor settles on the sea floor with its fluke pointing to the bottom is a longish stone attached crosswise to the shank and always attached on the same side as the arm. On some of these anchors one can see that the stone has been attached asymmetrically: it is longer at one side, which consequently would be the heavier side.

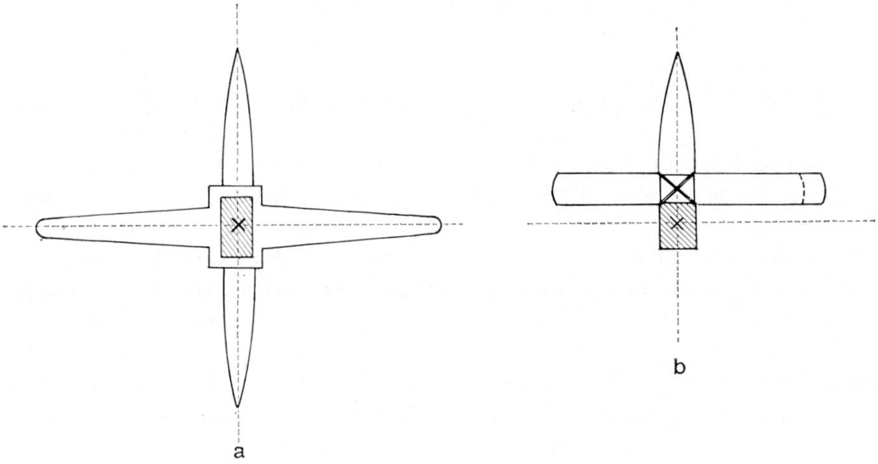

Figure 5. Sketches of the distribution of weight (*a*) in a two-armed anchor with fixed lead stock; (*b*) in a one-armed anchor with unbalanced stone stock.

For a better understanding of this particular feature a comparison with the two-armed anchor will be helpful. In the common two-armed anchor with a balanced stock in an axial position, the weight is equally distributed to the four quadrants formed by the crossing axes of stock and arms (Fig. 5*a*). Consequently such an anchor when lowered falls approximately equally often into each of its two possible working positions. On a single-armed anchor with an asymmetrical stock attached unbalanced to the same side

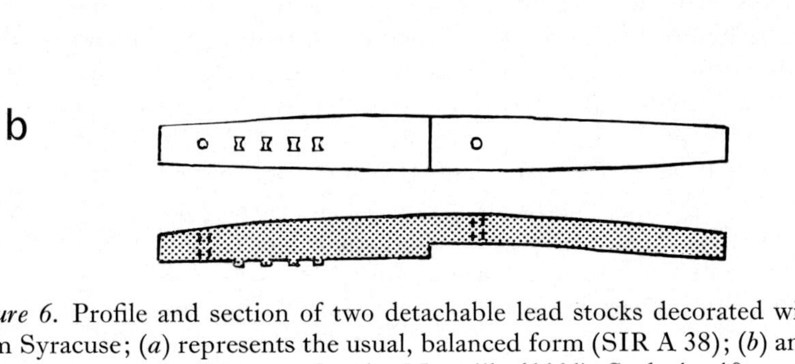

Figure 6. Profile and section of two detachable lead stocks decorated with astragals, from Syracuse; (*a*) represents the usual, balanced form (SIR A 38); (*b*) an unbalanced example, now in the Museum Borély, Marseille (6666). Scale 1 : 10.

of the shank as the arm, we find an excess of weight in one of the two quadrants flanking the arm (Fig. 5*b*). This imbalance made it more certain that the anchor landed "where the single prong stood out" (van Nouhuys, 1951, 29).

In other words, if we find asymmetrical stocks, it is fairly certain that we are dealing with one-armed anchors. Now from the ancient world we have examples of an unbalanced form of the detachable lead stock. In the common, balanced stock of this type, which is stopped against the shank usually by means of a step protruding on one side, both halves are kept to the same thickness (Fig. 6*a*). The unbalanced form can be made up of a thinner and a thicker half separated by a stopping step. An example of this shape is a small stock from Syracuse which was found several years ago by the divers of Cousteau's *Calypso* and then handed over to the Museum Borély at Marseille (Fig. 6*b*; Benoit, 1955, 122ff, Figs. 7 & 8.1). The stock was found together with an assembly-piece with three holes. The stock could, of course, have been used with a two-armed anchor; on the other hand, the context could be accidental, since at that time the sea floor at Syracuse was dotted with leaden parts of anchors.

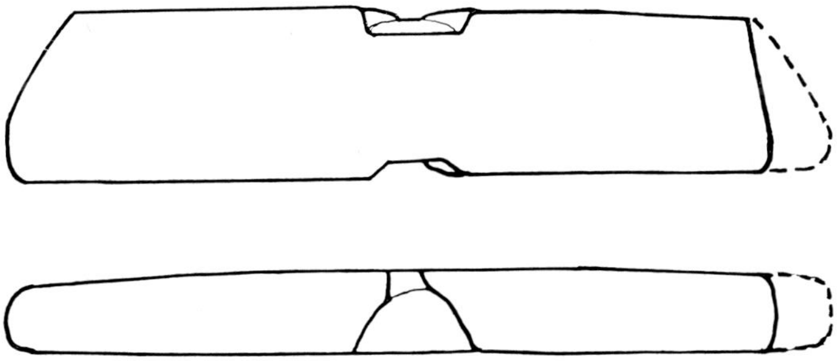

Figure 7. Unbalanced stone stock in the anchor collection at Syracuse (SIR A 116). The dotted line indicates the portion by which the stock differs from the shape of a balanced stock. Scale 1 : 8.5.

Perhaps more frequent were asymmetrical stocks of stone. They may, of course, sometimes be only unintentionally so, when an intended symmetrical arrangement did not work out right or was not possible because of some unevenness of the rough material. Some specimens may appear asymmetrical now because parts of the ends are missing. However, we have specimens without any damage whatsoever, on which the notch for adaptation and attachment to the shank is obviously intentionally cut not in the centre but strikingly off-centre. An example is a stock from the anchor collection at Syracuse (Fig. 7). Specimens of this kind have also been found elsewhere: unbalanced stone stocks are clearly identifiable in the group that was found in the Bay of Marathon (Braemer & Marcadé, 1953, Fig. 12, especially the stocks *a*, *b* and *g*, perhaps also *e* and *f*).

There is even less room for doubt in the case of unbalanced wooden stocks with leaden cores. Several pairs of such leads are known whose two parts have different lengths and weights; not seldom these are so different that an unbalanced stock must have been intended. Both the pairs of lead fillings from the Kyrenia wreck may be cited as typical specimens found in a clear-cut and unmistakable context (Fig. 8; see above, p. 384. Precise drawings of these leads will be published by the excavator, M. L. Katzev).

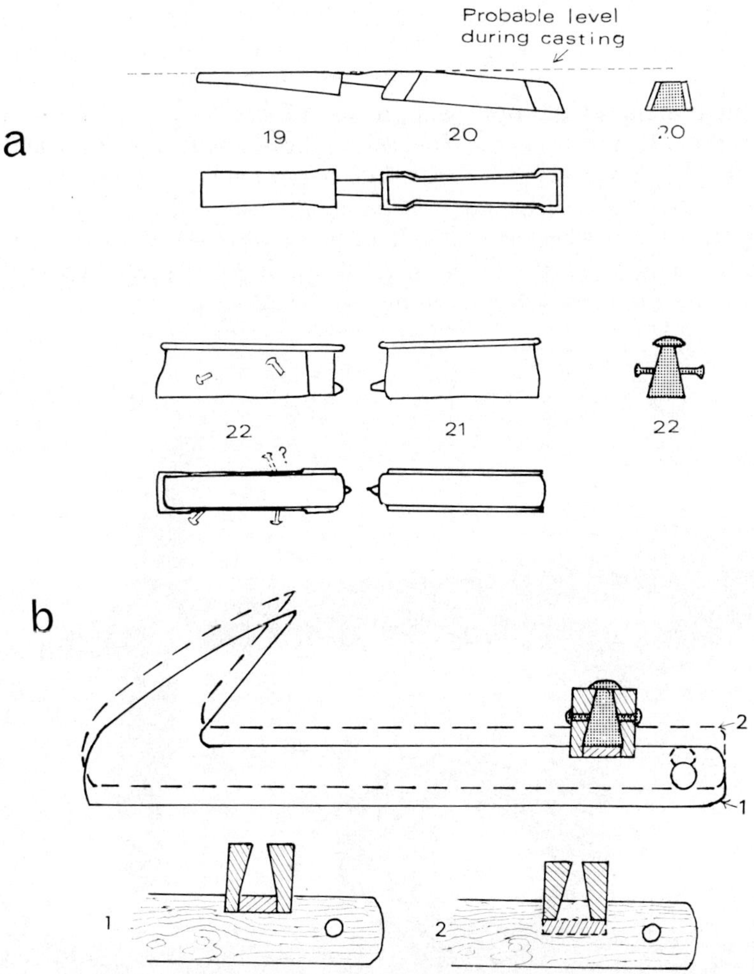

Figure 8. Sketches showing (*a*) profiles and sections of the two pairs of leaden fillings found in the Greek wreck off Kyrenia, Cyprus (rough sketch based on some measurements and photographs provided by courtesy of M. L. Katzev; scale 1 : 15); (*b*) the presumed position of the anchor during the casting of the leaden cores 21 and 22 from the Kyrenia wreck, and two suggested reconstructions of how the boards of the stock were attached to the shank.

I am inclined to believe that lead-filled wooden stocks and stone stocks were quite commonly used with single-armed anchors. On the other hand, the use of asymmetrical massive lead stocks on one-armed anchors seems to have been rather restricted. Why was this?

An experiment which I conducted perhaps gives the answer. I have tested a model of a single-armed anchor provided with an assembly-piece like that found at Brindisi and a detachable lead stock of the shape described (Fig. 9). This model was built approximately to a scale of 1 : 4. The test was carried out in water only 1 m deep, corresponding to a depth of 4 m for a small anchor of natural size. Hence the test conditions could be considered rather difficult, as the anchor had a very short distance in which to sink and land in the proper position. When thrown with the arm ahead or swung out on its line, the model settled in almost the right way; in several series of such throws the positive result was 90–95%. If, however, the model was thrown with the stock ahead, it often fell on its back, and almost every time the line became fouled around the stock. When the model was lowered slowly hanging on its line, it was still more certain to settle in the right way. If ever it fell on its back, it turned easily into the required position as soon as the line was lifted a little. Under natural conditions the rope would move in this way when kept fairly taut from a boat riding on the swell.

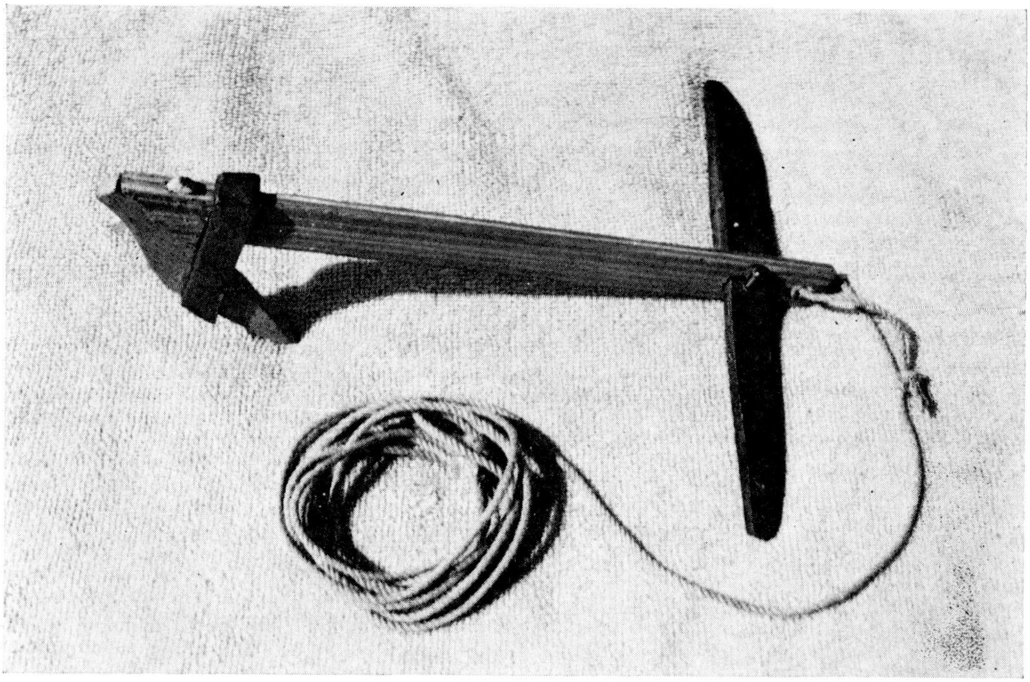

Figure 9. Model of the wooden one-armed anchor equipped with assembly-piece and detachable lead stock, used for experiments.

The model, however, had a certain defect. For it to work efficiently in the tests, the shank had to be kept relatively short, or, to put it another way, the stock had to be longer than it would usually be for an anchor of this size. First experiments on dry land with a stock 2 cm shorter had given a far less satisfactory result. If we look again at the sketches of the distribution of weight (Fig. 5) we can understand the problem: the imbalance is small in the model because the detachable stock is not fixed on one side of the shank, but inserted through the axis. Moreover, the assembly-piece works as a counterbalance. I have tested the same leaden model stock on another, slightly longer anchor model without assembly-piece. On dry land this arrangement works even more efficiently; in water the results depend also on the precise weight of the wooden parts.

As a result, it seems that the employment of solid lead parts on single-armed anchors could not have been very advantageous. The unbalanced detachable stock produces a comparatively small effect. A fixed lead stock attached laterally to the shank has yet to be found; it would have been possible if formed without the usual box but, like a stone stock, with a simple notch.[7] However, there could have been no cogent reason to use lead for such a type. A fixed lead stock attached to one side of the shank by means of a box would be technically almost impossible; the box would inevitably break by reason of the unbalanced weight situation. The box was the weak point on the two-armed anchor, as we have learned from numerous broken pieces. Because it is a soft metal, lead is obviously not suited for forming into heavy pieces of unbalanced shape.

Summarizing, I think that the following preliminary conclusions are possible: the one-armed anchor was known in antiquity, but was probably used preponderantly in an early period together with stone stocks or with filled wooden stocks; it is likely to have been almost abandoned on seagoing ships when anchor stocks of massive lead became very common; it must, however, have been retained for use on small vessels, such as fishing-boats, with perhaps some attempt to apply solid lead fittings to this type.

ACKNOWLEDGEMENTS

I am much indebted to the excavator of the Kyrenia wreck, Prof. Michael L. Katzev, for data and photographs of the leads from this wreck and the kind permission to cite them here, though they have not yet been published in an excavation report. I am indebted also to Sig. Gaetano Chiaramento of Syracuse, who kindly constructed the model of a single-armed anchor for me.

REFERENCES

Benoit, F. 1952 L'archéologie sous-marine en Provence. *RivStLig*, **18**, 237–307.

Benoit, F. 1955 Jas d'ancre et pièces d'outillages des épaves de Provence. *RivStLig*, **21**, 117–28.

Benoit, F. 1958 Nouvelles épaves de Provence. *Gallia*, **16**, 5–39.

Benoit, F. 1961 *Fouilles sous-marines. L'épave du Grand Congloué à Marseille* [*Gallia*, Suppl. XIV], 211 pp. Paris.

Braemer, F. & Marcadé, J. 1953 Céramique antique et pièces d'ancres trouvées en mer à la pointe de la Kynosoura (Baie de Marathon). *Bulletin dc Correspondance Hellénique*, **77**, 139–54.

Foerster, F. 1969 Un ancla romana de hierro. *CRIS*, *Revista de la Mar*, No. 122 (May 1969), 22–3.

Frost, H. 1970 Bronze Age Stone-anchors from the Eastern Mediterranean. *Mariner's Mirror*, **56**, 377–94.

Kapitän, G. 1967 Ein wichtiger Fund in Syrakus. *Delphin*, **14** No. 7, 6–7; **14** No. 8, 21–2.

Kapitän, G. 1968*a* A new type of ancient anchor stock. *Archaeology*, **21**, 63.

Kapitän, G. 1968*b* Der Ankerfund von Syrakus. Zur Frage der Datierung des bleigefüllten hölzernen Ankerstocks . . . . *Delphin*, **15** No. 3, 14–16, 32.

Kapitän, G. 1971 New Evidence of Ancient Anchors. *Archaeology*, **24**, 52–3.

Kapitän, G. (forthcoming) Some ancient anchors and plummets in the National Maritime Museum, Haifa. *Sefunim*, **3–4**.

Kapitän, G. (in press) Rinvenimento di un'ancora del tipo a ceppo smontabile all' Isola Lunga (Marsala). *Atti del IV Congresso Int. di Archeologia sottomarina, Nice 1970*. [See *Sicilia Archeologica*, No. 16 (Dec. 1971) 13–22].

[7] Last year there was a report of the discovery of such a lead stock by an Italian diver, and a sketch of the piece with a few measurements was published in *Mondo Sommerso*, **12**, No. 4 (April 1970), 487; the find is still on the sea floor.

Lamboglia, N. 1964 La campagna 1963 sul relitto di Punta Scaletta all'Isola di Giannutri (Relazione preliminare). *RivStLig*, **30**, 229–57.
Magon, L. 1894 Essai de reconstitution de l'ancre du Musée d'archéologie de Marseille. *RA*, 1894.II, 220–30.
Martin Avila, G. & Saludes, J. 1966 Hallazgos arqueológicos submarinos en la zone de El Saler (Valencia). *Archivo de Prehistoria Levantina*, **11**, 155–69.
Moll, F. 1929 Ein Bleianker. *Archäologischer Anzeiger*, **44**, 266–72.
Owen, D. I. 1971. Excavating a Classical Shipwreck. *Archaeology*, **24**, No. 2 (April 1971), 118–29.
Pallarés, F. 1971 Tipologia y cronologia preliminar de las anclas antiguas. *Atti del III Congresso Int. di Archeologia sottomarina, Barcellona 1961*, 384–93. Bordighera.
Rohlfs, G. 1963 *Antikes Knöchelspiel im einstigen Grossgriechenland*, 24 pp. Tübingen.
Torr, C. 1894 *Ancient Ships*, 139 pp. Cambridge. [Reprinted Chicago, 1964].
Tusa, V. 1961 Ricerche archeologiche sottomarine sulla costa nord-occidentale della Sicilia. *Atti del II Congresso Int. di Archeologia sottomarina, Albenga 1958*, 73–9. Bordighera.
Tusa, V. 1971 I rinvenimenti archeologici nella Sicilia Nord-Occidentale. *Atti del III Congresso Int. di Archeologia sottomarina, Barcellona 1961*, 263–95. Bordighera.
Ucelli, G. 1950 *Le Navi de Nemi*, 416 pp. Rome.
van Doorninck, F. H. 1967 *The Byzantine Shipwreck at Yassı Ada*, Univ. of Pennsylvania Dissertation.
van Nouhuys, J. W. 1951. The Anchor, *Mariner's Mirror*, **37**, 17–47.

Bulletin 1880 *Bulletin de la Société Nationale des Antiquaires de France*, 1880, 85–6.

POSTSCRIPT

by G. Kapitän

In 1972 I saw in France two other assembly-pieces with two holes only. They are of approximately the same shape as the one from Brindisi (above, p. 387), but somewhat larger in size. One is in the Musée de Docks Romains at Marseille (No. 6404); the other, found recently at the Presqu'Ile de St Tropez, has been acquired by M. J.-P. Joncheray of Fréjus, who kindly allowed me to study it.

Discussion

Green Could you comment on the finding of these lead stocks in pairs?
Kapitän They are probably the kind that are made in two pieces.

Throckmorton Your model asymmetric anchor is fine except for the way in which the cable is attached. When I was a child in the Far East we used similar anchors. The cable was attached at the crown; then it passed through a loop of rope coming from the top of the shank. Geared like this, the fluke always engaged itself on the bottom.

Swiny Have you found in Sicily any tips for the flukes of an anchor made of bronze or any other metal? And if so, are they dated?
Kapitän No. On the anchor found at Isola Lunga there was neither any metal, nor any trace of holes by which metal might have been attached to the tips of the arms, but I think metal-tipped arms must have existed.
Swiny They were found on the fifth-century B.C. ship in the Straits of Messina. The tips for the flukes were made of bronze and were well preserved (Owen, 1971, 126–7).
Kapitän There was a similar find in France, but I can't remember where; all that remained of the iron tips to the arms were concretions.

Anchors, the potsherds of marine archaeology: on the recording of pierced stones from the Mediterranean

by

HONOR FROST

INTRODUCTION

A GENERAL principle is difficult to communicate, especially in terms that are equally meaningful to archaeologists and to amateurs who also dive; yet without such exchanges marine archaeology will progress on a very superficial level.

To the archaeologist, anchors and other pierced stones found on the seabed are comparable with potsherds, because both serve as evidence in systems of deduction. On land, the sherds which an archaeologist picks up lead him to excavate a particular patch of ground, because to his trained eye they showed that antiquities of a certain period are probably buried there. Once his excavation has begun, he studies more sherds from all the occupation levels through which he digs. From these he assesses the differing degrees of culture and the trade relations of the civilizations in question, and he also deduces their dates. The discovery of a beautiful pot is a welcome bonus, but it is not the search for such museum objects that makes archaeologists study sherds, nor is the collecting of objects their main motive for digging.

In the sea there is, as yet, no equivalent routine. Divers are only faintly aware of one discipline; they realize that archaeologists can date wrecks from amphorae, on the basis of a typology painstakingly built up over the years. Today, the responsiblity for amassing an equivalent corpus of information on submarine finds devolves on divers.

REGISTERING AND RECORDING CONTEXTS

The stone anchors which are my subject have neither value nor meaning except by function of their contexts; they therefore cannot adequately be recorded by non-diving scholars who are unable to see where they were found.

A *corpus ancorarum* would be well worth producing. One section would be made up of land finds, but, though of basic importance, it would be small by comparison with the list of submarine finds.

The significance of the land material is easy to explain. The dates and provenances of stone anchors from excavations, especially those from Bronze Age excavations in the Levant, can be established. It follows therefore that similar anchors found on the seabed can be interpreted as marking the passage of specific kinds of ancient ships.

The implications are considerable. On land, excavators will automatically register stone anchors found, in the same way as any other artifact on their site, by

1. a measured drawing showing the anchor in elevation and section (very important);
2. a photograph with a scale;
3. the weight of the stone in kilogrammes;
4. a description of its dressing and piercing (the tools used, etc.);
5. the name of the stone and a sample thereof, for analysis;
6. its provenance and context: that is, whether it was in a temple, tomb or stone-mason's workshop, and whether it had deliberately been set up as a sacred object, or merely been reused as building stone, etc.

Initially, anchors on the seabed should be registered in exactly the same way. This can be done without lifting the anchor, the weight of a known kind of stone being calculable from its measurable volume (as long as a sample has been taken to determine the density of the material). The diver's difficulties start with the description of the context.

By "marine context" I mean the nature of the bottom, together with its potential significance in relation to ancient navigation. For example, does the find-spot represent a now silted or submerged proto-harbour, or an occasional, natural anchorage? If the latter, what are the possible reasons why it was so used (for example, a landfall at the end of a long sea crossing, a watering-stop, etc.)? The relation of the find-spot to any Bronze Age site on land, especially one where imports and exports have been recorded, will also be significant.

At sea the most important category of site where quantities of pre-medieval anchors are found is the shallows where ships that could not sail against the wind were forced, by calms or contrary winds, to drop anchor and wait until they could resume course. They had to do this at places which modern shipping would avoid as dangerous: on shoals, or by rocks overhanging submarine cliffs, in fact at any point along their course where the depth was not too great for their anchor cables to reach.

Divers who record anchors must therefore know, or find out about, not only archaeology but also local geography (fishermen are good informants). Because too many variables are involved, it is impossible or at least difficult to produce a short questionnaire for the diver, like the "finds sheet" used on land. Ultimately, the recording of the full facts about a marine context will also depend on the diver's grasp of the archaeological questions which his evidence is intended to answer or illuminate.

NAUTICAL PROBLEMS WHICH LOST ANCHORS COULD SOLVE

There are many archaeological questions that can never be solved from land findings alone. One of them is the "nationalities" of the dominant Bronze Age sea powers. Excavators can no more deduce from imported pottery the nationality of the ships that carried it, than archaeologists 6,000 years from now could deduce the existence now of a fleet of Greek-owned tankers from the remains of petrol engines found in Europe, or from ruined oil-wells in Arabia. Theoretically this sort of information could be got from excavation of wrecks; in practice Bronze Age wrecks are unlikely to be either found or excavated in sufficient number to produce statistically significant results at least in our lifetime, whereas the number of anchors lost at sea by ancient ships appears to be inexhaustible. A count of twenty-third-century B.C. Byblian, Ugaritic and Egyptian anchor types off any part of the Levant coast would, for instance, give us a good idea as to which of the three powers possessed most ships at that period.

Another nautical question which, paradoxically, grows more obscure as marine archaeology progresses is the attribution of a wreck to a place of construction. Now that ancient hulls are accessible and their carpentry is being studied, archaeologists find that they have less grounds for distinguishing between the build of a Phoenician and of a Greek ship than they had when they knew only formalized representations on gemstones, coins, sculpture and the like. This is because cargo provides evidence for ports of call, but never for a shipyard or port of origin. Again one of the most likely clues to a wreck's origin would be its identifiable anchors.

In a wider sense, lost stone anchors, like clues in a paper-chase, both mark the sea-lanes of antiquity and hint at the navigational habits of ancient seafarers. The question of whether early ships habitually sailed at night could, for instance, be answered if the anchors found on a site such as Lara Point in Cyprus (marked in the *Mediterranean Pilot* as the landfall for ships sailing from Rhodes) were predominantly of Aegean type. If, for good measure, the corresponding landfall in Rhodes produced Levantine-type anchors, the conclusion would be that the ships that made this long sea crossing could not have avoided night sailing. Unfortunately what usually happens to anchors on such sites is that, over the years, they are removed by different groups of divers, very often without being registered. Some anchors end up in private gardens and garages, a few in museum courtyards, but with the provenance usually lost by that time. Occasionally, and at best, the visiting specialist may be able to find out that one anchor was found by a Mr. so-and-so, on 4 June, in 6 m of water, near the town of . . . . When, as is preferable, an anchor has been photographed and left on the bottom, it is rare to find that a scale has been included in the picture, or that a sample of its stone has been taken. Size, weight and context remain obscure, but at least no information will have been lost to posterity.

Despite destruction by sporting amateurs and student expeditions, anchor evidence has already explained some nautical puzzles. For instance, the existence of nineteenth-century B.C. half-ton anchors at Ugarit (and in the sea) proved that a number of Bronze Age ships were far larger than hitherto supposed—so large, indeed, that they would have been unbeachable. As a corollary, a few major proto-harbours must have existed along the shelterless Levant coast, in order to have ensured trading by such large vessels. The deduction is interesting, in view of the paucity of dating evidence for the rock-cut harbour installations at such important sites as Arwad, Sidon, Tyre and Pharos.

THE ACCESSIBILITY AND DIFFUSION OF RECORDS

Such is the variety of problems that could be solved if anchors were recorded meaningfully and in sufficient number to allow statistical analysis. It is at this point that gatherings of divers usually vote pious resolutions about founding central archives in the Mediterranean. But the machinery for communicating archaeological findings, whether about potsherds or pierced stones, already exists.

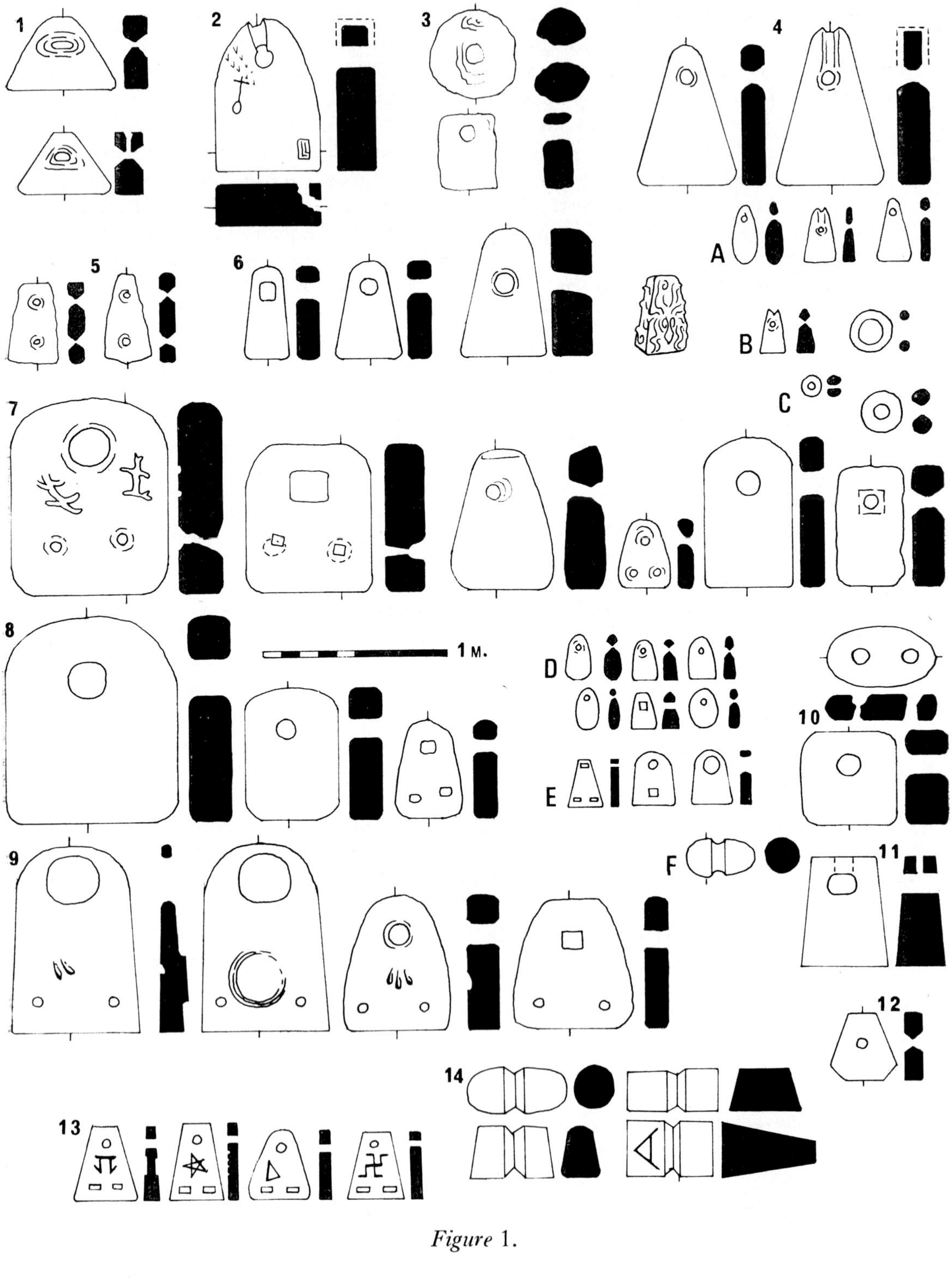

Figure 1.

Figure 1. The drawings on this table have been simplified so as to stress typological differences: e.g. damaged anchors of known shape and date have been shown as unbroken. Similarly, for ease of comparison, datings are based on excavators' estimates and current chronologies (excavation levels having been published elsewhere, see references). The groupings are numbered according to geographical provenance, while tackle is similarly identified, but by letters. Within these groups, specimens are commented upon from left to right, with the exception of 1 and 10, which read from top to bottom.

1. MALTA: (top) Ta Hajarat Temple, *c.* 3000 B.C., coralline limestone, 56 kg; (below) Tarxien Temple, *c.* 2200–2000 B.C., limestone (globigerina), 43.26 kg. Both in the National Museum, Valletta. Note the intercommunicating piercings; as yet no anchors of this date have been found in the sea around Malta.

2. EGYPT: inscribed with the hieroglyph NFR (meaning: perfect, good, beautiful); excavated in the "Sacred Enclosure", Byblos, 2200 B.C., limestone, 188.5 kg (Beirut National Museum). An uninscribed, but otherwise identical specimen was found near the Temple of Baal at Ugarit. The L-shaped piercing through one corner of the base was probably intended for a supplementary rope.

3. LHOTAL (India): two of the seven anchors excavated by Dr. S. R. Rao, *c.* 2000–1900 B.C. (personal communication).

4. BYBLOS (Lebanon): (i) one of two anchors found upright among votive obelisks and a stela dedicated to Rescheph, in a nineteenth-century B.C. Amorite chapel adjoining the main Temple of the Obelisks; limestone, estimated weight 30 kg. (ii) Excavated on a sixteenth-century, post-Hyksos wall surrounding the cella of the same temple; this cella was also filled with obelisks, and the anchor had probably fallen from among them; limestone, estimated weight 60 kg.

This isosceles triangle with a single apical piercing is typically Byblian, accounting for 9 out of the 28 anchors found there. The remainder were more roughly hewn, but none had more than one piercing and all were of medium weight, i.e. under 100 kg.

5. PANTELLERIA: excavated by Paolo Orsi at the end of the last century in a *capanna* which, by current datings, would be attributed to the second half of the second millennium; made of volcanic *tufa*, the anchors probably weigh *c.* 20 kg.

6. CRETE: (i) & (ii) excavated at Mallia by A. Dessenne, in a stonemason's workshop; nineteenth century B.C., local sandstone, estimated weight 25 and 40 kg. (iii) excavated on the same site, in an unidentified building of *c.* 1750 B.C., by O. Pelon; local sandstone, estimated weight 60 kg. (iv) found by Sir Arthur Evans in the Treasury of the Palace of Minos, seventeenth century B.C. Decorated with an octopus in bas-relief, the stone has been described as porphyrite (Evans) or breccia (Marinatos); probable weight 40 kg. Heraklion Museum.

Few anchors have as yet been found in Crete, so that no clear typology emerges; in view of theories about a "Minoan Thalassocracy", more evidence is urgently needed.

7. UGARIT (Syria): (i)–(iv) all from the Temple of Baal. (i) is inscribed with signs from an unidentified "Aegean-type" script; made of conglomerate, it weighs 700 kg; the piercings are conic-cupular in section. (ii) white limestone, 500 kg; the rope-hole is squared by chisel, the fluke-holes are pierced with a bow-drill, but squared on one face. (iii) black basalt, 160 kg. (iv) white limestone, estimated weight 25 kg. The

temple was in use between the nineteenth and thirteenth centuries B.C. Prof. C. F. A. Schaeffer has suggested that the anchors belong to the nineteenth-century level; this is uncertain in the case of the half-ton specimens, which were found before his excavation. (v) one of an identical pair flanking the dromos leading to a tomb used first in the late nineteenth and again in the late fifteenth centuries B.C. (Prof. Schaeffer attributes the anchors to the earlier use); local chalk, estimated weight 100 kg. (vi), from the port town of Ugarit, founded in the fourteenth and destroyed in the thirteenth century B.C., white limestone, 100 kg.

At first sight, the Ugaritic anchors appear to be too varied in shape to allow an overall classification; certain characteristics do, however, distinguish them from other groups: many piercings are either square-cut or cupular in section (i.e. a stone bit having been mounted on the point of a wooden bow-drill); some anchors are composite (i.e. with fluke-holes at either side of the base); the stones are generally squatter and thicker than at Byblos; and, as already observed, there are several half-ton anchors, more than twice as heavy as the largest Byblian anchors.

8. KITION (Cyprus): these three anchors are from a group (still *in situ* when recorded) that was excavated on a late thirteenth-century B.C. level where they had been reused as building stone; they may therefore be earlier, though they are unlikely to antedate the foundation of the town in the fourteenth century B.C. Made of conglomerate, local white limestone and sandstone respectively; though as yet unweighed, the largest is evidently a half-tonner. All have affinities with the Ugaritic shapes, but the Cypriot anchors are characterised by the regularity of their piercings.

9. HALA SULTAN TEKKE (Cyprus): (i) is of the indigenous "basket shape": narrow in section and tapering towards the top, broad in elevation with an unfunctionally large rope-hole. All three anchors were found at the base of the sea-wall surrounding this unexcavated port site. Nos. (i) and (ii) bear incised signs from a Cypro-Minoan syllabary not used earlier than the fourteenth century B.C. The sandstone, "basket-shaped" anchor had, in addition, a raised disk on one face; being fragmentary, this anchor was unweighed. The other two (limestone) anchors weighed 118.34 and 84.3 kg respectively.

10. MOTYA (Sicily): the contexts of these anchors, found during the earliest excavations, are not known, but the anchors probably antedate the destruction of this Phoenician colony by Dionysius of Syracuse in 398 B.C. There is a parallel at Byblos for the two-holed net-weight or anchor; unfortunately the Byblian example was also found out of context. Modern versions of the shape are associated with fishing rather than navigation.

11. SWANSEA: from the defensive bank surrounding an Iron Age enclosure at Kilvey Hill (1.2 km from the river Tawe and a natural harbour); local red sandstone, *c.* 25 kg. I am obliged to Mr. Bernard Morris for personally communicating this information.

12. PIRAEUS: a typical example of the shape of the anchors dredged up from Pasha (Zea) Limani, the traditional site of the Athenian trireme fleet; now in the Maritime Museum at Piraeus. Note the intercommunicating piercings, presumably to take double cables.

13. AGDE (Hérault, France): all made of the same local volcanic stone, these medieval anchors weigh some 20 kg. The signs which they bear have been identified as mason's marks by M. Aris, of the Adge Museum, from others which he found

in the eleventh- to thirteenth-century structure of the local cathedral (mason's marks from the nearby cathedral of St. Gilles also appear on anchors). The first three anchors are in the Agde Museum, the fourth in the Béziers Museum.

14. AMBONNE (Hérault, France): examples of a large group of stones, probably net-weights rather than anchors, found on a wreck by M. Bouscaras of Béziers, who suggests that they were made at Ambonne; of the same local stone as the Agde anchors, they are surprisingly heavy, weighing as much as 40 kg (personally communicated).

LINE-WEIGHTS AND TACKLE

A. BYBLOS: found out of context on the excavation, but since the shapes are miniature versions of Bronze Age anchors it can be assumed that they too are of Bronze Age date; the average weight is 6 kg.

B. CRETE: (i) Myrtos (excavated by G. Cadogan in 1970), possibly 1500 B.C. (ii) "messenger" stones (used to free fouled ropes) as found at Mallia. See also Discussion.

C. UGARIT: net-weight and "messenger" from the area of the Temple of Baal. See also Discussion.

D. ENKOMI (Cyprus): the town not having been rebuilt after the eleventh century, these otherwise undated miniature anchors are certainly of Bronze Age date.

E. APOSTOLOS ANDREAS BAY (Cyprus): some twenty of these set-long-line-weights were found *in situ* on a fishing-ground.

F. BYBLOS (Hellenistic level): a typical egg-shaped line-weight of the type also used in Old Kingdom Egypt, *c.* 2560 B.C.

Throughout the Mediterranean permission from the host country is needed for either surveying or excavation. A condition of such permits is that findings be deposited with the Antiquities Department in question; there they will always be available for inspection by local archaeologists and visiting scholars. In addition, most Departments produce Reports or Bulletins and it is an accepted courtesy that foreign expeditions should supply these with material for publication, such as a list of anchor finds.

British expeditions, when aided by university or public money, should produce a few facts at the end of a season for their sponsors. If each expedition that had asked for the blessing of the Council for Nautical Archaeology had, in return, produced a register of anchor finds, we might now be publishing the first volume of a *corpus*! Further, there is no lack of British archaeological journals covering the Mediterranean area: for example, those of the British Schools at Rome, Athens, Ankara and Jerusalem; none refuse good articles. The pages of *The Mariner's Mirror* have always been open to research on nautical history. Now, an even more specialized outlet exists in the newly founded *International Journal of Nautical Archaeology* (the first number to be published next year by Seminar Press for the Council for Nautical Archaeology), for which notes, queries and short reports, as well as long articles, are needed.

May I add that personally communicated records of individual anchors are always welcome as additions to my own card index, which, in return, might provide finders with identifications.

WHEN IS A PIERCED STONE NOT AN ANCHOR?

At this juncture, the "how" and the "why" of recording are a more urgent topic of discussion than details of anchor shapes. It would also be repetitious to summarize the important groups of dated anchors from Ugarit, Byblos and Kition, together with many ungrouped but identified anchors from places as far apart as Agde in France and Alexandria in Egypt, for they have already been published (representative specimens are illustrated in Fig. 1). Instead, and with recording in mind, I add some remarks on the less well-defined pierced stones.

Obviously any pierced stone found under water warrants recording, because it would not be in the sea if it did not have some nautical association. On shore sites, however, pierced stones have other known uses: as sockets for door-posts, tethering-posts for animals, mooring-stones, torch-holders, counter-weights for olive-presses (from the Hellenistic period on), etc.; the position being less clear, such objects should, when possible, be published in groups. This is because many stones, after becoming obsolete as anchors, were reused for other purposes. It is not unusual to find a well known fifteenth-century type of anchor serving some different purpose in a thirteenth-century B.C. level. The reverse is also possible: I have seen olive-pressweights at the bottom of the sea; they must have been snatched up on land in an emergency by some ship's captain who had lost his anchor.

WEIGHT AND DATE

Pierced stones at either extreme of the weight range, wherever they are found, are the easiest to date and identify; they are consequently the most significant, but (particularly on land) they are often cast aside. Not fitting in with preconceived notions, they are considered to be too big or too small to have served as anchors. Anchor-stones that are too heavy for one man to handle (i.e. in the 50–700 Kg range) will, however, almost certainly antedate the introduction of metal and wooden anchors during the Iron Age. Once lead-stocked anchors became current on all important craft, stones became the poor man's anchor and, since the poor man had a small boat, the size of stone anchors diminished accordingly; ones of the smaller sizes are very numerous.

Anchors in the 20 Kg range, which can be handled by one man, are still used and manufactured throughout the Mediterranean. Similar stones served until quite recently as net-weights in certain forms of fishing. They also carried sponge-divers to the bottom, though for obvious reasons diver's stones were rarely lost on the seabed. It follows that anchors within this weight range are almost impossible to date unless they are of exceptionally distinctive shape, or happen to be inscribed, or are associated with identifiable artifacts on the seabed.

At the opposite extreme of the weight range, miniature anchors of some 6 Kg are almost certain to date from the Bronze Age, when set-long-line-weights were often miniature replicas of contemporary anchor shapes; consequently such stones are often found in groups on the seabed. Fishing by means of a line whereon weights alternate with baited floats is still practised, but modern fishermen use any conveniently shaped or naturally pierced pebble. The miniature anchors have been found in dated contexts along the Levant cost and in Crete, but egg-shaped line-weights also appear to have been used in the third millenium B.C. in Egypt: they appear in a bas-relief showing a fishing-boat, on the Sixth-Dynasty Mastaba of Akhetep in the Louvre. Similar egg-shaped stones, with an encircling belt-like groove for lodging the rope, occur at Byblos, but in Hellenistic levels.

It has been suggested that some of the 6 Kg conical miniature anchors could have been sounds, because they are superficially of much the same shape and size as classical lead sounds, but I have yet to see one with the concave base characteristic of Mediterranean sounds, or holes for putting in grease. The suggestion is, however, worth keeping in mind; the only Bronze Age sounds at present known are those on Egyptian model boats, and these are lozenge-shaped. A variety of other stone tackle, such as the quoit-shaped "messengers" (still used by fishermen for disentangling ropes), has been found in the sea and excavated in datable contexts on land. All would contribute to the understanding of nautical history, and a great deal of research is still needed. But first the objects must be meaningfully recorded.

REFERENCES

Catling, H. W. & Nikolaou, K. 1967 Composite Anchors in Late Bronze Age Cyprus. *Antiquity*, **42**, 225–9.

Frost, H. 1963*a* *Under the Mediterranean*, 278 pp. London.

Frost, H. 1963*b* From Rope to Chain: on the development of the anchor in the Mediterranean. *Mariner's Mirror*, **49**, 1–20.

Frost, H. 1969*a* The Stone-anchors of Byblos. *Mélanges de l'Univ. St.-Joseph, Beyrouth*, **45**, 425–42.

Frost, H. 1969*b* The Stone-anchors of Ugarit, in *Ugaritica* VI [Mission archéologique de Ras Shamra, Tome XVII] 235–45. Paris.

Frost, H. 1970*a* Some Cypriot stone-anchors from land sites and from the sea. *Report of the Dept. of Antiquities, Cyprus*, 1970, 14–24.
Frost, H. 1970*b* Bronze-Age Stone-anchors from the Eastern Mediterranean: dating and identification. *Mariner's Mirror*, **56**, 377–94.
Frost, H. 1970*c* Stone-anchors as Indications of Early Trade Routes, *in* Mollat, M. (ed.) *Sociétés et Compagnies de Commerce en Orient et dans l'Ocean indien* [Actes du 8ième Colloque International d'Histoire Maritime, Beirut 1966] 55–61. Paris.
Moll, F. 1927 The history of the anchor. *Mariner's Mirror*, **13**, 293–332
van Nouhuys, J. W. 1951 The Anchor. *Mariner's Mirror*, **37**, 17–47

Discussion

Frost We must be very grateful to Jeremy Green for his group of recorded anchors; archaeologists must now get on with considering them. I agree with Peter Throckmorton that we must study the people still actually involved with sailing: stone anchors are still in use in native boats in the Mediterranean.

Green As you said, we do not know much about Bronze Age ships. That is why I suggested in my paper that we should experiment with dummy stone anchors to find out how much they dragged, because from this we could determine the size of Bronze Age ships.

Frost I disagree. I take your point and I have often said myself that half-ton Bronze Age stone anchors (which would obviously sink a fishing-boat) prove the existence of ships of at least 200 tons; more detailed deductions of this kind would, however, be misleading, because it is the way these anchors were and are used that matters.

Green I agree that these stone anchors may hold on a rock bottom, but what about sand?

Frost I repeat that you must learn from primitive sailors who still use them. There are two kinds of stone anchor: the one- and the three-holed (which have two wooden flukes so that they can be used on either sand or rock). Today Mediterranean fishermen put their ears to the bottom of the boat and listen for the "swish" or the "clicks" which tell them whether they are over sand or rock; then they anchor accordingly.

Green You are here talking about modern fishing-boats with engines, which have the ability at any time to sail into the wind or extract themselves from nasty situations. My question is whether Bronze Age ships had the ability to choose the places where they anchored in unfavourable situations.

Frost I too was thinking of boats without engines. Mediterranean seamen catch fish and pick sponges in calm weather when they do not mind the anchor dragging a little. If a squall blows up, or the anchor gets caught, they cut it loose. If a sailing boat is *forced* to anchor by a contrary wind, they may deploy several anchors (they carry more than one) so as to hold better. But their main preoccupation is always to know what kind of bottom they are on. For this reason they also depend on soundings. They put fat, such as lard, in the hollow bottom of the sound, and then examine the mud particles, sand, rock-scratches, weed, etc., that show on it. We have even found wrecks in this way by the traces of pottery on the sound.

Parker May I ask you to define the "marine context" of anchors.

Frost My point is that this is difficult to define. The man on the spot has to find out whether he is looking at an offshore shallow where ships that could not sail against the wind were forced to anchor, or a fishing-ground, or a sheltered mooring, or a wreck-site (where the ship may be covered with sand from which only the anchors protrude), and so on.

Parker I think that what you are asking from divers is not recording but interpretation. It should be sufficient for the diver to record the find-spot.
Frost I disagree. Jeremy Green has recorded a lost-anchor-site in such a way that it can be interpreted without the interpreter having to go there himself. Up to now, and at best, I have only seen marks on Admiralty Charts and descriptions of landmarks, etc. These tell someone in London absolutely nothing. It is easier for the person who has just found an anchor either to survey the area, or, by making enquiries locally, to find out the nature of the site.

Marsh Has any attempt ever been made to apply statistical analysis to the anchors which you have in your card index?
Frost I am constantly doing this, but it would be premature to publish these deductions before I have a statistically significant number of well-recorded underwater anchor-sites. The main aim of my index is to provide a typology, based on dated anchors from land sites, which will enable us to interpret the submarine finds.
Marsh Have you ever compared weight against depth, in order to discover what sort of anchors were used on certain types of bottom and depth?
Frost It would be simpler to ask fishermen. All would depend on the size of the ship that lost the anchor. On the offshore, shallows type of site the anchors which one sees range from 20 Kg to half a ton. Weight bears little relation to loss; in an emergency anything would be thrown overboard.
Marsh If statistical methods were used to compare these groups some kind of pattern might emerge.
Frost So far the records which you made with Jeremy Green are unique. If everyone turned out records like that, we could start on statistics. Furthermore, to apply statistical methods the records have to be absolutely accurate and even yours may not be—as Green said yesterday, one man in a line of swimmers may well be thinking of other things and miss small, half-buried anchors. The *smaller* sizes will always be more camouflaged by time on any bottom.
Marsh The virtue of statistics is surely that one can get some information out of incomplete data.
Frost I do, of course, have some information, but up to now I do not think there is enough to make analyses any good.

Davison You have suggested that one can identify the nationality of a ship from its anchor, but is it not possible that a ship could have picked up an anchor in a foreign port?
Frost Ships carried a complement of anchors, not just one. Further, we know that anchors were considered sacred during the Bronze Age. Of course "any port (or anchor) in a storm", but given half a chance, Bronze Age seamen would have been choosey about their replacements. Apollonius Rhodius tells how the Argonauts replaced an anchor (*Argonautica*, I. 950); the implication is that they carved it themselves to their own pattern.

Frost I should like to add an explanation which Throckmorton has given me for the quoit-shaped stones (my Fig. 1, B & C). He says that fishermen use the larger ones to attract fish. By leaning over the side and dragging the "quoit" quickly through the water, they produce a noise similar to that of a shoal of small fish; this, in turn, attracts the big fish. The explanation that I had been given by Cretan fishermen was that when their lines became entangled, they sent a quoit down one of the ropes to disentangle it from the rest. Both uses are possible.

Throckmorton says that the smaller "quoits" (about 12 cm in diameter) were used for catching groupers. Once hooked, a grouper will retreat into his hole, but if one of these stones is sent down over the line so that it hits him on the nose, he will straighten out so that he can be pulled out of the hole.

Ancore antiche nel Museo di Palermo

da

V. TUSA

SUMMARY

The anchor collection in the National Museum at Palermo is particularly interesting because of the richness of types and the great number of anchor-stocks with inscriptions and figured reliefs. Almost all these finds were made in the waters of Western Sicility, mainly on anchorages near Palermo. Unfortunately none is datable from context.

A complete catalogue is given of the stone anchors found, comprising fourteen pieces: primitive anchor-stones and stone anchors with holes; also four stone stocks from ancient wooden anchors. The anchor with stone stock is of a primitive type, perhaps following straight after the stone anchors and before the anchors with lead stocks (though continuing in use at the same time as the latter). In the second group are nineteen selected lead anchor-stocks, belonging to four different main types of fixed and movable stocks:

(1) fixed stocks of squat proportions with a rectangular central box containing no fastening-device;
(2) fixed stocks with a rounded central box containing no fastening-device;
(3) fixed stocks with a rectangular central box containing a fastening-device;
(4) movable stocks.

Most of them have inscriptions or reliefs or both; those on stocks of type (1) are different from the rest, but it is not certain whether this is due to difference in date or in place of origin. The dating of a few inscriptions (on epigraphical criteria) is included in the descriptions, with explanation of typological peculiarities and discussion of the persons and deities named in the inscriptions. The iron anchors in the Museum's collection are not included in the discussion in in this paper; their condition does not allow adequate presentation.

Some more detailed technological considerations and conclusions are appended about differences in the shape and in the fastening-device in the central box of fixed lead stocks.

INTRODUZIONE

Il Museo Nazionale archeologico di Palermo possiede una considerevole raccolta di ancore antiche rinvenute da alcuni anni a questa parte lungo le coste della Sicilia Occidentale: costituiscono nel loro complesso una notevole testimonianza di questo aspetto della marineria antica, non solo per la varietà delle forme e per i particolari costruttivi ma anche, e direi soprattutto, per i simboli, le decorazioni e le iscrizioni che spesso recano.

Ne presentiamo quì alcune tra le più interessanti: di esse daremo tutte le notizie in nostro possesso, purtroppo però non abbiamo dati sufficienti per indicarne l'esatta cronologia. Esse infatti provengono tutte da rinvenimenti casuali fatti da varî sommozzatori locali[1] che, com'è noto, s'immergono principalmente per praticare lo sport

[1] Ricordo con la più viva simpatia alcuni di essi, che cito a caso, scusandomi per eventuali, involontarie omissioni: Enzo Sole, Fratelli Michelini, Sergio Rocca, Ubaldo Cipolla, Mario Savona, Vincenzo Paladino, Francesco Colosimo.

subacqueo: questo fatto, se può essere apprezzabile per l'aspetto agonistico e anche umano, non lo è certo per lo aspetto archeologico. Questo materiale quindi non è frutto di ricerche sistematiche, quali ci saremmo augurati di poter fare ma che purtroppo, per varie ragioni, non ci è stato possibile poter eseguire: trattandosi di rinvenimenti sporadici le notizie che si danno sui varî pezzi sono sempre poche e spesso aleatorie.

Forse non è superfluo che anche in questa sede io insista sull'opportunità, anzi sulla necessità ormai, che ci si attrezzi convenientemente per eseguire anche in acqua quelle ricerche sistematiche che eseguiamo sulla terra: le possibilità ci sono, bisogna soltanto che noi adeguiamo a questa esigenza la nostra mentalità anzitutto convincendoci che nessuna differenza esiste tra la archeologia terrestre e l'archeologia sottomarina.[2] L'archeologia sottomarina invece è pure, come dice la stessa parola, archeologia e, come tale, fa parte di questa disciplina, non è affatto un'altra; cambiano i mezzi di ricerca e, per così dire, i mezzi di comunicazione per giungere allo scavo; al posto della zappetta dello scavatore si dovrà usare qualche altro mezzo per togliere il fango accumulato nel relitto, ed invece di andare in macchina o a piedi sul luogo dello scavo bisogna andarci a nuoto. In realtà però il metodo di scavo deve essere lo stesso di quello che si pratica in superficie, identici i risultati che s'intendono trarre dallo scavo, identico il metodo di studio dei reperti. Per concludere queste parole introduttive dirò che dovrà essere questo il terzo tempo dell'archeologia sottomarina: dopo le scoperte puramente fortuite e occasionali, dopo le scoperte avvenute finora per ricerche eseguite senza alcun metodo archeologico ma con intenti sportivi, dobbiamo ora passare, se vogliamo rendere veramente proficua questa branca dell'archeologia, all'adozione del metodo dello scavo archeologico anche per i relitti marini: cosa che del resto è stata fatta da varî colleghi archeologi altrove (Spargi, Baia, etc.: Lamboglia, 1961, *a* & *b* & *c*; Tursini, 1971). Il mancato uso del metodo archeologico e quindi la mancanza di dati che si ricavano da uno scavo sistematico, ancor di più sentiamo per i reperti archeologici sottomarini del Museo di Palermo, data la loro grande importanza e, spesso, la loro singolarità: quanto sarebbero stati più interessanti se avessimo potuto corredarli con i normali dati di scavo!

CATALOGO

Il materiale che qui si presenta proviene tutto dal mare antistante le coste della Sicilia nord-occidentale, come specificheremo per ogni pezzo: le ancore che presentiamo sono di pietra o di piombo; non manca nella collezione del Museo qualche ancora di ferro, ma per lo stato in cui s'è rinvenuta, che non permette una presentazione adeguata, non si ritiene opportuno publicarla in questa sede.

Delle ancore di pietra presentiamo la raccolta completa esistente nel Museo di Palermo: questo facciamo perchè riteniamo che sia opportuno far conoscere oggi tutta la collezione dato l'incremento che allo studio di questo particolare tipo di ancora è stato dato in questi ultimi tempi per merito della dott.ssa Honor Frost.[3]

[2] Diolé (1953, 200) sostiene invece che "l'archeologia subacquea è una disciplina indipendente, avente leggi proprie e metodi di ricerca particolari." A me pare che questa affermazione contrasti con quello che lo stesso autore dice nello stesso capitolo sull'opportunità di ricerche sistematiche in mare e che pienamente condividiamo.

[3] Mi è particolarmente gradito in questa occasione esprimere il mio più vivo riconoscimento per la competenza, la serietà e l'impegno con cui Miss Honor Frost conduce il suo lavoro e che io ho avuto modo di sperimentare a Mozia: mi auguro che questa collaborazione con la Soprintendenza possa continuare proficuamente negli anni venturi. Della stessa studiosa cito qui i seguenti lavori relativi alle ancore di pietra: Frost, 1969*a* & *b*; 1970*a* & *b*.

A(I) *Ancore di pietra con un foro*

1) Grossa pietra informe con un foro (Fig. 1). Inv. n.3361.
Lunghezza cm.92, largh. mass. cm.56,5, spessore cm.18 circa, diametro del foro cm.16–19. Peso Kg.110.

Rinvenuta da Mario Savona nella acque di Isola delle Femine (PA) alla profondità di m.31, nel versante ovest dell'Isola, in posizione eretta, non incagliata, ma in una fenditura, nella stessa zona di ritrovamenti di elementi plumbei di ancore. Pietra calcarea porosa con erosioni varie. Presenta concrezioni sulla superficie e una patina grigiastra con chiazze bluastre. Si tratta forse del tipo più primitivo di ancora, senza voler dare alla parola "primitivo" un valore cronologico assoluto (Torr, 1964, 70 sgg.; Frost, 1963, 27 sgg.): non è escluso però che questo pezzo sia abbastanza antico. La stessa incertezza cronologica dimostra il Diolè che ce ne presenta un esemplare simile (1952, 244–5 e Tav. XVI); a due pezzi simili al nostro accenna F. Benoit (1952, 269).

Figura 1.

Il nostro pezzo presenta ai lati del foro, in senso diagonale, due avvallamenti causati in maniera molto chiara dall'uso, verosimilmente dallo sfregamento di corde; inoltre, lungo tutto lo spessore, corre una scanalatura per la quale passava certamente una corda.

Volendo tentare una ricostruzione (Fig. 2) ritengo che si debba pensare ad una lunga trave di legno passante attraverso il buco, tenuta stretta da funi, avanti e dietro, che passavano per quelle parti oggi avallate e quindi giravano attorno alla pietra entro la scanalatura dello spessore per poi ritornare nella trave e finire in alto con un anello di corda per il quale la pietra veniva issata e abbassata.

Il Museo di Palermo conserva altre ancore simili a questa, tutte ricostruibili per l'uso all'incirca allo stesso modo; se ne dà qui di seguito la descrizione e la documentazione fotografica.

2) Grossa pietra di forma quasi quadrangolare, con un foro verso il centro (Fig. 3). Inv. n.6903.

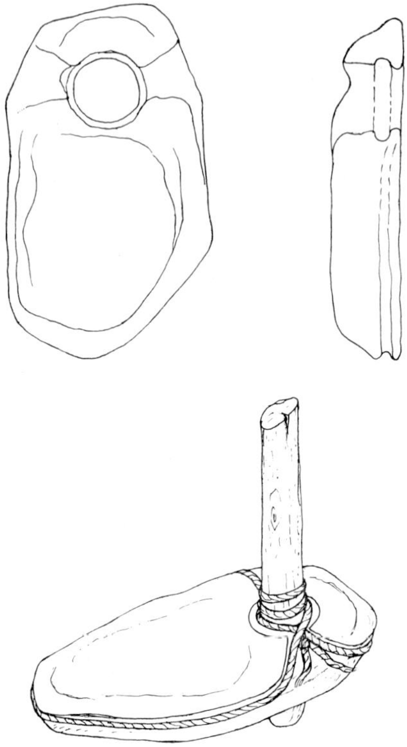

Figura 2. Rapporto 1 : 20.

Lunghezza cm.70, larghezza cm.55, spessore cm.21 circa, diametro del foro cm.12 circa. Peso Kg.90.
Pietra lavica con fitti e piccoli pori, di colore grigio scuro. È coperta da concrezioni biancastre con chiazze color grigiastro e ruggine.
Provenienza: come per l'ancora seguente (n.3).

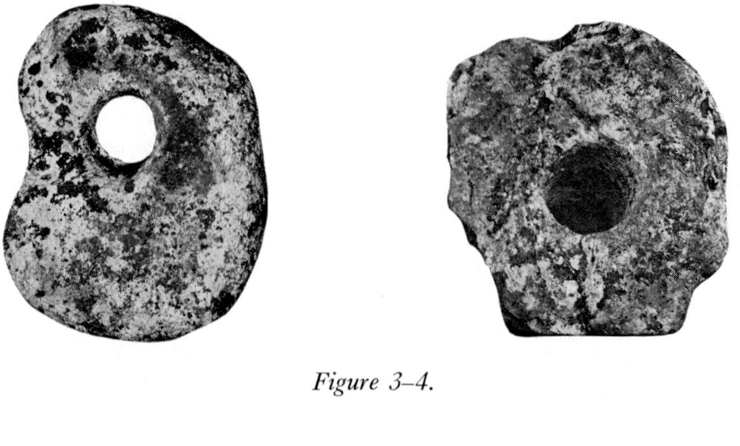

Figure 3–4.

3) Lastra informe di pietra calcarea con un foro verso la parte più stretta (Fig. 4). Inv. n.7265.
La parte terminale è definita a piano inclinato e levigata, per il resto della superficie presenta larghe scheggiature in più parti.
Lunghezza cm.61, larghezza cm.46, spessore cm.21 circa, diametro del foro cm.11 circa. Peso Kg.76.
Provenienza: ignota, è pervenuta al Museo a seguito di un sequestro effettuato dalla Guardia di Finanza presso la Dogana di Palermo su merce proveniente da Mazara del Vallo: di questa merce, oltre ad altri oggetti archeologici, faceva parte quest'ancora.

5 6 7

8 9

Figure 5–9.

4) Lastra di forma quasi piramidale, con un foro nella parte più stretta (Fig. 5). Inv. n.7266.
È una pietra biancastra, molto compatta. È rotta in tre punti e restaurata, presenta varie scheggiature.
Lunghezza cm.65, larghezza cm.60. Peso Kg.108.
Provenienza: come per l'ancora n.3.

o*

5) Lastra di pietra lavica quasi ovoidale, con foro praticato vicino all'orlo (Fig. 6). Inv. n.7191.
Lunghezza cm.45, larghezza cm.33 circa, spessore cm.18 circa; anche il foro è ovoidale ed ha le seguenti dimensioni: lunghezza cm.5, larghezza cm.3,5. Peso Kg.22.
È stata rinvenuta dai Sigg. C. Sacco e V. Sole nel giugno 1968, in località "Secca della Colombaia" nei pressi del'Isola di Ustica.

6) Lastra informe di pietra vulcanica porosa con un foro ad una estremità (Fig. 7). Inv. n.7324.
Lunghezza cm.52 circa, larghezza cm.41 circa, spessore cm.10 circa, diametro del foro cm.7 circa.
È molto abrasa specie alle estremità, presenta inoltre varî tratti coperti da concrezioni. Peso Kg.17.
È stata rinvenuta a m.50 circa dalla costa di Sferracavallo (ad Ovest di Palermo), dal sig. Vittorio Emanuele Cracchiolo, il 29 novembre 1968.

7) Lastra di pietra arrotondata con tendenza all'ovale e con un foro al centro (Fig. 8). Inv. n.3467.
Diametro cm.40–52,5, spessore cm.16 circa, diametro del foro cm.11.
È in buono stato di conservazione.
È stata rinvenuta da Enzo Sole nelle acque di Mondello (PA), alla profondità di m.25 circa, nclla zona "Gallo".

8) Frammento di ancora litica con foro centrale: è meno della metà di tutta l'ancora (Fig. 9). Inv. n.7267.
Si tratta di una lastra di pietra vulcanica dall'apparente forma triangolare con foro centrale passante.
Dimensioni: cm.60 × 33, spessore cm.11 circa, diametro del foro cm.18 circa.
La provenienza è ignota essendo pervenuta al Museo di Palermo da un sequestro eseguito a Mazara del Vallo.

A(II) *Ancore di pietra con due fori*

9) Grossa pietra calcarea quasi quadrangolare, con due fori (Figg. 10 e 11). Inv. n.5824.

Figure 10–11.

Lunghezza cm.41, larghezza max. cm.25, all'altezza del foro cm.16, spessore cm.15. Peso Kg. 12.
La superficie si presenta in parte compatta ed in parte coperta da pori più o meno grossi; presenta inoltre varie concrezioni biancastre e tracce di ruggine.
È stata rinvenuta nei pressi di Isola delle Femine (ad Ovest di Palermo) dai sigg. A. Nicitra e G. Armaforte.

Presenta due buchi, uno in basso, sulla fronte, ovale, l'altro circolare, in alto, lungo lo spessore. Volendo ricostruire la funzionalità di quest'ancora si può verosimilmente presumere che il foro ovale, sulla fronte, contenesse una trave di legno in funzione di marra, possibilmente appuntita, tale da rendere possibile il fissaggio sul fondo marino; nel foro praticato sullo spessore passava verosimilmente un'altra trave di legno cui doveva essere legata una fune per issare o abbassare l'ancora.

A(III) *Ancore di pietra con tre fori*

10) Lastra di pietra quasi quadrangolare, con tre fori (Fig. 12). Inv. n.3439.
Lunghezza cm.68,5, larghezza max. cm.51,5, spessore max. cm.13–14, diam. del foro grande cm.11 circa, dei fori piccoli cm.5,5 e 6,5. Peso Kg.60. Pietra calcarea compatta. È in parte coperta da concrezioni e da una patina chiara che si alterna con chiazze scure.
È stata rinvenuta da F. Colosimo nelle acque dell'Isola di Ustica, nei pressi di Punta Priola, a circa m.800 dalla costa, a m.26–27 di profondità.

Si presenta come una lastra di forma trapezoidale, ma arrotondata agli angoli; il foro più grande nella parte alta e più stretta serviva verosimilmente per l'attacco del cavo dell'ancora mentre i due più piccoli in basso contenevano pioli in legno in funzione di marre (Fig. 13; Bouscaras, 1964, Fig. 20; Benoit, 1961, 170 e Fig. 90). Si può anche pensare ad un altro modo di usare questo tipo di ancora: tre pioli di legno, sempre in funzione di marre, avrebbero attraversato i tre buchi riunendosi poi in un punto in cui sarebbe stata legata una fune per abbassare e sollevare l'ancora (Gargallo, 1961, 31 sgg., Fig. 1): per questa soluzione però non trova giustificazione il maggior diametro del buco in alto.

Figura 12.

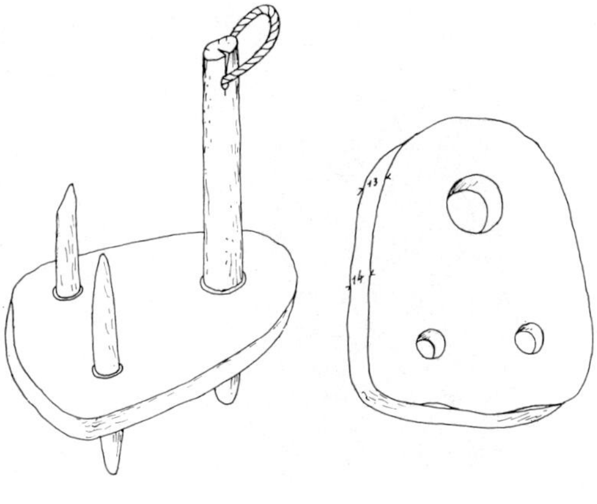

Figura 13. Rapporto 1 : 20.

Figure 14–15.

11) Lastra di pietra vulcanica con tre fori (Figg. 14 e 15). Inv. n.5825.
È lievemente porosa. Si presenta coperta da concrezioni biancastre con chiazze grigiastre.
Lunghezza cm.45, larghezza cm.29, spessore cm.11. Peso Kg.36.
È stata rinvenuta nelle acque di Palermo, verso Ovest, dal dott. Gianbenedetto Carcò.

La lastra è pressocchè triangolare, senza la punta in alto. Presenta tre buchi, due quadrati in basso sulla fronte (cm.5 per lato) ed uno, pure quadrato (cm.4 per lato), in alto sullo spessore: quest'ultimo evidentemente conteneva una trave di legno cui era legato un cavo per sollevare e abbassare l'ancora; gli altri due invece dovevano pure contenere travi di legno, ma in funzione di marre.

È da osservare che, contrariamente ai buchi delle altre ancore, questi sono quadrati, evidentemente per trattenere meglio il legno che passava in essi.

12) Lastra di pietra pressocchè triangolare, con tre fori (Fig. 16). Inv. n.7213.
Lunghezza cm.43, larghezza da cm.36 a cm.24, spessore cm.10,5 circa, diam. dei fori cm.3,3 circa. Peso Kg.17.
Pietra lavica compatta, di colore grigiastro, coperta da patina chiara e da concrezioni.

Presenta tre fori, tutti e tre rotondi e tutti sulla fronte.

Figure 16–17.

13) Lastra di terracotta con tre fori (Fig. 17). Inv. n.3357.
Lunghezza cm.46,5, larghezza cm.35, spessore da cm.6,5 a cm.8,5, i fori inferiori quadrati, misurano cm.3,5 per lato, quello superiore cm.3 × 4. Peso Kg.12.
È stata rinvenuta nelle acque antistanti Solunto, nei pressi dello "Scoglio della Formica".
Presenta qua e là concrezioni calcaree.

Pur essendo l'argilla molto compatta e quindi abbastanza pesante, si ha qualche dubbio circa la sua utilizzazione come áncora: presenta però, come appare chiaramente, tutte le caratteristiche delle áncore di questo tipo, tra l'altro anche il particolare dei fori quadrati per contenere meglio il legno.

Figura 18.

A(IV) *Ancore di pietra con scanalature*

14) Lastra parallelepipeda di pietra lavica, con scanalature (Fig. 18). Inv. n.7264.
Lunghezza cm.48,5, larghezza cm.27, spessore cm.15,3; scanalature, larghezza cm.4, profondità cm.1,7 circa. Peso Kg.20.
Provenienza, ignota: è pervenuta al Museo a seguito di un sequestro effettuato dalla Guardia di Finanza presso la Dogana di Palermo, su merce, costituita in parte da materiale archeologico, proveniente da Mazara del Vallo.
Pietra lavica compatta, poco porosa.

Presenta quattro scanalature, tre su una faccia ed una sull'altra opposta. Non mi risulta che siano state rinvenute altre ancore in tutto simili a questa, che solo per il tipo può essere avvicinata ad alcune rinvenute ad Agde (Bouscaras, 1964, Figg. 30–2). È verosimile che per le scanalature passassero le funi.

B *Ceppi d'ancora di pietra*

15) Ceppo d'ancora in pietra (Fig. 19). Inv. n.3331.
Lunghezza cm.98,5, sezione nel centro cm.10 × 18,5, larghezza dell'incavo cm.9, profondità dell'incavo cm.1, larghezza cm.18, spessore cm.10.
È formato da due pezzi giustapposti formatisi per rottura e constituiti da pietra lavica compatta con concrezioni biancastre. Peso Kg.20.

È stato rinvenuto probabilmente nel mare antistante Naxos (Sicilia Orientale), dove sono stati segnalati varî ceppi d'ancora di pietra (Papò, 1961).

Appartiene al tipo di ceppo di pietra con incavo piatto centrale e faccia superiore leggermente arcuata. È simile ad un altro rinvenuto nel mare di Siracusa (Gargallo, 1961, 32, Figg. 2–3), la cui ricostruzione mi sembra abbastanza valida. Si tratta certamente di un tipo primitivo di áncora (Ucelli, 1950, 243) che forse, in sede di cronologia relativa, viene subito dopo i tipi che abbiamo presentato sopra e prima di quelli in piombo.

Figura 19.

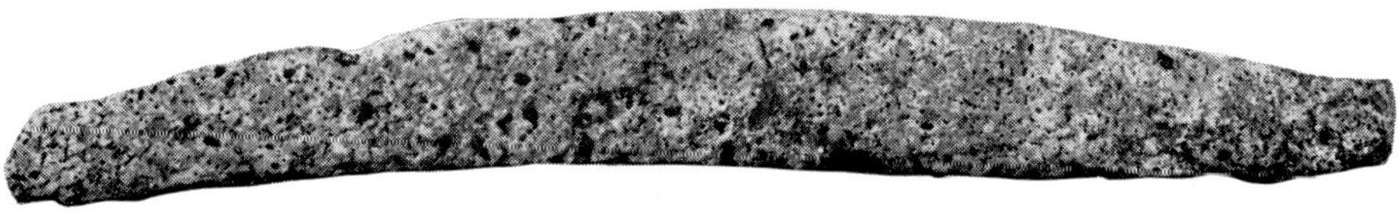

Figura 20.

Figura 21.

Figura 22.

16) Ceppo d'ancora in pietra (Fig. 20). Inv. n.3449.
Lunghezza cm.144,5, sezione nel centro cm.11 × 17, larghezza dell'incavo centrale cm.12 (non è determinabile la profondità dell'incavo stesso).
Pietra lavica porosa; presenta le superfici molto erose e coperte da patina grigio-chiara con chiazze di color ruggine e verdastro.

È stato rinvenuto da Sergio Rocca e Giovanni Michelini nelle acque dell'Isola di Ustica, presso Punta S. Paolo, a circa m.300 dalla costa, alla profondità di m.45. Peso Kg.22.

È del tipo simile al precedente, con una superficie forse meno convessa.

17) Ceppo d'ancora in pietra (Fig. 21). Inv. n.4651.
Lunghezza cm.74,5, sezione al centro cm.7 × 13. È del tipo senza incavo centrale. La forma è un pò arcuata e arrotondata alle estremità, forse per l'uso.
È stata rinvenuta da M. Savona presso Isola delle Femine, alla profondità di m.35.

18) Ceppo d'ancora in pietra (Fig. 22). Inv. n.7186.
Lunghezza m.1,04, larghezza cm.15, spessore cm.10 circa: trattasi in realtà di un frammento.
È di pietra lavica porosa; nella parte centrale, dov'è spezzata, presenta un ingrossamento.

Come appare dai pezzi che abbiamo presentato, l'uso dell'ancora in pietra, pur avendo origini molto antiche, dovette perdurare a lungo, anche quando erano molto usate quelle in piombo: questo noi diciamo, sia pure a titolo d'ipotesi, per la somiglianza tipologica stretta che c'è tra i ceppi d'ancora in piombo e alcuni di quelli in pietra: si direbbe che questi ultimi modificarono la loro forma quando apparveró i modelli in piombo. È interessante notare inoltre, anche per questi pochi pezzi presentati, la considerevole varietà di forma e di particolari che le varie áncore presentano. Purtroppo, come abbiamo detto all'inizio, non è possibile dare a questo materiale una sistemazione cronologica precisa mancando di precisi dati di scavo: la componente tipologica infatti non è determinante ai fini della cronologia. Auguriamoci che questo possa avvenire qualche volta, se e quando si attueranno quelle condizioni che abbiamo auspicato all'inizio del nostro discorso.

C *Ancore di piombo*: (I) *Ceppi d'ancora di tipo fisso*[4]

1) Ceppo d'ancora di piombo con cassetta centrale rettangolare (Figg. 23 e 24). Inv. n.3347.
Lunghezza totale m.1,79, lunghezza di ognuno dei bracci m.0,77, della cassetta m.0,24, altezza massima al centro m.0,11, altezza delle lettere cm.5–6.
Ben conservato. È stato rinvenuto da Sergio Rocca nelle acque di Isola delle Femine ad una profondità di m.55.

Colpisce soprattutto in questo ceppo di ancora e negli altri quattro che seguiranno uno straordinario appiattimento della forma in confronto ai ceppi più comunemente noti. È tutto di piombo massiccio. L'anello entro cui veniva infilata la marra di legno è quadrangolare e non aveva l'asse centrale.

[4] Con questa denominazione intendiamo indicare quei ceppi che presentano al centro un anello (cassetta), rotondo, ovale o quadrato, con asse o meno, entro cui passa la marra di legno; e questo per distinguerli dai ceppi di tipo mobile, pure di piombo, che passano attraverso un'apertura rettangolare praticata nella marra.

Su uno dei bracci, in una delle facce laterali, reca a rilievo la seguente iscrizione: BEOF; in basso, accanto alla F, è un piccolo triangolo, verosimilmente con funzione di punto.

Dalla forma delle lettere, e particolarmente dalla O perfettamente circolare, si potrebbe classificare questa iscrizione come "capitale quadrata" del tempo di Augusto, o anche più antica: ognuno sa però quanto sia aleatorio questo sistema di datazione basato esclusivamente sui caratteri epigrafici.

Figura 23.

Figura 24.

Figura 25.

Figura 26.

2) Ceppo d'ancora in piombo con cassetta centrale rettangolare (Figg. 25 e 26). Inv. n.3343.
Lunghezza totale m.1,45, lunghezza dei bracci m.0,63 e m.0,58, lunghezza della cassetta m.0,24, altezza massima al centro m.0,09, altezza delle lettere m.0,05–0,06. È ben conservato. È stato rinvenuto da Giuseppe Michelini nelle acque di Isola delle Femine.

È di forma ancora più appiattita della precedente; i bracci, alle estremità, hanno subito movimenti di torsione dovuti probabilmente ad urti. È tutto di piombo massiccio; nella parte superiore di uno dei bracci, quello senza iscrizione, si nota un solco irregolare dovuto ad un difetto di fusione, quello che F. Benoit (1955, 121) chiama "retassure de fonderie." L'anello è quadrangolare ed è privo dell'asse centrale.

Sulla parte superiore di uno dei bracci reca la seguente iscrizione, incavata e coperta d'incrostazioni: CLAU BIO. Verosimilmente si può integrare cosi: CLAU(DIO) BIO(S). Se così, si tratterebbe di una dedica greca scritta in caratteri latini, in omaggio all'imperatore Claudio: "a Claudio vita"; evidentemente il nome può riferirsi ad una qualsiasi persona. Ma se si dovesse trattare veramente dell'Imperatore Claudio, questo dato epigrafico ci autorizza a pensare che la nave cui apparteneva quest'ancora e le altre simili, siano appartenute a navi da guerra dell'epoca di Claudio (41–54 d.C.).[5] Penso a navi da guerra anzitutto per la dedica dell'ancora, se si dovesse proprio riferire all'imperatore Claudio, e poi anche per spiegare la differenza che esiste tra questo tipo appiattito e tutte le altre più comuni.

I caratteri epigrafici, quantunque abbiano poca importanza ai fini della datazione e, nel caso particolare, data anche la natura del materiale, siano mal resi, non contrastano tuttavia con l'età di Claudio.

Figura 27.

Figura 28.

3) Ceppo d'ancora di piombo con cassetta centrale rettangolare (Figg. 27 e 28). Inv. n.3344.
Lunghezza m.1,45, dei bracci m.0,61 e 0,62, della cassetta m.0,22, altezza massima al centro m.0,11, altezza delle lettere m.0,07.
È discretamente conservato, le lettere sono un pò abrase.
È stato rinvenuto da Giuseppe Michelini nelle acque di Isola delle Femine, ad una profondità di m.55.

È di forma appiattita; anche i bracci di questo ceppo hanno subito qualche movimento di torsione dovuto forse ad urti. È tutto di piombo massiccio. L'anello è rettangolare ed è privo dell'asse centrale.

[5] I rinvenitori mi assicurano che le ancore di questo tipo facevano parte di uno stesso gruppo.

In uno dei bracci, su una delle facce laterali, reca la seguente iscrizione, scritta da destra verso sinistra, a rilievo e doppia incisione:

Non c'è nessun segno di punteggiatura, tutta l'iscrizione dà l'impressione di essere stata poco curata; il tipo della L, col tratto inferiore rimboccato, s'incontra, sia pure raramente, in certe iscrizioni del II sec. d.C. e oltre: questa considerazione però non vuole costituire un'indicazione cronologica in questo caso. L'identificazione della penultima lettera è incerta.

Sulla faccia opposta dell'altro braccio reca quattro astragali in rilievo.

Figura 29.

Figura 30.

4) Ceppo d'ancora in piombo con cassetta centrale rettangolare (Figg. 29 e 30). Inv. n.3346.
   Lunghezza totale m.1,48, dei bracci m.0,62, dell'anello m.0,24, altezza massima al centro m.0,11, delle lettere m.0,09–0,10.
   È discretamente conservato, le lettere, a causa delle molte incrostazioni, sono appena visibili.
   È stato rinvenuto nelle acque di Isola delle Femine, alla profondità di m.55.

È di forma appiattita; anche i bracci di questo ceppo hanno subito movimenti di torsione dovuti probabilmente ad urti. È tutto di piombo massiccio. L'anello è quadrangolare ed è privo di asse centrale.

In uno dei bracci, su una delle facce laterali, è incisa con la stessa tecnica della precedente, con due linee leggermente incavate, e forse anche da destra verso sinistra, un'iscrizione che occupa forse, come la precedente, tutta la superficie della faccia: l'interpretazione però è molto difficoltosa dato lo stato in cui si trova l'iscrizione, specie a causa delle incrostazioni: s'intravvede appena alle estremità una I e forse una K.

Nella faccia opposta a quella dell'iscrizione e nell'altro braccio sono rese a rilievo sei borchie rotonde, forse astragali secondo l'uso comune nelle ancore: mi pare però che tra questi e i noti ossicini che, com'è noto, avevano valore apotropaico, non ci sia alcuna rassomiglianza; anche queste borchie però potrebbero avere un valore simbolico o indicativo che a noi sfugge.

5) Ceppo d'ancora in piombo con cassetta centrale rettangolare (Figg. 31–34). Inv. n.3345.
Lunghezza totale m.1,62, dei bracci m.0,69, dell'anello m.0,24, altezza massima al centro m.0,115, altezza delle lettere m.0,07.
È discretamente conservato.
È stato rinvenuto nelle acque di Isola delle Femine da Giovanni Michelini.

Figura 31.

Figura 32.

Figura 33.

Figura 34.

È di forma appiattita; anche i bracci di questo ceppo hanno subito movimenti di torsione alle estremità dovuti forse ad urti. È tutto di piombo massiccio. L'anello è quadrangolare ed è privo di asse centrale. Sulla faccia laterale di uno dei bracci reca un'iscrizione a rilievo costituita dalle seguenti lettere: C. F. M.; si tratta forse delle iniziali dell'armatore della nave (Figg. 32–33). Sulla stessa faccia inoltre è riprodotto a rilievo un oggetto di non chiara interpretazione in cui forse è da riconoscere una lucerna; lo stesso oggetto troviamo riprodotto in una delle facce laterali dell'altro braccio dello stesso ceppo (Fig. 34) ed in altri ceppi di cui diremo in seguito.

6) Ceppo d'ancora in piombo con cassetta centrale arrotondata (Fig. 35). Inv. n.3096. Lunghezza totale m.1,10, lunghezza di ognuno dei bracci m.0,49, larghezza dell'anello all'esterno m.0,12, lunghezza dell'anello all'interno m. 0,13, all'esterno m.0,20, altezza massima al centro m.0,135.
È discretamente conservato.
È stato rinvenuto nelle acque di Capo Zafferano, a circa 20 m. dalla punta, nei pressi di Solunto.

È del tipo a ceppo fisso con anima di legno e cassetta centrale arrotondata esternamente; non presenta altri segni particolari.

Figura 35.

Figura 36.

7) Ceppo d'ancora in piombo con cassetta centrale arrotondata (Fig. 36). Inv. n.3332. Lunghezza totale m.0,83, di ognuno dei bracci m.0,36, dell'anello m.0,11, altezza massima al centro m.0,095.
È discretamente conservato, nella cassetta è rotto in due pezzi.
Proviene da Capo Zafferano, come il precedente.

È del tipo a ceppo fisso con anima di legno in parte conservata. L'anello è di forma irregolare arrotondato esternamente. Presenta su un braccio un segno inciso (vedi Fig. 36).

Questi ceppi d'ancora con l'anello ovale presentano una certa rozzezza di lavorazione, ben lontana dalla rifinitura perfetta, e direi dalla eleganza che presentano invece alcuni ceppi con anello quadrangolare, tra cui principalmente quello proveniente dalle acque di Levanzo (qui al n.12, inv. n.3358); allo stato attuale delle nostre conoscenze non può essere questo un indizio cronologico (Bouscaras, 1954).

8) Ceppo d'ancora in piombo con cassetta centrale rettangolare (Figg. 37–38). Inv. n.3342.
Lunghezza totale m.1,14, di ognuno dei bracci m.0,51, dell'anello m.0,12, altezza massima al centro m.0,145, larghezza dell'anello m.0,17.
È ben conservato.
È stato rinvenuto da Giuseppe Michelini nelle acque di Isola delle Femine, alla profondità di m.55.

Figura 37.

Figura 38.

È di forma allungata, l'anello è quadrangolare ed è fornito di asse centrale.

Sulle facce dei due bracci, sullo stesso lato, sono riprodotte due lucerne simili a quella che abbiamo notato nel ceppo n.5 (inv. n.3345). Le estremità dei due bracci sono arrotondate.

La presenza delle lucerne in questo ceppo permette qualche indizio di datazione: per quanto se ne possa ricavare dalla imperfetta riproduzione nel piombo il tipo di lucerna qui riprodotto appartiene al 1° sec. d.C.

9) Ceppo d'ancora in piombo con cassetta centrale rettangolare (Figg. 39–41). Inv. n.3333.
Lunghezza totale m.1,44, di ognuno dei bracci m.0,62, dell'anello m.0,20, larghezza dell'anello m.0,29, altezza m.0,17, delle lettere m.0,08—0.09.
È ben conservato.
È stato rinvenuto nelle acque di Isola delle Femine da Francesco Renda alla profondità di m.45 circa.

Figura 39.

Figura 40.

Figura 41.

È del tipo a ceppo fisso con perno trasversale fuso nella cassetta centrale rettangolare.
Sulla faccia laterale di uno dei bracci reca l'iscrizione a leggero rilievo VENERI; sulla faccia opposta dell'altro braccio IOVI, resa allo stesso modo.

È chiaro che queste due iscrizioni siano votive, anche per la forma al dativo dei nomi, e che indichino verosimilmente la consacrazione della nave alle due divinità. L'uso di consacrare le navi ad Afrodite e a Zeus, e quindi a Venere e a Giove, il quale, com'è noto, era anche protettore dei marinai, era un uso praticato nell'antichità (Benoit, 1952, 237 sgg; Torr, 1964, tav. 8, 46): mi pare però che sia la prima volta che il nome delle due divinità ricorra insieme nello stesso ceppo e nella forma latina.

L'accostamento delle due divinità però, in altra sede e in altro ambiente, è attestato per alcuni luoghi dell'Italia antica, Apulia, Campania, Roma (Koch, 1955, coll. 834, 837, 839). Un'iscrizione da Pompei inoltre, oggi dispersa, riportava una dedica a Giove da parte di una certa "Antistia Methe", fatta per comando di "Venus fisica"(*C.I.L.*,X, 928; Onorato, 1957, n.66).

Per i caratteri epigrafici il ceppo si potrebbe datare all'epoca augustea.

Figura 42.

10) Ceppo d'ancora in piombo con cassetta centrale rettangolare (Fig. 42). Inv. n.3090. Lunghezza m.1,60, dei due bracci m.0,69 e 0,70, dell'anello m.0,21, altezza massima m.0,18, altezza delle lettere m.0,04–0,05.
È ben conservato.
È stato rinvenuto da Sergio Rocca a circa m.300 dalla costa di Isola delle Femine.

È del tipo a ceppo fisso con perno trasversale fuso nella cassetta.

Sulle due facce laterali opposte dei due bracci reca la seguente iscrizione a rilievo (nell'originale scritta da destra a sinistra): L · FVLVI · EVTI.

L'iscrizione è compresa tra due punte di tridente.[6] È chiaro che si tratta di un'iscrizione

[6] L'abitudine di decorare con un tridente gli oggetti attinenti all'uso marinaro era comune (Benoit, 1952, 253, Fig. 20).

Figura 43.

latina, completa di "praenomen, nomen e cognomen", da riferire molto probabilmente all'armatore della nave.

11) Ceppo d'ancora in piombo con cassetta centrale rettangolare (Fig. 43). Inv.n.3089. Lunghezza totale m.1,40, di ognuno dei bracci m.0,58, dell'anello m.0,24, altezza massima m.0,19.
È ben conservato.
È stato rinvenuto da Ubaldo Cipolla a circa m.1.500 dalla costa, in località Arenella, nei pressi di Palermo, al largo della torre antica: era isolata a circa 50 m. di profondità.

È del tipo a ceppo fisso con perno trasversale fuso nella cassetta centrale.

Tutte e quattro le facce laterali dei due bracci sono decorate, alternativamente e rispettivamente, con un delfino ed un astragalo, di piccole proporzioni. L'astragalo, com'è noto, aveva valore apotropaico e riccorre spesso nei ceppi d'ancora (Benoit, 1952, 237 sgg.), il delfino invece è più raro: evidentemente ricorda l'elemento marino.

Figura 44.

12) Ceppo d'ancora in piombo con cassetta centrale rettangolare (Fig. 44). Inv. n.3358. Lunghezza totale m.0,15, altezza massima m.0,165.
È ben conservato.
Proviene dalle acque antistanti l'Isola di Levanzo.

È di forma allungata con cassetta quadrangolare e perno fuso al centro della cassetta stessa. Non presenta alcun segno particolare se non l'estrema sottigliezza dei bracci relativamente agli altri ceppi: mentre in questo ceppo infatti hanno una larghezza massima di mm.7 e minima di mm.3, negli altri le due misure variano rispettivamente da mm.11 a mm.9 e da mm.7 a mm.4.

13) Ceppo d'ancora in piombo con cassetta centrale rettangolare (Fig. 45). Inv. n.3348. Lunghezza totale m.1,26, altezza m.0,13, larghezza massima m.0,19, "anima" di legno in sezione cm.8,5 × 6.
È mal conservato essendo rotto in più punti, i resti sono sostenuti da un' "anima" di legno che sostituisce quella antica.
È stato rinvenuto da Giuseppe Michelini, nelle acque di Isola delle Femine, alla profondità di m.55.

Si tratta di un tipo nuovo di ceppo d'ancora: era effettivamente di legno, perfettamente orizzontale, rivestito di piombo; il piombo esistente infatti si può considerare come un tubo quadrangolare, spesso mm.5–10, che racchiudeva l'anima di legno; al centro poi, e questa è la caratteristica più notevole, il rivestimento di piombo continua ad un livello leggermente inferiore (cm.2); nel punto in cui il livello della lamina di piombo si abbassa, si dipartono dal corpo del ceppo due alette, così come le vediamo oggi, ma che molto probabilmente costituiscono quel che è rimasto di un anello, forse ovale, o anche rettangolare, che doveva contenere e restringere il fuso di legno verticale il quale, a differenza dei ceppi d'ancora più comuni, incontrava all'esterno dell'anello non un'asse sottile, ma una grossa quasi quanto tutto il ceppo: in sostanza il ceppo era costituito da una sbarra di legno unica rivestita di piombo che al centro si assottigliava leggermente per dar modo al fuso verticale d'innestarvisi.

Non è escluso che il fuso verticale sia stato costruito, all'inizio, ben innestato al ceppo e che quindi la colata del piombo abbia rivestito contemporaneamente il ceppo e parte del fuso: questo sarebbe confermato da un frammento di ceppo di ancora di piombo, di cui ho avuto conoscenza ma di cui non mi è possibile presentare una documentazione adeguata, dal centro del quale si parte, in senso perpendicolare al ceppo stesso, una sottile lamina di piombo che serviva certamente a rivestire, almeno in parte, il fuso nel senso della lunghezza.

Quanto sopra è detto confermerebbe, sia pure per un altro tipo di ancora, quanto giustamente suppone F. Benoit (1955, 120–1), a proposito della fabbricazione dei ceppi di ancora.

Figura 45.

Figura 46.

14) Ceppo d'ancora di piombo con cassetta centrale leggermente arrotondata (Fig. 46). Inv. n.3098.

Lunghezza totale m.1,23, lunghezza dei bracci m.0,55 e m.0,56, dell'anello m.0,12, altezza massima m.0,10.

Mal conservata, manca di gran parte del rivestimento superiore, è conservata però parte dell'anima di legno.

È stato rinvenuto nelle acque di Favignana, a circa 150 m. dalla costa di punta sottile, su un fondale roccioso, alla profondità di m.43 circa.

La caratteristica principale di questo pezzo è data dal fatto che all'interno di esso è conservata una parte del legno che ne costituiva l'anima, e che è di rovere; a differenza del ceppo precedente però questo non è perfettamente orizzontale in quanto l'anima di legno era costituita da due pezzi distinti per i due bracci: questi, per la parte in piombo, risultavano dalla giustapposizione di due semicassette di lamina di piombo saldate al centro in senso orizzontale.

Al centro c'era l'anello, senza legno, ma con l'asse comune a tanti altri ceppi, di solo piombo.

Figura 47.

Figura 48.

15) Ceppo d'ancora in piombo con cassetta centrale rettangolare (Figg. 47–48). Inv. n.3452.
Lunghezza totale m.1,74, la cassetta misura all'interno cm.14 × 16.
Buono lo stato di conservazione; il piombo si è raggrinzito su una faccia durante la fusione; l'iscrizione è in parte corrosa.
È stato rinvenuto da Giuseppe Michelini nelle acque di Capo Zafferano.

È del tipo a ceppo fisso senza perno nella cassetta pressocchè quadrangolare. Reca sulla faccia laterale di un braccio la seguente iscrizione in caratteri greci, a rilievo (nell'originale scritta da destra a sinistra): ΗΡΑΚΛΗΣ.

Il nome di Eracle in questo ceppo ha evidentemente un significato dedicatorio, da parte dell'armatore della nave probabilmente: è raro però che sia stata scritta in greco.[7]

Qualche lettera di questa iscrizione può offrirci forse un indizio cronologico: mi riferisco principalmente all'incurvamento della linea retta mediana dell'alfa che diventa triangolare: questo fenomeno si verifica, com'è noto, nel III sec. a.C. (Guarducci, 1967, 371 e Fig. 196); d'altro canto la regolarità delle altre lettere, e principalmente del sigma, non ancora lunato, non ci consente di ritenere più tarda questa iscrizione.

[7] Per altre iscrizioni in greco nelle ancore, forse più tarde della nostra a giudicare dai caratteri epigrafici, v. C. Torr (1964, tav.8, 46 e 47).

16) Ceppo d'ancora in piombo con cassetta centrale rettangolare (Fig. 49). Inv. n.4646. Lunghezza totale m.1,26, interno della cassetta cm.12,5 × 16,5.
È ben conservato, solo l'iscrizione è un pò corrosa.
È stato rinvenuto da Enzo Sole nelle acque di Mondello (Palermo) a circa tre miglia dalla costa, sulla secca, ad una profondità di m.25 circa.

È di forma allungata, l'anello è quadrangolare ed è fornito dell'asse centrale fuso nella cassetta. I due bracci del ceppo sono angolati e rivolti verso l'alto.

Figura 49.

Su una delle facce laterali di uno dei bracci è la seguente iscrizione, a rilievo, resa da sinistra verso destra: CASIUS; si tratta dello appellativo di Zeus che, com'è noto, non è nuovo nei ceppi d'ancora: mi pare però che sia questa la prima volta in cui viene usato nella forma latina e da solo, non accompagnato cioè da Zeus o da Juppiter;[8] il riferimento a Giove però è certo e quindi è da presumere che la nave che portava quest'ancora fosse posta sotto la protezione di Giove stesso.

Nel ceppo qui riportato al n.9 (inv. n.3333) abbiamo notato le due iscrizioni dedicatorie a Venere e Giove, al dativo, chiaramente dedicatorie ed invocatrici; in questa invece il nominativo stava probabilmente ad indicare che Juppiter Casius, in prima persona, proteggeva la nave. L'iscrizione non è affatto curata, si può anzi dire che sia stata scritta male: anche per questo motivo non ci dà alcuna indicazione di carattere epigrafico e, conseguentemente, nessuna indicazione cronologica.

17) Ceppo d'ancora in piombo con cassetta centrale rettangolare (Fig. 50). Inv. n.3337. Lunghezza totale m.1,72, dimensioni della cassetta all'interno cm.15 × 20.
Stato di conservazione ottimo, manca il perno centrale nella cassetta.

Figura 50.

[8] Benoit, 1952, 272–3; un altro ceppo d'ancora con l'iscrizione ΖΕΥΣ ΚΑΣΙΟΣ ΣΩΖΩΝ si trova nel Museo di Cartagena (Moll, 1929); in Filone di Biblo troviamo menzione di Zeus Kasios che è verosimilmente identico a Baal Safon (Moscati, 1966, 67).

È stato rinvenuto nelle acque di Isola delle Femine da Ottavio Zanca. Forse il perno centrale era originariamente di legno: attualmente, nelle pareti interne della cassetta, si presentano due buchi poco profondi nel posto dove in altri esemplari è il perno di piombo. L'attuale mancanza del perno può significare che è stato fuso in un secondo tempo e cioè prima sarebbe stato fabbricato il ceppo, poi sarebbe stato montato sul fusto dell'ancora e quindi fissato meglio per mezzo della fusione del perno per il quale erano stati lasciati liberi i buchi corrispondenti nel ceppo e nel fusto.

Sulle facce laterali opposte dei due bracci presenta, a rilievo, il segno del caducéo: questo, simbolo di Ermete (Mercurio), dio del commercio, è connesso con una nave oneraria cui forse apparteneva l'ancora; ma il caducéo, com'è noto, è un simbolo usato anche dai punici (Tusa, 1964–65, 589 sgg., tav. LXXI) e pertanto l'ancora che lo portava può essere appartenuta ad una nave punica.

C(II) *Ceppi d'ancora in piombo di tipo mobile*
(Un esemplare simile in Gargallo, 1961, Figg. 9–10)

18) Ceppo d'ancora in piombo con sbarramento al centro (Fig. 51). Inv. n.3427.
Lunghezza cm.79,5, sezione al centro cm.3,5 × 9, larghezza della sede del fusto d'ancora cm.7 circa.
È ben conservato.
È stato rinvenuto nelle acque di Terrasini.

Figura 51.

Appartiene al tipo dal ceppo smontabile (o mobile o "ammiragliato") con la faccia superiore (posta verso il cavo d'ancora) arcuata e con sbarramento in forma di una barra a sezione rettangolare, lunga tanto quanto il ceppo è largo. I due fori, sulla faccia laterale, sono nella posizione usuale per questo tipo di ancora: quello verso il centro

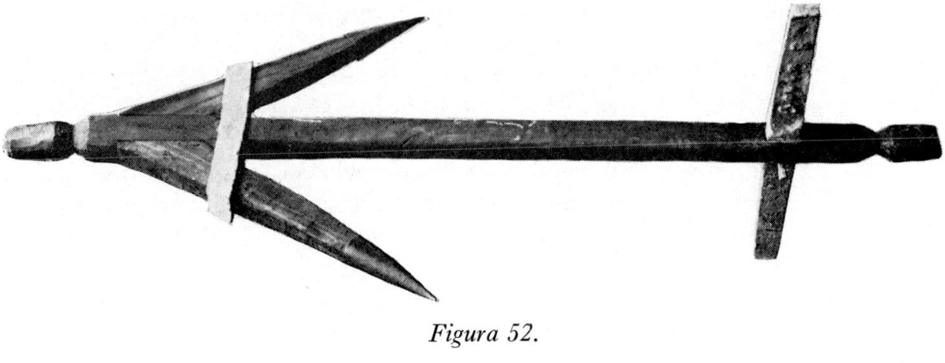

Figura 52.

serviva a fermare il fuso della marra che conteneva il ceppo mentre in quello all'estremità si faceva passare la fune che serviva per tirare o abbassare l'ancora o anche per tirare fuore il ceppo dal fusto. Su una delle facce laterali reca una decorazione costituita da tre foglie poste quasi a circolo: non mi risulta che esistano su ancore altre decorazioni simili.

19) Ceppo d'ancora di piombo con sbarramento al centro (Fig. 52). Inv. n.7276.
Lunghezza cm.97, sezione al centro (senza sbarramento) cm.4,5 × 9, larghezza della sede del fusto dell'ancora (fra sbarramento e foro) cm.9.
Buono lo stato di conservazione.
È stato rinvenuto da Ubaldo Cipolla nelle acque di Arenella, nei pressi di Palermo.

Appartiene al tipo di ancore a ceppo smontabile (o mobile o "ammiragliato"). È simile al precedente, qui si presenta la ricostruzione eseguita dal rinvenitore.

Presenta sul braccio con sbarramento sei astragali a rilievo, quattro più piccoli di diverse posizioni e due più grandi ai lati.

COMMENTARIO

Ritengo opportuno far seguire alcune considerazioni al catalogo dei pezzi sopra presentati, specialmente per quel che riguarda i ceppi d'ancora di piombo che costituiscono certamente il gruppo più numeroso ed interessante.

Debbo anzitutto dire che nel presentare questo catalogo ho inteso portare all'attenzione degli studiosi e di un pubblico più vasto alcuni pezzi che compongono la collezione archeologica sottomarina del Museo Nazionale di Palermo, corredati da tutti i dati archeologici in mio possesso, senza la pretesa di aver dato soluzioni definitive: gli studi riguardanti l'archeologia sottomarina sono veramente agli inizi, se ne ha proprio la sensazione immettendovisi dentro: perchè essi proseguano è assolutamente necessario e indispensabile conoscere quanto più materiale è possibile, anche in forma non definitiva.

A proposito dei ceppi d'ancora di piombo mi sembra opportuno far risaltare ancora la differenza profonda che esiste tra i ceppi di forma appiattita o a "ceppo mobile" e quelli di forma allungata o a "ceppo fisso": si ha proprio la sensazione di trovarsi di fronte a due tipi diversi per quel che riguarda il sistema di lavorazione del piombo, quasi due concezioni opposte dell'ancora. L'appiattimento che nei primi è in senso orizzontale, negli altri invece è in senso verticale, in quelli inoltre i bracci hanno subíto alle estremità, evidentemente per urti, dei movimenti di torsione che gli altri non mostrano di aver subíto: questo è dovuto però ad una diversa qualità del piombo oppure ad una diversa lavorazione. Inoltre i ceppi di forma appiattita hanno tutti l'anello quadrangolare privo di asse centrale, quelli di forma allungata invece hanno alcuni l'anello ovale, ed in questo caso è pure privo di asse centrale, mentre la maggior parte ha l'anello quadrangolare fornito sempre dell'asse centrale; i ceppi di forma appiattita danno infine una sensazione di rozzezza di lavorazione che gli altri certamente non danno.

A proposito dell'asse centrale dell'anello ho potuto fare le seguenti considerazioni nel ceppo di forma allungata, decorato con caducéo, e di cui al n.17 (inv. n.3337): in questo ceppo l'asse c'era in origine, ma oggi manca; ha lasciato i segni però, costituiti da due buchi che s'immettono all'interno dei bracci per una profondità di 4 cm. circa. Dall'esame accurato di questi buchi si nota che l'asse non faceva corpo unico con tutto il ceppo ma era aggiunto dopo. Da questa constatazione si può forse dedurre che l'asse veniva "colato" dopo che nell'anello stesso, fino a metà della sua altezza, era stato immesso il fuso di legno; il piombo evidentemente colava su una scanalatura del legno e su questi buchi all'interno dei bracci che erano nello stesso piano. Poi veniva posta la parte superiore del fuso ed il tutto legato fortemente con le funi. Può essere questa un'ipotesi tra le altre.

La "retassure de fonderie" si nota in quasi tutti i ceppi, molto di meno però in quelli di forma appiattita, negli altri invece di forma allungata, si trova in quasi tutti; questo particolare però non è dovuto all'anima di legno bensì a qualche particolare tecnico: ho attentamente esaminato i varî ceppi che presentano in maniera più evidente la "retassure de fonderie" e posso testimoniare che non c'è in essi anima di legno; quando questa c'è, come nei ceppi nn.13 e 14, troviamo le lamine di piombo quasi completamente distaccate dal legno e in parte perdute.

I ceppi di forma appiattita inoltre recano quasi tutti, come abbiamo visto, iscrizioni e simboli di non facile interpretazione, che non troviamo nei ceppi dell'altro tipo: anche questo particolare ci autorizza a pensare e ad affermare che tra i due tipi di ancore c'è una profonda differenza: è etnica? è cronologica? allo stato attuale delle nostre conoscenze, pur potendo formulare al riguardo qualche ipotesi suggestiva, preferiamo lasciare senza riposta questi interrogativi non avendo elementi sufficienti nemmeno per una ipotesi probante.

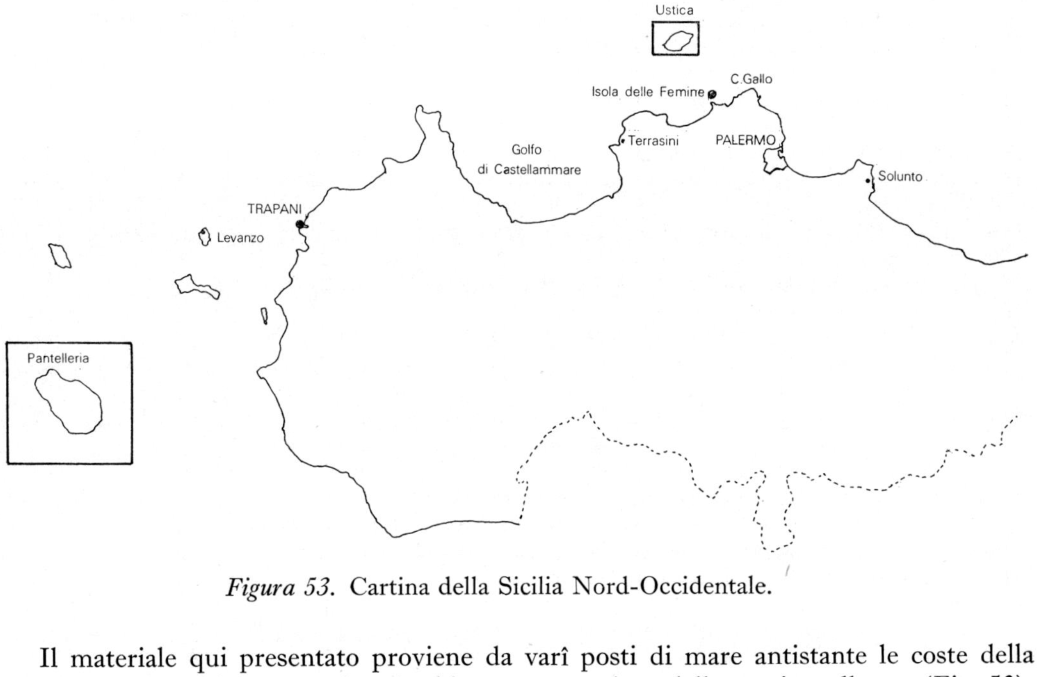

Figura 53. Cartina della Sicilia Nord-Occidentale.

Il materiale qui presentato proviene da varî posti di mare antistante le coste della Sicilia Occidentale, come si può chiaramente vedere dalla cartina allegata (Fig. 53);

la maggior parte dei pezzi però, e tra essi tutti i ceppi di forma appiattita, provengono dalla località detta "Isola delle Femine", sulla costa a 15 Km. ad Ovest di Palermo[9] esattamente ad Est nel golfo. Da questo posto sono state tratte molte ancore, e forse ancora molte ce ne sono. Questo si può spiegare con l'esistenza di un porto o, quanto meno, di un ancoraggio abituale in caso di tempesta, in quanto questo posto offre un buon ridosso meteorologico, molto calmo e sicuro particolarmente per i venti di maestrale e tramontana; malgrado la vicinanza con Palermo era difficile, per chi proveniva da Ovest, doppiare Capo Gallo, molto esposto ai venti e dove c'è anche una corrente di ritorno.[10]

Ai relitti originati da affondamento per cause meteorologiche sono da aggiungere quelli per cause belliche, che non dovettere essere certo inferiori: si pensi alle guerre puniche e alle altre numerose battaglie combattute su questo mare dai varî popoli che in questo mare navigarono e a queste coste si avvicinarono: auguriamoci che altri monumenti vengano alla luce dal nostro mare perchè servano a rendere sempre più completo il quadro storico della nostra terra e ad aumentare le nostre conoscenze in questo particolare settore dell'Archeologia.

BIBLIOGRAFIA

Benoit, F. 1952 L'archéologie sous-marine en Provence. *RivStLig*, **18**, 237–307.

Benoit, F. 1955 Jas d'ancre et pièces d'outillage des épaves de Provence. *RivStLig*, **21**, 117–28.

Benoit, F. 1961 *L'épave du Grand Congloué à Marseille* [*Gallia*, Suppl. XIV], 211 pp. Paris.

Bouscaras, A. 1954 Recherches sous-marines au large d'Agde (1951–53). *RivStLig*, **20**, 47–54.

Bouscaras, A. 1964 Notes sur les recherches sous-marines d'Agde. *RivStLig*, **30**, 267–87.

Diolé, P. 1952 *Promenades d'Archéologie sous-marine*, 272 pp. Paris.

Diolé, P. 1953 *L'avventura sottomarina*, 200 pp, Torino.

Frost, H. 1963 *Under the Mediterranean*, 278 pp. London.

Frost, H. 1969*a* The stone-anchors of Ugarit, in *Ugaritica* VI, 235–45. Paris.

Frost, H. 1969*b* The stone-anchors of Byblos. *Mélanges de l'Université Saint-Joseph*, **45**, 425–42,

Frost, H. 1970*a* Bronze-age Stone-anchors from the Eastern Mediterranean. *Mariner's Mirror*. **56**, 377–94.

Frost, H. 1970*b* Some Cypriot stone-anchors from land sites and from the sea. *Report of the Department of Antiquities, Cyprus*, 1970, 14–24.

Gargallo, P. N. 1961 Anchors of Antiquity. *Archaeology*, **14** No. 1, 31–5.

Guarducci, M. 1967 *Epigrafia greca*, I, 580 pp. Roma.

Koch, C. 1955 Venus. *R.E.* VIII A 1, 828–87.

Lamboglia, N. 1961*a* Lo stato attuale dell'archeologia sottomarina in Italia. *Atti del II Congresso Internazionale di Archeologia sottomarina, Albenga 1958*, 12–17. Bordighera.

Lamboglia, N. 1961*b* La Nave romana di Spargi (La Maddalena). Campagna di scavo 1958. *Atti del II Congresso Internazionale di Archeologia sottomarina, Albenga 1958*, 143–66. Bordighera.

Lamboglia, N. 1961*c* Tecnica del rilievo archeologico sottomarino. *Atti del II Congresso Internazionale di Archeologia sottomarina, Albenga 1958*, 275–84. Bordighera.

Moll, F. 1929 Ein Bleianker. *Archäologischer Anzeiger*, **44**, 266–72.

Moscati, S. 1966 *Il Mondo dei Fenici*, 497 pp. Milano.

[9] Questa località deriva il suo nome dall'arabo "fim" (bocca, imboccatura) o "fimi" (Eufemio), corrotto poi e scambiato col dialettale "fimmini" (femine).

[10] Devo queste informazioni al Capitano di lungo corso G. Voltolina, che cordialmente ringrazio.

Onorato, G. O. 1957 *Iscrizioni pompeiane. La vita pubblica*, 215 pp. Firenze.
Papò, F. 1961 Ancore all'ingrosso. *Mondo Sommerso*, **2**, No. 7, 52.
Torr, C. 1964 *Ancient Ships*, 222 pp. Chicago.
Tursini, L. 1971 Parole di guida ai ricercatori subacquei. *Atti del III Congresso Internazionale di Archeologia sottomarina, Barcellona 1961*, 335–41. Bordighera.
Tusa, V. 1964–65 Testimonianze fenicio-puniche. *Kokalos*, **10–11**, 589–602.
Ucelli, G. 1950 *Le navi di Nemi*, 416 pp. Roma.

The Spanish Armada expedition, 1968-70

by

COLIN J. M. MARTIN

1. INTRODUCTION

THE IDEA OF applying archaeological method to the search for, survey, and excavation of Spanish Armada shipwrecks around the British Isles was conceived by Mr. Sydney Wignall in the early 1960s after experience of underwater archaeology on Mediterranean sites. Though documentary evidence of the Armada campaign is abundant from both Spanish and English sources, technical evidence complementary to it had hitherto been almost non-existent, and lack of such evidence has raised difficulties in interpreting much of the historical material. From a broader standpoint, a study of Armada technologies based on archaeological discovery might be expected to add materially to the understanding of maritime affairs of the late sixteenth century, particularly in the fields of ship construction and armament. It was with the aim of recovering evidence of this kind that, in April 1968, Mr. Wignall organized, financed, and led an expedition to Blasket Sound, County Kerry, to seek the remains of the *Santa Maria de la Rosa*, vice-flagship of the Guipuzcoan squadron, lost there during a storm in September 1588 (Wignall, 1968).

After an area search of unprecedented magnitude, directed by Commander John Grattan of the Royal Navy, the site of an ancient shipwreck was located in deep water at the eye of a tide-race in the Sound's narrow neck (Wignall, 1968; 1969). During the remaining part of the 1968 season, and for a full six months in 1969, survey and limited excavation programmes were carried out on this difficult site (Martin, 1969*a* & *b*; 1970). It was discovered that much of the vessel's lower hull remains intact, pinned by the stone ballast which had lined the hold. A considerable amount of associated evidence has been recovered, including positive identification of the wreck as that of the *Santa Maria*.

On completion of the 1969 season it was decided temporarily to leave the *Santa Maria* site, and to seek a second Armada wreck in less difficult waters. This was occasioned in part by the limitations and expense of operating in Blasket Sound, and in part by a failure to find any of the ship's main armament there. After some research it was felt that the flagship of the Armada's supply squadron, *El Gran Grifon*, which had been wrecked on Fair Isle, offered the most promising prospects. A small-scale expedition to Fair Isle was launched in June 1970, and by following the evidence of strong local traditions the wreck site was found without difficulty. Though no structural remains appear to have survived, many artifacts have been located including, as had been hoped, a number of the ship's guns (Martin, 1972).

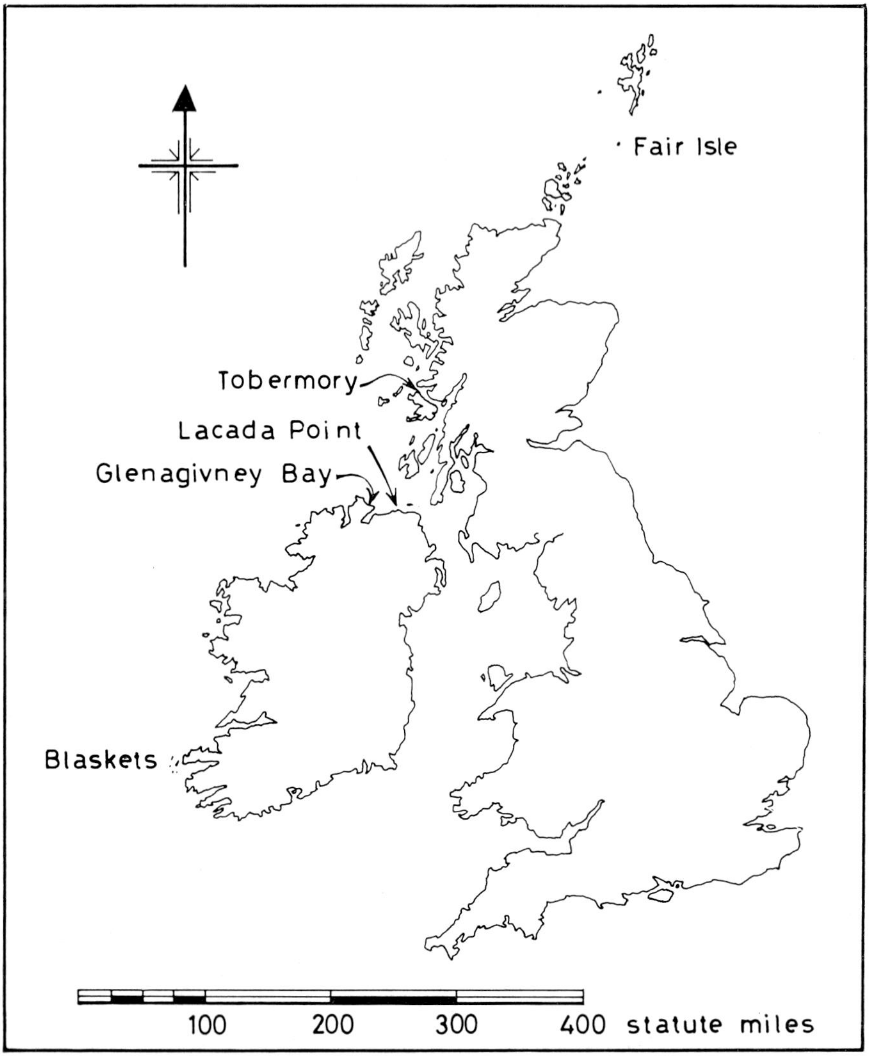

Figure 1. Armada wreck sites in the British Isles: *Santa Maria de la Rosa* (Blaskets); *Trinidad Valencera* (Glenagivney Bay, Donegal); *Girona* (Lacada Point, Antrim); *San Juan de Sicilia* (?) (Tobermory Bay); *El Gran Grifon* (Fair Isle).

Work on both sites is incomplete, and it is intended to spend at least one more full season on each before attempting to present the evidence and its interpretation in complete and final form. Nonetheless, some tentative historical conclusions have been drawn from the evidence so far recovered, and it is the aim of this paper to summarize the most important of these. It is also hoped to demonstrate how this kind of maritime archaeology, if read in conjunction with available documentary material, can illuminate and sometimes add to the understanding of history.

2. SANTA MARIA DE LA ROSA

Historical sources are silent concerning the origin of this ship, or her date of building. Mention of her is first made on 7 January 1588, when she was berthed at Lisbon as flagship to the Guipuzcoan squadron under Miguel de Oquendo (Duro I, No. 48, p. 405). By 19 March, however, when a progress report on the state of the fleet was sent to the king, she had lost her flag status to the *Santa Ana*, in which Oquendo ultimately sailed, and had become the squadron's *almiranta*, or vice-flagship (Duro I, No. 69, p. 441). In May, when a final muster before sailing was called, the ship is listed with a tonnage of 945, an armament of 26 guns of unspecified type and size, and a complement of 297 men (Duro II, No. 109, p. 63).

After a difficult start to the voyage, the Armada was forced to put into Corunna for revictualling and repair. The *Santa Maria* was one of those most badly damaged, having lost her mainmast during a storm (Duro II, No. 126, pp. 127–8; II, No. 128, p. 132). On 10 July the major operation of stepping a new mast was completed under the personal supervision of the Duke of Medina Sidonia (Duro II, No. 141, p. 174). While the *Santa Maria* was non-operational because of these repairs the vice-flag evidently passed to her Guipuzcoan sister-ship *San Salvador* (Duro II, No. 126, p. 127), though when a muster was held before the Armada left Corunna the *Santa Maria* is once again listed as "almiranta" (Duro II, No. 150, p. 196). As such, too, is she rated when her loss off Ireland is finally recorded in Spain (Duro II, No. 181, p. 331).

No direct reference to the ship's part in the Channel battles appears to exist, though that she was heavily engaged is implicit in her survivor's statement that "this ship was shot through four times, and one of the shots was between the wind and the water, whereof they thought she would have sunk, and most of her tackle was spoiled with shot". The dramatic and terrible story of her wrecking in Blasket Sound is to be found in the accounts of her only survivor, of an eye-witness on shore, and of an officer on board a neighbouring Spanish ship (C.S.P. [Ireland] Vol. CXXXVI, 41. iv. p. 40; *ibid.* 43. x. p. 42; Duro II, No. 178, pp. 319–21).

3. THE WRECK SITE

The wreck discovered in Blasket Sound on 6 July 1968 lies on a flat shingle bottom at a mean high water depth of 110 feet, and its position represents the south-eastern terminus of a NW–SE line across the Sound, indicated first by a sequence of iron anchors and then by the main pinnacle of an underwater reef close to the centre of the Sound's narrowest part (Fig. 2). From the evidence of Marcos de Aramburu, who commanded one of the two Spanish ships already at anchor in the lee of Great Blasket Island when the *Santa Maria* came in during a westerly gale at noon on 21 September 1588, it is reasonable to identify the two north-western anchors with ground tackle lost by these ships (Wignall, 1968). A third anchor possibly indicates the position at which, after drifting, the ships managed to re-anchor. The final anchor in the sequence undoubtedly belongs to the *Santa Maria* herself. On entering the Sound, as Aramburu's log records, the ship "cast her single anchor, for she was not carrying more". She held on for two hours until the ebb tide began to run, when she dragged to strike an unseen hazard and sink almost at once. The survivor's testimony confirms that the wrecking was caused by a submerged rock. This can only have been the tip of the main pinnacle

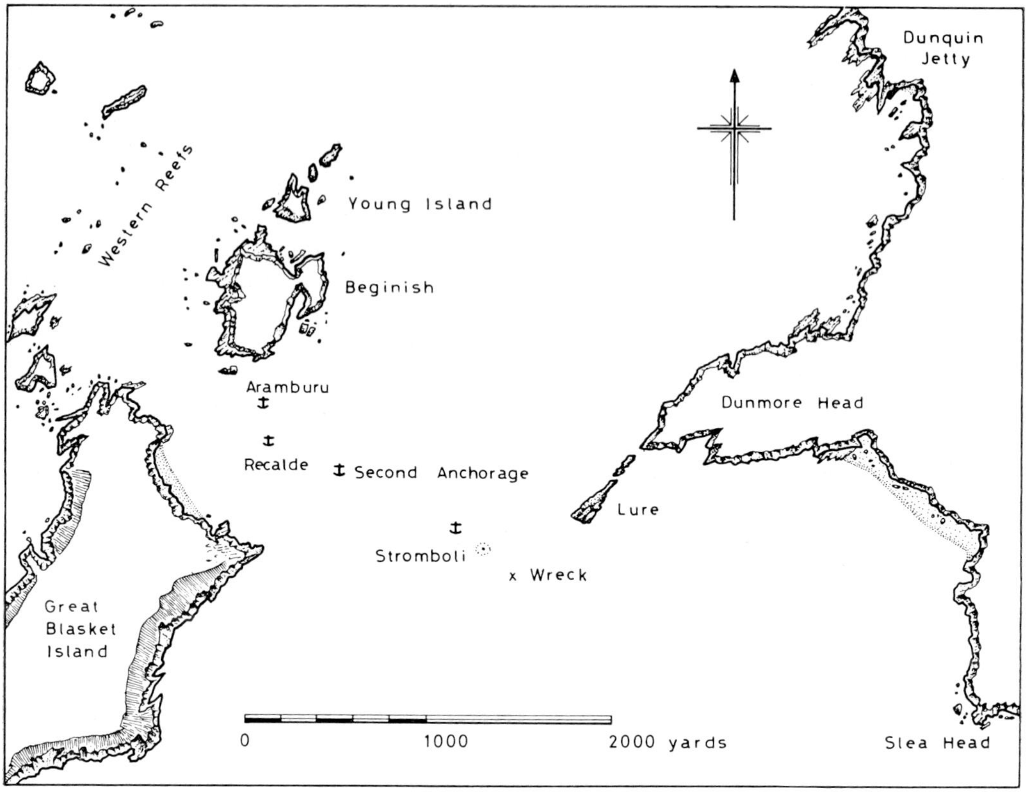

Figure 2. Blasket Sound, County Kerry, showing the positions of anchors associated with the Spanish ships, the main pinnacle of Stromboli Reef, and the *Santa Maria de la Rosa* wreck site.

of Stromboli Reef, which is still not adequately marked on Admiralty Chart 2790 (1966) and which at low water lies not much more than a fathom below the surface. At high water, not long after which the *Santa Maria* struck, the depth of the rock is still considerably less than the draught of a ship of her size and type.

The linear progression towards the wreck indicated by these various features, which were discovered during a systematic visual search of the entire Sound, corresponds with the mean influence of wind and tidal components at the time of the disaster and with the sequence of events leading to it, all of which are clearly noted in Aramburu's account.

The visible remains of the wreck comprise a mound of packed limestone ballast 100 feet long and 40 feet broad at the widest part. Excavation was to show that the average depth of ballast was in the order of two and a half feet, suggesting a mass in air of about 200 tons. The central ridge of the mound runs lengthwise in a north–south direction although, as will be seen, this does not reflect the main longitudinal axis of the wreck.

Towards the south of the mound its eastern and western edges draw together to form a marked "tail", the tip of which merges gradually with the natural shingle. On the north and north-western edges of the mound massive concretions of piled iron shot form a solid, larva-like crust, while seven lead ingots were found lying on top of the ballast at its highest point.

Thought was given to the question of identifying bow and stern ends. There exists a description of the well-known Tobermory Armada wreck (Fig. 1), probably that of the *San Juan de Sicilia* (Hardie, 1912), as it appeared to a salvor working on it in the late seventeenth century. The salvor, Archibald Miller of Greenock, had this to say of the remains: "There is no deck upon her except in ye hinder part . . . in the fore part of the ship lie many great ballast stones, and some shot amongst them" (Miller, 1683). The latter part of this description implies a configuration remarkably similar to that observed at the northern end of the Blasket wreck. Miller speaks of a concentration of ballast in the fore part of his ship, just as occurs in the broad head and narrowing tail of the Blasket mound. A consideration of factors involved in ballasting a ship of this kind suggests an explanation. The massive castlework of the stern, with its associated armament and fortification, must have exerted a considerable stern-down component in the trim of such a vessel. Ballast concentrated forward, tapering aft with the run of the hull, would correct this imbalance and would leave on a wreck site a spread of ballast of a kind noted by Miller at Tobermory and now evident in the Blasket mound. Miller also notes the presence of shot in the fore part of the Tobermory ship, and this is paralleled by the shot concretions at the broad northern end of the *Santa Maria*'s wreck. Structural evidence was subsequently to confirm the identification of this end as the bow.

4. IDENTITY OF THE WRECK

Though circumstantial and physical indications that the wreck is that of the *Santa Maria de la Rosa* are overwhelmingly strong, it was nonetheless gratifying to recover, in the course of the 1969 excavations, clear documentary proof of the ship's identity: two matching pewter campaign plates, 8 inches in diameter, inscribed on their lower rims with the name "Matute". Spanish and English sources confirm that a man of this name sailed with the Armada as an infantry captain, and the English sources, derived from the interrogation of the ship's survivor, identify him specifically as having perished aboard the *Santa Maria* (Duro II, No. 109, p. 77; C.S.P. [Ireland] Vol. CXXXVI, 41. iv. p. 40).

5. METAL DETECTOR SURVEY

Little was achieved during the 1968 season beyond location, survey, and exploratory trenching. Since the disposition of large metal objects, particularly guns, seemed a likely indicator of the way in which the hull had collapsed, arrangements were made with the Research Laboratory for Archaeology at Oxford to carry out a metal detector survey on the ballast mound and over the surrounding seabed. This operation was conducted in April 1969 under the direction of Mr. Jeremy Green of the Laboratory, and although later excavation confirmed the detector's ability to locate small metal objects, ferrous and non-ferrous, up to a buried depth of at least two feet, no large contacts which could be identified as guns were recorded (Green & Martin, 1970). The metal detector survey, though leading to the discovery of a number of widely

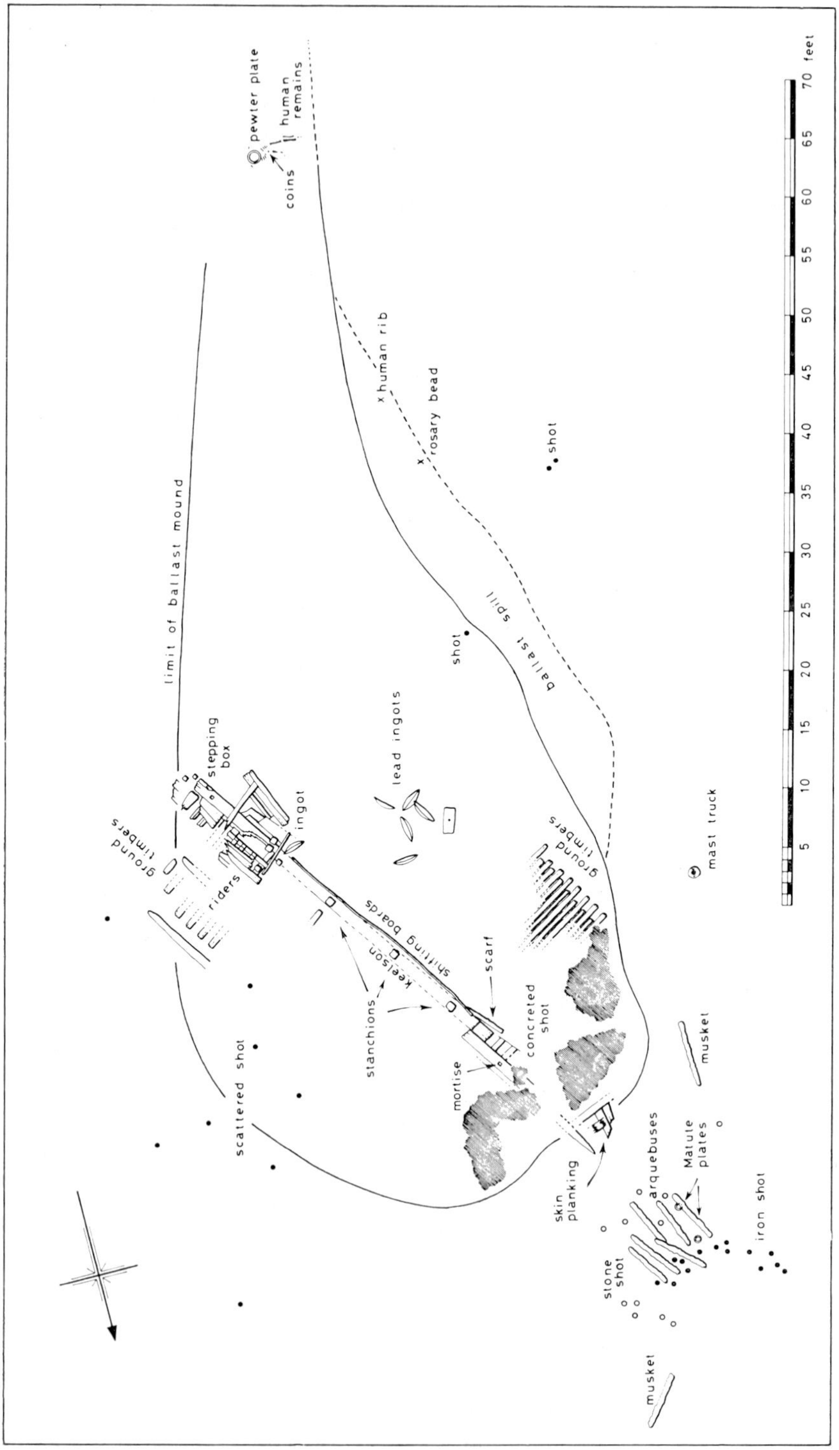

Figure 3. Santa Maria de la Rosa: general plan of the wreck.

scattered artifacts, thus added little to what was already known about the lie of the wreck, and it was felt that selective excavation of the structural remains pinned below the ballast mound should proceed. The interim stage which these excavations have reached is summarized in Figure 3, and the nature of the evidence uncovered is described below.

6. EXCAVATION OF THE HULL STRUCTURE

Excavation was first directed along a structural line of axis running NW–SE which proved to be the keelson of the forward part of the ship. This feature had been constructed in scarf-jointed lengths, 10 inches broad by 8 inches deep, with rib slots cut out of the underside. At 7-foot intervals the stanchions which carried the orlop beams were tenoned into the keelson, and some of these posts have survived up to the level of the ballast. Others can be identified by mortises cut into the keelson to receive them.

Hard against the port side of the forward stanchions and running along the axis of the keelson are two 20-foot planks, each 1 foot broad by 2 inches thick, set on edge one atop the other. They are not fastened in any way, being held in place against the uprights solely by pressure of ballast. They can thus be recognized as shifting boards, used when the ballast was moved from one side of the hold to the other during careening, or for the routine trenching which was necessary to check the floor timbers for leaks. They will also have helped to prevent the ballast from shooting sideways in heavy seas, or when the ship was sailing upon a tack. Mainwaring (*c*. 1623) describes the use of such boarding, which he calls "pouching".

Thirty-five feet from the bow end of the ballast, on the keelson axis, a complex structural arrangement was uncovered (Fig. 4). Here a series of uprights and boards had formed a rectangular box, now partly collapsed, set lengthwise directly above the keelson. The box had been constructed to withstand pressure from without, which suggests that its function had been to hold an open well within the ballast. Where it passes under this well, and for some distance fore and aft, the keelson is 16 inches deep—double its normal thickness. Under the forward part of the box the keelson is massively torn and splintered, as though by the ripping out of a heavy structure bolted to it. On either side the keelson had been supported by a 4-inch-square longitudinal sleeper, the starboard one being now considerably displaced. The floor of the box is packed flush with the level of keelson and sleepers with two runs of ceiling planking, evidently in order to secure a flat, firm base for seating a solid structural unit now no longer in place.

Three heavy timbers were then uncovered, riding athwartships above the main hull frames from the starboard side of the box. Their inboard ends, which are squared off and slightly tapered, lie over the displaced starboard sleeper. Clearly these ends had mated with recesses in a now vanished component, which analogy and structural considerations alike identify as the mainmast step. The "box" arrangement around the mast step is paralleled in the remains of a large ship excavated at Woolwich in 1912, variously identified but certainly belonging to the first half of the sixteenth century (Salisbury, 1961). The thickening of the keelson at this point of heavy stress is prescribed in a shipbuilding treatise of *c*. 1620 (Anderson & Salisbury, 1958). Finally, the supporting riders, intended to buttress the step athwartships, are closely paralleled in the arrangement noted by Lovegrove (1964) on the remains of a vessel recently discovered at Rye and believed by him to date from not later than the end of the sixteenth century.

Structural distortion in the area surrounding the *Santa Maria*'s mast step, and the ripping out of the long iron bolts which had bound the step itself to the keelson fore and aft, suggest that the mast toppled towards the south, the direction in which a strong ebb tide was running when the wrecking occurred. The collapse of the mast in this direction may also explain the absence of corresponding riders in position on the port side.

A reconstruction of the mast step and the related structures has been attempted in Figure 5. It is of particular interest to compare the makeshift appearance of the shoring around the step with the solid shipwrightry of the other components, for it will be recalled that the *Santa Maria* underwent a remasting operation not long before she sank. It is therefore not unreasonable to see in this shoring a temporary arrangement intended to clear the stepping area of ballast in preparation for the new mast which was fitted at Corunna.

After the keelson sequence and mast step had been examined, a transverse trench was begun on the port bow quarter of the ballast mound in order to locate frame timbers.

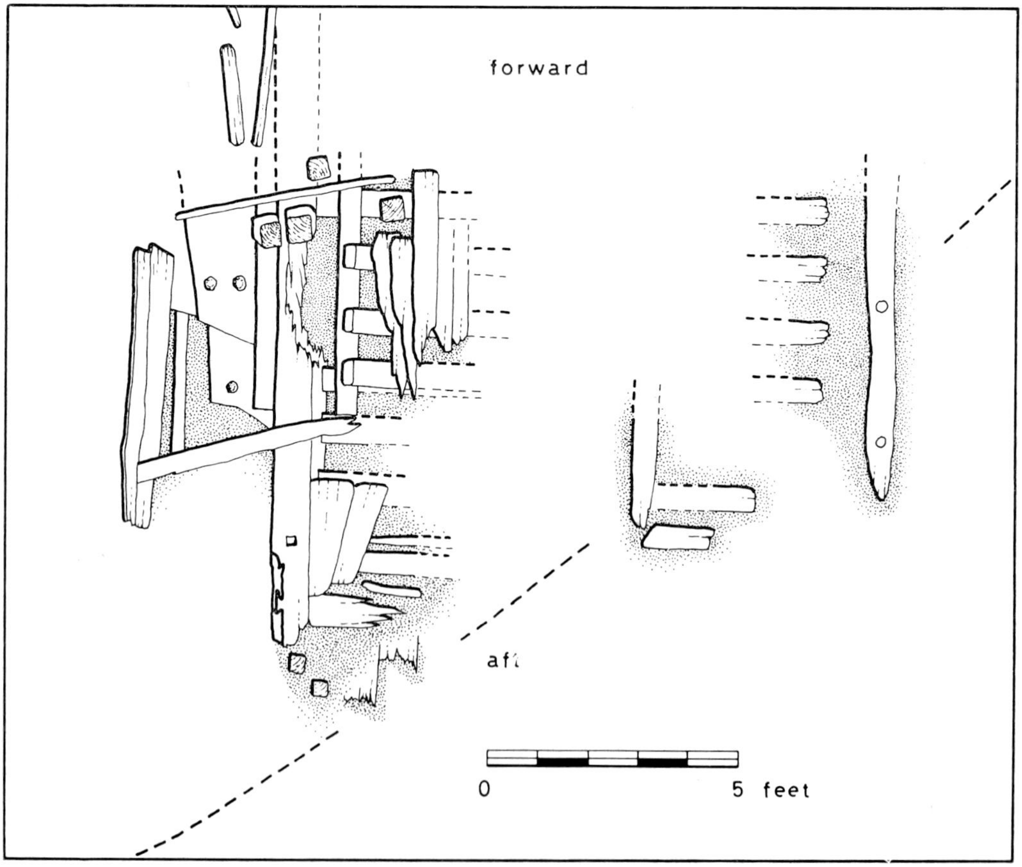

Figure 4. Santa Maria de la Rosa: excavations midships at the mainmast step, showing evidence of the after break.

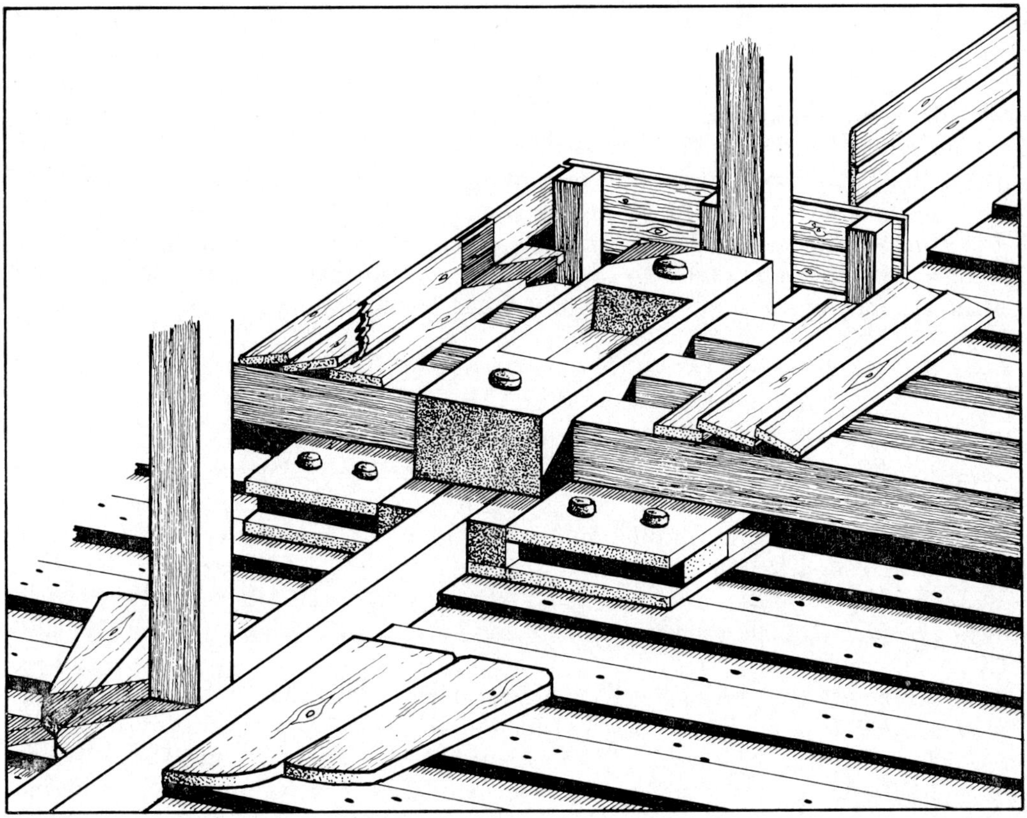

Figure 5. Santa Maria de la Rosa: reconstruction of the mainmast step and related structures.

Fifteen closely spaced ground timbers were uncovered. Every second timber is 8 inches wide and 1 foot deep, and these main members are spaced on average 6 inches apart. Between each pair of main timbers lies a filling timber, fitting tightly into the gap between its neighbours with its top just below the level of theirs. The lower hull thus appears to have been solid-framed throughout, without internal strengthening other than the mast step riders.

The skin planking, in the several places where it could be examined, is 4 inches thick. Except in the region of the mast step there appears to be no ceiling planking inside the hull. The outer planks are pinned to the frames with long trenails, 1 inch in diameter, studded in groups of two and three. The plank ends, or butts, where springing stresses are strongest, are bolted with iron just as Mainwaring (*c.* 1623) prescribes. These bolts are clenched on oakum or leather washers as a protection against salt water corrosion ("iron-sickness", as Mainwaring calls it). Evidence was found of lead patching over leaky trenails.

Just aft of the mast step the structural sequence along the keelson ceases abruptly, while the last few feet of structure show evidence of distortion and fracture. At this point the ballast mound sharply changes direction, trailing off some 50 degrees to port of the wreck's forward axis. From this it was concluded that the hull had broken aft of the mainmast, and that the stern section had pivoted to match the run of the ebbing tide. Whether this part of the ship actually broke free, spilling its ballast and drifting down tide, is not yet known; only further excavation will tell. It is possible, however, that the starboard side of the hull was extensively broken when the ship hit Stromboli, and that this break was continued to port by the subsequent ripping out of the mast. It may, then, be that the stern has gone completely and, if so, it is not inconceivable that this break-away may have taken with it much of the upper decks with their contents and guns. All that can be said with certainty at present is that the entire lower forward hull and the bulk of the ship's ballast are still on the site.

7. THE STRUCTURAL EVIDENCE

The mainmast step lies, by the line of the keelson, 37½ feet from the forward edge of the ballast, which must in turn be on or very close to the bow end of the keel. If the mast position be presumed to lie midway between stem and sternpost, as a historically closely parallel example of Atlantic shipbuilding traditions in Spain suggests (Palacio, 1587), then an overall keel length of 75 feet is obtained. This figure is patently too short to accommodate the *Santa Maria*'s listed 945 tons, even allowing for the Spanish tendency to over-estimate tonnages by contemporary English standards (Lewis, 1960). Such an interpretation must therefore be wrong, and in order to find a convincing solution it is necessary to seek parallels in a geographical rather than an historical setting.

In about 1445 Giorgio Timbotta, a Venetian merchant, wrote a treatise on shipbuilding which includes this passage: "To fix the mast step . . . divide the keel into five parts and leave three (less 1 foot) aft" (Anderson, 1925). If this formula be applied to the *Santa Maria*, assuming the 37½ feet between the mast step and the estimated position of the stem scarf to be two parts *plus* 1 foot forward, the following calculation emerges:

$$\begin{array}{llll} \text{1 part} & = \dfrac{37.5 - 1}{2} & & = 18.25 \\ \text{Therefore keel length} & = 18.25 \times 5 & & = 91.25 \\ \text{Keel length forward of step} & = 18.25 \times 2 + 1 & & = 37.5 \\ \text{Keel length aft of step} & = 18.25 \times 3 - 1 & & = 53.75 \end{array}$$

If the *Santa Maria* was a broad-beamed vessel, as the spread of ballast appears to confirm, then a keel length of 91 feet would well accommodate her tonnage. The figure, moreover, obtains powerful support from the fact that the run of ballast aft of the mast step (that is, the postulated broken stern section) closely agrees with the theoretical measurement of the stern according to this formula.

The inference is clear: the *Santa Maria de la Rosa*, vice-flagship of the Atlantic-based Guipuzcoan squadron, shows the characteristics of a Mediterranean build. Perhaps it was for this reason that she failed to cope well with Atlantic conditions (cf. the loss of her mainmast off Corunna). Captain Duro (Vol. I) has pointed out that many Armada ships were over-masted in relation to their structural strength, and indeed one finds trouble with masts cropping up time and again in Spanish narratives and reports of the campaign and its aftermath. The very slightness of the *Santa Maria*'s construction, evident in the dimensions of keelson, frames, and outer skin, and her apparent lack of internal strengthening members, further point to Mediterranean influence.

The writer recognizes full well the pitfalls inherent in attempting to distinguish categorically between "Atlantic" and "Mediterranean" shipbuilding traditions, for by their nature ships travel widely and developments in shipwrightry and fundamental design quickly spread and intermingle beyond purely geographic boundaries. None the less, long evolutions in different environments tend to produce underlying traditions which are very strong, and this is where the "Atlantic" and "Mediterranean" distinction is best drawn, however wavy and uncertain the resultant line must be. Broadly speaking, the Mediterranean shipbuilding tradition was much the older, and tended to rely on an overall structural integrity based on many small and closely fitting components which, though individually slight, locked together to form a relatively solid self-stressing "shell". In contrast, shipwrights following the newer "Atlantic" methods apparently favoured an internally stressed framework of fewer but more massive structural members, each of which possessed considerable strength even in isolation.

Mediterranean-type hulls could certainly be strong, but their strength was, as it were, the strength of an egg-shell, which, while intact, can resist great external pressure, but which, if only slightly cracked in one part, easily collapses overall. Such a vessel would indeed be prone to strain if over-masted and, perhaps more than anything else, would be desperately vulnerable to gunfire. In this connection it is worth noting that the group of ships which suffered the lowest casualty figures in the Armada campaign was the squadron of ten newly-built "Atlantic" galleons of Castile (10% losses), while the heaviest losses (80%) were sustained by the Levant squadron—the only squadron in the Armada all of whose ships are known *definitely* to have been of Mediterranean origin.

An instance of the inherent weakness of a Mediterranean build is to be found in the Proceedings of a Court Martial about the loss of H.M.S. *Daedalus*, a 40-gun frigate wrecked on the Little Basses, S. Ceylon, in 1813 (Clarke, 1964). She had been captured from the French, runs her captain's narrative, and had been "built at Venice, and perhaps never intended by the Enemy to go out of that Narrow Guelph; for when taken into dock at Deptford she was found to possess the Timbers, and Scantlings, of an 18-gun ship . . . the weight of her Upper Works and Guns, when she touched (the reef), crushed her slender Frame to pieces".

That the *Santa Maria* should appear to be of Mediterranean-type build is interesting, but far from inexplicable. Confusion has in the past arisen from the fact that two of the Armada's four auxiliary squadrons were supplied by the wholly Atlantic provinces of Guipuzcoa and Biscay, and in consequence an Atlantic origin has been assumed for all their ships. This of course need not have been so, and in fact there is strong reason to suppose that most of the indigenous merchant ships of these provinces were too small to mount the heavy battery artillery with which, almost at the last moment, the Spaniards equipped their auxiliary fleet in order to bring its armament up to front-line standards. Merchant ships of sufficient size to carry batteries of heavy guns were, for the most part, to be found in Mediterranean ports. In the 1586 Armada "Proposals" (Duro I, No. 7, pp. 250–1) it is stated that ships earmarked from Mediterranean sources had an average tonnage of 600 tons apiece, while those available from the provinces of Guipuzcoa and Biscay averaged only 350 tons. The same proposals (p. 290) also indicate the character of armament intended for these relatively small Atlantic vessels. It is an extremely light, essentially defensive armament, one in utter contrast to the heavy offensive batteries with which the auxiliary squadrons actually sailed. In 1588 the front-line ships of Guipuzcoa and Biscay set out with an average tonnage of 650 tons—a figure almost twice the average size of the provinces' indigenous ships in 1586, but one remarkably close to that of ships available from Mediterranean sources at the same date. Philip II's reply to Medina Sidonia's complaints about some of the Armada's ships seems to sum the matter up: "I see plainly the truth of what you say, that the Levant ships are less free and staunch in heavy seas than the vessels built here . . . it is true that if we could have things exactly as we wished, we would have other vessels . . ." (C.S.P. [Spanish] No. 332, p. 328).

Dr. de Courcy Ireland (1966) has recently shown that at least 12 large vessels intended for the Armada campaign sailed from the port of Ragusa (Dubrovnik) alone; these will have been under direct charter, for the Ragusan Republic owed no allegiance to the Spanish Crown. Vessels from this port had, moreover, already served Spain against Portugal in 1580 and against Strozzi and the French in 1582. The practice of hiring Mediterranean ships for naval operations in the Atlantic was evidently well established by 1588.

Even if the Armada's Levant squadron had drawn its entire front-line strength from this one source, which it did not, two Mediterranean ships would still have remained to be, in Dr. Ireland's words, "integrated with the squadrons of mainland Spain". But these twelve Ragusans were by no means the only Mediterranean ships to sail with the Armada; others are known to have come from Venice, Sicily, Naples and ports on the Mediterranean coast of Spain. Forty large converted merchantmen made up the auxiliary squadrons of Guipuzcoa, Biscay, Andalusia and Levant, with four attached to the squadron of Castile. Just how many of these were of Mediterranean origin is unlikely ever to be known with certainty, but the proportion is higher than has often been supposed. It amounted to half at least, and probably considerably more. Sir John Hawkins, who as the energetic reformer of Queen Elizabeth's Navy Royal can be relied upon to recognize ship-types when he sees them, was able to count, in the confusion of battle, "twenty great Venetians and argosies [i.e., Ragusans] of the seas within the Strait" among the Armada (Laughton I, p. 360). An oblique contemporary reference to the *Santa Maria* herself seems to clinch the point that she was one of them. It is to be found in the log of Pedro Calderon of the hulk *San Salvador* who, out in the North Atlantic, saw far to leeward "the ship Villafranca of Oquendo [i.e., the *Santa Maria*, for Villafranca was her captain, Oquendo her squadron commander] and *another* Levantine ship" (C.S.P. [Spanish] No. 439, p. 449).

8. EL GRAN GRIFON

El Gran Grifon is first named in the Lisbon muster of 7 January 1588 as flagship of the squadron of supply-hulks, a status confirmed by all subsequent lists. Like almost all of the other Armada hulks, she was a Hanseatic trader under charter to Spain. She herself came from Rostock, the emblem of which is a *griffin*. In the muster before sailing she is listed with a tonnage of 650, an armament of 38 unspecified guns, and a complement of 286 men (Duro II, No. 109, p. 64).

Though the hulks were not intended to act as combatant vessels, *El Gran Grifon* was heavily engaged during the Channel battles, in which she received severe hull damage (Mattingly, 1959). Because of this damage, and perhaps also because of her poor sailing qualities (Baltic hulks were notoriously clumsy vessels) she lagged behind the main body of the fleet during the north-about voyage. After a harrowing series of adventures in the North Atlantic and off the Irish coast she was driven back to the north, eventually fetching up into the lee of Fair Isle in a sinking condition (Duro II, No. 171, pp. 279–93). There, on 28 September 1588, her crew drove her ashore, escaping themselves by climbing up the cliff against which the masts leaned.

The site of the wreck, long pointed out by tradition, lies in the small cave-ended *geo* (inlet) of Stroms Hellier, close to the south-east corner of the island (Fig. 6). In here the

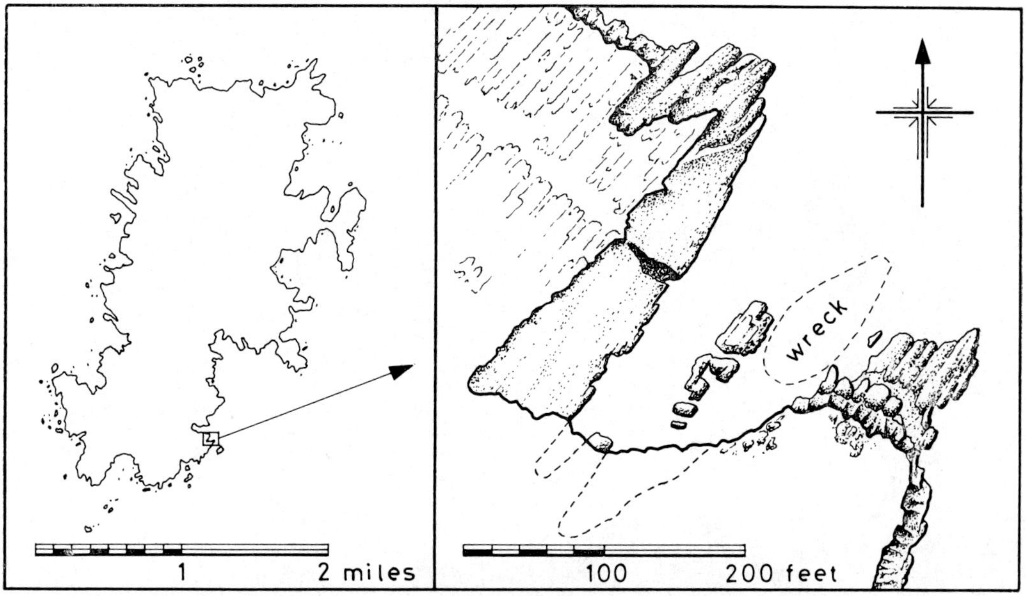

Figure 6. Fair Isle: the wreck of *El Gran Grifon* at Stroms Hellier.

scattered remains of an ancient shipwreck were located without difficulty. Though no absolute proof of identity has so far been recovered, the accumulation of evidence—traditional, circumstantial, and physical—is such that there can be no doubt at all that the remains are those of a sixteenth-century warship connected with the Armada, and in consequence they can only be those of *El Gran Grifon*.

Though the site has shown no evidence of the survival of any hull, it has yielded a rich deposit of artifacts and promises to produce much more. A record of what has so far been recovered is published elsewhere (Martin, 1972), together with an assessment of the evidence concerning the ship's armament. Twelve individual guns have now been identified, almost a third of the ship's known complement (Fig. 7). The hundred or so pieces of iron shot recovered from the site form a group well suited to serve guns of the types

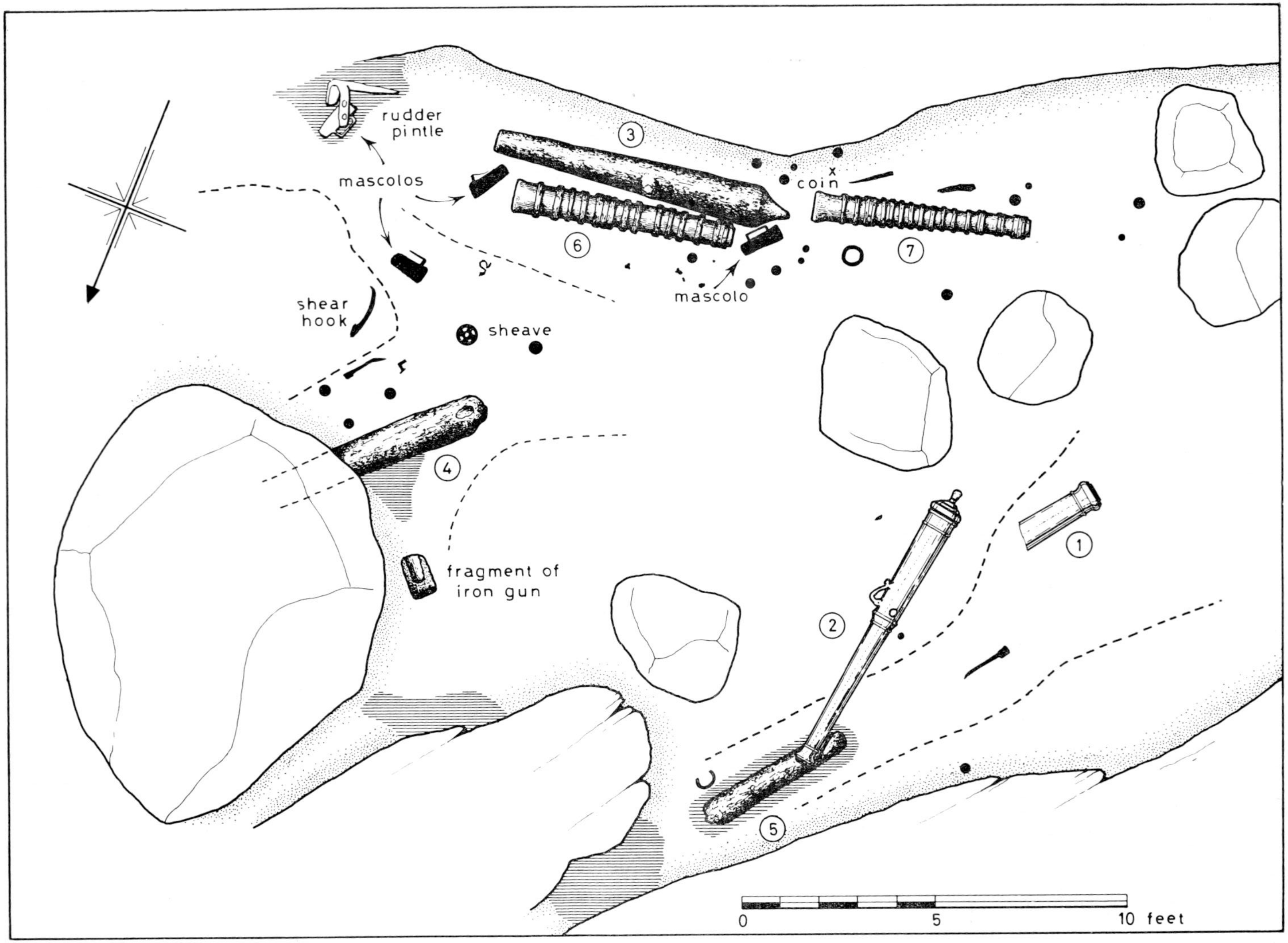

Figure 7. Leon Gully, Stroms Hellier, with guns from *El Gran Grifon*: (1) broken bronze *media-culebrina* (4.20-in.); (2) bronze *media-sacre* (2.92-in.); (3) *cuarto de canon* (*c.* 4-in.); (4) *cuarto de canon* (bore uncertain); (5) cast-iron "*pieza*" (*c.* 2-in.); (6) wrought-iron *esmeril largo* (*c.* 4-in.); (7) *esmeril largo* (*c.* 3.5-in.). *Mascolos* are breech-blocks for small swivel pieces (*esmeriles*).

identified, with none of other calibres. With this statistical evidence from two independent sources a tentative calculation has been made of the ship's gun-strength as a whole; an estimate which, however likely it is to err in detail, convincingly demonstrates the underlying character and purpose of the vessel's armament. This is the first concrete evidence to be recovered of the guns carried by a "second-line" Armada ship, and the interpretation of this evidence appears to throw some new light on the concepts of Spanish naval strategy in 1588.

9. SPANISH ARMAMENT STRATEGY IN 1588

From the first it should be stated that the basic conclusions of Professor Lewis's monumental study on Armada guns (1961) stand firmly unaltered in the face of this new evidence; no mean testimony, indeed, to its authority. In the classification of the guns Lewis's own system has been adopted, though in Table 1 the type-names are translated (albeit somewhat arbitrarily) into Spanish. Approximate English equivalents are given in brackets. It must, however, be stressed that sixteenth-century gun types were by no means standardized, and that even within the types very considerable variations may occur between individual guns.

Professor Lewis's thesis, in essence, is that between 1586 and 1588 Spanish naval thinking underwent a drastic change, a change which resulted in the equipping of the fighting ships with much heavier guns. This, he argues, was due to a sudden realization that gun-power rather than the ability to close and board had become the decisive factor in naval strategy. The Spaniards, however, still tended to regard boarding as the ultimate tactic, and so concentrated on short-range heavy artillery (cannons and perriers) intended to cripple an enemy into immobility before they came alongside to grapple and deliver the final *coup de grâce* in cold steel.

The English, on the other hand, who possessed faster and more manoeuvrable ships, but whose military steel, in terms both of sword blade and spirit, was less well tempered than that of the Spaniards, tended to utilize their superior mobility to keep out of range of the heavy Spanish ship-smashers and away from the danger of disablement and boarding. They therefore concentrated on the lighter-shotted but longer-range class of guns (culverins) with which they could hit the enemy from a safe distance.

There can no longer be doubt as to the basic truth of this hypothesis. It may be, however, that Professor Lewis has gone too far in suggesting that all the Spanish front-line ships were lightly armed in 1586, and that the entire "heavy gun" policy is subsequent to that date. What little evidence there is concerning the armament of the Spanish royal ships (the "Atlantic" squadrons of Portugal and Castile) suggests that they had been carrying heavy "ship-smashing" batteries for several years, and that even old-fashioned conservatives like the Marquis of Santa Cruz (who was to have commanded the Armada) had long realized that the broadside gun, however distasteful its inability to distinguish gentleman from commoner, had nonetheless come to stay (Waters, 1949).

The dramatic changes in armament policy between 1586 and 1588 seem, in every case for which there is evidence, to be confined to the auxiliary fleet. That the squadrons of this fleet appear to have been, at the same time, substantially re-equipped with large ships of Mediterranean type cannot be coincidence. The smaller "Atlantic" ships of

TABLE 1

Provisional comparative armament estimates of the *San Salvador* (of Guipuzcoa (952 tons, 24 guns) and *El Gran Grifon*, *capitana* of the *Urcas* (650 tons, 38 guns).

Role	Gun-Type	"Indicative" Weight	"Indicative" Shot	Brief Description	*San Salvador* (After Lewis)	*El Gran Grifon* (1970 estimate)
Short-Range Heavy Battery	*cañon* (cannon and demi-cannon)	*c.* 8,500 lb. (full cannon) *c.* 4,500 lb. (demi-cannon)	*c.* 50 lb. iron *c.* 32 lb. iron	*c.* 18–22 calibres in length	6	nil
	pedrero (perrier)	*c.* 2,850 lb.	*c.* 24 lb. stone	*c.* 8 calibres in length	5	nil
Long-Range Light Battery	*culebrina* (culverin)	*c.* 4,000 lb.	*c.* 18 lb. iron	*c.* 28 calibres in length	6	nil
	media-culebrina (demi-culverin)	*c.* 2,850 lb.	*c.* 9 lb. iron	*c.* 30 calibres in length	1	4
	sacre (saker)	*c.* 1,800 lb.	*c.* 6 lb. iron	*c.* 30–32 calibres in length	nil	4
	media-sacre (small minion)	*c.* 1,000 lb.	*c.* 4 lb. iron	*c.* 32 calibres in length	4	3

Tackle-Disablement and Anti-Personnel	*cuarto de cañon* (no direct equivalent)	*c.* 1,200 lb.	*c.* 7 lb. iron	*c.* 24 calibres in length	nil	6
	small cast-iron pieces (not identified)	*c.* 200 lb.	*c.* 1 lb. iron	(?) "piezas de hierro collado" (Duro I, p. 290)	nil	6
	esmeril largo (great base)	*c.* 700 lb.	*c.* 4 lb. iron or (?) bar shot	Wrought-iron breech-loaders (obsolescent)	nil	9
	esmeril (fowler or murderer)	*c.* 150 lb.	*c.* 1 lb. iron; $1\frac{1}{2}$ lb. lead; (?) assorted "case"	breech-loading swivel piece "mascolo" = breech-block	2	6

Guipuzcoa and Biscay were abandoned, it is here suggested, because they were unable to carry the proposed new armament. It is a question of cause and effect, and the cause must undoubtedly have been the decision, some time during 1587 (in which year the Cadiz galleys made a pathetic showing against the fire-power and manoeuvrability of Drake's ships on his famous raid), to abandon the 40-strong galley fleet which was to have sailed against England in direct support of the royal squadrons of Atlantic-built galleons. A supporting arm of such strength, if abandoned because of proved obsolescence, must somehow be replaced, and it is surely in this context that the Armada's reformed auxiliary fleet, with its new and heavy armament, is to be seen.

When the Armada sailed in 1588 the actual armament of the front-line auxiliaries was formidable indeed. Two of these ships—the *San Salvador* of Guipuzcoa and the *Nuestra Señora del Rosario*, flagship of Andalusia—were captured by the English, and from contemporary inventories Professor Lewis has calculated their full armament strengths. They were both, he concluded, extremely heavily gunned. Evidence of other auxiliary ship armaments, though less complete, points in the same direction. The *San Juan de Sicilia* of the Levant squadron, if indeed it is her remains which lie in the mud of Tobermory Bay, carried at least two 50-pounder full cannons (Miller, 1683). At "Borreis" in County Mayo, perhaps Tourglas on the Currawn peninsula (Spotswood Green, 1906) a great ship was wrecked with "50 pieces of brass, beside four great cannon" aboard her (C.S.P. [Ireland] Vol. CXXXVI, No. 37, p. 36). A wreck off Dunbeg in County Clare, perhaps that of the *San Esteban* of Guipuzcoa (Danahar, 1956), yielded to the Queen's Commissioner Sir George Carew in 1589 "a cannon of battery or basalyke so huge that it break our cables" (Carew Papers, 18, p. 8). *La Trinidad Valencera*, of Levant, had on board her "four cannons of brass" (Laughton II, p. 271) when she sank in Glenagivney Bay, Donegal, and two of these, at least, were full cannons of $7\frac{1}{4}$-inch bore, as the very recent discovery of her wreck by members of the City of Derry Sub-Aqua Club has now shown. The *Santa Maria* site (Martin, 1969*b*) has produced roundshot of a size so suitable to serve the known guns of her sister Guipuzcoan *San Salvador* that it is safe to assume that the general character of the two ships' armaments was much the same. In short, wherever evidence of the armament of an Armada front-line auxiliary is to be found, it invariably includes heavy, offensive guns.

The essential differences between "front-line" and "second-line" armaments are best seen in a tabulated comparison of guns belonging to an actual ship in each class (Table 1). The figures for the "front-line" ship are taken from Professor Lewis's estimate of the guns of the *San Salvador* (Lewis, 1961), while those for the "second-line" vessel are provided by the recently acquired evidence concerning the guns of *El Gran Grifon*—the guns, that is, of a large and important ship, but one unquestionably of non-combatant status (Martin, 1972). While the overall character of the armaments set out in the table is beyond serious doubt it must be stressed that the figures of both estimates, but particularly those of *El Gran Grifon*, are to be treated as indicative and not absolute. At best, they are a gross simplification of a truth which can never be known in all its detail. The force of the argument lies, however, not in detail but in trend.

The guns actually carried in 1588 by the *San Salvador*, and evidently also by the *Santa Maria de la Rosa* and other major ships in the auxiliary squadrons, were, as has already been shown, uniformly strong and aggressive. The *San Salvador* mounted a strong main battery of cannon-types and perriers, clearly intended to deliver ship-smashing broadsides at close range. Even in the long-range "culverin" group her guns are at the heavy end of the scale, as though intended for softening up an enemy while closing rather than for holding him off or annoying him at a distance. It is only in the final group of guns, the small tackle-disablers and anti-personnel pieces, that the *San Salvador* was noticeably lacking. Such weapons are essentially defensive, and negative self-defence was apparently no part of a front-line Armada ship's intended battle tactics.

In comparison, therefore, the most important point to be made about *El Gran Grifon*'s armament is that it is wholly defensive. She has no heavy battery pieces at all. Demi-culverins and sakers are long-range guns and, at any range, are not real ship-killers; thus the ship's main armament seems intended for holding off rather than destruction. For the same weight of main gun she could have carried perriers, 8-inch stone-throwers which would have given her a formidable close-range fire-power. But, as certainly as negative evidence can make it, she carried no perriers, and instead relied on a hotch-potch of small and partly obsolescent guns which could, at best, do little more than protect her from boarders. This is an armament tailored to a defensive, second-line role, and it is worth noting that it is one which bears a strong family resemblance to the guns proposed for the "pre-reformation" auxiliary squadrons of Guipuzcoa and Biscay in 1586 (Duro I, No. 7, pp. 289–90).

The figures, then, whatever their detailed inaccuracies, make one point quite clear. The ships of the Armada were armed to fulfil carefully planned roles, and the available guns were distributed amongst them accordingly. This may seem to be no more than plain common sense. But so clear and sensible a policy is in direct contrast to the chaotic state known to have pervaded the fleet and especially the distribution of armament under Santa Cruz, until the marquis's death precipitated the Duke of Medina Sidonia into unwilling command in February 1588 (Mattingly, 1959). Then, and only then, is reason seen to prevail. That the urgent reorganization which took place at this eleventh hour was due to the Duke's personal initiative and administrative competence there can be no doubt; there is simply no other explanation. Nor was it only in the redistribution of guns that his influence was felt. Under him, the quota of roundshot went up to the unprecedented average of 100 shots per gun for the front-line ships, supplies of small-arms ammunition were increased beyond recognition and the fleet's once abysmal morale was replaced by a pious fervour to sail. That the Armada which he had done his best to restore to fighting trim was given an impossible operational task was not his fault, but that of his king, and the Duke must take full credit for attempting, under appalling circumstances, to carry it out to the letter. Hostile and emotional critics may damn him, but the facts do not, and historians are still prone to follow the outbursts of the former while ignoring the evidence of the latter.

10. CONCLUSIONS

The Armada seems to have failed primarily because the fundamental plan was unrealistic and its execution unco-ordinated. Other reasons, however, appear to have played a considerable part. Spain, as Cipolla (1965) has recently stressed, was not a technologically advanced nation in the sixteenth century, and this failing is reflected in the equipment with which the Spaniards attempted to fight what was to be the first large-scale naval battle in which mobility and fire-power were the decisive factors. Their ships were not the monsters which a contemporary observer thought they were, "framed of planks and ribs four or five foot in thickness" (Hakluyt, 1589); on the contrary, their hulls seem to have been, in many instances at least, of eggshell-thin Mediterranean build. Spanish guns, though in some cases large, were, as Professor Cipolla's study shows, often obsolescent and generally of poor quality. *El Gran Grifon* has herself yielded a gun for which Robert Norton's criticisms of "forreigne foundings" (1628) would be well justified; it is "bored awry, crooked in the chase, and of unequall bore". The Armada is perhaps more correctly seen as a technological failure than as a naval defeat, though here Mr. Wignall's own paper is being anticipated (see below, pp. 463–81).

11. DATES AND UNITS OF MEASUREMENT

All dates have been adjusted to conform with the New (Gregorian) Calendar which the Spaniards, but not the English, were using in 1588. Contemporary English dates which were based on the Old (Julian) Calendar, appear to fall ten days earlier than their Spanish equivalents.

Because so much contemporary and later material concerning shipbuilding and gunnery has been expressed in figures at least closely approximating to the modern foot unit and pound weight it has been decided to retain, for the purposes of this study, the now obsolescent Imperial units of measurement and weight.

REFERENCES

Anderson, R. C. 1925 Italian naval architecture about 1445. *Mariner's Mirror*, **11**, 135–63.

Anderson, R. C. & Salisbury, W. (ed.) 1958 *A treatise on shipbuilding and a treatise on rigging written about 1620–1625*, 63 pp. London.

Cipolla, C. M. 1965 *Guns and Sails in the Early Phase of European Expansion 1400–1700*, 192 pp. London.

Clarke, A. 1964 *The Treasure of the Great Reef*, 194 pp. London.

Danahar, K. 1956 Armada losses on the Irish coast. *Irish Sword*, **2**, 320–31.

Duro, C. F. 1884–85 *La Armada Invencible*. See below.

Green, J. N. & Martin, C. J. M. 1970 Metal Detector Survey of the Armada Ship "Santa Maria de la Rosa". *Prospez. Archeol.* **5**, 95–100.

Green, W. Spotswood 1906 The wrecks of the Spanish Armada on the coast of Ireland. *Geographical Journal*, **27**, 429–51.

Hakluyt, R. 1589 *Principal Navigations, etc.*, vol. II (Everyman edition). London, 1907–09.

Hardie, R. P. 1912 *The Tobermory Argosy*, 68 pp. Edinburgh.

Ireland, J. de Courcy 1966 Review of E. Hardy, *Survivors of the Armada* (London, 1966). *Irish Historical Studies*, **15**, No. 57, 317–22.

Lane, F. C. 1934 Venetian naval architecture about 1550. *Mariner's Mirror*, **20**, 25–49.

Lewis, M. A. 1960 *The Spanish Armada*, 216 pp. London.

Lewis, M. A. 1961 *Armada Guns*, 243 pp. London.

Lovegrove, H. 1964 Remains of two old vessels found at Rye. *Mariner's Mirror*, **50**, 115–22.

Mainwaring, Sir H. *c.* 1623 *Seaman's Dictionary*, ed. with notes by G. E. Mainwaring & W. G. Perrin. London, 1920.

Martin, C. J. M. 1969*a* "Santa Maria de la Rosa"—Interim Report 1968. *C.N.A. Newsletter*, **3**, 5–8.

Martin, C. J. M. 1969*b* Surveying underwater on a wreck site, in *Surveying in Archaeology Underwater* (Colt Monograph V), 49–63. London.

Martin, C. J. M. 1970 Spanish Armada Expedition—Annual Report 1969. *C.N.A. Newsletter*, **4**, 30–5.
Martin, C. J. M. 1972. "El Gran Grifon". An Armada wreck on Fair Isle. *International Journal of Nautical Archaeology*, **1**, 59–71.
Mattingly, G. 1959 *The Defeat of the Spanish Armada*, 382 pp. London.
Miller, A. 1683 (MS.) *Informacion by Archibald Miller Anent the ship sunck in Tippermorie in ye Sound of Mull.* Rawlingson MSS, Bodleian Library, A. 189. f. 423.
Norton, R. 1628 *The Gunner, showing the whole Practice of Artillery, with all the appurtenances thereunto belonging. By Robert Norton, one of his Majesty's gunners.* London.
Palacio, Diego Garcia de 1587 (MS.): *see* Artinano, G. de 1920 *La Architectura Naval Española*, p. 115 and pp. 306–12. Madrid.
Salisbury, W. 1961 The Woolwich Ship. *Mariner's Mirror*, **47**, 81–90.
Stenuit, R. 1970 Excavation of the Galeass "Girona". *C.N.A. Newsletter*, **4**, 23–8; report in *Ulster Journal of Archaeology* forthcoming.
Tenison, E. 1940 *Elizabethan England*, Vol. VII. London
Waters, D. W. 1949 The Elizabethan navy and the Armada campaign. *Mariner's Mirror*, **35**, 90–138.
Wignall, S. 1968 *Santa Maria de la Rosa: Interim Report*, 128pp. Privately circulated. Dublin.
Wignall, S. 1969 Underwater search systems, in *Surveying in Archaeology Underwater* (Colt Monograph V), 81–94. London.

PUBLISHED CONTEMPORARY DOCUMENTS AND STATE PAPERS

La Armada Invencible (Vols. I and II): *State Papers and letters relating to the Spanish Armada, mostly in Simancas*, compiled by C. F. Duro, Madrid 1884 and 1885 (Duro I and II).
State Papers relating to the defeat of the Spanish Armada, 1588 (Vols. I and II), compiled by Sir John Laughton, London 1894 (Laughton I and II).
Calendar of (Spanish) letters and State Papers relating to English affairs, Vol. IV (Elizabeth) 1587–1603, ed. M. Hume. London 1899 (C.S.P. [Spanish]).
Calendar of State Papers (Ireland) Elizabeth, August 1558–September 1592, London 1885 (C.S.P [Ireland]).
Calendar of the Carew manuscripts 1589–1600, London 1869 (Carew Papers).

Discussion

Hague I am interested in the pieces of lead you found (on *El Gran Grifon*) which you thought had been cut from the ingots. Can you tell me from which type of ingot they were cut?
Martin No. The pieces are too small. They had evidently been hacked off with an axe, for the marks of cutting are quite clear.

Kennedy Do you have evidence of how the mast truck of the *Santa Maria de la Rosa* was fitted at the masthead? It looked as if there was some kind of sleeve on top of the mast, lining the truck.
Martin Yes. There was a sleeved construction which had evidently mated with the top of the mast.
Kennedy Was the top of the truck continuous or did the hole run right through?
Martin I don't know. The top part was destroyed. It seems possible that the top of the truck was decorated in some way—perhaps carved into the form of a crown, or something of that nature. But it is impossible on the evidence to say with certainty.
Kennedy It was certainly a truck, as it had what looks like a sheave for a flag-halyard.

McKee The question of the size of shipboard guns is of interest here. The *Mary Rose* of the earlier reign of Henry VIII included among her armament 68-pounder cannons-royal. These were apparently found to be unnecessarily heavy and difficult to handle when tried at sea during the first half of the sixteenth century, for reasons we do not understand. The relatively small-calibre 32-pounders (demi-cannons) were then tried, and found to be much more satisfactory. By 1588 the English fleet seems to have been using no guns larger than these.
Martin Yes. Henry VIII's navy seems to have been doing in the 1540s much as the Spaniards were doing at the time of the Armada—concentrating on the heavier types of battery gun. Indeed, many of Henry's ships were large Mediterranean vessels, as many of the Armada ships appear to have been 40 years later. This tends to support my original hypothesis—if you wanted very heavy batteries of guns at sea, then you needed large ships to carry them. As I have said, most really large ships at the time were of Mediterranean origin, or at least of Mediterranean-type build.
Lyon In the case of the Armada it was surely a matter of getting ships of any kind?
Martin Up to a point. The Marquis of Santa Cruz's "Armada Proposal" of 1586 is interesting in this respect, for it amounts rather to a list of the whole naval and military resources of the Spanish Empire than to a serious practical proposition for a single campaign. We can therefore get from it a clear impression of where the ships were available, with indications of number, type, and size. The ships from the Mediterranean—almost all of them merchant vessels, it should be remembered—are demonstrably larger than those from Atlantic provenances. Later, there are several distinct references by

Philip II himself to the great need for very large vessels. I think the Spaniards were much more "gun-conscious" than they were "ship-conscious"—perhaps this was their greatest mistake.

Throckmorton One point might be worth investigating. The small traditional ships of the Mediterranean have heavily cambered decks. Northern European types have flatter decks. I have heard that the mounting of cannons on wheeled trucks may have had something to do with the origin of this characteristic flat deck.
Naish All wooden ships have cambered decks. Look at *Victory*. This is not a Mediterranean speciality.
Martin In large ships you lose a great deal of structural strength if you have a flat deck.
Throckmorton But traditional Mediterranean ships have decks like half a barrel! It would be very difficult to handle wheeled guns on them.
Corney Is there any real evidence of guns on wheeled carriages in the sixteenth century?
Martin There is very little evidence about Armada-period shipboard gun-carriages. In the first half of the seventeenth century Sir Henry Mainwaring describes truck-carriages apparently identical to those now to be seen aboard *Victory*, and so one supposes that the type had reached a fair stage of development in 1588. *Wasa*'s gun-carriages, which date to 1628, are of this type.
Naish A painting of the Armada in the National Maritime Museum shows guns on small truck-carriages and guns on large-wheeled field-carriages. The ships are depicted without spritsail topmasts, and since large vessels started to carry these after about 1600 the picture must have been painted very close to the date of the Armada.
Martin I think contemporary Spanish shipboard guns were often mounted on two-wheeled field-carriages. Mainwaring himself says so, and suggests that the reason was that elm suitable for truck-carriages was not available in Spain or Italy. (See note).
McKee I believe that the earliest gun-carriage so far known is from a mid-sixteenth century wreck in the Baltic: the Jussaro wreck found in 1967 by Finnish divers, which may be a Swedish galley, from which were raised three bronze guns—a demi-culverin and two double-falconets—plus an iron gun concreted to the remains of a low oak carriage which had holes to take the shafts of four wheels (Report of the Bureau of Maritime Archaeology, Helsinki, January 1969, and personal communication and photographs from Lt. Cmdr. Christoffer H. Ericsson, February, 1969).
Martin This is interesting.

Note: Since this discussion took place six large-spoked field-carriage wheels have been identified on the wreck of the Armada ship *La Trinidad Valencera*, in Glenagivney Bay, Donegal.—C.M.

The Armada shot controversy

by

SYDNEY WIGNALL

AFTER YEARS OF confrontation and a state of undeclared war, the naval might of England and Spain met head-on in the Battle of the Narrow Seas in 1588.

The earlier skirmishes off the English coast were fought at beyond point-blank range and no serious damage was done to the vessels of either side.[1] The English captured two galleons, the *Nuestra Señora del Rosario* and the *San Salvador*, both of which were lost by accidental damage, the *Rosario* losing her bowsprit and foremast after colliding with another vessel and the *San Salvador* being shattered by an internal explosion, caused when a lighted linstock was dropped into a powder barrel. English gunnery could not take any credit for eliminating these two galleons from the battle.

When the English sent in the fireships at Calais and scattered the Spaniards from their anchorage, the galleas *San Lorenzo*, having fouled and damaged her rudder against the anchor-cable of the *San Juan de Sicilia*, drifted ashore and grounded. She was then attacked by Lord Howard of Effingham in his flagship, but she was already incapacitated. Once again English gunnery had scored no victory.

Off Gravelines both sides were presented with the opportunity to force the battle to a conclusion. The fight raged for five hours. We have it on authority of Sir William Wynter in the Vanguard that the range was down to point-blank.[2] This is confirmed from the Spanish side by Purser Calderon (C.S.P. [Spanish] Vol. IV, pp. 444–5). As the battle drew to a close the *Maria Juan*, a 665-ton galleon of the Armada squadron of Biscay, sank with most of her crew on board. A strong offshore wind then blew the Armada away from the danger of the Flemish shoals. Two badly damaged galleons of the squadron of Portugal, the *San Felipe* and the *San Mateo*, unable to keep up with the Armada and wishing to avoid capture by the English, ran themselves aground, to be boarded and taken by the Dutch "sea beggars".

The Spanish Armada of 130 vessels failed in its task, which was to transport the army of the Duke of Parma from the Low Countries to England. The English fleet of approximately 170 ships had mauled the Armada, but had failed to inflict a decisive defeat. Both sides were bedevilled by shortage of shot in the final stages of the fight. The Spaniards, with 123,790 rounds, had by their estimation sufficient for a five-day fight. The English, according to a letter from Sir Francis Drake to the Council, dated March

[1] C.S.P. (Dom.) ccxiii; 30 July 1588. Cecil to Burghley: "There was few men hurt with any shot, nor any vessel sunk, for as this man reporteth, they shoot very far off".

Ibid, ccxii; 21 July 1588. Howard to Walsingham: "We durst not venture to put in amongst them, their fleet being so strong".

[2] Ibid, ccxiv; 1 August 1588. Wynter to Walsingham: "When I was furthest off in discharging any of the pieces, I was not out of shot of their arquebuss, and most times within speech of one another".

1588, entered battle with powder and shot sufficient for only one and a half days of fighting (C.S.P. [Dom.] ccix, 40; 30 March 1588).

The very detailed analysis by the late Professor Michael Lewis of the armament carried by both fleets provided conclusive evidence that the Spaniards were better armed than the English (Lewis, 1961, 186). The Armada's main armament consisted of whole cannon and demi-cannon firing 50-pound and 32-pound shot. The English battery pieces were in the main the lighter-shotted long-range 18-pounder and 9-pounder culverins. The Spaniards held a further advantage: their gunpowder consisted entirely of "fine-corned" or pistol-quality powder (Duro, 1885, No. 110, p. 83), whereas the major proportion of the English powder was "serpentine", which had a much lower maximum pressure when ignited, with a consequent reduction in muzzle velocity.

The Spanish galleons most closely engaged ran out of shot, as did their English counterparts. A redistribution of shot among the Spanish ships might have allowed a further few hours of battle, but the prevailing weather conditions made this impossible. The English, with shot-lockers empty, followed the Armada up into the North Sea, keeping at all times out of gunnery range. In the words of Lord Howard of Effingham, they "put on a brag countenance" (Bruce, 1798, App. LX, p. cclxxxiv).

The Battle of the Narrow Seas then drew to a close. The English could claim to have sunk only one Spanish galleon and mortally wounded two others. English ship losses were nil and their total casualties, according to Captain Edward Fenner, who saw close action in the *Nonpareil*, were under one hundred.[3]

Could it be that the Spanish 50-pound and 32-pound cannon shot, when fired at point-blank range, was ineffective against the sides of a well built oak ship? Proof of the effectiveness of point-blank gunnery was provided by a series of tests carried out at Woolwich Arsenal in 1651 by Professor John Greaves (Ffoulkes, 1937, 97). At that time there had been no improvement in the quality of smooth-bore guns or the propellant. Iron shot ranging from 32-pound demi-cannon to 9-pound demi-culverin were fired at point-blank range at butts of oak and elm. Three butts were set up, each 19 inches in thickness. The distance between the first and second butts was 42 feet, and between the second and third 24 feet. Nearly all the shots fired burst through the first and second butts and struck the third. These tests confirmed the devastating effect of iron shot when fired at point-blank range.

The remarkable degree of penetration of iron shot fired from a smooth-bore gun is further confirmed by the fact that during the Napoleonic Wars, when ships of the Royal Navy attacked a French vessel from both sides (the manoeuvre known as "doubling"), the gunnery officers were ordered to reduce the powder charges by as much as 50 per cent. It had been learned by experience that a 32-pound ball, propelled by a full charge of powder, could smash through both sides of an enemy vessel and still possess sufficient velocity to damage seriously an allied ship on the far side.

In July 1968 an expedition organized by the writer located the wreck of an Armada Vice-Flagship, the *Santa Maria de la Rosa*, of the Squadron of Guipuzcoa, a 945-ton, 26-gun Nao, which sank in Blasket Sound, off the west coast of Ireland, in September 1588.

[3] Ibid., ccxiv; 4 August 1588. Fenner to Walsingham: "God hath mightily protected Her Majesty's forces with the least losses that have ever been heared of, being within the compass of so many great volleys of shot both great and small. I verily believe there is not three score lost in Her Majesty's forces".

Analysis of the first samples of shot by the Department of Chemistry, University College, Dublin, suggested that the iron was rich in sulphur (a negative factor in the casting of iron). This proved to be a "red herring". The high sulphur content had been induced by the action of the sea during the 380 years that the shot had lain on the sea bed. It did, however, provide the impetus for the writer's present line of enquiry: was there anything wrong with the shot fired by the Armada in 1588?

The quality of the shot used by both sides has never before been called into question; historians had therefore created a constant, the "Ballistic Constant", which assumes that all iron shot is of identical quality.

Because of the lack of sixteenth-century data on shot performance I pursued the matter on a theoretical mathematical basis. I had to take into consideration the acceleration of the shot due to the propellant forces in the barrel of the piece, and the decelerating forces as the shot struck the ship's timber sides. When it is fired the forces are uniformly spread over half the surface of the spherical shot. But when it strikes the target, the decelerating forces are applied initially over a very small area. From this we can surmise that although a badly smelted and cast iron shot might be weakened by the massive blow imparted by *high charge density* and *high maximum pressure* fine-corned black powder, the odds are that its complete disintegration would more probably take place when the first terminal contact was made with the target.

Later battles have shown that the quality of the projectiles fired often had a direct bearing on the outcome of a battle. A perfect example is the Battle of Jutland in 1916. In that battle Britain lost three battle-cruisers, three cruisers and eight destroyers, with a loss of over 6,000 lives. Though, as was later established, the British gunnery had established three hits to the German two, German losses in ships and men were much lower. The reason for this lay in the poor quality of the British armour-piercing shot, which broke up on striking the German ships. The defective quality of the British shot was in fact known before the 1914–18 war commenced, but nothing was done to correct it.

All samples of Armada shot examined proved to have been quenched, that is, they had been rapidly chilled from the hot state immediately after casting. This was shown by masses of concentric rings, which gave the appearance of a shot within a shot (Fig. 1). This process would make the ball brittle. Why had the Spaniards quenched their shot? There could be two reasons: one, that they had an inadequate knowledge of the craft of iron-founding; the other, that a crash programme of shot-moulding forced them to adopt a dangerous procedure.

An examination of the Spanish records for the year 1588 provided confirmation that Spain had undertaken a rapid expansion in shot-casting. In March of that year the Duke of Medina Sidonia, Commander-in-Chief of the Armada, complained to Philip II that the shot allowance of 30 rounds per gun was inadequate (Duro, 1885, No. 110, p. 83). He raised the shot allowance from 70,000 to 123,000 rounds in only two months. This would amount to a production of 350–400 tons of cast iron—a remarkable achievement in itself. The total annual output of iron guns and shot in England in that period never exceeded 1,000 tons (Schubert, 1957, 250). The Spaniards were able to produce perhaps a third of that amount, entirely in shot, in only two months, in a period when Spain in fact had no viable industry for the production of good-quality cast iron. An examination of the structure of Spain's iron industry in the sixteenth century suggests that her knowledge of iron-founding and metallurgy was slight.

Figure 1. Sample of Spanish 7-in 50-lb "whole cannon" iron shot from the wreck of the *Santa Maria de la Rosa.* This shot had been quenched when still red-hot.

In the early sixteenth century bronze guns were most in favour and cast-iron guns were looked upon with a jaundiced eye. Cast-iron guns often blew up under proof test, while a gun which stood a proof test was often of such enormous weight that it was unsuitable for shipboard use. Spain's advent into the field of colonial and European expansion found her with practically no capacity for smelting and casting good-quality iron—a state of affairs that was to last well into the seventeenth century. Attempts to establish foundries for gun-making were a dismal failure. The volume of production was lower than that of England and the quality of the products was poor. The arsenal town of Medina del Campo was one of Spain's largest commercial centres and boasted the largest iron-foundry in the country. By the middle of the sixteenth century it fell into a decline. The one other large foundry, at Malaga, produced cast iron of such poor quality that its production fell to almost nothing by 1590 (Carrasco, 1887, 185).

Philip II had within the boundaries of his kingdom some of the finest bronze gun-founders in Europe. His subjects in Flanders and in Italy produced guns equal in quality to those cast in the Tower of London. None of these master gun-founders lived in the Iberian peninsula and, as a consequence, Philip was forced either to order his guns from abroad or to invite foreign master founders to set up industry in Spain

(Yernaux, 1937, 6–13). The gun-founders of the Low Countries, being predominantly Protestant, avoided service in Spain owing to fear of the Inquisition. As a result, a first-class indigenous Spanish iron-founding industry did not emerge until 1622, thirty-four years after the Armada had sailed.

This state of affairs can be attributed to several causes, one of which was the lack of a commercially-minded middle class. Another cause was Spain's great wealth, which flowed in from the Indies in the Plata Flota, the Fleets of Tierra Firme and the Carreira da India. As long as Philip could purchase his guns from wherever he pleased the need for a home industry was not apparent. Spain, as a consequence, was bedevilled by a constant balance of payments problem. In the words of the Venetian ambassador, Vendramin, "this gold that comes from the Indies does on Spain as rain does on a roof; it pours on her and flows away".

Opposite economic factors brought about the rapid development of both bronze and iron gun-founding in England. Henry VIII rapidly dissipated the fortune left to him by his father. This is confirmed by the fact that after the continental gun-founder Poppenruyter had cast a number of guns for Henry VIII, he was unable to obtain payment (Ffoulkes, 1937, 109). The war with the French forced Henry, now almost bankrupt, to turn to home industry. The French gun-maker Peter Baude was sent to the Weald of Sussex, the seat of the English iron-founding industry. There he instructed the master iron-founder, Ralph Hogge, in the art of casting ordnance. Hogge's first cast-iron gun was produced in the same year, 1543 (Schubert, 1957, 171–2).

Years of iron-founding in a small way had long since taught the Sussex craftsmen like Hogge the negative influence of quenching hot cast iron. The English also had an accident of nature acting as their ally in the smelting of the iron ore: the presence in the ore of tiny fossilized sea shells, known as "greys", which provided the "flux" that was necessary to extract the maximum quantity of slag from the smelted ore (Schubert, 1957, 229). Thus the term "grey iron" for good-quality cast iron came into use in the iron industry, and is still in use to this day. Grey iron was described thus: "always a fine, genuine, good sort of metal; possessed of every good quality that can be desired" (Horne,1773, 62). Iron smelted from an ore without the use of a flux produced a very brittle product which was known in the trade as "cold-short". (Schubert, 1957, 233–4).

A further improvement in quality was obtained by "fining" or "refining" the iron after it had been smelted. This was effected by re-heating and the removal of all impurities and dross at the liquid stage. It was recognised in England as early as 1496 that it was essential that iron intended for the casting of shot should be refined *before* it was despatched to the shot-moulder. Otherwise the unrefined iron, containing many impurities, might produce a poor-quality shot (Schubert, 1957, 273).

So desperate were the Spaniards for good-quality guns and shot that in 1574 the Spanish governor of the Netherlands placed an order with English gun-makers for 38 cast-iron guns. Elizabeth reacted immediately and passed an ordinance forbidding the casting of guns other than for the use of the realm. The governor of the Netherlands then turned to the gun-makers of Liège, one of the most prominent of whom, Wathier Godefrin, undertook in 1575 to produce 300 guns and 46,000 rounds of iron shot. The guns were delivered within six months as per contract, but they blew up when subjected to test proof and Godefrin was thrown into prison (Lejeune, 1939, 185). Presumably his shot was as deficient in quality as his guns.

In the same year, 1574, an attempt was made to influence Flemish iron-founders to set up industry in Spain, but they refused, and Spain reacted by offering panic prices of £20 per ton for iron guns in the Low Countries.

In 1587 disloyal English merchants smuggled 140 bronze culverins to Naples, thereby allowing Philip II to dismount many larger pieces from the fortifications of Naples to equip his ships (Lewis, 1961, 137).

In 1603, fifteen years after the Armada failure, a number of Flemish gun-founders set up industry in Spain at the expense of the state; but the quality of their cast-iron guns was so poor that the scheme was abandoned with heavy financial loss (Carrasco, 1887, 187). It was not until about 1622 that Spain for the first time produced good-quality cast-iron guns and shot (Carrasco, 1889, 67).

Six years later, the English master gun-founder John Browne was able to cast an iron gun which was lighter than a bronze gun and which withstood double the proof-test charge of powder (C.S.P. [Domestic] Charles I, 1625/26, Vol. 25, No. 79). England had led the field in the production of good-quality cast iron for nearly eighty years. Proof of this is available, for there are in existence today culverins and whole cannons cast in iron in the sixteenth century (Schubert, 1957, 251 & Pl. 12). The Spaniards were unable to cast iron guns of such size until well into the seventeenth century.

Was the poor quality of Spanish cast iron attested in any field other than that of guns and shot? There is ample evidence that Spanish cast-iron anchors of the period were of poor quality. The Netherlanders, as subjects of Philip II, sailed in their thousands in Spanish ships, and they originated the saying "as meagre as a Spanish anchor".

Positive identification of several Armada anchors during recent years has provided the confirmation required.

During the 1968 search for the wreck of the *Santa Maria de la Rosa*, my team of 43 divers systematically searched 3,200 acres of the sea bed in Blasket Sound, using a search system known as the "Swim Line" (Wignall, 1968, 28–37). We located several ancient anchors, two of which we can positively identify by means of the meticulous log kept by Marcos de Aramburu, of the squadron of Castile, who witnessed the sinking of the *Santa Maria de la Rosa* (Spanish text in Duro, 1885, No. 178, pp. 315–26; English translation in Wignall, 1968, 114–22).

Aramburu described how his galleon, the *San Juan*, was dragging on two anchors, and about to collide with the sinking *Santa Maria*, when the *San Juan* fouled an anchor which held. Aramburu raised his other anchor and found that it had broken in two, leaving the lower part of the shank and the two arms and flukes on the sea bed. We located and raised this half-anchor (Figs. 2A and 3). On a line from it to the wreck of the *Santa Maria* we found another huge anchor, lying hooked under a ledge of rock, at the foot of the uncharted reef on which the *Santa Maria* broke her back. This could only be the main anchor of the sunken *Santa Maria de la Rosa*. It had one complete arm and fluke missing (Figs. 2B and 4).

The poor quality of the casting of the anchor had sealed the ship's doom. It has been suggested (van Nouhuys, 1951, 44) that the Dutch saying "as meagre as a Spanish anchor" was related to the thin or light construction of the anchors. The construction of the Aramburu and *Santa Maria* anchors belies this. The *Santa Maria* anchor still had its ring intact. The ring, and perhaps the tip of a fluke, would be the weakest part of an anchor. A well cast anchor would not break in the shank or at the crown of the arm.

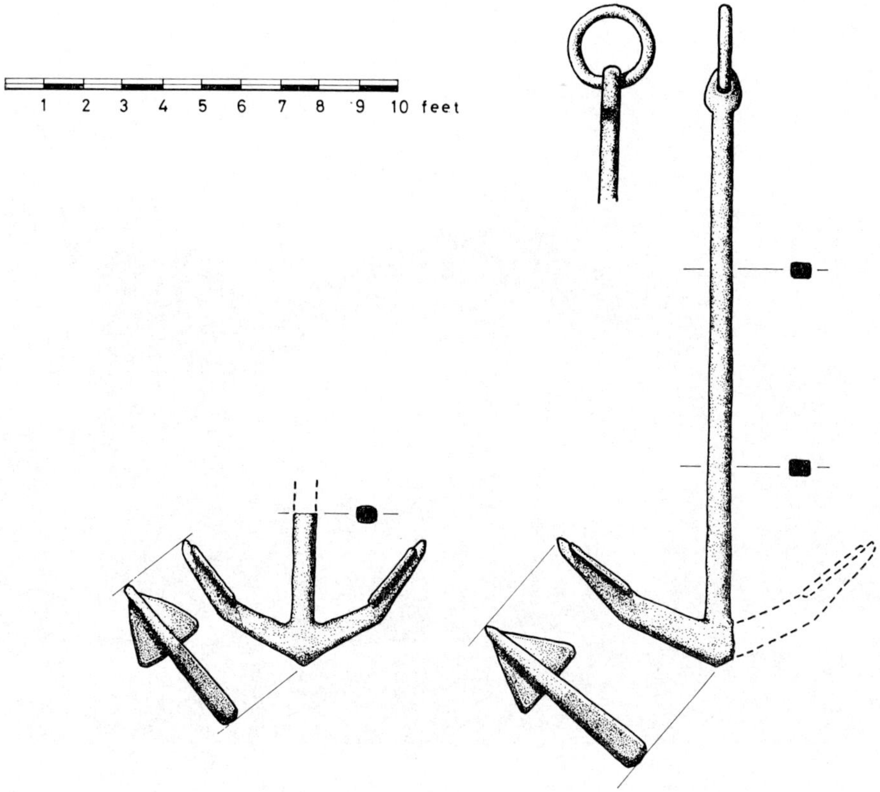

Figure 2A. Spanish medium-sized anchor, broken in half at the shank, left in Blasket Sound, Co. Kerry, by Marcos de Aramburu of the galleon *San Juan* of the squadron of Castile, 21 September 1588.
Figure 2B. Main anchor of the *Santa Maria de la Rosa*, found with one arm and fluke missing.

In 1968–9 Robert Stenuit located and excavated the wreck of the Armada galleas *Girona* off the north coast of Ireland. The only anchor found in the vicinity of the *Girona* had part of one arm and the fluke missing.

We obtained proof of the poor quality of Spanish gun-founding during our 1969 and 1970 expeditions. In 1969, during a period of bad weather which precluded diving, Mr. J. N. Green of the Oxford University Research Laboratory for Archaeology, operating a metal detector supplied by Dr. E. T. Hall, made at my suggestion a survey of the site of Dun an Oir, County Kerry, where a papal force of Spanish and Italian mercenaries had landed in 1580. After disembarking, the soldiers had erected temporary fortifications and installed several artillery pieces. They were invested by the English and eventually surrendered, after which the 600 odd survivors of the battle were massacred by armed bands commanded by a Captain Walter Raleigh. The metal-detector survey exposed part of the shattered breech of a bronze gun which had disintegrated on firing (Fig. 5; Green & Martin, 1970, 102).

Figure 3. The half-anchor of the *San Juan* (cf. Fig. 2A).

In 1970 Colin Martin and I located off Fair Isle, Scotland, the wreck of the Armada flagship of the squadron of *Urcas* or Hulks, *El Gran Grifon* (Martin, 1971; 1972). One of the finds consisted of part of the muzzle of a bronze demi-culverin. Its 4.20-inch bore was well out of true (Figs. 6 and 7). It must be remembered that the casting of guns in the solid and the boring-out of the barrel did not take place until the early eighteenth century (Ffoulkes, 1937, 17). Prior to this the gun was cast on a core, or kernel, to which was attached a "Crown Iron" which prevented the core from moving in the mould. If the core moved, the bore would be off-centre. The *Gran Grifon* demi-culverin, cast off-centre, was thus a product of poor workmanship. The gun would be highly inaccurate, and being so thin on one side of the breech might easily burst on firing.

Samples of shot from the *Grifon*, when analysed by the Royal Armaments Research and Development Establishment at Sevenoaks, were found to have suffered very little from their 380 years' immersion in the sea, in marked contrast to the shot of the *Santa Maria de la Rosa*, which was reduced to a mass of crystalline iron oxide—a phenomenon for which we have no explanation. The *Grifon* was a Baltic hulk from the Hanseatic port of Rostock. Although badly mauled in the earlier stages of the channel battle, she took no great part in the final close-range mélée off Gravelines. Her armament was of the lightest and she carried none of the heavier range of cannon. The largest sample of shot found matched the broken gun.

Figure 4. The main anchor of the *Santa Maria de la Rosa*, lying at the foot of the reef on which the *Santa Maria* broke her back, 21 September 1588 (cf. Fig. 2B).

There now remained one other source of historical information which could prove or disprove the poor quality of Spanish iron shot: the English royal galleons. How much damage had they suffered in the battle at point-blank range off Gravelines?

The matter was summed up very clearly by Sir John Hawkins, Treasurer to the Navy, in a letter to Secretary Walsingham, written a few days after the battle had ceased: "Our ships, God be thanked, have received little hurt" (C. S. P. [Dom.] Elizabeth, ccxiii, 71; 31 July 1588). Proof of the lack of damage to Elizabeth's galleons is contained in the report on the survey of the Navy completed on 28 September 1588 (Laughton, 1894, II. 250–54). The survey was carried out by the two most able marine architects of their day, Peter Pett and Mathew Baker. The only mention of damage to a royal galleon was contained in the reference to a new mast for *Revenge*, which had been "spoiled by great shot". The survey was minutely detailed: new rigging, new sails, replacement of rotten knees and ribs. There was no mention of even minor hull damage. The total estimate for repairs, over and above the ordinary annual maintenance account, was only £1,300, and the major part of this was for victualling shipwrights and for careening and caulking, etc. (Bruce, 1798, App. XLI, p. cxcvi).

Why had the Spanish shot failed to inflict any serious damage on the English galleons? The majority of historians have evaded this question. One fallacious hypothesis put

Figure 5. Exploded breech of a bronze gun, and other objects found during a metal-detector survey at Dun an Oir, Co. Kerry, in 1969.

forward was that the Spanish ships were built so high out of the water that their shot flew over the top of the English ships (Froude, 1901, 266). This theory, accepted without question, is still presented, not as an unqualified assumption, but as a matter of historical fact.

In his book *The Spanish Armada* (1960, 166–67) the late Michael Lewis suggested that the English with their superior seamanship were able to keep the range open, so that they remained outside the range of the Spanish cannons, but close enough for their own culverins to punish their opponents.

Professor Lewis had, however, already destroyed this hypothesis by proving that the Spaniards in point of fact carried more of the 18-pounder whole culverins than did the English (1961, table opp. p. 162). The latter hypothesis, however, still ignored the final point-blank mêlée off Gravelines, where the Spaniards could bring into play their 50-pounder whole cannon, a size of ordnance with which the English were not equipped.

An examination of all the recorded engagements between English and Spanish vessels in the sixteenth century suggests that something was very much amiss with the Spanish artillery. The first gunnery battle took place at the Caribbean port of San Juan de Ulua in 1568 (Corbett, 1898, I. 114). John Hawkins, in the *Jesus of Lubeck*, anchored between Spanish galleons, perceived that an attack was about to take place. He therefore

Figure 6. Muzzle of a cast-bronze "demi-culverin" from the wreck of *El Gran Grifon*, Fair Isle; bore 4.20-in (cf. Fig. 7).

warped his vessel off shore and opened fire with his main armament. Although greatly outnumbered, and armed only with culverins and stone-firing perriers (Lewis, 1936, 324–6), he put at least 60 shot into the Spanish admiral's galleon, setting her on fire. The Spanish vice-admiral's galleon blew up. In the face of Spanish fire-ships and attempts at boarding, Hawkins retreated to a smaller vessel and escaped. The *Jesus* fell into the hands of the Spaniards.

In 1583 a decisive battle was fought at the port of San Vicente on the coast of Brazil between the English galleon *Leicester*, of 400 tons, and three Spanish Biscayans, of 300, 400 and 500 tons. Captain Edward Fenton was anchored offshore in the galleon *Leicester* and he later described how the *Santa Maria de Begona* bore down on him in an attempt to board. Both vessels engaged with broadside artillery and in due course the *Begona* sank, while the *Leicester* suffered no great damage. The battle is well documented in Fenton's narrative of his voyage (Hakluyt Society, 1959, 269–70), and also in the journal of the Spanish explorer and hydrographer Don Pedro Sarmiento de Gamboa, who arived at San Vicente a few days after the battle had taken place (Hakluyt Society, 1895, 269).

In 1589 the Spanish Plata Flota, arriving in the Azores from the West Indies, was beset by numerous English "reprisal pirates". One such encounter was witnessed by the Dutch chronicler Jan Huyghen van Linschoten, who watched the battle from the quayside

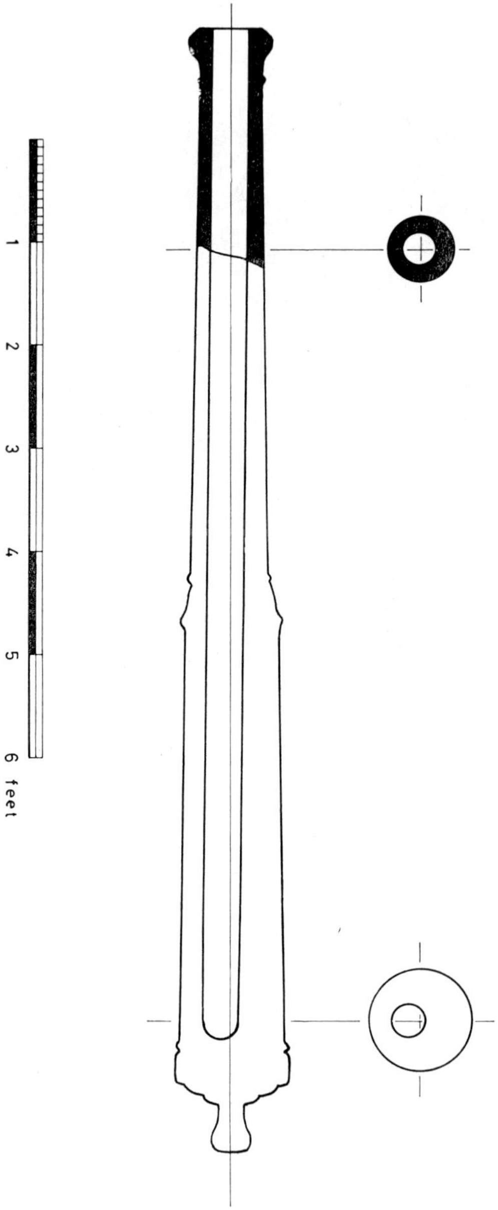

Figure 7. Restored section of the "demi-culverin" from *El Gran Grifon*. The piece had been cast on a core which had moved out of alignment and made the bore off-centre. The casting error is shown projected to the breech (cf. Fig. 6).

at Angra on the island of Terceira (Hakluyt Society, 1885, 293). A Spanish galleon was attacked by an English raider close inshore. The Spanish ship was armed with twelve guns, while according to Linschoten the English ship had no more than three pieces of artillery. Before two pinnaces armed with arquebusiers were able to put out from the shore the Spanish galleon sank.

In 1591 Sir Richard Grenville in the galleon *Revenge*, of 500 tons, took on the whole might of the Spanish "Indian Guard" of over 50 ships. In a sixteen-hour battle, fought at all times at point-blank range, *Revenge* sank two Spanish galleons, one of which was of 1,200 tons and the other of 1,000 tons. *Revenge*, armed with 39 bronze guns, fought galleons which carried from 30 to 90 pieces of artillery. An English survivor of the battle informed Sir Walter Raleigh that *Revenge* had been hit by at least 800 Spanish shot (Hakluyt, 1589, V. 7). When *Revenge* struck her colours to Don Martin de Bertandona off the Azores island of Flores, she was dismasted and dead in the water, with most of her crew dead or wounded and the last round of shot expended. She was not in sinking condition. About a week later, under jury-rig and with a Spanish prize-crew aboard, she was caught in a typhoon and wrecked against the cliffs of the island of Terceira (Hakluyt Society, 1885, 313).

The last fight of the *Revenge* completely disproved Froude's hypothesis that since the Spanish ships were so high out of the water their shot flew over the English galleons. The Spanish galleons of the Indian Guard faced by *Revenge* in 1591 included the huge *Twelve Apostles*, some of which displaced 1,500 tons; they were far bigger than any of the Armada vessels of 1588.

A most revealing engagement was that fought in 1593 by Sir Richard Hawkins in the *Dainty* against two Spanish galleons off the coast of Peru. In that action the *Dainty* was armed with demi-cannon and the Spaniards with culverins (Hakluyt Society, 1847, 214), a complete reversal of the artillery situation in the Channel in 1588. The action was fought at all times at point-blank range. Hawkins suffered grave handicaps from the very beginning of the fight. His master gunner was incompetent and allowed the Spaniards to pass close alongside the *Dainty*, while one of her complete broadsides lay unloaded. On one occasion this same gunner was seen to place a ball down the barrel of a gun, and the charge of powder after it. Hawkins' crew, by his own admission, refused on the second day to put on their body-armour, being intoxicated with wine, and therefore suffered many needless casualties (Hakluyt Society, 1847, 215–7). The general level of incompetence of the crew, Hawkins himself not excluded, lost the *Dainty* to the Spaniards. She surrendered when there were insufficient unwounded men left to man the guns or trim the sails. The battle had raged for three days and two nights, "In which time the enemy never left us, day nor night, beating continually upon us with his great and small shot" (Hawkins in Hakluyt Society, 1847, 212).

The loss of the *Dainty* highlighted the fact that a badly handled English galleon could not be sunk by Spanish gunnery, even though the range was down to point-blank and the odds two to one. In over thirty years of face-to-face gunnery battles between English and Spanish ships not one of Elizabeth's galleons was sunk by the Spaniards.

I have deliberately neglected the attacks made by Drake on Cadiz in 1587 and Corunna in 1589. In the former, oar-propelled galleys were massacred by broadside English gunnery; in the latter, the only Spanish ship of consequence was at anchor and therefore helpless.

In conclusion, it is possible that the true quality of sixteenth-century Spanish shot will never be known. The samples of shot from the *Santa Maria de la Rosa* and the *Girona* are badly deteriorated spheres of crystalline iron oxide, which we know to have been quenched, but they tell us nothing about the smelting and iron-casting methods of the Spaniards in the reign of Philip II. We know that the Spaniards used a good-quality haematite ore. Of their smelting and casting techniques we know very little. That they produced poor-quality cast-iron guns and anchors is an established historical fact. A mass of circumstantial and historical evidence would suggest that it was in the fluxing and smelting of the ore, the refining after smelting, and the quenching and other casting techniques, that the Spaniards were years behind the English.

The English ore-smelting and gun- and shot-founding techniques were kept a close secret in the sixteenth century, but the secrets could not last for ever. Eventually agents from the Low Countries pieced together the details of how the English were able to cast good-quality iron, and on 13 July 1619 Jan Andries Moerbeek was granted a patent to cast cannon which were to be produced from imported ore, ore which came from the Weald of Sussex. The importance of a high degree of fluxing in the smelting of the ore had been discovered (Doorman, 1942, 118). The techniques spread to Germany, and by 1630 a new Spanish gun-foundry at Lierganes, near Santander, operated by Germans, was producing first-class quality cast-iron guns and shot (Carrasco, 1889, 67). For the "Invincible Armada" they arrived forty-two years too late.

REFERENCES

Bruce, J. 1798 *Report on the Arrangements which were made for the Internal Defence of these Kingdoms, etc.*, 97 + cccxxxviii pp. London.

Carrasco, A. 1887 *Memorial de Artilleria de Bronze*, Madrid.

Carrasco, A. 1889 *Memorial de Artilleria de Hierro*, Madrid.

Corbett, J. G. 1898 *Drake and the Tudor Navy*, 2 vols., 436 + 488 pp. London.

Doorman, G. 1942 *Patents for Inventions in the Netherlands during the 16th, 17th and 18th centuries*, 228 pp. The Hague.

Duro, C. F. 1885 *La Armada Invencible*, Vol. II, 539 pp. Madrid.

Ffoulkes, C. J. 1937 *The Gun-Founders of England*, xvi + 134 pp. Cambridge. Reprinted 1969.

Froude, J. A. 1901 *English Seamen in the XVIth Century*, 309 pp. London.

Green, J. N. & Martin, C. J. M. 1970 Metal detector survey at Dun an Oir. *Prospezioni Archeologiche*, **5**, 101–4.

Hakluyt, R. 1589 *The Principal Navigations, Voyages, Traffiques and Discoveries of the English Nation.* Quoted from Everyman edition, 8 vols., 1907–09. London.

Horne, H. 1773 *Essays concerning Iron and Steel*, 223 pp. London.

Laughton, J. Knox (ed.) 1894 *State papers relating to the defeat of the Spanish Armada*, 2 vols., lxxxiv + 365 pp. Navy Records Society Publications, 1–2. London.

Lejeune, J. 1939 *La formation du capitalisme moderne dans la Principauté du Liège au XVI siècle*, 364 pp. Bibliothèque de la Faculté de philosophie et lettres de l'Université de Liège, Fasc. 87. Liège & Paris.

Lewis, M. A. 1936 The guns of the Jesus of Lubeck. *Mariner's Mirror*, **22**, 324–45.

Lewis, M. A. 1960 *The Spanish Armada*, 216 pp. London.

Lewis, M. A. 1961 *Armada Guns: a comparative study of English and Spanish armaments*, 243 pp. London.

Martin, C. J. M. 1971 *El Gran Grifon: Interim Report 1970*, 21 pp. Privately circulated.

Martin, C. J. M. 1972 "El Gran Grifon". An Armada wreck on Fair Isle. *International Journal of Nautical Archaeology*, **1**, 59–71.

Schubert, H. R. 1957 *History of the British Iron and Steel Industry from c. 450 B.C. to A.D. 1775*, xxi + 445 pp. London.
van Nouhuys, J. W. 1951 The Anchor. *Mariner's Mirror*, **37**, 17–47.
Wignall, S. 1968 *Santa Maria de la Rosa: Interim Report*, 128 pp. Privately circulated. Dublin.
Yernaux, J. 1937 Fondeurs de cloches et artillerie à Liège au XVIe Siecle; *Chronique archéologiqeu du pays de Liège*, **28** (Jan.–March 1937) 6–13.

PUBLISHED CONTEMPORARY DOCUMENTS AND STATE PAPERS

Calendar of State Papers (*Domestic*), (C.S.P. [Dom.]).
Calendar of (*Spanish*) *letters and State Papers relating to English affairs*, Vol. IV (Elizabeth) 1587–1603, ed. M. Hume. London 1899 (C.S.P. [Spanish]).

Publications of the Hakluyt Society:

The observations of Sir Richard Hawkins, Knt, in his voyage into the South Sea in the year 1593, ed. C. R. Drinkwater Bethune. First series, Vol. I, xvi + 246 pp. (Hakluyt Society, 1847).
The voyage of John Huyghen van Linschoten to the East Indies, Vol. II, ed. P. A. Tiele. First series, Vol. LXXI, xv + 341 pp. (Hakluyt Society, 1885).
Narratives of the voyages of Pedro Sarmiento de Gamboa to the straits of Magellan, ed. Clements R. Markham. First series, Vol. XCI, xxx + 401 pp. (Hakluyt Society, 1895).
The Troublesome Voyage of Captain Edward Fenton, 1582–1583, ed. E. G. R. Taylor. Second Series, Vol. CXIII, lvii + 333 pp. (Hakluyt Society, 1959).

See also Duro, 1885; Laughton, 1894.

Discussion

Higgs Is it not true that a cannon-ball will punch a neat circular hole in English oak whereas most European wood will split completely? English oak ships would then have the considerable advantage that cannon-ball holes could be temporarily filled with large wads of cotton waste carried specially for that purpose, while split planks in other European ships could not be repaired so effectively or so quickly.

Wignall There is no evidence to suggest that the Spanish galleons were constructed of inferior timbers. The Spaniards and the Portuguese relied mainly on oak for ship-construction, but it was recognised in the sixteenth century that the best constructed ships and those with the longest life were the Portuguese caracks built in Goa, the timbers of which were entirely of teak.

There is evidence that prior to John Hawkins' term of office as Treasurer to the Navy the Queen was systematically defrauded by her officers. Hawkins exposed the fact that Sir William Wynter had ordered the very best timber for the construction of the Queen's royal galleons and had then exchanged this fine-quality oak for green unseasoned timber with which the Queen's ships were built. Wynter then used the good-quality timber for building his own ships. There was similar corruption with regard to the supply of Baltic cordage, canvas and ship's masts. The survey of the English fleet after the battle highlighted the fact that many of the ships went into the 1588 action with rotten ribs, knees and frames. Most of the Queen's ships were suffering from dry rot before they even left the slipway. The Spaniards no doubt had similar problems.

Johnstone In our experiments at the Royal Armaments Research and Development Establishment the ball when fired at high velocity made a small hole in the 18-inch thick timber butts on entry and a small hole on exit. When fired at about 600 feet per second, a velocity which simulated the approximate muzzle velocity of a sixteenth-century gun, the ball made a small hole on entry but a very wide one on exit, shattering the timbers at the rear facing of the butts.

Higgs I have heard of experiments with English oak which demonstrated the properties which I mentioned above.

Anon. Were other woods ever used?

Wignall The English and the Spaniards used oak in the main. The Portuguese occasionally used teak. The *Santa Maria de la Rosa* was not designed as a fighting ship. She was an armed merchant ship, built on the coast of Yugoslavia and constructed of Adriatic oak.

McKee You must hit below the waterline if you want to sink a battleship easily. As a result of repeated hits a frame might be smashed and that might start a slow leak below the waterline, and in that way a big ship might eventually be sunk by gunfire, but I do not believe that they actually set out to sink ships. The purpose of the guns was to smash the upperworks, ruin the boarding-nets and disorganize and shock the defenders, prior to the assault. It was a matter of attrition.

Wignall In the battle off Flores in September 1591 the tiny 500-ton *Revenge* showed that a number of Spanish ships could be sunk by point-blank gunfire.
McKee That is quite true.
Wignall The question of poor-quality missiles or shot is not confined to the sixteenth century alone. At the battle of Jutland many of the British armour-piercing shells hit the German battleships and did not explode. Long before the 1914–18 war commenced a committee of inquiry had reported that British armour-piercing shells were of poor quality, but nothing was done to correct this fault. After Pearl Harbour the only offensive weapon which the U.S. Navy had in the Pacific was the long-range ocean-going submarine. For months they sank very few ships, until the Americans realised that the magnetic pistols in their torpedoes were faulty. In 1970 the Royal Navy discovered that the majority of detonators in their conventional submarine torpedoes were faulty. There was a danger of their blowing up when fired. This problem took almost a year to put right.

Lyon For me the most important objection to your theory is that there is no documentary evidence from either Spanish or English sources to show that Spanish shot did fail. Surely in thirty years of continuous warfare someone would have noticed and recorded such a drastic failure if it had happened.

I feel that you have not considered enough that a warship and her crew are as much a part of the weapon system as are the guns which the ship carried. English warships probably handled better, and would therefore have been better able to reach a position on bow, stern or quarter of their enemies from where they could hit without being hit back. Is there any real evidence that the British ships were actually broadside to broadside with the Spaniards, even in the hottest part of the Armada Fight?

As for the battle of Jutland, recent researches seem to show that British shells penetrated German ships' main armour belts, which is more than the vaunted German shells did. Our heavier losses in that battle were probably due mostly to poor stowage of propellant in our magazines. Although German ships were hit as often and as badly as ours they were less likely to blow up from fire reaching a magazine.

To return to the Armada, the fact that the English ships carried fewer cannon-balls does not mean that they therefore fired them at a slower rate. I suspect the opposite. Certainly one of the secrets of victory in later wars against the French was the ability of English ships to fire two or three broadsides to the enemy's one.

Your theory is a stimulating one, but unless you can produce more evidence it remains a highly dubious extrapolation from disparate and unsatisfactory fragments of information.
Wignall The evidence from the Spanish side is that they never sank any English galleon in thirty years of war. There is ample evidence that the Spaniards fired their guns as quickly as the English. For example, the *Relacion*, flagship of the Duke of Medina Sidonia, was attacked by several English ships sailing one after the other in line ahead. As they fired their broadsides and passed by, the Duke's gunners were able, according to him, to load, fire and reload fast enough for him to engage every one of the English ships, and his fire was so hot that the galleons at the end of the English line hauled off and opened the range. Once a ship had fired a broadside of ordnance loaded with black powder, there would be a great cloud of smoke. At point-blank range it would be impossible to

see what damage had been effected on an enemy ship. The Duke of Medina Sidonia stated that at the height of the battle off Gravelines there was so much gun-smoke that he could not follow the course of the battle even though he had climbed right up into the tops.

During the Napoleonic Wars there was an instance of an English frigate attacking another vessel at point-blank range in broad daylight. On seeing that his adversary was dismasted and in dire straits, the English captain shouted "Will you strike your colours?", only to be answered in English. If owing to gun-smoke they could not recognise ships of their own nationality, they were hardly likely to look for individual hits or shot-holes.

There was another parallel in the battle of the Falkland Islands in December 1914 when an English battle-cruiser pulled out of the line because she could not see the German cruisers because of her own gun-smoke.

Lyon I think that this was more probably due to smoke from funnels than smoke from guns.

Tilley Did you not make some test firings of iron shot against butts?

Wignall Tests were carried out at very short notice by the Royal Armaments Research and Development Establishment with cast-iron shot provided by a foundry in North Wales. The foundry concerned had been asked to provide shot of poor quality. When tested the shot pierced the butts again and again. The shot samples were afterwards subjected to a compression test and they withstood the enormous pressure of 76 tons. The shot provided by the foundry was in fact superior to anything we had at Trafalgar and the tests were therefore a complete waste of time.

Hague When did Toledo steel come into prominence?

Wignall Toledo steel was forged. The sword-makers of Toledo made superb products. It was in the art of founding cast iron that the Spaniards were so many years behind the English. Although the gun-makers of the Low Countries could make good-quality cast-bronze guns or fine pistols, they could not cast iron guns of an acceptable quality until the early 1620s.

Baker If there were such problems in casting, I wonder whether the Spaniards may have found that iron cannon of obsolete design (that is, iron rods welded together to form the barrel, as found on the *Gran Grifon* site) were easier to make and more reliable in operation.

Wignall Investigations by Dr. W. H. F. Tickle of the British Steel Corporation have led him to the conclusion that my hypothesis is correct. He is of the opinion that the Spanish shot used in 1588 technically did not consist of pure cast iron. He believes that the Spanish shot-moulders, knowing that their iron was poor in quality, decided that a further reduction in quality would matter little; they therefore used a trick in both the smelting and the casting of iron shot, one that Dr. Tickle believes was quite widespread in Spain in that period. Further experiments are in hand.

Corney Your premise is founded in the supposition that the quality of iron shot could be a decisive factor in sixteenth-century naval warfare. In attempting to establish this, you cite Jutland as an example of a battle in which the quality of the projectiles was decisive. I submit that comparisons with twentieth-century naval battles, with iron ships and armour-piercing high-explosive shell, are wholly inappropriate for this purpose. Your choice of Jutland emphasizes your difficulty in establishing your proposition.

Wooden battleships could founder; they could be sunk by burning; they could be battered into surrender or captured by boarding; but they could hardly ever be sunk by gunfire. At best, early guns could be expected to immobilise a vessel by causing superficial damage and by cutting rigging and bringing down yards and possibly masts, leaving the hulk accessible for closing and boarding or battering into surrender at the assailants' discretion.

I suggest that seen in these terms the physical quality of iron shot would be of little more than academic interest.

Wignall It is true that the Spaniards used their ships as floating infantry-platforms, but it is said that the English revolutionized naval warfare in 1588 by breaking away from this concept and concentrating on broadside gunnery. This was not a matter of choice for the English and it cannot be attributed to naval genius. The plain fact was that England, having fought very few land battles, had no standing army until the New Model Army of Cromwell and Fairfax in the seventeenth century. England could not muster the trained soldiers necessary to meet the Spaniards on equal terms. It is obvious that if the wind had turned to the north or north-west after the Gravelines battle and the Spaniards had, as they had agreed they would, turned and fought the English, it would have been the latter who would have been destroyed and not the Spaniards. If both sides were out of shot then the English would have had to fight on Spanish terms, that is, by "boarding and entering". Since the English ships had hardly any soldiers and the Spanish ships were crammed with the best trained and most experienced army in the world, the outcome of such a conflict would have been the complete destruction of those English ships which stayed to fight.

McKee The only really effective way of sinking battleships is to obtain an underwater hit—and that means mines, torpedoes and aircraft bombs dropped just alongside. Wooden battleships were very rarely sunk by each other's gunfire; the purpose of the preliminary bombardment was to create psychological shock as well as to inflict physical damage on the ship and crew. The psychological effect of bombardment is a vital factor in battle.

Green If it was so difficult to sink ships, what was the point in the English sending in the fire-ships at Calais?

Wignall The sending in of the fire-ships was the one brilliant stroke of the English in 1588. Its purpose was to scatter the Spanish ships from their anchorage and destroy their very successful crescent-shaped defensive formation. None of the Spanish ships was set on fire.

The investigation of the wreck of the "Amsterdam"

by

PETER MARSDEN

SUMMARY

This ship, built in 1748 in Amsterdam, was a Dutch East Indiaman. She lost her rudder in the English Channel while sailing to Batavia in Java, was beached near Hastings in January 1749, and quickly sank deep into the sand and clay of the beach.

In 1969 a contractor building a sewer nearby dug into the ship when it was visible at low tide in order to hunt for treasure, and unearthed a remarkable collection of antiquities ranging from bronze guns to pins. The Committee for Nautical Archaeology was told of the discovery, and an investigation of the wreck under my direction was commenced. With a considerable amount of assistance, especially from the BBC, this investigation has now been successfully completed.

The purpose of the investigation was

(a) to discover how much of the ship had survived, and in what condition;
(b) to make a full record of the objects discovered in 1969;
(c) to determine to what extent the ship still contains objects;
(d) to investigate fully the English and Dutch records.

The investigation in 1969–71 has shown that about three-quarters of the Amsterdam survives in the beach at Hastings; that she probably still contains the bulk of her cargo, stores, and many of the personal possessions of the people on board; and that contemporary documentary records relating to the ship in this country and in the Netherlands are exceptionally complete.

THE *Amsterdam* was a Dutch East Indiaman, built for the Amsterdam Chamber of the Dutch East India Company in 1748. She was about 150 feet long, was armed with 52 or 54 guns, and carried a considerable amount of canvas on three large masts. Her purpose was to carry cargo between the Netherlands and the Company's port of Batavia, now Djakarta, in Java. 335 people were crammed into her confined hull, comprising 203 officers and crew, 127 soldiers, and 5 passengers. After two attempts to sail from Texel at the mouth of the Zuyder Zee, which proved abortive because contrary winds blew soon after they had set sail, the *Amsterdam* finally set sail on 8 January 1749 (New Style dates only are used in this paper). The weather quickly worsened as the wind veered to the south-west and began to blow strongly. At the same time this brought heavy rainfall with it. By about 20–22 January the *Amsterdam* had reached Pevensey Bay, and Captain Willem Klump steered for the shelter of this bay which is protected from the worst of the south-westerly gales by Beachy Head. Unfortunately the ship's log seems to have been destroyed, so that we have to reconstruct the last fateful days of the voyage from other sources. As she sailed into the bay she apparently struck a shoal and lost her rudder, and at this critical stage she began to drift or be blown north-eastwards towards the shore. To save his ship Captain Klump dropped anchor off the very small village of Bexhill, hoping that the wind would veer around to the east and allow the *Amsterdam* to sail on to Portsmouth for repairs. Presumably by this stage he had erected a temporary rudder. The weather did not improve, however, and he could hold out no longer than Sunday, 26 January. During the previous 18 days nearly 50 men had died, and 40 more lay very sick on the ship's ill-ventilated lower deck. While firing her guns as a distress signal, the *Amsterdam* sailed straight towards a desolate beach between Bexhill and the small port of Hastings. The tide was high when she ran aground, but the point at which she stopped lay between ordinary low water mark and spring low water mark.

We have been especially lucky with this ship, for on four separate occasions good fortune, archaeologically and historically speaking, has protected the *Amsterdam* and her story. The first of these occurred when William Klump the Captain sailed his ship towards the beach, for he could not have known that she sailed through a narrow gap in a rocky outcrop on the seabed which would probably have torn a hole in her bottom. The second occurred minutes later, when the ship ran aground. Had it been almost anywhere else in the area she would have grounded on a firm beach, but just at that point a thick bed of clay crops out and allowed the ship to ground gently; heavy with cargo and stores, she began sinking into the beach. A few weeks later she stopped sinking when her keel lay about 8 m below the beach, and her upper deck was level with the beach. She had sunk so quickly that the salvage of her cargo proved to be almost completely impossible.

The third stroke of good fortune was discovered early in 1971 by Mr. Joop Reinboud, who searched the official Dutch East India Company records for details relating to the *Amsterdam.* Most of these are in the minutes of the meetings of the directors of the Company, but Mr. Reinboud did discover the ship's paybook, giving not only the names of every individual on board, but also his rank, pay, and other details. This was especially fortunate, since for the period of nearly two centuries during which the company was in existence all the annual paybooks, with the exception of just seven years, have been destroyed. The fourth stroke of good fortune dates from September 1748, when a local dignitary of Hastings, John Collier, suffered a stroke which partly paralysed him. He was sent to Bath to recover for the winter, but as he was the agent of the Duke of Newcastle, then Vice-Admiral of the coast of Sussex, his family and friends kept up a steady flow of correspondence describing local happenings, and one of these was the loss of the *Amsterdam.* These letters survive and thus we have eye-witness accounts of the loss of the ship, and of the subsequent attempts to salvage her.

Ever since 1749 the ship has been visible at extremely low tides, its timbers just projecting out of the beach. On a few occasions during the early nineteenth century there were attempts to recover her cargo, but these had very little success as low tide is not of sufficient duration to allow really deep holes to be dug, and in any case the sand is completely waterlogged so that any hole quickly fills up with water.

In July 1969 a contractor, William Press & Son Ltd., building a sewer outfall near the wreck site, decided to hunt for treasure. Using two powerful mechanical excavators they dug deeply into the ship: at the bow they dug up pulley-blocks, barrels, and brushes; amidships they found five bronze cannons, dozens of glass bottles of wine, and stoneware

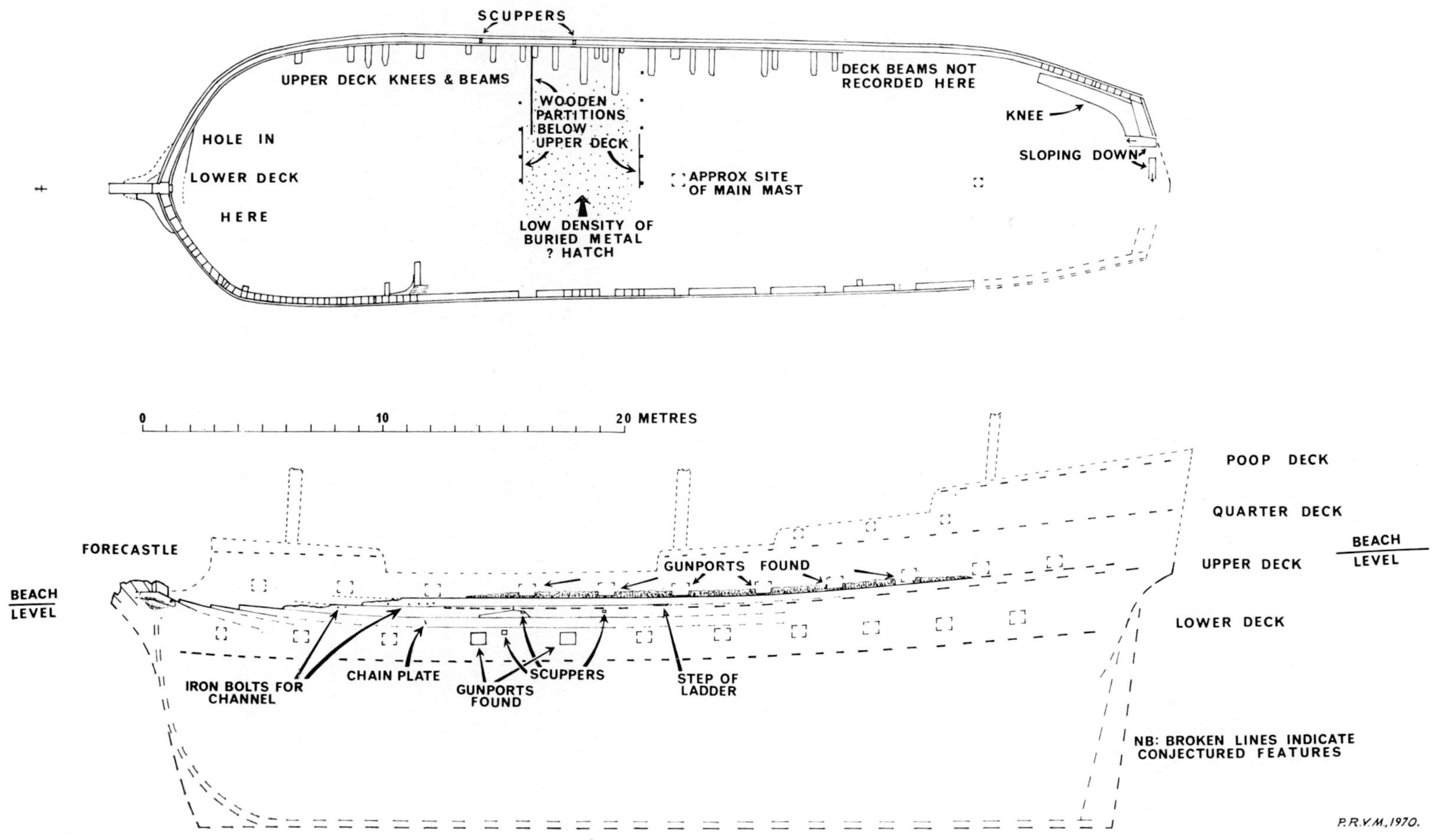

Figure 1. Plan and side elevation of the *Amsterdam*.

jugs; and near the stern they found cooking-utensils, military belts, and many of the personal possessions of the people who were on board. The Committee for Nautical Archaeology was told of this discovery, and in September 1969 an investigation was started under my direction.

At the beginning it was decided not to excavate the ship, and to do only such digging as was necessary to establish how much of the ship had survived. This work would require financial backing and practical help, and in this the B.B.C. "Chronicle" programme, through Mr. P. Johnstone and Mr. R. Sutcliffe, has been the major contributor, not only financially but also in finding someone to search and translate the relevant Dutch records. Mr. Joop Reinboud did this work magnificently.

The first step was to make a detailed plan of the visible part of the wreck during the last week of September 1969; since then other parts have been added to the plan. The method used was to stretch a long base-line, graduated in half-metre sections, along the axis of the ship from a nail on the stem-post to another nail at the stern. At 1 m intervals measurements to the sides of the ship were taken from the base-line, to give an outline plan of the ship. To this the details were added, such as the thickness of the inner and outer skins of planking, and the positions of some of the frames which formed a solid wall of timber between the skins. From the beginning it was clear that the ship is not lying horizontally in the beach, but is heeling to her port side (west). On the starboard side the knees and beams of one deck are visible, while on the other side most of the deck-beams are buried and much of the side is exposed up to the lower parts of a series of gunports. All of these features were carefully measured to complete the plan of the visible structure of the ship, but as time was extremely limited at each low tide all this work was backed up with a comprehensive photographic coverage (Fig. 1).

This could not be done at one group of tides only, and measurements and photographs of the ship's structure continued to be taken until the survey was terminated in March 1971. From the beach level it is impossible to get a general view of the ship as a whole; but it was only when Hy-mac Ltd. offered to assist the survey that it was decided that this particular problem could be solved. This company make not only mechanical excavators, but also mobile high-level platforms which are frequently used for repairing street lights. During the very low spring tides of March 1970 two mobile platforms, one 50 feet high and another 30 feet high, were assembled at Hastings. Hy-mac also provided a mechanical excavator on wide caterpillar tracks whose prime job was to drag the other vehicles through the deep shingle at high-water mark, and also to pull them out of the quicksand around the ship should they get stuck. Another company, Itt Flygt Pumps Ltd., which makes submersible pumps, also agreed to help free of charge; it agreed to pump all of the sea-water out of the hollow scoured in and around the ship, to expose details of the vessel's structure not normally seen. This meant that not only did great lengths of hose and the pumps have to be taken down to the wreck in a lorry, but also a powerful generator had to be dragged down, and once again the excavator proved invaluable as a crane to lower the pumps into position in the ship. In about half-an-hour these pumps drained an estimated 80,000 gallons of water from the hollow, thus enabling a very full photographic record to be made of the normally obscured upper part of the ship's interior (Fig. 2). As a result the true nature of the transverse partitions amidships could be defined more precisely.

Figure 2. The *Amsterdam*, looking aft. This view was taken from a 50-ft high mobile platform at low tide, and shows the proton magnetometer survey in progress.

The investigations as a whole showed that the remains of a deck lay at beach level, and that on the west or port side of the ship were preserved the lower parts of several gunports. The next problem was to identify the deck. The lower parts of several gunports, visible on the west (port) side, showed that it must be either the upper or lower deck, where the main armament was situated; but the only way of definitely solving the problem was to dig a hole immediately outside the ship to look for a lower row of gunports. If there were no more present, then the visible deck must be the lower deck, but if there was a lower row of gunports, then it must be the upper deck.

The excavation was carried out by a mechanical excavator during an especially long low tide one night in September 1969, and soon two closed gunports were revealed on the port side, thus showing that the visible deck must be the upper deck. The inward slope or "tumble-home" of the side was carefully measured, as were all other features revealed, such as the iron bolts which once secured the foremast channel; the bottom of foremast chain-plate; and the one rung of a ladder up the ship's side. These were very important details which made it possible for a side elevation of the ship to be reconstructed with a reasonable degree of certainty. The instrument used for quickly measuring

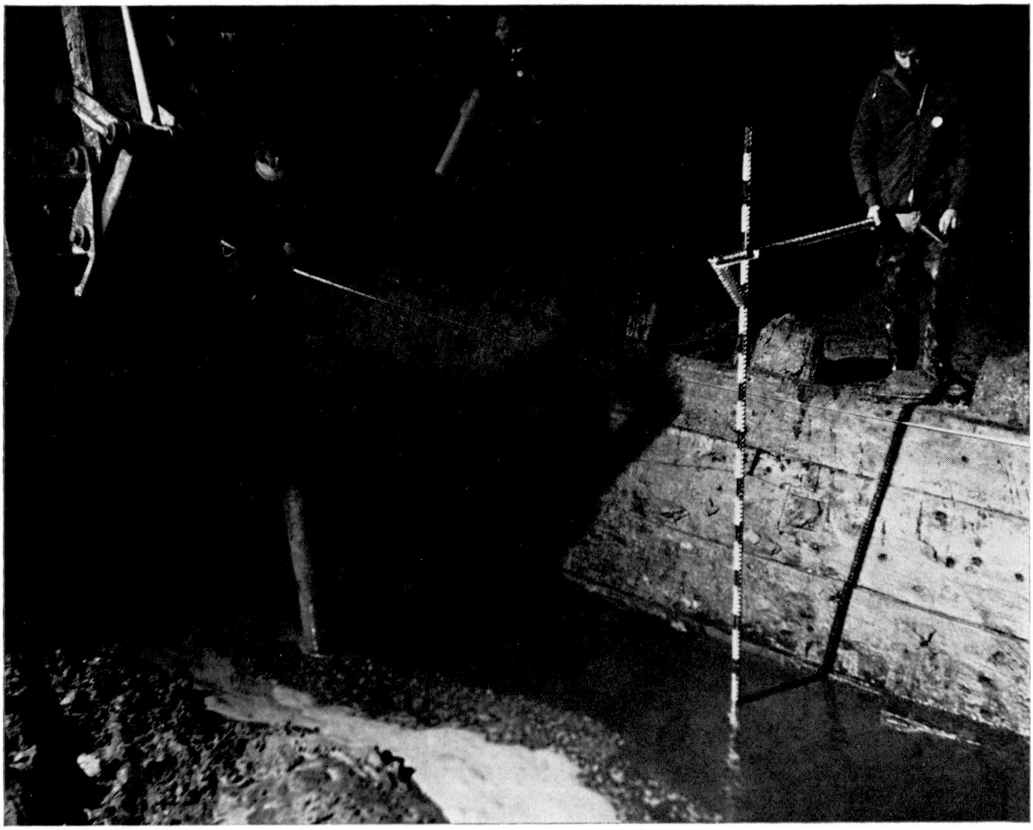

Figure 3. Instrument designed and made by Mr. W. St. John Wilkes for measuring the "tumble-home" of the *Amsterdam.*

the "tumble-home" was devised by Mr. W. St. John Wilkes. Two pieces of angle-iron, one longer than the other, were rigidly bolted together to form a right-angled L-shape. A spirit-level was fastened to the shorter arm, while the long arm was painted in alternating black and white lengths each of exactly 10 cm. Guilded by the spirit-level the long arm could be made to stand vertically, and measurements could be taken to the ship's side (Fig. 3).

A second hole was dug next morning on the east or starboard side of the ship, but unfortunately here the outside of the hull was found to be coated with a layer of iron-pan which completely obscured the outside of the hull. This hole was about 3 m deep, and its excavation revealed one unexpected feature about the ship—that the iron bolts fastening the *Amsterdam*'s frames and planks together had corroded away. The rising tide filled the interior of the ship before it filled the hole we had dug, and for a few seconds before the hole was filled the increased pressure inside the ship began pushing the planks and frames into the hole, but when the hole filled up this movement was stopped. Although it is regrettable that this happened, the extent of the distortion to the hull is very localised and not very great; and we did learn that any total excavation of the ship must take into consideration the corrosion of the iron bolts. Another very important feature is the iron-pan, which has formed not only on the outside of the starboard side, but also, as far as one can judge, at the junction of most timbers. As a result it would seem that at present probably the most practical way to raise and preserve the ship would be to take it apart, clean and preserve each timber, and put the vessel together again elsewhere. If the ship were bolted together again *in situ* and raised as a whole, the conservation problems would be enormous. The argument for taking the ship apart as its excavation proceeds is strengthened by the discovery from the probing in 1971 that the starboard side has almost certainly been considerably distorted, probably owing to the pressure of sand and clay outside the ship long ago. Also, dismembering the ship *in situ* seems to be the only practical way of avoiding technical problems posed by the siting of internal cross-beams or struts bracing the sides of the coffer-dam in which it is presumed that the ship would be excavated.

The investigation of the structure of the ship was further aided by the use of a metal rod to probe into the sand filling the interior of the ship. Four transverse sections were probed across the ship, and a further probed section was made across the stern along the ship's long axis. These have shown that the lower deck is undoubtedly present, but that it seems to have been damaged on the starboard half. It seems likely that parts of it may have collapsed into the hold below.

Messrs. William Press had recovered hundreds of objects from within the ship, and part of our job was to try to establish whether or not there were many more objects. The eighteenth-century English records both tell of the impossibility of being able to recover the cargo, as the ship was quickly filling with sand; and the Dutch records specifically mention that, apart from the treasure of silver, only three cases containing merchandise were recovered and returned to the Netherlands. It was decided not to dig down inside the ship, as this would disturb objects lying on the lower deck. Of the many objects of pottery, glass, wood, leather and metal, only the presence of those made of metal could be detected by highly sensitive instruments. The presence and density of the metal objects would therefore be a valuable indicator of the presence and density of other objects. A request for assistance was sent to Dr. E. T. Hall, Director of the

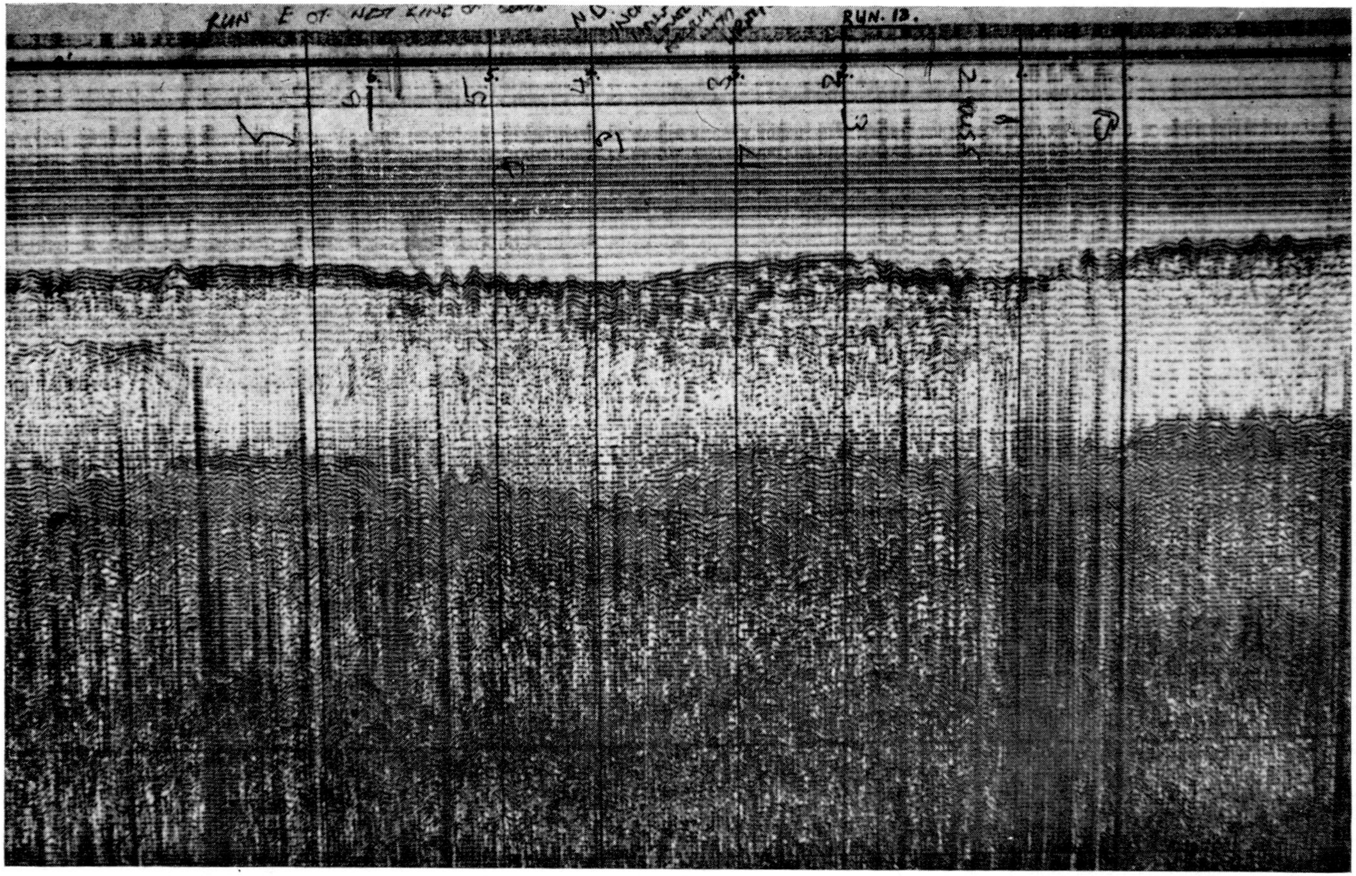

Figure 4. Part of the sonar record of the *Amsterdam*, showing a long section through the ship. The seabed is plainly visible, and immediately beneath it the dark area in the centre of the photograph is caused by reflections from objects lying within the ship. The vertical lines indicate the positions of marker-buoys positioned around the wreck. The ship's bow is on the right side of the photograph.

Research Laboratory for Art and Archaeology, Oxford University and he kindly replied by allowing Mr. Jeremy Green to carry out the survey free of charge.

First, a metal detector was used, which showed that there was a scatter of objects on the lower deck, and an interesting absence of objects amidships which must be due to the presence of the main hatch to the hold.

Secondly, the ship and its surrounding area were surveyed with a proton magnetometer, with very important results (Fig. 2). It revealed the presence of a number of ferrous objects in and around the ship, especially beyond its west side. It also revealed two "linear features" west of the ship, one of which was the fallen mainmast, the end of which is visible projecting up out of the sand; the other feature may be the foremast or bowsprit. It also recorded the presence of two separate masses of iron ballast in the bottom of the ship, each of the order of perhaps 50 tons.

Finally, the wreck site has been examined geologically, and for this a survey using sonar has been carried out by Mr. I. Bowyer and Mr. A. Cameron of EG&G Geophysical Ltd. The wreck is situated in a heavily faulted area in which clay overlies hard sandstone, and it seems that the weight of this heavily-laden ship on the clay caused her to sink into the beach. The south-westerly gales of 1749 scoured a hollow in the clay on the west side of the ship, and the vessel heeled over a little towards the hollow; she therefore sank into the beach at that angle, which is clearly visible nowadays in the exposed part of the ship. As the upper part of the ship broke up, masts collapsed and decks were smashed by the early salvors and the heavy seas, and many loose parts of the ship fell into the hollow.

The sonar record showed not only many objects in the ship, but also geological formations around the wreck (Fig. 4). What it did not show clearly was the vessel itself. The two sides of the ship are certainly visible on the sonar graphs, but the lower deck is only possibly visible. As there were only 20 feet of water over the ship when the record was made, the penetration of the sonar was only 20 feet into the beach.

This is merely a brief account of part of the investigation of the *Amsterdam*, and, as much work still has to be carried out on the results of the research described above, the conclusions reached here must remain tentative to some extent. The survey has, however, enabled us to evaluate the significance and remarkable state of preservation of this wreck, and to give the Dutch Government, who now own her, sufficient information with which to decide what they should do with her; in this connection a special Anglo-Dutch Committee has now been formed by the Dutch Ministry of Culture.

REFERENCES

Marsden, P. 1972 The wreck of the Dutch East Indiaman *Amsterdam* near Hastings, 1749. An interim report. *International Journal of Nautical Archaeology*, **1**, 73–96.

Discussion

McKee What type of clay is there around the *Amsterdam*? Blue, or what? I should like a comparison with the clay at the *Mary Rose* site at Spithead.
Marsden It is bluish-grey clay; it is soft and should be very heavy.
McKee When you put in a rod, can you move it sideways quite easily?
Marsden No.
McKee We can do this at the *Mary Rose* site.
Marsden It is almost impossible for us to do this around the *Amsterdam*.

Lewis What sonar frequency was used, and what was the depth of the water over the wreck and sand?
Green A 12 kc. "pinger" was used, and the depth was 20 feet.
Lewis Was the sand mixed with mud, and how much sand was there?
Marsden There was a layer of sand over pure mud. The sand was generally inside the ship, but it is difficult to tell the difference between sand and mud from the sonar record.
McKee The two "pingers" which we were lent by EG&G were 5 kc. and 12 kc. The 5 kc. one gives deep penetration, but little fine detail. The 12 kc. one gives better definition near the surface of the seabed, but does not penetrate so far.

Marsh Are the general public breaking the law by digging on this site?
Marsden Yes. They can be accused of malicious damage to wreck, under salvage law.
Richards Will this apply to other sites at a later date?
Blackman The CNA has been campaigning for a long time for legislation to protect underwater archaeological sites in British waters in the same way as land sites.
Johnstone There is a bye-law at Hastings which forbids vehicles being taken on the foreshore. Therefore as long as we can keep vehicles away the *Amsterdam* will be fairly well protected.
Marsden People have been trying for years to dig on the *Amsterdam* with buckets and spades, and they are no great threat; but a machine will do the job much better, and will do a considerable amount of damage.

Ships and shipwrecks: the archaeology of ships

by

PETER THROCKMORTON

WE HAVE COME a long way in the thirteen years since I began work in marine archaeology and in the eleven years since Joan du Plat Taylor and I helped to excavate the Bronze Age ship at Cape Gelidonya. I am very moved and honoured by the prominence you have given me in asking me to speak this evening and begin this conference.*

I show a twelfth-century A.D. plate from the Kyra Panagia wreck which we surveyed on behalf of the Greek Archaeological Service last summer (see now Throckmorton & Kritzas, 1971, 176 Fig. 1). The beautiful graffito ware plates with their vivid geometric and realistic patterns were well preserved when we found them under 50 cm of mud. Excavations of this kind have now become a familiar story, so I shall not discuss the techniques of this excavation, except to say that we have progressed to the point where the scientific and scrupulous excavation of the shattered bones of a sunken shipwreck is now technically possible to the same standards as are reached in land excavations.

All of you know that the bottom of the Mediterranean has produced most of the beautiful bronze statues of Classical and Hellenistic times which survive to this day. It has been reliably estimated that perhaps a third of the exported products of nations which have engaged in sea trade was lost at sea. It would be a rash person who today would argue that marine archaeology is not a valuable branch of that great family of archaeologies which began when General Pitt Rivers excavated in the last century.

I should explain to you why I personally am interested in marine archaeology. I am not a classicist, nor do I have any pretensions to being an academic of any description. I am a seaman. It is the ships of the past that bring me to marine archaeology and thus to this meeting.

To understand the ships of the past, we must understand and love and work with ships today. It says in the Bible that the two most beautiful things in the world are a woman with a child and a ship in the sea. I agree. I am fascinated by the continuing challenge of learning to sail my own boat. Sailing her and handling her under sail in all weathers in the Aegean has given us a great insight into the lives of the ancient mariners of the Mediterranean. I would rather have you see me as I prefer to see myself, as a man in dirty dungarees and a fearnought jacket aboard my own ship, than as the caricature in a monkey-suit who appears here.

* Editor's note: This paper, though delivered as prologue, has been printed as epilogue, to join the other papers on ships.

Figure 1. The schooner *Heraclea*, at anchor off Methone in about 1940.

We must distinguish between the archaeology of ships and marine archaeology. The archaeology of sailing ships begins with the Bronze Age and ends with schooners like the beautiful three-masted schooner *Heraclea*, which you see here at anchor off Methone in about 1940 (Fig. 1). A few years after that time I had the opportunity as a young boy to sail a little bit in schooners like this on the coast of Maine and Nova Scotia and as far south as the West Indies, never knowing then that I was playing at an art and a trade which began some 4,000 years ago and which would disappear in my lifetime. Today the *Heraclea* is a shattered mass of broken timbers and worm-eaten planking, half-buried under the mud in the little harbour of Porto Longo in the south-western Peloponnese (Fig. 2; Throckmorton, 1965; Frey, above, 181–4). It is the job of the ship archaeologist to recreate from junk like this the beautiful reality of the actual ship so that she can be studied and remembered.

Wrecks like the *Heraclea* are obviously not worth the time and effort of excavating, except for some specialist reason such as the study of preservation, which is why we

Figure 2. Divers studying the wreck of the *Heraclea* in Porto Longo.

investigated her. Other wrecks are important. Ones like the sarcophagi wrecks which we studied at Methone (Throckmorton & Bullitt, 1963) can be investigated at little cost by teams of amateur divers led by a competent architect who understands archaeology, or a competent archaeologist who understands how to make underwater drawings. This is not strictly ship archaeology, but the end product, a good drawing of the wreck, is equally useful to both "ship" and "classical" archaeologists. The size of the ship can be estimated from drawings of the bulk cargo. The sarcophagi can be identified and much other information can be extracted about Mediterranean voyaging at the time of the shipwreck, which in this case was the third century A.D.

Excavations like the one we made at Torre Sgarrata near Taranto are much more interesting. Here we had large elements of the frames and planking of a Roman ship of the second century A.D., lost with her cargo of rough-cut marble on her way, perhaps, to Rome from Asia Minor (Figs. 3–6; Throckmorton, 1969). As you can see, the wreck was badly broken up and we only found small parts of it. However, scrupulous drawing of these wooden elements of the ship will allow us to make a valid reconstruction of the ship herself. One of the things that we are increasingly conscious of in this field is the beauty of the carpentry which went into these ships, hinting at the expertise that went into their design.

The Byzantine ship which we excavated at the Pantano Longarini in 1965 is a beautiful example of very well preserved portions of the hull of a large ship of the fifth or sixth century A.D. (Throckmorton & Kapitän, 1968). The Pantano wreck was a cargo-carrier of perhaps 400 tons burden. The technique of her construction is very similar to that

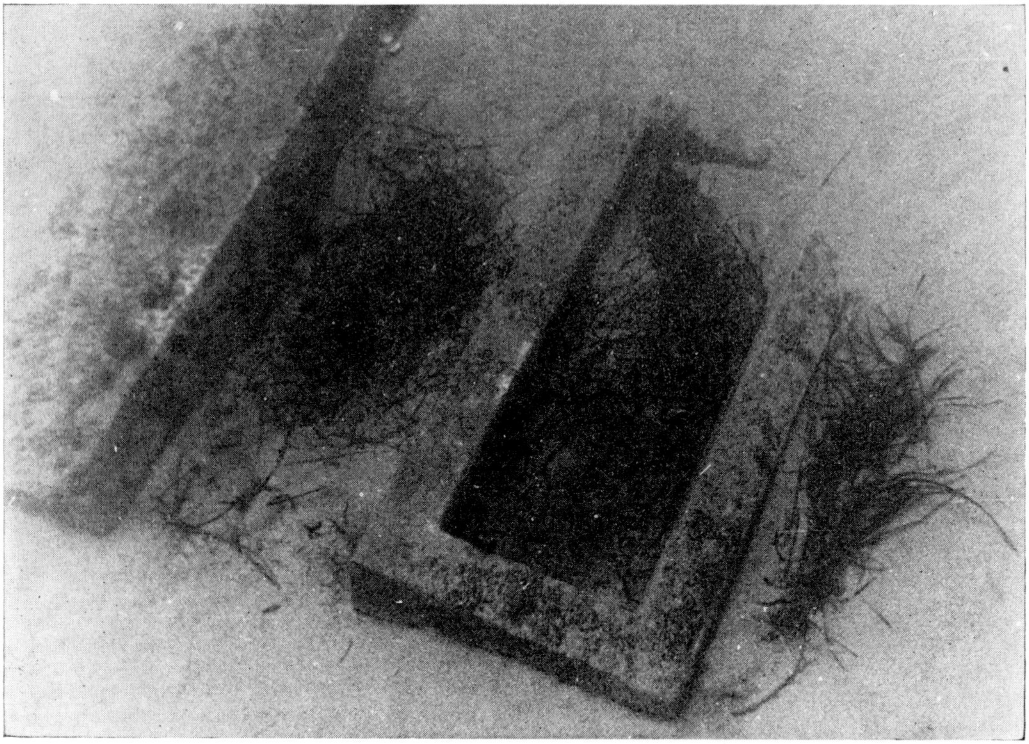

Figure 3. Torre Sgarrata: all that was visible of the wreck when discovered. Photo: G. Kapitän.

Figure 4. Torre Sgarrata: a rough-cut sarcophagus, with the marble sheets as stowed; planking is visible underneath.

Figure 5. Torre Sgarrata: the west end of the site during air-lifting.

Figure 6. Torre Sgarrata: hull planking, frames and (extreme left) inner stringer.

seen in the shipwrecks excavated by Bass and van Doorninck in Turkey (Bass & van Doorninck, 1971). To me the wonder of this vessel is that in her construction we see massive longitudinal strength incorporated into the construction in a manner reminiscent of the technique used by Isambard Kingdom Brunel in the *Great Britain*.

Here at the Pantano we see in an actual wreck the use of through-beams, which protruded outside the massive longitudinal wales, which girdled the ship at the waterline and above. These are familiar from ancient bas-reliefs and pictures. Here we see them for the first time in an actual ship (Figs. 7–9).

Figure 7. Pantano Longarini wreck: through-beam 8. Its inner rider timbers are visible in the upper part of the picture. Photo: G. Kapitän.

We have succeeded in making a reconstruction of the Pantano ship, using techniques which I believe to be new. About a quarter or less of the ship is preserved: only the stern transom (Fig. 10) and a bit of the starboard side which joins it. We made a 1 : 10 drawing of each timber. If you have the parts of a model of all the pieces of a ship, including their fastening-holes, it follows that you can assemble the model like putting together a Meccano set. Thus from the model we are able to extend our knowledge of the shape of the vessel to a point near the midships section.

The Pantano ship is not a unique find. There are thousands of such partially preserved ships under the surface of the protecting mud all over the world. We are presently preoccupied, with the help of our colleagues, Professors Hall, Frey and Edgerton and

Figure 8. Pantano Longarini wreck: a through-beam towards midships, seen from above.

Figure 9. Pantano Longarini wreck: a through-beam, its outer end on the left.

Figure 10. Pantano Longarini wreck: the stern transom. Photo: G. Kapitän.

many others, with working with electronic methods—magnetometers, metal detectors, etc.—which will enable us to detect such wrecks.

It is a moving experience to see and handle the timbers of a ship that a seaman from the bad old days of one or two hundred years ago served his time in. However, we have here a terrible problem. Ships can be excavated. They can be studied and drawn and what is left of them can be permanently recorded on paper. Yet up to now I have not succeeded, undoubtedly because of mismanagement on my part, in arranging for the preservation of any of the shipwrecks that I have found and excavated, and I must conclude that it would be most unprincipled and unprofessional if I were to attempt another excavation unless I had figured out in advance how the valuable and interesting timber which remains can be saved. (On preservation see especially Barkman, 1967).

I confess that every time I think of the wood of the Torre Sgarrata ship, now rotting away in tanks in Taranto, I blush. It is perhaps too easy to argue the responsibility of the Italian Archaeological Service, which has neither the time, nor the money, nor the interest, perhaps, to send a workman once a week to the tanks where the wood is rotting, in order to top up the tanks with fresh water and put in fungicide. This neglect would not happen in England nor in America. However, it is I who excavated the wreck. If I had not removed the timbers from the sea after excavating them, they would have been lost in the first winter storms of 1968. But if I had not excavated the wreck at all I would be considerably in pocket and the wreck would be preserved for ever.

Figure 11. The wreck of H.M.S. *Nautilus*: a cannon, so battered by the rock and the surf that its trunnions have been knocked off.

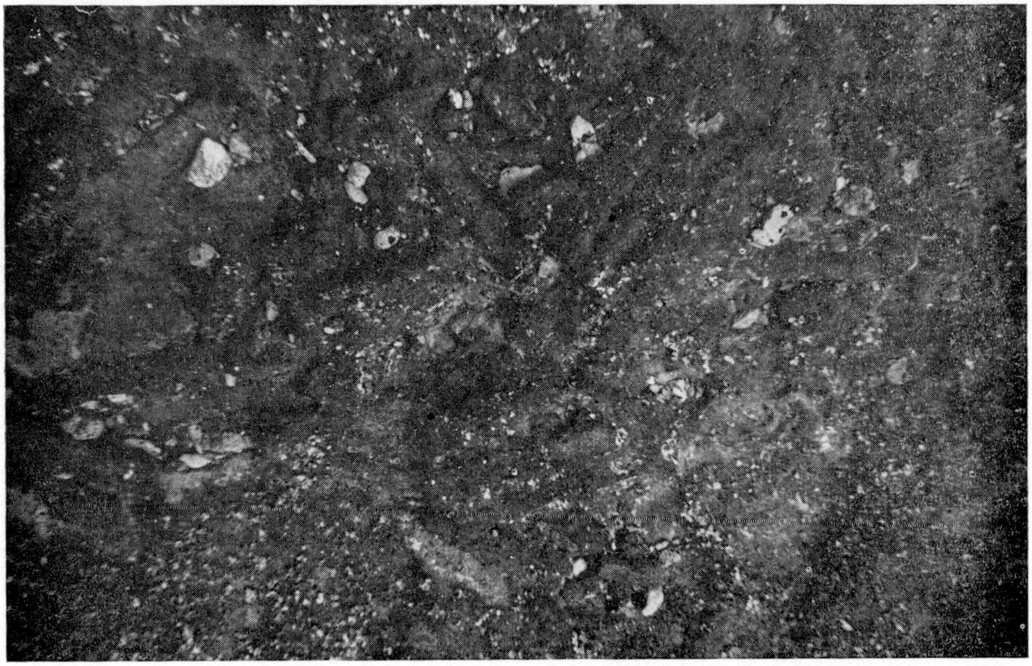

Figure 12. The wreck of H.M.S. *Nautilus*: iron ballast bars.

Eighteenth-century wrecks like the wreck of H.M.S. *Nautilus* at Nautilus Rock in the Aegean, between Kythera and Crete, are interesting because of their historical associations. Divers should study them because, with the advent of skin-diving as a sport, such remnants will disappear completely in the very near future. Using the eighteenth- and early nineteenth-century archives of the Royal Navy in order to find wrecks is a fascinating study in itself. In the case of H.M.S. *Nautilus*, we found the court martial documents of the surviving officers and men of the ship, and when we visited the site we were able vividly to recreate in our minds that night in January 1807, when *Nautilus*, with the north wind behind her, driving at nine knots under reefed topsails, smashed on a corner of Nautilus Rock and in ten minutes became a total wreck (Throckmorton, 1970, Chapter III).

The *Nautilus* incident brings us back to Nelson's navy, and to Admiral Collingwood, who was destined never to receive the despatches that the *Nautilus* carried.

As can be seen from the photographs (Figs. 11–12), nothing of the ship herself remains. No matter: we have her plans. A silver spoon that we discovered in the heap of ballast bars, which is all that remains, was identified as having belonged to her captain. If wrecks of this kind are forgotten, the small objects which remain will soon disappear into the hands of skin-divers, where they have a good chance of being lost or of disintegrating completely through lack of conservation. Although no great historical problems can be resolved by such investigations, it is my belief that the scattered

Figure 13. Lake Bolsena: modern rowing-boat.

souvenirs of this dramatic and fascinating period of naval history should be preserved in museums, where everybody can see them.

In 1965 we excavated the site of an eighth- or ninth-century B.C. village, submerged in Lake Bolsena, about 100 km north of Rome. We were struck by the apparent resemblance in life-style between the lake fishermen, whose village we used as a base for our excavation, and the ancient Villanovan lake-villagers, whose submerged houses we were excavating.

I do not know what kind of boats the ancient Villanovans had—and I would obviously very much like to know—but the modern Villanovans have curious boats which are rowed in a curious way, with the rower standing sideways in the boat looking over the starboard side (Fig. 13). The port oar is lashed to a steel thole-pin at the extreme after end of the boat. The starboard oar is lashed to a thole-pin 6 feet forward on the starboard side. The rower works the starboard oar with his left hand, the port oar with his right, using a sculling motion which I have never seen anywhere else except in Vietnam, where there are similar boats with similar rowing arrangements. I do not wish to make any comment, except that this seems to me a very interesting phenomenon which should be analytically investigated by somebody competent to do so. I should very much like to know the result of such a study. A good friend who is a prominent anthropologist advised me not to mention this boat or my interest in it at a talk I gave at an American university a few weeks ago. I fail to understand this attitude. Are they related, or aren't they? If they are related, why?

Figure 14. A *caravoscaro*—cut down, motorized, worn out and abandoned. Such ships will never be seen again.

Figure 15. The stern of a *varkhalass*.

The Eastern Mediterranean is one of the last strongholds of traditional shipbuilding in the world. In the Greek islands, in Turkey and in Syria, the locals are constructing the last generation of wooden sailing boats, which belong to what is undoubtedly a very old tradition.

There are many different boat types in the Eastern Aegean. One of the most common is the *caravoscaro* (Fig. 14). These beautiful clipper-bowed, round-sterned ships are probably descended from the fast American topsail schooners, which the piratical traders of Hydra, Spetsai, and Psara saw in the south of France when they and the Americans were filling their pockets by running contraband through the Royal Navy's blockade of Napoleonic France.

Figure 16. A large sailing *perama*, now a motor ship (compare Fig. 17). A tradition 3,000 years old will end when this ship disappears.

Another common type which survives in the Eastern Aegean is the *varkhalass.* These have a transom stern (Fig. 15) and a straight, heavily raked bow. It is a curious coincidence that the Arab *baggala* has similar characteristics.

Another common type is the *perama* (Figs. 16–18). *Peramas* are traditional in the easternmost corners of the Aegean and the Sea of Marmara, and I believe that they are direct descendants of Roman ship types like the wrecks we have excavated at Yassı Ada, the Pantano Longarini, and Torre Sgarrata.

The most ubiquitous of all Aegean types is the perennial *trehandiri.* These *trehandiria* are seen everywhere in the Aegean, and are undoubtedly very ancient.

Figure 17. The lovely stern of the *Perama* illustrated in Figure 16.

Figure 18. The *Evangelistria* of Mykonos at sea. Though motorized, she is the last Aegean *perama* to carry most of her original rig. Her mainsail wore out in 1961, and was not replaced.

No Mediterranean equivalent of Basil Greenhill has documented the last of these little sailing ships. The ancient formulas, handed down from father to son for hundreds of years, are fast being forgotten. The classical shapes are being bastardized, as the Aegean seamen convert from sail to power. My own boat, *Stormie Seas*, is, I think, the last large-sized traditional Greek sailing boat still able to manoeuvre without her engine, and she is rigged as a staysail schooner rather than with the traditional Aegean lugsail, the *bratsera* (Fig. 19).

Figure 19. Stormie Seas.

In our lifetimes, then, the memory of these beautiful ships will have completely disappeared unless we are able to record them (Figs. 20–23).

The distinguished American nautical writer, Lincoln Colcord, said of the beautiful ships of the last days of sail that

> "The sailing ship stood for a sociological achievement of the highest order. She stood for a means whereby men were brought to their fullest development. She stood for a profession which only merit could endure. She stood for a real efficiency of spirit and character. She stood for things the world cannot afford to lose."

I propose that the world cannot afford to lose the last of these vessels, which stand at the end of so many thousands of years of development of the sailing ship. In the year that I was born there were nearly one hundred square-rigged ships under the American

Figure 20. Kaïkis in St. George harbour, Piraeus, in 1961. Since then most of these vessels have been scrapped.

Figure 21. Once abandoned, hulls disintegrate in a few years in the warm, teredo-infested waters of the Mediterranean.

flag. Today there are six. One, the ex-German training ship *Eagle*, belongs to the United States Coast Guard and still sails. *Kaiulani*, the last surviving American-built square-rigged ship, is a ruined hulk in Manila, and we face many years of hard work and vast expense before her restoration is accomplished and she can be preserved as a monument to the thousands of men who built our country with such ships.

Figure 22. Pithoi at Koroni. Ancient trades such as this will have been forgotten completely in twenty years.

Two of the ships we have saved in America are British—the full-rigged ships *Balclutha* and the *Falls of Clyde*. The *Balclutha* is an extremely successful museum-ship in San Francisco (Fig. 24). Now restored to her original state as an ocean carrier of 1886, she earns nearly $200,000 a year, which pays both for her own maintenance and for much of the staff and most of the expenses of the San Francisco Maritime Museum. The *Falls of Clyde* is now being restored in Honolulu (Fig. 25).

The *Charles Morgan*, last survivor of the hundreds of whaling barques which Herman Melville described so eloquently, and the Danish training ship *Joseph Conrad* (ex-*George Stage*) survive in Mystic, Connecticut, as successful museum-ships.

It seems, then, from our experience in America that preserving these ships not only is a culturally and historically valuable thing to do, but also can be guaranteed to pay for itself. The *Balclutha* has earned more money as a museum at Fisherman's Wharf than she ever earned in her arduous voyages around Cape Horn. Here in Bristol the *Great Britain* is already proving to be one of the most prominent tourist attractions

Fig. 23. Argyris, the last amphora-trader, in 1961. Since then he has scrapped his boat and bought a truck.

Figure 24. The *Balclutha* crossing San Francisco Bay after restoration. Photo: Karl Kortum.

of the city and I understand that she has earned several tens of thousands of pounds over and above her day-to-day expenses, since her arrival here.

These ships appeal to the public because the very sight of them strikes a chord in the hearts of nearly everyone who sees them. They are beautiful. *Elissa*, the little iron barque that we have just bought for the San Francisco Maritime Museum, has hardly a straight line in her ironwork (Fig. 26). The craftsmanship in the ships is something inconceivable today. These ships, then, should be considered not as ships any longer, but as great works of art.

Figure 25. The *Falls of Clyde* with her lower rigging in place, 1970. Photo: San Francisco Maritime Museum.

Samuel Eliot Morison once wrote (1921, 370–1)

> "Never, in these United States, has the brain of man conceived, or the hand of man fashioned, so perfect a thing as the clipper ship. In her, the long-suppressed artistic impulse of a practical, hard-worked race burst into flower. The *Flying Cloud* was our Rheims, the *Sovereign of the Seas* our Parthenon, the *Lightning* our Amiens; but they were monuments carved from snow. For a brief moment of time they flashed their splendor around the world, then disappeared with the sudden completeness of the wild pigeon."

If Professor Morison had been interested, he could have saved the last Donald McKay ship, *Glory of the Seas*, burnt for her copper in 1922 (Mjelde, 1970). The value realized was less than the price of a ticket to England to see the *Cutty Sark*.

Now, when it comes to the last of the great ships of sail, we have almost come to the very end of the line. The reason that we have gone so far is that up to the beginning of the Second World War, the backwaters of the maritime world were clogged with abandoned sailing ships which were, for good commercial reasons, scrapped or burnt or otherwise disposed of. Today there are perhaps only between 40 and 50 square-rigged ships of pre-1914 vintage remaining afloat. Of these about 20 are stabilized in permanent homes; twenty more are in danger of being scrapped in the fairly near future. More than 20 important sailing ships have been scrapped in the past ten years. This includes the famous *Lawhill*, the lovely *British Isles*, the *Pax* in Noumea, and the *Mary Moore*.

Figure 26. The only extant photograph of the iron barque *Elissa* under sail, taken in about 1929, after she had been partially cut down. Photo: Lars Grönstrand.

Through the initiative of the San Francisco Maritime Museum, *Polly Woodside*, once known as the prettiest ship ever built in Belfast, has been saved in Australia. Alexander Hall's lovely little barque *Elissa*, the last surviving ship in the whole world which closely resembles Joseph Conrad's first command, the *Otago*, is now laid up in Piraeus. I am proud to say that I am her last owner of register, in a chain which began with an obscure Liverpool shipowner named Henry Fowler Watt in 1878. We are now campaigning to save the great French iron four-masted barque, the *Ville de Mulhouse*, which survives intact and unconverted in the Straits of Magellan, the lovely iron barque *Lady Elizabeth*, and the last American-built Western Ocean packet ship, *Charles Cooper* (Fig. 27), which are hulks at Port Stanley.

The last decade of ship archaeology has been very successful. Workers like George Bass, Fred van Doorninck and Michael Katzev have carried out ship excavations which

Figure 27. The stern of the *Charles Cooper*, the last American packet ship. Photo: Karl Kortum.

show us the construction of Mediterranean ships of thousands of years ago and give us a startling insight into the lives of their seamen and the trades in which they were engaged. However, our investigations in ancient naval architecture have created tremendous technical and administrative problems which must somehow be solved. We are now in the last decade of hope for the survivors of the climactic period of sailing ship naval architecture, which ends in the late 1900s with the great grain and nitrate clippers. Very shortly the last wooden traditional ships will have disappeared for ever.

Ship archaeology is a vast interdisciplinary subject with great interest for the research student, for the historian, for the archaeologist, for the amateur diver and the volunteer. If this meeting serves its purpose, we can hope that the coming decade will be even more productive than the last.

One thing is certain: if we as a group, archaeologists, classicists, historians and engineers, do not work together, then in the decade before us an important part of man's heritage will be lost for ever.

REFERENCES

Barkman, L. 1967 *On Resurrecting a Wreck*, 31 pp. Statens Sjöhistoriska Museum, Stockholm: Wasastudier, No. 6.

Bass, G. F. 1966 *Archaeology under Water*, 224 pp. London & New York. [Revised paperback edit., 1970].

Bass, G. F. & others 1967 Cape Gelidonya: a Bronze Age Shipwreck. *Trans. Am. Phil. Soc.* (*N.S.*) **57** Part 8, 177 pp.

Bass, G. F. & Katzev, M. L. 1968 New Tools for Underwater Archaeology. *Archaeology*, **21** No. 3, 164–73.

Bass, G. F. & van Doorninck, F. H. 1971 A Fourth-Century Shipwreck at Yassı Ada. *AJA*, **75**, 27–37.

Morison, S. E. 1921 *The Maritime History of Massachusetts, 1783–1860*, 400 pp. Boston & New York.

Mjelde, M. J. 1970 *Glory of the Seas*, 303 pp. Middletown, Conn.

Owen, D. I. 1970 Picking up the pieces: the salvage excavation of a looted 5th century B.C. shipwreck in the Straits of Messina. *Expedition*, **13** No. 1 (Fall 1970) 24–9.

Throckmorton, P. 1965 Wrecks at Methone. *Mariner's Mirror*, **51**, 305–20.

Throckmorton, P. 1969 Ancient Shipwreck Yields New Facts—and a Strange Cargo. *Natn. geogr. Mag.*, **135** No. 2 (Feb. 1969) 282–300.

Throckmorton, P. 1970 *Shipwrecks and Archaeology: the Unharvested Sea*, 270 pp. London.

Throckmorton, P. & Bullitt, J. 1963 Underwater surveys in Greece, 1962. *Expedition*, **5** No. 2 (Winter 1963) 16–23.

Throckmorton, P. & Kapitän, G. 1968 An Ancient Shipwreck at Pantano Longarini. *Archaeology*, **21** No. 3, 182–7.

Throckmorton, P. & Kritzas, Ch. B. 1971 Exploration of a Byzantine Wreck at Pelagos Island near Alonnesos. *Athens Annals of Archaeology*, **4** No. 2, 176–85.

Discussion

Throckmorton There are about forty square-rigged ships left in the world which were built before 1914. Of these about twenty are in danger of being scrapped in the next ten years, just as about twenty have been scrapped in the last decade. The peak of traditional sailing ship development was reached in about 1860 and the great period ended by 1890. Only about a dozen ships now survive from this great period.

There are forty to fifty square-rigged ships left which were built after 1914. Some ten of these are period reproductions, like the *Mayflower*, and about ten are Russian.

My point is that the archaeology of sailing ships begins in the Bronze Age and ends with these lovely iron sailing ships—a period of 4,000 years of nautical tradition which ends in our own time.

Lewis Are we going to find an economical way of conserving wrecks which have been recovered, and if so, when?

Throckmorton There is much work being done on this, although people and governments do not realize how difficult it is. Until a government is prepared to give financial backing, say £200,000, no institution or individual can handle a large shipwreck. There must also be adequate museum facilities to deal with the finds. However beautiful drawings may be, they are an inadequate substitute, especially when one is trying to reconstruct a fragmentary mess as at Torre Sgarrata or the Pantano. I don't say that we *must* preserve miles of identical hull planking, and so on. But I do believe that, in the case of a difficult wreck where every clue counts, one does need everything to hand, stored in fresh water at least, with a rot-resisting chemical. After reconstruction on paper has been completed, after the material has been published, and after every expert has had his say, then it is reasonable to consider what should be thrown away and what preserved. From my limited experience I should say that, of the wrecks which I have worked on, one would want to preserve a fairly large amount for exhibition purposes. I don't think one should start work on any underwater wreck without having prepared for the worst: that is, having arranged for the transportation and safe storage of vast quantities of material.

Blackman Is there not a difference between a rescue job and a deliberate project? The former clearly must be done at once or not at all; the latter must not be done unless fully backed financially.

Throckmorton Exactly. But one should add that these projects can pay off. If the British Government were to put up £1 million for a *Mary Rose* excavation and museum, the money and the interest would be paid back within twenty years.

Flemming Given that there are a very large number of wrecks similar for similar periods, is it possible to excavate some and save them by re-covering with the sand?

Throckmorton Probably not, for chemical changes occur immediately the wreck is uncovered. In half-an-hour the wood begins to turn black, as we found at Torre Sgarrata.
Swiny One of the reasons for raising the wood of the Kyrenia ship in the second season was that disintegration had taken place over the first winter. The cargo of grinding-stones had been left in place by us on purpose, to hold the wood on the bottom. We even covered the hull with plastic sheeting and sand, but the disintegration was considerable.
Lewis Once oxygen gets into the wood it starts to disintegrate.
Throckmorton If £10–20,000 is available for excavation, surely much more should be available for conservation. These ships have great public appeal, for their carpentry is incredible.

Flemming In the present situation money is available only for the big sites. There must be a lot of wrecks worth studying archaeologically, but not worth preserving for exhibition. Would it be possible just to preserve the smaller wrecks under water to avoid disintegration?
Throckmorton All of these wrecks should be kept in water indefinitely. It must all be thought out very carefully from the beginning. We should have vast preserving tanks, and then all models and types of ships could be saved.

Green How important are the sea people and their way of life in this field of archaeology? Are we not losing touch with these people and their lore and sailing methods, and do you not think we ought to get as much knowledge as possible from them before they die out, and the knowledge with them?
Throckmorton Yes, this is my main point. I feel that a ship archaeologist ought to start with the "living" past and go right back into the "dead" past, for I believe that the whole is connected. The recording of the last sailing ships in the Mediterranean and also the last sailing ships in British waters is very important. In this connection nineteenth-century records are very important too.

McKee Very little of the original *Victory* is left (and that ship has 600,000 visitors a year). Re-rigging takes place fairly frequently, and there you have the old techniques still maintained. Deterioration will take place above the water as well as below, and that ship was never sunk.
Throckmorton Any ship replaces all her parts many times during her lifetime, but she does live on if this is done properly. No matter how many times the planking is changed, the ship is still the same.

Flemming Are all ships in the Aegean built with templates, and how old are the templates?
Throckmorton The formulas from which the templates are made are very old. I have a suspicion that some of these date back to Roman times, although there is no proof of this. Shapes are seldom new.

Hague Is there a strong case for people to give up diving, except for rescue work, and turn to recording ships which are becoming extinct?
Throckmorton My feeling is that these two activities are one and the same. If you are going to dive and work on ships of unknown shapes, you should know about ships of known shape. Money should be spent on encouraging students to research and record what is on the surface.
Hague Are students encouraged to do this?
Throckmorton I hope so. We should not lose the chain of study. We should never give up the diving, but neither should we give up recording the surviving traditional ships.

Tayless Do you not think that sailing ships, for example the *Cutty Sark*, should be sailing and not dying in a museum?
Throckmorton San Francisco Maritime Museum has just bought the ex-barque *Elissa* of 1877. It is our intention to re-rig *Elissa* and use her as a working youth-training ship in San Francisco Bay. We feel that a totally "dead" museum is wrong. If one is going to be a ship archaeologist one should work on ships—preferably square-rigged ones. There is, unfortunately, at present no way of licensing officers commanding square-rigged ships in America, for the Mills Law prevents the licensing of anything built under a foreign flag.
Lyon I wish to take issue with you over "dead" ships. It is all very well to talk about using one of the very few survivors from the great age of sail as a training ship—but remember the case of Nelson's *Foudroyant*, which was bought for this purpose, and which ended as a wreck on Blackpool Sands. Have we the right to do this to an irreplaceable original? Surely this is the job for the replica.
Throckmorton Of course some ships are so valuable that they should never be taken to sea. But connected with these ships there should always be a "living" ship to work. This is a case for a replica which sails. The *Balclutha* is another example. It is too big and has no engine.

Lyon Does the ship archaeologist's task end with the great period of sailing ships? The era of the big-gun ship is now ending—witness the fate of the *Belfast*. Even the knowledge of how to fire heavy naval artillery is fast vanishing. Surely these techniques should also be recorded, and some of the ships preserved.
Throckmorton Ship archaeology means learning about sailing ships and how to sail them, and therefore it ends with the iron ship at the end of the nineteenth century. After that time the subject should be referred to as the history of technology and not archaeology. There is very little possibility of learning anything from later ships about the long nautical traditions of the past.

Singmaster There are people still living in America and Great Britain who sailed on square-riggers. Is anything being done to preserve the technology of the sailing ship, knowledge of which is being lost as these people die, along with the old mariners of the Mediterranean?

Throckmorton Many people have done a great deal of systematic recording in this field. The situation, however, is pretty desperate in Britain and America, since nobody is learning to sail square-riggers from people who really know about it.
Green The Norwegian marine archaeology section have an excellent arrangement—they spend time searching for wrecks, but more important, they spend time recording information about sailing ships: how many people sailed these ships, what amounts and types of provisions they carried, etc. This surely is the way we must progress, before all the knowledge dies with the people who have it.
Throckmorton Nautical archaeologists must know all these things; they must be seamen.

Davidson It is all very well to suggest leaving wrecks on the bottom and not raising them, but then they will just be pillaged. Do you see any way to end the pillaging of wrecks during the process of excavation and before?
Throckmorton Laws must be passed to stop this.
Davidson Do laws effectively stop pillaging?
Throckmorton They do where they are strictly enforced, for example in Greece. The situation is serious because not only are the cargoes lost but the ships' hulls are gradually exposed by looting, and suffer badly from this.
McKeone As I see it, there is a useful function which keen amateur divers can carry out: the accurate survey of surface features without excavation. In the first place, this gives valuable information to archaeologists who have to choose between possible sites for a more ambitious expedition; secondly, accurate surveys give information which could help in the estimate of any subsequent looting by less scrupulous divers.
Throckmorton Without the protection of a strong law little can be done to save wrecks. Very many people are interested in looting, often on a small scale.

Singmaster If governments were willing to allow the sale and export of, say, three quarters of the amphorae from a wreck, which otherwise only clutter up local museums, this would help to depress the inflated prices on the antique market (now about $100 for an amphora) and to discourage looting. Furthermore, expeditions could be financed with the proceeds to save more wrecks.
Throckmorton What you suggest might well have the desired effect. But we must not and cannot interfere in the affairs of foreign governments which are independent and have each their differing problems. Where we can work for change is in the legislation of our own countries.

Members of the Symposium

Bailey, D. M., British Museum, London.
Baker, P., Institute of Geological Sciences, Leeds.
Baldwin, E. A., Royal Navy.
Bax, A. D., Fort Bovisand, Plymouth.
Betts, J. H., University of Bristol.
Blackman, D. J., University of Bristol.
Branigan, K., University of Bristol.
Christie, R., Aberystwyth.
Clamp, J. R., University of Bristol.
Clarke, H., Bramhall, Cheshire.
Cook, J. M., University of Bristol.
Corney, A., Portsmouth City Museum.
Croome, A., Daily Telegraph, London.
Davidson, D. P., Derby.
Davies, R., B.B.C., London.
Davison, K., University of Birmingham.
Eichholz, D. E., University of Bristol.
Evans, A. C., British Museum, London.
Evans, G., Imperial College of Science & Technology, London.
Farrell, R., Cornell University.
Fenwick, V., National Maritime Museum, Greenwich.
Fischer, M., University of Oxford.
Flemming, N. C., National Institute of Oceanography, Wormley.
Frey, D. A., Robert College, Istanbul.
Frost, H., London.
Fryer, J., University of Keele.
Gill, J., Bristol.
Green, J., University of Oxford.
Hague, D. B., R.C.A.M., Wales & Monmouthshire, Aberystwyth.
Hall, E. T., University of Oxford.
Hamilton, D., University of Bristol.
Hawkins, A. B., University of Bristol.
Higgs, K., University of Aston.
Hill, P. A., Carleton University, Ottawa.
Humphreys, S. C., University College, London.
Johnstone, P., B.B.C., London.
Kapitän, G., Syracuse.
Kennedy, R. A., County Museum, Haverfordwest.
Lawrence, S., University of Bristol.
Leigh, D., University of Southampton.

Lewis, E., Portsmouth City Museum.
Lewis, J. D., U.S. Army.
Linder, E., University of Haifa.
Lyon, D. J., National Maritime Museum, Greenwich.
McKee, A., Hayling Island.
McKeone, D. H., Polytechnic of the South Bank, London.
Marsden, P., Guildhall Museum, London.
Marsh, R. H. K., University of Oxford.
Marshall, B., Baltimore.
Martin, C. J. M., Kelso, Roxburghshire.
Morgan, R. G., University of Bristol.
Naish, G. P. B., National Maritime Museum, Greenwich.
Parker, A. J., University College, Dublin.
Peel, R. F., University of Bristol.
Quare, D., University of Bristol.
Richards, B., Royal Air Force.
Rule, M. H., Fishbourne.
Saxon, E. C., University Museum, Philadelphia.
Sherborne, J. W., University of Bristol.
Singmaster, D., Polytechnic of the South Bank, London
Squire, D. M., Esher.
Sutcliffe, R., B.B.C., London.
Swiny, H. Wylde, Kyrenia.
Tayless, J., University of Bristol.
Taylor, J. du Plat, Balsham, Cambridge.
Throckmorton, P., Piraeus.
Tilley, A. F., Royal Navy.
Waite, D., University of Bristol.
Wallace, H., British Sub-Aqua Club, Kingston.
Wignall, S., Old Colwyn, Denbighshire.
Wilkes, W. G. St. J., Eastbourne.
Wilms-Posen, H., Bonn.

Contributors unable to be present:
Jameson, M. H., University of Pennsylvania.
Tusa, V., National Archaeological Museum, Palermo.